D0832806

TIMES BOOKS
London

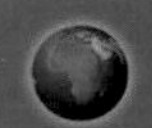

CONTENTS

Times Books,
77-85 Fulham Palace Road,
London W6 8JB

First published 1991
First published as
The Times Atlas of the World
Mini Edition 1994
Second Edition 1999
Reprinted 1999, 2000, 2001
Revised Edition 2003
Reprinted with changes 2003
Reprinted 2004

Printed and bound in
Singapore by Imago

British Library Cataloguing
in Publication Data.
A catalogue record for
this book is available from
the British Library.

ISBN 0 00 714500 4

RH11826 Imp 003

www.harpercollins.co.uk
visit the book lover's website

Pages Title

IMAGES OF EARTH

6-7 OCEANIA
8-9 ASIA
10-11 EUROPE
12-13 AFRICA
14-15 NORTH AMERICA
16-17 SOUTH AMERICA
18-19 ANTARCTICA

THE WORLD TODAY

20-21 CLIMATE
22-23 LAND COVER
24-25 POPULATION
26-27 URBANIZATION
28-29 CITIES

GEOGRAPHICAL INFORMATION

30-35 STATES AND TERRITORIES OF THE WORLD
36-37 CONTINENTS, ISLANDS AND MOUNTAINS
38-39 OCEANS, SEAS, LAKES AND RIVERS

40-41 INTRODUCTION TO THE ATLAS
42-43 SYMBOLS AND ABBREVIATIONS

CONTENTS

Pages	Title	Scale
	WORLD	
44-45	**WORLD** Physical Features	1:170 000 000
46-47	**WORLD** Countries	1:170 000 000
48-49	**OCEANIA**	1:70 000 000
50-51	**AUSTRALIA**	1:25 000 000
52-53	**AUSTRALIA** Southeast	1:10 000 000
54	**NEW ZEALAND**	1:10 000 000
55	**ANTARCTICA**	1:60 000 000
56-57	**ASIA**	1:70 000 000
58-59	**SOUTHEAST ASIA**	1:30 000 000
60-61	**MALAYSIA** and **INDONESIA WEST**	1:15 000 000
62-63	**CONTINENTAL SOUTHEAST ASIA**	1:15 000 000
64	**PHILIPPINES**	1:15 000 000
65	**NORTH KOREA** and **SOUTH KOREA**	1:9 000 000
66-67	**JAPAN**	1:10 000 000
68-69	**CHINA** and **MONGOLIA**	1:30 000 000
70-71	**CHINA** Central	1:15 000 000
72-73	**SOUTH ASIA**	1:20 000 000
74-75	**PAKISTAN, INDIA** and **BANGLADESH**	1:15 000 000
76-77	**CENTRAL ASIA**	1:20 000 000
78-79	**ARABIAN PENINSULA**	1:15 000 000

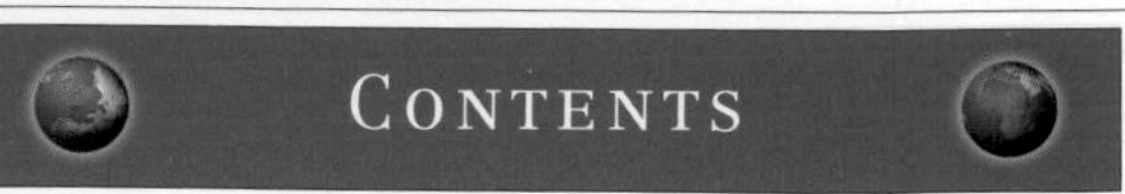

CONTENTS

Pages	Title	Scale
80-81	**EAST MEDITERRANEAN**	1:15 000 000
82-83	**RUSSIAN FEDERATION**	1:42 000 000
84-85	**EUROPE**	1:40 000 000
86-87	**EUROPEAN RUSSIAN FEDERATION**	1:20 000 000
88-89	**NORTHEAST EUROPE**	1:8 000 000
90-91	**UKRAINE AND MOLDOVA**	1:8 000 000
92-93	**SCANDINAVIA AND ICELAND**	1:10 000 000
94-95	**BRITISH ISLES**	1:8 000 000
96	**SCOTLAND**	1:4 000 000
97	**IRELAND**	1:4 000 000
98-99	**ENGLAND AND WALES**	1:4 000 000
100-101	**NORTHWEST EUROPE**	1:4 000 000
102-103	**CENTRAL EUROPE**	1:8 000 000
104-105	**FRANCE AND SWITZERLAND**	1:8 000 000
106-107	**SPAIN AND PORTUGAL**	1:8 000 000
108-109	**ITALY AND THE BALKANS**	1:8 000 000
110-111	**GREECE, ROMANIA AND BULGARIA**	1:8 000 000
112-113	**AFRICA**	1:60 000 000
114-115	**NORTHWEST AFRICA**	1:26 000 000
116-117	**NORTHEAST AFRICA**	1:26 000 000
118-119	**CENTRAL AFRICA**	1:20 000 000
120-121	**SOUTHERN AFRICA**	1:20 000 000
122-123	**REPUBLIC OF SOUTH AFRICA**	1:10 000 000

CONTENTS

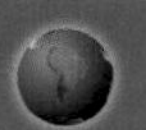

Pages	Title	Scale
124-125	**NORTH AMERICA**	1:70 000 000
126-127	**CANADA**	1:30 000 000
128-129	**CANADA** West	1:15 000 000
130-131	**CANADA** East	1:15 000 000
132-133	**UNITED STATES OF AMERICA**	1:25 000 000
134-135	**USA** West	1:11 000 000
136-137	**USA** North Central	1:11 000 000
138-139	**USA** South Central	1:11 000 000
140-141	**USA** Northeast	1:11 000 000
142-143	**USA** Southeast	1:11 000 000
144-145	**MEXICO**	1:15 000 000
146-147	**CARIBBEAN**	1:20 000 000
148-149	**SOUTH AMERICA**	1:70 000 000
150-151	**SOUTH AMERICA** North	1:25 000 000
152-153	**SOUTH AMERICA** South	1:25 000 000
154-155	**BRAZIL** Southeast	1:10 000 000
	OCEANS	
156-157	**PACIFIC OCEAN**	1:120 000 000
158	**ATLANTIC OCEAN**	1:120 000 000
159	**INDIAN OCEAN**	1:120 000 000
160	**ARCTIC OCEAN**	1:60 000 000
	INDEX	161-256

6

OCEANIA

Australia and the vast expanse of the Pacific Ocean dominate this satellite image of Oceania. The islands of Indonesia lie to the northwest of Australia and New Guinea to the north, with the islands of the Solomon Islands chain, Vanuatu and New Caledonia stretching southeast from New Guinea towards New Zealand. The Hawaiian Islands appear top right of the image.

Data from the 1 km AVHRR Global Land dataset project by ESA, CEOS, IGBP, NASA, NOAA, USGS, IONIA processed by ESA/ESRIN distributed by Eurimage S.p.A.

ASIA

This image shows the continent of Asia from the Mediterranean Sea and the distinctive shape of The Gulf in the west, to Japan in the east, and from snow-covered Siberia in the north to the tropical islands of Indonesia in the south. The shapes of the Caspian and Aral Seas appear in the northwest.

© Bartholomew Ltd

Data from the 1 km AVHRR Global Land dataset project by ESA, CEOS, IGBP, NASA, NOAA, USGS, IONIA processed by ESA/ESRIN distributed by Eurimage S.p.A.

EUROPE

The distinctive shapes of Scandinavia, the British Isles, Spain and Italy can be clearly seen on this image; Greenland lies to the northwest with Svalbard top centre. The huge land mass of the Russian Federation stretches from the Gulf of Bothnia and the Black Sea in the centre right of the image, northeast into Asia and beyond the horizon.

Data from the 1 km AVHRR Global Land dataset project by ESA, CEOS, IGBP, NASA, NOAA, USGS, IONIA processed by ESA/ESRIN distributed by Eurimage S.p.A.

AFRICA

This view of Africa looks north, with South America just appearing in the southwest, the island of Madagascar to the southeast and Arabia and Asia to the northeast.

Data from the 1 km AVHRR Global Land dataset project by ESA, CEOS, IGBP, NASA, NOAA, USGS, IONIA processed by ESA/ESRIN distributed by Eurimage S.p.A.

NORTH AMERICA

This image views North America from above the centre of the continent and includes most of the Arctic Ocean. The Aleutian Islands in the northwest stretch in an arc toward the Kamchatka Peninsula in eastern Asia, and western Europe and northwest Africa appear to the northeast. The islands of the Caribbean lie east and south of Florida in the bottom right of the image.

Data from the 1 km AVHRR Global Land dataset project by ESA, CEOS, IGBP, NASA, NOAA, USGS, IONIA processed by ESA/ESRIN distributed by Eurimage S.p.A.

South America

South and Central America appear in the centre of this image with the Pacific Ocean to the west and the Atlantic Ocean to the east, and Africa appearing on the northeast and southeast horizons. The Galapagos Islands lie off the coast of Ecuador and the Falkland Islands, South Georgia and the Antarctic Peninsula off the southern tip of the continent.

Data from the 1 km AVHRR Global Land dataset project by ESA, CEOS, IGBP, NASA, NOAA, USGS, IONIA processed by ESA/ESRIN distributed by Eurimage S.p.A.

ANTARCTICA

This image positions the Antarctic continent with the Greenwich meridian to the top centre. The distinctive shape of the Antarctic Peninsula lies to the top left and the prominent Ross Ice Shelf can be identified to the bottom of the image, below the Transantarctic Mountains range.

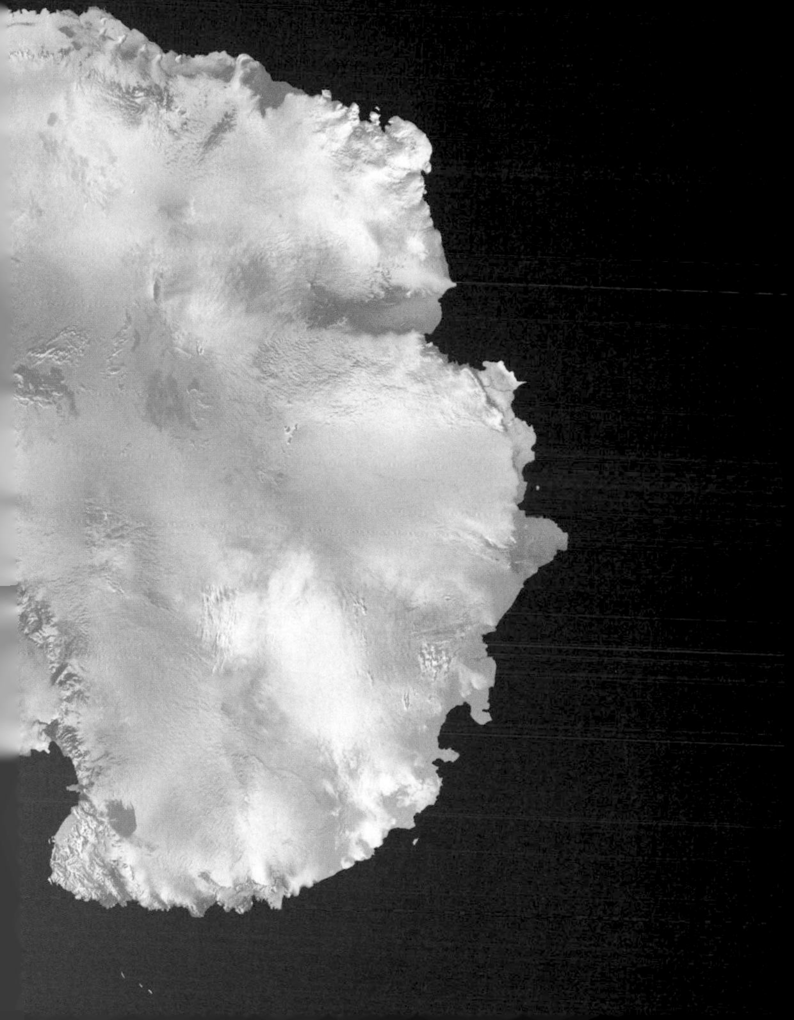

CLIMATE

MAJOR CLIMATIC REGIONS AND SUB-TYPES

Köppen classification system

Winkel Tripel Projection
scale 1:200 000 000

Polar

EF	Ice cap
ET	Tundra

Dry

BS	Steppe
BW	Desert

Tropical humid

Aw As	Savanna
Af Am	Rain forest

Cooler humid

Dc Dd	Subarctic
Db	Continental cool summer
Da	Continental warm summer

Warmer humid

Cb Cc	Temperate
Ca	Humid subtropical
Cs	Mediterranean

A Rainy climate with no winter: coolest month above 18°C (64.4°F).

B Dry climates; limits are defined by formulae based on rainfall effectiveness:
- **BS** Steppe or semi-arid climate.
- **BW** Desert or arid climate.

*C Rainy climates with mild winters: coolest month above 0°C (32°F), but below 18°C (64.4°F); warmest month above 10°C (50°F).

*D Rainy climates with severe winters: coldest month below 0°C (32°F) warmest month above 10°C (50°F).

E Polar climates with no warm season: warmest month below 10°C (50°F).
- **ET** Tundra climate: warmest month below 10°C (50°F) but above 0°C (32°F).
- **EF** Perpetual frost: all months below 0°C (32°F).

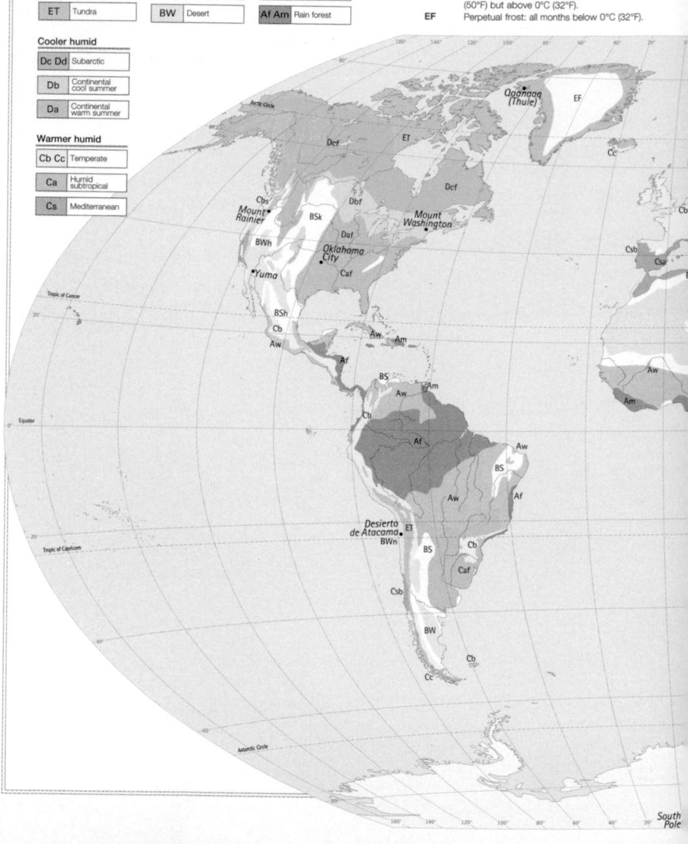

a	Warmest month above 22°C (71.6°F).
b	Warmest month below 22°C (71.6°F).
c	Less than four months over 10°C (50°F).
d	As 'c', but with severe cold: coldest month below -38°C (-36.4°F).
f	Constantly moist rainfall throughout the year.
*h	Warmer dry: all months above 0°C (32°F).
*k	Cooler dry: at least one month below 0°C (32°F).
m	Monsoon rain: short dry season, compensated by heavy rains during rest of the year.
n	Frequent fog.
s	Dry season in summer.
w	Dry season in winter.
*	Modification of Köppen definition.

World weather extremes

Highest shade temperature	57.8°C/136°F Al 'Azīzīyah, Libya (13th September 1922)
Hottest place – Annual mean	34.4°C/93.9°F Dalol, Ethiopia
Driest place – Annual mean	0.1 mm/0.004 inches Desierto de Atacama, Chile
Most sunshine – Annual mean	90% Yuma, Arizona, USA (over 4 000 hours)
Least sunshine	Nil for 182 days each year, South Pole
Lowest screen temperature	-89.2°C/-128.6°F Vostok Station, Antarctica (21st July 1983)
Coldest place – Annual mean	-56.6°C/-69.9°F Plateau Station, Antarctica
Wettest place – Annual mean	11 873 mm/467.4 inches Meghalaya, India
Highest surface wind speed	
– High altitude	372 km per hour/231 miles per hour Mount Washington, New Hampshire, USA, (12th April 1934)
– Low altitude	333 km per hour/207 miles per hour Qaanaaq (Thule), Greenland (8th March 1972)
– Tornado	512 km per hour/318 miles per hour Oklahoma City, Oklahoma, USA (3rd May 1999)
Greatest snowfall	31 102 mm/1 224.5 inches Mount Rainier, Washington, USA (19th February 1971 – 18th February 1972)

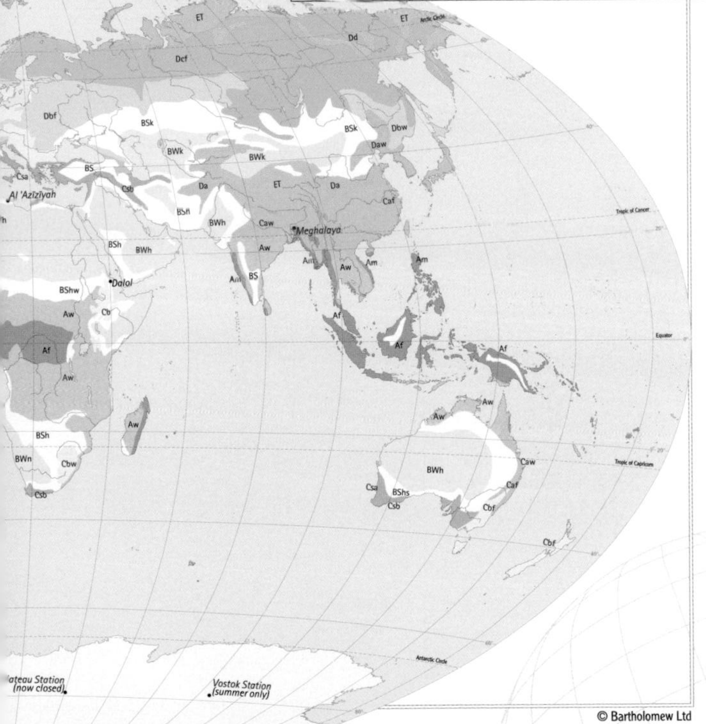

LAND COVER

WORLD LAND COVER

Goode Interrupted Homolosine Projection
scale: approximately 1:200 000 000

1. Evergreen needleleaf forest
2. Evergreen broadleaf forest
3. Deciduous needleleaf forest
4. Deciduous broadleaf forest
5. Mixed forest
6. Closed shrublands
7. Open shrublands

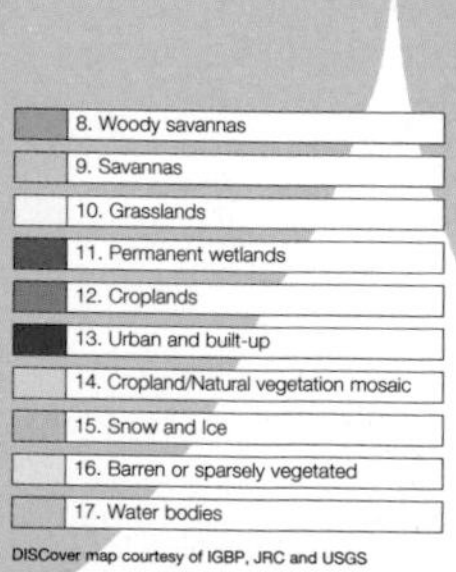

DISCover map courtesy of IGBP, JRC and USGS

LAND COVER GRAPHS - CLASSIFICATION

Class description	Map classes (IGBP/DISCover)
Forest/Woodland	1 Evergreen needleleaf forest 2 Evergreen broadleaf forest 3 Deciduous needleleaf forest 4 Deciduous broadleaf forest 5 Mixed forest
Shrubland	6 Closed shrublands 7 Open shrublands
Grass/Savanna	8 Woody savannas 9 Savannas 10 Grasslands
Wetland	11 Permanent wetlands
Crops/Mosaic	12 Croplands 14 Cropland/Natural vegetation mosaic
Urban	13 Urban and built-up
Snow/Ice	15 Snow and Ice
Barren	16 Barren or sparsely vegetated

Continental land cover composition

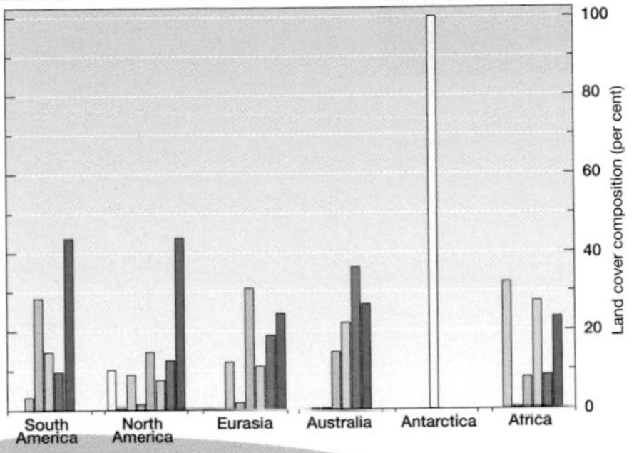

Land cover composition (per cent)

100
80
60
40
20
0

South America
North America
Eurasia
Australia
Antarctica
Africa

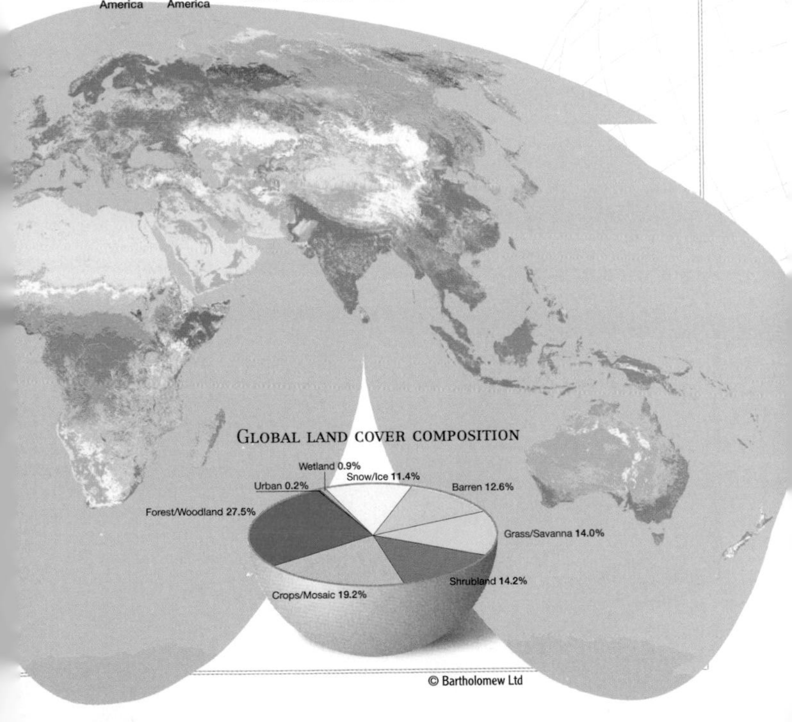

Global land cover composition

Wetland 0.9%
Snow/Ice 11.4%
Urban 0.2%
Barren 12.6%
Forest/Woodland 27.5%
Grass/Savanna 14.0%
Shrubland 14.2%
Crops/Mosaic 19.2%

POPULATION

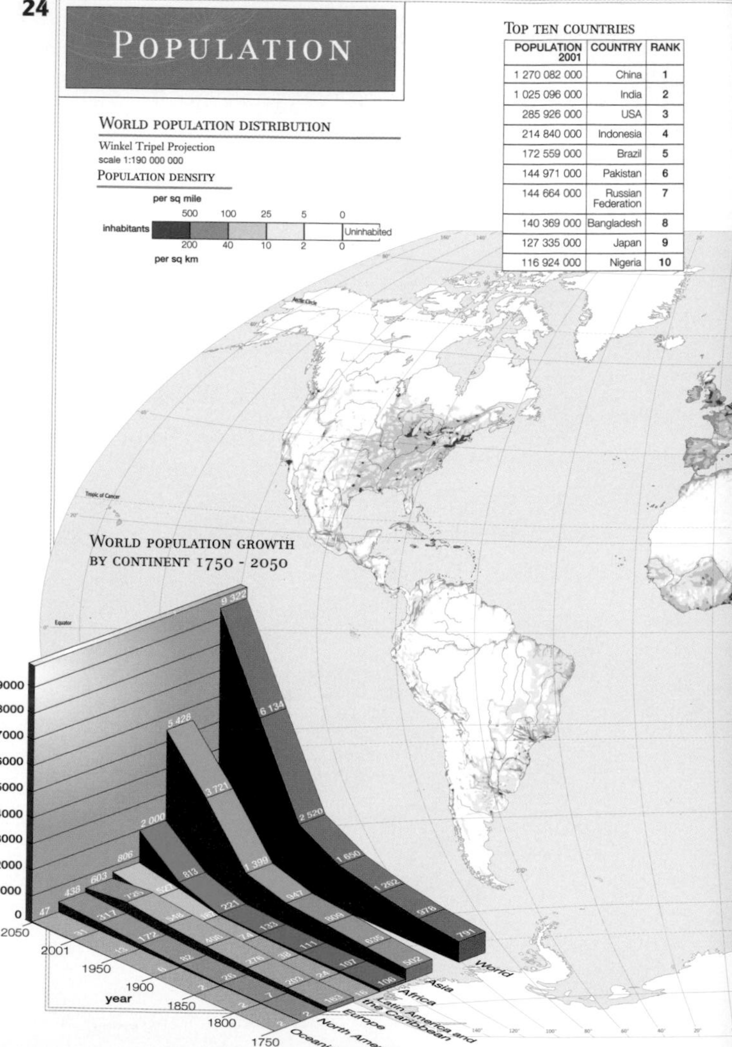

TOP TEN COUNTRIES

POPULATION 2001	COUNTRY	RANK
1 270 082 000	China	1
1 025 096 000	India	2
285 926 000	USA	3
214 840 000	Indonesia	4
172 559 000	Brazil	5
144 971 000	Pakistan	6
144 664 000	Russian Federation	7
140 369 000	Bangladesh	8
127 335 000	Japan	9
116 924 000	Nigeria	10

KEY POPULATION STATISTICS FOR MAJOR REGIONS

	Population (millions) 2001	Growth (per cent)	Infant mortality rate	Total fertility rate	Life expectancy
World	6 134	1.23	57	2.82	65.0
More developed regions[1]	1 194	0.16	9	1.57	74.9
Less developed regions[2]	4 940	1.48	63	3.10	63.0
Africa	813	2.33	87	5.27	51.4
Asia	3 721	1.26	57	2.70	65.8
Europe[3]	726	-0.18	12	1.41	73.2
Latin America and the Caribbean[4]	527	1.42	36	2.69	69.3
North America	317	0.88	7	2.00	76.7
Oceania	31	1.24	24	2.41	73.5

Except for population (2001,and growth (2000-2005), the data are annual averages projected for the period 1995-2000.

1. Europe, North America, Australia, New Zealand and Japan.
2. Africa, Asia (excluding Japan), Latin America and the Caribbean, and Oceania (excluding Australia and New Zealand).
3. Includes Russian Federation.
4. South America, Central America (including Mexico) and all Caribbean Islands.

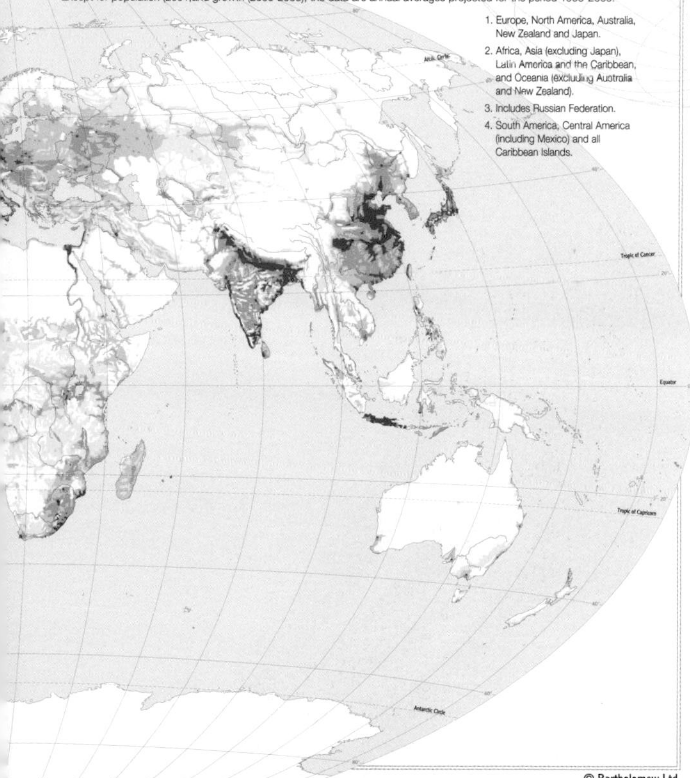

URBANIZATION

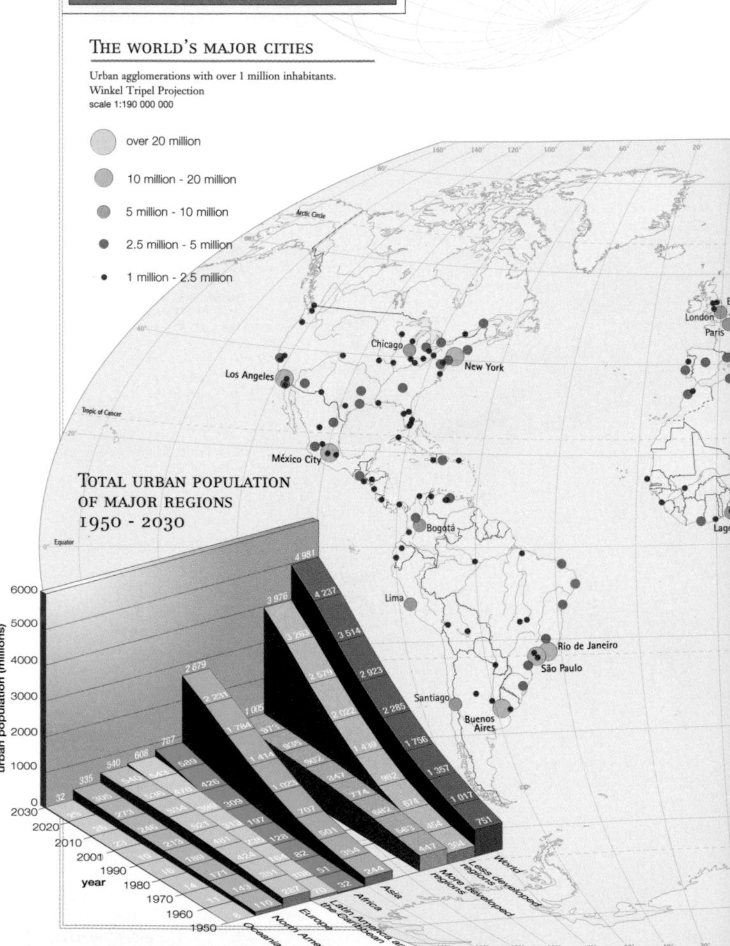

LEVEL OF URBANIZATION BY MAJOR REGION 1970-2030

Urban population as a percentage of total population

	1970	2001	2030
World	37	48	60
More developed regions[1]	68	76	83
Less developed regions[2]	25	41	56
Africa	23	38	53
Asia	23	38	54
Europe[3]	65	74	81
Latin America and the Caribbean[4]	58	76	84
North America	74	78	85
Oceania	71	74	71

1. Europe, North America, Australia, New Zealand and Japan.
2. Africa, Asia (excluding Japan), Latin America and the Caribbean, and Oceania (excluding Australia and New Zealand).
3. Includes Russian Federation.
4. South America, Central America (including Mexico) and all Caribbean Islands.

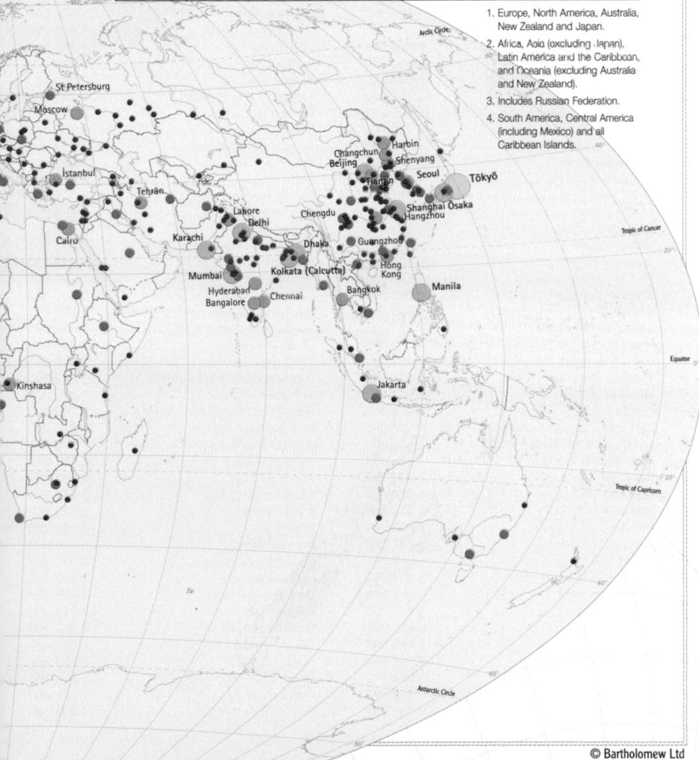

CITIES

THE WORLD'S LARGEST CITIES 2001

Figures are for the urban agglomeration, defined as the population contained within the contours of a contiguous territory inhabited at urban levels without regard to administrative boundaries. They incorporate the population within a city plus the suburban fringe lying outside of, but adjacent to, the city boundaries.

Tōkyō Japan	26 444 000
Mexico City Mexico	18 066 000
São Paulo Brazil	17 962 000
New York USA	16 732 000
Mumbai (Bombay) India	16 086 000
Los Angeles USA	13 213 000
Kolkata (Calcutta) India	13 058 000
Shanghai China	12 887 000
Dhaka Bangladesh	12 519 000
Delhi India	12 441 000
Buenos Aires Argentina	12 024 000
Jakarta Indonesia	11 018 000
Ōsaka Japan	11 013 000
Beijing China	10 839 000
Rio de Janeiro Brazil	10 652 000
Karachi Pakistan	10 032 000
Manila Philippines	9 950 000
Seoul South Korea	9 888 000
Paris France	9 630 000
Cairo Egypt	9 462 000
Tianjin China	9 156 000
İstanbul Turkey	8 953 000
Lagos Nigeria	8 665 000
Moscow Russian Federation	8 367 000
London United Kingdom	7 640 000
Lima Peru	7 443 000
Bangkok Thailand	7 372 000
Chicago USA	6 989 000
Tehrān Iran	6 979 000
Hong Kong China	6 860 000
Bogotá Colombia	6 771 000
Essen Germany	6 531 000
Chennai (Madras) India	6 353 000
Bangalore India	5 567 000
Santiago Chile	5 467 000
Lahore Pakistan	5 452 000
Hyderabad India	5 445 000
Wuhan China	5 169 000
Kinshasa Dem. Rep. Congo	5 054 000
Chongqinq China	4 900 000
Baghdād Iraq	4 865 000
Shenyang China	4 828 000
Toronto Canada	4 752 000
St Petersburg Russian Federation	4 635 000
Ho Chi Minh City Vietnam	4 619 000
Riyadh Saudi Arabia	4 549 000
Ahmadabad India	4 427 000
Philadelphia USA	4 427 000
Rangoon (Yangôn) Myanmar	4 393 000
Milan Itlay	4 251 000
Belo Horizonte Brazil	4 224 000
San Francisco USA	4 077 000
Singapore Singapore	4 018 000
Madrid Spain	3 976 000
Washington USA	3 952 000
Dallas USA	3 937 000
Sydney Australia	3 907 000
Guangzhou China	3 893 000
Lisbon Portugal	3 861 000
Pusan South Korea	3 830 000
Detroit USA	3 809 000
Abidjan Côte d'Ivoire	3 790 000
Porto Alegre Brazil	3 757 000
Hanoi Vietnam	3 751 000
Guadalajara Mexico	3 697 000
Frankfurt Germany	3 681 000
Pune India	3 655 000
Chittagong Bangladesh	3 651 000
Alexandria Egypt	3 506 000
Katowice Poland	3 494 000
Montréal Canada	3 480 000
Bandung Indonesia	3 409 000
Houston USA	3 386 000
Casablanca Morocco	3 357 000
Recife Brazil	3 346 000
Berlin Germany	3 319 000
Chengdu China	3 294 000
Monterrey Mexico	3 267 000
Guatemala City Guatemala	3 242 000
Salvador Brazil	3 238 000
Düsseldorf Germany	3 233 000
Melbourne Australia	3 232 000
Jeddah Saudi Arabia	3 192 000
Nagoya Japan	3 157 000
Ankara Turkey	3 155 000
Caracas Venezuela	3 153 000
P'yŏngyang North Korea	3 124 000
Xi'an China	3 123 000
Athens Greece	3 116 000
Changchun China	3 093 000
Fortaleza Brazil	3 066 000
Cologne Germany	3 050 000
Naples Italy	3 012 000
San Diego USA	3 002 000
Johannesburg South Africa	2 950 000
Boston USA	2 934 000
Cape Town South Africa	2 930 000
Harbin China	2 928 000
Inch'ŏn South Korea	2 884 000

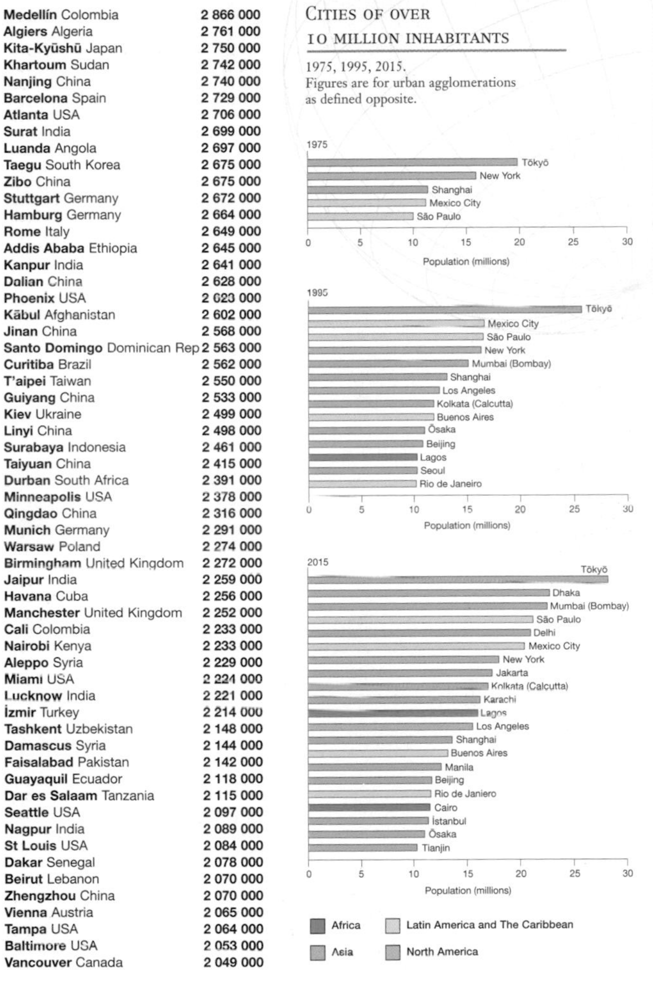

City	Population
Medellín Colombia	2 866 000
Algiers Algeria	2 761 000
Kita-Kyūshū Japan	2 750 000
Khartoum Sudan	2 742 000
Nanjing China	2 740 000
Barcelona Spain	2 729 000
Atlanta USA	2 706 000
Surat India	2 699 000
Luanda Angola	2 697 000
Taegu South Korea	2 675 000
Zibo China	2 675 000
Stuttgart Germany	2 672 000
Hamburg Germany	2 664 000
Rome Italy	2 649 000
Addis Ababa Ethiopia	2 645 000
Kanpur India	2 641 000
Dalian China	2 628 000
Phoenix USA	2 623 000
Kābul Afghanistan	2 602 000
Jinan China	2 568 000
Santo Domingo Dominican Rep	2 563 000
Curitiba Brazil	2 562 000
T'aipei Taiwan	2 550 000
Guiyang China	2 533 000
Kiev Ukraine	2 499 000
Linyi China	2 498 000
Surabaya Indonesia	2 461 000
Taiyuan China	2 415 000
Durban South Africa	2 391 000
Minneapolis USA	2 378 000
Qingdao China	2 316 000
Munich Germany	2 291 000
Warsaw Poland	2 274 000
Birmingham United Kingdom	2 272 000
Jaipur India	2 259 000
Havana Cuba	2 256 000
Manchester United Kingdom	2 252 000
Cali Colombia	2 233 000
Nairobi Kenya	2 233 000
Aleppo Syria	2 229 000
Miami USA	2 224 000
Lucknow India	2 221 000
İzmir Turkey	2 214 000
Tashkent Uzbekistan	2 148 000
Damascus Syria	2 144 000
Faisalabad Pakistan	2 142 000
Guayaquil Ecuador	2 118 000
Dar es Salaam Tanzania	2 115 000
Seattle USA	2 097 000
Nagpur India	2 089 000
St Louis USA	2 084 000
Dakar Senegal	2 078 000
Beirut Lebanon	2 070 000
Zhengzhou China	2 070 000
Vienna Austria	2 065 000
Tampa USA	2 064 000
Baltimore USA	2 053 000
Vancouver Canada	2 049 000

CITIES OF OVER 10 MILLION INHABITANTS

1975, 1995, 2015.
Figures are for urban agglomerations as defined opposite.

States and Territories of the World

State/Territory Name	Population	Capital	Area sq km	Area sq miles
A				
AFGHANISTAN	22 475 000	Kābul	652 225	**251 825**
ALBANIA	3 145 000	Tirana (Tiranë)	28 748	**11 100**
ALGERIA	30 841 000	Algiers (Alger)	2 381 741	**919 595**
American Samoa	70 000	Fagatogo	197	**76**
ANDORRA	90 000	Andorra la Vella	465	**180**
ANGOLA	13 527 000	Luanda	1 246 700	**481 354**
Anguilla (U.K.)	12 000	The Valley	155	**60**
ANTIGUA AND BARBUDA	65 000	St John's	442	**171**
ARGENTINA	37 488 000	Buenos Aires	2 766 889	**1 068 302**
ARMENIA	3 788 000	Yerevan (Erevan)	29 800	**11 506**
Aruba (Netherlands)	104 000	Oranjestad	193	**75**
AUSTRALIA	19 338 000	Canberra	7 682 395	**2 966 189**
AUSTRIA	8 075 000	Vienna (Wien)	83 855	**32 377**
AZERBAIJAN	8 096 000	Baku (Bakı)	86 600	**33 436**
B				
THE BAHAMAS	308 000	Nassau	13 939	**5 382**
BAHRAIN	652 000	Manama (Al Manāmah)	691	**267**
BANGLADESH	140 369 000	Dhaka (Dacca)	143 998	**55 598**
BARBADOS	268 000	Bridgetown	430	**166**
BELARUS	10 147 000	Minsk	207 600	**80 155**
BELGIUM	10 264 000	Brussels (Bruxelles)	30 520	**11 784**
BELIZE	231 000	Belmopan	22 965	**8 867**
BENIN	6 446 000	Porto-Novo	112 620	**43 483**
Bermuda (U.K.)	63 000	Hamilton	54	**21**
BHUTAN	2 141 000	Thimphu	46 620	**18 000**
BOLIVIA	8 516 000	La Paz/Sucre	1 098 581	**424 164**
BOSNIA-HERZEGOVINA	4 067 000	Sarajevo	51 130	**19 741**
BOTSWANA	1 554 000	Gaborone	581 370	**224 468**
BRAZIL	172 559 000	Brasília	8 547 379	**3 300 161**
BRUNEI	335 000	Bandar Seri Begawan	5 765	**2 226**
BULGARIA	7 867 000	Sofia (Sofiya)	110 994	**42 855**
BURKINA	11 856 000	Ouagadougou	274 200	**105 869**
BURUNDI	6 502 000	Bujumbura	27 835	**10 747**
C				
CAMBODIA	13 441 000	Phnum Pénh (Phnom Penh)	181 000	**69 884**
CAMEROON	15 203 000	Yaoundé	475 442	**183 569**
CANADA	31 015 000	Ottawa	9 970 610	**3 849 674**
CAPE VERDE	437 000	Praia	4 033	**1 557**

State/Territory Name	Population	Capital	Area sq km	Area sq miles
Cayman Islands (U.K.)	40 000	George Town	259	**100**
CENTRAL AFRICAN REPUBLIC	3 782 000	Bangui	622 436	**240 324**
CHAD	8 135 000	Ndjamena	1 284 000	**495 755**
CHILE	15 402 000	Santiago	756 945	**292 258**
CHINA	1 270 082 000	Beijing (Peking)	9 584 492	**3 700 593**
Christmas Island (Australia)	2 135	The Settlement	135	**52**
Cocos Islands (Australia)	637	Home Island	14	**5**
COLOMBIA	42 803 000	Bogotá	1 141 748	**440 831**
COMOROS	727 000	Moroni	1 862	**719**
CONGO	3 110 000	Brazzaville	342 000	**132 047**
CONGO, DEMOCRATIC REPUBLIC OF	52 522 000	Kinshasa	2 345 410	**905 568**
Cook Islands (N.Z.)	20 000	Avarua	293	**113**
COSTA RICA	4 112 000	San José	51 100	**19 730**
CÔTE D'IVOIRE	16 349 000	Yamoussoukro	322 463	**124 504**
CROATIA	4 655 000	Zagreb	56 538	**21 829**
CUBA	11 237 000	Havana (La Habana)	110 860	**42 803**
CYPRUS	790 000	Nicosia (Lefkosia)	9 251	**3 572**
CZECH REPUBLIC	10 260 000	Prague (Praha)	78 864	**30 450**

D

State/Territory Name	Population	Capital	Area sq km	Area sq miles
DENMARK	5 333 000	Copenhagen (København)	43 075	**16 631**
DJIBOUTI	644 000	Djibouti	23 200	**8 958**
DOMINICA	71 000	Roseau	750	**290**
DOMINICAN REPUBLIC	8 507 000	Santo Domingo	48 442	**18 704**

E

State/Territory Name	Population	Capital	Area sq km	Area sq miles
EAST TIMOR	750 000	Dili	14 874	**5 743**
ECUADOR	12 880 000	Quito	272 045	**105 037**
EGYPT	69 080 000	Cairo (Al Qāhirah)	1 000 250	**386 199**
EL SALVADOR	6 400 000	San Salvador	21 041	**8 124**
EQUATORIAL GUINEA	470 000	Malabo	28 051	**10 831**
ERITREA	3 816 000	Asmara	117 400	**45 328**
ESTONIA	1 377 000	Tallinn	45 200	**17 452**
ETHIOPIA	64 459 000	Addis Ababa (Ādīs Ābeba)	1 133 880	**437 794**

F

State/Territory Name	Population	Capital	Area sq km	Area sq miles
Falkland Islands (U.K.)	2 000	Stanley	12 170	**4 699**
Faroe Islands (Denmark)	47 000	Tórshavn (Thorshavn)	1 399	**540**
FIJI	823 000	Suva	18 330	**7 077**
FINLAND	5 178 000	Helsinki (Helsingfors)	338 145	**130 559**
FRANCE	59 453 000	Paris	543 965	**210 026**
French Guiana	170 000	Cayenne	90 000	**34 749**
French Polynesia	237 000	Papeete	3 265	**1 261**

G

State/Territory Name	Population	Capital	Area sq km	Area sq miles
GABON	1 262 000	Libreville	267 667	**103 347**
THE GAMBIA	1 337 000	Banjul	11 295	**4 361**
GAZA (including occupied West Bank)	3 311 000	Gaza	6 223	**2 403**
GEORGIA	5 239 000	T'bilisi	69 700	**26 911**
GERMANY	82 007 000	Berlin	357 028	**137 849**

State/Territory Name	Population	Capital	Area sq km	Area sq miles
GHANA	19 734 000	Accra	238 537	**92 100**
Gibraltar (U.K.)	27 000	Gibraltar	7	**3**
GREECE	10 623 000	Athens (Athina)	131 957	**50 949**
Greenland (Denmark)	56 000	Nuuk (Godthåb)	2 175 600	**840 004**
GRENADA	94 000	St George's	378	**146**
Guadeloupe (France)	431 000	Basse-Terre	1 780	**687**
Guam (U.S.A.)	158 000	Hagåtña	541	**209**
GUATEMALA	11 687 000	Guatemala City	108 890	**42 043**
Guernsey (U.K.)	64 555	St Peter Port	78	**30**
GUINEA	8 274 000	Conakry	245 857	**94 926**
GUINEA-BISSAU	1 227 000	Bissau	36 125	**13 948**
GUYANA	763 000	Georgetown	214 969	**83 000**

H

HAITI	8 270 000	Port-au-Prince	27 750	**10 714**
HONDURAS	6 575 000	Tegucigalpa	112 088	**43 277**
HUNGARY	9 917 000	Budapest	93 030	**35 919**

I

ICELAND	281 000	Reykjavík	102 820	**39 699**
INDIA	1 025 096 000	New Delhi	3 065 027	**1 183 414**
INDONESIA	214 840 000	Jakarta	1 919 445	**741 102**
IRAN	71 369 000	Tehrān	1 648 000	**636 296**
IRAQ	23 584 000	Baghdād	438 317	**169 235**
IRELAND, REPUBLIC OF	3 841 000	Dublin (Baile Átha Cliath)	70 282	**27 136**
Isle of Man (U.K.)	76 000	Douglas	572	**221**
ISRAEL	6 172 000	Jerusalem (Yerushalayim) (El Quds)	20 770	**8 019**
ITALY	57 503 000	Rome (Roma)	301 245	**116 311**

J

JAMAICA	2 598 000	Kingston	10 991	**4 244**
Jammu and Kashmir	13 000 000	Srinagar	222 236	**85 806**
JAPAN	127 335 000	Tōkyō	377 727	**145 841**
Jersey (U.K.)	89 136	St Helier	116	**45**
JORDAN	5 051 000	'Ammān	89 206	**34 443**

K

KAZAKHSTAN	16 095 000	Astana (Akmola)	2 717 300	**1 049 155**
KENYA	31 293 000	Nairobi	582 646	**224 961**
KIRIBATI	84 000	Bairiki	717	**277**
KUWAIT	1 971 000	Kuwait (Al Kuwayt)	17 818	**6 880**
KYRGYZSTAN	4 986 000	Bishkek (Frunze)	198 500	**76 641**

L

LAOS	5 403 000	Vientiane (Viangchan)	236 800	**91 429**
LATVIA	2 406 000	Rīga	63 700	**24 595**
LEBANON	3 556 000	Beirut (Beyrouth)	10 452	**4 036**
LESOTHO	2 057 000	Maseru	30 355	**11 720**

State/Territory Name	Population	Capital	Area sq km	Area sq miles
LIBERIA	3 108 000	Monrovia	111 369	**43 000**
LIBYA	5 408 000	Tripoli (Ţarābulus)	1 759 540	**679 362**
LIECHTENSTEIN	33 000	Vaduz	160	**62**
LITHUANIA	3 689 000	Vilnius	65 200	**25 174**
LUXEMBOURG	442 000	Luxembourg	2 586	**998**
M				
MACEDONIA (Former Yugoslav Republic of Macedonia - F.Y.R.O.M.)	2 044 000	Skopje	25 713	**9 928**
MADAGASCAR	16 437 000	Antananarivo	587 041	**226 658**
MALAWI	11 572 000	Lilongwe	118 484	**45 747**
MALAYSIA	22 633 000	Kuala Lumpur	332 965	**128 559**
MALDIVES	300 000	Male	298	**115**
MALI	11 677 000	Bamako	1 240 140	**478 821**
MALTA	392 000	Valletta	316	**122**
MARSHALL ISLANDS	52 000	Delap-Uliga-Djarrit	181	**70**
Martinique (France)	386 000	Fort-de-France	1 079	**417**
MAURITANIA	2 747 000	Nouakchott	1 030 700	**397 955**
MAURITIUS	1 171 000	Port Louis	2 040	**788**
Mayotte (France)	144 944	Dzaoudzi	373	**144**
MEXICO	100 368 000	Mexico City (México)	1 972 545	**761 604**
MICRONESIA, FEDERATED STATES OF	126 000	Palikir	701	**271**
MOLDOVA	4 285 000	Chişinău (Kishinev)	33 700	**13 012**
MONACO	34 000	Monaco-Ville	2	**1**
MONGOLIA	2 559 000	Ulaanbaatar (Ulan Bator)	1 565 000	**604 250**
Montserrat (U.K.)	3 000	Plymouth	100	**39**
MOROCCO	30 430 000	Rabat	446 550	**172 414**
MOZAMBIQUE	18 644 000	Maputo	799 380	**308 642**
MYANMAR (Burma)	48 364 000	Rangoon (Yangôn)	676 577	**261 228**
N				
NAMIBIA	1 788 000	Windhoek	824 292	**318 261**
NAURU	13 000	Yaren	21	**8**
NEPAL	23 593 000	Kathmandu	147 181	**56 827**
NETHERLANDS	15 930 000	Amsterdam/The Hague ('s-Gravenhage)	41 526	**16 033**
Netherlands Antilles	217 000	Willemstad	800	**309**
New Caledonia (France)	220 000	Nouméa	19 058	**7 358**
NEW ZEALAND	3 808 000	Wellington	270 534	**104 454**
NICARAGUA	5 208 000	Managua	130 000	**50 193**
NIGER	11 227 000	Niamey	1 267 000	**489 191**
NIGERIA	116 929 000	Abuja	923 768	**356 669**
Niue (N.Z.)	2 000	Alofi	258	**100**
Norfolk Island (Australia)	2 000	Kingston	35	**14**
Northern Mariana Islands (U.S.A.)	76 000	Saipan	477	**184**
NORTH KOREA	22 428 000	P'yŏngyang	120 538	**46 540**
NORWAY	4 488 000	Oslo	323 878	**125 050**
O				
OMAN	2 622 000	Muscat (Masqaţ)	309 500	**119 499**

State/Territory Name	Population	Capital	Area sq km	Area sq miles
P				
PAKISTAN	144 971 000	Islamabad	803 940	**310 403**
PALAU	20 000	Koror	497	**192**
PANAMA	2 899 000	Panama City (Panamá)	77 082	**29 762**
PAPUA NEW GUINEA	4 920 000	Port Moresby	462 840	**178 704**
PARAGUAY	5 636 000	Asunción	406 752	**157 048**
PERU	26 093 000	Lima	1 285 216	**496 225**
PHILIPPINES	77 131 000	Manila	300 000	**115 831**
Pitcairn Islands (U.K.)	68	Adamstown	45	**17**
POLAND	38 577 000	Warsaw (Warszawa)	312 683	**120 728**
PORTUGAL	10 033 000	Lisbon (Lisboa)	88 940	**34 340**
Puerto Rico (U.S.A.)	3 952 000	San Juan	9 104	**3 515**
Q				
QATAR	575 000	Doha (Ad Dawḩah)	11 437	**4 416**
R				
Réunion (France)	732 000	St-Denis	2 551	**985**
ROMANIA	22 388 000	Bucharest (București)	237 500	**91 699**
RUSSIAN FEDERATION	144 664 000	Moscow (Moskva)	17 075 400	**6 592 849**
RWANDA	7 949 000	Kigali	26 338	**10 169**
S				
St Helena and Dependencies (U.K.)	6 000	Jamestown	121	**47**
ST KITTS AND NEVIS	38 000	Basseterre	261	**101**
ST LUCIA	149 000	Castries	616	**238**
St Pierre and Miquelon (France)	7 000	St-Pierre	242	**93**
ST VINCENT AND THE GRENADINES	114 000	Kingstown	389	**150**
SAMOA	159 000	Apia	2 831	**1 093**
SAN MARINO	27 000	San Marino	61	**24**
SÃO TOMÉ AND PRÍNCIPE	140 000	São Tomé	964	**372**
SAUDI ARABIA	21 028 000	Riyadh (Ar Riyāḑ)	2 200 000	**849 425**
SENEGAL	9 662 000	Dakar	196 720	**75 954**
SERBIA AND MONTENEGRO	10 538 000	Belgrade (Beograd)	102 173	**39 449**
SEYCHELLES	81 000	Victoria	455	**176**
SIERRA LEONE	4 587 000	Freetown	71 740	**27 699**
SINGAPORE	4 108 000	Singapore	639	**247**
SLOVAKIA	5 403 000	Bratislava	49 035	**18 933**
SLOVENIA	1 985 000	Ljubljana	20 251	**7 819**
SOLOMON ISLANDS	463 000	Honiara	28 370	**10 954**
SOMALIA	9 157 000	Muqdisho (Mogadishu)	637 657	**246 201**
SOUTH AFRICA, REPUBLIC OF	43 792 000	Pretoria/Cape Town	1 219 090	**470 693**
SOUTH KOREA	47 069 000	Seoul (Sŏul)	99 274	**38 330**
SPAIN	39 921 000	Madrid	504 782	**194 897**
SRI LANKA	19 104 000	Sri Jayewardenepura Kotte	65 610	**25 332**
SUDAN	31 809 000	Khartoum	2 505 813	**967 500**
SURINAME	419 000	Paramaribo	163 820	**63 251**
SWAZILAND	938 000	Mbabane	17 364	**6 704**
SWEDEN	8 833 000	Stockholm	449 964	**173 732**

State/Territory Name	Population	Capital	Area sq km	Area sq miles
SWITZERLAND	7 170 000	Bern (Berne)	41 293	**15 943**
SYRIA	16 610 000	Damascus (Dimashq)	185 180	**71 498**

T

State/Territory Name	Population	Capital	Area sq km	Area sq miles
TAIWAN	22 300 000	T'aipei	36 179	**13 969**
TAJIKISTAN	6 135 000	Dushanbe	143 100	**55 251**
TANZANIA	35 965 000	Dodoma	945 087	**364 900**
THAILAND	63 584 000	Bangkok (Krung Thep)	513 115	**198 115**
TOGO	4 657 000	Lomé	56 785	**21 925**
Tokelau (N.Z.)	1 000	none	10	**4**
TONGA	99 000	Nuku'alofa	748	**289**
TRINIDAD AND TOBAGO	1 300 000	Port of Spain	5 130	**1 981**
TUNISIA	9 562 000	Tunis	164 150	**63 379**
TURKEY	67 632 000	Ankara	779 452	**300 948**
TURKMENISTAN	4 835 000	Ashgabat (Ashkhabad)	488 100	**188 456**
Turks and Caicos Islands (U.K.)	17 000	Grand Turk (Cockburn Town)	430	**166**
TUVALU	10 000	Vaiaku	25	**10**

U

State/Territory Name	Population	Capital	Area sq km	Area sq miles
UGANDA	24 023 000	Kampala	241 038	**93 065**
UKRAINE	49 112 000	Kiev (Kyiv)	603 700	**233 090**
UNITED ARAB EMIRATES	2 654 000	Abu Dhabi (Abū Ẕabī)	83 600	**32 278**
UNITED KINGDOM	59 542 000	London	244 082	**94 241**
UNITED STATES OF AMERICA	285 926 000	Washington	9 809 378	**3 787 422**
URUGUAY	3 361 000	Montevideo	176 215	**68 037**
UZBEKISTAN	25 257 000	Tashkent	447 400	**172 742**

V

State/Territory Name	Population	Capital	Area sq km	Area sq miles
VANUATU	202 000	Port Vila	12 190	**4 707**
VATICAN CITY	480	Vatican City	0.5	**0.2**
VENEZUELA	24 632 000	Caracas	912 050	**352 144**
VIETNAM	79 175 000	Hanoi (Ha Nôi)	329 565	**127 246**
Virgin Islands (U.K.)	24 000	Road Town	153	**59**
Virgin Islands (U.S.A.)	122 000	Charlotte Amalie	352	**136**

W

State/Territory Name	Population	Capital	Area sq km	Area sq miles
Wallis and Futuna Islands (France)	15 000	Matā'utu	274	**106**
Western Sahara	260 000	Laâyoune	266 000	**102 703**

Y

State/Territory Name	Population	Capital	Area sq km	Area sq miles
YEMEN	19 114 000	Şan'ā'	527 968	**203 850**

Z

State/Territory Name	Population	Capital	Area sq km	Area sq miles
ZAMBIA	10 649 000	Lusaka	752 614	**290 586**
ZIMBABWE	12 852 000	Harare	390 759	**150 873**

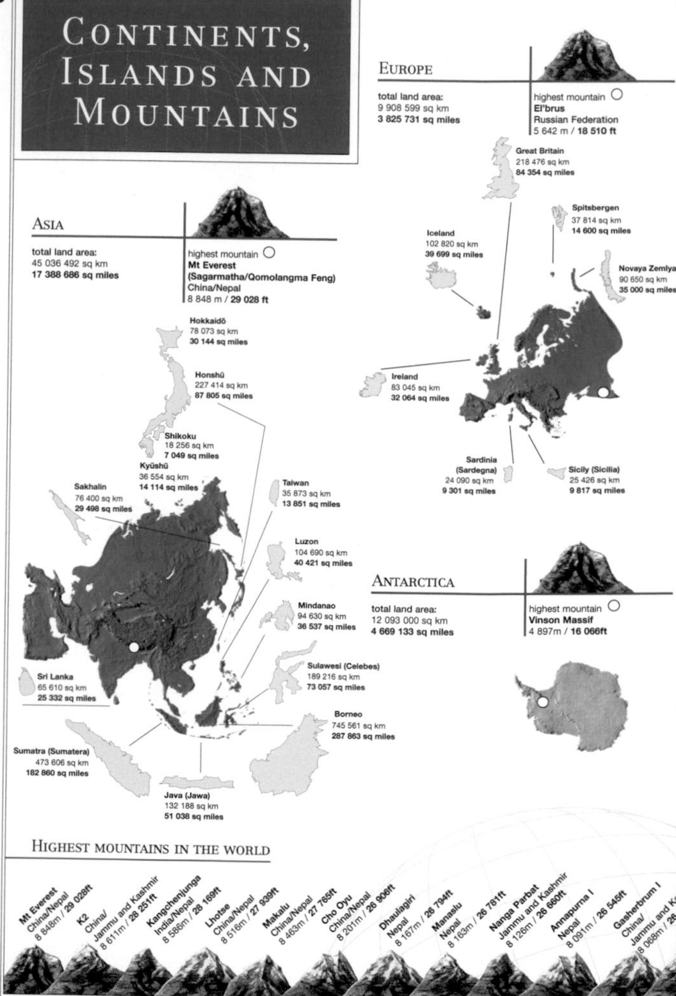
CONTINENTS, ISLANDS AND MOUNTAINS
EUROPE
total land area:
9 908 599 sq km
3 825 731 sq miles
highest mountain
El'brus
Russian Federation
5 642 m / 18 510 ft
Great Britain
218 476 sq km
84 354 sq miles
Spitsbergen
37 814 sq km
14 600 sq miles
Iceland
102 820 sq km
39 699 sq miles
Novaya Zemlya
90 650 sq km
35 000 sq miles
Ireland
83 045 sq km
32 064 sq miles
Sardinia
(Sardegna)
24 090 sq km
9 301 sq miles
Sicily (Sicilia)
25 426 sq km
9 817 sq miles
ASIA
total land area:
45 036 492 sq km
17 388 686 sq miles
highest mountain
Mt Everest
(Sagarmatha/Qomolangma Feng)
China/Nepal
8 848 m / 29 028 ft
Hokkaidō
78 073 sq km
30 144 sq miles
Honshū
227 414 sq km
87 805 sq miles
Shikoku
18 256 sq km
7 049 sq miles
Kyūshū
36 554 sq km
14 114 sq miles
Sakhalin
76 400 sq km
29 498 sq miles
Taiwan
35 873 sq km
13 851 sq miles
Luzon
104 690 sq km
40 421 sq miles
Mindanao
94 630 sq km
36 537 sq miles
Sulawesi (Celebes)
189 216 sq km
73 057 sq miles
Sri Lanka
65 610 sq km
25 332 sq miles
Borneo
745 561 sq km
287 863 sq miles
Sumatra (Sumatera)
473 606 sq km
182 860 sq miles
Java (Jawa)
132 188 sq km
51 038 sq miles
ANTARCTICA
total land area:
12 093 000 sq km
4 669 133 sq miles
highest mountain
Vinson Massif
4 897m / 16 066ft
HIGHEST MOUNTAINS IN THE WORLD
Mt Everest
China/Nepal
8 848m / 29 028ft
K2
China/
Jammu and Kashmir
8 611m / 28 251ft
Kangchenjunga
India/Nepal
8 586m / 28 169ft
Lhotse
China/Nepal
8 516m / 27 939ft
Makalu
China/Nepal
8 463m / 27 765ft
Cho Oyu
China/Nepal
8 201m / 26 906ft
Dhaulagiri
Nepal
8 167m / 26 794ft
Manaslu
Nepal
8 163m / 26 781ft
Nanga Parbat
Jammu and Kashmir
8 126m / 26 660ft
Annapurna I
Nepal
8 091m / 26 545ft
Gasherbrum I
China/
Jammu and Kash
8 068m / 26 46

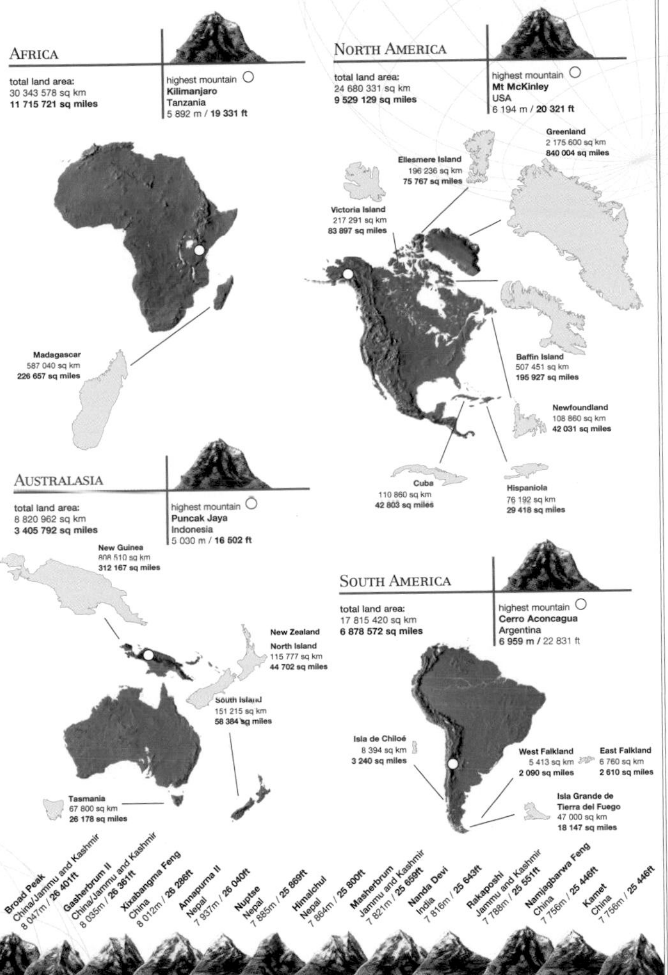
AFRICA
total land area:
30 343 578 sq km
11 715 721 sq miles
highest mountain
Kilimanjaro
Tanzania
5 892 m / 19 331 ft
Madagascar
587 040 sq km
226 657 sq miles
NORTH AMERICA
total land area:
24 680 331 sq km
9 529 129 sq miles
highest mountain
Mt McKinley
USA
6 194 m / 20 321 ft
Greenland
2 175 600 sq km
840 004 sq miles
Ellesmere Island
196 236 sq km
75 767 sq miles
Victoria Island
217 291 sq km
83 897 sq miles
Baffin Island
507 451 sq km
195 927 sq miles
Newfoundland
108 860 sq km
42 031 sq miles
Cuba
110 860 sq km
42 803 sq miles
Hispaniola
76 192 sq km
29 418 sq miles
AUSTRALASIA
total land area:
8 820 962 sq km
3 405 792 sq miles
highest mountain
Puncak Jaya
Indonesia
5 030 m / 16 502 ft
New Guinea
808 510 sq km
312 167 sq miles
New Zealand
North Island
115 777 sq km
44 702 sq miles
South Island
151 215 sq km
58 384 sq miles
Tasmania
67 800 sq km
26 178 sq miles
SOUTH AMERICA
total land area:
17 815 420 sq km
6 878 572 sq miles
highest mountain
Cerro Aconcagua
Argentina
6 959 m / 22 831 ft
Isla de Chiloé
8 394 sq km
3 240 sq miles
West Falkland
5 413 sq km
2 090 sq miles
East Falkland
6 760 sq km
2 610 sq miles
Isla Grande de Tierra del Fuego
47 000 sq km
18 147 sq miles
Broad Peak China/Jammu and Kashmir 8 047m / 26 401ft
Gasherbrum II China/Jammu and Kashmir 8 035m / 26 361ft
Xixabangma Feng China 8 012m / 26 286ft
Annapurna II Nepal 7 937m / 26 040ft
Nuptse Nepal 7 885m / 25 869ft
Himalchul Nepal 7 864m / 25 800ft
Masherbrum Jammu and Kashmir 7 821m / 25 659ft
Nanda Devi India 7 816m / 25 643ft
Rakaposhi Jammu and Kashmir 7 788m / 25 551ft
Namjagbarwa Feng China 7 756m / 25 446ft
Kamet China 7 756m / 25 446ft

Oceans, Seas, Lakes and Rivers

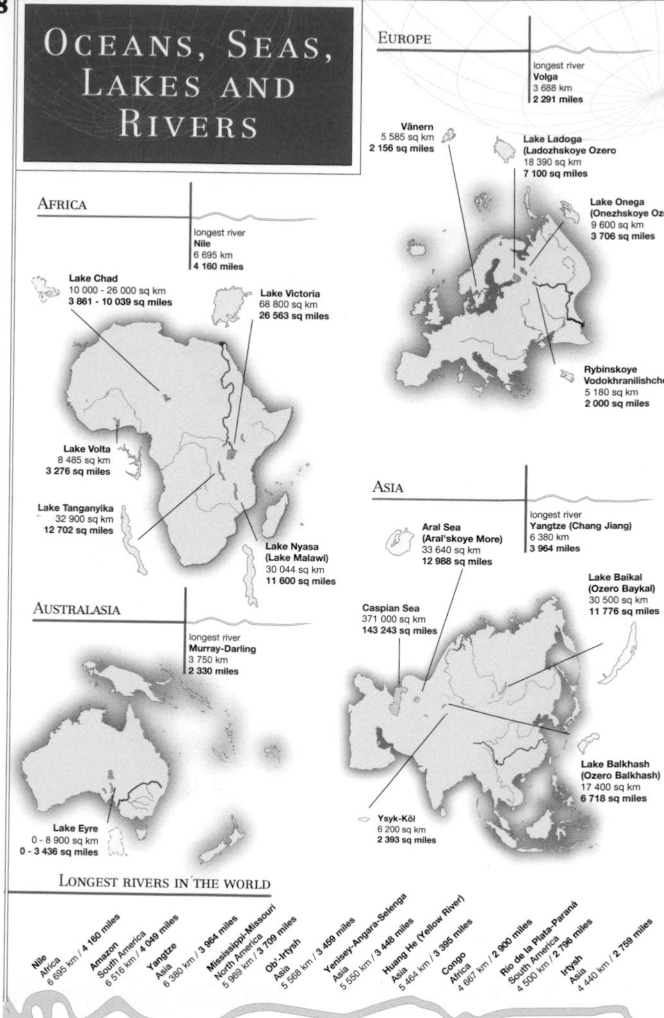
Europe
longest river
Volga
3 688 km
2 291 miles
Vänern
5 585 sq km
2 156 sq miles
Lake Ladoga
(Ladozhskoye Ozero
18 390 sq km
7 100 sq miles
Lake Onega
(Onezhskoye Ozero)
9 600 sq km
3 706 sq miles
Rybinskoye
Vodokhranilishche
5 180 sq km
2 000 sq miles
Africa
longest river
Nile
6 695 km
4 160 miles
Lake Chad
10 000 - 26 000 sq km
3 861 - 10 039 sq miles
Lake Victoria
68 800 sq km
26 563 sq miles
Lake Volta
8 485 sq km
3 276 sq miles
Lake Tanganyika
32 900 sq km
12 702 sq miles
Lake Nyasa
(Lake Malawi)
30 044 sq km
11 600 sq miles
Australasia
longest river
Murray-Darling
3 750 km
2 330 miles
Lake Eyre
0 - 8 900 sq km
0 - 3 436 sq miles
Asia
longest river
Yangtze (Chang Jiang)
6 380 km
3 964 miles
Aral Sea
(Aral'skoye More)
33 640 sq km
12 988 sq miles
Caspian Sea
371 000 sq km
143 243 sq miles
Lake Baikal
(Ozero Baykal)
30 500 sq km
11 776 sq miles
Lake Balkhash
(Ozero Balkhash)
17 400 sq km
6 718 sq miles
Ysyk-Köl
6 200 sq km
2 393 sq miles
Longest rivers in the world
Nile Africa 6 695 km / 4 160 miles
Amazon South America 6 516 km / 4 049 miles
Yangtze Asia 6 380 km / 3 964 miles
Mississippi-Missouri North America 5 969 km / 3 709 miles
Ob'-Irtysh Asia 5 568 km / 3 459 miles
Yenisey-Angara-Selenga Asia 5 550 km / 3 448 miles
Huang He (Yellow River) Asia 5 464 km / 3 395 miles
Congo Africa 4 667 km / 2 900 miles
Río de la Plata-Paraná South America 4 500 km / 2 796 miles
Irtysh Asia 4 440 km / 2 759 miles

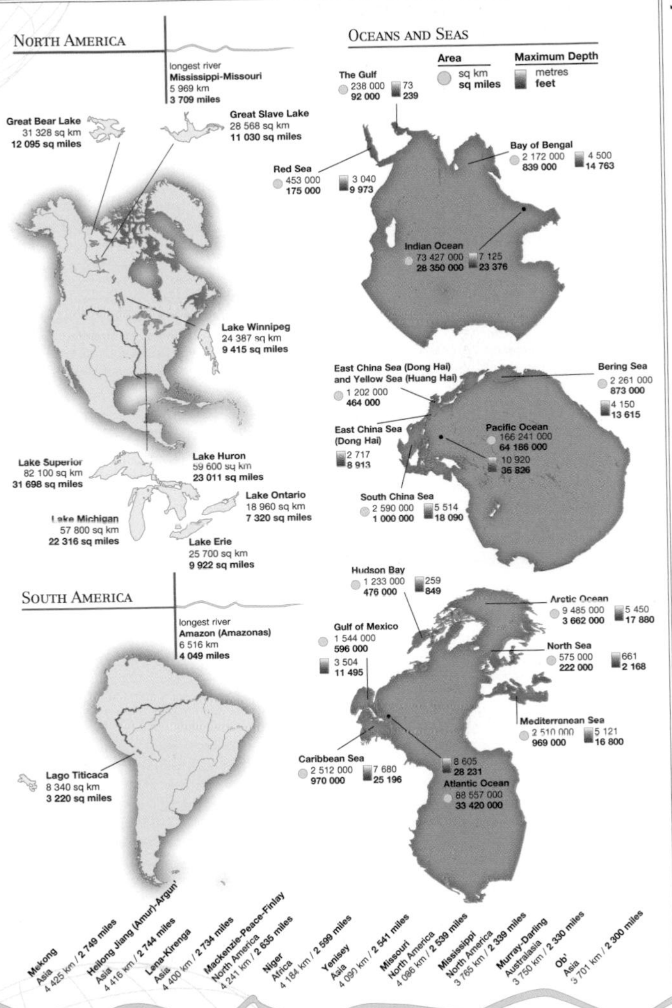
North America
longest river
Mississippi-Missouri
5 969 km
3 709 miles
Great Bear Lake
31 328 sq km
12 095 sq miles
Great Slave Lake
28 568 sq km
11 030 sq miles
Lake Winnipeg
24 387 sq km
9 415 sq miles
Lake Superior
82 100 sq km
31 698 sq miles
Lake Huron
59 600 sq km
23 011 sq miles
Lake Ontario
18 960 sq km
7 320 sq miles
Lake Michigan
57 800 sq km
22 316 sq miles
Lake Erie
25 700 sq km
9 922 sq miles
South America
longest river
Amazon (Amazonas)
6 516 km
4 049 miles
Lago Titicaca
8 340 sq km
3 220 sq miles
Oceans and Seas
Area
sq km
sq miles
Maximum Depth
metres
feet
The Gulf
238 000
92 000
73
239
Red Sea
453 000
175 000
3 040
9 973
Bay of Bengal
2 172 000
839 000
4 500
14 763
Indian Ocean
73 427 000
28 350 000
7 125
23 376
East China Sea (Dong Hai)
and Yellow Sea (Huang Hai)
1 202 000
464 000
Bering Sea
2 261 000
873 000
4 150
13 615
East China Sea
(Dong Hai)
2 717
8 913
Pacific Ocean
166 241 000
64 186 000
10 920
35 826
South China Sea
2 590 000
1 000 000
5 514
18 090
Hudson Bay
1 233 000
476 000
259
849
Arctic Ocean
9 485 000
3 662 000
5 450
17 880
Gulf of Mexico
1 544 000
596 000
3 504
11 495
North Sea
575 000
222 000
661
2 168
Mediterranean Sea
2 510 000
969 000
5 121
16 800
Caribbean Sea
2 512 000
970 000
7 680
25 196
8 605
28 231
Atlantic Ocean
88 557 000
33 420 000
Mekong
Asia
4 425 km / 2 749 miles
Heilong Jiang (Amur)-Argun'
Asia
4 416 km / 2 744 miles
Lena-Kirenga
Asia
4 400 km / 2 734 miles
Mackenzie-Peace-Finlay
North America
4 241 km / 2 635 miles
Niger
Africa
4 184 km / 2 599 miles
Yenisey
Asia
4 090 km / 2 541 miles
Missouri
North America
4 086 km / 2 539 miles
Mississippi
North America
3 765 km / 2 339 miles
Murray-Darling
Australasia
3 750 km / 2 330 miles
Ob'
Asia
3 701 km / 2 300 miles

Introduction to the Atlas

In the tradition of The Times Atlas of the World, the map sequence in this edition starts at the International Date Line in the Pacific Ocean and broadly works westwards, moving from Oceania through Asia, Europe, Africa, North America and finally to South America. Each continent is introduced by a politically coloured map on the same projection as the satellite images on pages 6-17 at the beginning of the atlas.

The map pages include a key to the relief layer-colouring and scale bars. The measurements on the relief key are given in both metric and imperial units and there are separate metric and imperial scale bars. The symbols and place name abbreviations used on the maps are fully explained on pages 42-43. The alphanumeric reference system used in the index is based on latitude and longitude, and the number and letter for each graticule square is shown along the sides, top and bottom of each map, within the map frame, in red.

Projections

The creation of new computer-generated maps presented the opportunity to review the map projections used and to select projections specifically for the area and scale of each map, or suite of maps. As the only way to show the Earth with absolute accuracy is on a globe, all map projections are compromises. Some projections seek to maintain correct area relationships (equal area projections), true distances and bearings from a point (equidistant projections) or correct angles and shapes (conformal projections); others attempt to achieve a balance between these properties. The choice of projections used in this atlas has been made on an individual continental and regional basis. Projections used, and their individual parameters, have been defined to minimize distortion and to reduce scale errors as much as possible.

The selection of projections for the series of regional maps within each continent has been made on an individual basis for that region. The Albers Conic Equal Area projection has been selected for Asia; in Europe the Conic Equidistant projection has been used and the Lambert Azimuthal Equal Area projection has been employed in North America, South America, Africa and Australia. The projection used is indicated at the bottom left of each map page.

Place Names

The spelling of place names on maps has always been a matter of great complexity, because of the variety of the world's languages and the systems used to write them down. There is no standard way of spelling names or of converting them from one alphabet, or symbol set, to another. Instead, conventional ways of spelling have evolved in each of the world's major languages, and the results often differ significantly from the name as it is spelled in the original language. Familiar examples of English conventional names include Munich (München), Florence (Firenze) and Moscow (from the transliterated form, Moskva).

In this atlas, local name forms are used where these are in the Roman alphabet, though for major cities, and main physical features, conventional English names are given first. The local forms are those which are officially recognized by the government of the country concerned, usually as represented by its official mapping agency. This is a basic principle laid down by the United Kingdom government's Permanent Committee on Geographical Names (PCGN) and the equivalent United States Board on Geographic Names, (BGN).

The names of continents, oceans, seas and under-water features in international waters

Boundaries

The status of nations, their names and their boundaries, are shown in this atlas as they are at the time of going to press, as far as can be ascertained. Where an international boundary symbol appears in the sea or ocean it does not necessarily infer a de jure maritime boundary, but shows which off-shore islands belong to which country. The extent of island nations is shown by a short boundary symbol at the extreme limits of the area of sea or ocean within which all land is part of that nation.

Where international boundaries are the subject of dispute it may be that no portrayal of them will meet with the approval of any of the countries involved, but it is not seen as the function of this atlas to try to adjudicate between the rights and wrongs of political issues. Although reference mapping at atlas scales is not the ideal medium for indicating the claims of many separatist and irredentist movements, every reasonable attempt is made to show where an active territorial dispute exists, and where there is an important difference between 'de facto' (existing in fact, on the ground) and 'de jure' (according to law) boundaries. This is done by the use of a different symbol where international boundaries are disputed, or where the alignment is unconfirmed, to that used for settled international boundaries. Cease-fire lines are also shown by a separate symbol. For clarity, disputed boundaries and areas are annotated where this is considered necessary. The atlas aims to take a strictly neutral viewpoint of all such cases, based on advice from expert consultants.

Jammu and Kashmir

The territory is de facto divided between India and Pakistan along a cease-fire line established following hostilities in 1948 and formalized in 1972 as the Line of Control. It terminates at a grid reference known as NJ9842: between that point and the Chinese border there is no agreed dividing line. The area known as Aksai Chin is regarded by India as an integral part of Jammu and Kashmir and therefore of Indian territory, but is de facto controlled by China.

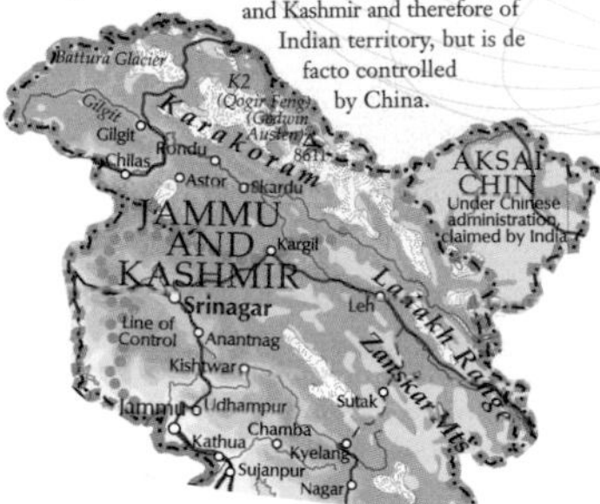

appear in English throughout the atlas, as do those of other international features where such an English form exists and is in common use. International features are defined as features crossing one or more international boundary.

Country names are shown in conventional English form, but include changes promulgated by national governments and adopted by the United Nations – Myanmar (replacing Burma), Belarus (replacing Belorussia and a variety of other versions including the traditional White Russia), Kyrgyzstan (for Kirghizia or Kirgizia), Moldova (Moldavia), and Côte d'Ivoire (Ivory Coast).

Scale

In order to directly compare like with like throughout the world it would be necessary to maintain a single scale throughout the atlas. However, the desirability of mapping the more densely populated areas of the world at larger scales, and other geographical considerations, such as the need to fit a homogeneous physical region within a uniform rectangular page format, mean that a range of scales have been used. Scales for continental maps range between 1:40 000 000 and 1:70 000 000, depending on the size of the continental land mass being covered. Scales for regional maps are typically in the range 1:20 000 000 to 1:30 000 000. Mapping for most countries is at scales between 1:8 000 000 and 1:15 000 000.

Symbols and Abbreviations

Map symbols used on the map pages are explained here. The depiction of relief follows the tradition of layer-colouring, with colours depicting altitude bands. Ocean pages have a different contour interval. Settlements are classified in terms of both population and administrative significance. The abbreviations listed are those used in place names on the map pages and within the index.

LAND AND WATER FEATURES

Lake

Impermanent lake

Salt lake or lagoon

Impermanent salt lake

Dry salt lake or salt pan

River

Impermanent river

Ice cap / Glacier

123 Pass
height in metres

Site of special interest

Wall

RELIEF

Contour intervals used in layer-colouring for land height and sea depth

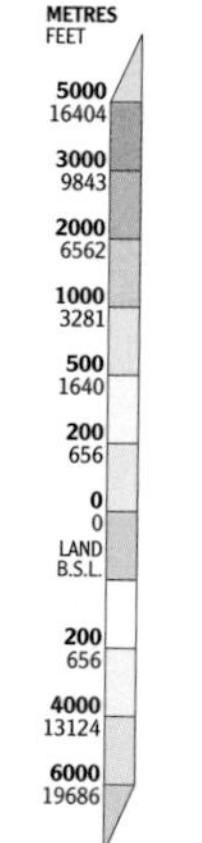

1234 Summit
Height in metres

Ocean pages

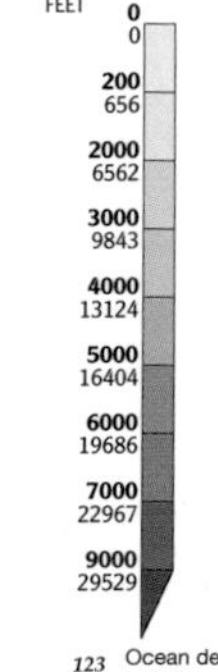

123 Ocean deep
In metres.

BOUNDARIES

International boundary

Disputed international boundary or alignment unconfirmed

Undefined international boundary in the sea.
All land within this boundary is part of state or territory named.

Administrative boundary
Shown for selected countries only.

Ceasefire line or other boundary described on the map

TRANSPORT

Motorway

Main road

Track

Main railway

Canal

Main airport

CITIES AND TOWNS

Population	National Capital	Administrative Capital Shown for selected countries only	Other City or Town
over 1 million	**BEIJING** □	**Sydney** ○	**New York** ○
500 000 to 1 million	**BANGUI** □	**Edmonton** ○	**Jeddah** ○
100 000 to 500 000	WELLINGTON □	Edinburgh ○	Apucarana ○
50 000 to 100 000	PORT OF SPAIN □	Bismarck ○	Invercargill ○
under 50 000	MALABO □	Charlottetown ○	Ceres ○

Built-up area
Scale 1:4 000 000 only

STYLES OF LETTERING

Cities and towns are explained separately

Country	**FRANCE**
Overseas Territory/Dependency	**Guadeloupe**
Disputed Territory	AKSAI CHIN
Administrative name Shown for selected countries only.	**SCOTLAND**
Area name	PATAGONIA

Physical features

Island	*Gran Canaria*
Lake	*Lake Erie*
Mountain	*Mt Blanc*
River	*Thames*
Region	*LAPPLAND*

CONTINENTAL MAPS

BOUNDARIES

——— International boundary

------ Disputed international boundary

•••••••• Ceasefire line

CITIES AND TOWNS

Population	National capital	Other city or town
Over 1 million	**Beijing** □	**New York** ○
500 000 to 1 million	**Bangui** □	**Irkutsk** ○
100 000 to 500 000	Wellington □	Iquitos ○
under 100 000	Malabo □	Inuvik ○

ABBREVIATIONS

Arch.	Archipelago		
B.	Bay Bahia, Baía Bahía Baie	 Portuguese Spanish French	 bay bay bay
C.	Cape Cabo Cap	 Portuguese, Spanish French	 cape, headland cape, headland
Co	Cerro	Spanish	hill, peak, summit
E.	East, Eastern		
Est.	Estrecho	Spanish	strait
Gt	Great		
I.	Island, Isle Ilha Islas	 Portuguese Spanish	 island island
Is	Islands, Isles Islas	 Spanish	 islands
Khr.	Khrebet	Russian	mountain range
L.	Lake Loch Lough Lac Lago	 (Scotland) (Ireland) French Portuguese, Spanish	 lake lake lake lake
M.	Mys	Russian	cape, point
Mt	Mount Mont	 French	 hill, mountain
Mt.	Mountain		
Mte	Monte	Portuguese, Spanish	hill, mountain
Mts	Mountains Monts	 French	 hills, mountains
N.	North, Northern		
O.	Ostrov	Russian	island
Pt	Point		
Pta	Punta	Italian, Spanish	cape, point
R.	River Rio Río Rivière	 Portuguese Spanish French	 river river river
Ra.	Range		
S.	South, Southern Salar, Salina, Salinas	 Spanish	 salt pan, salt pans
Sa	Serra Sierra	Portuguese Spanish	mountain range mountain range
Sd	Sound		
S.E.	Southeast, Southeastern		
St	Saint Sankt Sint	 German Dutch	 saint
Sta	Santa	Italian, Portuguese, Spanish	saint
Ste	Sainte	French	saint
Str.	Strait		
W.	West, Western Wadi, Wādī	 Arabic	 watercourse

ARCTIC

Greenland

Mt McKinley 6194
Mt Logan 5959
Baffin Island
Aleutian Islands
Gulf of Alaska
NORTH AMERICA
Hudson Bay
Iceland
Labrador
Rocky Mountains
British Isles
Missouri
Great Lakes
Newfoundland
St Lawrence
EU
Alps
Rio Grande
Mississippi
Appalachian Mts
Med
Azores
Atlas Mountains
Hawaiian Islands
Sa Madre Occidental
ATLANTIC OCEAN
Gulf of Mexico
Cuba
Canary Islands
Saha
PACIFIC OCEAN
Hispaniola
Caribbean Sea
Cape Verde
AFR
Niger
Orinoco
Line Islands
Gulf of Guinea
Galapagos Islands
Amazon
Andes
SOUTH AMERICA
Ascension
Polynesia
Brazilian Highlands
St Helena
Tuamotu Islands
Parana
Tubuai Islands
Pitcairn Is
Easter Island
Cerro Aconcagua 6959
Tristan da Cunha
Patagonia
Falkland Islands
Tierra del Fuego
South Georgia
South Sandwich Islands
Cape Horn
Antarctic Peninsula
Amundsen Sea
Weddell Sea
Vinson Massif 4897
ANTAR

160° 120° 80° 40° 0°
80° 60° 40° 20° 0° 20° 40° 60° 80°

METRES	FEET
6000	19686
4000	13124
2000	6562
1000	3281
500	1640
200	656
0	0
LAND B.S.L.	
200	656
3000	9843
5000	16404
7000	22967

Winkel Tripel Projection

1:170 000 000

MILES 0 1000 2000 3000

CTIC OCEAN
Arctic Circle
Central Siberian Plateau
Siberia
Lena
Yenisey
West Siberian Plain
Ob
Bering Sea
Sea of Okhotsk
Scandinavia
North European Plain
Ural Mountains
Lake Baikal
Amur
Irtysh
ROPE
Volga
Aral Sea
Gobi
Sea of Japan
Danube
Black Sea
El'brus 5642
Caspian Sea
ASIA
Tien Shan
Honshu
PACIFIC
terranean Sea
Zagros Mts
Indus
Himalaya
Mt Everest 8848
Yangtze
East China Sea
Tropic of Cancer
Nile
The Gulf
Ganges
Mariana Trench
Arabian Peninsula
Red Sea
Deccan
Bay of Bengal
South China Sea
Mekong
Philippines
Challenger Deep 10920
OCEAN
Arabian Sea
ICA
Micronesia
Sri Lanka
Ethiopian Highlands
Maldives
Great Rift Valley
Lake Victoria
Congo
Congo Basin
Kilimanjaro 5892
Borneo
Sumatra
Celebes
Puncak Jaya 5030
New Guinea
Equator
Melanesia
Java
Seychelles
INDIAN
Arafura Sea
Zambezi
Madagascar
Coral Sea
Kalahari Desert
OCEAN
AUSTRALIA
Great Victoria Desert
Tropic of Capricorn
Great Dividing Ra.
Darling
Murray
Great Australian Bight
Cape of Good Hope
Tasman Sea
New Zealand
Tasmania
Îles Kerguélen
Davis Sea
Antarctic Circle
Ross Sea
TICA
40°
80°
120°
160°
80°
60°
40°
20°
0 1000 2000 3000 4000 5000 KILOMETRES

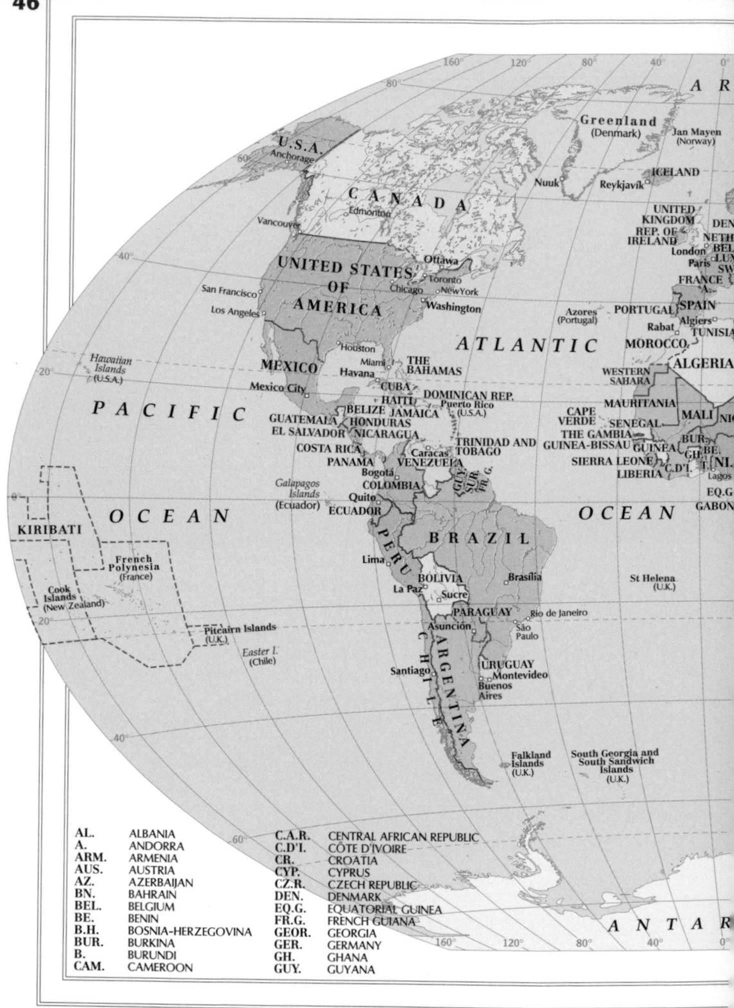

Winkel Tripel Projection

1:170 000 000

MILES 0 1000 2000 3000

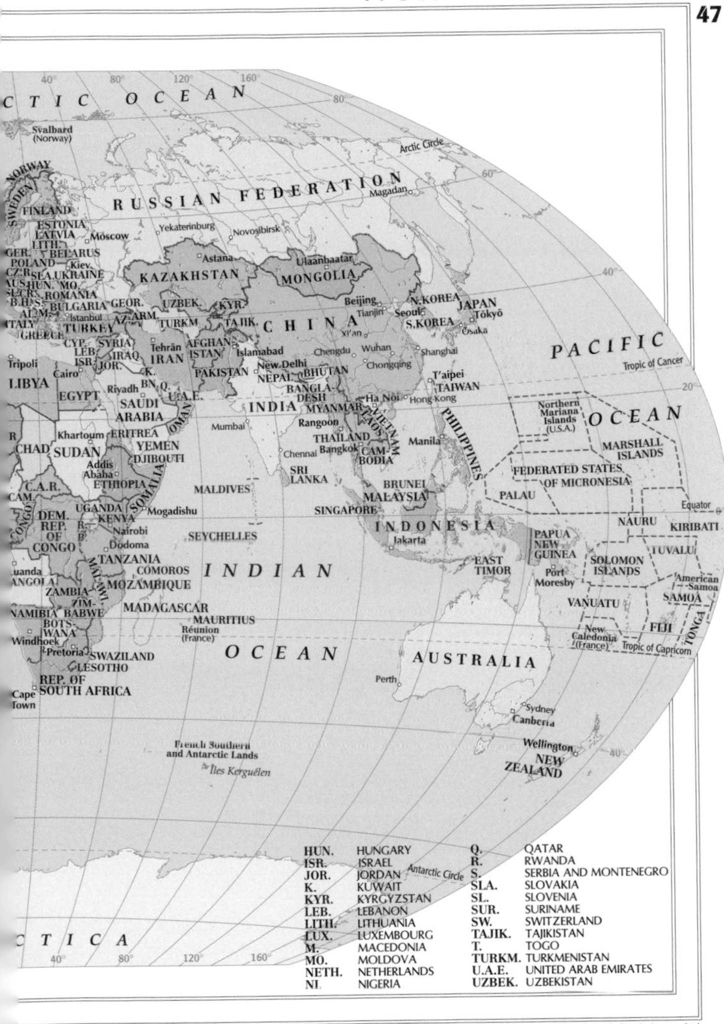

0 1000 2000 3000 4000 5000 KILOMETRES

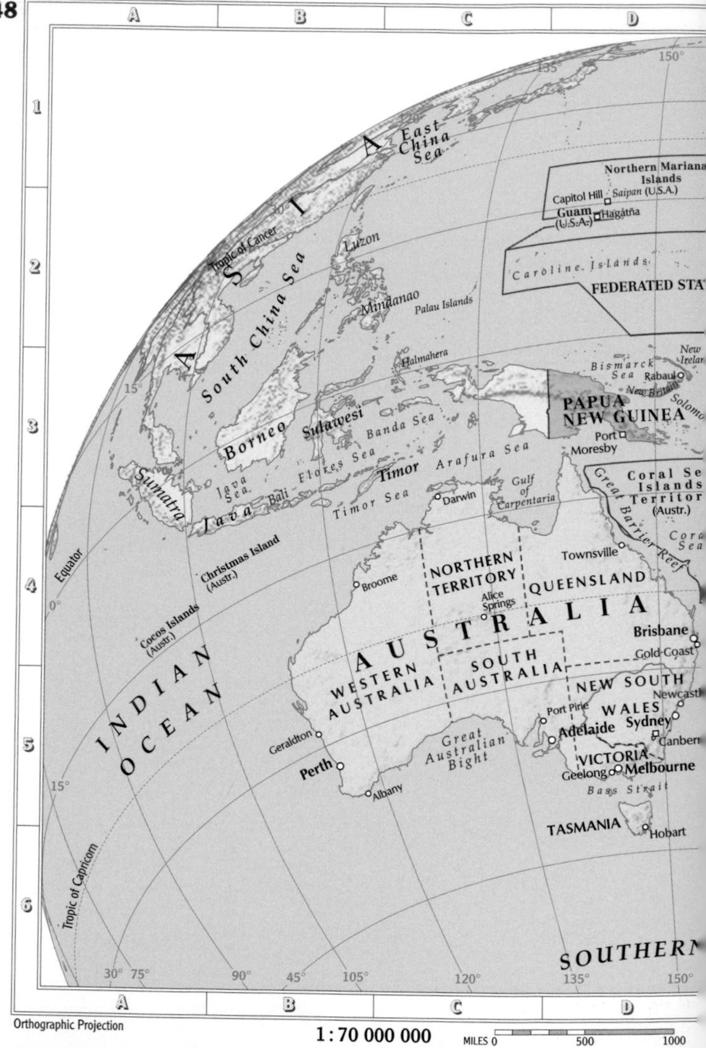

Orthographic Projection

1:70 000 000

MILES 0 500 1000

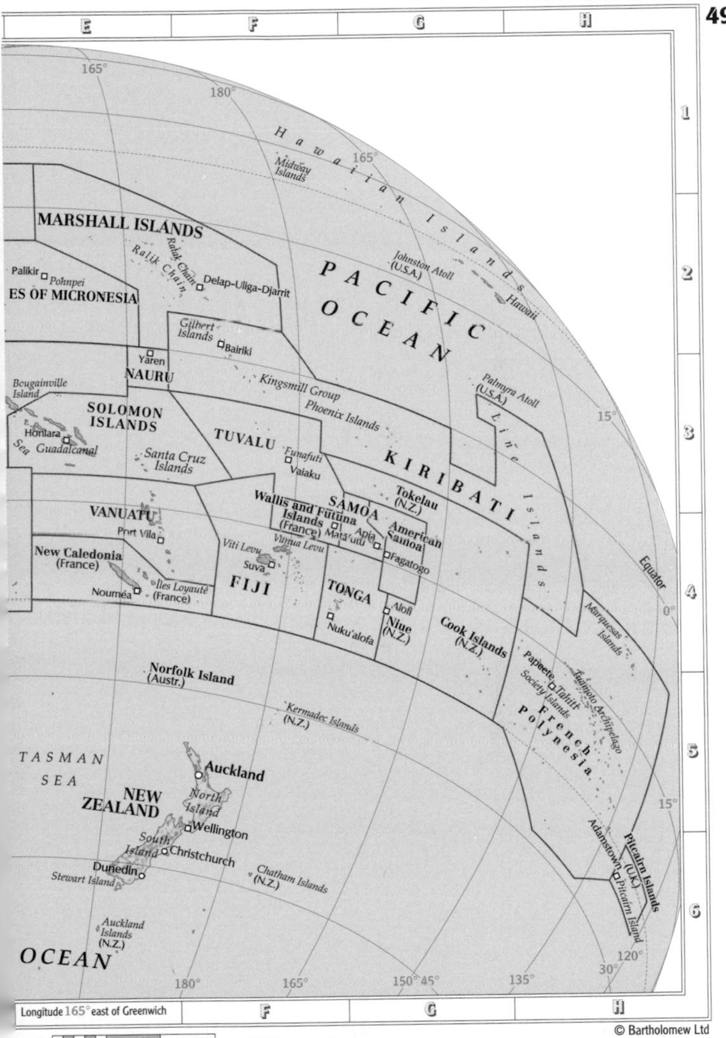
E
F
G
H
1
2
3
4
5
6
165°
180°
165°
150°
45°
135°
120°
30°
15°
0°
15°
Hawaiian Islands
Midway Islands
MARSHALL ISLANDS
Ralik Chain
Ratak Chain
Palikir
Pohnpei
ES OF MICRONESIA
Delap-Uliga-Djarrit
PACIFIC OCEAN
Johnston Atoll (U.S.A.)
Hawaii
Gilbert Islands
Bairiki
Yaren
NAURU
Kingsmill Group
Phoenix Islands
Palmyra Atoll (U.S.A.)
Line Islands
Bougainville Island
SOLOMON ISLANDS
Honiara
Guadalcanal
Sea
Santa Cruz Islands
TUVALU
Funafuti
Vaiaku
KIRIBATI
Tokelau (N.Z.)
Wallis and Futuna Islands (France)
Mata'utu
SAMOA
Apia
American Samoa
Fagatogo
VANUATU
Port Vila
Viti Levu
Vanua Levu
Suva
FIJI
New Caledonia (France)
Nouméa
Îles Loyauté (France)
TONGA
Nuku'alofa
Alofi
Niue (N.Z.)
Cook Islands (N.Z.)
Equator
Marquesas Islands
Papeete
Tahiti
Society Islands
Tuamotu Archipelago
French Polynesia
Norfolk Island (Austr.)
Kermadec Islands (N.Z.)
TASMAN SEA
Auckland
NEW ZEALAND
North Island
Wellington
South Island
Christchurch
Dunedin
Stewart Island
Chatham Islands (N.Z.)
Auckland Islands (N.Z.)
OCEAN
Adamstown
Pitcairn Islands (U.K.)
Pitcairn Island
Longitude 165° east of Greenwich
0
500
1000
1500 KILOMETRES

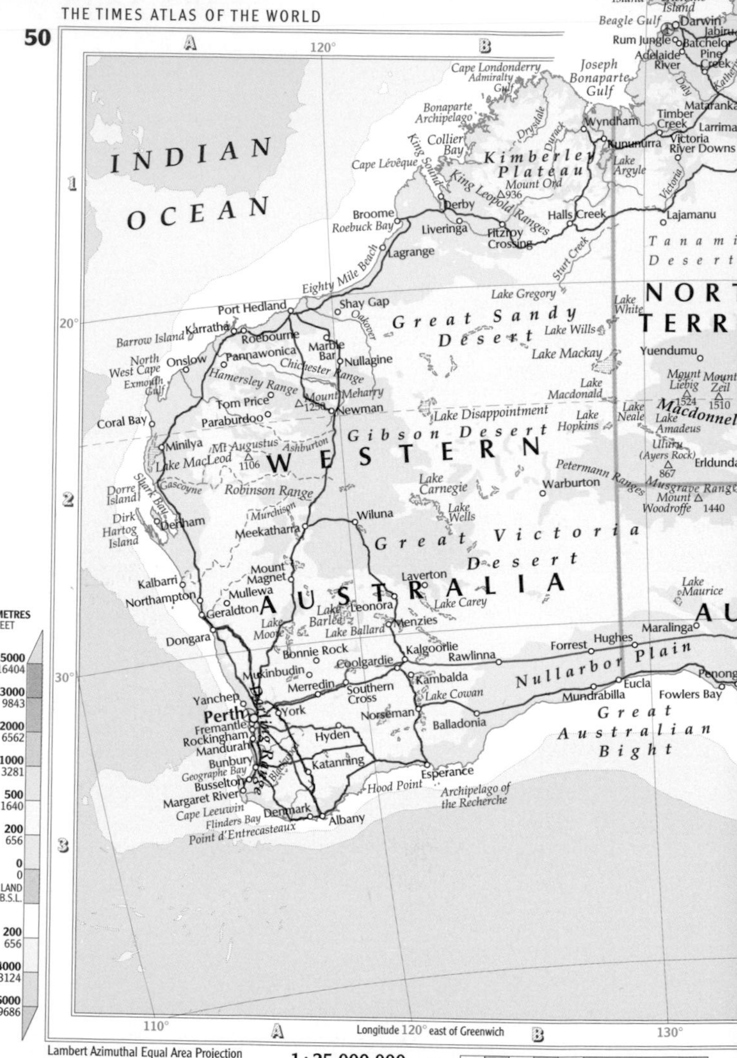

Lambert Azimuthal Equal Area Projection

1:25 000 000

MILES 0 250 500

Wessel Is
Cape Wessel
Buckingham Bay
Nhulunbuy
Cape Arnhem
Arnhem Bay
Arnhem Land
Isle Woodah
Alyangula
Groote Eylandt
Gulf of Carpentaria
Sir Edward Pellew Group
Borroloola
Mornington Island
Wellesley Islands
Daly Waters
Lake Woods
Barkly Tableland
Burketown
Normanton
Tennant Creek
Camooweal
Kajabbi
Leichhardt
Flinders
Gregory Range
Forsayth
Gilbert
Mitchell
Cape York
Bamaga
C. Grenville
Albatross Bay
Weipa
Cape York Peninsula
Archer
Coen
C. Direction
Princess Charlotte Bay
Cape Melville
Cape Flattery
Laura
Cooktown
Mossman
Cairns
Mount Bartle Frere
1612
Innisfail
Tully
Hinchinbrook Island
Townsville
Ayr
Bowen
Whitsunday I.
Proserpine
Mt Dalrymple
1277
Mackay
Percy Islands
Arthur Point
Charters Towers
GREAT BARRIER REEF
CORAL SEA
HERN TORY
Mount Isa
Cloncurry
Richmond
Selwyn Range
Barrow Creek
Georgina
Winton
QUEENSLAND
Boulia
Longreach
Barcaldine
Clermont
Rockhampton
Yeppoon
Curtis I.
Tropic of Capricorn
Emerald
Gladstone
Moura
Biloela
Bundaberg
Hervey Bay
Sandy Cape
Fraser Island
Monto
Maryborough
Gympie
Tewantin
Nambour
Caboolture
Kingaroy
Brisbane
Beenleigh
Gold Coast
Byron Bay
Ballina
Alice Springs
Ranges
Simpson Desert
Cluny
Diamantina
Yaraka
Blackall
Windorah
Bilpa Morea Claypan
Birdsville
Buckland Tableland
Warrego
GREAT DIVIDING RANGE
Charleville
Quilpie
Mitchell
Roma
Balonne
Dalby
Toowoomba
Alberga
Oodnadatta
Lake Eyre (North)
Macumba
Warburton
Cooper Creek
Sturt Stony Desert
Lake Blanche
SOUTH STRALIA
Coober Pedy
Lake Eyre (South)
Grey Range
Hungerford
St George
Cunnamulla
Dirranbandi
Darling
Goondiwindi
Downs
Mungindi
Warwick
Tibooburra
Brewarrina
Barwon
Moree
Glen Innes
Casino
Bourke
Walgett
Inverell
Grafton
Narrabri
Armidale
Macksville
Tarcoola
Lake Torrens
Flinders Ranges
Lake Frome
Barrier Range
Darling
Lake Gairdner
Woomera
Island Lagoon
Ceduna
Broken Hill
Wilcannia
Cobar
Macquarie
Tamworth
Streaky Bay
Whyalla
Port Augusta
Port Pirie
Jamestown
Burra
Warren
Dubbo
Muswellbrook
Port Macquarie
Taree
Anxious Bay
Kyancutta
Eyre Peninsula
Spencer Gulf
NEW SOUTH WALES
Ivanhoe
Lachlan
Parkes
Orange
Newcastle
Garnpung Lake
Murray
Port Lincoln
Cape Carnot
Gawler
Adelaide
Murray Bridge
Mildura
Hay
Griffith
Cowra
Sydney
Investigator Strait
Swan Hill
Wagga Wagga
Goulburn
Yass
Botany Bay
Wollongong
Nowra
CANBERRA
A.C.T.
Kangaroo Island
Lake Tyrrell
Nhill
Wangaratta
Albury
Bendigo
Batemans Bay
Cape Jaffa
VICTORIA
Mount William
1167
Ballarat
Mt Kosciuszko
2230
Bega
Eden
Mount Gambier
Discovery Bay
Geelong
Colac
Melbourne
Cape Howe
TASMAN SEA
Portland
Warrnambool
Moe
Sale
Bairnsdale
Cape Otway
Bass Strait
Wilson's Promontory
Currie
King Island
Flinders Island
Furneaux Group
Cape Barren I.
Hunter Islands
Burnie
Devonport
Eddystone Pt
Mount Ossa
1617
Launceston
Queenstown
Fingal
TASMANIA
Lake Gordon
Sorell
Hobart
Port Arthur
140°
150°
20°
30°
40°
C
D
E
1
2
3
0
250
500 KILOMETRES
© Bartholomew Ltd

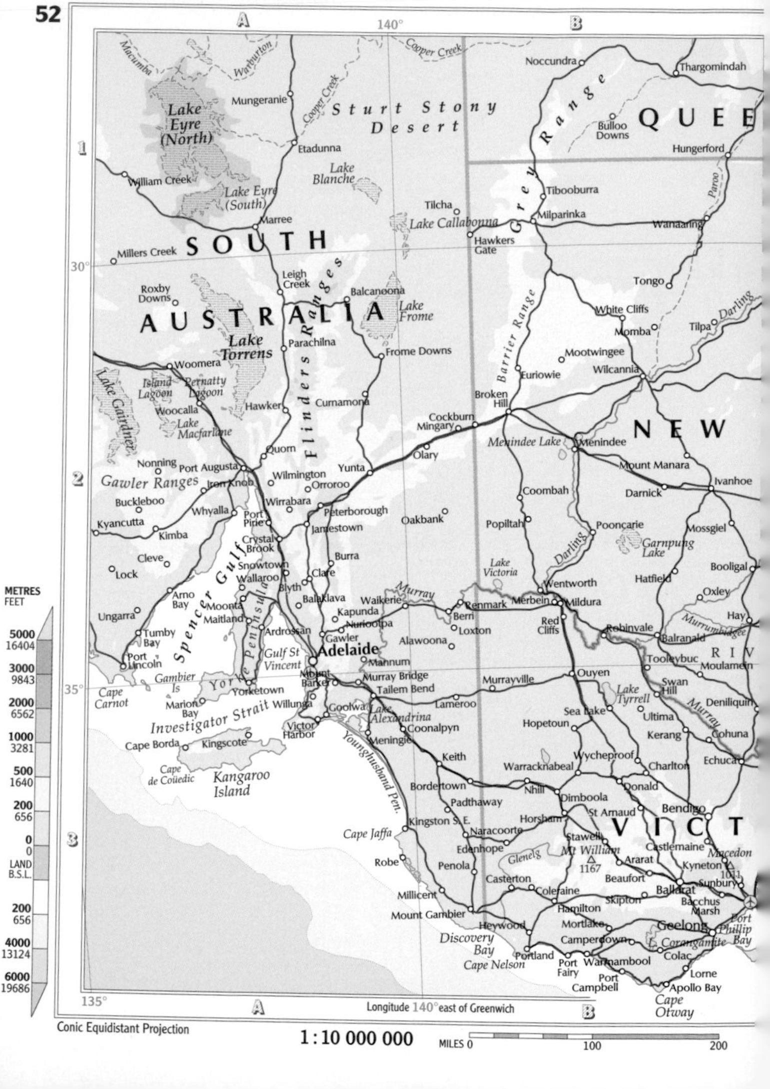

A 140° B

Macumba
Warburton
Cooper Creek
Cooper Creek
Noccundra
Thargomindah
Lake Eyre (North)
Mungeranie
Sturt Stony Desert
Grey Range
Bulloo Downs
QUEE
1
Etadunna
Hungerford
Lake Blanche
William Creek
Lake Eyre (South)
Tibooburra
Paroo
Tilcha
Milparinka
Marree
Lake Callabonna
Wanaaring
Millers Creek
SOUTH
Hawkers Gate
30°
Leigh Creek
Tongo
Roxby Downs
Balcanoona
AUSTRALIA
Lake Frome
Barrier Range
White Cliffs
Darling
Flinders Ranges
Momba
Tilpa
Lake Torrens
Parachilna
Frome Downs
Mootwingee
Woomera
Wilcannia
Euriowie
Island Lagoon
Pernatty Lagoon
Lake Gairdner
Broken Hill
Hawker
Curnamona
Woocalla
Lake Macfarlane
Cockburn
Mingary
NEW
Menindee Lake
Menindee
Quorn
Olary
Nonning
Port Augusta
Mount Manara
2
Gawler Ranges
Yunta
Wilmington
Orroroo
Ivanhoe
Iron Knob
Coombah
Darnick
Buckleboo
Whyalla
Wirrabara
Port Pirie
Peterborough
Oakbank
Popiltah
Pooncarie
Mossgiel
Kyancutta
Kimba
Jamestown
Crystal Brook
Garnpung Lake
Darling
Burra
Cleve
Snowtown
Lake Victoria
Booligal
Lock
Wallaroo
Clare
Hatfield
Wentworth
Spencer Gulf
Blyth
Murray
Oxley
Arno Bay
Moonta
Balaklava
Waikerie
Renmark
Merbein
Mildura
Ungarra
Maitland
Yorke Peninsula
Kapunda
Berri
Hay
Nuriootpa
Red Cliffs
Murrumbidgee
Tumby Bay
Ardrossan
Loxton
Robinvale
Gawler
Alawoona
Balranald
Port Lincoln
Gulf St Vincent
Adelaide
RIV
Mannum
Tooleybuc
Moulamein
Gambier Is
Mount Barker
Murray Bridge
Murrayville
Ouyen
Swan Hill
35°
Cape Carnot
Yorke
Yorketown
Tailem Bend
Lake Tyrrell
Murray
Marion Bay
Willunga
Goolwa
Lameroo
Deniliquin
Investigator Strait
Lake Alexandrina
Sea Lake
Ultima
Victor Harbor
Coonalpyn
Hopetoun
Kerang
Cohuna
Cape Borda
Kingscote
Meningie
Younghusband Pen.
Keith
Wycheproof
Echuca
Cape de Couëdic
Kangaroo Island
Warracknabeal
Charlton
Bordertown
Nhill
Donald
Padthaway
Dimboola
Bendigo
Kingston S.E.
Horsham
St Arnaud
VICT
3
Cape Jaffa
Naracoorte
Stawell
Castlemaine
Edenhope
Mt William
Macedon
Robe
Glenelg
1167
Ararat
Kyneton
Penola
1011
Casterton
Beaufort
Sunbury
Millicent
Coleraine
Ballarat
Skipton
Bacchus Marsh
Mount Gambier
Hamilton
Port Phillip Bay
Heywood
Mortlake
Geelong
Discovery Bay
Camperdown
L. Corangamite
Portland
Colac
Cape Nelson
Port Fairy
Warrnambool
Lorne
Port Campbell
Apollo Bay
Cape Otway

METRES
FEET
5000
16404
3000
9843
2000
6562
1000
3281
500
1640
200
656
0
0
LAND B.S.L.
200
656
4000
13124
6000
19686

135° A Longitude 140° east of Greenwich B

Conic Equidistant Projection

1:10 000 000

MILES 0 100 200

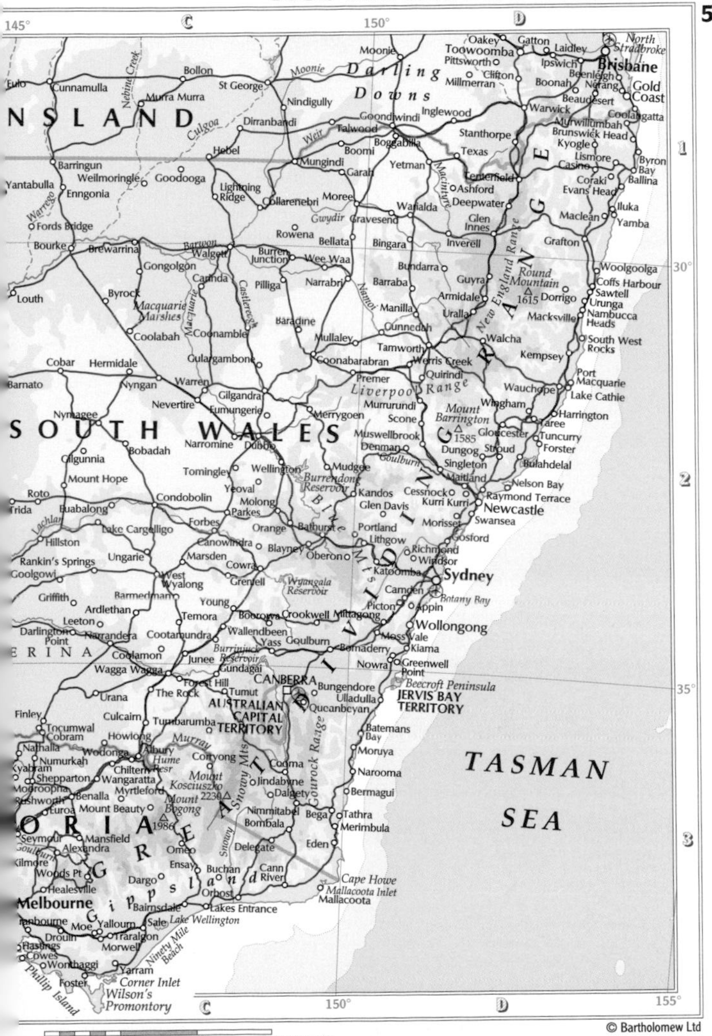

NEW ZEALAND

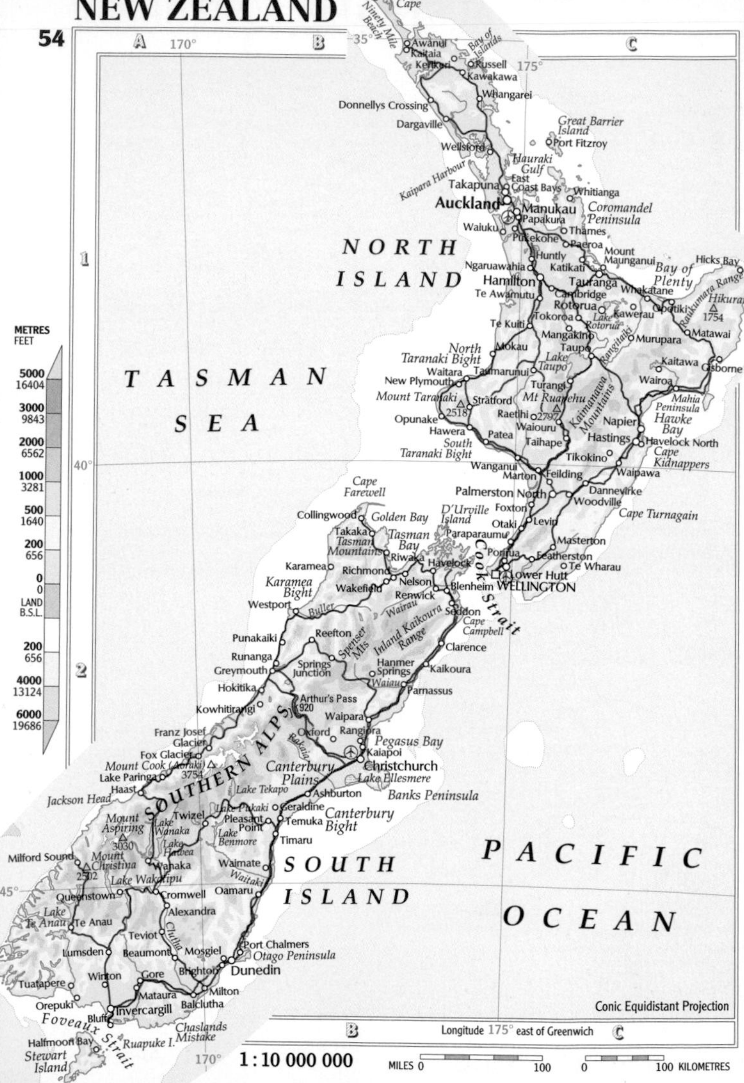

A
B
C
170°
175°
35°
40°
45°
1
2
METRES
FEET
5000
16404
3000
9843
2000
6562
1000
3281
500
1640
200
656
0
0
LAND
B.S.L.
200
656
4000
13124
6000
19686
TASMAN SEA
PACIFIC OCEAN
NORTH ISLAND
SOUTH ISLAND
Te Paki
North Cape
Ninety Mile Beach
Awanui
Kaitaia
Bay of Islands
Kerikeri
Russell
Kawakawa
Whangarei
Donnellys Crossing
Dargaville
Great Barrier Island
Port Fitzroy
Wellsford
Kaipara Harbour
Hauraki Gulf
Takapuna
East Coast Bays
Whitianga
Auckland
Manukau
Coromandel Peninsula
Papakura
Waiuku
Thames
Pukekohe
Paeroa
Huntly
Mount Maunganui
Ngaruawahia
Katikati
Hicks Bay
Hamilton
Tauranga
Bay of Plenty
Te Awamutu
Cambridge
Whakatane
Raukumara Range
Rotorua
Kawerau
Opotiki
Hikurangi
1754
Lake Rotorua
Tokoroa
Te Kuiti
Mangakino
Murupara
Matawai
Rangitaiki
North Taranaki Bight
Mokau
Taupo
Lake Taupo
Kaitawa
Gisborne
Waitara
Taumarunui
Wairoa
New Plymouth
Turangi
Mount Taranaki
Stratford
Mt Ruapehu
Kaimanawa Mountains
Mahia Peninsula
2518
2797
Opunake
Raetihi
Napier
Hawke Bay
Hawera
Waiouru
Patea
Hastings
South Taranaki Bight
Taihape
Havelock North
Cape Kidnappers
Tikokino
Wanganui
Marton
Feilding
Waipawa
Cape Farewell
Palmerston North
Dannevirke
Woodville
D'Urville Island
Foxton
Collingwood
Golden Bay
Cape Turnagain
Otaki
Levin
Takaka
Tasman Bay
Paraparaumu
Tasman Mountains
Masterton
Cook Strait
Riwaka
Havelock
Porirua
Featherston
Karamea
Richmond
Te Wharau
Lower Hutt
Nelson
Karamea Bight
Wakefield
Blenheim
WELLINGTON
Renwick
Westport
Buller
Wairau
Inland Kaikoura Range
Seddon
Cape Campbell
Punakaiki
Reefton
Spenser Mts
Clarence
Runanga
Hanmer Springs
Greymouth
Springs Junction
Kaikoura
Waiau
Hokitika
Parnassus
Arthur's Pass
920
Kowhitirangi
Waipara
Franz Josef Glacier
Oxford
Rangiora
Pegasus Bay
Fox Glacier
Rakaia
Kaiapoi
Mount Cook (Aoraki)
3754
Christchurch
SOUTHERN ALPS
Lake Paringa
Canterbury Plains
Lake Ellesmere
Haast
Lake Tekapo
Ashburton
Banks Peninsula
Jackson Head
Lake Pukaki
Geraldine
Canterbury Bight
Mount Aspiring
Twizel
Pleasant Point
Temuka
Lake Wanaka
3030
Lake Benmore
Timaru
Lake Hawea
Milford Sound
Mount Christina
Wanaka
Waimate
2502
Lake Wakatipu
Waitaki
Oamaru
Queenstown
Cromwell
Lake Te Anau
Te Anau
Alexandra
Teviot
Clutha
Port Chalmers
Otago Peninsula
Lumsden
Beaumont
Mosgiel
Dunedin
Winton
Gore
Brighton
Tuatapere
Mataura
Milton
Orepuki
Balclutha
Invercargill
Foveaux Strait
Bluff
Chaslands Mistake
Halfmoon Bay
Ruapuke I.
Stewart Island
Conic Equidistant Projection
Longitude 175° east of Greenwich
1:10 000 000
MILES 0
100
0
100 KILOMETRES

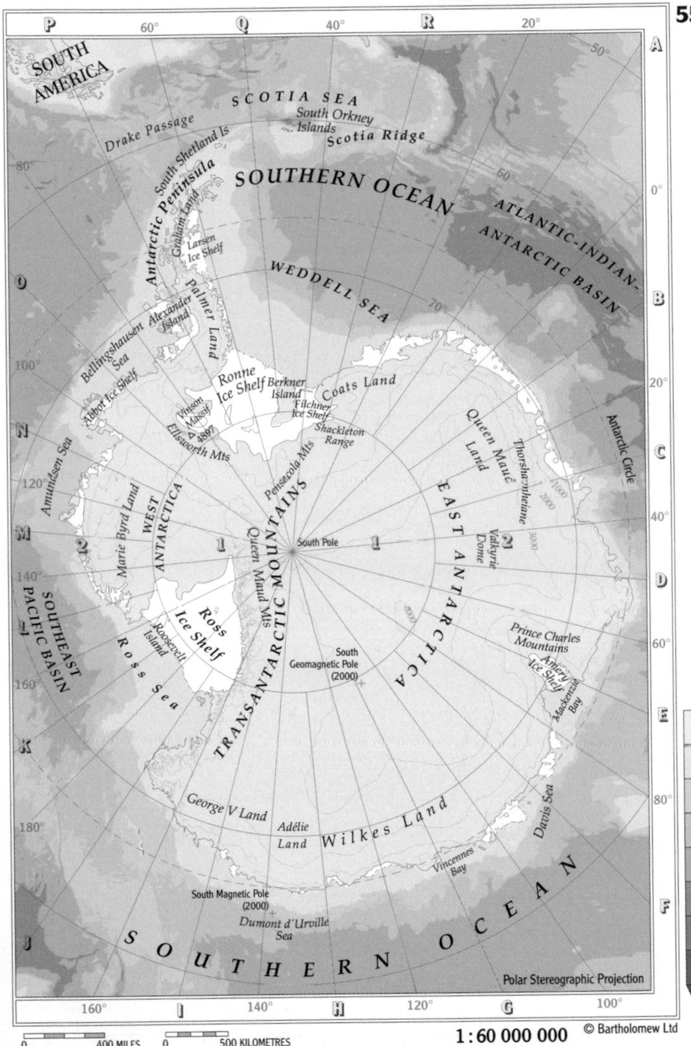

SOUTH AMERICA
SCOTIA SEA
South Orkney Islands
Scotia Ridge
Drake Passage
South Shetland Is
Antarctic Peninsula
Graham Land
SOUTHERN OCEAN
ATLANTIC-INDIAN-ANTARCTIC BASIN
Larsen Ice Shelf
WEDDELL SEA
Palmer Land
Alexander Island
Bellingshausen Sea
Ronne Ice Shelf
Berkner Island
Coats Land
Filchner Ice Shelf
Abbot Ice Shelf
Vinson Massif 4897
Ellsworth Mts
Shackleton Range
Queen Maud Land
Thorshavnheiane
Antarctic Circle
Amundsen Sea
Pensacola Mts
WEST ANTARCTICA
Marie Byrd Land
TRANSANTARCTIC MOUNTAINS
Queen Maud Mts
South Pole
EAST ANTARCTICA
Valkyrie Dome
SOUTHEAST PACIFIC BASIN
Ross Ice Shelf
Roosevelt Island
Ross Sea
South Geomagnetic Pole (2000)
Prince Charles Mountains
Amery Ice Shelf
Mackenzie Bay
George V Land
Adélie Land
Wilkes Land
Davis Sea
Vincennes Bay
South Magnetic Pole (2000)
Dumont d'Urville Sea
SOUTHERN OCEAN
Polar Stereographic Projection
METRES
FEET
0 0
200 656
2000 6562
3000 9843
4000 13124
5000 16404
6000 19686
7000 22967
9000 29529
0 400 MILES
0 500 KILOMETRES

1:60 000 000

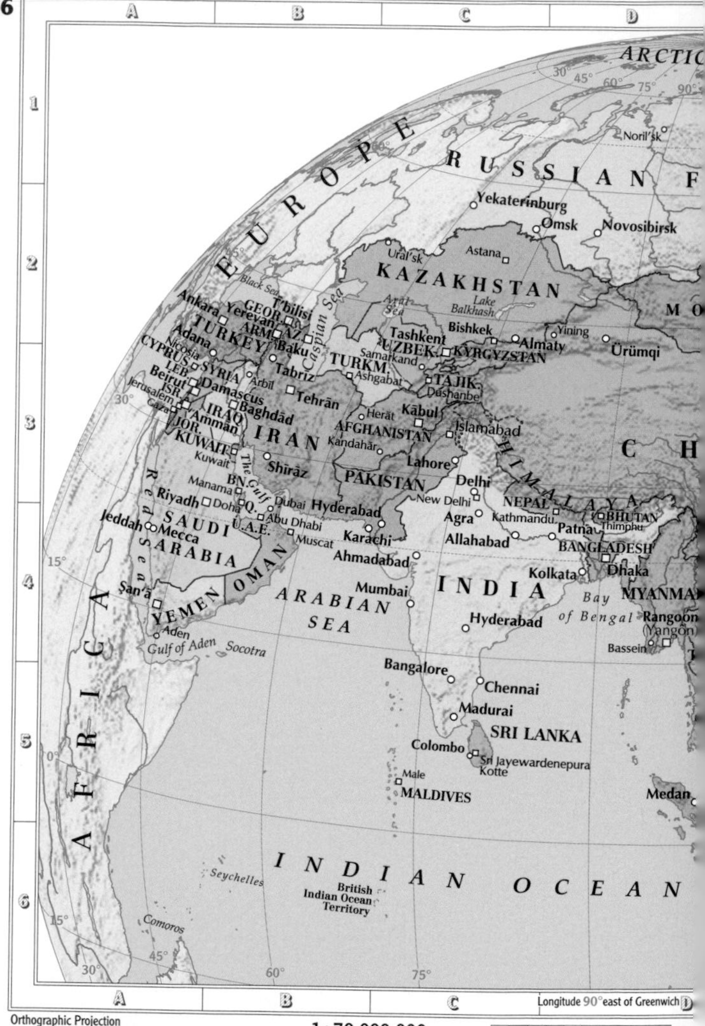

Orthographic Projection

1:70 000 000

MILES 0 500 1000

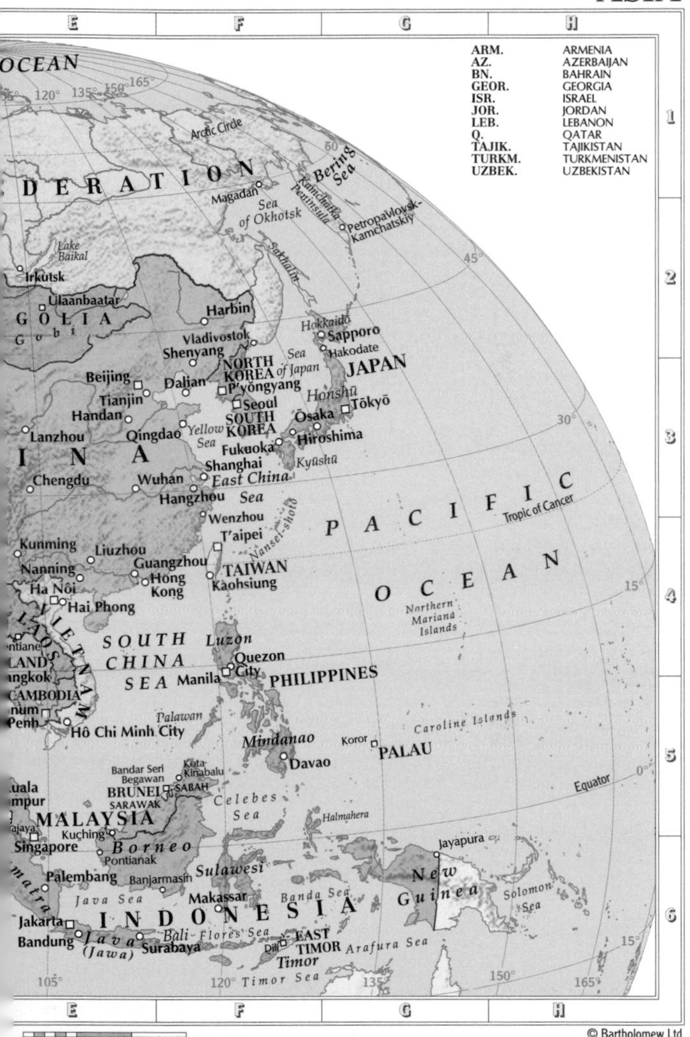
ARM. ARMENIA
AZ. AZERBAIJAN
BN. BAHRAIN
GEOR. GEORGIA
ISR. ISRAEL
JOR. JORDAN
LEB. LEBANON
Q. QATAR
TAJIK. TAJIKISTAN
TURKM. TURKMENISTAN
UZBEK. UZBEKISTAN
OCEAN
DERATION
Arctic Circle
Bering Sea
Magadan
Sea of Okhotsk
Kamchatka Peninsula
Petropavlovsk-Kamchatskiy
Lake Baikal
Sakhalin
Irkutsk
Ulaanbaatar
GOLIA
Gobi
Harbin
Vladivostok
Hokkaidō
Sapporo
Hakodate
Shenyang
NORTH KOREA
Sea of Japan
JAPAN
Beijing
Dalian
P'yŏngyang
Tianjin
Seoul
Honshū
Tōkyō
Handan
SOUTH KOREA
Ōsaka
Lanzhou
Qingdao
Yellow Sea
Hiroshima
Fukuoka
INA
Shanghai
Kyūshū
Chengdu
Wuhan
East China Sea
Hangzhou
Wenzhou
Nansei-shotō
PACIFIC
Tropic of Cancer
T'aipei
Kunming
Liuzhou
Guangzhou
TAIWAN
Nanning
Hong Kong
Kaohsiung
OCEAN
Ha Nôi
Hai Phong
Northern Mariana Islands
LAOS
VIETNAM
SOUTH CHINA SEA
Luzon
Quezon City
Manila
PHILIPPINES
CAMBODIA
Palawan
Hô Chi Minh City
Caroline Islands
Mindanao
Koror
PALAU
Davao
Bandar Seri Begawan
Kota Kinabalu
BRUNEI
SABAH
SARAWAK
Equator
Celebes Sea
MALAYSIA
Halmahera
Kuching
Singapore
Borneo
Pontianak
Jayapura
Palembang
Banjarmasin
Sulawesi
New Guinea
Java Sea
Makassar
Banda Sea
Solomon Sea
Jakarta
INDONESIA
Bandung
Java (Jawa)
Bali
Flores Sea
Surabaya
Dili
EAST TIMOR
Arafura Sea
Timor
Timor Sea
120°
135°
150°
165°
105°
60°
45°
30°
15°
0°
E
F
G
H
1
2
3
4
5
6
0
500
1000
1500 KILOMETRES

A 105° B 120°

1

Pyinmana Toungoo Chiang Rai Phayao Nan Chiang Mai Phrae Lampang Pegu Uttaradit Thaton Tak Phitsanulok Moulmein Khon Kaen

Louangphrabang Xiangkhoang Thanh Hoa Vinh Ha Tinh Udon Thani VIENTIANE (Viangchan) Dông Hôi Savannakhet Huê Đa Năng Sarayan

Nam Đinh Gulf of Tongking Xuwen Haikou Chengmai Wenchang Qionghai Dongfang Wanning Hainan (China)

Luzon Strait Batan Islands Babuyan Islands Laoag Aparri Tuguegarao Vigan Bontoc Ilagan San Fernando Luzon Dagupan Tarlac Quezon City MANILA Lucena Batangas Mindoro Romblon Calamian Group Cuyo Islands Panay Taytay Iloilo Negros

15°

THAILAND Lop Buri Tavoy Ayutthaya Surin Nakhon Ratchasima Ubon Ratchathani Pakxe BANGKOK (Krung Thep) Pattaya Mergui Palaw Chanthaburi CAMBODIA Batdambang Tenasserim Prachuap Khiri Khan Gulf of Thailand Kampong Spoe PHNUM PENH Takêv Sihanoukville Chumphon Ranong Surat Thani

LAOS VIETNAM Quang Ngai Qui Nhon Buôn Mê Thuôt Nha Trang Đa Lat Phan Rang Phan Thiêt Biên Hoa Tây Ninh Hô Chi Minh City (Saigon) Long Xuyen Can Tho Rach Gia Ca Mau Bac Lieu Mui Ca Mau Mouths of the Mekong

SOUTH CHINA SEA

Puerto Princesa Palawan Brooke's Point Sulu Sea Balabac Strait Banggi Kudat Zamboanga Isabela Basilan Jolo

2

Takua Pa Nakhon Si Thammarat Krabi Phuket Phatthalung Songkhla Hat Yai Yala Kangar Kota Bharu Alor Setar Georgetown Sungei Petani Pasir Putih Taiping Kuala Terengganu Ipoh Kuala Lipis

MALAYSIA

Banda Aceh Sigli Bireun Langsa Pangkalansusu Medan Simeulue Prapat Strait of Malacca PUTRAJAYA KUALA LUMPUR Labuhanbilik Gunungsitoli Sibolga Melaka Keluang Nias Dumai Muar Johor Bahru Pulau-pulau Batu Minas SINGAPORE Payakumbuh Bukittinggi Sijunjung Padang Siberut

Kepulauan Anambas Natuna Besar Kepulauan Natuna Kepulauan Tambelan Kepulauan Riau

Gunung Kinabalu 4101 Kota Kinabalu Sandakan SABAH BANDAR SERI BEGAWAN BRUNEI Lahad Datu Semporna Miri Banjaran Crocker Tawau Tarakan Bintulu Igan Mukah Sibu SARAWAK Tanjungselor Tanjungredeb Liku Kuching Sambas Debak Serian Sri Aman Singkawang Lubok Antu Mempawah Sambaliung Sangkulirang

Sulu Archipelago Celebes Sea Semenanjung Tolitoli Moutong Teluk Tomini Donggala Palu Poso Uekuli SULAWESI (CELEBES) Wotu 3074 Malili Makale Parepare Kolaka Watampone Makassar Bulukumba Bontosunggu Benteng Salayar Tanahjampea Kep. Bonerate Flores Sea Flores

SUMATRA (SUMATERA) G. Kerinci 3805 Sipura Pagai Utara Pagai Selatan Kepulauan Mentawai Jambi Bangko Pangkalpinang Sungailiat Bangka Belinyu Palembang Sekayu Tebingtinggi Bengkulu G. Dempo 3159 Bukit Barisan Lahat Bintuhan Krui Enggano Bandar Lampung

Kepulauan Lingga Selat Karimata Pontianak Sukadana Ketapang Manggar Belitung Toboali Kendawangan Pangkalanbuun Seruyan Sampit Kahayan Banjarmasin Martapura BORNEO Samarinda Balikpapan Amuntai Kotabaru Laut Macassar Strait Tg Selatan

INDONESIA

3

Java Sea Selat Sunda JAKARTA Cirebon Semarang Sukabumi Bandung Tk Palabuhanratu Cilacap Surakarta Surabaya Madura Kepulauan Kangean Jember Malang Bali Sea Bali Denpasar Mataram Lombok Selat Lombok Praya Dompu Raba Sumbawa Reo Ende Waikabubak Waingapu Sumba Timor

JAVA (JAWA)

INDIAN OCEAN

Christmas I. (Australia)

METRES / FEET
5000 / 16404
3000 / 9843
2000 / 6562
1000 / 3281
500 / 1640
200 / 656
0 / 0
LAND B.S.L.
200 / 656
4000 / 13124
6000 / 19686

A Longitude 105° east of Greenwich B 120°

Albers Equal Area Conic Projection

1:30 000 000

MILES 0 200 400 600

PACIFIC OCEAN
PHILIPPINE SEA
PHILIPPINES
Northern Mariana Islands (U.S.A.)
Pagan
Saipan
Tinian
CAPITOL HILL
Rota
Guam (U.S.A.)
HAGÅTÑA
Polillo Islands
Daet
Catanduanes
Sorsogon
Catarman
Samar
Catbalogan
Tacloban
Bacolod
Cebu
Tagbilaran
Surigao
Bohol Sea
Butuan
Cagayan de Oro
Oroquieta
Pagadian
Mindanao
Davao
Mati
Cotabato
Moro Gulf
General Santos
Ulithi
Fais
Yap
FEDERATED STATES OF MICRONESIA
Ngulu
Sorol
Eauripik
Caroline Islands
PALAU
KOROR
Kepulauan Talaud
Kepulauan Sangir
Morotai
Molucca Sea
Manado
Tobelo
Tondano
Ternate
Halmahera
Gorontalo
Sao-Siu
Equator
Pelleluhu Is
Hermit Is
Waigeo
Kwoka
Jazirah Doberai
Manokwari
Biak
Numfoor
Selat Yapen
Tg d'Urville
Sorong
Ransiki
Labuna
Bacan
Obi
Salawati
Misool
Fafanlap
Inanwatan
Yapen
Sarmi
Jayapura
Vanimo
Aitape
Schouten Islands
Pegunungan Van Rees
Taritatu
Wewak
Manam I.
Long Island
Madang
Luwuk
Peleng
Taliabu
Mangole
Banggai
Kepulauan Sula
Seram
Teluk Berau
Babo
Teluk Cenderawasih
Nabire
Pk Jaya
Pk Trikora
Pk Mandala
Sepik
PAPUA
Central Ra.
Umboi
Huon Peninsula
Namlea
Buru
Piru
Binaija
Seram Sea
Fakfak
Kaimana
Enarotali
5030
4730
4700
4000
4309
Goroka
Kendari
Ambon
Saparua
3019
Adi
NEW GUINEA
Mendi
Mount Hagen
Lae
Wowoni
Raha
Buton
Kepulauan Banda
Kepulauan Watubela
Kepulauan Kai
Amamapare
Tual
Dobo
Wokam
Kai Kecil
Kai Besar
Benjina
Kikori
NEW GUINEA
Wau
Morobe
Kepulauan Tukangbesi
Banda Sea
Kepulauan Aru
Kobroör
Trangan
Sia
Tg Deyong
Digul
Kerema
Mt Victoria
Bereina
4073
P. Dolak
Balimo
Gulf of Papua
Kepulauan Barat Daya
Damar
Wuliaru
Larat
Kepulauan Tanimbar
Tg Vals
Merauke
Morehead
Daru
PORT MORESBY
Kepulauan Alor
Alor
Roma
Babar
Kalabahi
Wetar
Huaki
Kaiwatu
Saumlakki
Kepulauan Sermata
Selaru
Leti
DILI
Manatuto
2960
EAST TIMOR
Arafura Sea
C. York
Bamaga
Kefamenanu
Timor
Kupang
Rote
Melville Island
AUSTRALIA
Croker I.
Wessel Is
C. Wessel
Gulf of Carpentaria
Weipa
Bathurst Island
Van Diemen Gulf
Nhulunbuy
C. Arnhem
Beagle Gulf
Darwin
Jabiru
Coen
135°
15°
0°
0
500
1000 KILOMETRES

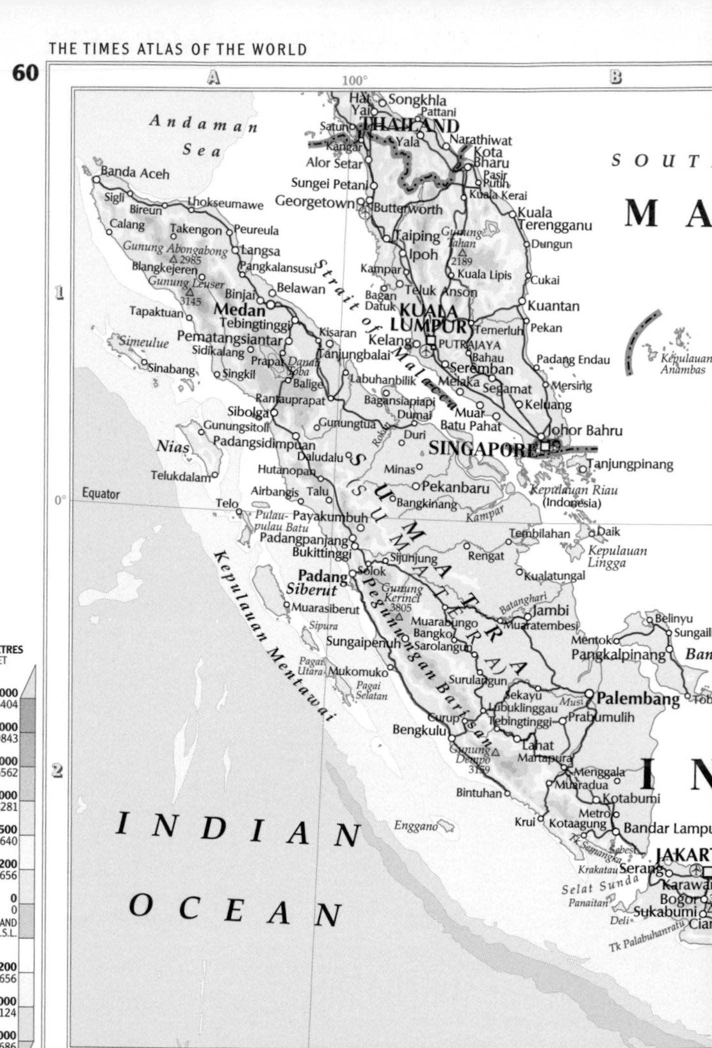
Andaman Sea
SOUTH
MA
Banda Aceh
Sigli
Bireun
Lhokseumawe
Calang
Takengon
Peureula
Gunung Abongabong 2985
Langsa
Blangkejeren
Gunung Leuser 3145
Pangkalansusu
Binjai
Belawan
Medan
Tapaktuan
Tebingtinggi
Pematangsiantar
Simeulue
Sidikalang
Sinabang
Singkil
Prapat
Danau Toba
Balige
Kisaran
Tanjungbalai
Labuhanbilik
Rantauprapat
Sibolga
Gunungsitoli
Nias
Padangsidimpuan
Telukdalam
Hat Yai
Songkhla
Pattani
THAILAND
Satun
Kangar
Yala
Narathiwat
Kota Bharu
Alor Setar
Pasir Putih
Sungei Petani
Kuala Kerai
Georgetown
Butterworth
Kuala Terengganu
Taiping
Gunung Tahan 2189
Dungun
Ipoh
Kampar
Kuala Lipis
Cukai
Strait of Malacca
Bagan Datuk
Teluk Anson
Kuantan
KUALA LUMPUR
Temerluh
Pekan
Kelang
PUTRAJAYA
Bahau
Padang Endau
Kepulauan Anambas
Seremban
Melaka
Segamat
Mersing
Bagansiapiapi
Muar
Keluang
Dumai
Batu Pahat
Johor Bahru
Gunungtua
Duri
SINGAPORE
Rokan
Tanjungpinang
Daludalu
Hutanopan
Minas
SUMATERA
Equator
Airbangis
Talu
Pekanbaru
Kepulauan Riau (Indonesia)
Telo
Bangkinang
Pulau-pulau Batu
Payakumbuh
Kampar
Tembilahan
Daik
Padangpanjang
Rengat
Kepulauan Lingga
Bukittinggi
Sijunjung
Kepulauan Mentawai
Solok
Kualatungal
Padang
Siberut
Gunung Kerinci 3805
Batanghari
Jambi
Muarasiberut
Pegunungan Barisan
Muarabungo
Muaratembesi
Belinyu
Sipura
Bangko
Sungailiat
Mentok
Sungaipenuh
Sarolangun
Pangkalpinang
Bangka
Pagai Utara
Mukomuko
Pagai Selatan
Surulangun
Sekayu
Palembang
Toboali
Musi
Lubuklinggau
Curup
Tebingtinggi
Prabumulih
Bengkulu
Lahat
Gunung Dempo 3159
Martapura
IN
Menggala
Muaradua
Bintuhan
Kotabumi
Metro
INDIAN OCEAN
Enggano
Krui
Kotaagung
Bandar Lampung
Tk Semangka
Sabesi
JAKARTA
Krakatau
Serang
Selat Sunda
Karawang
Panaitan
Bogor
Sukabumi
Deli
Cianjur
Tk Palabuhanratu
METRES FEET
5000 16404
3000 9843
2000 6562
1000 3281
500 1640
200 656
0 0
LAND B.S.L.
200 656
4000 13124
6000 19686
Longitude 100° east of Greenwich
Albers Equal Area Conic Projection
1:15 000 000
MILES 0 100 200 300

MALAYSIA AND INDONESIA WEST

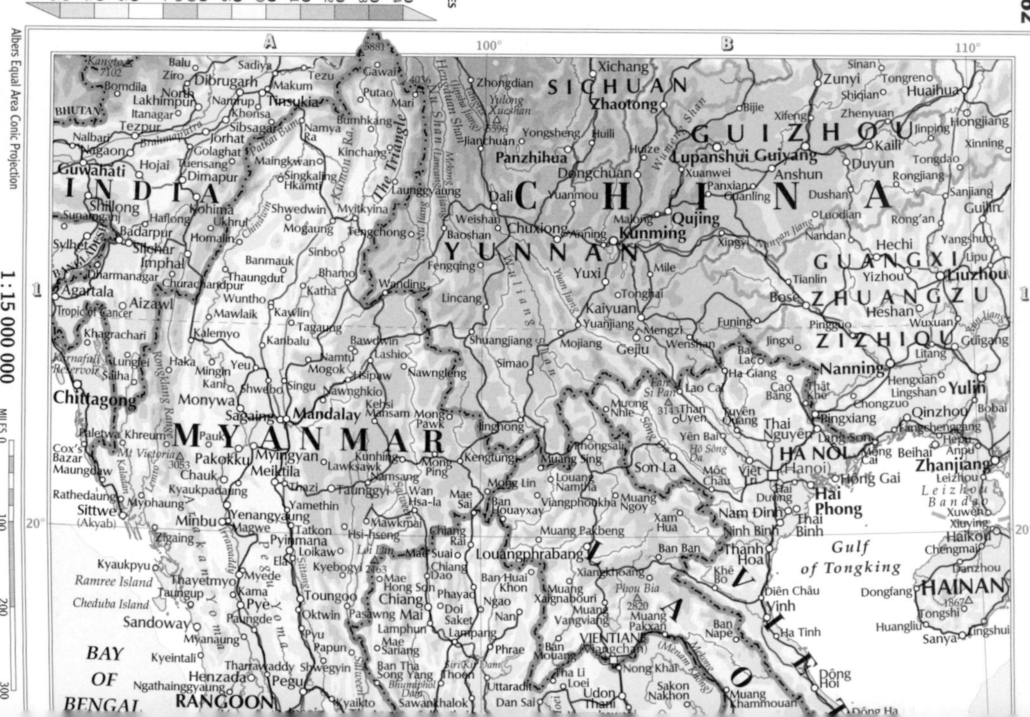

Albers Equal Area Conic Projection

1:15 000 000

MILES 0 100 200 300

0 250 500 KILOMETRES

Albers Equal Area Conic Projection

1:15 000 000

MILES 0 100 0 250 KILOMETRES

NORTH KOREA AND SOUTH KOREA

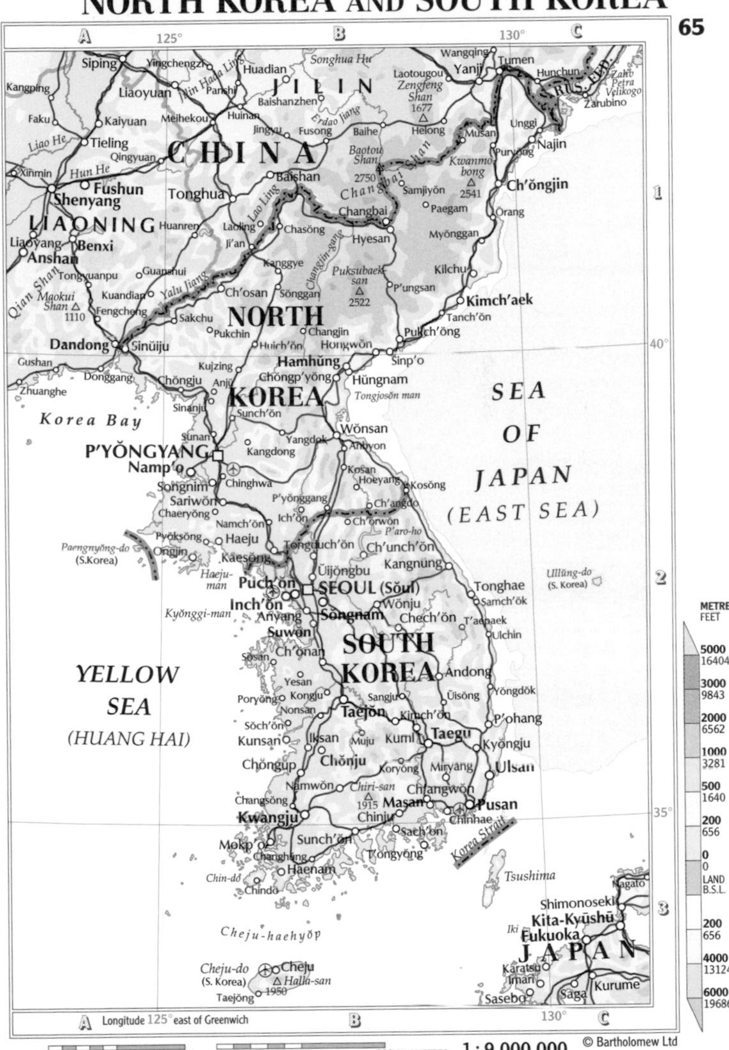

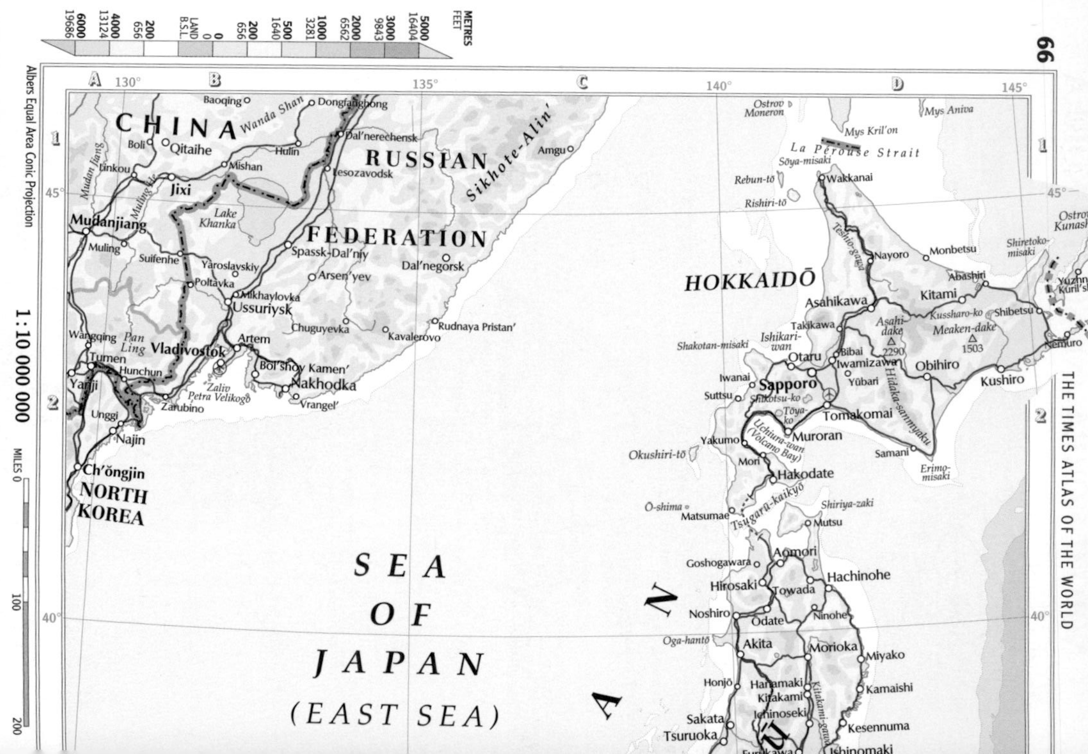

Albers Equal Area Conic Projection

1:10 000 000

MILES 0 100 200

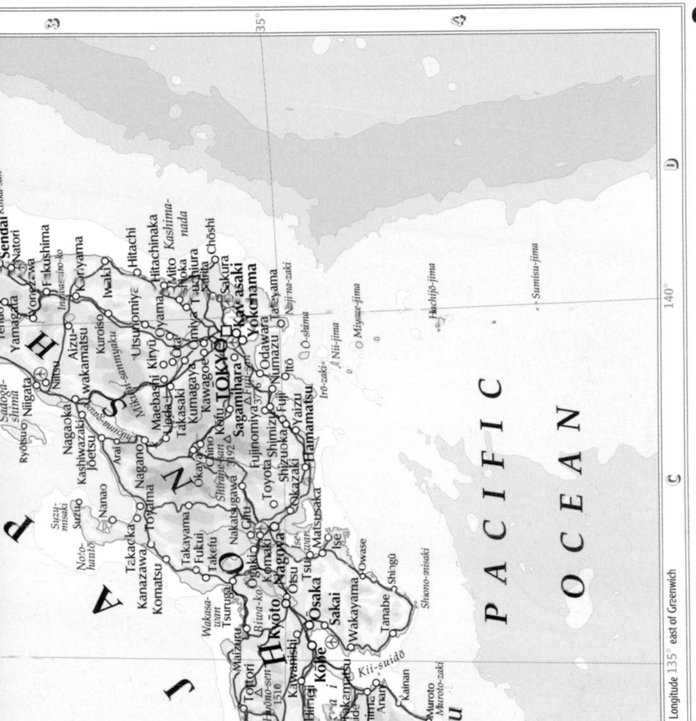

PACIFIC OCEAN
JAPAN
HONSHU
SHIKOKU
KYŪSHŪ
TŌKYŌ
Yokohama
Kawasaki
Sendai
Natori
Fukushima
Yamagata
Tendō
Yonezawa
Kōriyama
Iwaki
Hitachi
Hitachinaka
Mito
Chōshi
Sakura
Narita
Tateyama
Niigata
Nagaoka
Kashiwazaki
Jōetsu
Nagano
Toyama
Kanazawa
Komatsu
Fukui
Takefu
Tsuruga
Nanao
Suzu
Takaoka
Takayama
Gifu
Nagoya
Toyota
Okazaki
Hamamatsu
Shizuoka
Shimizu
Fujinomiya
Fuji
Numazu
Odawara
Sagamihara
Kōfu
Maebashi
Takasaki
Kumagaya
Kawagoe
Ōmiya
Utsunomiya
Oyama
Kiryū
Ōta
Kuroiso
Aizu-wakamatsu
Kyōto
Ōsaka
Sakai
Kōbe
Himeji
Kawanishi
Wakayama
Tanabe
Shingū
Owase
Ise
Matsusaka
Tsu
Ōtsu
Ōgaki
Komaki
Maizuru
Tottori
Kurayoshi
Matsue
Izumo
Gōtsu
Hamada
Masuda
Hagi
Nagato
Yamaguchi
Shimonoseki
Kita-Kyūshū
Okayama
Kurashiki
Tsuyama
Hiroshima
Kure
Iwakuni
Hōfu
Ube
Tokushima
Takamatsu
Sakaide
Anan
Kainan
Muroto
Kōchi
Niihama
Matsuyama
Uwajima
Yawatahama
Fukuoka
Kurume
Saga
Sasebo
Nagasaki
Isahaya
Ōmura
Imari
Karatsu
Kumamoto
Arao
Yatsushiro
Ōita
Beppu
Usa
Saiki
Nobeoka
Miyazaki
Miyakonojō
Kagoshima
Kanoya
Sendai
Makurazaki
Nishino-omote
Tsushima
Iki
Oki-shotō
Dōgo
Dōzen
Liancourt Rocks
Ullŭng-do
(S. Korea)
Sadoga-shima
Noto-hantō
Biwa-ko
Kii-suidō
Bungo-suidō
Ōsumi-kaikyō
Ōsumi-shotō
Hachijō-jima
Miyake-jima
Ō-shima
Nii-jima
Sumisu-jima
Fuji-san 3776
Longitude 135° east of Greenwich
0 100 200 KILOMETRES
© Bartholomew Ltd

METRES
FEET

METRES	FEET
5000	16404
3000	9843
2000	6562
1000	3281
500	1640
200	656
0	0
LAND B.S.L.	
200	656
4000	13124
6000	19686

Albers Equal Area Conic Projection

1:30 000 000

MILES 0 200 400 600

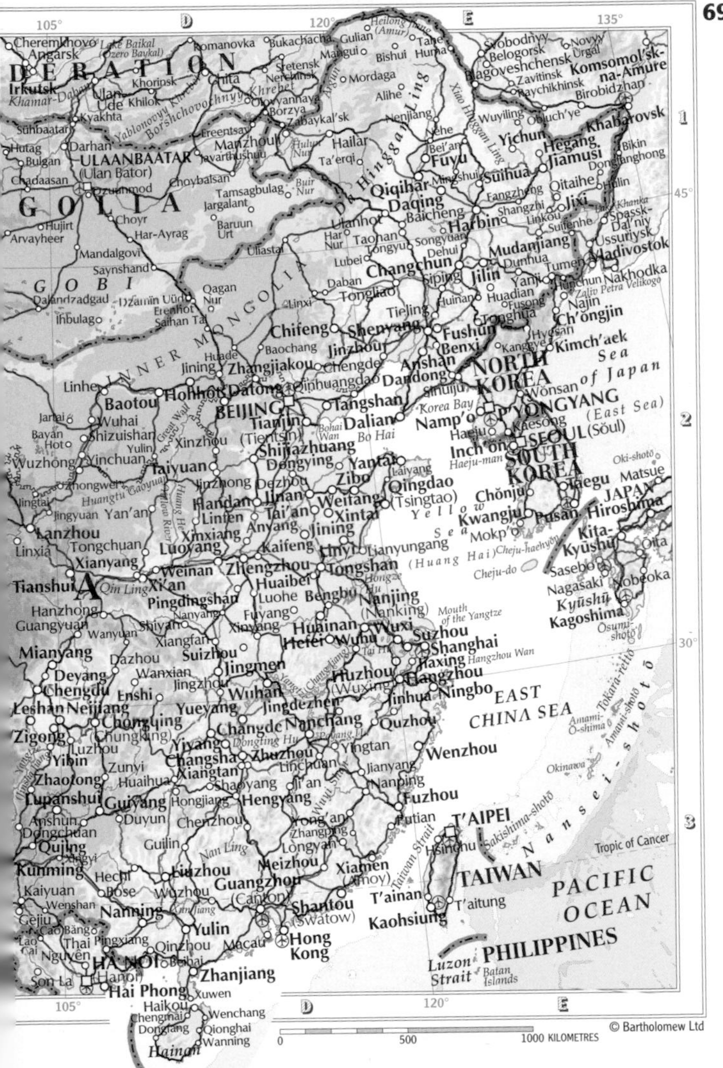
105°
D
120°
E
135°
1
2
3
45°
30°
Cheremkhovo
Angarsk
Lake Baikal
(Ozero Baykal)
Romanovka
Bukachacha
Gulian
Heilong Jiang
(Amur)
Tahe
Svobodnyy
Novyy Urgal
Belogorsk
Irkutsk
Khamar-Daban
Ulan-Ude
Khilok
Khorinsk
Chita
Sretensk
Nerchinsk
Mangui
Bishui
Huma
Blagoveshchensk
Zavitinsk
Raychikhinsk
Komsomol'sk-na-Amure
Birobidzhan
Yablonovyy Khrebet
Borshchovochnyy Khrebet
Mordaga
Alihe
Borzya
Zabaykal'sk
Kyakhta
Sühbaatar
Nenjiang
Wuyiling
Obluch'ye
Khabarovsk
Bikin
Darhan
Hutag
Bulgan
ULAANBAATAR
(Ulan Bator)
Ereentsav
Manzhouli
Hulun Nur
Hailar
Ta'erqi
Nehe
Bei'an
Fuyu
Yichun
Hegang
Jiamusi
Dongfanghong
Xiao Hinggan Ling
Da Hinggan Ling
Chadaasan
Dzuunmod
Choybalsan
Buir Nur
Tamsagbulag
Jargalant
Qiqihar
Mingshui
Suihua
Qitaihe
Hulin
MONGOLIA
Choyr
Hujirt
Arvayheer
Har-Ayrag
Baruun Urt
Daqing
Baicheng
Fangzheng
Shangzhi
Linkou
Jixi
Khanka
Spassk-Dal'niy
Harbin
Suifenhe
Ussuriysk
Ulanhot
Har Nur
Taonan
Tongyu
Songyuan
Dehui
Mudanjiang
Vladivostok
Mandalgovi
Saynshand
Uliastai
Lubei
Changchun
Dunhua
Tumen
Nakhodka
GOBI
Dalandzadgad
Dzamïn Üüd
Erenhot
Saihan Tal
Qagan Nur
Daban
Tongliao
Linxi
Siping
Jilin
Yanji
Hunchun
Zaliv Petra Velikogo
Inbulag
Huinan
Huadian
Fusong
Najin
Tieling
Tonghua
Ch'ŏngjin
Chifeng
Shenyang
Fushun
Hyesan
Kimch'aek
INNER MONGOLIA
Baochang
Jinzhou
Benxi
Kanggye
Huade
Jining
Zhangjiakou
Chengde
Anshan
NORTH KOREA
Sea of Japan
(East Sea)
Linhe
Baotou
Hohhot
Datong
Qinhuangdao
Dandong
Sinuiju
Wŏnsan
BEIJING
Tangshan
Korea Bay
P'YONGYANG
Jartai
Wuhai
Tianjin
(Tientsin)
Bohai Wan
Bo Hai
Dalian
Namp'o
Kaesŏng
Bayan Hot
Shizuishan
Great Wall
Xinzhou
Haeju
SEOUL (Sŏul)
Yulin
Shijiazhuang
Inch'ŏn
SOUTH KOREA
Wuzhong
Yinchuan
Taiyuan
Dongying
Yantai
Laiyang
Haeju-man
Oki-shotō
Zhongwei
Jinzhong
Dezhou
Zibo
Qingdao
(Tsingtao)
Taegu
Matsue
Huangtu Gaoyuan
Handan
Jinan
Weifang
Chŏnju
JAPAN
Jingtai
Jingyuan
Yan'an
Huang He
(Yellow River)
Linfen
Tai'an
Xintai
Yellow Sea
(Huang Hai)
Kwangju
Pusan
Hiroshima
Lanzhou
Xinxiang
Anyang
Jining
Mokp'o
Kita-Kyūshū
Oita
Linxia
Tongchuan
Luoyang
Kaifeng
Linyi
Lianyungang
Cheju-haehyŏp
Xianyang
Zhengzhou
Tongshan
Cheju-do
Sasebo
Tianshui
Weinan
Xi'an
Qin Ling
Huaibei
Hongze Hu
Nagasaki
Nobeoka
Pingdingshan
Luohe
Bengbu
Nanjing
(Nanking)
Kyūshū
Hanzhong
Guangyuan
Nanyang
Shiyan
Fuyang
Mouth of the Yangtze
Kagoshima
Wanyuan
Xinyang
Huainan
Wuxi
Suzhou
Ōsumi-shotō
Xiangfan
Hefei
Wuhu
Tai Hu
Shanghai
Mianyang
Dazhou
Suizhou
Jiaxing
Hangzhou Wan
Deyang
Wanxian
Jingmen
Huzhou
(Wuxing)
Hangzhou
Chengdu
Enshi
Jingzhou
Wuhan
Jinhua
Ningbo
EAST CHINA SEA
Leshan
Neijiang
Yueyang
Jingdezhen
Chongqing
(Chungking)
Nanchang
Quzhou
Amami-Ō-shima
Tokara-rettō
Amami-shotō
Zigong
Luzhou
Changde
Yiyang
Dongting Hu
Poyang Hu
Yingtan
Yibin
Changsha
Zhuzhou
Wenzhou
Xiangtan
Zunyi
Linchuan
Jianyang
Okinawa
Zhaotong
Huaihua
Shaoyang
Ji'an
Nanping
Liupanshui
Guiyang
Hongjiang
Hengyang
Wuyi Shan
Fuzhou
Nansei-shotō
Sakishima-shotō
Anshun
Duyun
Chenzhou
Yong'an
Zhangping
Putian
T'AIPEI
Qujing
Guilin
Nan Ling
Longyan
Hsinchu
Taiwan Strait
Tropic of Cancer
Kunming
Hechi
Liuzhou
Meizhou
Xiamen
(Amoy)
TAIWAN
Kaiyuan
Bose
Wuzhou
Guangzhou
(Canton)
T'ainan
T'aitung
PACIFIC OCEAN
Wenshan
Nanning
Xun Jiang
Shantou
(Swatow)
Kaohsiung
Gejiu
Cao Bang
Yulin
Pingxiang
Qinzhou
Macau
Hong Kong
PHILIPPINES
Thai Nguyen
Beihai
HA NOI
(Hanoi)
Luzon Strait
Batan Islands
Son La
Hai Phong
Zhanjiang
Xuwen
Haikou
Chengmai
Wenchang
Dongfang
Qionghai
Wanning
Hainan
0
500
1000 KILOMETRES

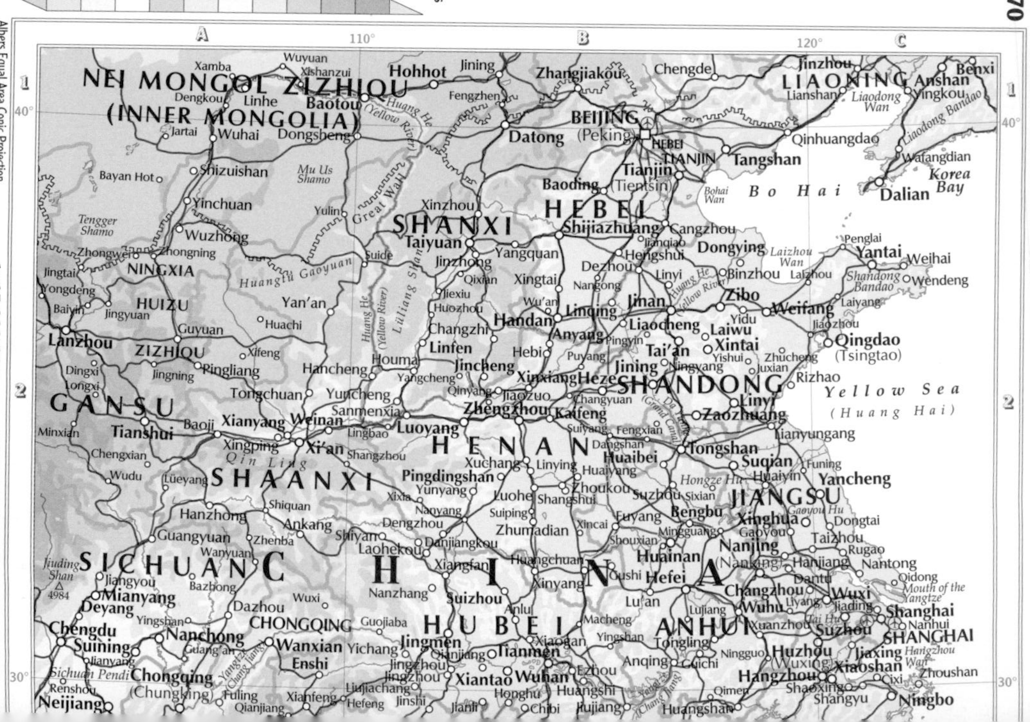

METRES	FEET
5000	16404
3000	9843
2000	6562
1000	3281
500	1640
200	656
0	0
LAND B.S.L.	
200	656
4000	13124
6000	19686

Albers Equal Area Conic Projection

1:15 000 000

MILES 0 100 200 300

EAST
CHINA
SEA
SOUTH
CHINA
SEA
Luzon
Strait
Taiwan Strait
Gulf
of Tongking
Tropic of Cancer
ZHEJIANG
FUJIAN
JIANGXI
HUNAN
GUIZHOU
GUANGDONG
GUANGXI
ZHUANGZU
ZIZHIQU
HAINAN
TAIWAN
HONG KONG
VIETNAM
LAOS
LUZON
PHILIPPINES
Leizhou Bandao
Dongting Hu
Poyang Hu
Nan Ling
Wuyi Shan
Jinhua
Wenzhou
Quzhou
Jingdezhen
Nanchang
Changsha
Zhuzhou
Xiangtan
Hengyang
Pingxiang
Ji'an
Ganzhou
Yueyang
Changde
Yiyang
Shaoyang
Yongzhou
Fuzhou
Sanming
Xiamen
(Amoy)
Zhangzhou
Meizhou
Shantou
(Swatow)
Chaozhou
Guangzhou
(Canton)
Shenzhen
Hong Kong
Macau
Shaoguan
Zhanjiang
Maoming
Guilin
Liuzhou
Nanning
Wuzhou
Yulin
Beihai
Haikou
Sanya
Guiyang
Zunyi
Anshun
Duyun
Kaili
Qujing
Zhaotong
Liupanshui
Zigong
Yibin
Luzhou
HA NÔI
(Hanoi)
Hai Phong
Nam Đinh
Thanh Hoa
Vinh
TAIPEI
Chilung
(Keeling)
Hsinchu
T'aichung
Chiai
T'ainan
Kaohsiung
Hualien
T'aitung
P'ingtung
Laoag
Aparri
Batan Islands
Babuyan Islands
Longitude 110° east of Greerwich
0
250
500 KILOMETRES
© Bartholomew Ltd

METRES	FEET
5000	16404
3000	9843
2000	6562
1000	3281
500	1640
200	656
0	0
LAND B.S.L.	
200	656
4000	13124
6000	19686

Albers Equal Area Conic Projection

1 : 20 000 000

MILES 0 100 200 300 400

MYANMAR
BAY OF BENGAL
INDIAN OCEAN
ARABIAN SEA
SRI LANKA
MALDIVES
Deccan
Western Ghats
Eastern Ghats
Mumbai
(Bombay)
Pune
(Poona)
Hyderabad
Bangalore
Chennai
(Madras)
Colombo
SRI JAYEWARDENEPURA KOTTE
Nagpur
Surat
Nashik
Aurangabad
Solapur
Secunderabad
Vishakhapatnam
Vijayawada
Madurai
Coimbatore
Cochin
Trivandrum
Calicut
Salem
Dharwad
Hubli
Cuttack
Bhubaneshwar
Sittwe
Sandoway
Andaman Islands
(India)
Nicobar Islands
(India)
Laccadive
Islands
(India)
Ten Degree Channel
Nine Degree Channel
Eight Degree Channel
Gulf of Mannar
Gulf of Khambhat
Mouths of the Ganges
Mouths of the Godavari
Mouths of the Krishna
Longitude 90° east of Greenwich
0
200
400
600 KILOMETRES

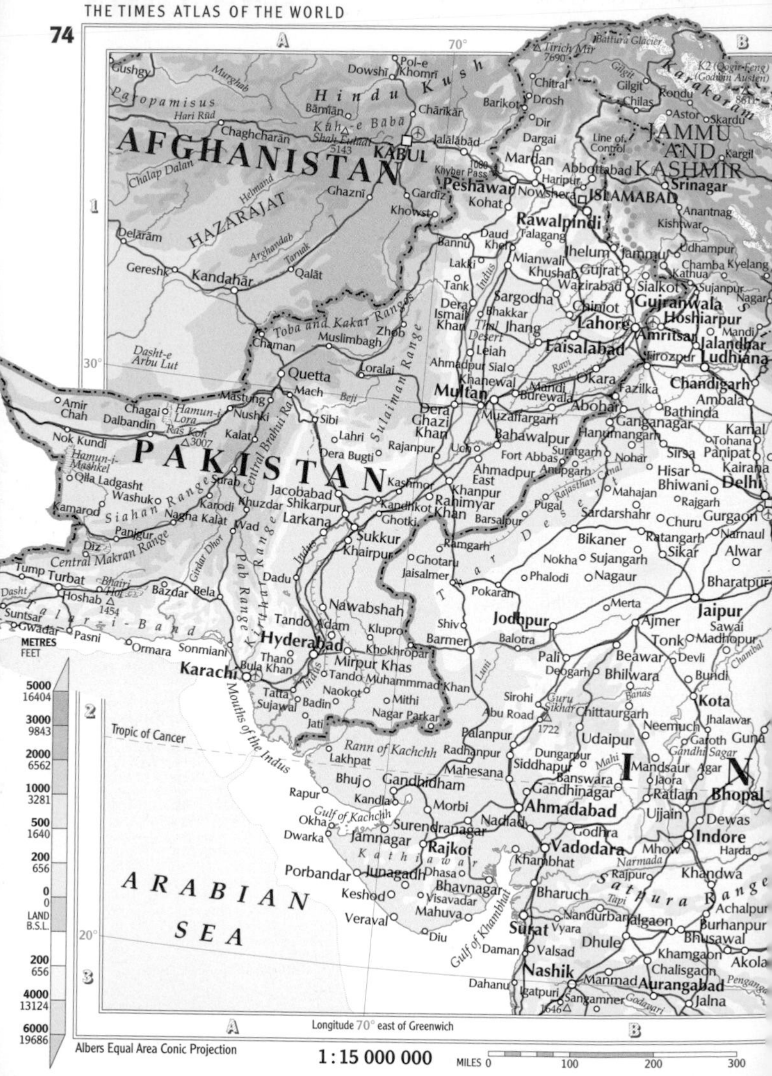

Albers Equal Area Conic Projection

1:15 000 000

PAKISTAN, INDIA AND BANGLADESH

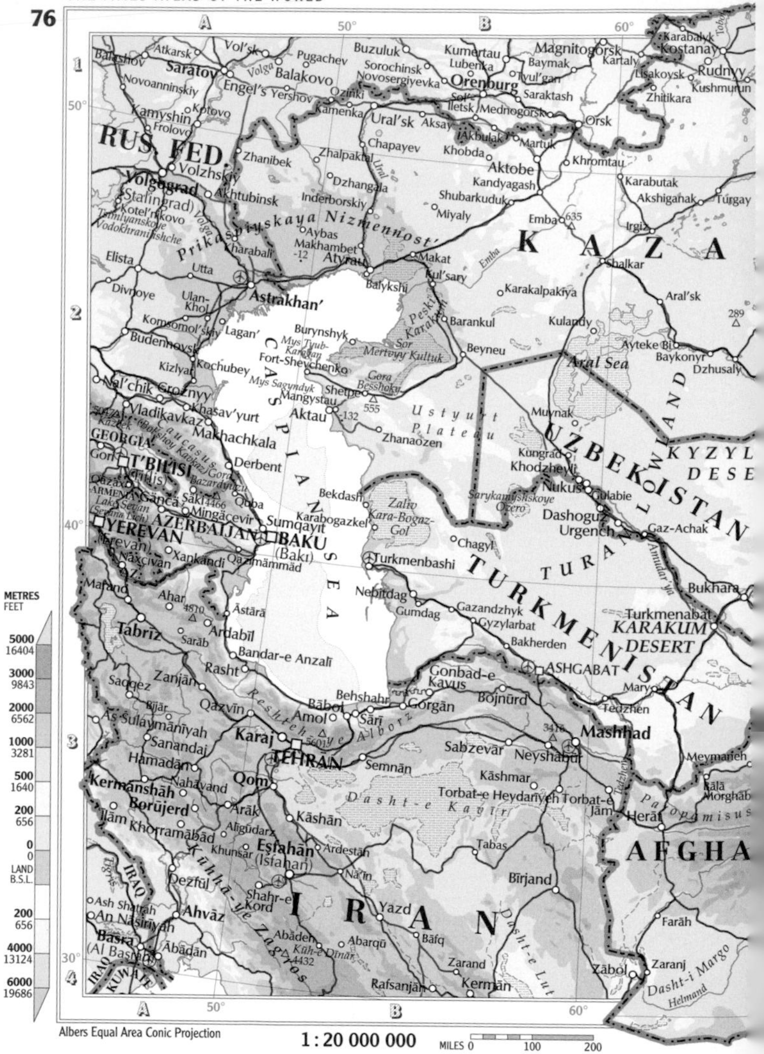

METRES	FEET
5000	16404
3000	9843
2000	6562
1000	3281
500	1640
200	656
0	0
LAND B.S.L.	
200	656
4000	13124
6000	19686

Albers Equal Area Conic Projection

1:20 000 000

MILES 0 100 200

RUS. FED.
KAZAKHSTAN
KYRGYZSTAN
TAJIKISTAN
CHINA
PAKISTAN
INDIA
NEPAL
AFGHANISTAN
ASTANA (Akmola)
BISHKEK
TASHKENT
DUSHANBE
KABUL
ISLAMABAD
Petropavlovsk
Kokshetau
Pavlodar
Semipalatinsk
Ust'-Kamenogorsk
Karaganda
Temirtau
Zhezkazgan
Balkhash
Taldykorgan
Almaty
Kyzylorda
Shymkent
Taraz
Turkestan
Namangan
Andizhan
Osh
Fergana
Kokand
Khujand
Samarkand
Karshi
Termez
Mazar-e Sharif
Kulob
Kashi
Aksu
Yining
Karamay
Shihezi
Kuqa
Hotan
Gilgit
Srinagar
Peshawar
Rawalpindi
Lahore
Faisalabad
Amritsar
Ludhiana
Chandigarh
Kandahār
Kazakhskiy Melkosopochnik
Betpak-Dala
Lake Balkhash (Ozero Balkhash)
TIEN SHAN
Pamir
Hindu Kush
KUNLUN SHAN
HIMALAYA
XINJIANG UYGUR ZIZHIQU
Tarim Pendi
Taklimakan Shamo
XIZANG ZIZHIQU (TIBET)
Qingzang Gaoyuan
JAMMU AND KASHMIR
AKSAI CHIN
Line of Control
K2 (Qogir Feng) (Godwin Austen)
Longitude 70° east of Greenwich
0 200 400 600 KILOMETRES
© Bartholomew Ltd

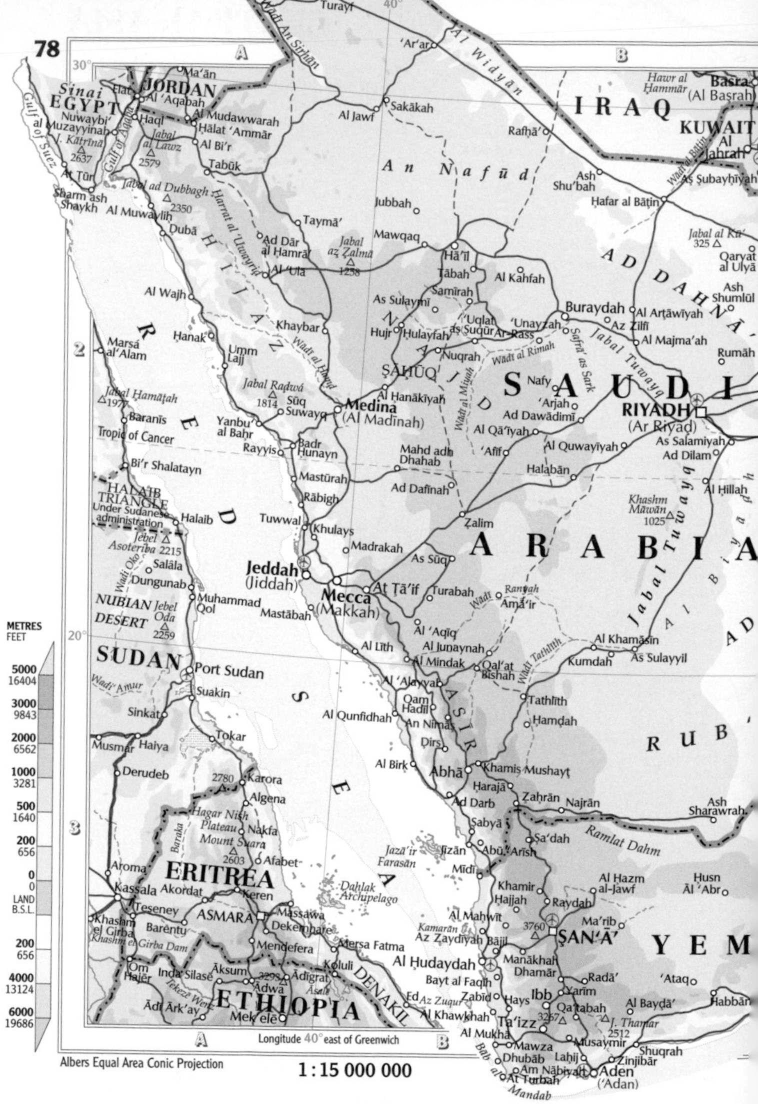

A
B
2
3
30°
40°
20°
Sinai
EGYPT
JORDAN
IRAQ
KUWAIT
SAUDI ARABIA
SUDAN
ERITREA
ETHIOPIA
YEMEN
RED SEA
Gulf of Suez
Gulf of Aqaba
Tropic of Cancer
Elat
Ma'ān
Al 'Aqabah
Nuwaybi'
al Muzayyinah
Haql
Al Mudawwarah
Ḩālat 'Ammār
Al Bi'r
J. Kātrīnā
2637
Jabal al Lawz
2579
Tabūk
At Ţūr
Sharm ash Shaykh
Jabal ad Dubbagh
2350
Al Muwayliḩ
Dubā
Harrat al 'Uwayrid
Turayf
'Ar'ar
Al Widyān
Wādī As Sirḩān
Sakākah
Al Jawf
An Nafūd
Jubbah
Taymā'
Ad Dār al Ḩamrā'
Jabal az Zalmā
1258
Al 'Ulā
Mawqaq
Ḩā'il
Ţābah
Al Kahfah
Samīrah
As Sulaymī
Hawr al Ḩammār
Basra
(Al Başrah)
Rafḩā'
Ash Shu'bah
Ḩafar al Bāţin
Wādī al Bāţin
Al Jahrah
Aş Şubayḩīyah
Jabal al Ku'
325
Qaryat al Ulyā
Ash Shumlūl
AD DAHNĀ'
Buraydah
Al Arţāwīyah
Az Zilfī
Al Majma'ah
Rumāh
'Unayzah
'Uqlat aş Şuqūr
Ar Rass
Hujr
Ḩulayfah
Nuqrah
Wādī al Rimah
Şafrā' as Sark
Jabal Ţuwayq
HIJAZ
NAJD
Al Wajh
Khaybar
Wādī al Ḩamḑ
Ḩanak
Marsá al 'Alam
Umm Lajj
Jabal Raḑwá
1814
Jabal Ḩamāţah
1977
Sūq Suwayq
Medina
(Al Madīnah)
Al Ḩanākīyah
ŞAHŪQ
Wādī al Miyah
Nafy
'Arjah
Ad Dawādimī
RIYADH
(Ar Riyāḑ)
Baranīs
Yanbu' al Baḩr
Rayyis
Badr Ḩunayn
Al Qā'īyah
'Afīf
Al Quwayīyah
As Salamiyah
Ad Dilam
Mahd adh Dhahab
Bi'r Shalatayn
Mastūrah
Halabān
HALAIB TRIANGLE
Under Sudanese administration
Halaib
Ad Dafīnah
Al Ḩillah
Rābigh
Khashm Māwān
1025
Tuwwal
Khulays
Ẓalim
Madrakah
Jebel Asoteriba
2215
Salâla
Wadi Oko
As Sūq
Jeddah
(Jiddah)
Mecca
(Makkah)
Aţ Ţā'if
Turabah
Wādī Ranyah
Amā'ir
Dungunab
Muhammad Qol
Mastābah
NUBIAN DESERT
Jebel Oda
2259
Al 'Aqīq
Al Junaynah
Al Līth
Al Mindak
Qal'at Bīshah
Wādī Tathlīth
Al Khamāsīn
Kumdah
As Sulayyil
Al Biyāḑ
Port Sudan
Wadi Amur
Suakin
Al 'Alayyah
Qam Hadīl
'ASIR
Al Qunfidhah
An Nimāş
Tathlīth
Ḩamḑah
Sinkat
Tokar
Musmar
Haiya
Dirs
RUB'
Al Birk
Abhā
Khamīs Mushayţ
Derudeb
2780
Karora
Algena
Ḩarajā
Ad Darb
Ẓahrān
Najrān
Ash Sharawrah
Hagar Nish Plateau
Nakfa
Baraka
Mount Suara
2603
Afabet
Şabyā
Şa'dah
Ramlat Dahm
Jazā'ir Farasān
Jīzān
Abū 'Arīsh
Mīdī
Aroma
Kassala
Akordat
Keren
Dahlak Archipelago
Khamir
Ḩajjah
Al Ḩazm al-Jawf
Ḩusn Āl 'Abr
Raydah
Teseney
ASMARA
Massawa
Khashm el Girba
Barentu
Dekemhare
Al Maḩwīt
Kamarān
Az Zaydīyah
Bājil
3760
ŞAN'Ā'
Ma'rib
Khashm el Girba Dam
Mendefera
Mersa Fatma
Manākhah
Dhamār
Al Ḩudaydah
Om Hajer
Inda Silasē
Āksum
3298
Ādīgrat
Adwa
Koluli
DENAKIL
Asale
Tekezē Wenz
Bayt al Faqīh
Raḑā'
'Ataq
Yarīm
Ed
Az Zuqur
Zabīd
Ḩays
Ibb
Ādī Ārk'ay
Mek'elē
Al Khawkhah
Ta'izz
Qa'ţabah
3267
Al Bayḑā'
Ḩabbān
J. Thamar
2512
Al Mukhā
Mawza
Musaymīr
Shuqrah
Dhubāb
Laḩij
Zinjibār
Bāb al Mandab
Am Nābiyah
Aţ Turbah
Aden
('Adan)
METRES
FEET
5000
16404
3000
9843
2000
6562
1000
3281
500
1640
200
656
0
0
LAND B.S.L.
200
656
4000
13124
6000
19686
Longitude 40° east of Greenwich
Albers Equal Area Conic Projection
1:15 000 000

Khorramshahr
Bandar-e Emām Khomeynī
Ābādān
Al Fāw
KUWAIT (Al Kuwayt)
Al Aḩmadī
Kāzerūn
Shīrāz
Ganāveh
Būshehr
Borāzjān
Farrāshband
Ahram
Khvormūj
Dowlatābād
Zīr Rūd
Kangān
Firūzābād
Qīr
Jahrom
Jūyom
Khonj
Evaz
Lār
Lamard
Hāleh
Gāvbandī
Bastak
Bandar-e Maqām
Bandar-e Chārak
Bandar-e Lengeh
Kūh-e Tābask 3218
Zarqān
Arsenajān
Daryācheh-ye Tashk
Kherāmeh
Estahbān
Fasā
Neyrīz
Dārāb
Rostāq
Ḩājjīābād
Sa'ādatābād
Rafsanjān
Bardsīr
Kermān
Sīrjān
Zeydābād
Bāft
Kūh-e Ilazārān 4420
'Alīābād
Kūh-e Fūrgun 3279
Dowlatābād
Kahnūj
Bandar-e 'Abbās
Fāryāb
Lāft
Qeshm
Sūzā
Mīnāb
Sīrīk
Jaghīn
IRAN
Nosratābād
Hormak
Kahūrak
Zāhedān
Mīrjāveh
Tahrūd
Bam
Vakīlābād
Rīgān
Jīroft
Kharān
Kūh-e Lādīz
Taftān 4042
Khāsh
SARHAD
Kūh-e Bazmān 3489
Bazmān
Saravan
Hāmūn-e Jaz Mūrīān
Īrānshahr
Zābolī
Kūh-e Kūhrān 2161
Espakeh
Remeshk
Sarbāz
MAKRAN
Angohrān
Marākī
Nīkshahr
Qasr-e Qand
Pīshīn
Bāhū Kalāt
Pozm Tīāb
Kalāt
Jāsk
Chābahār
Strait of Hormuz
OMAN
Al Khasab
Dibā al Ḩişn
Ra's al Khaymah
Ash Shāriqah
Adh Dhayd
Al Fujayrah
Dubai (Dubayy)
Mina Jebel Ali
Ash Shināş
Gulf of Oman
Şuḩār
ABU DHABI (Abū Zabī)
Trucial Coast
Tarīf
Al Buraymī
Ruweis
UNITED ARAB EMIRATES
Al Mariyyah
Al Ḩajar al Gharbī
Al Khābūrah
As Suwayq
MUSCAT (Masqaţ)
Barka
Ar Rustāq
Sunaynah
J. Akhḑar
Sumāil
Qurayat
'Ibrī
Nazwá
Ibrā'
Ţīwī
Şūr
Ra's al Ḩadd
NU'AYM
Al Mudaibī
Adam
Al Kāmil
Bilād Banī Bū 'Alī
An Nu'ayrīyah
Al Mish'āb
Manīfah
Al Jubayl
Al Ḩinnāh
Ras Tannūrah
Ad Dammām
Dhahran
MANAMA
BAHRAIN
Fuwayriţ
Al Khawr
Al Mubarrez
Al Jamaliyah
Dukhān
QATAR
DOHA (Ad Dawḩah)
Khurays
Al Hufūf
Ghwaybiyah
Al Kir'ānah
Salwah
THE GULF
Ḩaraḑh
Al Khunn
DAHNĀ'
Aş Şanām
AR RIMĀL
AL KHĀLĪ
Al Ḩibāk
Al Qu'āmīyāt
OMAN
Maşīrah
Khalīj Maşīrah
Hajmā'
Jiddat al Ḩarāsīs
Dawqah
Thamarīt
Şalālah
Mirbāţ
Juzur al Ḩalāniyāt
Al Ghayḑah
Ghubbat al Qamar
Tarīm
Shibām
Al Qaţn
Wādī al Masīlah
YEMEN
Sayḩūt
Ash Shiḩr
Al Mukallā
ARABIAN SEA

50°
60°
20°
C
D
2
3
MILES 0 100 200
0 250 500 KILOMETRES

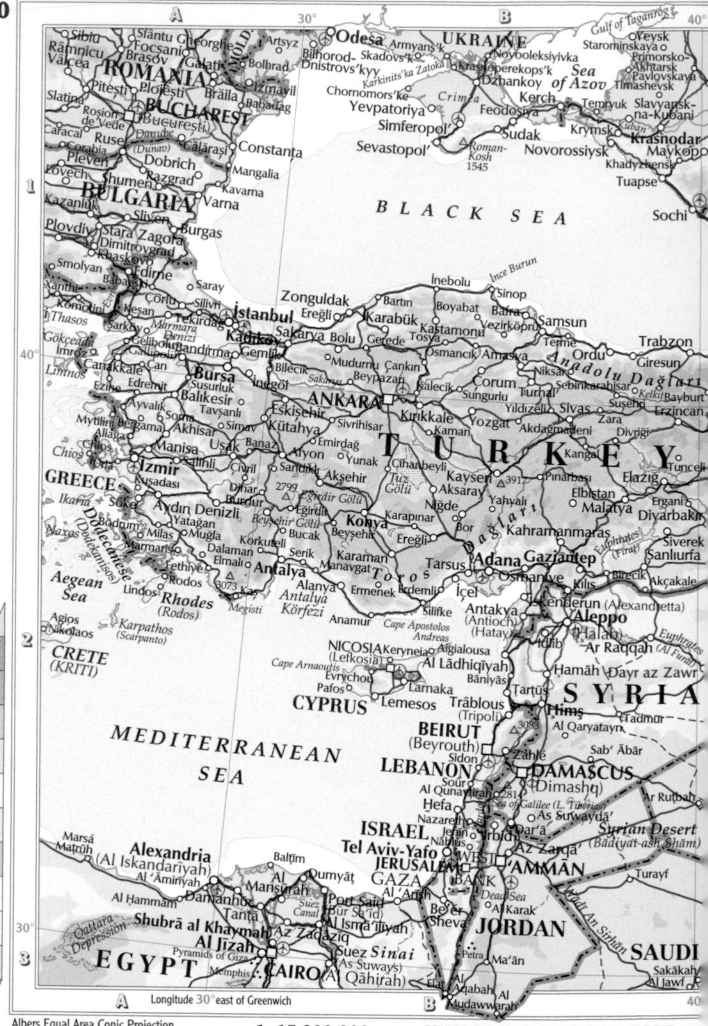

METRES	FEET
5000	16404
3000	9843
2000	6562
1000	3281
500	1640
200	656
0	0
LAND B.S.L.	
200	656
4000	13124
6000	19686

Albers Equal Area Conic Projection

1:15 000 000

MILES 0 100 200 300

C
D
50°
40°
30°
1
2
3
RUSSIAN FEDERATION
Sal'sk
Ozero Manych-Gudilo
Elista
Utta
Astrakhan'
Tikhoretsk
Ipatovo
Divnoye
Ulan-Khol
Kropotkin
Stavropol'skaya
Komsomol'skiy
Lagan'
Stavropol'
Vozvyshennost'
Budennovsk
Armavir
Labinsk
Nevinnomyssk
Kochubey
Psebay
Georgiyevsk
Kizlyar
Cherkessk
Pyatigorsk
Kislovodsk
Prokhladnyy
Nal'chik
Groznyy
Khasav'yurt
Makhachkala
Gagra
Alagir
Vladikavkaz
Sokhumi
Tqvarch'eli
Izberbash
Buynaksk
Zugdidi
Samtredia
Derbent
GEORGIA
K'ut'aisi
T'elavi
P'ot'i
Gori
T'BILISI
(Tiflis)
Bat'umi
Gora Bazardyuzyu
4466
Şäki
Quba
Pazar
Artvin
Ardahan
Qazax
Rize
Mingäçevir
Göyçay
Şamaxı
Sumqayıt
Abşeron Yarımadası
3932
Yusufeli
Gyumri
Gäncä
Kaçkar Dağı
Kars
ARMENIA
AZERBAIJAN
BAKU
(Bakı)
Oltu
Sarıkamış
YEREVAN
(Erevan)
Qazımämmäd
Horasan
Iğdır
Araks
Ağdam
Älät
Erzurum
Ağrı
Mt Ararat
5165
Xankändi
Salyan
Hınıs
Doğubeyazıt
AZER.
Sisian
Naxçıvan
Patnos
Bingöl
Malazgirt
Erciş
Mākū
Länkäran
Āstārā
Murat
Ahlat
4058
Muş
Khvoy
Marand
4810
Ahar
Ardabīl
Silvan
Tatvan
Van Gölü
Van
Salmās
Sarāb
Tabrīz
Siirt
Başkale
Daryācheh-ye Orūmīyeh
Mīāneh
Bandar-e Anzalī
Lāhījān
Batman
Şırnak
Hakkâri
3711
Mardin
Al 'Amādīyah
Semdīnlī
Marāgheh
Rasht
Now Shahr
Bābol
Behshahr
Gorgān
Gonbad-e Kāvus
Al Qāmishlī
Zākhō
Oshnoviyeh
Miandowāb
Mahābād
Zanjān
Qazvīn
Amol
Sārī
Reshteh-ye Alborz
Emāmrūd
Damghān
Tall Afar
Al Ḩasakah
Saqqez
5601
Al Mawşil
Arbīl
Bījār
Karaj
TEHRĀN
Semnān
As Sulaymānīyah
Sanandaj
Halabja
Ash Sharqāţ
Kirkūk
Tigris
Tuz Khurmātū
Hamadān
Qom
Ravānsar
Dasht-e Kavīr
Bayjī
Tikrīt
Qasr-e Shīrīn
Kermānshāh
Malāyer
IRAN
Kāshān
Jandaq
Abū Kamāl
'Ānah
Kerend
Sāmarrā'
Nahāvand
Arāk
Al Ḩadīthah
Eslāmābād-e Gharb
Borūjerd
Golpāyegān
Ardestān
Buḩayrat ath Tharthār
Hīt
Ba'qūbah
Īlām
Khunsar
Dārān
Ar Ramādī
BAGHDAD
Khorramābād
Alīgūdarz
Esfahān
(Isfahan)
Nā'īn
Hawr al Ḩabbānīyah
Buḩayrat ar Razāzah
Kūhhā-ye Zāgros
Najafābād
Karbalā'
Al Ḩillah
Dezfūl
Shahr-e Kord
IRAQ
Al Kūt
Shushtar
Shahrezā
Yazd
Al Ḩayy
Masjed Soleymān
An Najaf
Ad Dīwānīyah
Ash Shaţrah
Ābādeh
Abarqū
Euphrates
Ahvāz
Rāmhormoz
Kūh-e Dīnār
4432
As Samāwah
Sūq ash Shuyūkh
An Nāşirīyah
Khorramshahr
Bandar-e Emām Khomeynī
Arsenajān
Ar'ar
Hawr al Ḩammār
Basra
(Al Başrah)
Ābādān
Kūh-e Tābask
3218
Zargān
Daryācheh-ye Tashk
ARABIA
Al Fāw
KUWAIT
Ganāveh
Kāzerūn
Shīrāz
Kherāmeh
CASPIAN SEA
Mys Tyub-Karagan
Burynshyk
Peski Karakum
Sor Mertvyy Kultuk
Barankul
Beyneu
KAZAKHSTAN
Fort-Shevchenko
Gora Besshoky
Ustyurt Plateau
Mys Sagyndyk
Shetpe
555
Aktau
Mangystau
-132
Zhanaozen
Kazakhskiy Zaliv
TURKMENISTAN
Bekdash
Zaliv Kara-Bogaz-Gol
Karabogazkel'
Dzhanga
Turkmenbashi
Nebitdag
Cheleken
Gumdag
0
250
500 KILOMETRES

METRES
FEET
5000
16404
3000
9843
2000
6562
1000
3281
500
1640
200
656
0
0
LAND
B.S.L.
200
656
4000
13124
6000
19686
ARCTIC
BARENTS SEA
Norwegian Sea
Greenland Sea
Kara Sea
(Karskoye More)
White Sea
(Beloye More)
Gulf of Bothnia
Gulf of Finland
Caspian Sea
Black Sea
Sea of Azov
Aral Sea
Svalbard
(Norway)
Spitsbergen
LONGYEARBYEN
Nordaustlandet
Edgeøya
Bjørnøya
Jan Mayen
(Norway)
ICELAND
Faroe Islands
(Denmark)
TÓRSHAVN
Shetland
Zemlya Frantsa-Iosifa
Zemlya Aleksandry
Ostrov Rudol'fa
Ostrov Greem-Bell
O. Ushakova
Zemlya Vil'cheka
Mys Zhelaniya
Novaya Zemlya
O-va Arkticheskogo Instituta
O. Belyy
Mezhdusharskiy Ostrov
Ostrov Kolguyev
Poluostrov Kanin
Poluostrov Yamal
Obskaya Guba
Gydanskiy Poluostrov
Khrebet Pay-Khoy
Ural Mountains
(Ural'skiy Khrebet)
Timanskiy Kryazh
Altai Mountains
NORWAY
SWEDEN
FINLAND
ESTONIA
LATVIA
LITHUANIA
BELARUS
UKRAINE
RUSSIAN
GEORGIA
KAZAKHSTAN
UZBEKISTAN
TURKMEN.
IRAN
Bergen
Trondheim
OSLO
STOCKHOLM
HELSINKI
RIGA
VILNIUS
MINSK
MOSCOW
(Moskva)
St Petersburg
(Sankt-Peterburg)
(Leningrad)
Lofoten
Tromsø
Hammerfest
Nordkapp
(North Cape)
Mehamn
Kirkenes
Murmansk
Kola Peninsula
Kandalaksha
Arkhangel
(Arkhangel'sk)
Mezen'
Nar'yan-Mar
Vorkuta
Salekhard
Usinsk
Pechora
Ukhta
Syktyvkar
Kotlas
Vel'sk
Plesetsk
Onega
Petrozavodsk
Yaroslavl'
Kostroma
Rybinsk
Tver'
Smolensk
Tula
Bryansk
Orel
Kursk
Kharkiv
(Khar'kov)
Homyel'
Donets'k
Mariupol'
Rostov-na-Donu
Krasnodar
Maykop
Stavropol'
Elista
Groznyy
Budennovsk
Bat'umi
T'BILISI
(Tiflis)
YEREVAN
BAKU
(Bakı)
Tabriz
Rasht
Qazvin
Astrakhan'
Volgograd
(Stalingrad)
Kamyshin
Saratov
Voronezh
Tambov
Penza
Ryazan'
Vladimir
Nizhniy Novgorod
Kazan'
Ul'yanovsk
Samara
Orenburg
Ufa
Perm'
Kirov
(Vyatka)
Glazov
Berezniki
Solikamsk
Sarapul
Yekaterinburg
(Sverdlovsk)
Chelyabinsk
Magnitogorsk
Orsk
Kostanay
Kurgan
Tobol'sk
Omsk
Petropavlovsk
Novosibirsk
Tomsk
Kemerovo
Barnaul
Biysk
Serov
Ivdel'
Sovetskiy
Nyagan'
Khanty-Mansiysk
Surgut
Nefteyugansk
Nizhnevartovsk
Noyabr'sk
Nadym
Novyy Urengoy
Tarko-Sale
Berezovo
Dudinka
Noril'sk
Igarka
Kolpashevo
Podgornoye
Asino
Bogotol
Iskitim
Kiselevsk
Abaza
Slavgorod
Aleysk
Rubtsovsk
Semipalatinsk
Ust'-Kamenogorsk
Pavlodar
Kokshetau
ASTANA
(Akmola)
Karaganda
Balkhash
Lake Balkhash
(Ozero Balkhash)
Taldykorgan
Ushtobe
Sarkand
Ucharal
Karamay
Tacheng
Altay
Ayagoz
Kokpekti
Ozero Zaysan
Aktogay
Kentau
Turkestan
Kyzylorda
Dzhusaly
Aral'sk
Betpak-Dala
Kyzylkum Desert
Urgench
Nukus
Turkmenbashi
Nebitdag
Zhanaozen
Aktau
Fort-Shevchenko
Ustyurt Plateau
Kul'sary
Atyrau
Ural'sk
Aktobe
Emba
Khromtau
Arkalyk
Turgay
Irgiz
Zhitikara
Rudnyy
Ural
Volga
Irtysh
Ob'
Pur
Taz
Ket'
Chulym
Ishim
Tobol
Longitude 75° east of Greenwich
Conic Equidistant Projection
1:42 000 000
MILES 0
250
500
750

OCEAN
O. Shmidta
O. Komsomolets
Ostrov Oktyabr'skoy Revolyutsii
O. Bol'shevik
Severnaya Zemlya
Laptev Sea
(More Laptevykh)
Arkhipelag Nordenshel'da
Poluostrov Taymyr
Ozero Taymyr
Anabarskiy Zaliv
Novosibirskiye Ostrova
(New Siberian Islands)
Ostrova De-Longa
O. Bennetta
O. Zhokhova
Kotel'nyy
Ostrov Novaya Sibir'
East Siberian Sea
O. Bol. Lyakhovskiy
O. Malyy Lyakhovskiy
O. Bel'kovskiy
Yanskiy Zaliv
Tiksi
Ostrov Vrangelya
Chukchi Sea
Point Hope
Bering Strait
U.S.A.
St Lawrence Island
Mys Shmidta
Iul'tin
Arctic Circle
Chukotskiy P-ov
Provideniya
Egvekinot
Anadyr'
M. Navarin
Proliv Longa
Pevek
M. Shelagskiy
O. Ayon
Bilibino
Malyy Anyuy
Bol'shoy Anyuy
O-va Medvezh'i
Chokurdakh
Kolymskaya Nizmennost'
Yano-Indigirskaya Nizmennost'
Deputatskiy
Srednekolymsk
Yukagirskoye Ploskogor'ye
Seymchan
Khrebet Kolymskiy
Kamenskoye
Koryakskiy Khrebet
Ossora
Karaginskiy Zaliv
Ust'-Kamchatsk
Komandorskiye Ostrova
Ostrov Bering
Nikol'skoye
Mil'kovo
Sredinnyy Khrebet
Petropavlovsk-Kamchatskiy
Ozernovskiy
Ostrov Paramushir
Palana
Evensk
Zaliv Shelikhova
Mys Alevina
Sea of Okhotsk
Oktyabr'skiy
Batagay
Khonuu
Zyryanka
3003
Khrebet Cherskogo
Ust'-Nera
Susuman
Omsukchan
Ust'-Omchug
Magadan
2984
Okhotsk
Allakh-Yun'
Khandyga
Verkhoyanskiy Khrebet
Khrebet Orulgan
Olenek
Anabar
Saskylakh
Popigay
Kheta
Kotuy
Ozero Khantayskoye
Zhigansk
Sangar
Yakutsk
Namtsy
Pokrovsk
Amga
Aldan
Vilyuy
Lena
SIBERIA
FEDERATION
Sredne-Sibirskoye Ploskogor'ye
Tura
Nizh. Tunguska
Mirnyy
Suntar
Chernyshevskiy
Olekminsk
Lensk
Yerbogachen
Podkamennaya Tunguska
Ayan
Khrebet Dzhugdzhur
Chumikan
Maya
Uchur
Okha
M. Marii
Sakhalin
Aleksandrovsk-Sakhalinskiy
Poronaysk
Tatarskiy Proliv
Yuzhno-Sakhalinsk
Neryungri
Stanovoy Khrebet
2482
Stanovoye Nagor'ye
Tynda
Zeya
Zeyskoye Vdkhr.
Mayskiy
Khrebet Turana
Svobodnyy
Blagoveshchensk
Birobidzhan
Khabarovsk
Vanino
Sikhote-Alin'
Bodaybo
Kirensk
Ust'-Ilimsk
2618
Boguchany
Angara
Yenisey
Lesosibirsk
Bratsk
Ust'-Kut
Krasnoyarsk
Kansk
Uyar
Nizhneudinsk
Zima
Kachug
Baykal'skiy Khr.
Lake Baikal
Kurumkan
Mogocha
Vitim
Sretensk
Chita
Karymskoye
Borzya
Olovyannaya
Zabaykal'sk
Hailar
Hulun Nur
Buir Nur
Abakan
Vostochnyy Sayan
Ust'-Ordynskiy
Angarsk
Irkutsk
Ulan-Ude
Gusinoozersk
Yablonovyy Khrebet
Kyzyl
Teeli
Hövsgöl Nuur
Sühbaatar
Darhan
Uvs Nuur
Ulaangom
Mörön
Bulgan
ULAANBAATAR
(Ulan Bator)
Hyargas Nuur
Hovd
4021
Tsetserleg
Dzuunmod
Baruun Urt
Har Us Nuur
Uliastay
4231
MONGOLIA
Arvayheer
Mandalgovi
Bayanhongor
Altay
Gichgeniyn Nuruu
GOBI
Saynshand
Xilinhot
Da Hinggan Ling
Mangui
Gulian
Heilong Jiang
Xiao Hinggan Ling
Yichun
Hegang
Jiamusi
Bikin
Qiqihar
Suihua
Harbin
Jixi
Mudanjiang
Vladivostok
Nakhodka
Zaliv Petra Velikogo
Daqing
Baicheng
Jilin
CHINA
Ch'ŏngjin
N. KOREA
Changchun
Siping
Yanji
Hyesan
Shenyang
Fushun
Benxi
Hamhŭng
P'YŎNGYANG
SEOUL
(Sŏul)
S. KOREA
Chifeng
Jinzhou
Anshan
Sinuiju
90°
180°
75°
165°
180°
165°
150°
45°
135°
105°
120°
0
500
1000
1500 KILOMETRES

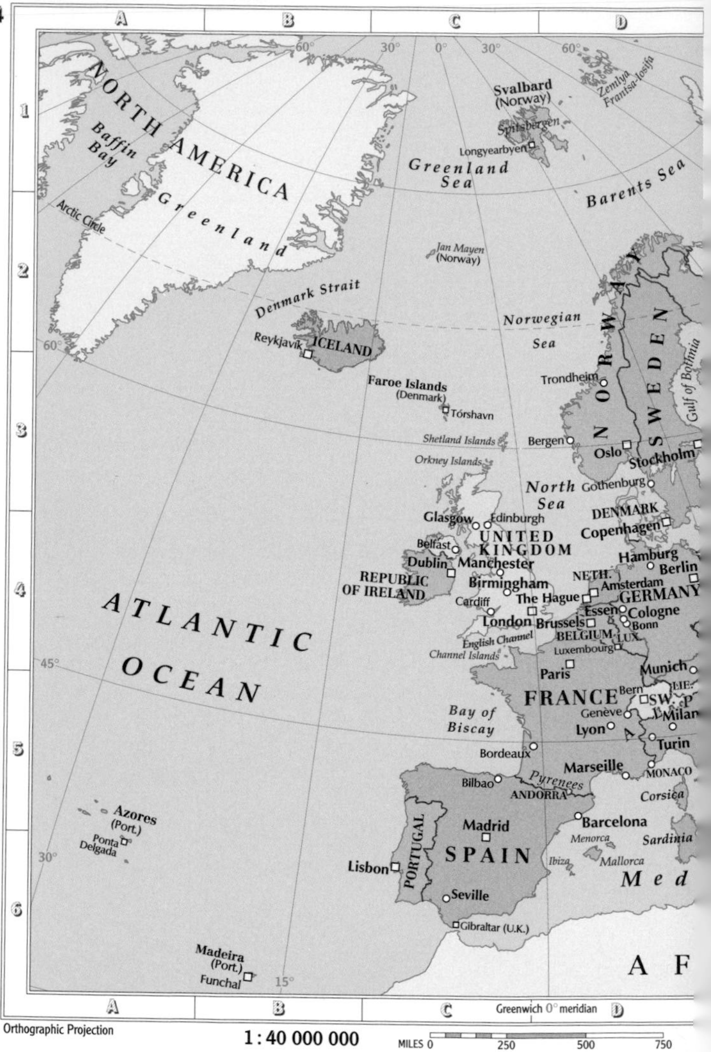

A B C D

1 2 3 4 5 6

NORTH AMERICA
Baffin Bay
Greenland
Arctic Circle
Denmark Strait
Svalbard (Norway)
Spitsbergen
Longyearbyen
Zemlya Frantsa-Iosifa
Greenland Sea
Barents Sea
Jan Mayen (Norway)
Norwegian Sea
Reykjavík
ICELAND
Faroe Islands (Denmark)
Tórshavn
Trondheim
NORWAY
SWEDEN
Gulf of Bothnia
Shetland Islands
Orkney Islands
Bergen
Oslo
Stockholm
North Sea
Gothenburg
DENMARK
Copenhagen
Glasgow
Edinburgh
UNITED KINGDOM
Belfast
Dublin
Manchester
REPUBLIC OF IRELAND
Birmingham
Cardiff
London
The Hague
NETH.
Amsterdam
Hamburg
Berlin
GERMANY
Essen
Cologne
Bonn
Brussels
BELGIUM
LUX.
Luxembourg
English Channel
Channel Islands
Paris
Munich
LIE.
FRANCE
Bern
SW.
Genève
Milan
Lyon
Turin
Bay of Biscay
Bordeaux
Marseille
MONACO
Pyrenees
ANDORRA
Bilbao
Corsica
Barcelona
Menorca
Sardinia
Madrid
PORTUGAL
SPAIN
Lisbon
Ibiza
Mallorca
Med
Seville
Gibraltar (U.K.)
ATLANTIC OCEAN
Azores (Port.)
Ponta Delgada
Madeira (Port.)
Funchal
AF

60° 30° 0° 30° 60° 60° 45° 30° 15°

Greenwich 0° meridian

Orthographic Projection

1:40 000 000

MILES 0 250 500 750

AL. ALBANIA
B.H. BOSNIA-HERZEGOVINA
CR. CROATIA
CZ.R. CZECH REPUBLIC
HUN. HUNGARY
LIE. LIECHTENSTEIN
LUX. LUXEMBOURG
M. MACEDONIA
NETH. NETHERLANDS
RUS.FED. RUSSIAN FEDERATION
S. SERBIA AND MONTENEGRO
SL. SLOVENIA
SLA. SLOVAKIA
SW. SWITZERLAND
Arctic Circle
Novaya Zemlya
Murmansk
Archangel
Ural Mountains
RUSSIAN FEDERATION
FINLAND
Perm'
Kazan'
Samara
Helsinki
St Petersburg
Tallinn
ESTONIA
Moscow
Baltic Sea
LATVIA
Riga
LITHUANIA
Vilnius
Minsk
RUS. FED.
Kaliningrad
BELARUS
POLAND
Warsaw
Kiev
Kharkiv
Volgograd
Rostov-na-Donu
Astrakhan'
Aral Sea
UKRAINE
Donets'k
Katowice
Prague
CZ.R.
SLA.
Vienna
Bratislava
MOLDOVA
Odesa
Chişinău
Budapest
AUSTRIA
HUN.
ROMANIA
Caspian Sea
ASIA
SL.
Ljubljana
Zagreb
Bucharest
Black Sea
Belgrade
CR.
B.H.
BULGARIA
SAN MARINO
Sarajevo
S.
Sofia
İstanbul
Skopje
TURKEY
ITALY
Tirana
AL.
Rome
GREECE
Athens
Tigris
Euphrates
Rhodes
Sicily
Cyprus
The Gulf
Crete
Mediterranean Sea
Valletta
MALTA
AFRICA
90°
45°
30°
60°
15°
E F G H
1 2 3 4 5 6
0 500 1000 KILOMETRES

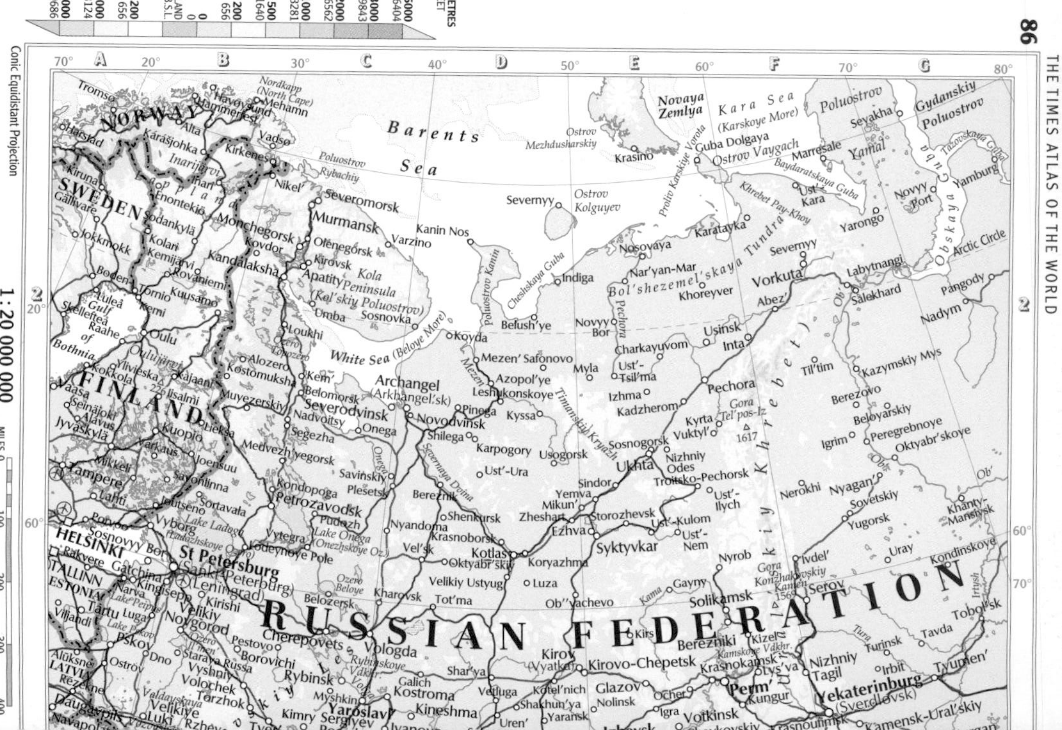

1:20 000 000

MILES 0 100 200 300 400

EUROPEAN RUSSIAN FEDERATION

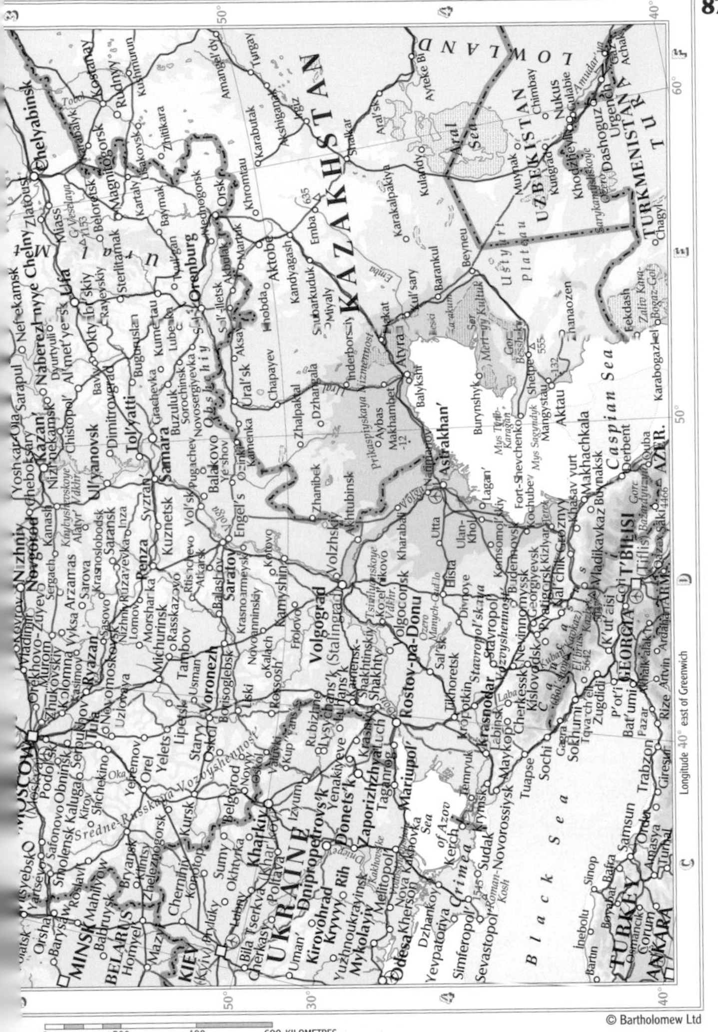

0 200 400 600 KILOMETRES

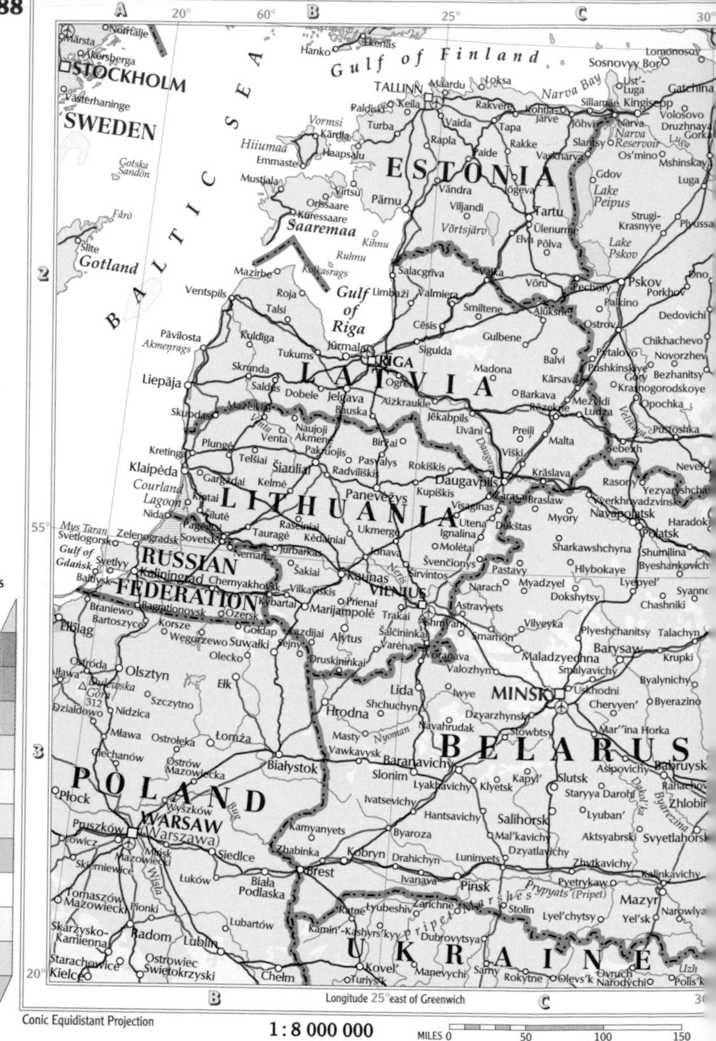

Conic Equidistant Projection

1:8 000 000

MILES 0 50 100 150

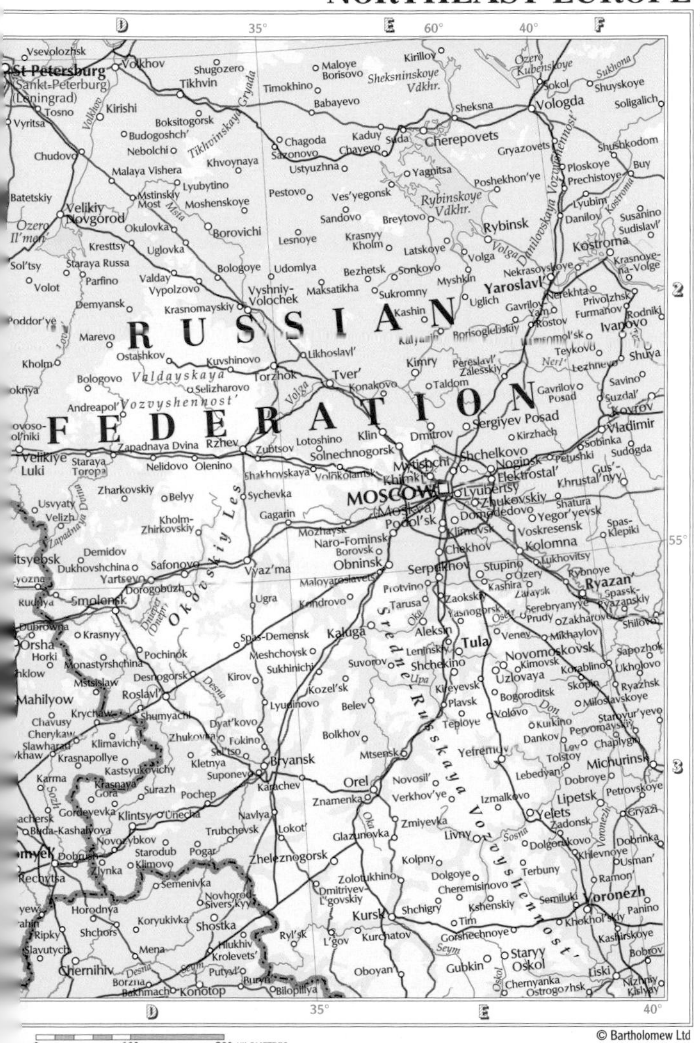

METRES
FEET

METRES	FEET
5000	16404
3000	9843
2000	6562
1000	3281
500	1640
200	656
0	0
LAND B.S.L.	
200	656
4000	13124
6000	19686

Conic Equidistant Projection

1:8 000 000

MILES 0 50 100 150

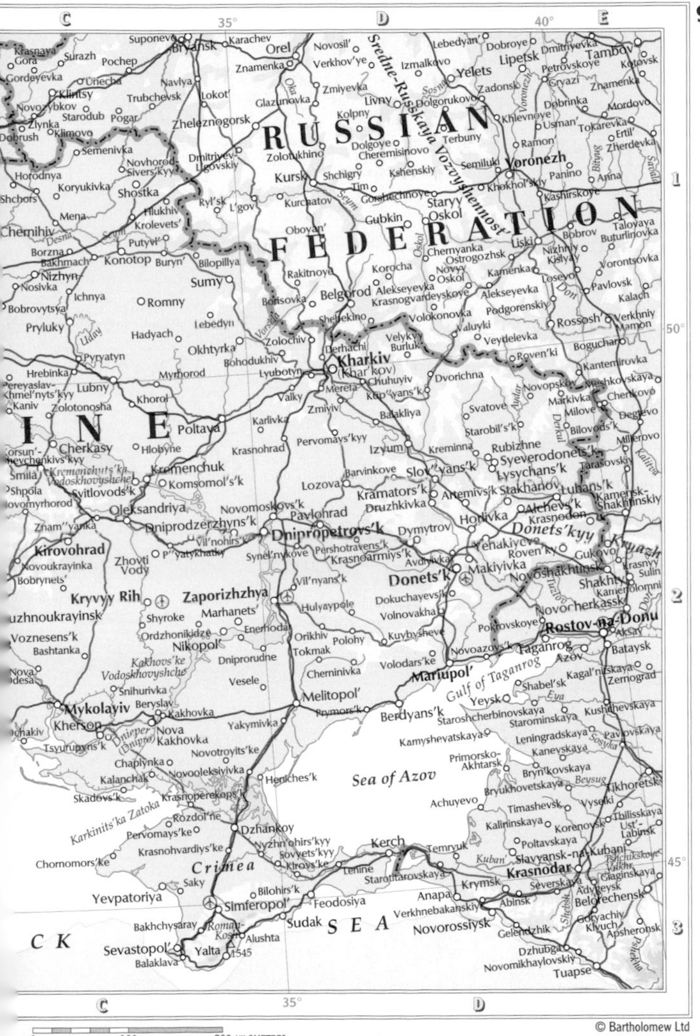

0 100 200 KILOMETRES

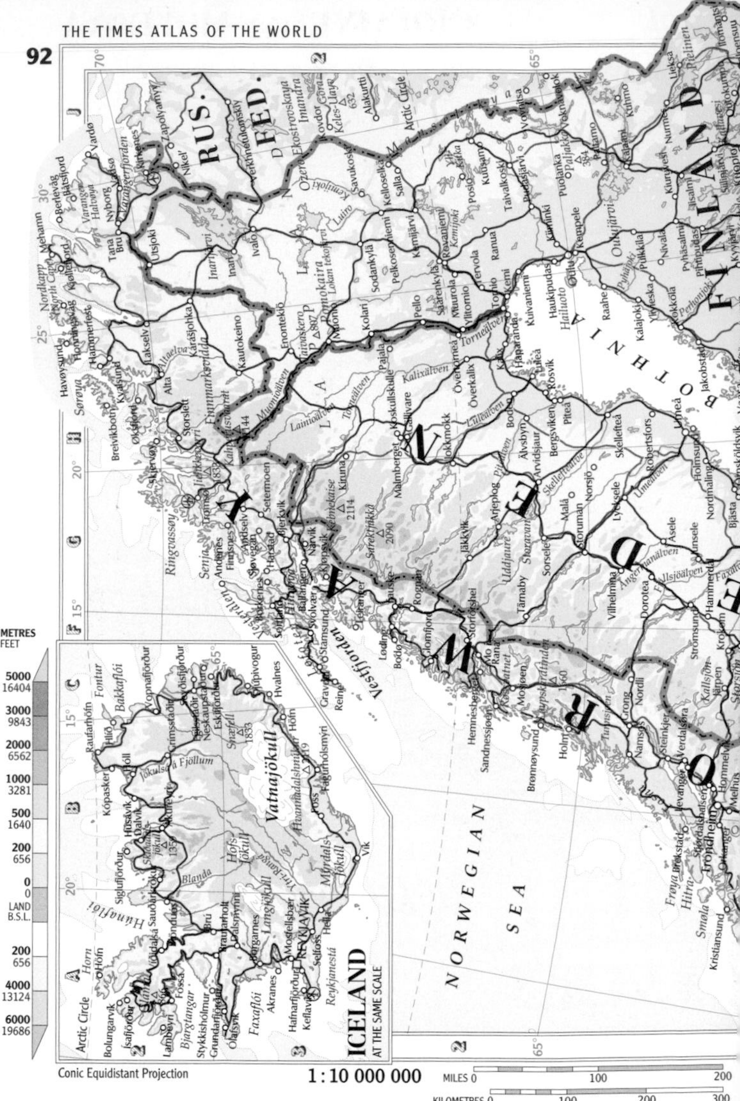
METRES
FEET
5000
16404
3000
9843
2000
6562
1000
3281
500
1640
200
656
0
0
LAND
B.S.L.
200
656
4000
13124
6000
19686
ICELAND
AT THE SAME SCALE
NORWEGIAN SEA
Conic Equidistant Projection
1:10 000 000
MILES 0
100
200
KILOMETRES 0
100
200
300

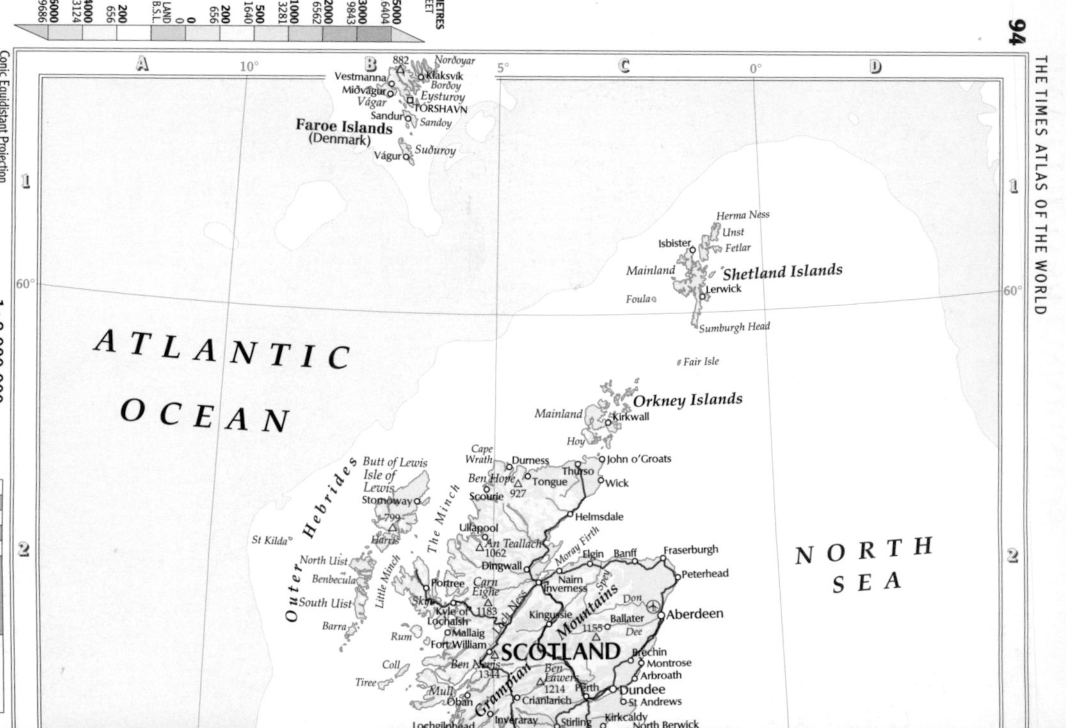

Conic Equidistant Projection

1:8 000 000

MILES 0 50 100 150

UNITED KINGDOM
ENGLAND
WALES
LONDON
NORTHERN IRELAND
REPUBLIC OF IRELAND
FRANCE
DUBLIN
PENNINES
Southern Uplands
Irish Sea
CELTIC SEA
English Channel
(La Manche)
North Channel
St George's Channel
Bristol Channel
Strait of Dover
Isle of Man (U.K.)
Channel Islands (Îles Normandes)
Guernsey (U.K.)
Jersey (U.K.)
Isle of Wight
Isles of Scilly
Birmingham
Manchester
Liverpool
Leeds
Sheffield
Bristol
Cardiff
Newcastle upon Tyne
Kingston upon Hull
Belfast
Cork
Limerick
Galway
Longitude 5° west of Greenwich
0 100 200 KILOMETRES

SCOTLAND

A
6°
B
4°
C
2°
D
1
2
3
58°
56°
60°
North Ronaldsay
Westray
Sanday
Rousay
Loth
Stronsay
Birsay
Orkney Islands
Mainland
Kirkwall
Stromness
Gritley
Ward Hill
479
Scapa Flow
Hoy
South Ronaldsay
Pentland Firth
Dunnet Head
John o' Groats
Duncansby Head
Thurso
Wick
Herma Ness
Unst
Yell
Isbister
450
Ronas Hill
Ulsta
Fetlar
Toft
Whalsay
Walls
Mainland
Lerwick
Foula
Shetland Islands
Bressay
Sumburgh
Sumburgh Head
Fair Isle
Cape Wrath
Durness
Ben Hope
927
Tongue
Naver
Thurso
Dunbeath
Helmsdale
Helmsdale
Scourie
Point of Stoer
Ben More Assynt
998
Loch Shin
Cassley
Lochinver
Lairg
Golspie
Dornoch
Dornoch Firth
Loch Broom
Ullapool
An Teallach
1062
Loch Maree
Ben Wyvis
1046
Invergordon
Alness
Moray Firth
Gairloch
Achnasheen
Dingwall
Black Isle
Torridon
Inverness
Nairn
Forres
Elgin
Lossiemouth
Buckie
Banff
Fraserburgh
Rattray Head
Aberchirder
Peterhead
Deveron
Huntly
Dufftown
Ellon
Strathspey
Spey
Findhorn
Beauly
Carn Eighe
1183
Loch Ness
Grantown-on-Spey
Inverurie
Dyce
Aberdeen
Don
Aviemore
Cairngorm Mountains
Fort Augustus
Monadhliath Mountains
Kingussie
Ben Macdui
1309
Ballater
Dee
Braemar
Lochnagar
1155
Stonehaven
North Esk
GRAMPIAN MOUNTAINS
Glen Shee
Lochaber
Garry
Mallaig
Fort William
Ben Nevis
1344
SCOTLAND
Brechin
Montrose
Blair Atholl
Pitlochry
Kirriemuir
Forfar
Sidlaw Hills
Arbroath
Dundee
Firth of Tay
Blairgowrie
Tay
Ben Lawers
1214
Loch Tay
Rannoch Moor
Glen Coe
Killin
Crieff
Perth
St Andrews
NORTH SEA
Fife Ness
Cupar
Glenrothes
Buckhaven
Kirkcaldy
Firth of Forth
North Berwick
Dunbar
Crianlarich
Callander
Forth
Stirling
Alloa
Dunfermline
Cowdenbeath
Falkirk
Edinburgh
Haddington
St Abb's Head
Musselburgh
Dalkeith
Berwick-upon-Tweed
Holy Island (Lindisfarne)
Duns
Tweed
Penicuik
Coldstream
Kelso
Peebles
Galashiels
Selkirk
Newtown St Boswells
The Cheviot
815
Jedburgh
Alnwick
Hawick
Cheviot Hills
Rothbury
SOUTHERN UPLANDS
Broad Law
840
Biggar
Clyde
Lanark
Moffat
Ashington
Morpeth
Thornhill
Nith
Esk
North Tyne
Kielder Water
Newcastle upon Tyne
Lockerbie
Dumfries
Longtown
Hexham
Blaydon
Gateshead
Annan
Carlisle
Consett
Dalbeattie
Solway Firth
Durham
Wear
ENGLAND
Cockermouth
Workington
931
Penrith
Cross Fell
893
Spennymoor
Butt of Lewis
Port Ness
Loch a' Tuath
West Loch Roag
Isle of Lewis
Stornoway
The Minch
Clisham
799
Tarbert
Harris
Sound of Harris
Outer Hebrides
North Uist
Lochmaddy
Little Minch
Benbecula
Uig
Skye
Portree
Inner Sound
Beinn Mhòr
620
South Uist
Lochboisdale
Sgurr Alasdair
993
Kyle of Lochalsh
Barra
Castlebay
Canna
Cuillin Sound
Rum
Eigg
Point of Ardnamurchan
Salen
Loch Shiel
Coll
Arinagour
Tobermory
Morvern
Loch Linnhe
Tiree
Scarinish
Mull
Ben More
966
Firth of Lorn
Oban
Loch Awe
Iona
Fionnphort
Inveraray
Ben Lomond
974
Tarbet
Loch Lomond
Colonsay
Jura
Sound of Jura
Lochgilphead
Helensburgh
Greenock
Dumbarton
Cumbernauld
Clydebank
Glasgow
Johnstone
Coatbridge
Paisley
Motherwell
Hamilton
Port Askaig
785
Tarbert
Rothesay
Largs
East Kilbride
Islay
Gigha
Ardrossan
Kilmarnock
Goat Fell
874
Brodick
Arran
Irvine
Prestwick
Ayr
Cumnock
Mull of Oa
Port Ellen
Kintyre
Campbeltown
Firth of Clyde
Maybole
Rathlin Island
Giant's Causeway
Portrush
Ballycastle
Mull of Kintyre
Girvan
Merrick
843
Portstewart
Coleraine
Antrim Hills
North Channel
Ballymoney
Bann
Cairnryan
Newton Stewart
Castle Douglas
Cullybackey
Stranraer
Ballymena
Larne
Wigtown
NORTHERN IRELAND
Whitehead
Kirkcudbright
Luce Bay
Whithorn
Antrim
Ballyclare
Bangor
Newtownabbey
Donaghadee
Mull of Galloway
Longitude 4° west of Greenwich
METRES
FEET
5000
16404
3000
9843
2000
6562
1000
3281
500
1640
200
656
0
0
LAND B.S.L.
200
656
4000
13124
6000
19686
Conic Equidistant Projection
1:4 000 000
MILES 0
25
50
75

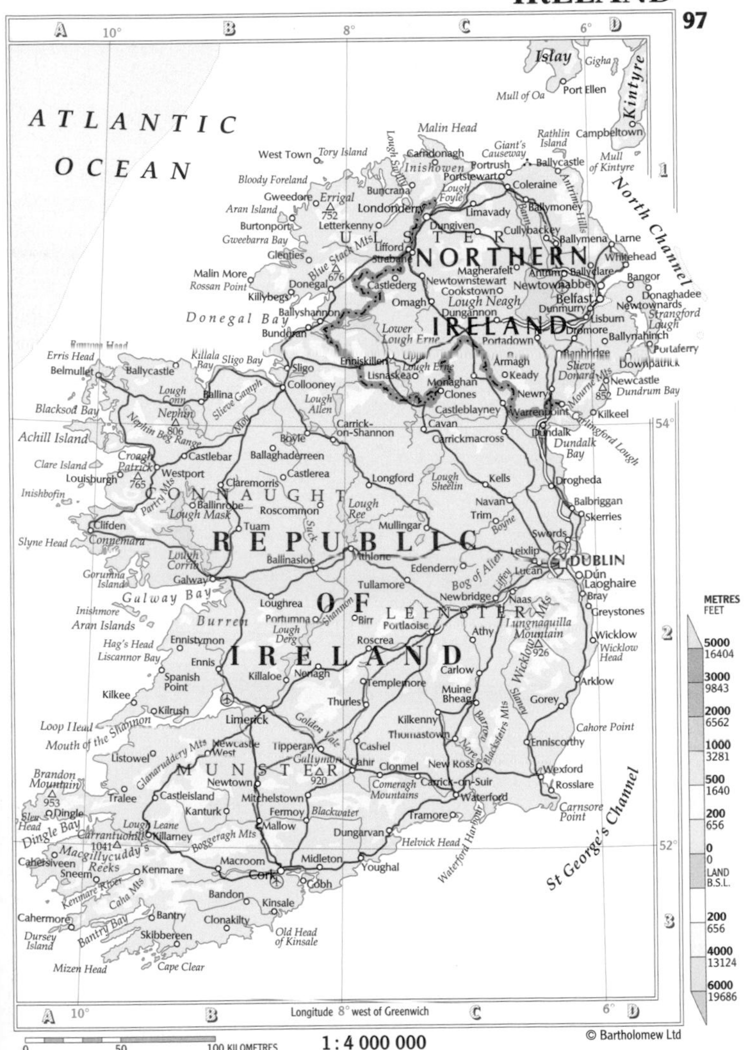
A
B
C
D
10°
8°
6°
1
2
3
54°
52°
Islay
Gigha
Kintyre
Port Ellen
Mull of Oa
Rathlin Island
Campbeltown
Mull of Kintyre
North Channel
ATLANTIC
OCEAN
Malin Head
Giant's Causeway
Ballycastle
West Town
Tory Island
Lough Swilly
Carndonagh
Inishowen
Portrush
Portstewart
Coleraine
Bloody Foreland
Gweedore
Errigal
752
Buncrana
Lough Foyle
Antrim Hills
Bann
Ballymoney
Aran Island
Londonderry
Limavady
Burtonport
Letterkenny
Dungiven
Cullybackey
Gweebarra Bay
ULSTER
Ballymena
Larne
Glenties
Blue Stack Mts
Lifford
Strabane
NORTHERN
Whitehead
676
Magherafelt
Antrim
Ballyclare
Bangor
Malin More
Rossan Point
Donegal
Castlederg
Newtownstewart
Newtownabbey
Donaghadee
Killybegs
Cookstown
Belfast
Newtownards
Omagh
Lough Neagh
Dunmurry
Strangford Lough
Ballyshannon
Dungannon
Lisburn
Donegal Bay
IRELAND
Dromore
Bundoran
Lower Lough Erne
Portadown
Ballynahinch
Erris Head
Portaferry
Killala Bay
Sligo Bay
Belmullet
Ballycastle
Sligo
Enniskillen
Upper Lough Erne
Armagh
Slieve Donard
Downpatrick
Lisnaskea
Keady
Newcastle
Collooney
Monaghan
Mourne Mts
Dundrum Bay
Lough Conn
Ballina
Slieve Gamph
Clones
Newry
852
Lough Allen
Blacksod Bay
Nephin
Castleblayney
Warrenpoint
Kilkeel
806
Nephin Beg Range
Moy
Carrick-on-Shannon
Cavan
Carlingford Lough
Achill Island
Boyle
Dundalk
Carrickmacross
Dundalk Bay
Croagh Patrick
Castlebar
Ballaghaderreen
Clare Island
Westport
Castlerea
Louisburgh
765
Claremorris
Longford
Lough Sheelin
Kells
Drogheda
Inishbofin
Partry Mts
CONNAUGHT
Ballinrobe
Roscommon
Lough Ree
Navan
Balbriggan
Lough Mask
Trim
Skerries
Clifden
Suck
Mullingar
Boyne
Tuam
Slyne Head
Connemara
REPUBLIC
Swords
Leixlip
Lough Corrib
Ballinasloe
Athlone
Edenderry
DUBLIN
Gorumna Island
Bog of Allen
Lucan
Dún Laoghaire
Galway
Tullamore
Liffey
Bray
Galway Bay
Newbridge
Naas
Inishmore
Loughrea
OF
Greystones
Aran Islands
Burren
Portumna
Shannon
Birr
LEINSTER
Lugnaquilla Mountain
Portlaoise
Lough Derg
Wicklow
Hag's Head
Ennistymon
Roscrea
Athy
Wicklow Mts
Wicklow Head
Liscannor Bay
926
Ennis
IRELAND
Carlow
Spanish Point
Killaloe
Nenagh
Arklow
Templemore
Kilkee
Muine Bheag
Slaney
Thurles
Gorey
Kilrush
Barrow
Blackstairs Mts
Loop Head
Limerick
Kilkenny
Golden Vale
Thomastown
Mouth of the Shannon
Cahore Point
Newcastle West
Tipperary
Enniscorthy
Nore
Listowel
Glanaruddery Mts
Galtymore
Cashel
Cahir
Clonmel
New Ross
MUNSTER
920
Wexford
Brandon Mountain
Newtown
Comeragh Mountains
Carrick-on-Suir
Rosslare
953
Castleisland
Mitchelstown
Waterford
Tralee
Kanturk
Fermoy
Blackwater
Carnsore Point
St George's Channel
Slea Head
Dingle
Tramore
Dingle Bay
Lough Leane
Mallow
Carrantuohill
Killarney
Boggeragh Mts
Dungarvan
Helvick Head
1041
Waterford Harbour
Macgillycuddy's Reeks
Cahersiveen
Midleton
Youghal
Sneem
Kenmare
Macroom
Cork
Cobh
Kenmare River
Caha Mts
Bandon
Kinsale
Cahermore
Bantry
Clonakilty
Bantry Bay
Dursey Island
Skibbereen
Old Head of Kinsale
Mizen Head
Cape Clear
Longitude 8° west of Greenwich
METRES
FEET
5000
16404
3000
9843
2000
6562
1000
3281
500
1640
200
656
0
0
LAND
B.S.L.
200
656
4000
13124
6000
19686
0
50
100 KILOMETRES
1:4 000 000
© Bartholomew Ltd

METRES
FEET

5000
16404

3000
9843

2000
6562

1000
3281

500
1640

200
656

0
0
LAND
B.S.L.

200
656

4000
13124

6000
19686

Conic Equidistant Projection

1:4 000 000

MILES 0 25 50 75

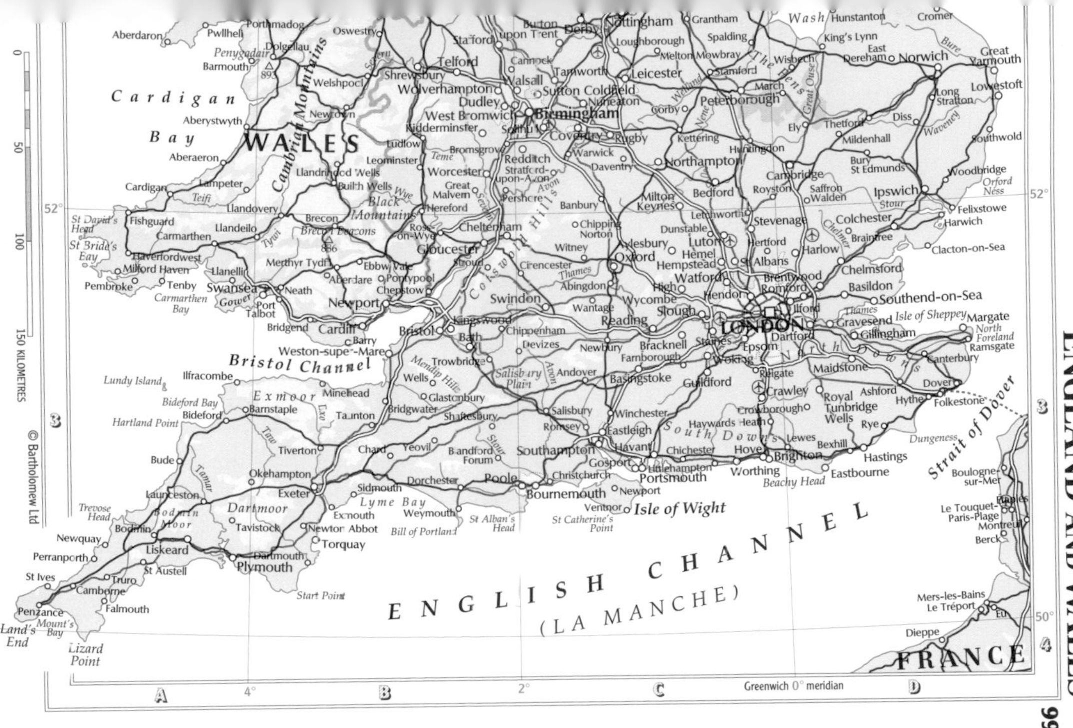

ENGLISH CHANNEL
(LA MANCHE)
Strait of Dover
FRANCE
WALES
Cardigan Bay
Bristol Channel
Isle of Wight
Cambrian Mountains
Black Mountains
Brecon Beacons
Exmoor
Dartmoor
Bodmin Moor
The Fens
Wash
North Downs
South Downs
Cotswold Hills
Salisbury Plain
Mendip Hills
Lyme Bay
St Bride's Bay
Carmarthen Bay
Bideford Bay
Mount's Bay
Gower
Lundy Island
Isle of Sheppey
Lizard Point
Land's End
Start Point
Hartland Point
Trevose Head
St David's Head
Bill of Portland
St Alban's Head
St Catherine's Point
Beachy Head
Dungeness
North Foreland
Orford Ness
Greenwich 0° meridian
52°
50°
2°
4°
A
B
C
D
3
4
LONDON
Birmingham
Bristol
Cardiff
Swansea
Newport
Plymouth
Exeter
Southampton
Portsmouth
Bournemouth
Poole
Brighton
Norwich
Ipswich
Cambridge
Oxford
Reading
Leicester
Nottingham
Derby
Coventry
Wolverhampton
Peterborough
Northampton
Gloucester
Cheltenham
Worcester
Hereford
Shrewsbury
Telford
Stafford
Swindon
Bath
Salisbury
Winchester
Guildford
Canterbury
Dover
Folkestone
Hastings
Eastbourne
Maidstone
Southend-on-Sea
Chelmsford
Colchester
Luton
Bedford
Milton Keynes
Aberystwyth
Carmarthen
Haverfordwest
Pembroke
Fishguard
Cardigan
Brecon
Llandovery
Llandeilo
Llanelli
Neath
Port Talbot
Bridgend
Merthyr Tydfil
Taunton
Barnstaple
Bideford
Ilfracombe
Torquay
Truro
Penzance
Newquay
St Ives
Falmouth
Bodmin
Liskeard
Launceston
Bude
Boulogne-sur-Mer
Le Touquet-Paris-Plage
Montreuil
Berck
Eu
Le Tréport
Mers-les-Bains
Dieppe
© Bartholomew Ltd
0
50
100
150 KILOMETRES

Conic Equidistant Projection

1:4 000 000

MILES 0 25 50 75

Longitude 10° east of Greenwich

METRES	FEET
5000	16404
3000	9843
2000	6562
1000	3281
500	1640
200	656
0	0
LAND B.S.L.	
200	656
4000	13124
6000	19686

Conic Equidistant Projection

1:8 000 000

MILES 0 50 100 150

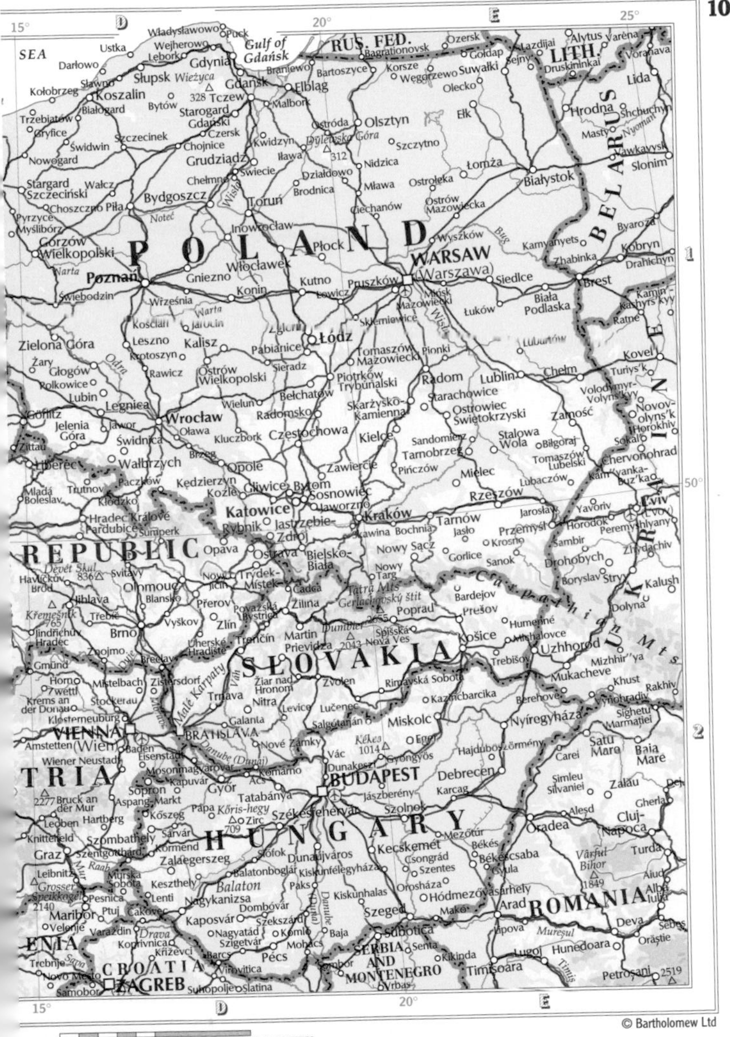

0 100 200 KILOMETRES

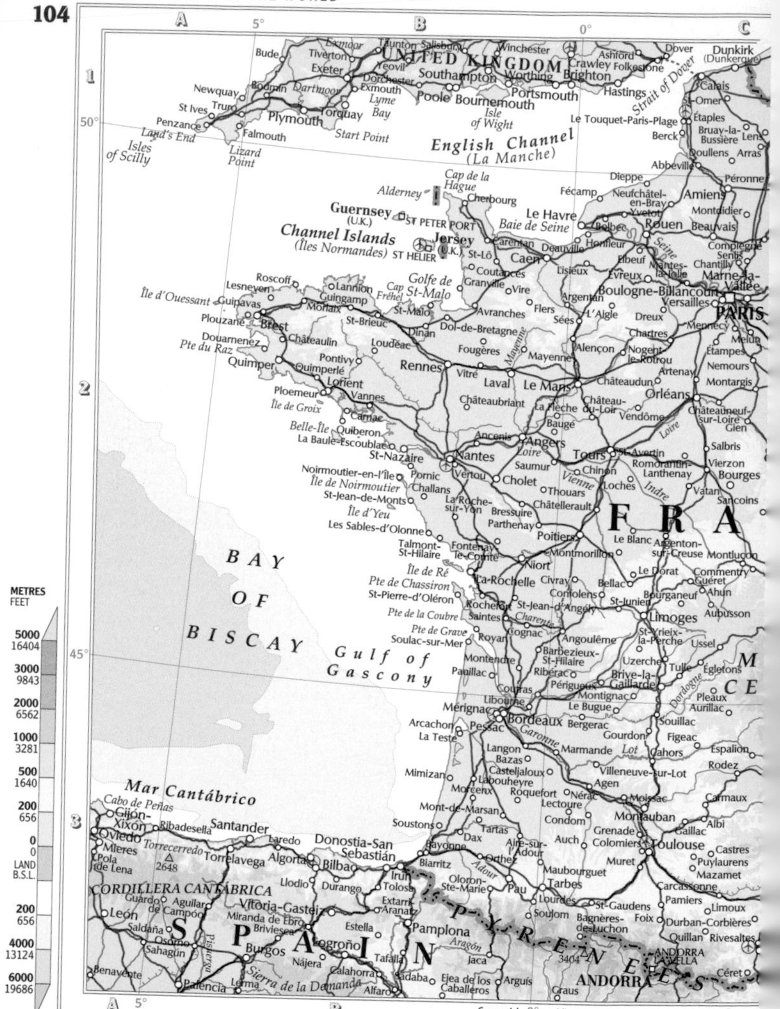

UNITED KINGDOM
English Channel (La Manche)
Channel Islands (Îles Normandes)
BAY OF BISCAY
Gulf of Gascony
Mar Cantábrico
FRANCE
SPAIN
ANDORRA
PYRENEES

METRES FEET
5000 16404
3000 9843
2000 6562
1000 3281
500 1640
200 656
0 0
LAND B.S.L.
200 656
4000 13124
6000 19686

Conic Equidistant Projection

1:8 000 000

MILES 0 50 100 150

Greenwich 0° meridian

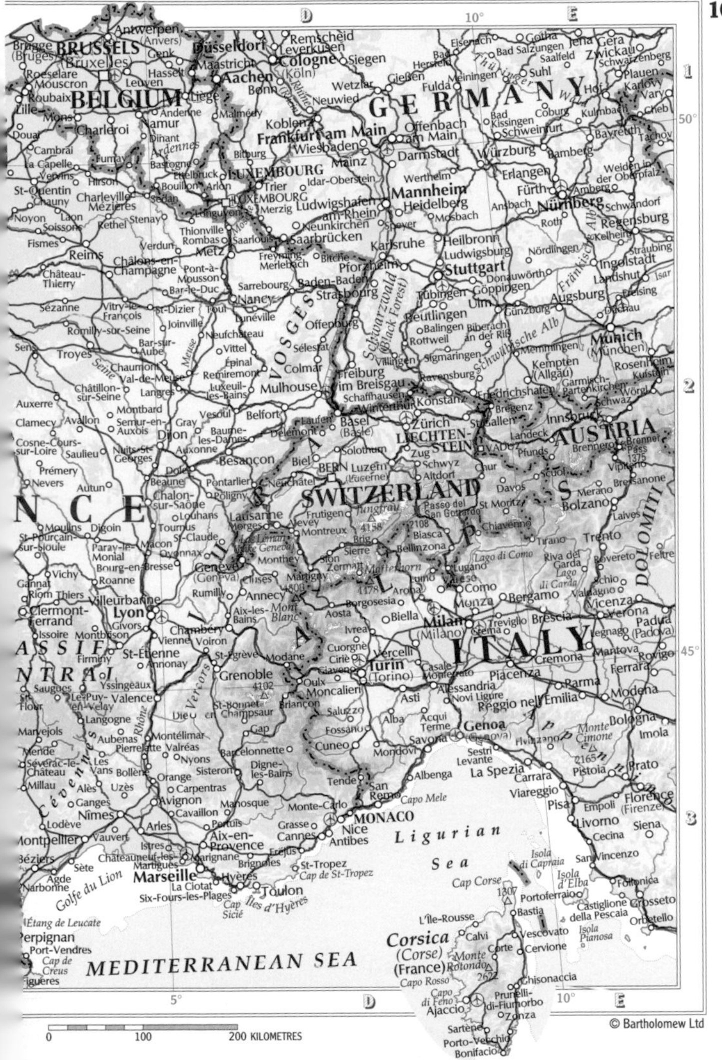

BRUSSELS
(Bruxelles)
BELGIUM
Antwerpen
(Anvers)
Brugge
(Bruges)
Genk
Hasselt
Leuven
Roeselare
Mouscron
Roubaix
Lille
Mons
Charleroi
Namur
Liège
Andenne
Dinant
Ardennes
Douai
Cambrai
La Capelle
Fumay
Bastogne
Hirson
Bouillon
Arlon
LUXEMBOURG
Trier
St-Quentin
Charleville-Mézières
Sedan
Chauny
Noyon
Laon
Soissons
Rethel
Stenay
Thionville
Rombas
Saarlouis
Merzig
Fismes
Reims
Verdun
Metz
Saarbrücken
Châlons-en-Champagne
Château-Thierry
Pont-à-Mousson
Bar-le-Duc
Sarrebourg
Nancy
Lunéville
Sézanne
Vitry-le-François
St-Dizier
Toul
Joinville
Romilly-sur-Seine
Neufchâteau
Bar-sur-Aube
Troyes
Sens
Vittel
Épinal
Chaumont
Val-de-Meuse
Remiremont
Luxeuil-les-Bains
Langres
Châtillon-sur-Seine
Auxerre
Montbard
Clamecy
Avallon
Semur-en-Auxois
Vesoul
Gray
Dijon
Belfort
Baume-les-Dames
Cosne-Cours-sur-Loire
Saulieu
Nuits-St-Georges
Auxonne
Besançon
Prémery
Nevers
Autun
Dole
Beaune
Pontarlier
Poligny
Chalon-sur-Saône
Louhans
Tournus
St-Claude
Moulins
Digoin
St-Pourçain-sur-Sioule
Paray-le-Monial
Mâcon
Oyonnax
Bourg-en-Bresse
Vichy
Roanne
Gannat
Riom
Thiers
Clermont-Ferrand
Villeurbanne
Lyon
Givors
Issoire
Vienne
Voiron
St-Étienne
Firminy
Annonay
Yssingeaux
Saugues
Le-Puy-en-Velay
St-Flour
Valence
Langogne
Marvejols
Aubenas
Montélimar
Mende
Pierrelatte
Valréas
Nyons
Sévérac-le-Château
Les Vans
Bollène
Millau
Alès
Uzès
Orange
Carpentras
Ganges
Avignon
Nîmes
Cavaillon
Lodève
Arles
Montpellier
Vauvert
Béziers
Sète
Agde
Narbonne
Golfe du Lion
Étang de Leucate
Perpignan
Port-Vendres
Cap de Creus
Figueres
MEDITERRANEAN SEA
Marseille
Martigues
Istres
Marignane
Aix-en-Provence
Pertuis
Manosque
La Ciotat
Six-Fours-les-Plages
Cap Sicié
Toulon
Îles d'Hyères
Hyères
Brignoles
St-Tropez
Cap de St-Tropez
Fréjus
Cannes
Grasse
Antibes
Nice
MONACO
Monte-Carlo
Sisteron
Digne-les-Bains
Barcelonnette
Gap
Die
Vercors
Grenoble
St-Égrève
Chambéry
Aix-les-Bains
Annecy
Rumilly
Genève
(Geneva)
Cluses
Lac Léman
(Lake Geneva)
Thonon
Lausanne
Morges
Vevey
Montreux
Monthey
Martigny
Sion
Sierre
Zermatt
Matterhorn
Mont Blanc
Aosta
Ivrea
Biella
Modane
Briançon
Oulx
Cuorgnè
Ciriè
Turin
(Torino)
Moncalieri
Saluzzo
Fossano
Cuneo
Mondovì
Tende
San Remo
Capo Mele
Albenga
Savona
Genoa
(Genova)
Alba
Asti
Acqui Terme
Alessandria
Novi Ligure
Casale Monferrato
Vercelli
Novara
Borgosesia
Arona
Varese
Como
Lugano
Lago di Como
Monza
Milan
(Milano)
Treviglio
Crema
Bergamo
Brescia
Cremona
Piacenza
Parma
Reggio nell'Emilia
Modena
Bologna
Imola
ITALY
Mantova
Legnago
Verona
Vicenza
Padua
(Padova)
Rovigo
Ferrara
Schio
Valdagno
Rovereto
Riva del Garda
Lago di Garda
Trento
Feltre
DOLOMITI
Bolzano
Merano
Bressanone
Laives
Tirano
Chiavenna
St Moritz
Davos
Scuol
Chur
Bellinzona
Biasca
Passo del San Gottardo
Brig
Frutigen
Jungfrau
Altdorf
Schwyz
Zug
Luzern
(Lucerne)
BERN
Biel
Solothurn
Neuchâtel
Delémont
Laufen
Basel
(Basle)
Zürich
Winterthur
Schaffhausen
Konstanz
St Gallen
LIECHTENSTEIN
VADUZ
SWITZERLAND
Bregenz
Landeck
Pfunds
Innsbruck
Brenner Pass
Vipiteno
AUSTRIA
Schwaz
Wörgl
Kufstein
Rosenheim
Garmisch-Partenkirchen
Kempten
(Allgäu)
Memmingen
Friedrichshafen
Ravensburg
Sigmaringen
Villingen
Rottweil
Balingen
Biberach an der Riß
Reutlingen
Tübingen
Schwäbische Alb
Ulm
Günzburg
Augsburg
Munich
(München)
Dachau
Freising
Landshut
Isar
Ingolstadt
Straubing
Kelheim
Regensburg
Schwandorf
Amberg
Nürnberg
Fürth
Erlangen
Roth
Ansbach
Nördlingen
Donauwörth
Fränkische Alb
Göppingen
Stuttgart
Ludwigsburg
Heilbronn
Mosbach
Heidelberg
Mannheim
Wertheim
Würzburg
Bamberg
Bayreuth
Weiden in der Oberpfalz
Tachov
Cheb
Karlovy Vary
Kulmbach
Hof
Plauen
Schwarzenberg
Zwickau
Gera
Jena
Saalfeld
Bad Salzungen
Gotha
Eisenach
Thüringer Wald
Suhl
Meiningen
Coburg
Bad Kissingen
Schweinfurt
Bad Hersfeld
Fulda
Gießen
Siegen
Wetzlar
Offenbach am Main
Frankfurt am Main
Darmstadt
Wiesbaden
Mainz
GERMANY
Koblenz
Neuwied
Bonn
Rhine
Cologne
(Köln)
Leverkusen
Remscheid
Düsseldorf
Aachen
Maastricht
Malmédy
Bitburg
Idar-Oberstein
Ludwigshafen am Rhein
Neunkirchen
Speyer
Karlsruhe
Pforzheim
Baden-Baden
Strasbourg
Offenburg
Schwarzwald
(Black Forest)
Freyming-Merlebach
Bitche
VOSGES
Sélestat
Colmar
Mulhouse
Freiburg im Breisgau
JURA
ALPS
Corsica
(Corse)
(France)
Cap Corse
Bastia
L'Île-Rousse
Calvi
Corte
Vescovato
Cervione
Monte Rotondo
2622
Capo Rosso
Capo di Feno
Ajaccio
Ghisonaccia
Prunelli-di-Fiumorbo
Zonza
Sartène
Porto-Vecchio
Bonifacio
Ligurian Sea
Isola di Capraia
Isola d'Elba
Portoferraio
Isola Pianosa
Castiglione della Pescaia
Grosseto
Orbetello
Follonica
San Vincenzo
Cecina
Livorno
Siena
Pisa
Empoli
Florence
(Firenze)
Prato
Pistoia
Viareggio
Carrara
La Spezia
Sestri Levante
Monte Cimone
2165
Apennines
MASSIF CENTRAL
Cévennes
Rhône
Seine
Meuse
Moselle
50°
45°
5°
10°
D
E
1
2
3
0
100
200 KILOMETRES

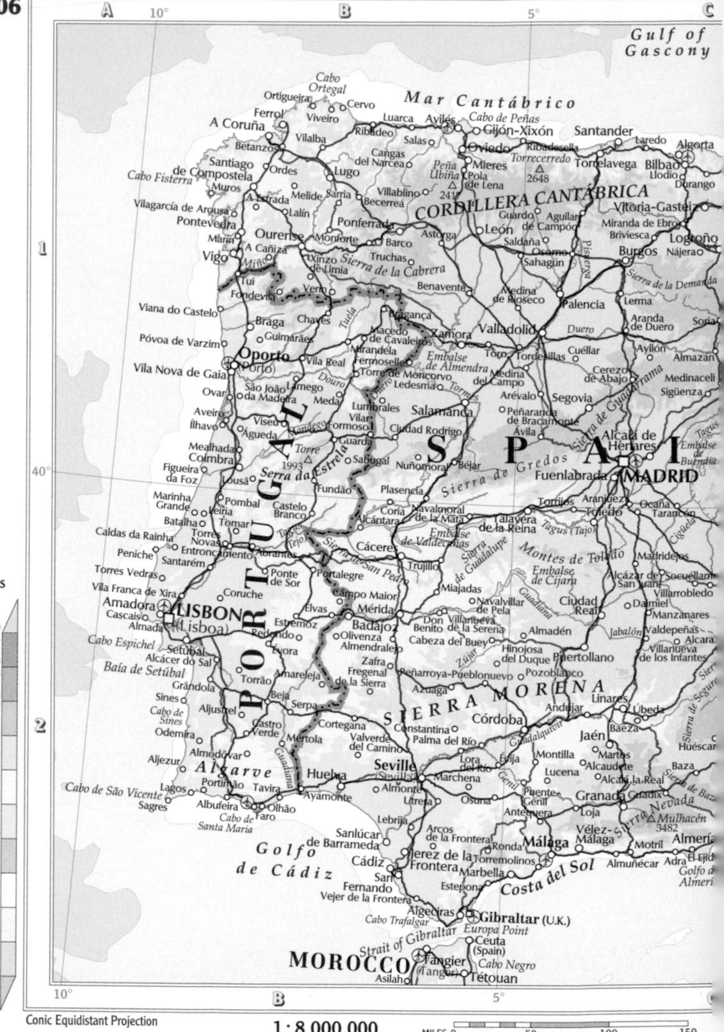

Conic Equidistant Projection

1:8 000 000

MILES 0 50 100 150

0°
D
5°
E
Langon
Bazas
Marmande
Lot
Cahors
Rodez
Villeneuve-sur-Lot
Sévérac-le-Château
Florac
Bollène
Orange
Sisteron
Casteljaloux
Agen
Moissac
Carmaux
Millau
Alès
Uzès
Carpentras
Digne-les-Bains
Mimizan
Morcenx
Labouheyre
Roquefort
Nérac
Montauban
Albi
Cévennes
Ganges
Avignon
Cavaillon
Manosque
Lectoure
Condom
Gaillac
Nîmes
Arles
Mont-de-Marsan
F R A N C E
Lodève
Vauvert
Pertuis
Aix-en-Provence
Soustons
Tartas
Colomiers
Toulouse
Castres
Montpellier
Istres
Marignane
Brignoles
Dax
Aire-sur-l'Adour
Auch
Puylaurens
Châteauneuf-les-Martigues
Bayonne
Orthez
Muret
Mazamet
Béziers
Sète
Marseille
Toulon
Adour
Maubourguet
Agde
Golfe du Lion
La Ciotat
Hyères
Irún
Biarritz
Carcassonne
Six-Fours-les-Plages
Cap Sicié
Donostia-San Sebastián
Oloron-Ste-Marie
Pau
Tarbes
Pamiers
Narbonne
Lourdes
St-Gaudens
Limoux
Durban-Corbières
Soulom
Bagnères-de-Luchon
Foix
Quillan
Rivesaltes
Étang de Leucate
P Y R E N E E S
Perpignan
Etxarri-Aranatz
Pamplona
Aragón
ANDORRA LA VELLA
Port-Vendres
Céret
Cap de Creus
Estella
3404
Tafalla
Jaca
ANDORRA
Figueres
1
Calahorra
Ejea de los Caballeros
Arguís
Graus
Ripoll
Banyoles
Olot
Cap de Begur
Sádaba
Huesca
Tremp
Berga
Torroella de Montgrí
Alfaro
Tudela
Barbastro
Monzón
Torelló
Vic
Girona
Costa Brava
Alto del Moncayo
Tarazona
Palamós
2316
Alagón
Binéfar
Tàrrega
Manresa
Sabadell
Blanes
Zaragoza
Igualada
Mataró
Fraga
Lleida
Martorell
El Prat de Llobregat
Barcelona
Quinto
Valls
Calatayud
Cariñena
Escatrón
Caspe
Ebro
Reus
Vilanova i la Geltrú
Esteras de Medinaceli
Daroca
Alcañiz
Tarragona
Molina de Aragón
Gandesa
Golf de Sant Jordi
Calamocha
Guadalope
Tortosa
(Tajo)
Tordesilos
Monreal del Campo
Amposta
Perales del Alfambra
Morella
N
Peñarroya
Vinaròs
Menorca
(Minorca)
2019
Pta Nati
Cap de Formentor
Ciutadella de Menorca
40°
Teruel
Torreblanca
Serranía de Cuenca
Sarrión
Alcora
Mahón
Cuenca
Santa Cruz de Moya
Castelló de la Plana
Mallorca
(Majorca)
Alcúdia
Burriana
Cap des Freu
Embalse de Alarcón
Cabriel
Turia
Vall de Uxó
Calvià
Sagunto
Llíria
Sa Dragonera
Manacor
Utiel
Requena
Valencia
Palma de Mallorca
Felanitx
Motilla del Palancar
Minglanilla
Torrent
Golfo de Valencia
Cap de ses Salines
La Roda
Júcar
Algemesí
Sueca
Cullera
San Juan Bautista
Ibiza
(Eivissa)
Cabrera
Carcaixent
Gandía
San Antonio Abad
Albacete
Xàtiva
Oliva
Eivissa
Almansa
Alcoy-Alcoi
Cabo de la Nao
San Francisco Javier
Alcaraz
Villena
Altea
Formentera
Hellín
Benidorm
BALEARIC ISLANDS
(ISLAS BALEARES)
(Spain)
Segura
Elda
Alicante-Alacant
Caravaca de la Cruz
Cieza
Elche-Elx
Orihuela
Costa Blanca
Murcia
El Moral
Torrevieja
2
Alhama de Murcia
Lorca
Cabo de Palos
Huércal-Overa
Cartagena
MEDITERRANEAN SEA
Águilas
Vera
Dellys
Tizi Ouzou
Bejaïa
ALGIERS
(Alger)
Aïn Taya
Boumerdes
Koléa
Cabo de Gata
Djebel Bissa
Larba
Bougaa
Ténès
Gouraya
Tipasa
Blida
Bouira
1157
Miliana
Médéa
Bordj Bou Arréridj
Ouled Farès
Aïn Defla
Khemis Miliana
Berrouaghia
Sidi Ali
Oued Chélif
Ech Chélif
Sour el Ghozlane
Sidi Aïssa
M'Sila
Mostaganem
Ksar el Boukhari
Aïn Tédélès
Bordj Bounaama
Gap Carbon
Oran
Arzew
Relizane
Oued Tlélat
Zemmora
Tissemsilt
A L G E R I A
Sig
Mohammadia
Greenwich 0° meridian
D
5°
0
100
200 KILOMETRES

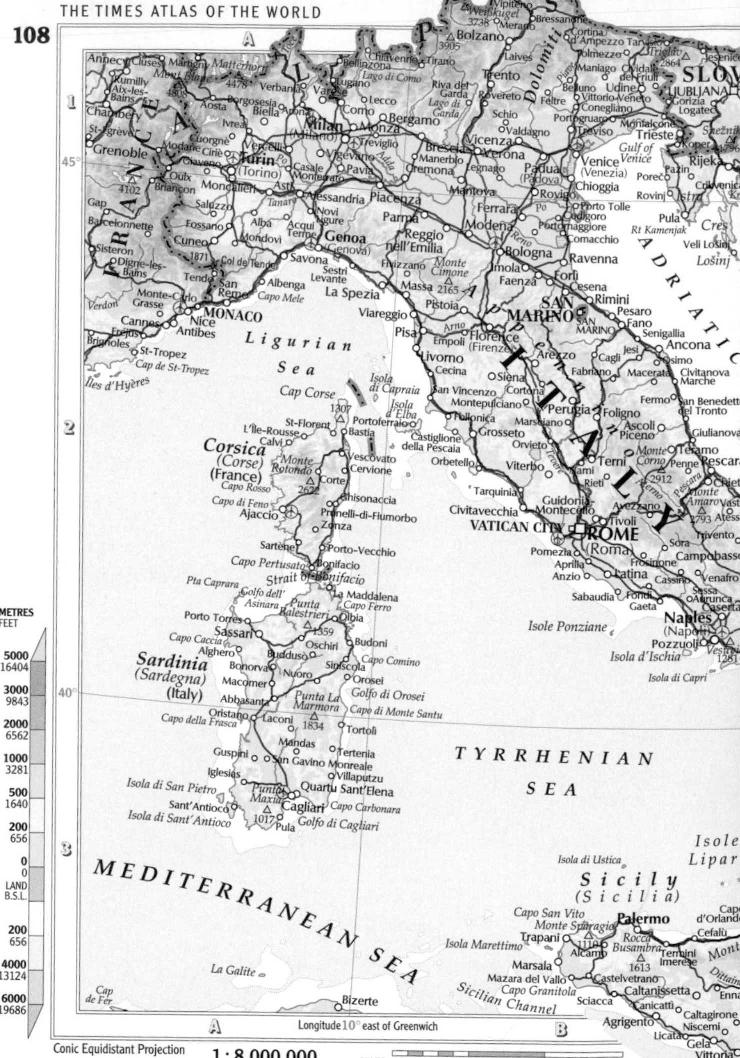

Conic Equidistant Projection

1:8 000 000

MILES 0 50 100 150

HUNGARY
CROATIA
BOSNIA-HERZEGOVINA
SERBIA AND MONTENEGRO
SRBIJA (SERBIA)
CRNA GORA (MONTENEGRO)
KOSOVO
VOJVODINA
ROMANIA
ALBANIA
MACEDONIA (F.Y.R.O.M.)
GREECE
BUL.
ZAGREB
BELGRADE (Beograd)
SARAJEVO
SKOPJE
TIRANA (Tiranë)
SOFIA (Sofiya)
DALMACIJA
Carpatii Meridionali
Vârful Svinecea Mare
Danube (Donau)
Drava
Drina
Tisa
Timiş
Mureşul
Stol
Durmitor
Korab
Olympus
Grammos
Parnassos
Kyllini
Pindos
Vardar
Pineios
Aliakmonas
Maribor
Murska Sobota
Varaždin
Koprivnica
Nagyatád
Kaposvár
Pécs
Mohács
Baja
Subotica
Sombor
Senta
Kikinda
Timişoara
Lugoj
Hunedoara
Deva
Orăştie
Sebeş
Petroşani
Lupeni
Caransebeş
Reşiţa
Târgu Jiu
Motru
Strehaia
Drobeta-Turnu Severin
Calafat
Băileşti
Poiana Mare
Karlovac
Ogulin
Senj
Bihać
Gospić
Zadar
Šibenik
Split
Makarska
Dubrovnik
Osijek
Vukovar
Novi Sad
Zrenjanin
Vršac
Pančevo
Smederevo
Požarevac
Kragujevac
Niš
Leskovac
Priština
Prizren
Peć
Podgorica
Cetinje
Shkodër
Durrës
Elbasan
Korçë
Vlorë
Sarandë
Ohrid
Bitola
Prilep
Kumanovo
Štip
Strumica
Blagoevgrad
Kyustendil
Montana
Thessaloniki
Kozani
Larisa
Ioannina
Kerkyra
Corfu (Kerkyra)
Lefkada
Kefallonia (Cephalonia)
Argostoli
Ionian Islands (Ionioi Nisoi)
Zakynthos (Zante)
Patra
Lamia
Karditsa
Kalamata
Tripoli
Megalopoli
Kyparissia
Pyrgos
Termoli
Vieste
Manfredonia
Foggia
Barletta
Bari
Molfetta
Monopoli
Brindisi
Lecce
Taranto
Matera
Potenza
Salerno
Avellino
Cosenza
Crotone
Catanzaro
Reggio di Calabria
Messina
Catania
Syracuse
Golfo di Taranto
Golfo di Squillace
Strait of Otranto
Stretta di Messina
IONIAN SEA
LA SILA
Le Murge
20°
40°
45°
15°
0
100
200 KILOMETRES
© Bartholomew Ltd

Conic Equidistant Projection

1 : 8 000 000

MILES 0 50 100 150

GREECE
TURKEY
AEGEAN SEA
IONIAN SEA
MEDITERRANEAN SEA
Krytiko Pelagos
Mirtoö Pelagos
Strait of Otranto
Mountains
CRETE (KRITI)
Rhodes (Rodos)
Dodecanese (Dodekanisos)
Cyclades (Kyklades)
Lesbos (Lesvos)
Chios
Evvoia (Euboea)
Ionian Islands (Ionioi Nisoi)
Kefallonia (Cephalonia)
Zakynthos (Zante)
Corfu (Kerkyra)
Lefkada
Limnos
Thasos
Samothraki
Gökçeada
Bozcaada
Samos
Ikaria
Fournoi
Patmos
Leros
Kalymnos
Kos
Naxos
Paros
Mykonos
Tinos
Andros
Syros
Kythnos
Serifos
Sifnos
Sikinos
Ios
Amorgos
Astypalaia
Milos
Kea
Ydra
Thira (Santorini)
Tilos
Symi
Chalki
Karpathos (Scarpanto)
Kasos
Kythira
Antikythira
Gavdos
Chrysi
Skyros
Skopelos
Alonnisos
Skiathos
Psara
Agios Efstratios
Marmara Denizi
Saros Körfezi
Edremit Körfezi
Kuşadası Körfezi
Thermaïkos Kolpos
Argolikos Kolpos
Saronikos Kolpos
Korinthiakos Kolpos
Lakonikos Kolpos
Messiniakos Kolpos
Kolpos Mirampelou
Akra Drepano
Akra Paliouri
Akra Kafireas
Akra Maleas
Akra Spatha
Akra Sideros
Akra Lithino
Akrathos
Athos
Olympus 2911
Parnassos 2457
Kyllini 2376
Parnon
Taygetos 2404
Pindos
Uludağ
Simav Dağları
Boz Dağları
Kara Ada
ATHENS (Athina)
Peiraias
Thessaloniki
Kalamaria
Larisa
Volos
Lamia
Patra
Ioannina
Kalamata
Tripoli
Sparti
Korinthos
Argos
Nafplio
Pyrgos
Kavala
Xanthi
Drama
Serres
Kilkis
Alexandroupoli
Komotini
Katerini
Veroia
Edessa
Florina
Kastoria
Kozani
Grevena
Trikala
Karditsa
Igoumenitsa
Preveza
Arta
Agrinio
Mesolongi
Nafpaktos
Amfissa
Delphi
Chalkida
Kymi
Karystos
Mytilini
Chios
Rhodes (Rodos)
Irakleio
Chania
Rethymno
Agios Nikolaos
Kastelli
Palaiochora
Sfakia
Ierapetra
Izmir
Istanbul
Bakırköy
Kadıköy
Kartal
Bursa
Balıkesir
Manisa
Aydın
Denizli
Kütahya
Uşak
Bodrum
Marmaris
Fethiye
Muğla
Milas
Datça
Söke
Kuşadası
Çeşme
Ayvalık
Bergama
Çanakkale
Gelibolu (Gallipoli)
Tekirdağ
Edirne
Yalova
Gemlik
Bandırma
Kalkan
TIRANA (Tiranë)
Durrës
Elbasan
Vlorë
Korçë
Fier
Berat
Sarandë
Gjirokastër
Bitola
Ohrid
Struga
Strumica
Prilep
Gevgelija
(F.Y.R.O.M.)
Longitude 20° east of Greenwich
© Bartholomew Ltd
0
100
200 KILOMETRES

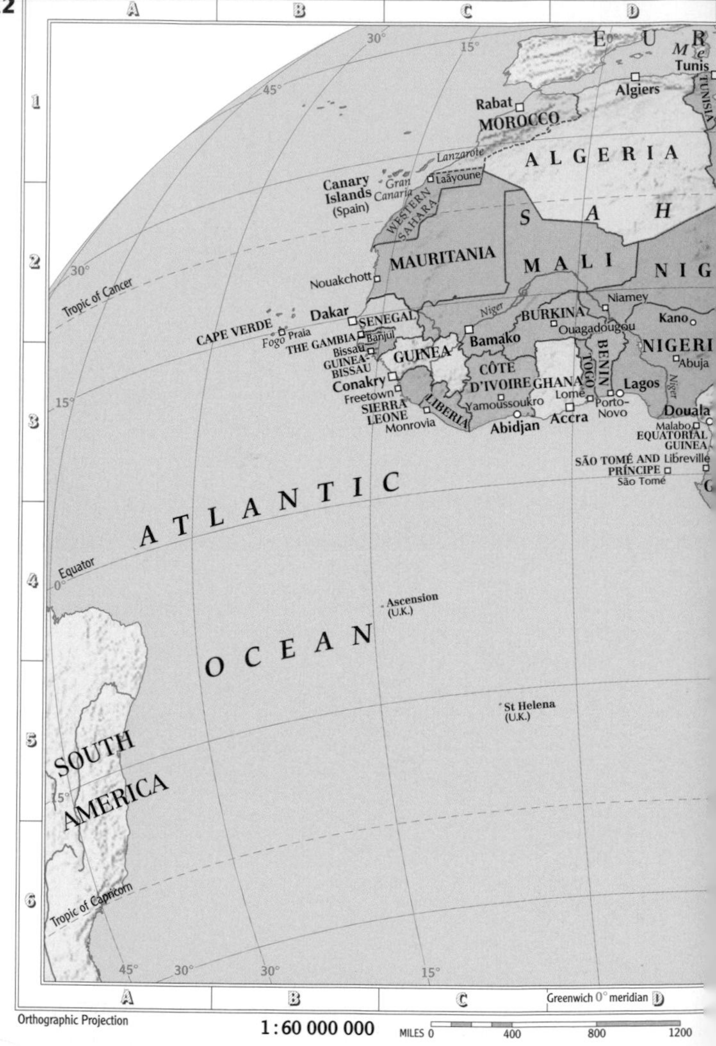
A
B
C
D
1
2
3
4
5
6
E U R
Tunis
TUNISIA
Algiers
Rabat
MOROCCO
ALGERIA
Lanzarote
Canary Islands (Spain)
Gran Canaria
Laâyoune
WESTERN SAHARA
S A H
MAURITANIA
MALI
NIG
Nouakchott
Tropic of Cancer
Niamey
Niger
Dakar
SENEGAL
BURKINA
Kano
CAPE VERDE
Praia
Fogo
THE GAMBIA
Banjul
Bamako
Ouagadougou
Bissau
GUINEA-BISSAU
GUINEA
BENIN
TOGO
NIGERI
Abuja
Conakry
CÔTE D'IVOIRE
GHANA
Lagos
Freetown
SIERRA LEONE
LIBERIA
Yamoussoukro
Lomé
Porto-Novo
Douala
Monrovia
Abidjan
Accra
Malabo
EQUATORIAL GUINEA
SÃO TOMÉ AND PRÍNCIPE
Libreville
São Tomé
ATLANTIC
OCEAN
Equator
Ascension (U.K.)
St Helena (U.K.)
SOUTH AMERICA
Tropic of Capricorn
Greenwich 0° meridian
Orthographic Projection
1:60 000 000
MILES 0 400 800 1200

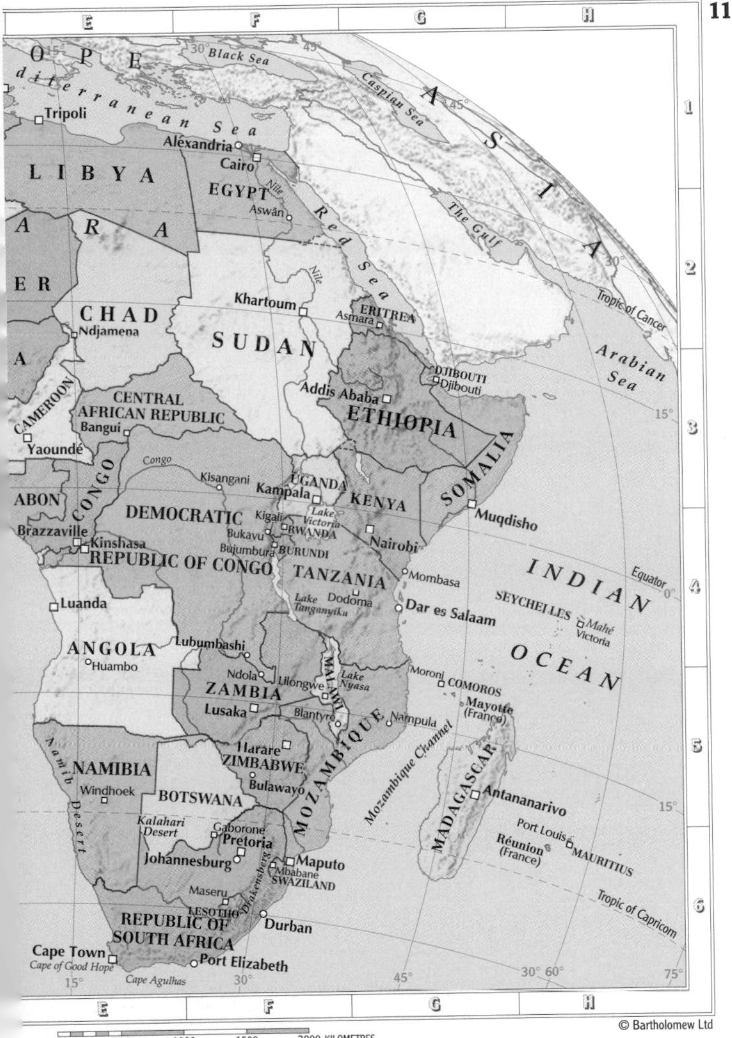
E
F
G
H
1
2
3
4
5
6
Black Sea
Caspian Sea
Mediterranean Sea
ASIA
Tripoli
Alexandria
Cairo
LIBYA
EGYPT
Nile
Aswân
Red Sea
The Gulf
Tropic of Cancer
Khartoum
CHAD
Ndjamena
SUDAN
ERITREA
Asmara
Arabian Sea
DJIBOUTI
Djibouti
Addis Ababa
ETHIOPIA
CAMEROON
CENTRAL AFRICAN REPUBLIC
Bangui
Yaoundé
SOMALIA
Congo
CONGO
Kisangani
UGANDA
Kampala
KENYA
GABON
DEMOCRATIC REPUBLIC OF CONGO
Lake Victoria
Kigali
RWANDA
Bukavu
Bujumbura
BURUNDI
Muqdisho
Nairobi
Brazzaville
Kinshasa
TANZANIA
Mombasa
INDIAN OCEAN
Equator
Luanda
Lake Tanganyika
Dodoma
Dar es Salaam
SEYCHELLES
Mahé
Victoria
ANGOLA
Huambo
Lubumbashi
Ndola
Lilongwe
MALAWI
Lake Nyasa
Moroni
COMOROS
ZAMBIA
Lusaka
Blantyre
Nampula
Mayotte (France)
Harare
ZIMBABWE
Bulawayo
MOZAMBIQUE
Mozambique Channel
MADAGASCAR
Namib Desert
NAMIBIA
Windhoek
BOTSWANA
Antananarivo
Kalahari Desert
Gaborone
Pretoria
Port Louis
Réunion (France)
MAURITIUS
Johannesburg
Maputo
Mbabane
SWAZILAND
Drakensberg
Maseru
LESOTHO
Durban
Tropic of Capricorn
REPUBLIC OF SOUTH AFRICA
Cape Town
Cape of Good Hope
Port Elizabeth
Cape Agulhas
0 500 1000 1500 2000 KILOMETRES

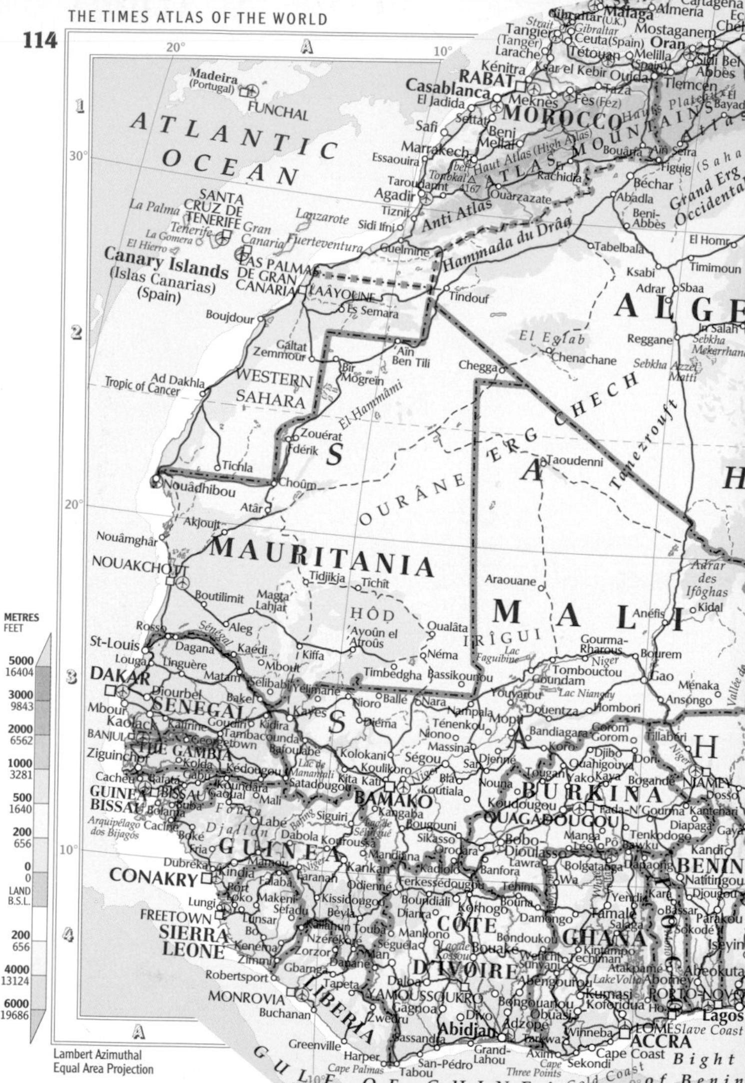

Lambert Azimuthal Equal Area Projection

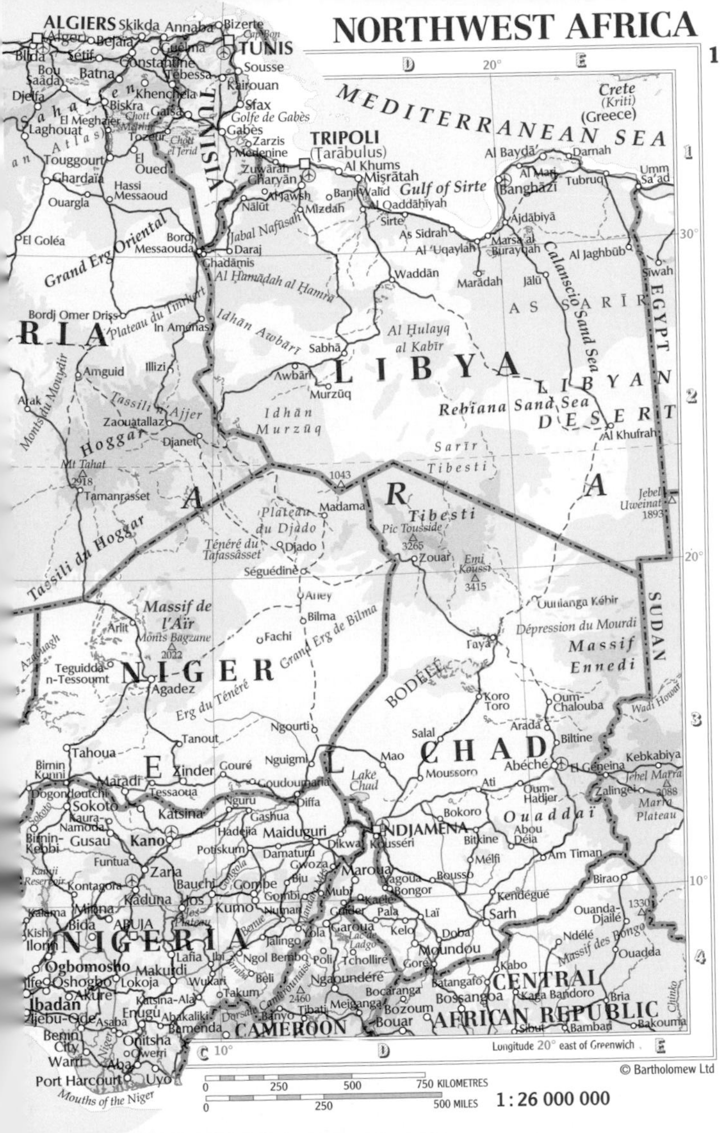

NORTHWEST AFRICA

Longitude 20° east of Greenwich

0 250 500 750 KILOMETRES

0 250 500 MILES

1 : 26 000 000

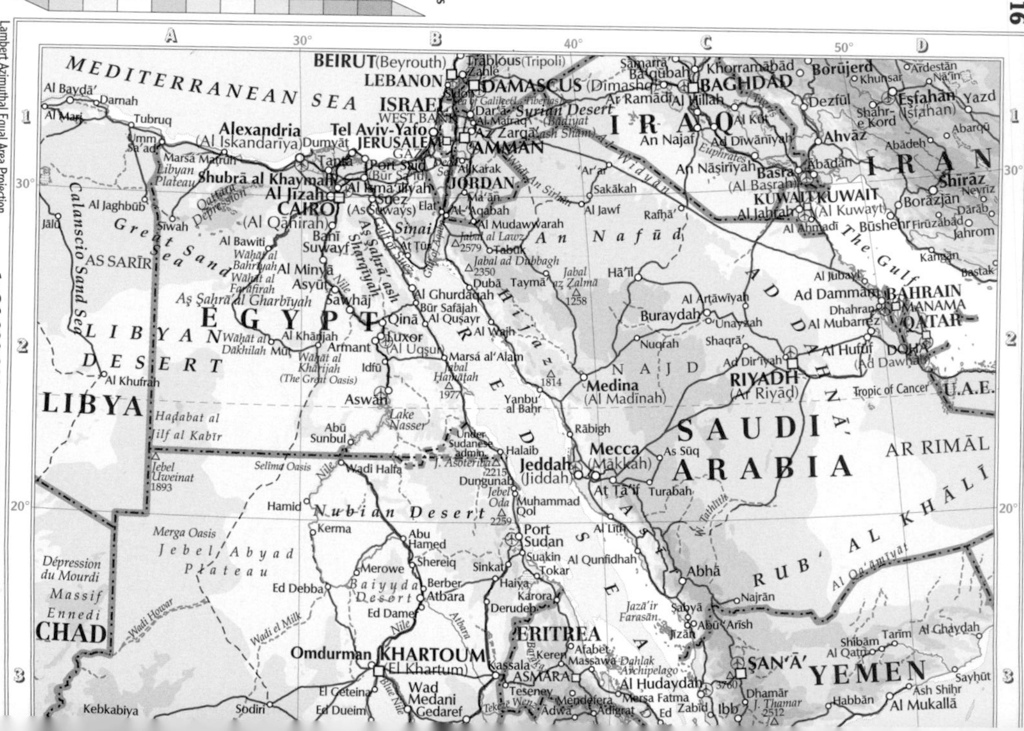

Lambert Azimuthal Equal Area Projection

1:26 000 000

MILES 0 250 500

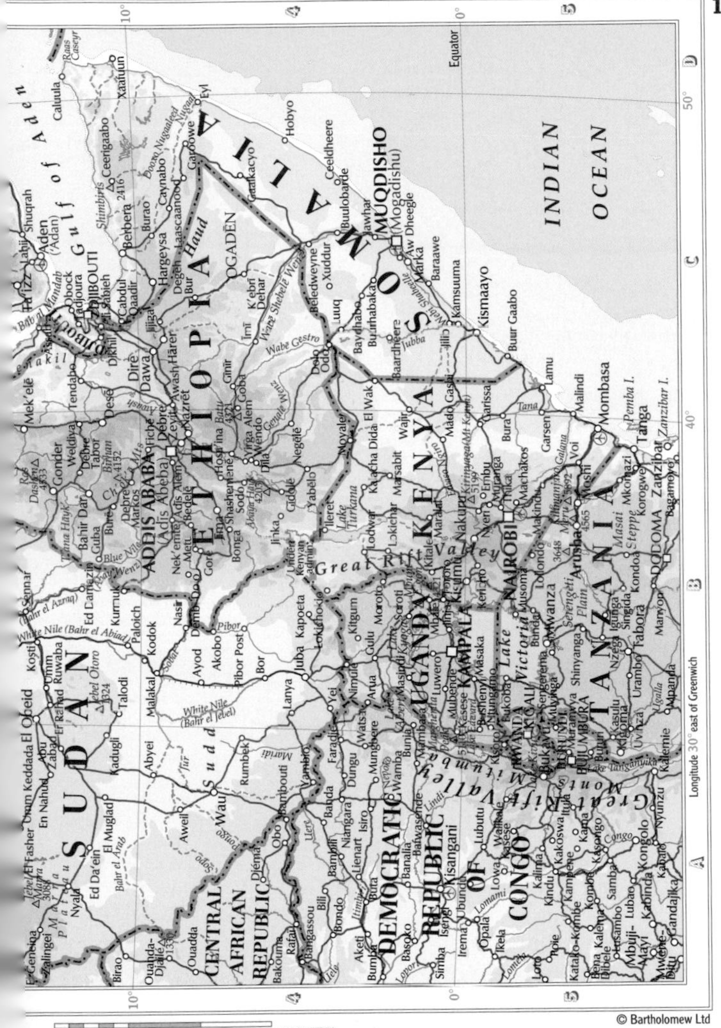

SUDAN
ETHIOPIA
SOMALIA
KENYA
UGANDA
TANZANIA
RWANDA
BURUNDI
DJIBOUTI
CENTRAL AFRICAN REPUBLIC
DEMOCRATIC REPUBLIC OF CONGO
INDIAN OCEAN
Gulf of Aden
ADDIS ABABA (Adis Abeba)
MUQDISHO (Mogadishu)
NAIROBI
KAMPALA
KIGALI
BUJUMBURA
DODOMA
Great Rift Valley
Lake Victoria
Lake Turkana
Lake Tanganyika
Mombasa
Zanzibar
Kisangani
Wau
Juba
Malakal
Kosti
El Obeid
Sennar
Gonder
Bahir Dar
Dire Dawa
Hargeysa
Berbera
Aden ('Adan)
Kismaayo
Equator
Longitude 30° east of Greenwich
0
250
500
750 KILOMETRES
© Bartholomew Ltd

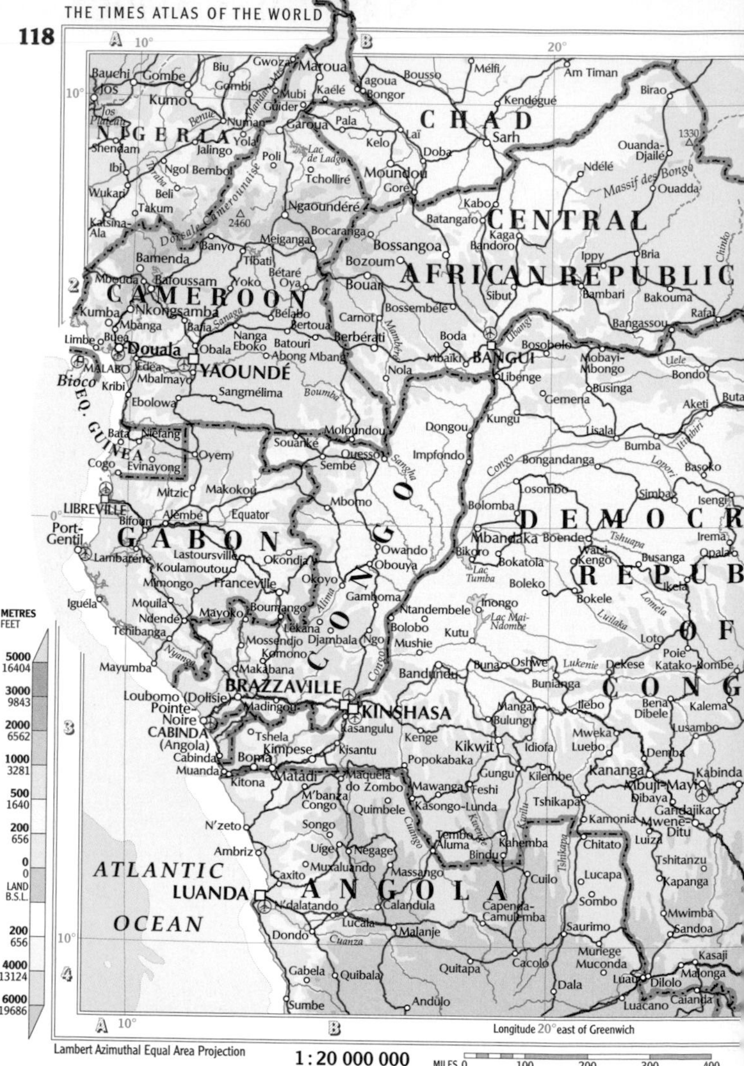

Lambert Azimuthal Equal Area Projection

1:20 000 000

MILES 0 100 200 300 400

C
30°
D
40°
10°
El Muglad
Kadugli
Talodi
Kurmuk
Blue Nile
(Abay Wenz)
Debre Markos
Ch'ok'e Mts
Bahr el Arab
Kodok
Paloich
Mendi
ADDIS ABABA
(Ādīs Ābeba)
Fichē
Awash
Abyei
Malakal
Nek'emtē
Debre Zeyit
Āwash
SUDAN
Sobat
Ādīs Alem
Nazrēt
Dembī Dolo
Bedelē
Aweil
Jur
White Nile
(Bahr el Jebel)
Ayod
Nasir
Metu
Gorē
ETHIOPIA
Jīma
Hosa'ina
Sopo
Sudd
Akobo
Batu
4321
Gīnīr
Wau
Pongo
Pibor
Bonga
Shashemenē
Goba
Yirga Alem
Wendo
Pibor Post
Sodo
Dila
Rumbek
Ābaya Hāyk'
4203
Genale Wenz
Bor
Djéma
Maridi
Jinka
Gidolē
Negēlē
2
Obo
Bambouti
Lanya
Under Kenyan admin.
Yabēlo
Juba
Kapoeta
Yambio
Lokichokio
Lotikipi Plain
Ileret
Uere
Yei
Lake Turkana
Moyale
Bili
Banda
Faradje
Bambili
Great Rift Valley
Niangara
Dungu
Nimule
Kitgum
Lodwar
Kalacha Dida
El Wak
Watsa
Lienart
Isiro
Arua
Gulu
Moroto
Mungbere
Marsabit
Lokichar
UGANDA
Nepoko
Lake Albert
Masindi
Mount Elgon
4321
KENYA
Wajir
Wamba
Soroti
Bunia
Mambasa
Banalia
Lindi
Lake Kyoga
Mbale
Maralal
Ewaso Ngiro
Mado Gashi
Kitale
Bafwasende
Luwero
Beni
Margherita Peak
Mubende
Jinja
Tororo
Kirinyaga
(Mt Kenya)
5199
Kisangani
Kakamega
Equator
0°
5110
KAMPALA
Kisumu
Nakuru
Garissa
ATIC
Kasese
Lake Edward
Masaka
Kericho
Nyeri
Embu
Ubundu
Lubutu
Bushenyi
Lake
Kisii
Naivasha
Muranga
Ntungamo
Bura
Kisoro
Victoria
NAIROBI
Thika
LIC
Walikale
Bukoba
Lomami
Kasese
Goma
Machakos
Tana
Lowa
RWANDA
Musoma
Lake Kivu
Gitarama
KIGALI
Lollondo
Congo
Bunda
Makindu
Garsen
Lamu
Kalima
Kabare
Cyangugu
Mwanza
Kilimanjaro
5892
Galana
Bukavu
Muyinga
3648
Meru
4565
Kindu
Bururi
Sengerema
BURUNDI
Moshi
Voi
Malindi
Kakoswa
Muramvya
Serengeti Plain
Kama
BUJUMBURA
Shinyanga
Arusha
Hai
Mombasa
Itula
Babati
Same
Kampene
Nzega
Igunga
O
Pemba I.
Rift
Bururi
Masai Steppe
Mkomazi
3
Mitumba
Kombe
Fizi
Kasulu
Singida
Kasongo
Samba
Kigoma
Urambo
Tabora
Kondoa
Korogwe
Tanga
Uvinza
Zanzibar I.
Lubao
Kongolo
TANZANIA
Nyunzu
Kalemie
Manyoni
DODOMA
Bagamoyo
Kabalo
Ugalla
Zanzibar
Mpanda
Morogoro
Congo
Great
Kitunda
Kilosa
Dar es Salaam
Kashyukulu
Luvua
Lake Tanganyika
Inyonga
Mbuyuni
Kibiti
Manono
Moba
Great Ruaha
Iringa
Rufiji
Kabongo
Kiambi
Lake Rukwa
Ifakara
Mohoro
Mafia I.
Piodi
Mwanza
2458
Mafinga
Kikondja
Sumbawanga
Makongolosi
Nangulangwa
Kilwa Masoko
Kamina
Lac Upemba
Mbeya
Chimala
Njinjo
Mitole
Matandu
Kilwa
Lake Mweru
Mbala
Mporokoso
Nakonde
Luhombero
Njombe
Kimambi
Kinda
Sampwe
Nchelenge
Chitipa
Karonga
Liwale
Lindi
Lubudi
Chaîne des Mitumba
ZAMBIA
10°
Mingoyo
Mtwara
Kasenga
Kasama
Songea
Masasi
Quionga
Tenke
Kambove
Mwenda
Chinsali
Lake Nyasa
(Lake Malawi)
4
Kolwezi
Minga
Chambeshi
Chama
MALAWI
Mbinga
Tunduru
Ruvuma
MOZAMBIQUE
Mocimboa da Praia
Likasi
Lake Bangweulu
Lupilichi
Lubumbashi
Mansa
Mzuzu
Mueda
Chililabombwe
30°
D
40°
C
Ndola
0
200
400
600 KILOMETRES
© Bartholomew Ltd

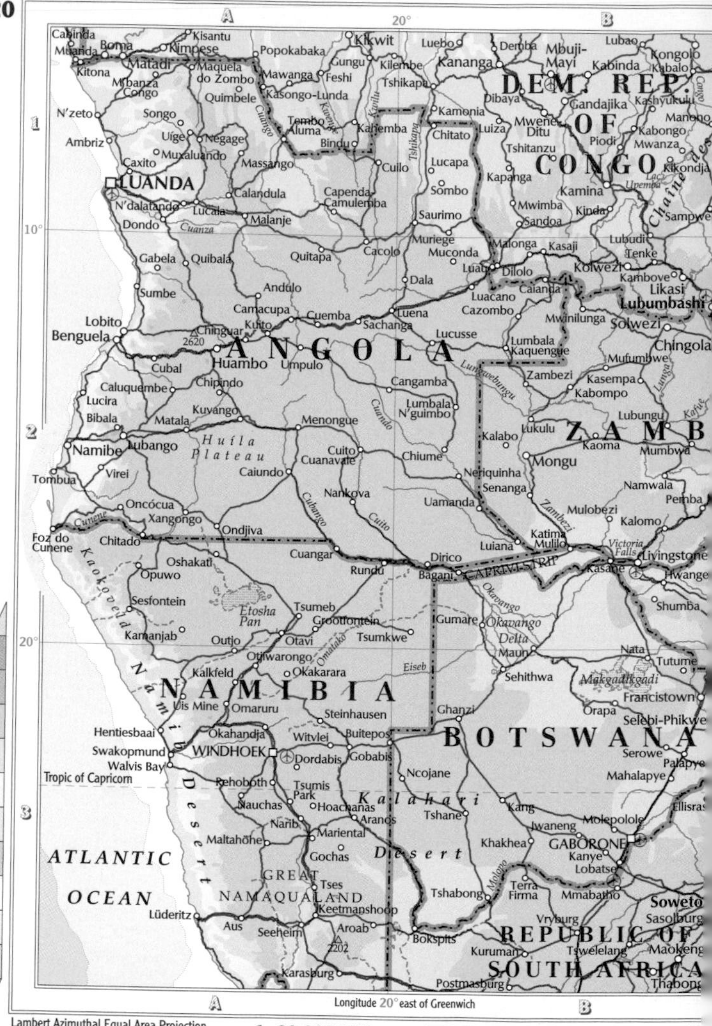

METRES
FEET

METRES	FEET
5000	16404
3000	9843
2000	6562
1000	3281
500	1640
200	656
0	0
LAND B.S.L.	
200	656
4000	13124
6000	19686

Lambert Azimuthal Equal Area Projection

1:20 000 000

MILES 0 100 200 300 400

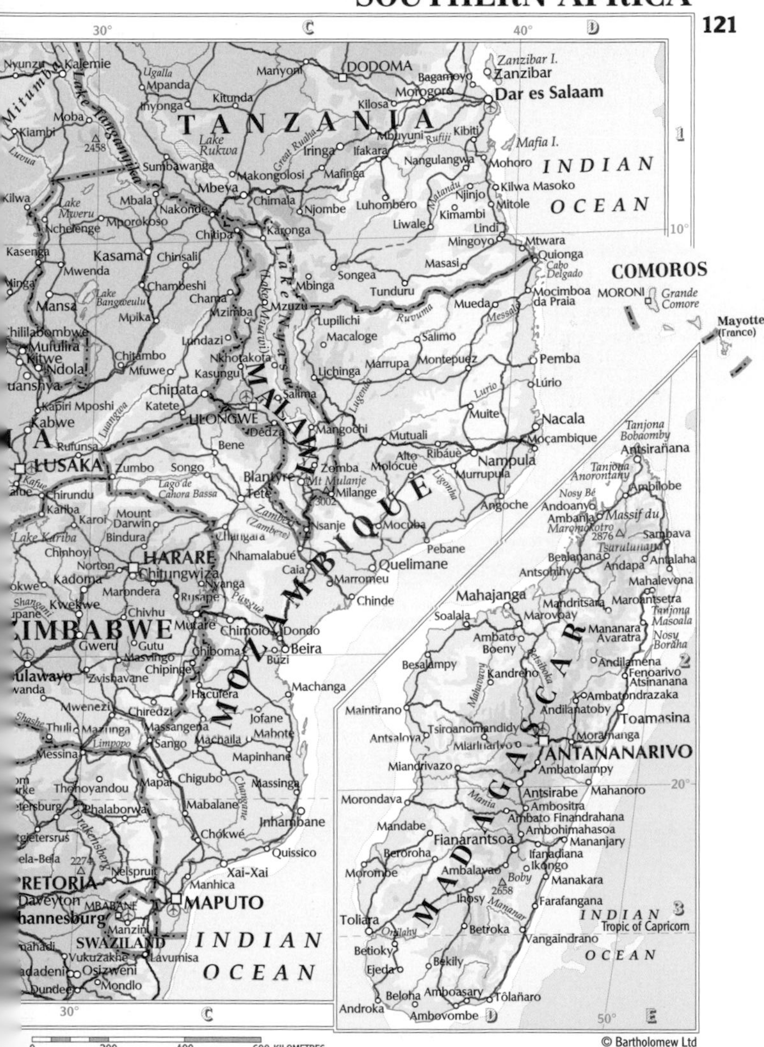

TANZANIA
DODOMA
Dar es Salaam
Zanzibar
INDIAN OCEAN
MALAWI
LILONGWE
MOZAMBIQUE
MAPUTO
ZIMBABWE
HARARE
LUSAKA
PRETORIA
SWAZILAND
MBABANE
COMOROS
MORONI
Mayotte (France)
MADAGASCAR
ANTANANARIVO
Tropic of Capricorn
0 200 400 600 KILOMETRES

REPUBLIC OF SOUTH AFRICA

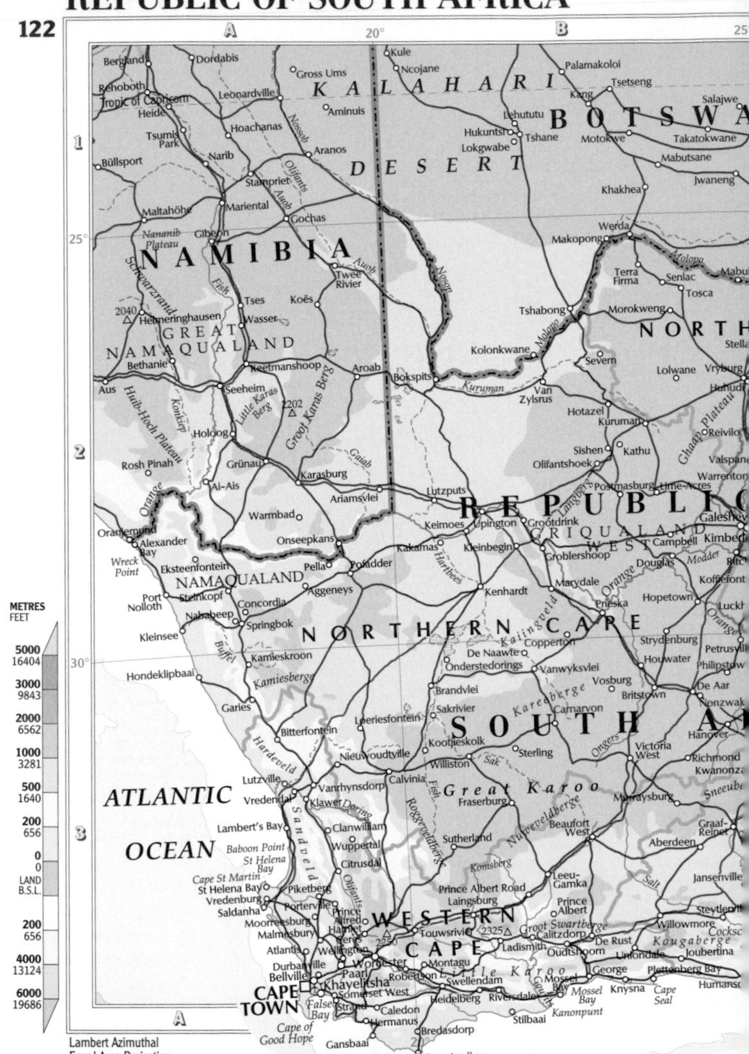

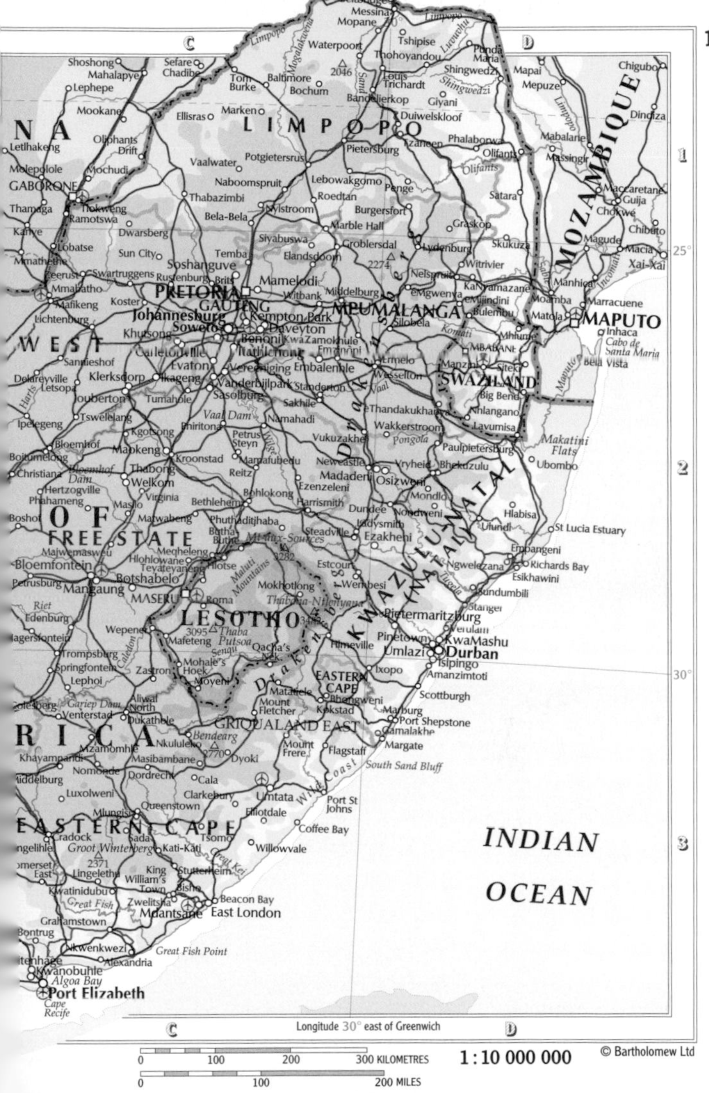
C
D
1
2
3
25°
30°
LIMPOPO
MPUMALANGA
GAUTENG
NORTH WEST
FREE STATE
KWAZULU-NATAL
EASTERN CAPE
GRIQUALAND EAST
LESOTHO
SWAZILAND
MOZAMBIQUE
INDIAN
OCEAN
Beitbridge
Messina
Mopane
Limpopo
Waterpoort
Tshipise
Thohoyandou
Punda Maria
Shingwedzi
Louis Trichardt
Tom Burke
Baltimore
Bochum
2046
Bandelierkop
Giyani
Mapai
Mepuze
Chigubo
Dindiza
Shoshong
Mahalapye
Sefare
Chadibe
Lephepe
Mookane
Ellisras
Marken
Duiwelskloof
Tzaneen
Phalaborwa
Olifants
Mabalane
Massingir
Letlhakeng
Oliphants Drift
Vaalwater
Potgietersrus
Pietersburg
Molepolole
Mochudi
GABORONE
Naboomspruit
Lebowakgomo
Penge
Satara
Macaretane
Guija
Chokwe
Chibuto
Thamaga
Mokweng
Ramotswa
Thabazimbi
Roedtan
Nylstroom
Burgersfort
Bela-Bela
Marble Hall
Graskop
Kanye
Dwarsberg
Lobatse
Siyabuswa
Groblersdal
Lydenburg
Skukuza
Magude
Macia
Xai-Xai
Mmathethe
Sun City
Temba
Elandsdoorn
2274
Witrivier
Soshanguve
Nelspruit
Zeerust
Swartruggens
Rustenburg
Brits
Mamelodi
Manhiça
Mmabatho
PRETORIA
Witbank
Middelburg
eMgwenya
KaNyamazane
Mafikeng
Koster
Moamba
Marracuene
Lichtenburg
Johannesburg
Kempton Park
eMjindini
Bulembu
Matola
MAPUTO
Soweto
Daveyton
Silobela
Khutsong
Benoni
KwaZamokhule
Mhlume
Inhaca
Cabo de Santa Maria
Carletonville
Ratanda
Emzinoni
MBABANE
Sannieshof
Evaton
Vereeniging
Embalenhle
Ermelo
Manzini
Siteki
Bela Vista
Delareyville
Letsopa
Klerksdorp
Ikageng
Vanderbijlpark
Standerton
Wesselton
Vaal
Harts
Jouberton
Sasolburg
Tumahole
Sakhile
Big Bend
Thandakukhanya
Nhlangano
Tswelelang
Vaal Dam
Namahadi
Lavumisa
Ipelegeng
Kgotsong
Phiritona
Wakkerstroom
Pongola
Makatini Flats
Bloemhof
Petrus Steyn
Vukuzakhe
Paulpietersburg
Boitumelong
Maokeng
Kroonstad
Mamafubedu
Newcastle
Vryheid
Bhekuzulu
Ubombo
Christiana
Bloemhof Dam
Thabong
Reitz
Madadeni
Osizweni
Welkom
Ezenzeleni
Hertzogville
Virginia
Bohlokong
Mondlo
Phahameng
Bethlehem
Harrismith
Dundee
Nondweni
Hlabisa
Boshof
Masilo
Matwabeng
Phuthaditjhaba
Ladysmith
Ulundi
St Lucia Estuary
Botha Bothe
Steadville
Ezakheni
Majwemasweu
Meqheleng
Mt-aux-Sources
3282
Empangeni
Hlohlowane
Teyateyaneng
Ficksburg
Richards Bay
Bloemfontein
Hlotse
Estcourt
Ngwelezana
Eskhawini
Petrusburg
Botshabelo
Maluti Mountains
Wembesi
Mangaung
MASERU
Roma
Mokhotlong
Sundumbili
Riet
Thabana-Ntlenyana
Stanger
Edenburg
Pietermaritzburg
Verulam
Wepener
3095
Thaba Putsoa
Pinetown
KwaMashu
Jagersfontein
Mafeteng
Senqu
Qacha's Nek
Himeville
Umlazi
Durban
Trompsburg
Caledon
Isipingo
Springfontein
Mohale's Hoek
Zastron
Ixopo
Amanzimtoti
Lephoi
Moyeni
Matatiele
Scottburgh
Aliwal North
Gariep Dam
Mount Fletcher
Bhongweni
Kokstad
Colesberg
Venterstad
Dukathole
Marburg
Port Shepstone
Gamalakhe
Bendearg
Nkululeko
2770
Mount Frere
Flagstaff
Margate
Mzamomhle
Khayamnandi
Masibambane
Dyoki
South Sand Bluff
Noupoort
Nomonde
Dordrecht
Cala
Wild Coast
Middelburg
Luxolweni
Clarkebury
Umtata
Port St Johns
Queenstown
Mlungisi
Elliotdale
Coffee Bay
Cradock
Sada
Tsomo
Groot Winterberg
Kati-Kati
Willowvale
2371
Great Kei
Lingelethu
King William's Town
Stutterheim
Kwatinidubu
Bisho
Great Fish
Zwelitsha
Beacon Bay
Mdantsane
East London
Grahamstown
Bontrug
Nkwenkwezi
Great Fish Point
Alexandria
Kwanobuhle
Algoa Bay
Port Elizabeth
Cape Recife
Longitude 30° east of Greenwich
0
100
200
300 KILOMETRES
0
100
200 MILES
1:10 000 000

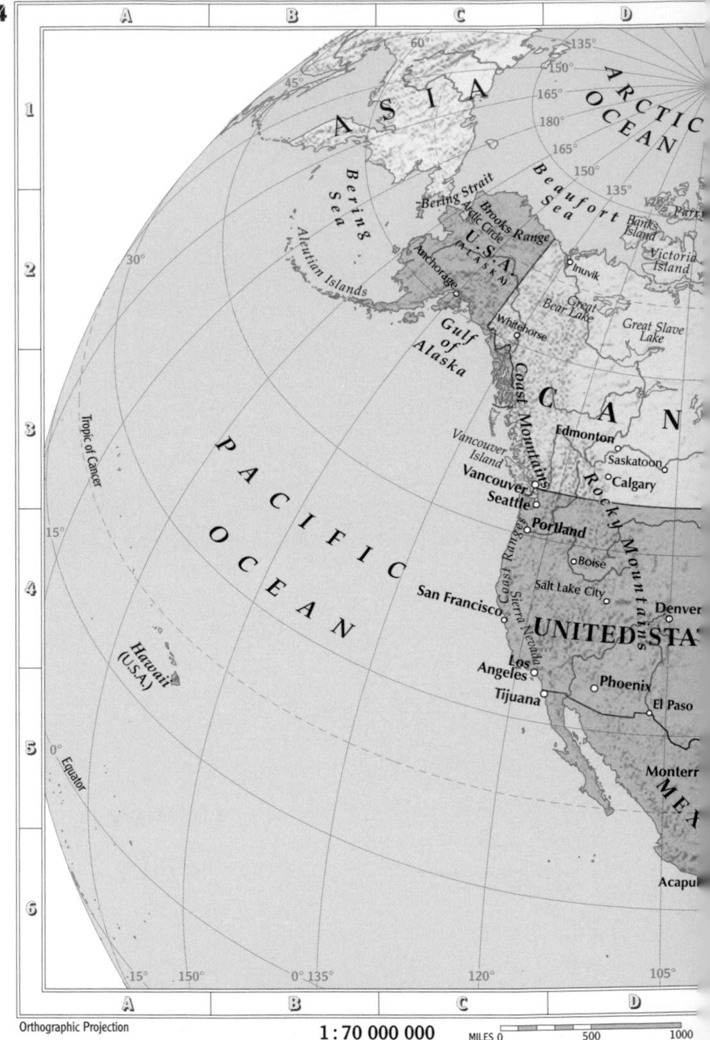

Orthographic Projection

1 : 70 000 000

MILES 0 500 1000

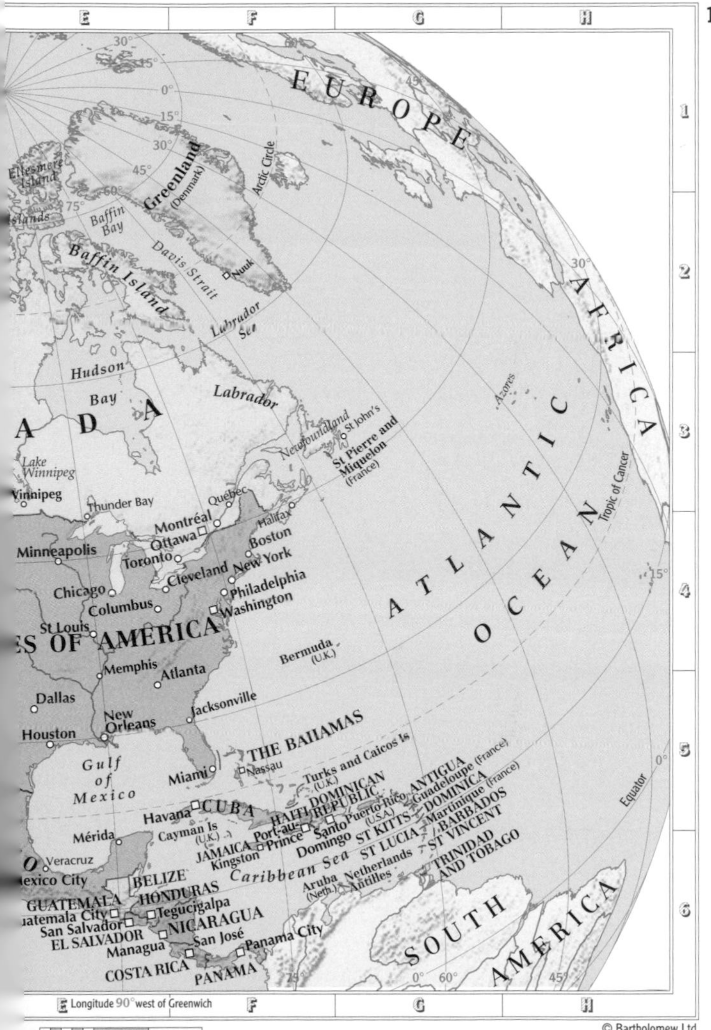
E
F
G
H
1
2
3
4
5
6
EUROPE
AFRICA
ATLANTIC OCEAN
SOUTH AMERICA
Greenland
(Denmark)
Ellesmere Island
Baffin Bay
Baffin Island
Davis Strait
Nuuk
Arctic Circle
Labrador Sea
Hudson Bay
Labrador
Newfoundland
St John's
St Pierre and Miquelon
(France)
Azores
Tropic of Cancer
Lake Winnipeg
Winnipeg
Thunder Bay
Québec
Montréal
Ottawa
Halifax
Boston
Minneapolis
Toronto
Cleveland
New York
Philadelphia
Chicago
Columbus
Washington
St Louis
ES OF AMERICA
Bermuda
(U.K.)
Memphis
Atlanta
Dallas
New Orleans
Jacksonville
Houston
THE BAHAMAS
Nassau
Miami
Gulf of Mexico
Turks and Caicos Is
(U.K.)
Havana
CUBA
HAITI
DOMINICAN REPUBLIC
ANTIGUA
Guadeloupe (France)
DOMINICA
Martinique (France)
BARBADOS
ST VINCENT
Equator
Mérida
Cayman Is
(U.K.)
JAMAICA
Kingston
Port-au-Prince
Santo Domingo
Puerto Rico
(U.S.A.)
ST KITTS
ST LUCIA
TRINIDAD AND TOBAGO
Veracruz
Caribbean Sea
Aruba
(Neth.)
Netherlands Antilles
BELIZE
HONDURAS
GUATEMALA
Guatemala City
Tegucigalpa
San Salvador
NICARAGUA
EL SALVADOR
Managua
San José
Panama City
COSTA RICA
PANAMA
Longitude 90° west of Greenwich
0
500
1000
1500 KILOMETRES

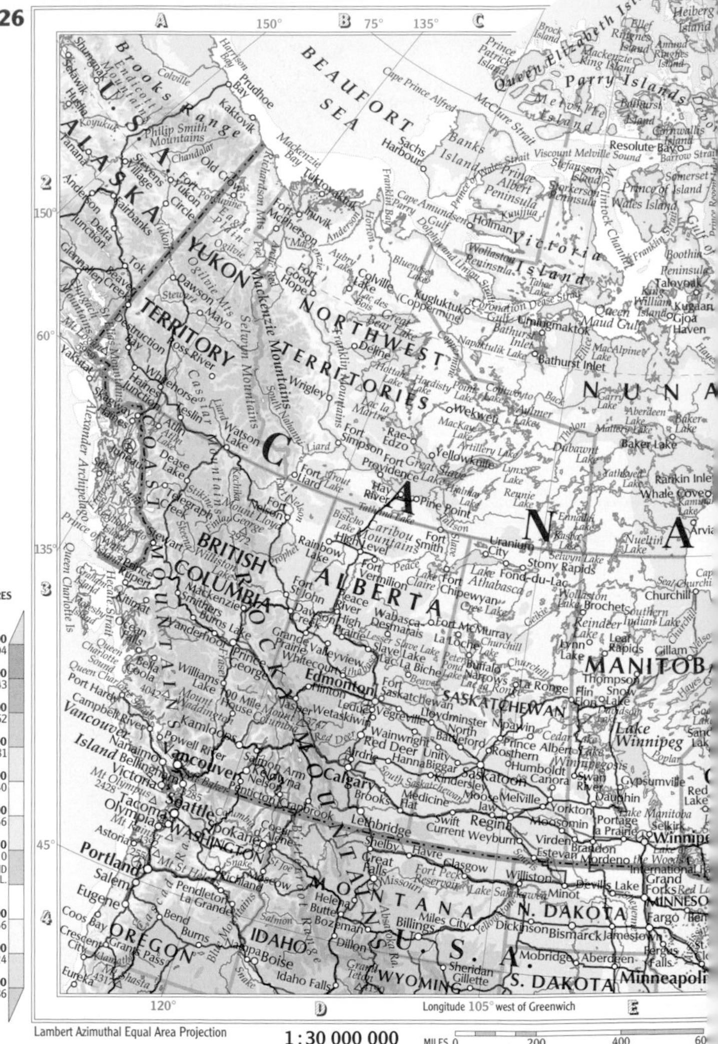

METRES
FEET
5000
16404
3000
9843
2000
6562
1000
3281
500
1640
200
656
0
0
LAND
B.S.L.
200
656
4000
13124
6000
19686

Lambert Azimuthal Equal Area Projection

1:30 000 000

MILES 0 200 400 600

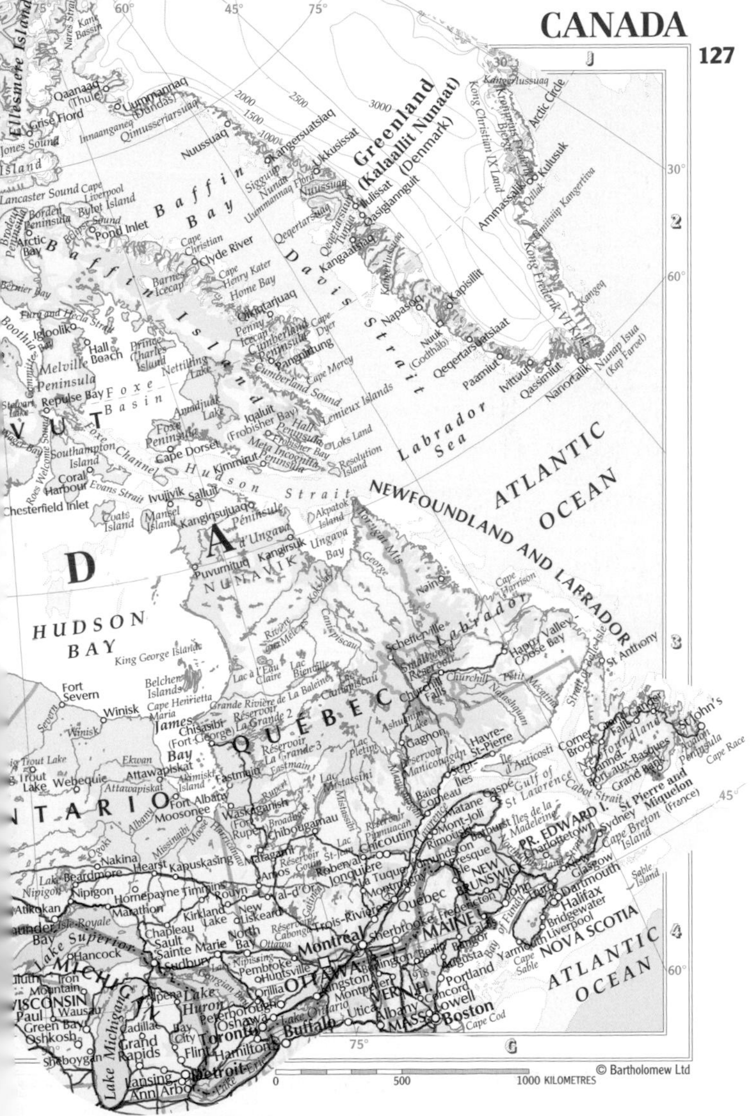
Ellesmere Island
Nares Strait
Kane Basin
Qaanaaq (Thule)
Uummannaq (Dundas)
Grise Fiord
Jones Sound
Innaanganeq
Qimusseriarsuaq
Nuussuaq
Kangersuatsiaq
Ukkusissat
Greenland (Kalaallit Nunaat) (Denmark)
Kangerlussuaq
Kong Christian IX Land
Kronprins Frederik Bjerge
Arctic Circle
Kulusuk
Qillak
Ammassalik
Uummannaq Fjord
Nuussuaq
Ilulissat
Qasigiannguit
Qeqertarsuaq
Qeqertarsuup Tunua
Kangaatsiaq
Lancaster Sound
Cape Liverpool
Bylot Island
Borden Peninsula
Brodeur Peninsula
Eclipse Sound
Pond Inlet
Arctic Bay
Baffin Bay
Baffin Island
Cape Christian
Clyde River
Cape Henry Kater
Home Bay
Barnes Icecap
Bernier Bay
Davis Strait
Kong Frederik VI Kyst
Kapisillit
Napasoq
Nuuk (Godthåb)
Qeqertarsuatsiaat
Paamiut
Ivittuut
Qassimiut
Nanortalik
Nunap Isua (Kap Farvel)
Kangeq
Fury and Hecla Strait
Boothia
Igloolik
Hall Beach
Prince Charles Island
Qikiqtarjuaq
Penny Icecap
Cumberland Peninsula
Cape Dyer
Pangnirtung
Cape Mercy
Cumberland Sound
Melville Peninsula
Committee Bay
Nettilling Lake
Foxe Basin
Repulse Bay
Stewart Lake
Amadjuak Lake
Iqaluit (Frobisher Bay)
Hall Peninsula
Frobisher Bay
Lemieux Islands
Loks Land
Meta Incognita Peninsula
Resolution Island
Labrador Sea
Foxe Peninsula
Cape Dorset
Foxe Channel
Southampton Island
Roes Welcome Sound
Wager Bay
Coral Harbour
Evans Strait
Kimmirut
Hudson Strait
Ivujivik
Salluit
Chesterfield Inlet
Coats Island
Mansel Island
Kangiqsujuaq
Péninsule d'Ungava
Akpatok Island
Ungava Bay
Kangirsuk
Puvurnituq
NUNAVIK
NEWFOUNDLAND AND LABRADOR
ATLANTIC OCEAN
Torngat Mts
George
Koksoak
Nain
Cape Harrison
Labrador
HUDSON BAY
King George Islands
Belcher Islands
Rivière aux Mélèzes
Caniapiscau
Lac à l'Eau Claire
Lac Bienville
Schefferville
Smallwood Réservoir
Churchill Falls
Churchill
Happy Valley-Goose Bay
Strait of Belle Isle
St Anthony
Fort Severn
Severn
Winisk
Cape Henrietta Maria
Grande Rivière de La Baleine
Réservoir La Grande 2
Chisasibi (Fort-George)
James Bay
QUÉBEC
Réservoir La Grande 3
Eastmain
Ashuanipi Lake
Gagnon
Réservoir Manicouagan
Lac Plétipi
Havre-St-Pierre
Île d'Anticosti
Corner Brook
Grand Falls
Gander
Newfoundland
St John's
Avalon Peninsula
Cape Race
Channel-Port-aux-Basques
Grand Bank
St Pierre and Miquelon (France)
Cabot Strait
Big Trout Lake
Ekwan
Attawapiskat
Akimiski Island
Fastmain
Lac Mistassini
Sept-Îles
Baie-Comeau
Gulf of St Lawrence
Gaspé
Matane
Mont-Joli
Rimouski
Îles de la Madeleine
PR. EDWARD I.
Charlottetown
Sydney
Cape Breton Island
Webequie
Fort Albany
Albany
Moosonee
Moose
Waskaganish (Fort Rupert)
Rupert
Broadback
Chibougamau
Réservoir Pipmuacan
Chicoutimi
ONTARIO
Ogoki
Nakina
Hearst
Kapuskasing
Missinaibi
Matagami
Réservoir Gouin
Lac St-Jean
Roberval
Jonquière
Amos
Val-d'Or
La Tuque
Montmagny
Edmundston
Presque Isle
NEW BRUNSWICK
Bathurst
Northumberland Strait
New Glasgow
Dartmouth
Halifax
Bridgewater
Liverpool
Sable Island
Lake Nipigon
Nipigon
Lake Beardmore
Hornepayne
Timmins
Rouyn
Atikokan
Marathon
Kirkland Lake
New Liskeard
Gatineau
Trois-Rivières
Québec
Fredericton
Saint John
Bay of Fundy
Yarmouth
NOVA SCOTIA
Cape Sable
Isle Royale
Thunder Bay
Lake Superior
Chapleau
Sault Sainte Marie
North Bay
Ottawa
Réservoir Cabonga
Montréal
Sherbrooke
MAINE
Bangor
Calais
Augusta
Portland
Hancock
MICHIGAN
Sudbury
Lake Nipissing
Pembroke
Huntsville
OTTAWA
Burlington
Berlin
Duluth
Iron Mountain
WISCONSIN
Wausau
Green Bay
Oshkosh
Sheboygan
Alpena
Lake Huron
Georgian Bay
Orillia
Peterborough
Kingston
Montpelier
VERMONT
N.H.
Concord
Lowell
Boston
Cape Cod
Lake Michigan
Cadillac
Bay City
Grand Rapids
Flint
Oshawa
Lake Ontario
Toronto
Hamilton
Buffalo
Utica
Albany
MASS.
Lansing
Ann Arbor
Detroit
Lake Erie
0
500
1000 KILOMETRES
© Bartholomew Ltd

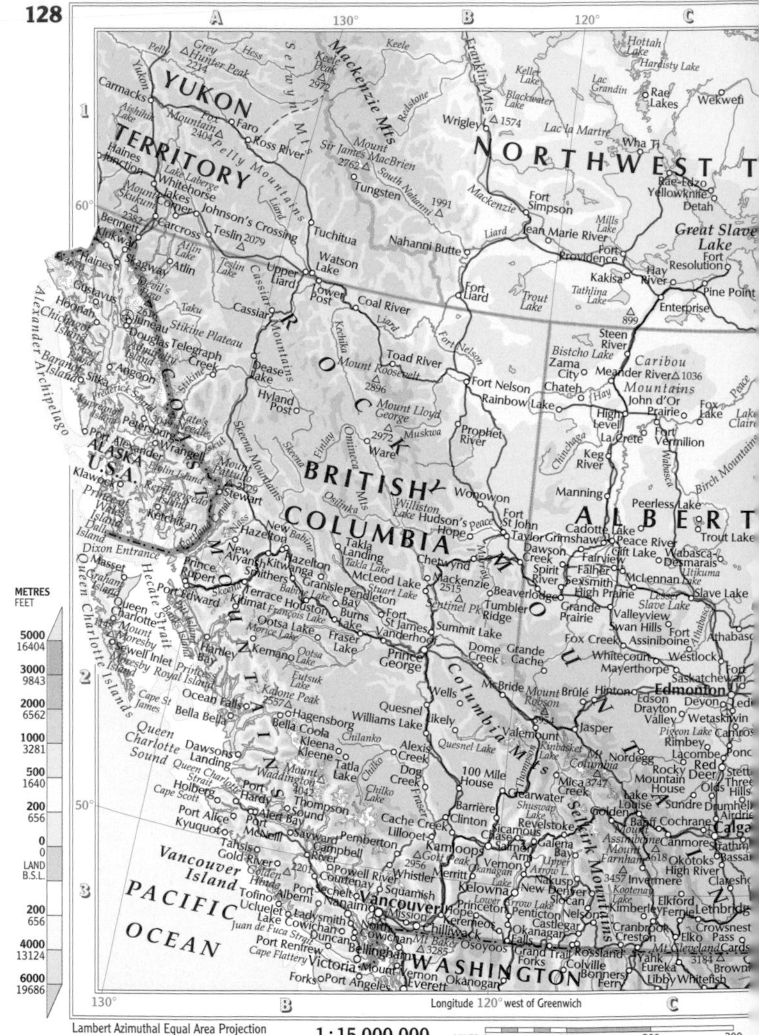
A
B
C
130°
120°
1
2
3
60°
50°
YUKON TERRITORY
NORTHWEST T
BRITISH COLUMBIA
ALBERT
ROCKY MOUNTAINS
COAST MOUNTAINS
ALASKA U.S.A.
WASHINGTON
PACIFIC OCEAN
Selwyn Mts
Mackenzie Mts
Pelly Mountains
Cassiar Mountains
Skeena Mountains
Columbia Mts
Selkirk Mountains
Caribou Mountains
Birch Mountains
Stikine Plateau
Alexander Archipelago
Queen Charlotte Islands
Vancouver Island
Queen Charlotte Sound
Hecate Strait
Dixon Entrance
Juan de Fuca Strait
Great Slave Lake
Carmacks
Faro
Ross River
Whitehorse
Haines Junction
Johnson's Crossing
Teslin
Carcross
Skagway
Haines
Atlin
Juneau
Sitka
Petersburg
Wrangell
Ketchikan
Stewart
Prince Rupert
Masset
Watson Lake
Upper Liard
Tuchitua
Tungsten
Cassiar
Dease Lake
Telegraph Creek
Toad River
Fort Nelson
Fort Simpson
Wrigley
Jean Marie River
Nahanni Butte
Fort Liard
Fort Providence
Hay River
Yellowknife
Rae-Edzo
Wha Ti
Wekweti
Rae Lakes
Enterprise
Pine Point
Fort Resolution
Kakisa
Steen River
Meander River
High Level
La Crete
Fort Vermilion
Manning
Peace River
Fort St John
Dawson Creek
Grande Prairie
Hudson's Hope
Chetwynd
Mackenzie
Tumbler Ridge
Prince George
Vanderhoof
Fort St James
Smithers
Terrace
Kitimat
Hazelton
Houston
Burns Lake
Quesnel
Williams Lake
Bella Coola
Bella Bella
Ocean Falls
Port Hardy
Port McNeill
Port Alice
Campbell River
Courtenay
Powell River
Nanaimo
Port Alberni
Tofino
Ucluelet
Duncan
Victoria
Vancouver
Squamish
Whistler
Chilliwack
Hope
Merritt
Kamloops
Kelowna
Vernon
Penticton
Nelson
Castlegar
Trail
Cranbrook
Golden
Revelstoke
Banff
Canmore
Calga
Edmonton
Jasper
Hinton
Edson
Whitecourt
Red Deer
Bellingham
Port Angeles
Everett
Mt Baker
Mount Robson
Mt Columbia 3747
Mount Waddington 4042
Longitude 120° west of Greenwich
METRES
FEET
5000 16404
3000 9843
2000 6562
1000 3281
500 1640
200 656
0 0
LAND B.S.L.
200 656
4000 13124
6000 19686
Lambert Azimuthal Equal Area Projection
1:15 000 000
MILES 0 100 200 300

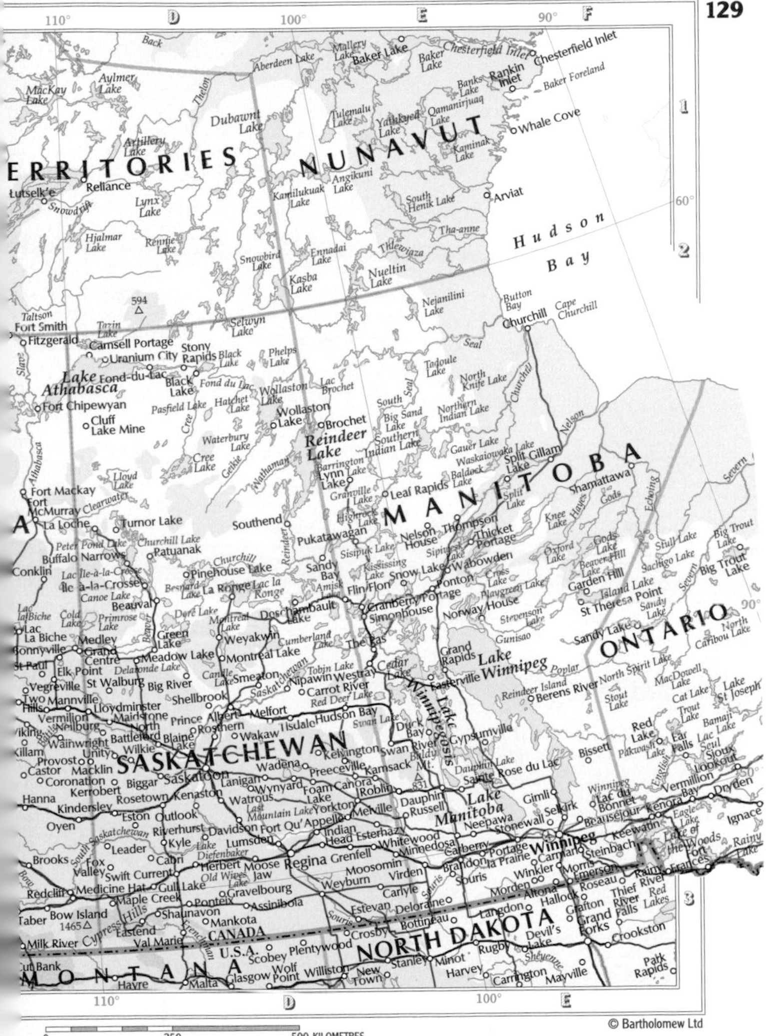
NUNAVUT
MANITOBA
SASKATCHEWAN
ONTARIO
NORTH DAKOTA
MONTANA
Hudson Bay
Lake Athabasca
Reindeer Lake
Lake Winnipeg
Lake Manitoba
Winnipegosis Lake
Chesterfield Inlet
Rankin Inlet
Whale Cove
Arviat
Churchill
Thompson
Flin Flon
The Pas
Prince Albert
Saskatoon
Regina
Moose Jaw
Swift Current
Medicine Hat
Lloydminster
Brandon
Winnipeg
Kenora
Dryden
Uranium City
Fort Chipewyan
Fort McMurray
Fort Smith
CANADA
U.S.A.
© Bartholomew Ltd
0 250 500 KILOMETRES

METRES / FEET

METRES	FEET
5000	16404
3000	9843
2000	6562
1000	3281
500	1640
200	656
0	0
LAND B.S.L.	
200	656
4000	13124
6000	19686

Longitude 80° west of Greenwich

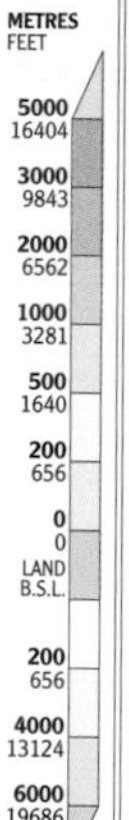

Lambert Azimuthal Equal Area Projection

1:15 000 000

MILES 0 100 200 300

0 250 500 KILOMETRES

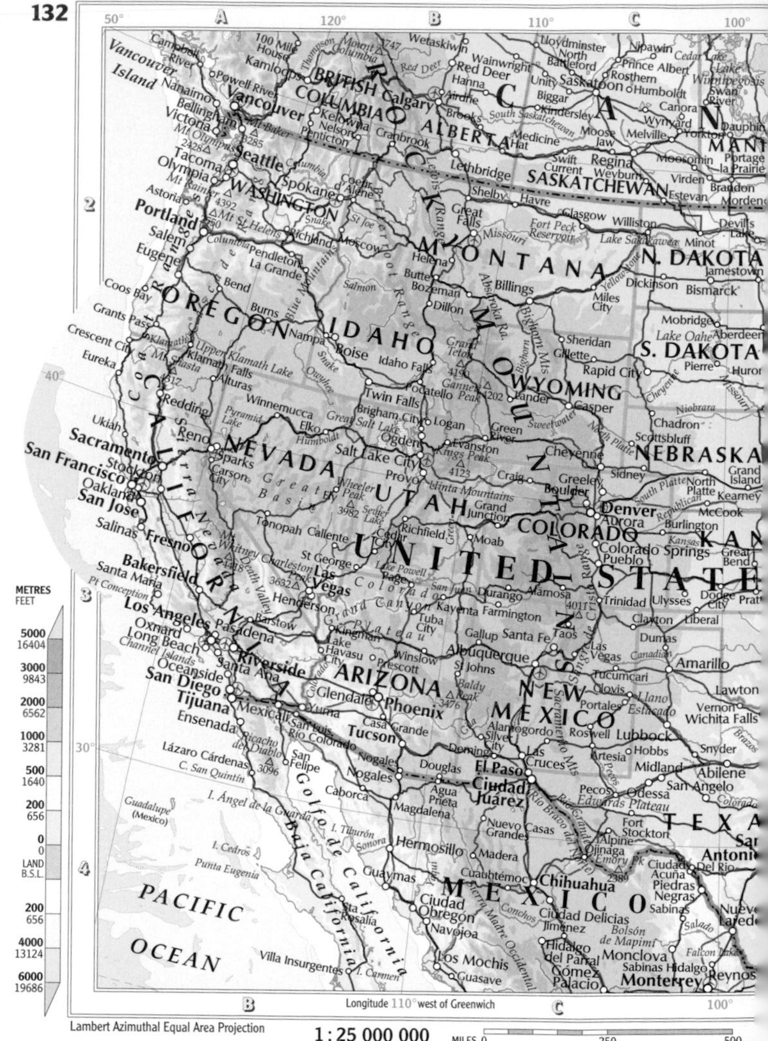

Lambert Azimuthal Equal Area Projection

1 : 25 000 000

MILES 0 250 500

METRES	FEET
6000	19686
4000	13124
200	656
LAND B.S.L.	
0	0
200	656
500	1640
1000	3281
2000	6562
3000	9843
5000	16404

UNITED STATES OF AMERICA

0 250 500 750 KILOMETRES

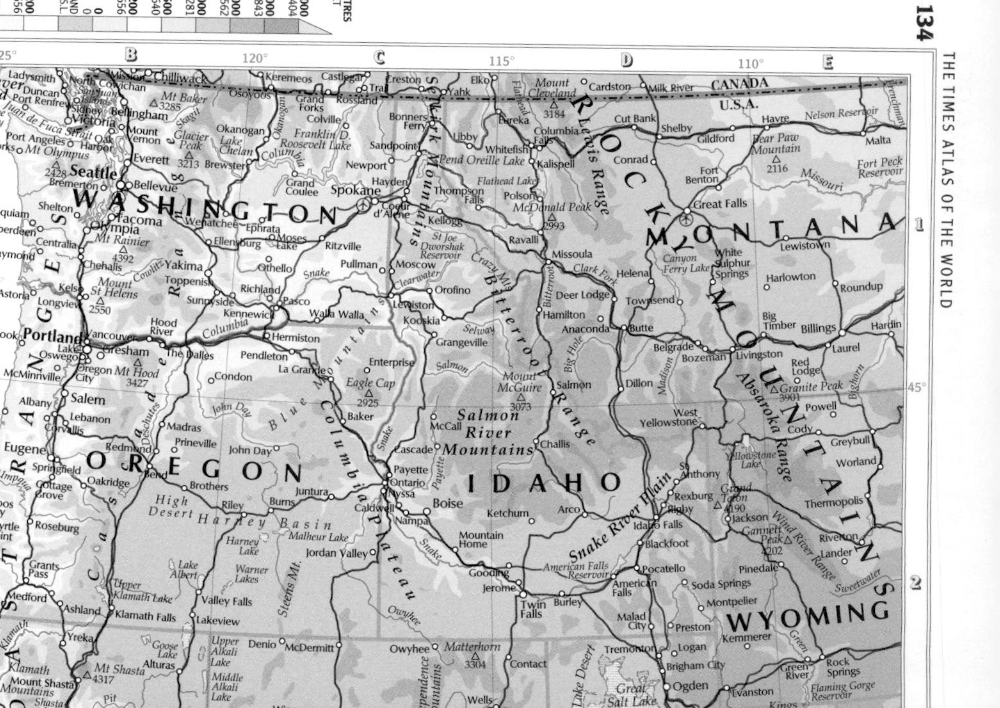

METRES	FEET
5000	16404
3000	9843
2000	6562
1000	3281
500	1640
200	656
0	0
LAND B.S.L.	
200	656
4000	13124
6000	19686

Lambert Azimuthal Equal Area Projection

1:11 000 000

MILES 0 100 200

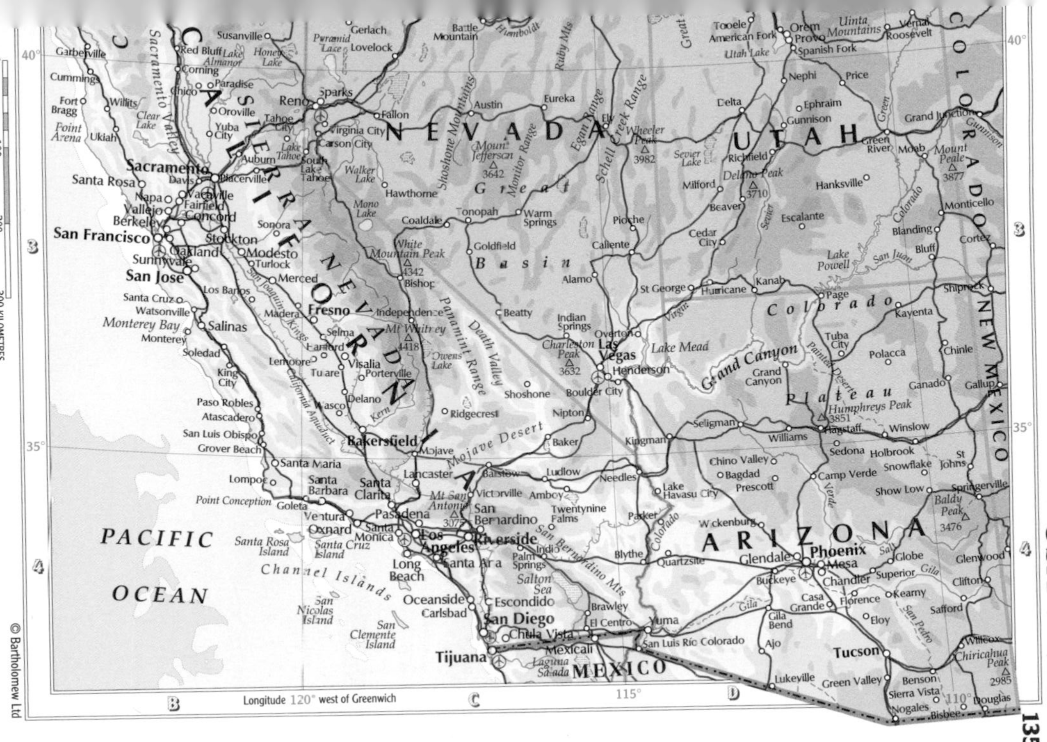

0 100 200 300 KILOMETRES

A 110° B 105° C 100°

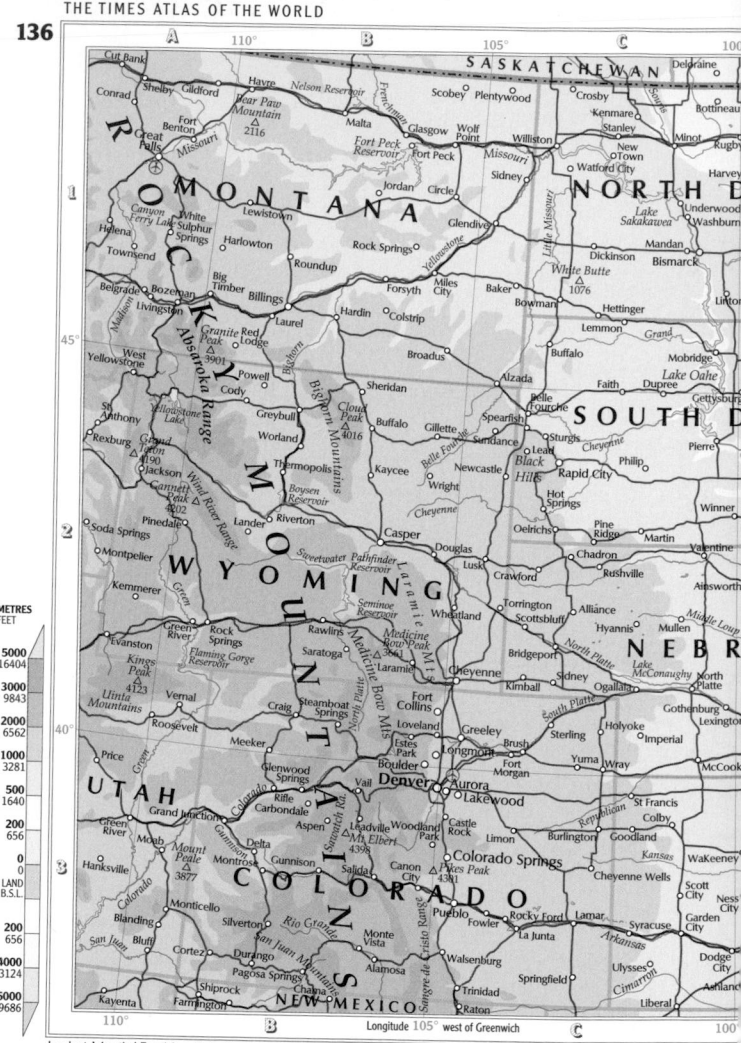

SASKATCHEWAN

Cut Bank, Shelby, Conrad, Gildford, Havre, Nelson Reservoir, Bear Paw Mountain 2116, Frenchman, Scobey, Plentywood, Deloraine, Crosby, Souris, Bottineau, Kenmare, Stanley, Fort Benton, Great Falls, Missouri, Malta, Glasgow, Wolf Point, Williston, Minot, Rugby, Fort Peck Reservoir, Fort Peck, New Town, Watford City, Harvey, Sidney, Jordan, Circle

ROCKY MOUNTAINS

MONTANA

NORTH D

1

Canyon Ferry Lake, White Sulphur Springs, Lewistown, Helena, Harlowton, Glendive, Little Missouri, Lake Sakakawea, Underwood, Washburn, Townsend, Rock Springs, Yellowstone, Roundup, Dickinson, Mandan, Bismarck, White Butte 1076, Belgrade, Bozeman, Big Timber, Billings, Miles City, Forsyth, Baker, Bowman, Linton, Madison, Livingston, Laurel, Hardin, Colstrip, Hettinger, Lemmon, Grand, Granite Peak 3901, Red Lodge, Absaroka Range, Broadus, Buffalo, Mobridge, 45°, West Yellowstone, Bighorn, Powell, Alzada, Lake Oahe, Faith, Dupree, Cody, Sheridan, Belle Fourche, Gettysburg, St Anthony, Yellowstone Lake, Greybull, Bighorn Mountains, Cloud Peak 4016, Buffalo, Gillette, Spearfish, SOUTH D, Rexburg, Grand Teton 4190, Worland, Sundance, Sturgis, Cheyenne, Pierre, Jackson, Thermopolis, Kaycee, Belle Fourche, Newcastle, Lead, Black Hills, Rapid City, Philip, Wind River Range, Gannett Peak 4202, Boysen Reservoir, Wright, Hot Springs, Winner, Cheyenne

2

Soda Springs, Pinedale, Lander, Riverton, Casper, Oelrichs, Pine Ridge, Martin, Valentine, Montpelier, Sweetwater, Pathfinder Reservoir, Douglas, Chadron, Rushville, WYOMING, Laramie Mts, Lusk, Crawford, Ainsworth, Kemmerer, Green, Seminoe Reservoir, Torrington, Wheatland, Scottsbluff, Alliance, Middle Loup, Hyannis, Mullen, Green River, Rock Springs, Rawlins, Medicine Bow Peak 3661, Evanston, NEBR, Kings Peak 4123, Flaming Gorge Reservoir, Saratoga, Medicine Bow Mts, Laramie, North Platte, Bridgeport, Cheyenne, Kimball, Sidney, Ogallala, Lake McConaughy, North Platte, Uinta Mountains, Vernal, Craig, Steamboat Springs, Fort Collins, South Platte, Gothenburg, Lexington, Roosevelt, 40°, Loveland, Greeley, Sterling, Holyoke, Imperial, Meeker, Estes Park, Longmont, Brush, Price, Green, Boulder, Fort Morgan, Yuma, Wray, McCook, Glenwood Springs, Vail, Denver, Aurora, Lakewood, UTAH, Colorado, Rifle, Carbondale, St Francis, Republican, Grand Junction, Colby, Green River, Aspen, Sawatch Ra., Leadville, Woodland Park, Castle Rock, Limon, Burlington, Goodland, Moab, Gunnison, Delta, Mt Elbert 4398, Mount Peale 3877, Montrose, Gunnison, Colorado Springs, Kansas, WaKeeney

3

Hanksville, Salida, Canon City, Pikes Peak 4301, Cheyenne Wells, COLORADO, Colorado, Scott City, Ness City, Monticello, Sangre de Cristo Range, Pueblo, Fowler, Rocky Ford, Lamar, Blanding, Silverton, Rio Grande, Syracuse, Garden City, San Juan, Bluff, Monte Vista, La Junta, Arkansas, Cortez, Durango, San Juan Mountains, Walsenburg, Alamosa, Dodge City, Pagosa Springs, Ulysses, Springfield, Shiprock, Chama, Trinidad, Cimarron, Ashland, Kayenta, Farmington, NEW MEXICO, Raton, Liberal

110° B Longitude 105° west of Greenwich C 100°

METRES / FEET
5000 / 16404
3000 / 9843
2000 / 6562
1000 / 3281
500 / 1640
200 / 656
0 / 0
LAND B.S.L.
200 / 656
4000 / 13124
6000 / 19686

Lambert Azimuthal Equal Area Projection

1 : 11 000 000

MILES 0 100 200

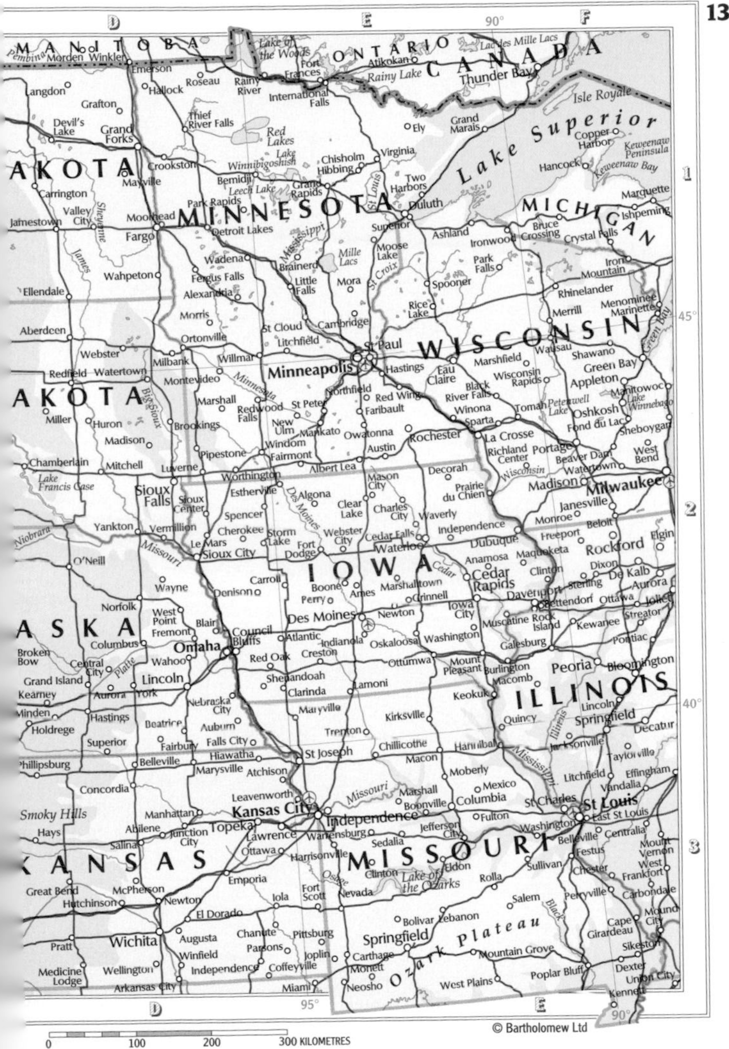

0 100 200 300 KILOMETRES

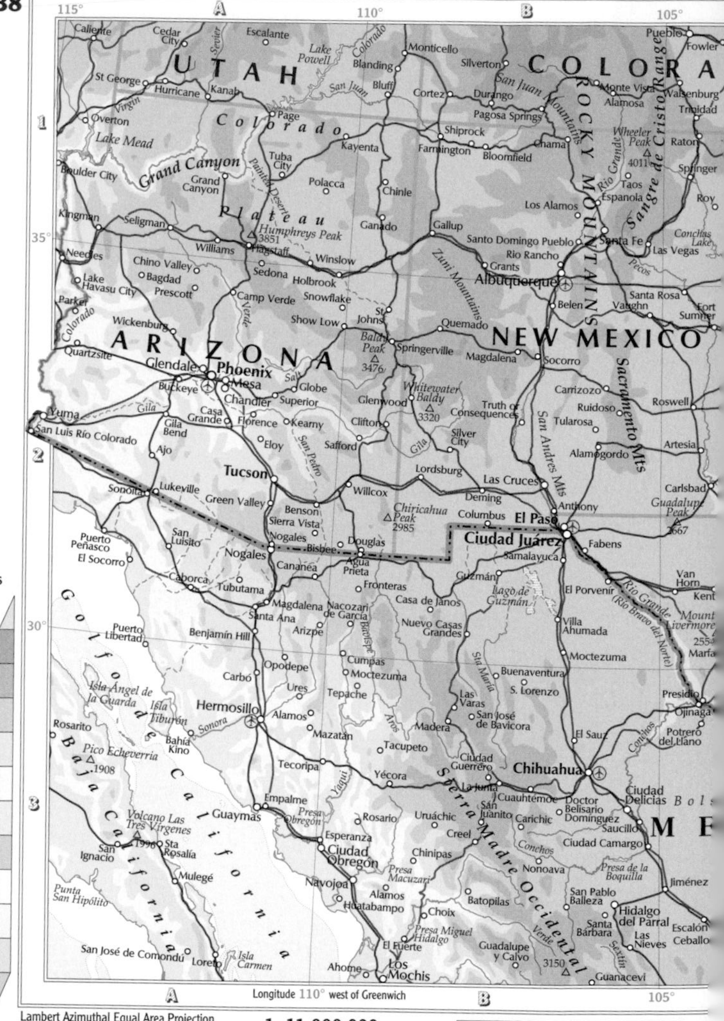

METRES
FEET

METRES	FEET
5000	16404
3000	9843
2000	6562
1000	3281
500	1640
200	656
0	0
LAND B.S.L.	
200	656
4000	13124
6000	19686

Lambert Azimuthal Equal Area Projection

1:11 000 000

MILES 0 100 200

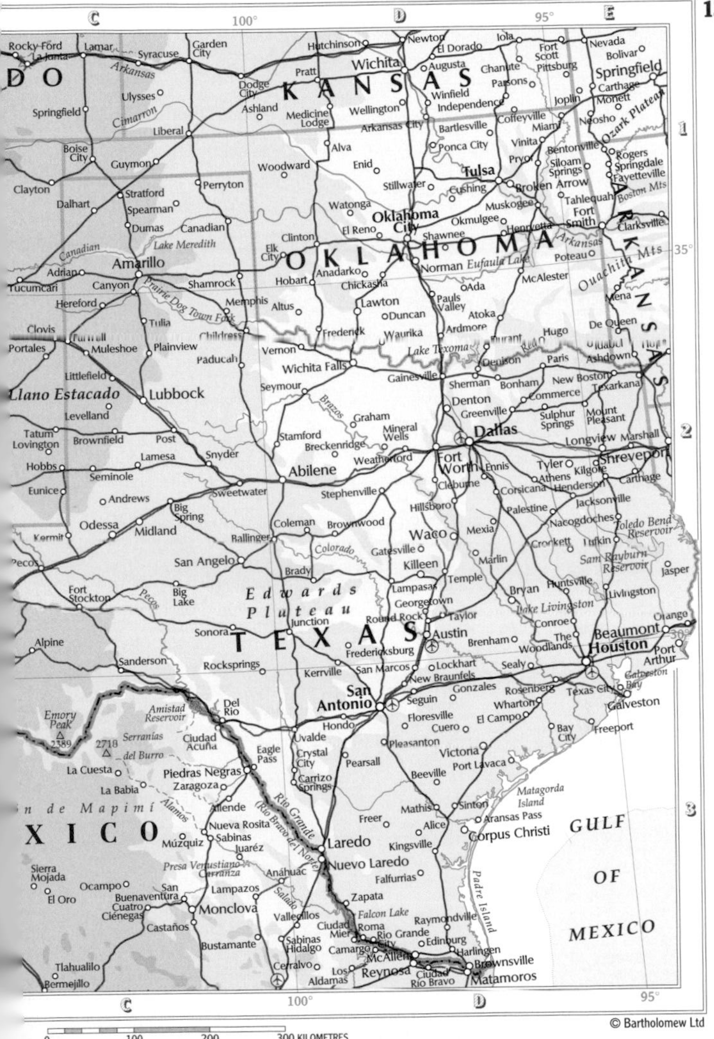

0 100 200 300 KILOMETRES

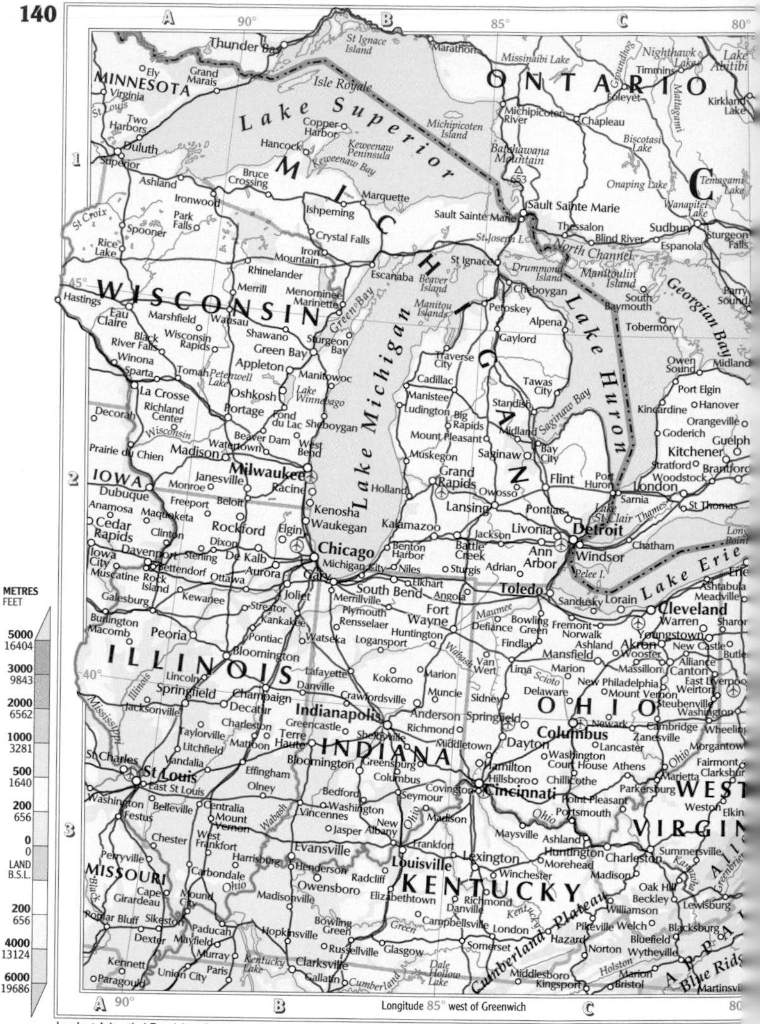

METRES
FEET

METRES	FEET
5000	16404
3000	9843
2000	6562
1000	3281
500	1640
200	656
0	0
LAND B.S.L.	
200	656
4000	13124
6000	19686

Longitude 85° west of Greenwich

Lambert Azimuthal Equal Area Projection

1:11 000 000

MILES 0 100 200

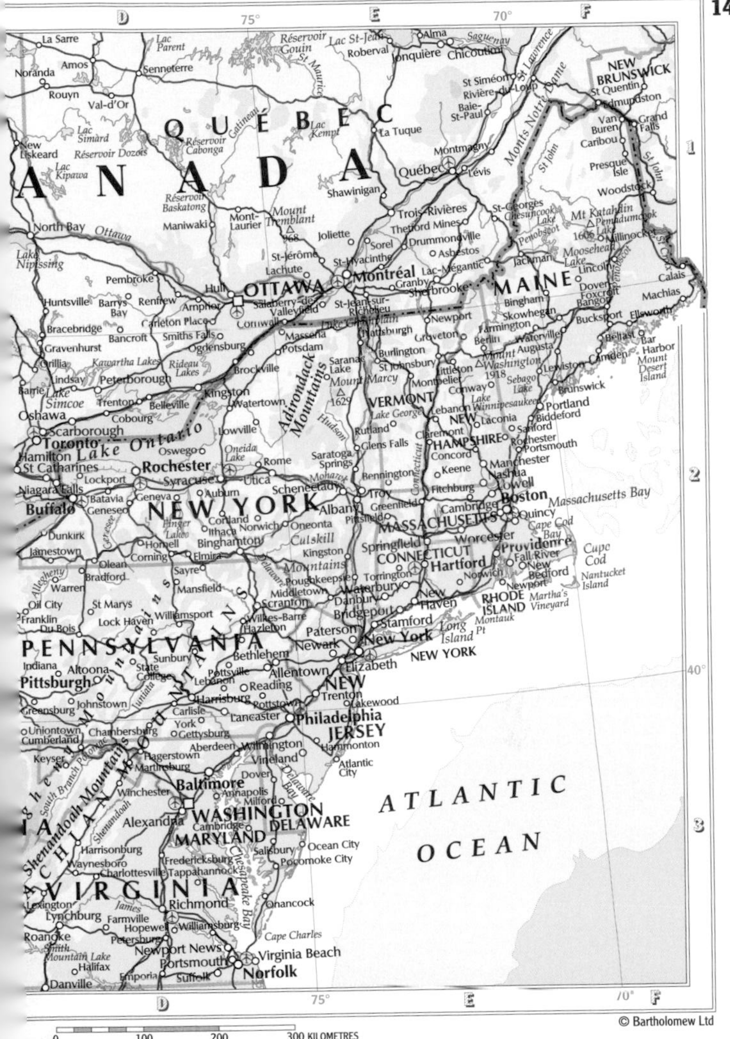
D
75°
E
70°
F
1
2
3
40°
CANADA
QUÉBEC
La Sarre
Lac Parent
Réservoir Gouin
St Maurice
Lac St-Jean
Alma
Saguenay
Roberval
Jonquière
Chicoutimi
St Lawrence
Noranda
Amos
Senneterre
Rouyn
Val-d'Or
St Siméon
Rivière-du-Loup
Baie-St-Paul
Monts Notre Dame
NEW BRUNSWICK
St Quentin
Edmundston
Van Buren
Grand Falls
Caribou
Presque Isle
Woodstock
St John
Lac Simard
Réservoir Cabonga
Gatineau
Lac Kempt
La Tuque
New Liskeard
Réservoir Dozois
Lac Kipawa
Montmagny
Québec
Lévis
Shawinigan
Réservoir Baskatong
Mount Tremblant
968
Mont-Laurier
Maniwaki
Trois-Rivières
Thetford Mines
St-Georges
Chesuncook Lake
Mt Katahdin
1606
Pemadumcook Lake
Millinocket
North Bay
Ottawa
Lake Nipissing
Joliette
Sorel
Drummondville
Asbestos
Penobscot
Moosehead Lake
St Croix
St-Jérôme
Lachute
St-Hyacinthe
Montréal
Lac-Mégantic
Jackman
Lincoln
Calais
Pembroke
Hull
OTTAWA
Granby
Sherbrooke
MAINE
Bingham
Dover Foxcroft
Bangor
Machias
Huntsville
Barrys Bay
Renfrew
Arnprior
Salaberry-de-Valleyfield
St-Jean-sur-Richelieu
Skowhegan
Bucksport
Ellsworth
Bracebridge
Bancroft
Carleton Place
Cornwall
Lake Champlain
Newport
Farmington
Waterville
Belfast
Bar Harbor
Mount Desert Island
Smiths Falls
Ogdensburg
Massena
Potsdam
Plattsburgh
Groveton
Berlin
Augusta
Camden
Gravenhurst
Kawartha Lakes
Rideau Lakes
Orillia
Lindsay
Peterborough
Brockville
Saranac Lake
Burlington
St Johnsbury
Littleton
Mount Washington
1918
Lewiston
Adirondack Mountains
Mount Marcy
1629
Montpelier
Conway
Sebago Lake
Brunswick
Barrie
Lake Simcoe
Trenton
Belleville
Kingston
Watertown
VERMONT
Lake Winnipesaukee
Portland
Oshawa
Cobourg
Lake George
Lebanon
NEW HAMPSHIRE
Laconia
Biddeford
Sanford
Scarborough
Toronto
Lake Ontario
Lowville
Hudson
Rutland
Claremont
Rochester
Portsmouth
Hamilton
Oswego
Oneida Lake
Glens Falls
Connecticut
Concord
St Catharines
Rochester
Rome
Saratoga Springs
Manchester
Nashua
Keene
Lockport
Syracuse
Utica
Mohawk
Bennington
Lowell
Niagara Falls
Geneva
Auburn
Schenectady
Troy
Fitchburg
Boston
Massachusetts Bay
Batavia
Buffalo
Geneseo
NEW YORK
Albany
Greenfield
Cambridge
Pittsfield
Quincy
MASSACHUSETTS
Cape Cod Bay
Finger Lakes
Cortland
Ithaca
Norwich
Oneonta
Genesee
Dunkirk
Catskill
Worcester
Providence
Cape Cod
Hornell
Binghamton
Kingston
Springfield
Jamestown
Corning
Elmira
CONNECTICUT
Hartford
Fall River
New Bedford
Nantucket Island
Olean
Delaware
Mountains
Bradford
Sayre
Poughkeepsie
Torrington
Norwich
Allegheny
Warren
Mansfield
Middletown
Waterbury
Newport
New Haven
Martha's Vineyard
RHODE ISLAND
Oil City
St Marys
Scranton
Danbury
Franklin
Lock Haven
Williamsport
Wilkes-Barre
Bridgeport
Stamford
Montauk Pt
Du Bois
Hazleton
Paterson
Long Island
PENNSYLVANIA
New York
Newark
Indiana
Altoona
Sunbury
State College
Bethlehem
Elizabeth
NEW YORK
Pittsburgh
Pottsville
Lebanon
Allentown
Juniata
Reading
NEW
Johnstown
Harrisburg
Pottstown
Trenton
Lakewood
Greensburg
Carlisle
Lancaster
Philadelphia
JERSEY
Uniontown
Chambersburg
York
Gettysburg
Cumberland
Potomac
Aberdeen
Wilmington
Hammonton
Keyser
Hagerstown
Vineland
Atlantic City
Martinsburg
South Branch Potomac
Dover
Delaware Bay
Baltimore
ATLANTIC
Winchester
Annapolis
Milford
Shenandoah Mountains
Shenandoah
WASHINGTON
Alexandria
Cambridge
DELAWARE
MARYLAND
OCEAN
Harrisonburg
Salisbury
Ocean City
Pocomoke City
Waynesboro
Fredericksburg
Chesapeake Bay
Charlottesville
Tappahannock
VIRGINIA
Onancock
Lexington
Richmond
James
Lynchburg
Farmville
Hopewell
Williamsburg
Roanoke
Petersburg
Cape Charles
Smith Mountain Lake
Newport News
Virginia Beach
Halifax
Portsmouth
Norfolk
Emporia
Suffolk
Danville
0
100
200
300 KILOMETRES

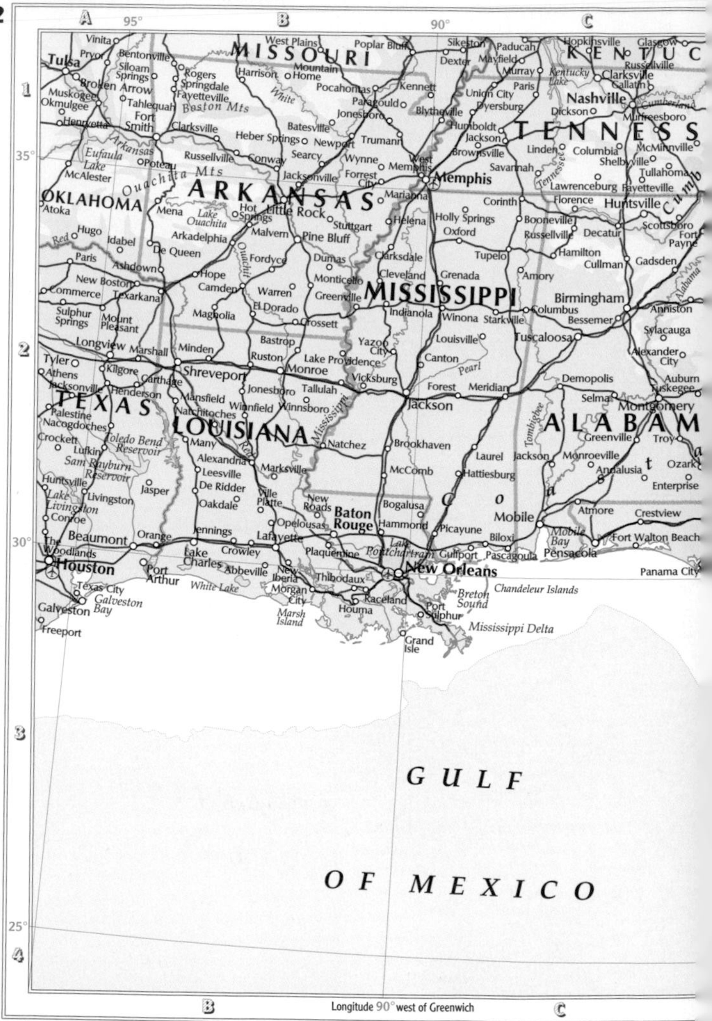

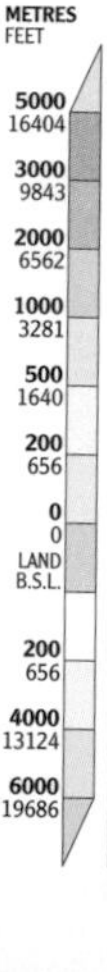

A B C
95° 90°
1 2 3 4
35° 30° 25°

MISSOURI
KENTUCKY
TENNESSEE
OKLAHOMA
ARKANSAS
MISSISSIPPI
ALABAMA
TEXAS
LOUISIANA

Vinita, Pryor, Tulsa, Bentonville, Siloam Springs, Rogers, Springdale, Fayetteville, Broken Arrow, Muskogee, Okmulgee, Tahlequah, Boston Mts, Henryetta, Fort Smith, Eufaula Lake, Poteau, McAlester, Ouachita Mts, Atoka, Hugo, Idabel, Red, Paris, Ashdown, De Queen, Mena, Lake Ouachita, Hot Springs, Arkadelphia, Hope, New Boston, Commerce, Texarkana, Sulphur Springs, Mount Pleasant, Longview, Marshall, Tyler, Athens, Kilgore, Carthage, Jacksonville, Henderson, Palestine, Nacogdoches, Crockett, Lufkin, Toledo Bend Reservoir, Sam Rayburn Reservoir, Huntsville, Lake Livingston, Livingston, Jasper, Conroe, The Woodlands, Houston, Beaumont, Orange, Port Arthur, Texas City, Galveston Bay, Galveston, Freeport

West Plains, Poplar Bluff, Sikeston, Dexter, Kennett, Mountain Home, Harrison, White, Pocahontas, Paragould, Jonesboro, Blytheville, Batesville, Heber Springs, Newport, Trumann, Searcy, Clarksville, Russellville, Conway, Wynne, Jacksonville, Forrest City, West Memphis, Memphis, Little Rock, Stuttgart, Marianna, Helena, Malvern, Pine Bluff, Fordyce, Dumas, Camden, Warren, Monticello, Magnolia, El Dorado, Greenville, Crossett, Ouachita

Paducah, Mayfield, Murray, Hopkinsville, Glasgow, Russellville, Kentucky Lake, Clarksville, Gallatin, Nashville, Cumberland, Union City, Dyersburg, Paris, Dickson, Murfreesboro, Humboldt, Jackson, Brownsville, Linden, Columbia, McMinnville, Shelbyville, Tullahoma, Savannah, Tennessee, Lawrenceburg, Fayetteville, Corinth, Florence, Huntsville, Holly Springs, Oxford, Booneville, Russellville, Decatur, Scottsboro, Fort Payne, Tupelo, Hamilton, Cullman, Gadsden, Clarksdale, Cleveland, Grenada, Amory, Alabama, Birmingham, Anniston, Indianola, Winona, Starkville, Columbus, Bessemer, Sylacauga, Yazoo City, Louisville, Tuscaloosa, Alexander City, Canton, Pearl, Demopolis, Auburn, Tuskegee, Forest, Meridian, Selma, Montgomery, Vicksburg, Jackson, Tombigbee, Greenville, Troy, Natchez, Brookhaven, Laurel, Monroeville, Ozark, McComb, Hattiesburg, Andalusia, Enterprise, Atmore, Crestview, Mobile, Biloxi, Fort Walton Beach, Mobile Bay, Pensacola, Panama City

Bastrop, Minden, Ruston, Lake Providence, Shreveport, Monroe, Jonesboro, Tallulah, Mansfield, Winnfield, Winnsboro, Natchitoches, Mississippi, Many, Alexandria, Red, Leesville, Marksville, De Ridder, Oakdale, Ville Platte, New Roads, Baton Rouge, Opelousas, Bogalusa, Hammond, Picayune, Jennings, Lafayette, Lake Charles, Crowley, Abbeville, New Iberia, Plaquemine, Lake Pontchartrain, Gulfport, Pascagoula, New Orleans, Thibodaux, Morgan City, Raceland, Houma, White Lake, Marsh Island, Port Sulphur, Breton Sound, Chandeleur Islands, Mississippi Delta, Grand Isle

GULF OF MEXICO

METRES / FEET
5000 16404
3000 9843
2000 6562
1000 3281
500 1640
200 656
0 0
LAND B.S.L.
200 656
4000 13124
6000 19686

Longitude 90° west of Greenwich

Lambert Azimuthal Equal Area Projection

1:11 000 000

MILES 0 100 200

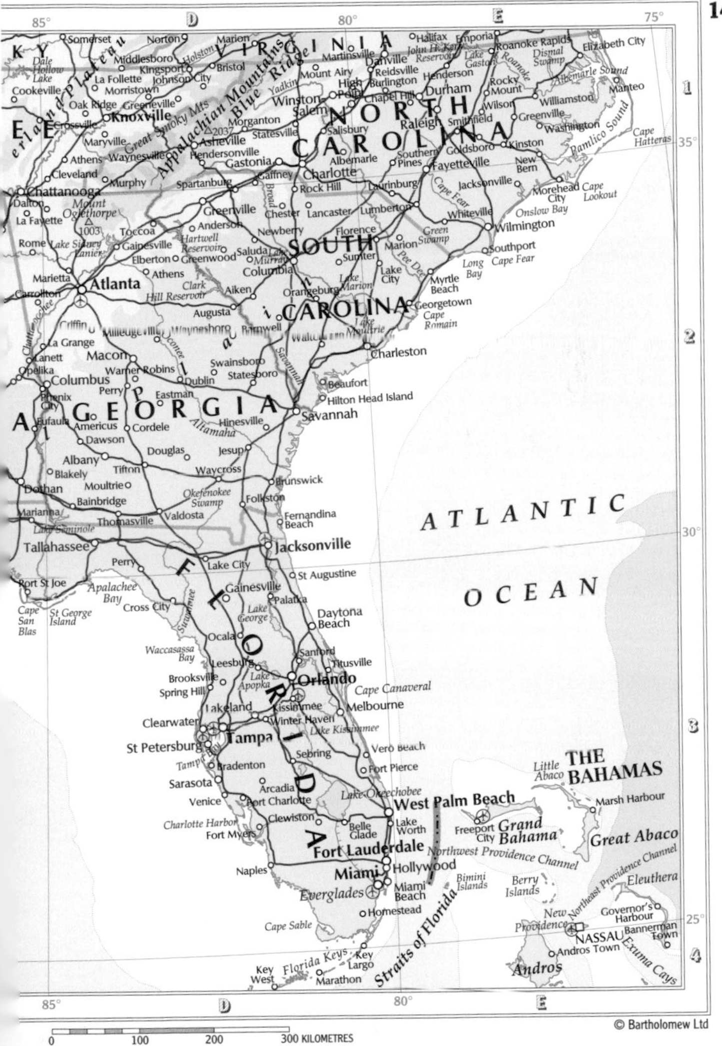

85°
D
80°
E
75°
1
2
3
4
35°
30°
25°
VIRGINIA
NORTH CAROLINA
SOUTH CAROLINA
GEORGIA
FLORIDA
KY
Appalachian Mountains
Blue Ridge
Great Smoky Mts
Cumberland Plateau
Somerset
Norton
Marion
Martinsville
Danville
Halifax
Emporia
Roanoke Rapids
Elizabeth City
Dale Hollow Lake
Middlesboro
Kingsport
Bristol
Johnson City
John H. Kerr Reservoir
Lake Gaston
Dismal Swamp
Cookeville
La Follette
Morristown
Mount Airy
Reidsville
Henderson
Albemarle Sound
Manteo
Oak Ridge
Greeneville
Winston-Salem
High Point
Burlington
Durham
Rocky Mount
Williamston
Knoxville
Crossville
Chapel Hill
Wilson
Greenville
Washington
Maryville
Morganton
Statesville
Salisbury
Raleigh
Smithfield
Pamlico Sound
Cape Hatteras
Asheville
Waynesville
2037
Hendersonville
Gastonia
Albemarle
Southern Pines
Goldsboro
Kinston
New Bern
Athens
Cleveland
Murphy
Spartanburg
Gaffney
Charlotte
Rock Hill
Laurinburg
Fayetteville
Jacksonville
Morehead City
Cape Lookout
Chattanooga
Dalton
La Fayette
Mount Oglethorpe
1003
Greenville
Chester
Lancaster
Lumberton
Whiteville
Onslow Bay
Wilmington
Toccoa
Anderson
Newberry
Florence
Green Swamp
Rome
Lake Sidney Lanier
Gainesville
Hartwell Reservoir
Saluda
Lake Murray
Sumter
Marion
Southport
Cape Fear
Elberton
Greenwood
Columbia
Long Bay
Marietta
Athens
Lake City
Myrtle Beach
Atlanta
Carrollton
Clark Hill Reservoir
Aiken
Orangeburg
Lake Marion
Augusta
Georgetown
Cape Romain
Griffin
Milledgeville
Waynesboro
Barnwell
Lake Moultrie
La Grange
Charleston
Lanett
Macon
Opelika
Warner Robins
Swainsboro
Statesboro
Columbus
Dublin
Beaufort
Perry
Eastman
Hilton Head Island
Phenix City
Savannah
Eufaula
Americus
Cordele
Hinesville
Altamaha
Dawson
Douglas
Jesup
Albany
Tifton
Blakely
Waycross
Brunswick
Dothan
Moultrie
Okefenokee Swamp
Folkston
Bainbridge
Marianna
Thomasville
Valdosta
Fernandina Beach
Lake Seminole
Tallahassee
Jacksonville
ATLANTIC
Perry
Lake City
St Augustine
Port St Joe
Apalachee Bay
Gainesville
OCEAN
Cape San Blas
St George Island
Cross City
Palatka
Lake George
Daytona Beach
Suwannee
Ocala
Waccasassa Bay
Sanford
Leesburg
Titusville
Brooksville
Lake Apopka
Orlando
Spring Hill
Cape Canaveral
Lakeland
Kissimmee
Melbourne
Clearwater
Winter Haven
Lake Kissimmee
Tampa
St Petersburg
Vero Beach
Tampa Bay
Sebring
THE BAHAMAS
Little Abaco
Bradenton
Fort Pierce
Sarasota
Arcadia
Venice
Port Charlotte
Lake Okeechobee
West Palm Beach
Marsh Harbour
Clewiston
Charlotte Harbor
Belle Glade
Lake Worth
Freeport City
Grand Bahama
Fort Myers
Great Abaco
Fort Lauderdale
Northwest Providence Channel
Naples
Miami
Hollywood
Miami Beach
Bimini Islands
Berry Islands
Northeast Providence Channel
Eleuthera
Everglades
Homestead
New Providence
Governor's Harbour
Cape Sable
NASSAU
Bannerman Town
Straits of Florida
Andros Town
Exuma Cays
Florida Keys
Key Largo
Key West
Marathon
Andros
0
100
200
300 KILOMETRES

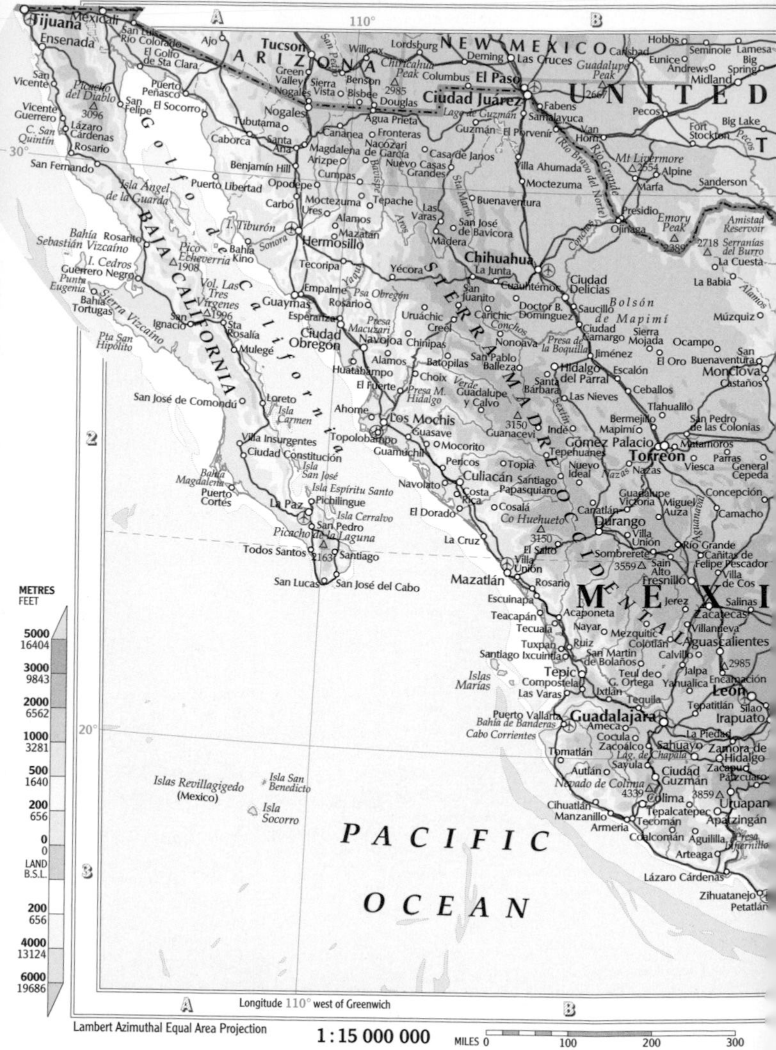

Lambert Azimuthal Equal Area Projection

1:15 000 000

MILES 0 100 200 300

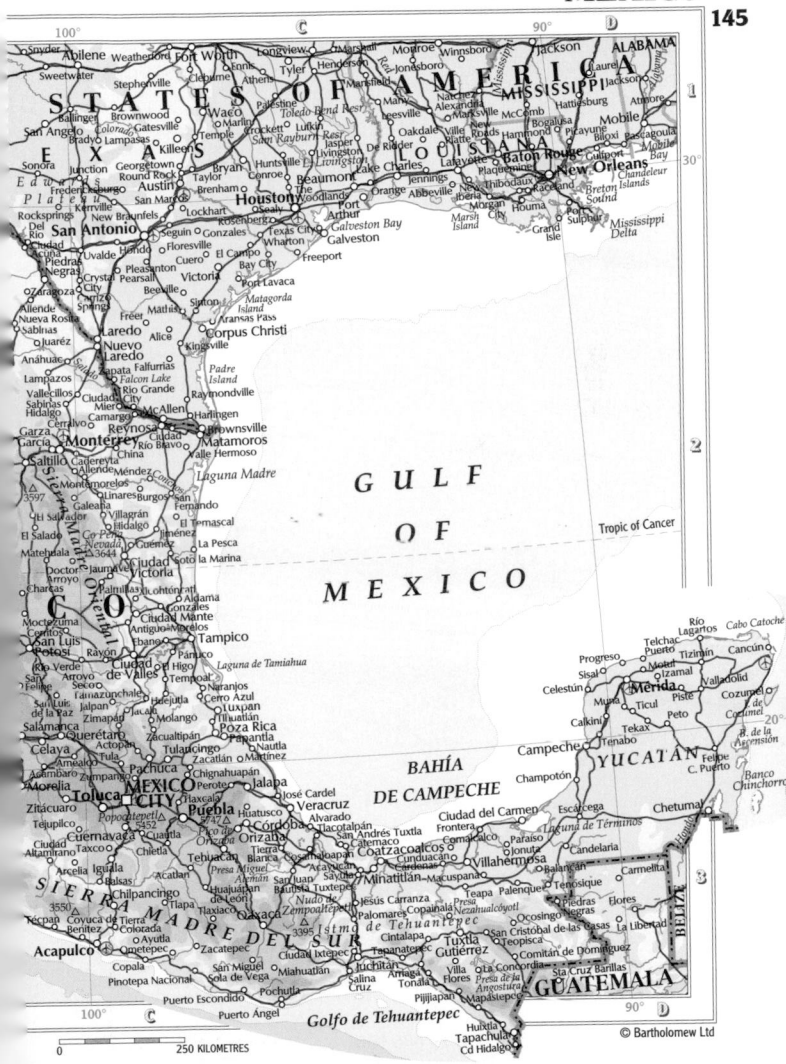

UNITED STATES OF AMERICA
TEXAS
LOUISIANA
MISSISSIPPI
ALABAMA
Snyder
Abilene
Weatherford
Fort Worth
Longview
Marshall
Monroe
Winnsboro
Jackson
Sweetwater
Stephenville
Cleburne
Ennis
Athens
Tyler
Henderson
Jonesboro
Laurel
Jackson
Palestine
Toledo Bend Resr.
Mansfield
Natchez
Alexandria
Marksville
McComb
Hattiesburg
Atmore
Ballinger
Brownwood
Waco
Marlin
Many
Leesville
Bogalusa
Mobile
San Angelo
Gatesville
Temple
Crockett
Lufkin
Oakdale
Ville Platte
New Roads
Hammond
Picayune
Pascagoula
Brady
Lampasas
Killeen
Sam Rayburn Resr.
Jasper
Livingston
De Ridder
Biloxi
Mobile Bay
Sonora
Junction
Georgetown
Bryan
Huntsville
L. Livingston
Lake Charles
Lafayette
Baton Rouge
Gulfport
Bay
Round Rock
Taylor
Conroe
Beaumont
Jennings
Plaquemine
New Orleans
Edwards Plateau
Fredericksburg
Austin
Brenham
The Woodlands
Orange
Abbeville
New Iberia
Thibodaux
Raceland
Chandeleur Islands
Kerrville
San Marcos
Houston
Port Arthur
Morgan City
Houma
Breton Sound
Rocksprings
New Braunfels
Lockhart
Sealy
Rosenberg
Marsh Island
Port Sulphur
Mississippi Delta
Del Rio
San Antonio
Seguin
Gonzales
Texas City
Galveston Bay
Galveston
Grand Isle
Ciudad Acuña
Uvalde
Hondo
Floresville
Wharton
Piedras Negras
Pleasanton
Cuero
El Campo
Bay City
Freeport
Crystal City
Pearsall
Victoria
Port Lavaca
Zaragoza
Carrizo Springs
Beeville
Matagorda Island
Allende
Nueva Rosita
Freer
Mathis
Sinton
Aransas Pass
Sabinas
Laredo
Alice
Corpus Christi
Juaréz
Nuevo Laredo
Kingsville
Anáhuac
Salado
Falfurrias
Padre Island
Lampazos
Zapata
Falcon Lake
Rio Grande City
Raymondville
Vallecillos
Sabinas Hidalgo
Ciudad Mier
McAllen
Harlingen
Cerralvo
Camargo
Reynosa
Brownsville
Garza García
Monterrey
Ciudad Río Bravo
Matamoros
Saltillo
Cadereyta
China
Valle Hermoso
Allende
Méndez
Conchos
Laguna Madre
Montemorelos
3597
Linares
Burgos
San Fernando
Sierra Madre Oriental
Galeana
El Salvador
Villagrán
Hidalgo
El Temascal
El Salado
Co Peña Nevada
3644
Jiménez
Guémez
La Pesca
Matehuala
Soto la Marina
Ciudad Victoria
Doctor Arroyo
Jaumave
Charcas
Palmillas
Xicohténcatl
Aldama
MEXICO
Gonzales
Ciudad Mante
Moctezuma
Cerritos
Antiguo Morelos
San Luis Potosí
Ébano
Tampico
Rayón
Pánuco
Río Verde
Ciudad de Valles
El Higo
Laguna de Tamiahua
Arroyo Seco
Tempoal
San Felipe
Naranjos
Tamazunchale
Huejutla
Cerro Azul
San Luis de la Paz
Jalpan
Jacala
Tuxpan
Zimapán
Molango
Tihuatlán
Salamanca
Poza Rica
Querétaro
Zacualtipán
Papantla
Celaya
Actopan
Nautla
Tula
Tulancingo
Martínez
Amealco
Zacatlán
Acámbaro
Pachuca
Chignahuapán
Zumpango
Morelia
MEXICO CITY
Perote
Jalapa
Toluca
Tlaxcala
José Cardel
Zitácuaro
Popocatépetl
5452
Puebla
Huatusco
Veracruz
Tejupilco
5747
Pico de Orizaba
Córdoba
Alvarado
Cuernavaca
Cuautla
Orizaba
Tlacotalpán
Ciudad Altamirano
Taxco
Chietla
San Andrés Tuxtla
Tehuacán
Catemaco
Tierra Blanca
Arcelia
Iguala
Presa Miguel Alemán
Cosamaloapan
Coatzacoalcos
Acayucan
Balsas
Acatlán
Sayula
Minatitlán
SIERRA MADRE DEL SUR
San Juan Bautista Tuxtepec
Chilpancingo
Huajuápan de León
Nudo de Zempoaltépetl
Jesús Carranza
3550
Tlapa
Tlaxiaco
Palomares
Técpan
Coyuca de Benítez
Tierra Colorada
Oaxaca
3395
Istmo de Tehuantepec
Ayutla
Acapulco
Ometepec
Zacatepec
Ciudad Ixtepec
Copala
San Miguel Sola de Vega
Miahuatlán
Juchitán
Pinotepa Nacional
Pochutla
Salina Cruz
Puerto Escondido
Puerto Ángel
Golfo de Tehuantepec
GULF OF MEXICO
Tropic of Cancer
BAHÍA DE CAMPECHE
Río Lagartos
Cabo Catoche
Telchac Puerto
Progreso
Tizimín
Cancún
Sisal
Motul
Izamal
Celestún
Mérida
Valladolid
Muna
Piste
Cozumel
I. de Cozumel
Ticul
Peto
Calkiní
Tekax
Tenabo
B. de la Ascensión
Campeche
YUCATÁN
Felipe C. Puerto
Champotón
Banco Chinchorro
Ciudad del Carmen
Escárcega
Chetumal
Frontera
Laguna de Términos
Hondo
Comalcalco
Paraíso
Jonuta
Candelaria
Cunduacán
Cárdenas
Villahermosa
Balancán
Carmelita
Macuspana
Tenosique
Teapa
Palenque
Piedras Negras
Flores
Copainalá
Presa Nezahualcóyotl
Ocosingo
Cintalapa
Tuxtla Gutiérrez
San Cristóbal de las Casas
La Libertad
BELIZE
Tapanatepec
Teopisca
Comitán de Domínguez
Arriaga
Villa Flores
La Concordia
Tonalá
Presa de la Angostura
Sta. Cruz Barillas
GUATEMALA
Pijijiapan
Mapastepec
Huixtla
Tapachula
Cd Hidalgo
100°
90°
30°
20°
C
D
1
2
3
0
250 KILOMETRES

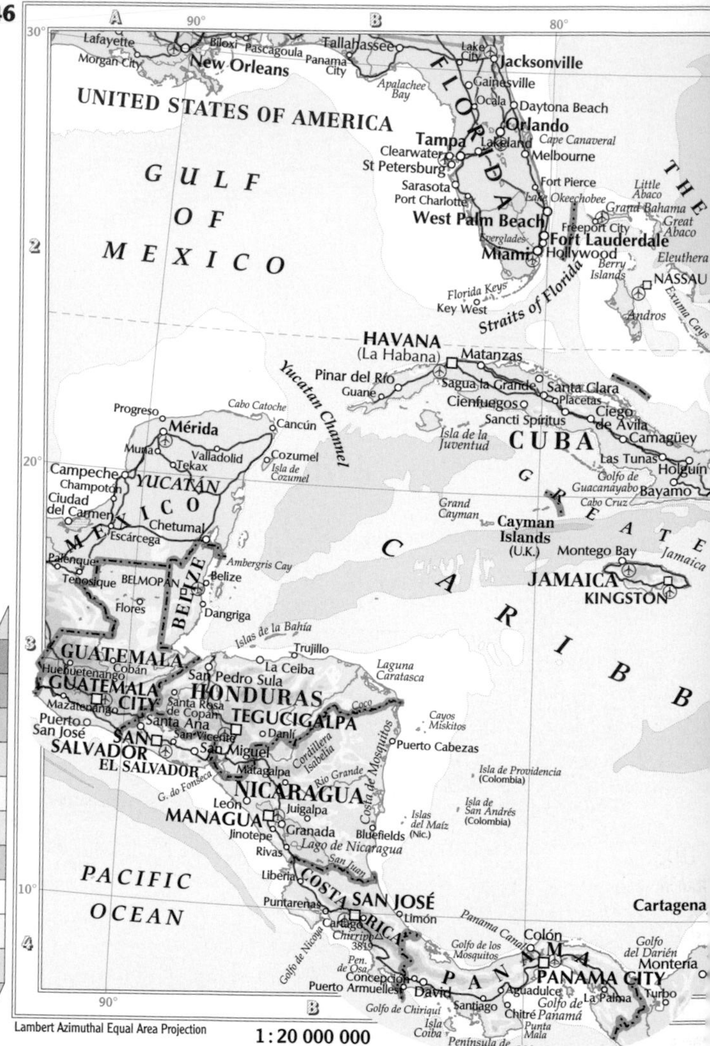

Lambert Azimuthal Equal Area Projection

1:20 000 000

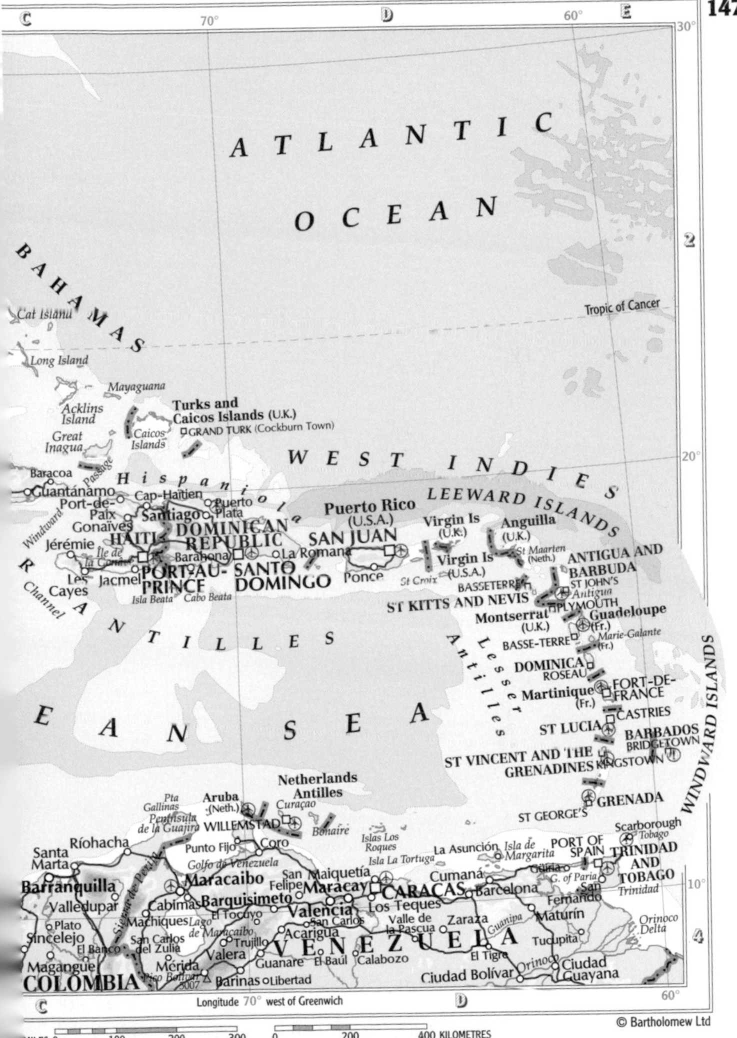
ATLANTIC
OCEAN
BAHAMAS
Cat Island
Long Island
Mayaguana
Acklins Island
Great Inagua
Turks and Caicos Islands (U.K.)
Caicos Islands
GRAND TURK (Cockburn Town)
WEST INDIES
LEEWARD ISLANDS
Tropic of Cancer
Baracoa
Windward Passage
Guantánamo
Hispaniola
Cap-Haïtien
Puerto Plata
Port-de-Paix
Gonaïves
Santiago
DOMINICAN REPUBLIC
HAITI
Jérémie
Île de la Gonâve
Barahona
PORT-AU-PRINCE
SANTO DOMINGO
La Romana
Les Cayes
Jacmel
Isla Beata
Cabo Beata
Puerto Rico (U.S.A.)
SAN JUAN
Ponce
Virgin Is (U.K.)
Virgin Is (U.S.A.)
St Croix
Anguilla (U.K.)
St Maarten (Neth.)
ANTIGUA AND BARBUDA
ST JOHN'S
Antigua
BASSETERRE
ST KITTS AND NEVIS
PLYMOUTH
Montserrat (U.K.)
Guadeloupe (Fr.)
Marie-Galante (Fr.)
BASSE-TERRE
DOMINICA
ROSEAU
Martinique (Fr.)
FORT-DE-FRANCE
CASTRIES
ST LUCIA
BARBADOS
BRIDGETOWN
ST VINCENT AND THE GRENADINES
KINGSTOWN
GRENADA
ST GEORGE'S
WINDWARD ISLANDS
Lesser Antilles
ANTILLES
Channel
CARIBBEAN SEA
Netherlands Antilles
Aruba (Neth.)
Curaçao
WILLEMSTAD
Bonaire
Pta Gallinas
Península de la Guajira
Islas Los Roques
Isla La Tortuga
La Asunción
Isla de Margarita
PORT OF SPAIN
Scarborough
Tobago
TRINIDAD AND TOBAGO
Trinidad
G. of Paria
Güiria
San Fernando
Santa Marta
Ríohacha
Punto Fijo
Coro
Golfo de Venezuela
Barranquilla
Maracaibo
San Felipe
Maiquetía
Maracay
CARACAS
Cumaná
Barcelona
Valledupar
Cabimas
Barquisimeto
El Tocuyo
Valencia
Los Teques
Valle de la Pascua
Zaraza
Maturín
Plato
Machiques
Lago de Maracaibo
San Carlos
Guanipa
Orinoco Delta
Sincelejo
San Carlos del Zulia
Trujillo
Acarigua
VENEZUELA
Tucupita
El Banco
Sierra de Perijá
Valera
Guanare
El Baúl
Calabozo
El Tigre
Magangué
Mérida
Pico Bolívar 5007
Barinas
Libertad
Ciudad Bolívar
Orinoco
Ciudad Guayana
COLOMBIA
70°
60°
30°
20°
10°
Longitude 70° west of Greenwich
MILES 0 100 200 300
0 200 400 KILOMETRES

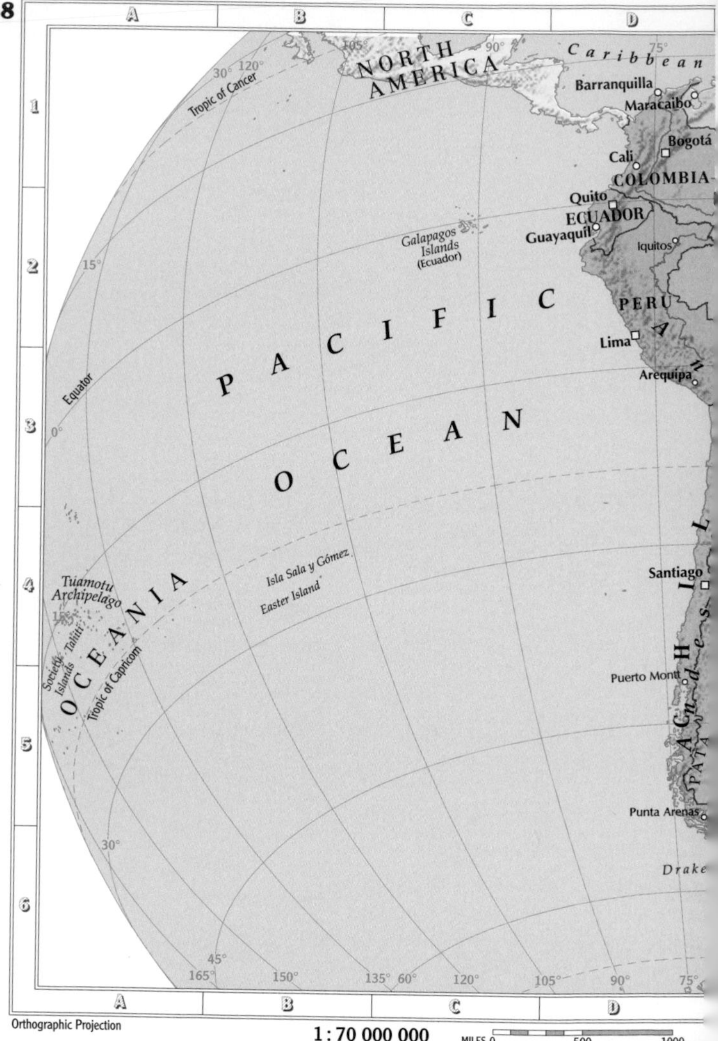

Orthographic Projection

1 : 70 000 000

MILES 0 500 1000

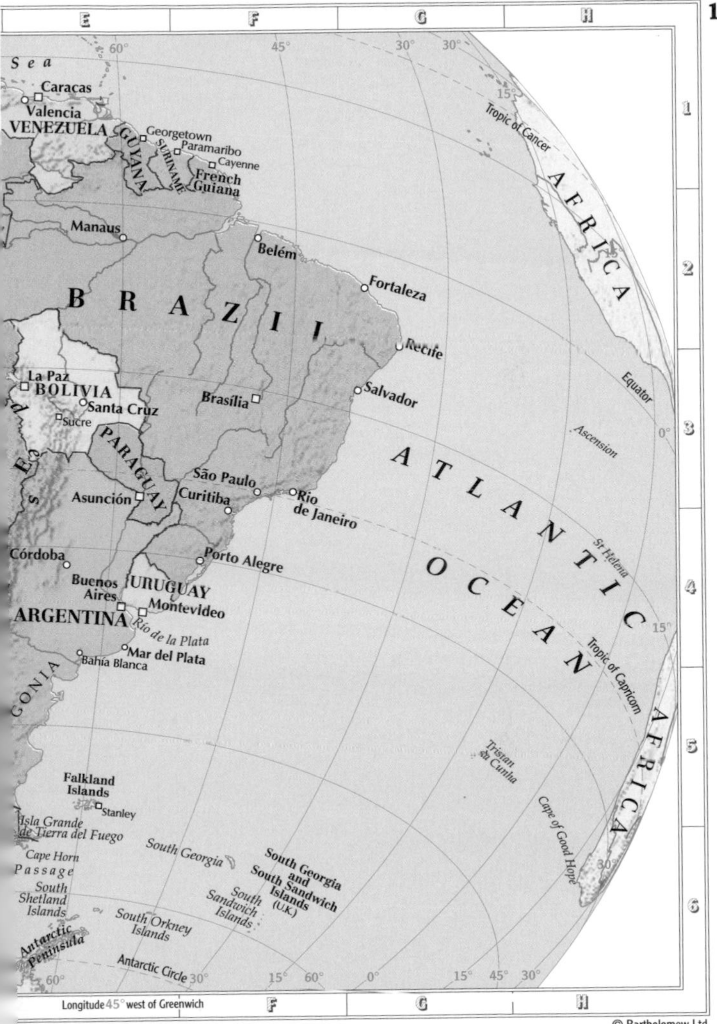
Sea
Caracas
Valencia
VENEZUELA
GUYANA
Georgetown
SURINAME
Paramaribo
Cayenne
French Guiana
Manaus
Belém
Fortaleza
BRAZIL
Recife
La Paz
BOLIVIA
Santa Cruz
Sucre
Brasília
Salvador
PARAGUAY
São Paulo
Asunción
Curitiba
Rio de Janeiro
Córdoba
Porto Alegre
Buenos Aires
URUGUAY
Montevideo
ARGENTINA
Río de la Plata
Mar del Plata
Bahía Blanca
GONIA
Falkland Islands
Stanley
Isla Grande de Tierra del Fuego
Cape Horn
Passage
South Georgia
South Georgia and South Sandwich Islands (U.K.)
South Sandwich Islands
South Shetland Islands
South Orkney Islands
Antarctic Peninsula
Antarctic Circle
ATLANTIC OCEAN
AFRICA
Tropic of Cancer
Equator
Ascension
St Helena
Tropic of Capricorn
Tristan da Cunha
Cape of Good Hope
Longitude 45° west of Greenwich
0 500 1000 1500 KILOMETRES
E F G H
1 2 3 4 5 6

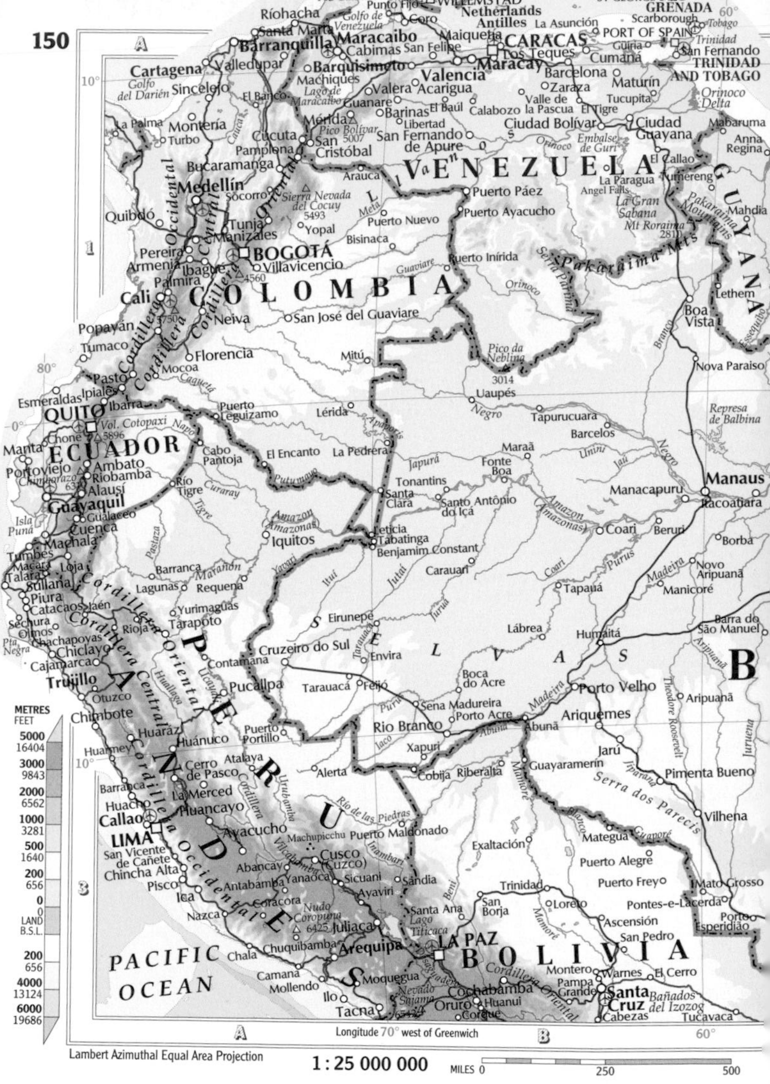
Pta Gallinas
Punto Fijo
WILLEMSTAD
Netherlands Antilles
ST GEORGE'S
GRENADA
Ríohacha
Golfo de Venezuela
Coro
La Asunción
Scarborough
Tobago
Santa Marta
Maracaibo
Maiquetía
CARACAS
PORT OF SPAIN
Trinidad
Barranquilla
Cabimas
San Felipe
Los Teques
Güiria
San Fernando
Cartagena
Valledupar
Barquisimeto
Maracay
Cumaná
TRINIDAD AND TOBAGO
Golfo del Darién
Sincelejo
Machiques
Valencia
Barcelona
Maturín
Lago de Maracaibo
El Banco
Valera
Acarigua
Zaraza
Valle de la Pascua
Tucupita
Orinoco Delta
Guanare
Barinas
El Baúl
Calabozo
El Tigre
La Palma
Montería
Turbo
Mérida
Libertad
Ciudad Bolívar
Ciudad Guayana
Mabaruma
Cauca
Pico Bolívar 5007
Cúcuta
San Cristóbal
San Fernando de Apure
Embalse de Guri
Orinoco
Anna Regina
Pamplona
Bucaramanga
El Callao
VENEZUELA
Llanos
Arauca
La Paragua
Tumereng
Angel Falls
Medellín
Socorro
Sierra Nevada del Cocuy 5493
Puerto Páez
La Gran Sabana
Mt Roraima 2810
Pakaraima Mountains
Mahdia
Quibdó
Cordillera Occidental
Cordillera Central
Cordillera Oriental
Tunja
Yopal
Meta
Puerto Nuevo
Puerto Ayacucho
GUYANA
Manizales
Pereira
Armenia
Bisinaca
BOGOTÁ
Villavicencio
Ibagué
4560
Puerto Inírida
Pakaraima Mts
Serra Parima
Palmira
Guaviare
Orinoco
Cali
COLOMBIA
Lethem
5750
Neiva
San José del Guaviare
Boa Vista
Popayán
Tumaco
Pico da Neblina 3014
Branco
Essequibo
Florencia
Mitú
Nova Paraiso
Pasto
Mocoa
Caquetá
Esmeraldas
Ipiales
Ibarra
Uaupés
QUITO
Vol. Cotopaxi 5896
Puerto Leguízamo
Lérida
Negro
Tapurucuara
Represa de Balbina
Napo
Apaporis
Barcelos
Chone
Manta
ECUADOR
Cabo Pantoja
El Encanto
La Pedrera
Maraã
Unini
Negro
Jaú
Portoviejo
Ambato
Riobamba
Chimborazo 6310
Japurá
Fonte Boa
Putumayo
Alausí
Río Tigre
Curaray
Tonantins
Manaus
Manacapuru
Guayaquil
Santa Clara
Santo Antônio do Içá
Itacoatiara
Gualaceo
Tigre
Amazon
Amazonas
Isla Puná
Cuenca
Pastaza
Leticia
Tabatinga
Coari
Beruri
Machala
Iquitos
Benjamim Constant
Borba
Tumbes
Loja
Barranca
Marañón
Carauari
Purus
Macará
Talara
Sullana
Lagunas
Requena
Yavari
Ituí
Jutaí
Coari
Madeira
Novo Aripuanã
Piura
Catacaos
Jaén
Tapauá
Manicoré
Sechura
Olmos
Yurimaguas
Tarapoto
Juruá
Rioja
Chachapoyas
Eirunepé
Lábrea
Barra do São Manuel
Pta Negra
Chiclayo
Cajamarca
Trujillo
Cruzeiro do Sul
Tarauacá
Envira
Humaitá
Aripuanã
SELVAS
Contamana
Otuzco
Pucallpa
Ucayali
Huallaga
Cordillera Central
Cordillera Oriental
Tarauacá
Feijó
Boca do Acre
Porto Velho
Theodore Roosevelt
Aripuanã
Juruena
Chimbote
Purus
Sena Madureira
Porto Acre
Ariquemes
Huaraz
Huánuco
Puerto Portillo
Rio Branco
Abunã
Iaco
Huarmey
Xapuri
Jarú
Cerro de Pasco
Atalaya
Alerta
Cobija
Riberalta
Guayaramerín
Pimenta Bueno
Barranca
La Merced
Urubamba
Mamoré
Ji-Paraná
Serra dos Parecis
Huacho
Huancayo
Río de las Piedras
Vilhena
Callao
LIMA
Ayacucho
Machupicchu
Puerto Maldonado
Guaporé
Blanco
San Vicente de Cañete
Vilcabamba
Cusco (Cuzco)
Inambari
Exaltación
Mategua
Chincha Alta
Abancay
Puerto Alegre
Pisco
Antabamba
Yanaoca
Sicuani
Sandia
Puerto Frey
Mato Grosso
Ica
Ayaviri
Trinidad
Coracora
Beni
San Borja
Loreto
Pontes-e-Lacerda
Nazca
Nudo Coropuna 6425
Juliaca
Santa Ana
Lago Titicaca
Ascensión
Porto Esperidião
Chuquibamba
Arequipa
LA PAZ
San Pedro
PACIFIC OCEAN
Chala
BOLIVIA
Camana
Mollendo
Moquegua
Montero
Warnes
El Cerro
Ilo
Tacna
Nevado Sajama 6542
Cochabamba
Pampa Grande
Santa Cruz
Bañados del Izozog
Oruro
Huanui
Cordillera Oriental
Corque
Cabezas
Tucavaca
ANDES
PERU
METRES
FEET
5000
16404
3000
9843
2000
6562
1000
3281
500
1640
200
656
0
0
LAND B.S.L.
200
656
4000
13124
6000
19686
10°
80°
0°
10°
60°
60°
A
B
1
2
3
Longitude 70° west of Greenwich
Lambert Azimuthal Equal Area Projection
1:25 000 000
MILES 0
250
500

ATLANTIC
OCEAN
SURINAME
French
Guiana
RAZIL
GEORGETOWN
New Amsterdam
PARAMARIBO
St-Laurent-du-Maroni
CAYENNE
Kourou
Oiapoque
Nieuw Nickerie
Professor van Blommestein Meer
Pontoetoe
Lourenço
Calçoene
Amapá
Ilha de Maracá
Serra Tumucumaque
Mouths of the Amazon
Porto Santana
Macapá
Mazagão
Cabo Maguarinho
Baía de Marajó
Chaves
Arere
Ilha de Marajó
Salinópolis
Bragança
Belém
Viseu
Castanhal
Óbidos
Oriximiná
Almeirim
Breves
Portel
Cametá
Acará
Monte Alegre
Urucara
Parintins
Urucurituba
Santarém
Altamira
Tucuruí
Represa Tucuruí
Jacunda
Marabá
Imperatriz
Tocantinópolis
Itaituba
Jacareacanga
Araras
São Félix
Manuelzinho
Cururupu
Baía de São Marcos
São Luís
Pinheiro
Viana
Parnaíba
Camocim
Itapicuru Mirim
Luzilândia
Fortaleza
Bacabal
Codó
Tianguá
Sobral
Caucaia
Pedreiras
Caxias
Piripiri
Campo Maior
Canindé
Aracati
Timon
Teresina
Quixada
Ponta do Calcanhar
Pres. Dutra
Buriti Bravo
Macau
Touros
Grajaú
Barra do Corda
Crateús
Mossoró
Natal
Açude Boa Esperança
Palmeirais
Taua
Porto Franco
Floriano
Iguatu
Sousa
João Pessoa
Araguaína
Jerumenha
Picos
Campina Grande
Balsas
Carolina
Uruçuí
Oeiras
Crato
Juazeiro do Norte
Olinda
Conceição do Araguaia
Canto do Buriti
Paulistana
Jaboatão
Floresta
Salgueiro
Caruaru
Recife
São Raimundo Nonato
Santa Maria das Barreiras
Pedro Afonso
Petrolina
Garanhuns
Caracol
Juazeiro
Paulo Afonso
Maceió
Palmas
Porto Nacional
Barragem de Sobradinho
Senhor do Bonfim
Arapiraca
Corrente
Ilha do Bananal
Xique Xique
Monte Santo
Dianópolis
Aracaju
São Félix
Jacobina
Irecê
Natividade
Serrinha
Estância
Barreiras
Ibotirama
Feira de Santana
Alagoinhas
Santana
Bom Jesus da Lapa
Itaberaba
Sto Antônio de Jesus
Salvador
Porangatu
Cavalcante
Correntina
Represa Serra da Mesa
Posse
Brumado
Jequié
Uruaçu
Niquelândia
Guanambi
Itabuna
Ubaitaba
Ilhéus
BRASÍLIA
Formosa
Espinosa
Vitória da Conquista
Una
Goiás
Anápolis
Arinos
Januária
Janaúba
Itapetinga
Iporá
Goiânia
Unaí
Montes Claros
Salinas
Almenara
Porto Seguro
Serra do Caiapó
Paraúna
Vianópolis
Jequitaí
Rio Verde
Paracatu
Teófilo Otôni
Alcobaça
Itumbiara
Patos de Minas
Araguari
Serra do Cachimbo
Serra dos Caiabis
Serra do Roncador
Serra Geral de Goiás
Chapada Diamantina
Serra do Espinhaço
Porto dos Gaúchos
Óbidos
Porto Artur
Diamantino
Rosário Oeste
Cuiabá
Barra do Garças
Cáceres
Rondonópolis
Alto Garças
Itiquira
Puerto Isabel
Coxim
Jataí
Rio Verde de Mato Grosso
Trombetas
Paru
Xingu
Tapajós
Iriri
Curuá
Tocantins
Capim
Gurupi
Pindaré
Araguaia
Parnaíba
Poti
Piauí
Gurgueia
São Francisco
Salgado
Piranhas
Itapicuru
Salitre
Culuene
Rio das Mortes
Paraguai
Cuiabá
Taquari
Claro
Corumbá
Velhas
Equator
0°
10°
50°
40°
C
D
E
1
2
3
0
250
500
750 KILOMETRES
© Bartholomew Ltd

METRES
FEET
5000
16404
3000
9843
2000
6562
1000
3281
500
1640
200
656
0
0
LAND
B.S.L.
200
656
4000
13124
6000
19686
B R A Z I L
B O L I V I A
P A R A G U A Y
P E R U
BRASÍLIA
ASUNCIÓN
LA PAZ
SUCRE
Rio de Janeiro
São Paulo
Belo Horizonte
Santos
Santo André
Campinas
Curitiba
Porto Alegre
Goiânia
Santa Cruz
Cochabamba
Córdoba
Salvador de Jujuy
San Miguel de Tucumán
Desierto de Atacama
Tropic of Capricorn
Serra Geral de Goiás
Serra do Espinhaço
Serra de Maracaju
Lagoa dos Patos
Lambert Azimuthal Equal Area Projection
1:25 000 000
MILES 0
250
500

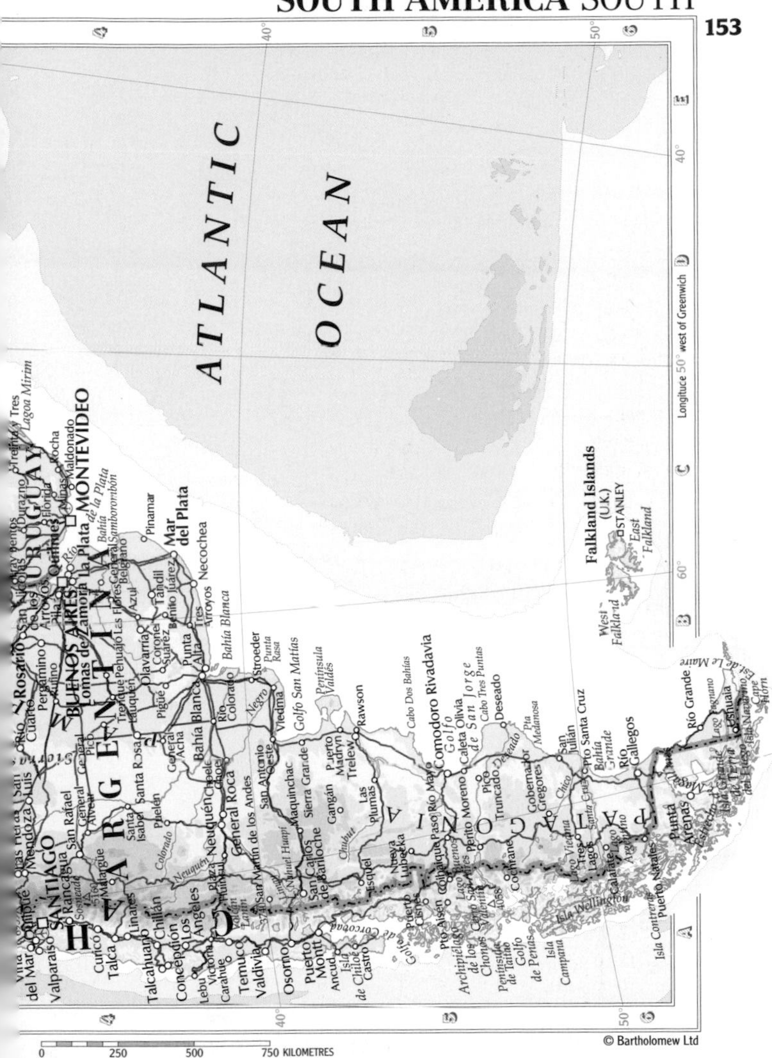
ATLANTIC
OCEAN
ARGENTINA
URUGUAY
CHILE
PATAGONIA
BUENOS AIRES
MONTEVIDEO
SANTIAGO
Mar del Plata
Bahía Blanca
Comodoro Rivadavia
Falkland Islands
(U.K.)
STANLEY
East Falkland
West Falkland
Tierra del Fuego
Cape Horn
Ushuaia
Punta Arenas
Río Gallegos
Estrecho de Magallanes
Golfo San Matías
Península Valdés
Golfo San Jorge
Isla de Chiloé
Puerto Montt
Valdivia
Concepción
Valparaíso
Mendoza
Rosario
Neuquén
Viedma
Rawson
Trelew
Longitude 50° west of Greenwich
0
250
500
750 KILOMETRES

METRES
FEET

METRES	FEET
5000	16404
3000	9843
2000	6562
1000	3281
500	1640
200	656
0	0
LAND B.S.L.	
200	656
4000	13124
6000	19686

Lambert Azimuthal Equal Area Projection

1:10 000 000

MILES 0 100 200

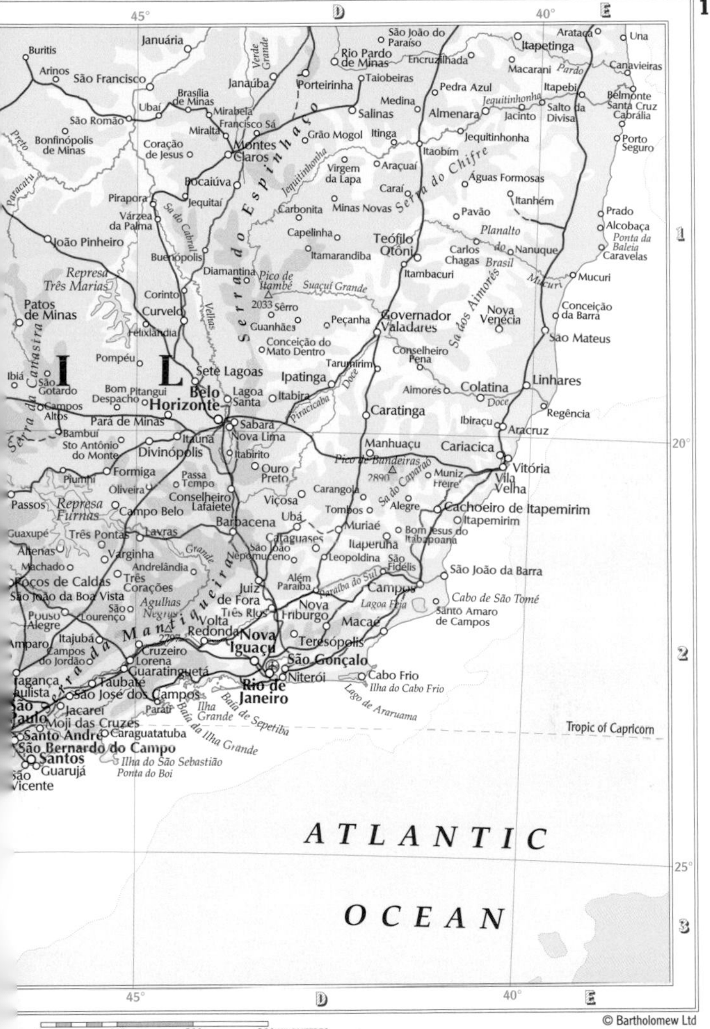

0 100 200 300 KILOMETRES

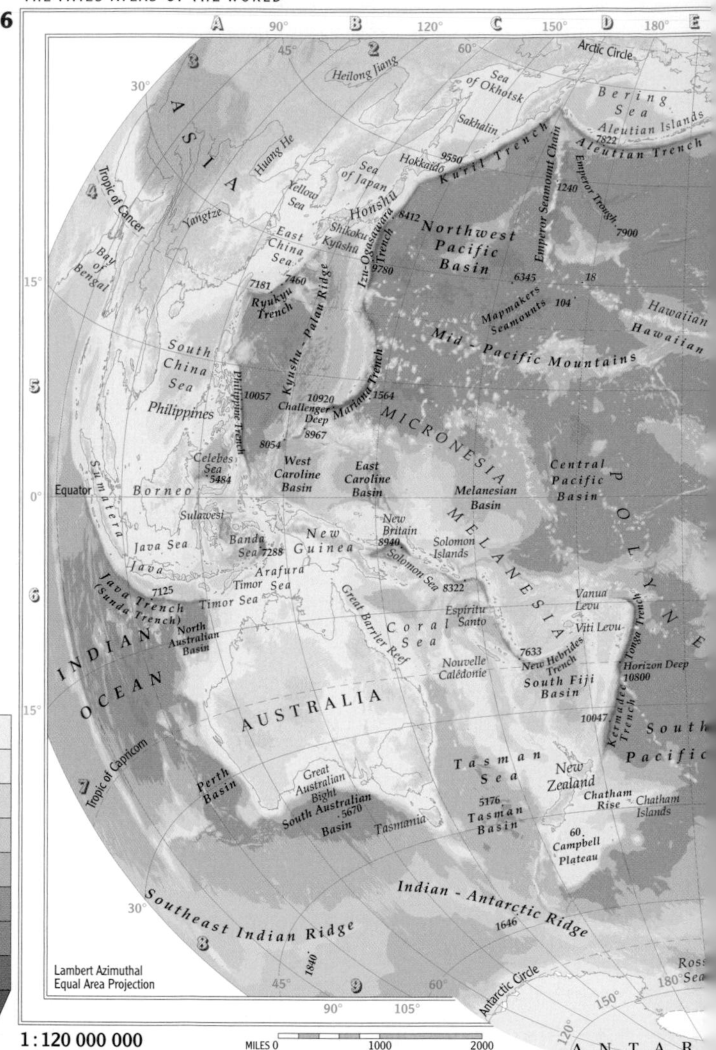
ASIA
Heilong Jiang
Sea of Okhotsk
Bering Sea
Sakhalin
Aleutian Islands
Aleutian Trench
Kuril Trench
Hokkaido
Sea of Japan
Honshu
Yellow Sea
Huang He
Yangtze
East China Sea
Shikoku
Kyushu
Izu-Ogasawara Trench
Northwest Pacific Basin
Emperor Seamount Chain
Emperor Trough
Tropic of Cancer
Bay of Bengal
Ryukyu Trench
Kyushu - Palau Ridge
Mapmakers Seamounts
Mid - Pacific Mountains
Hawaiian
South China Sea
Philippine Trench
Philippines
Challenger Deep
Mariana Trench
MICRONESIA
Celebes Sea
West Caroline Basin
East Caroline Basin
Central Pacific Basin
Melanesian Basin
Equator
Sumatera
Borneo
Sulawesi
New Britain
Solomon Islands
Java Sea
Banda Sea
New Guinea
Solomon Sea
MELANESIA
POLYNESIA
Java
Arafura Sea
Timor
Timor Sea
Java Trench (Sunda Trench)
North Australian Basin
Great Barrier Reef
Coral Sea
Espíritu Santo
Vanua Levu
Viti Levu
Tonga Trench
INDIAN OCEAN
Nouvelle Calédonie
New Hebrides Trench
Horizon Deep 10800
South Fiji Basin
AUSTRALIA
Kermadec Trench
South Pacific
Tropic of Capricorn
Perth Basin
Great Australian Bight
South Australian Basin
Tasmania
Tasman Sea
Tasman Basin
New Zealand
Chatham Rise
Chatham Islands
Campbell Plateau
Indian - Antarctic Ridge
Southeast Indian Ridge
Antarctic Circle
Arctic Circle
Ross Sea
ANTAR
METRES
FEET
0 0
200 656
2000 6562
3000 9843
4000 13124
5000 16404
6000 19686
7000 22967
9000 29529
Lambert Azimuthal Equal Area Projection
MILES 0 1000 2000

1 : 120 000 000

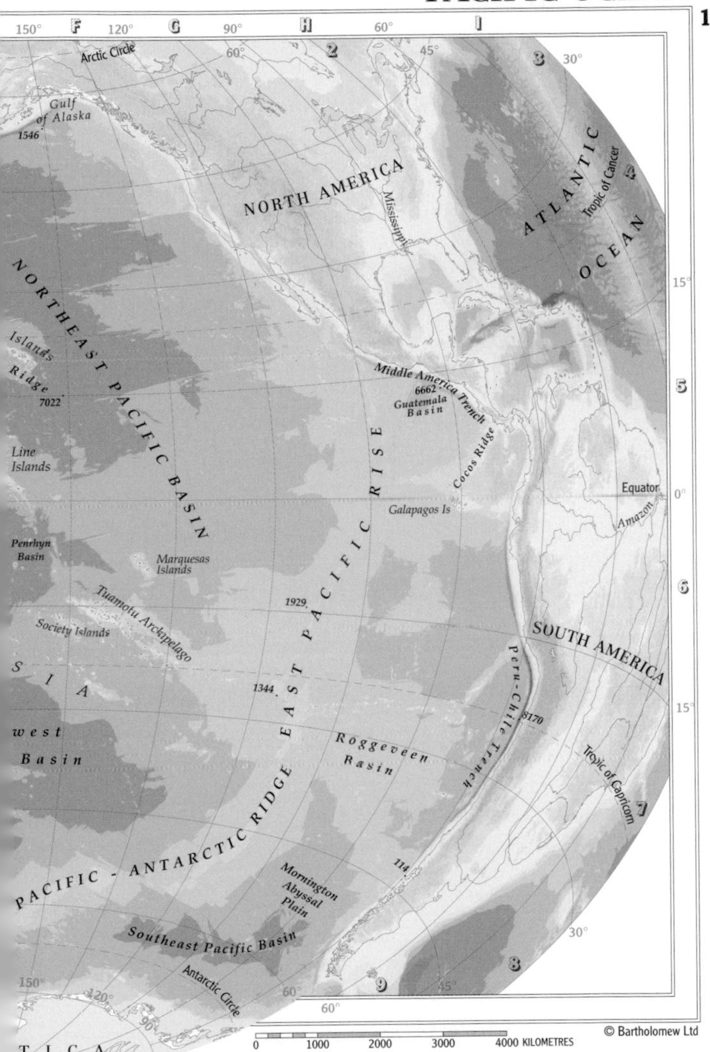
Arctic Circle
Gulf of Alaska
1546
NORTH AMERICA
Mississippi
ATLANTIC OCEAN
Tropic of Cancer
NORTHEAST PACIFIC BASIN
Islands Ridge
7022
Middle America Trench
6662
Guatemala Basin
Cocos Ridge
EAST PACIFIC RISE
Line Islands
Equator
Galapagos Is
Amazon
Penrhyn Basin
Marquesas Islands
Tuamotu Archipelago
Society Islands
1929
SOUTH AMERICA
Peru-Chile Trench
1344
8170
Roggeveen Basin
Tropic of Capricorn
PACIFIC - ANTARCTIC RIDGE
Mornington Abyssal Plain
Southeast Pacific Basin
Antarctic Circle
0
1000
2000
3000
4000 KILOMETRES

ATLANTIC OCEAN

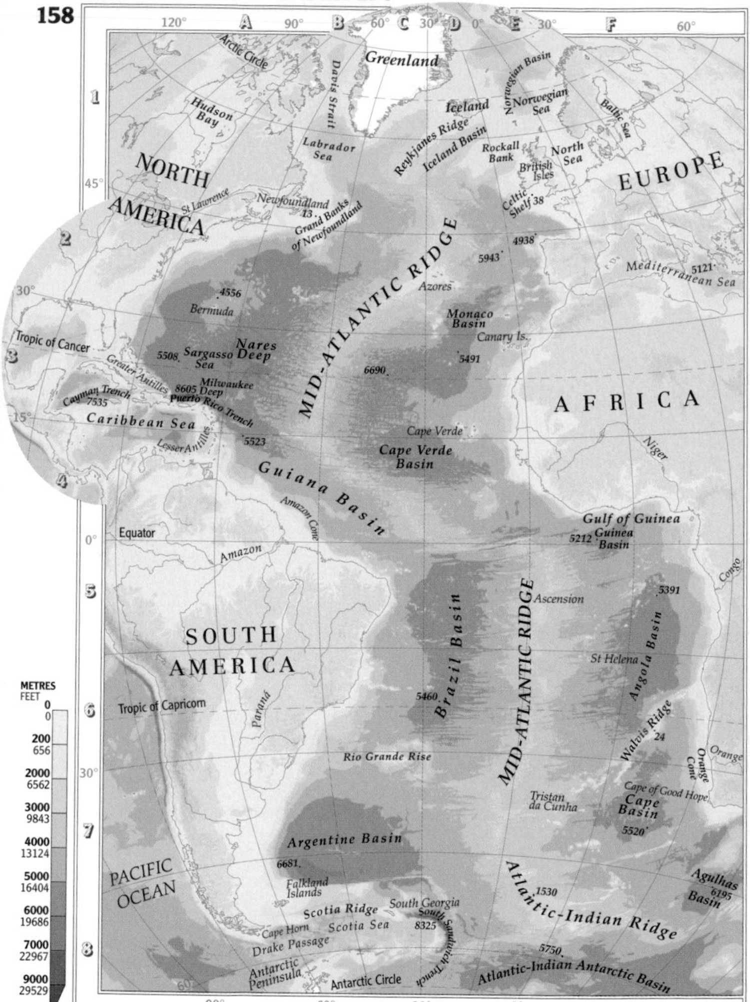

Lambert Azimuthal Equal Area Projection

1:120 000 000

MILES 0 1000 2000

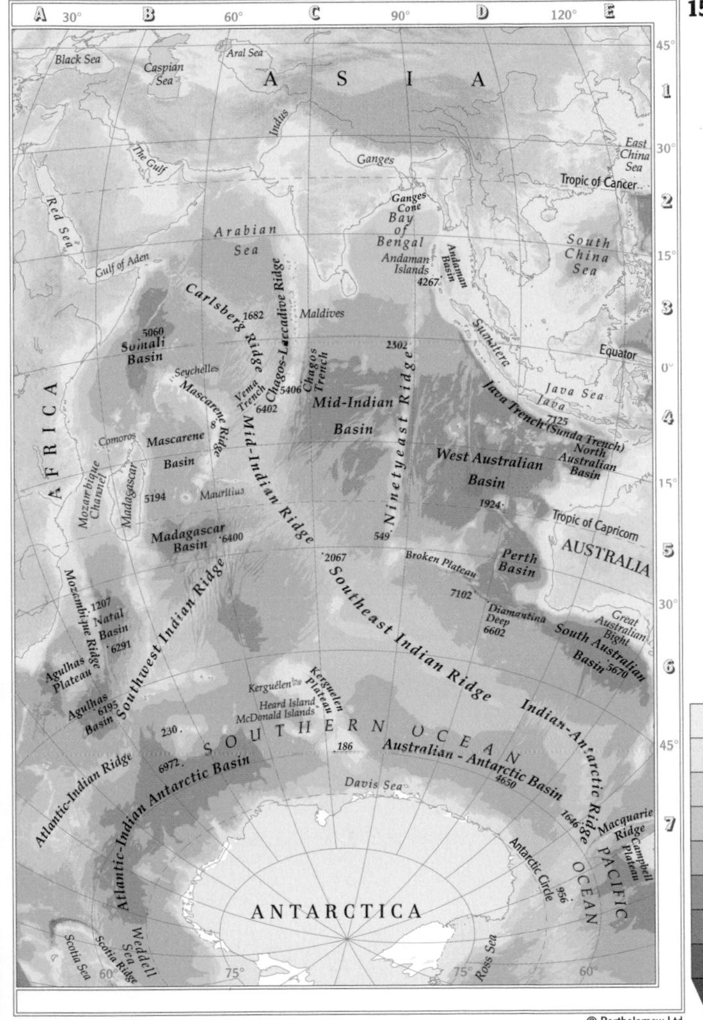
A S I A
Black Sea
Caspian Sea
Aral Sea
Indus
The Gulf
Ganges
East China Sea
Tropic of Cancer
Red Sea
Ganges Cone
Bay of Bengal
Arabian Sea
South China Sea
Gulf of Aden
Andaman Islands
Andaman Basin
4267
Carlsberg Ridge
Chagos-Laccadive Ridge
1682
Maldives
Sumatera
5060
Somali Basin
2302
Chagos Trench
Ninetyeast Ridge
Equator
Seychelles
Mascarene Ridge
Vema Trench
5406
6402
Mid-Indian Basin
Java Sea
Java
Java Trench (Sunda Trench)
7125
AFRICA
Comoros
Mascarene Basin
Mid-Indian Ridge
North Australian Basin
West Australian Basin
Mozambique Channel
Madagascar
5194
Mauritius
1924
Tropic of Capricorn
Madagascar Basin
6400
549
AUSTRALIA
2067
Broken Plateau
Perth Basin
Southwest Indian Ridge
Southeast Indian Ridge
7102
Mozambique Ridge
1207
Natal Basin
6291
Diamantina Deep
6602
Great Australian Bight
South Australian Basin
5670
Agulhas Plateau
Agulhas Basin
6195
Kerguélen
Kerguelen Plateau
Heard Island
McDonald Islands
Indian-Antarctic Ridge
230
SOUTHERN OCEAN
186
Australian - Antarctic Basin
Atlantic-Indian Ridge
6972
Atlantic-Indian Antarctic Basin
4650
Davis Sea
1646
Macquarie Ridge
Campbell Plateau
PACIFIC OCEAN
Antarctic Circle
956
ANTARCTICA
Scotia Sea
Scotia Ridge
Weddell Sea
Ross Sea
METRES
FEET
0
0
200
656
2000
6562
3000
9843
4000
13124
5000
16404
6000
19686
7000
22967
9000
29529
0
1000
2000
3000
4000 KILOMETRES

ARCTIC OCEAN

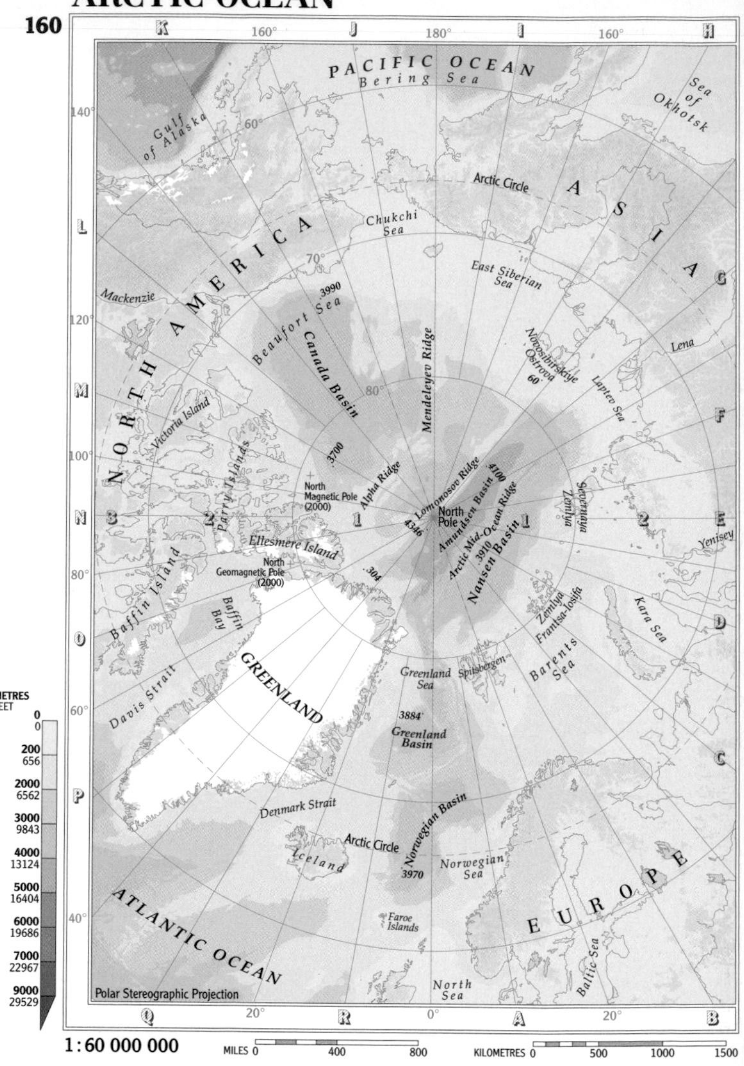

PACIFIC OCEAN
Bering Sea
Sea of Okhotsk
Gulf of Alaska
Arctic Circle
ASIA
Chukchi Sea
NORTH AMERICA
East Siberian Sea
Mackenzie
3990
Beaufort Sea
Canada Basin
Mendeleyev Ridge
Novosibirskiye Ostrova
60
Lena
Laptev Sea
Victoria Island
Parry Islands
3700
Alpha Ridge
North Magnetic Pole (2000)
Lomonosov Ridge
4100
North Pole
Amundsen Basin
Arctic Mid-Ocean Ridge
Severnaya Zemlya
Yenisey
4346
Ellesmere Island
3910
Nansen Basin
North Geomagnetic Pole (2000)
304
Baffin Island
Baffin Bay
Zemlya Frantsa-Iosifa
Kara Sea
GREENLAND
Greenland Sea
Spitsbergen
Barents Sea
Davis Strait
3884
Greenland Basin
Norwegian Basin
Denmark Strait
Arctic Circle
Iceland
3970
Norwegian Sea
EUROPE
Faroe Islands
ATLANTIC OCEAN
North Sea
Baltic Sea
Polar Stereographic Projection
METRES
FEET
0
0
200
656
2000
6562
3000
9843
4000
13124
5000
16404
6000
19686
7000
22967
9000
29529
1:60 000 000
MILES 0 400 800
KILOMETRES 0 500 1000 1500

INTRODUCTION TO THE INDEX

The index includes all names shown on the maps in the Atlas of the World. Names are referenced by page number and by a grid reference. The grid reference correlates to the alphanumeric values which appear within each map frame. Each entry also includes the country or geographical area in which the feature is located. Entries relating to names appearing on insets are indicated by a small box symbol: □, followed by a grid reference if the inset has its own alphanumeric values.

Name forms are as they appear on the maps, with additional alternative names or name forms included as cross-references which refer the user to the entry for the map form of the name. Names beginning with Mc or Mac are alphabetized exactly as they appear. The terms Saint, Sainte, etc, are abbreviated to St, Ste, etc, but alphabetized as if in the full form.

Names of physical features beginning with generic, geographical terms are permuted – the descriptive term is placed after the main part of the name. For example, Lake Superior is indexed as Superior, Lake; Mount Everest as Everest, Mount. This policy is applied to all languages.

Entries, other than those for towns and cities, include a descriptor indicating the type of geographical feature. Descriptors are not included where the type of feature is implicit in the name itself.

Administrative divisions are included to differentiate entries of the same name and feature type within the one country. In such cases, duplicate names are alphabetized in order of administrative division. Additional qualifiers are also included for names within selected geographical areas.

INDEX ABBREVIATIONS

admin. div.	administrative division
Afgh.	Afghanistan
Alg.	Algeria
Arg.	Argentina
Austr.	Australia
aut. reg.	autonomous region
aut. rep.	autonomous republic
Azer.	Azerbaijan
Bangl.	Bangladesh
Bol.	Bolivia
Bos.-Herz.	Bosnia Herzegovina
Bulg.	Bulgaria
Can.	Canada
C.A.R.	Central African Republic
Col.	Colombia
Czech Rep.	Czech Republic
Dem. Rep. Congo	Democratic Republic of Congo
depr.	depression
des.	desert
Dom. Rep.	Dominican Republic
esc.	escarpment
est.	estuary
Eth.	Ethiopia
Fin.	Finland
for.	forest
g.	gulf
Ger.	Germany
Guat.	Guatemala
hd	headland
Hond.	Honduras
imp. l.	impermanent lake
Indon.	Indonesia
isth.	isthmus
Kazakh.	Kazakhstan
Kyrg.	Kyrgyzstan
lag.	lagoon
Lith.	Lithuania
Lux.	Luxembourg
Madag.	Madagascar
Maur.	Mauritania
Mex.	Mexico
Moz.	Mozambique
mun.	municipality
N.	North
Neth.	Netherlands
Nic.	Nicaragua
N.Z.	New Zealand
Pak.	Pakistan
Para.	Paraguay
Phil.	Philippines
plat.	plateau
P.N.G.	Papua New Guinea
Pol.	Poland
Port.	Portugal
prov.	province
reg.	region
Rep.	Republic
Rus. Fed.	Russian Federation
S.	South
Serb. and Mont.	Serbia and Montenegro
Switz.	Switzerland
Tajik.	Tajikistan
Tanz.	Tanzania
terr.	territory
Thai.	Thailand
Trin. and Tob.	Trinidad and Tobago
Turkm.	Turkmenistan
U.A.E.	United Arab Emirates
U.K.	United Kingdom
Ukr.	Ukraine
Uru.	Uruguay
U.S.A.	United States of America
Uzbek.	Uzbekistan
val.	valley
Venez.	Venezuela

A

100 C2 **Aachen** Ger.
100 B2 **Aalst** Belgium
100 B2 **Aarschot** Belgium
68 C2 **Aba** China
115 C4 **Aba** Nigeria
81 C2 **Ābādān** Iran
81 D2 **Ābādeh** Iran
114 B1 **Abadla** Alg.
115 C4 **Abakaliki** Nigeria
83 H3 **Abakan** Rus. Fed.
150 A3 **Abancay** Peru
81 D2 **Abarqū** Iran
66 D2 **Abashiri** Japan
117 B4 **Ābaya Hāyk'** *l.* Eth.
Ābay Wenz *r.* Eth./Sudan *see* **Blue Nile**
82 G3 **Abaza** Rus. Fed.
108 A2 **Abbasanta** *Sardinia* Italy
104 C1 **Abbeville** France
142 B3 **Abbeville** U.S.A.
55 O2 **Abbot Ice Shelf** Antarctica
74 B1 **Abbottabad** Pak.
115 E3 **Abéché** Chad
114 B4 **Abengourou** Côte d'Ivoire
93 E4 **Åbenrå** Denmark
114 C4 **Abeokuta** Nigeria
99 A2 **Aberaeron** U.K.
96 C2 **Aberchirder** U.K.
99 B3 **Aberdare** U.K.
99 A2 **Aberdaron** U.K.
122 B3 **Aberdeen** S. Africa
96 C2 **Aberdeen** U.K.
141 D3 **Aberdeen** *MD* U.S.A.
137 D1 **Aberdeen** *SD* U.S.A.
134 B1 **Aberdeen** *WA* U.S.A.
129 E1 **Aberdeen Lake** Can.
134 B2 **Abert, Lake** U.S.A.
99 A2 **Aberystwyth** U.K.
86 F2 **Abez'** Rus. Fed.
78 B3 **Abhā** Saudi Arabia
Abiad, Bahr el *r.* Sudan/Uganda *see* **White Nile**
114 B4 **Abidjan** Côte d'Ivoire
137 D3 **Abilene** *KS* U.S.A.
139 D2 **Abilene** *TX* U.S.A.
99 C3 **Abingdon** U.K.
91 D3 **Abinsk** Rus. Fed.
130 B2 **Abitibi, Lake** Can.
Åbo Fin. *see* **Turku**
74 B1 **Abohar** India
114 C4 **Abomey** Benin
60 A1 **Abongabong, Gunung** *mt.* Indon.
118 B2 **Abong Mbang** Cameroon
64 A2 **Aborlan** Phil.
115 D3 **Abou Déia** Chad
106 B2 **Abrantes** Port.
152 B3 **Abra Pampa** Arg.
136 A2 **Absaroka Range** *mts* U.S.A.
81 C1 **Abşeron Yarımadası** *pen.* Azer.
78 B3 **Abū 'Arīsh** Saudi Arabia
79 C2 **Abu Dhabi** U.A.E.
116 B3 **Abu Hamed** Sudan
115 C4 **Abuja** Nigeria
81 C2 **Abū Kamāl** Syria
152 B1 **Abunã** *r.* Bol.
150 B2 **Abunã** Brazil
74 B2 **Abu Road** India
116 B2 **Abū Sunbul** Egypt
117 A3 **Abu Zabad** Sudan
Abū Ẓabī U.A.E. *see* **Abu Dhabi**
117 A4 **Abyei** Sudan
145 B2 **Acambaro** Mex.
106 B1 **A Cañiza** Spain
144 B2 **Acaponeta** Mex.
145 C3 **Acapulco** Mex.
151 D2 **Acará** Brazil
150 B1 **Acarigua** Venez.
145 C3 **Acatlan** Mex.
145 C3 **Acayucán** Mex.
114 B4 **Accra** Ghana
98 B2 **Accrington** U.K.
74 B2 **Achalpur** India
97 A2 **Achill Island** Rep. of Ireland
101 D1 **Achim** Ger.
96 B2 **Achnasheen** U.K.
91 D2 **Achuyevo** Rus. Fed.
111 C3 **Acıpayam** Turkey
109 C3 **Acireale** *Sicily* Italy
147 C2 **Acklins Island** Bahamas
153 B4 **Aconcagua, Cerro** *mt.* Arg.
106 B1 **A Coruña** Spain
108 A2 **Acqui Terme** Italy
103 D2 **Ács** Hungary
145 C2 **Actopán** Mex.
139 D2 **Ada** U.S.A.
79 C2 **Adam** Oman
49 H6 **Adamstown** Pitcairn Islands
'Adan Yemen *see* **Aden**
80 B2 **Adana** Turkey
Adapazari Turkey *see* **Sakarya**
108 A1 **Adda** *r.* Italy
78 B2 **Ad Dafīnah** Saudi Arabia
78 B2 **Ad Dahnā'** *des.* Saudi Arabia
78 B2 **Ad Dahnā'** *des.* Saudi Arabia
114 A2 **Ad Dakhla** Western Sahara
79 C2 **Ad Dammām** Saudi Arabia
78 A2 **Ad Dār al Ḥamrā'** Saudi Arabia
78 B3 **Ad Darb** Saudi Arabia
78 B2 **Ad Dawādimī** Saudi Arabia
Ad Dawḥah Qatar *see* **Doha**
78 B2 **Ad Dilam** Saudi Arabia
116 C2 **Ad Dir'īyah** Saudi Arabia
117 B4 **Addis Ababa** Eth.
81 C2 **Ad Dīwānīyah** Iraq
52 A2 **Adelaide** Austr.
50 C1 **Adelaide River** Austr.
101 D2 **Adelebsen** Ger.
55 J2 **Adélie Land** *reg.* Antarctica
78 B3 **Aden** Yemen
117 C3 **Aden, Gulf of** Somalia/Yemen
100 C2 **Adenau** Ger.
79 C2 **Adh Dhayd** U.A.E.
59 C3 **Adi** *i.* Indon.
78 A3 **Ādī Ārk'ay** Eth.
116 B3 **Ādīgrat** Eth.
75 B3 **Adilabad** India
141 E2 **Adirondack Mountains** U.S.A.
Ādīs Ābeba Eth. *see* Addis Ababa
117 B4 **Ādīs Alem** Eth.
110 C1 **Adjud** Romania
50 B1 **Admiralty Gulf** Austr.
128 A2 **Admiralty Island** U.S.A.
104 B3 **Adour** *r.* France
106 C2 **Adra** Spain
114 B2 **Adrar** Alg.
140 C2 **Adrian** *MI* U.S.A.
139 C1 **Adrian** *TX* U.S.A.
108 B2 **Adriatic Sea** Europe
116 B3 **Ādwa** Eth.
83 K2 **Adycha** *r.* Rus. Fed.
91 D3 **Adygeysk** Rus. Fed.
114 B4 **Adzopé** Côte d'Ivoire
111 B3 **Aegean Sea** Greece/Turkey
101 D1 **Aerzen** Ger.
106 B1 **A Estrada** Spain
116 B3 **Afabet** Eritrea
76 C3 **Afghanistan** *country* Asia
78 B2 **'Afīf** Saudi Arabia
80 B2 **Afyon** Turkey
115 C3 **Agadez** Niger
114 B1 **Agadir** Morocco
77 D2 **Agadyr'** Kazakh.
74 B2 **Agar** India
75 D2 **Agartala** India
81 C2 **Ağdam** Azer.
105 C3 **Agde** France
104 C3 **Agen** France
122 A2 **Aggeneys** S. Africa
111 C3 **Agia Vervara** Greece
111 B3 **Agios Dimitrios** Greece
111 C3 **Agios Efstratios** *i.* Greece
111 C3 **Agios Nikolaos** Greece
110 B1 **Agnita** Romania
75 B2 **Agra** India
81 C2 **Ağrı** Turkey
Ağrı Dağı *mt* Turkey *see* **Ararat, Mount**
108 B3 **Agrigento** *Sicily* Italy
111 B3 **Agrinio** Greece
109 B2 **Agropoli** Italy
154 B2 **Água Clara** Brazil
146 B4 **Aguadulce** Panama
144 B2 **Aguanaval** *r.* Mex.
144 B1 **Agua Prieta** Mex.
144 B2 **Aguascalientes** Mex.
155 D1 **Águas Formosas** Brazil
106 B1 **Águeda** Port.
106 C1 **Aguilar de Campóo** Spain
107 C2 **Águilas** Spain
144 B3 **Aguililla** Mex.
122 B3 **Agulhas, Cape** S. Africa
155 D2 **Agulhas Negras** *mt.* Brazil
111 C2 **Ağva** Turkey
81 C2 **Ahar** Iran
100 C1 **Ahaus** Ger.
81 C2 **Ahlat** Turkey
100 C2 **Ahlen** Ger.
74 B2 **Ahmadabad** India
73 B3 **Ahmadnagar** India
74 B2 **Ahmadpur East** Pak.
74 B1 **Ahmadpur Sial** Pak.
144 B2 **Ahome** Mex.
79 C2 **Ahram** Iran
101 E1 **Ahrensburg** Ger.
104 C2 **Ahun** France
81 C2 **Ahvāz** Iran
122 A2 **Ai-Ais** Namibia
80 B2 **Aigialousa** Cyprus
111 B3 **Aigio** Greece
143 D2 **Aiken** U.S.A.
155 D1 **Aimorés** Brazil
155 D1 **Aimorés, Serra dos** *hills* Brazil
114 B2 **'Aïn Ben Tili** Maur.
107 D2 **Aïn Defla** Alg.
114 B1 **Aïn Sefra** Alg.
136 D2 **Ainsworth** U.S.A.
Aintab Turkey *see* **Gaziantep**
107 D2 **Aïn Taya** Alg.
107 D2 **Aïn Tédélès** Alg.
60 A1 **Airbangis** Indon.
128 C2 **Airdrie** Can.
104 B3 **Aire-sur-l'Adour** France
101 E3 **Aisch** *r.* Ger.
128 A1 **Aishihik Lake** Can.
100 A3 **Aisne** *r.* France
59 D3 **Aitape** P.N.G.
110 B1 **Aiud** Romania
105 D3 **Aix-en-Provence** France
105 D2 **Aix-les-Bains** France
62 A1 **Aizawl** India
88 C2 **Aizkraukle** Latvia
67 C3 **Aizu-wakamatsu** Japan
105 D3 **Ajaccio** *Corsica* France
115 E1 **Ajdābiyā** Libya
74 B2 **Ajmer** India
138 A2 **Ajo** U.S.A.
87 E3 **Akbulak** Rus. Fed.
80 B2 **Akçakale** Turkey

111 C3 **Akdağ** *mt.* Turkey
80 B2 **Akdağmadeni** Turkey
88 A2 **Åkersberga** Sweden
118 C2 **Aketi** Dem. Rep. Congo
87 D4 **Akhalk'alak'i** Georgia
79 C2 **Akhḑar, Jabal** *mts* Oman
111 C3 **Akhisar** Turkey
87 D4 **Akhtubinsk** Rus. Fed.
130 B1 **Akimiski Island** Can.
66 D3 **Akita** Japan
114 A3 **Akjoujt** Maur.
77 D1 **Akkol'** Kazakh.
88 B2 **Akmeņrags** *pt* Latvia
Akmola Kazakh. *see* **Astana**
117 B4 **Akobo** Sudan
74 B2 **Akola** India
78 A3 **Akordat** Eritrea
127 G2 **Akpatok Island** Can.
92 □A3 **Akranes** Iceland
111 B2 **Akrathos, Akra** *pt* Greece
140 C2 **Akron** U.S.A.
75 B1 **Aksai Chin** *terr.* Asia
80 B2 **Aksaray** Turkey
76 B1 **Aksay** Kazakh.
91 D2 **Aksay** Rus. Fed.
80 B2 **Akşehir** Turkey
76 C2 **Akshiganak** Kazakh.
77 E2 **Aksu** China
78 A3 **Āksum** Eth.
76 B2 **Aktau** Kazakh.
76 B1 **Aktobe** Kazakh.
77 D2 **Aktogay** Kazakh.
88 C3 **Aktsyabrski** Belarus
115 C4 **Akure** Nigeria
92 □B2 **Akureyri** Iceland
142 C2 **Alabama** *r.* U.S.A.
142 C2 **Alabama** *state* U.S.A.
111 C3 **Alaçatı** Turkey
81 C1 **Alagir** Rus. Fed.
151 E3 **Alagoinhas** Brazil
107 C1 **Alagón** Spain
79 B2 **Al Aḩmadī** Kuwait
77 E2 **Alakol', Ozero** *salt l.* Kazakh.
92 J2 **Alakurtti** Rus. Fed.
78 B3 **Al 'Alayyah** Saudi Arabia
81 C2 **Al 'Amādīyah** Iraq
80 A2 **Al 'Āmirīyah** Egypt
135 C3 **Alamo** U.S.A.
138 B2 **Alamogordo** U.S.A.
144 A2 **Alamos** *Sonora* Mex.
144 B2 **Alamos** *Sonora* Mex.
144 B2 **Alamos** *r.* Mex.
136 B3 **Alamosa** U.S.A.
93 G3 **Åland** *is* Fin.
80 B2 **Alanya** Turkey
80 B3 **Al 'Aqabah** Jordan
78 B2 **Al 'Aqīq** Saudi Arabia
107 C2 **Alarcón, Embalse de** *resr* Spain
80 B2 **Al 'Arīsh** Egypt
78 B2 **Al Arţāwīyah** Saudi Arabia
61 C2 **Alas** Indon.
111 C3 **Alaşehir** Turkey
128 A2 **Alaska** *state* U.S.A.
124 C2 **Alaska, Gulf of** U.S.A.
81 C2 **Älät** Azer.
87 D3 **Alatyr'** Rus. Fed.
150 A2 **Alausí** Ecuador
93 H3 **Alavus** Fin.
52 B2 **Alawoona** Austr.
108 A2 **Alba** Italy
107 C2 **Albacete** Spain
110 B1 **Alba Iulia** Romania
109 C2 **Albania** *country* Europe
50 A3 **Albany** Austr.
130 B1 **Albany** *r.* Can.
143 D2 **Albany** *GA* U.S.A.
141 E2 **Albany** *NY* U.S.A.
134 B2 **Albany** *OR* U.S.A.
Al Başrah Iraq *see* **Basra**
51 D1 **Albatross Bay** Austr.
116 A2 **Al Bawīţī** Egypt
115 E1 **Al Bayḑā'** Libya
78 B3 **Al Bayḑā'** Yemen
143 D1 **Albemarle** U.S.A.
143 E1 **Albemarle Sound** *sea chan.* U.S.A.
108 A2 **Albenga** Italy
51 C2 **Alberga** *watercourse* Austr.
119 D2 **Albert, Lake** Dem. Rep. Congo/Uganda
128 C2 **Alberta** *prov.* Can.
100 B2 **Albert Kanaal** *canal* Belgium
137 E2 **Albert Lea** U.S.A.
104 C3 **Albi** France
78 A2 **Al Bi'r** Saudi Arabia
78 B3 **Al Birk** Saudi Arabia
78 B2 **Al Biyāḑh** *reg.* Saudi Arabia
93 E4 **Ålborg** Denmark
81 C2 **Alborz, Reshteh-ye** *mts* Iran
106 B2 **Albufeira** Port.
138 B1 **Albuquerque** U.S.A.
79 C2 **Al Buraymī** Oman
53 C3 **Albury** Austr.
106 B2 **Alcácer do Sal** Port.
106 C1 **Alcalá de Henares** Spain
106 C2 **Alcalá la Real** Spain
108 B3 **Alcamo** *Sicily* Italy
107 C1 **Alcañiz** Spain
106 B2 **Alcántara** Spain
106 C2 **Alcaraz** Spain
106 C2 **Alcaraz, Sierra de** *mts* Spain
106 C2 **Alcaudete** Spain
106 C2 **Alcázar de San Juan** Spain
91 D2 **Alchevs'k** Ukr.
155 E1 **Alcobaça** Brazil
107 C1 **Alcora** Spain
107 C2 **Alcoy-Alcoi** Spain
107 D2 **Alcúdia** Spain
145 C2 **Aldama** Mex.
83 J3 **Aldan** Rus. Fed.
83 J2 **Aldan** *r.* Rus. Fed.
95 C4 **Alderney** *i.* Channel Is
114 A3 **Aleg** Maur.
155 D2 **Alegre** Brazil
152 C3 **Alegrete** Brazil
83 K3 **Aleksandrovsk-Sakhalinskiy** Rus. Fed.
91 D1 **Alekseyevka** *Belgorodskaya Oblast'* Rus. Fed.
91 D1 **Alekseyevka** *Belgorodskaya Oblast'* Rus. Fed.
89 E3 **Aleksin** Rus. Fed.
109 D2 **Aleksinac** Serb. and Mont.
118 B3 **Alèmbé** Gabon
155 D2 **Além Paraíba** Brazil
93 F3 **Ålen** Norway
104 C2 **Alençon** France
80 B2 **Aleppo** Syria
150 A3 **Alerta** Peru
128 B2 **Alert Bay** Can.
105 C3 **Alès** France
110 B1 **Aleşd** Romania
108 A2 **Alessandria** Italy
93 E3 **Ålesund** Norway
124 B2 **Aleutian Islands** U.S.A.
83 L3 **Alevina, Mys** *c.* Rus. Fed.
128 A2 **Alexander Archipelago** *is* U.S.A.
122 A2 **Alexander Bay** S. Africa
142 C2 **Alexander City** U.S.A.
55 O2 **Alexander Island** Antarctica
53 C3 **Alexandra** Austr.
54 A3 **Alexandra** N.Z.
111 B2 **Alexandreia** Greece
Alexandretta Turkey *see* **İskenderun**
116 A1 **Alexandria** Egypt
110 C2 **Alexandria** Romania
123 C3 **Alexandria** S. Africa
142 B2 **Alexandria** *LA* U.S.A.
137 D1 **Alexandria** *MN* U.S.A.
141 D3 **Alexandria** *VA* U.S.A.
52 A3 **Alexandrina, Lake** Austr.
111 C2 **Alexandroupoli** Greece
131 E1 **Alexis** *r.* Can.
128 B2 **Alexis Creek** Can.
77 E1 **Aleysk** Rus. Fed.
107 C1 **Alfaro** Spain
81 C3 **Al Fāw** Iraq
101 D2 **Alfeld (Leine)** Ger.
155 C2 **Alfenas** Brazil
79 C2 **Al Fujayrah** U.A.E.
Al Furāt *r.* Iraq/Syria *see* **Euphrates**
106 B2 **Algeciras** Spain
107 C2 **Algemesí** Spain
78 A3 **Algena** Eritrea
Alger Alg. *see* **Algiers**
114 C2 **Algeria** *country* Africa
79 C3 **Al Ghayḑah** Yemen
108 A2 **Alghero** *Sardinia* Italy
116 B2 **Al Ghurdaqah** Egypt
79 B2 **Al Ghwaybiyah** Saudi Arabia
115 C1 **Algiers** Alg.
123 C3 **Algoa Bay** S. Africa
137 E2 **Algona** U.S.A.
106 C1 **Algorta** Spain
81 C2 **Al Ḩadīthah** Iraq
79 C2 **Al Ḩajar al Gharbī** *mts* Oman
115 D2 **Al Ḩamādah al Ḩamrā'** *plat.* Libya
107 C2 **Alhama de Murcia** Spain
80 A2 **Al Ḩammām** Egypt
78 B2 **Al Ḩanākīyah** Saudi Arabia
81 C2 **Al Ḩasakah** Syria
81 C2 **Al Ḩayy** Iraq
78 B3 **Al Ḩazm al-Jawf** Yemen
79 C3 **Al Ḩibāk** *des.* Saudi Arabia
81 C2 **Al Ḩillah** Iraq
78 B2 **Al Ḩillah** Saudi Arabia
79 B2 **Al Ḩinnāh** Saudi Arabia
78 B3 **Al Ḩudaydah** Yemen
79 B2 **Al Hufūf** Saudi Arabia
115 D2 **Al Ḩulayq al Kabīr** *hills* Libya
79 C2 **'Alīābād** Iran
111 C3 **Aliağa** Turkey
111 B2 **Aliakmonas** *r.* Greece
107 C2 **Alicante-Alacant** Spain
139 D3 **Alice** U.S.A.
109 C3 **Alice, Punta** *pt* Italy
51 C2 **Alice Springs** Austr.
75 B2 **Aligarh** India
81 C2 **Alīgūdarz** Iran
69 E1 **Alihe** China
118 B3 **Alima** *r.* Congo
111 C3 **Aliova** *r.* Turkey
117 C3 **Ali Sabieh** Djibouti
Al Iskandarīyah Egypt *see* **Alexandria**
116 B1 **Al Ismā'īlīyah** Egypt
123 C3 **Aliwal North** S. Africa
115 E2 **Al Jaghbūb** Libya
78 B2 **Al Jahrah** Kuwait
79 C2 **Al Jamalīyah** Qatar
78 A2 **Al Jawf** Saudi Arabia
115 D1 **Al Jawsh** Libya
106 B2 **Aljezur** Port.
116 B2 **Al Jīzah** Egypt
79 B2 **Al Jubayl** Saudi Arabia
78 B2 **Al Junaynah** Saudi Arabia
106 B2 **Aljustrel** Port.
78 B2 **Al Kahfah** Saudi Arabia
79 C2 **Al Kāmil** Oman
80 B2 **Al Karak** Jordan
79 C2 **Al Khābūrah** Oman
78 B2 **Al Khamāsīn** Saudi Arabia

116 B2 **Al Khārijah** Egypt
79 C2 **Al Khaṣab** Oman
78 B3 **Al Khawkhah** Yemen
79 C2 **Al Khawr** Qatar
115 E2 **Al Khufrah** Libya
115 D1 **Al Khums** Libya
79 B2 **Al Khunn** Saudi Arabia
79 C2 **Al Kir'ānah** Qatar
100 B1 **Alkmaar** Neth.
81 C2 **Al Kūt** Iraq
Al Kuwayt Kuwait *see* **Kuwait**
80 B2 **Al Lādhiqīyah** Syria
75 C2 **Allahabad** India
83 K2 **Allakh-Yun'** Rus. Fed.
141 D2 **Allegheny** *r.* U.S.A.
140 C3 **Allegheny Mountains** U.S.A.
97 B1 **Allen, Lough** *l.* Rep. of Ireland
145 B2 **Allende** *Coahuila* Mex.
145 B2 **Allende** *Nuevo León* Mex.
141 D2 **Allentown** U.S.A.
73 B4 **Alleppey** India
101 D1 **Aller** *r.* Ger.
136 C2 **Alliance** *NE* U.S.A.
140 C2 **Alliance** *OH* U.S.A.
78 B2 **Al Līth** Saudi Arabia
96 C2 **Alloa** U.K.
131 C2 **Alma** Can.
Alma-Ata Kazakh. *see* **Almaty**
106 B2 **Almada** Port.
106 C2 **Almadén** Spain
Al Madīnah Saudi Arabia *see* **Medina**
116 B1 **Al Mafraq** Jordan
78 B3 **Al Maḥwīt** Yemen
78 B2 **Al Majma'ah** Saudi Arabia
135 B2 **Almanor, Lake** U.S.A.
107 C2 **Almansa** Spain
80 B2 **Al Manṣūrah** Egypt
79 C2 **Al Mariyyah** U.A.E.
115 E1 **Al Marj** Libya
77 D2 **Almaty** Kazakh.
81 C2 **Al Mawṣil** Iraq
106 C1 **Almazán** Spain
151 C2 **Almeirim** Brazil
100 C1 **Almelo** Neth.
155 D1 **Almenara** Brazil
106 B1 **Almendra, Embalse de** *resr* Spain
106 B2 **Almendralejo** Spain
106 C2 **Almería** Spain
106 C2 **Almería, Golfo de** *b.* Spain
87 E3 **Al'met'yevsk** Rus. Fed.
78 B2 **Al Mindak** Saudi Arabia
116 B2 **Al Minyā** Egypt
79 B2 **Al Mish'āb** Saudi Arabia
106 B2 **Almodôvar** Port.
106 B2 **Almonte** Spain
75 B2 **Almora** India
79 B2 **Al Mubarrez** Saudi Arabia
79 C2 **Al Muḍaibī** Oman
80 B3 **Al Mudawwarah** Jordan
79 B3 **Al Mukallā** Yemen
78 B3 **Al Mukhā** Yemen
106 C2 **Almuñécar** Spain
78 A2 **Al Muwayliḥ** Saudi Arabia
111 B3 **Almyros** Greece
96 B2 **Alness** U.K.
98 C1 **Alnwick** U.K.
49 G4 **Alofi** Niue
111 B3 **Alonnisos** *i.* Greece
59 C3 **Alor** *i.* Indon.
59 C3 **Alor, Kepulauan** *is* Indon.
60 B1 **Alor Setar** Malaysia
Alost Belgium *see* **Aalst**
86 C2 **Alozero** Rus. Fed.
140 C1 **Alpena** U.S.A.
139 C2 **Alpine** U.S.A.
105 D2 **Alps** *mts* Europe
79 B3 **Al Qa'āmīyāt** *reg.* Saudi Arabia
115 D1 **Al Qaddāḥīyah** Libya
Al Qāhirah Egypt *see* **Cairo**
78 B2 **Al Qā'īyah** Saudi Arabia
81 C2 **Al Qāmishlī** Syria
80 B2 **Al Qaryatayn** Syria
79 B3 **Al Qaṭn** Yemen
80 B2 **Al Qunayṭirah** Syria
78 B3 **Al Qunfidhah** Saudi Arabia
116 B2 **Al Quṣayr** Egypt
78 B2 **Al Quwayīyah** Saudi Arabia
101 D2 **Alsfeld** Ger.
92 H2 **Alta** Norway
92 H2 **Altaelva** *r.* Norway
68 B1 **Altai Mountains** Asia
143 D2 **Altamaha** *r.* U.S.A.
151 C2 **Altamira** Brazil
109 C2 **Altamura** Italy
68 B1 **Altay** China
68 C1 **Altay** Mongolia
105 D2 **Altdorf** Switz.
107 C2 **Altea** Spain
101 F2 **Altenburg** Ger.
100 C2 **Altenkirchen (Westerwald)** Ger.
111 C3 **Altınoluk** Turkey
111 D3 **Altıntaş** Turkey
152 B2 **Altiplano** *plain* Bol.
154 B1 **Alto Araguaia** Brazil
107 C1 **Alto del Moncayo** *mt.* Spain
154 B1 **Alto Garças** Brazil
121 C2 **Alto Molócuè** Moz.
129 E3 **Altona** Can.
141 D2 **Altoona** U.S.A.
154 B1 **Alto Sucuriú** Brazil
102 C2 **Altötting** Ger.
68 B2 **Altun Shan** *mts* China
134 B2 **Alturas** U.S.A.
139 D2 **Altus** U.S.A.
88 C2 **Alūksne** Latvia
78 A2 **Al 'Ulā** Saudi Arabia
115 D1 **Al 'Uqaylah** Libya
Al Uqṣur Egypt *see* **Luxor**
91 C3 **Alushta** Ukr.
139 D1 **Alva** U.S.A.
145 C3 **Alvarado** Mex.
93 F3 **Älvdalen** Sweden
93 F3 **Älvdalen** *val.* Sweden
92 H2 **Älvsbyn** Sweden
78 A2 **Al Wajh** Saudi Arabia
74 B2 **Alwar** India
81 C2 **Al Widyān** *plat.* Iraq/Saudi Arabia
Alxa Youqi China *see* **Ehen Hudag**
Alxa Zuoqi China *see* **Bayan Hot**
51 C1 **Alyangula** Austr.
88 B3 **Alytus** Lith.
136 C1 **Alzada** U.S.A.
100 D3 **Alzey** Ger.
50 C2 **Amadeus, Lake** *salt flat* Austr.
127 G2 **Amadjuak Lake** Can.
106 B2 **Amadora** Port.
78 B2 **Amā'ir** Saudi Arabia
93 F4 **Åmål** Sweden
111 B3 **Amaliada** Greece
59 D3 **Amamapare** Indon.
154 A2 **Amambaí** Brazil
154 B2 **Amambaí** *r.* Brazil
69 E3 **Amami-Ō-shima** *i.* Japan
69 E3 **Amami-shotō** *is* Japan
77 C1 **Amangel'dy** Kazakh.
109 C3 **Amantea** Italy
123 D3 **Amanzimtoti** S. Africa
151 C1 **Amapá** Brazil
106 B2 **Amareleja** Port.
139 C1 **Amarillo** U.S.A.
108 B2 **Amaro, Monte** *mt.* Italy
80 B1 **Amasya** Turkey
150 C1 **Amazon** *r.* S. America
151 D1 **Amazon, Mouths of the** Brazil
Amazonas *r.* S. America *see* **Amazon**
74 B1 **Ambala** India
121 □D3 **Ambalavao** Madag.
121 □D2 **Ambanja** Madag.
150 A2 **Ambato** Ecuador
121 □D2 **Ambato Boeny** Madag.
121 □D3 **Ambato Finandrahana** Madag.
121 □D2 **Ambatolampy** Madag.
121 □D2 **Ambatondrazaka** Madag.
101 E3 **Amberg** Ger.
146 B3 **Ambergris Cay** *i.* Belize
75 C2 **Ambikapur** India
121 □D2 **Ambilobe** Madag.
98 B1 **Ambleside** U.K.
121 □D3 **Amboasary** Madag.
121 □D3 **Ambohimahasoa** Madag.
59 C3 **Ambon** Indon.
59 C3 **Ambon** *i.* Indon.
121 □D3 **Ambositra** Madag.
121 □D3 **Ambovombe** Madag.
135 C4 **Amboy** U.S.A.
120 A1 **Ambriz** Angola
68 C2 **Amdo** China
145 B2 **Amealco** Mex.
144 B2 **Ameca** Mex.
100 B1 **Ameland** *i.* Neth.
134 D2 **American Falls** U.S.A.
134 D2 **American Falls Reservoir** U.S.A.
135 D2 **American Fork** U.S.A.
49 G4 **American Samoa** *terr.* S. Pacific Ocean
143 D2 **Americus** U.S.A.
100 B1 **Amersfoort** Neth.
55 E2 **Amery Ice Shelf** Antarctica
137 E2 **Ames** U.S.A.
111 B3 **Amfissa** Greece
83 J2 **Amga** Rus. Fed.
66 C1 **Amgu** Rus. Fed.
115 C2 **Amguid** Alg.
83 K3 **Amgun'** *r.* Rus. Fed.
131 D2 **Amherst** Can.
104 C2 **Amiens** France
73 B3 **Amindivi Islands** India
122 A1 **Aminuis** Namibia
74 A2 **Amir Chah** Pak.
129 D2 **Amisk Lake** Can.
139 C3 **Amistad Reservoir** Mex./U.S.A.
98 A2 **Amlwch** U.K.
80 B2 **'Ammān** Jordan
127 I2 **Ammassalik** Greenland
78 B3 **Am Nābiyah** Yemen
81 D2 **Amol** Iran
111 C3 **Amorgos** *i.* Greece
142 C2 **Amory** U.S.A.
130 C2 **Amos** Can.
Amoy China *see* **Xiamen**
155 C2 **Amparo** Brazil
107 D1 **Amposta** Spain
75 B2 **Amravati** India
74 B1 **Amritsar** India
100 B1 **Amstelveen** Neth.
100 B1 **Amsterdam** Neth.
103 C2 **Amstetten** Austria
115 E3 **Am Timan** Chad
76 B2 **Amudar'ya** *r.* Asia
126 E1 **Amund Ringnes Island** Can.
126 C2 **Amundsen Gulf** Can.
55 M2 **Amundsen Sea** Antarctica
61 C2 **Amuntai** Indon.

Amur *r.* China/Rus. Fed. *see* **Heilong Jiang**
78 A3 **'Amur, Wadi** *watercourse* Sudan
83 I2 **Anabar** *r.* Rus. Fed.
83 I2 **Anabarskiy Zaliv** *b.* Rus. Fed.
134 D1 **Anaconda** U.S.A.
139 D1 **Anadarko** U.S.A.
80 B1 **Anadolu Dağları** *mts* Turkey
83 M2 **Anadyr'** *r.* Rus. Fed.
81 C2 **'Ānah** Iraq
145 B2 **Anáhuac** Mex.
60 B1 **Anambas, Kepulauan** *is* Indon.
137 E2 **Anamosa** U.S.A.
80 B2 **Anamur** Turkey
67 B4 **Anan** Japan
73 B3 **Anantapur** India
74 B1 **Anantnag** Jammu and Kashmir
90 B2 **Anan'yiv** Ukr.
91 D3 **Anapa** Rus. Fed.
154 C1 **Anápolis** Brazil
152 B3 **Añatuya** Arg.
65 B2 **Anbyon** N. Korea
104 B2 **Ancenis** France
108 B2 **Ancona** Italy
153 A5 **Ancud** Chile
Anda China *see* **Daqing**
93 E3 **Åndalsnes** Norway
142 C2 **Andalusia** U.S.A.
73 D3 **Andaman Islands** India
63 A2 **Andaman Sea** Indian Ocean
121 □D2 **Andapa** Madag.
100 B2 **Andelst** Neth.
92 G2 **Andenes** Norway
100 B2 **Andenne** Belgium
100 B2 **Anderlecht** Belgium
126 C2 **Anderson** *r.* Can.
126 B2 **Anderson** *AK* U.S.A.
140 B2 **Anderson** *IN* U.S.A.
143 D2 **Anderson** *SC* U.S.A.
153 A4 **Andes** *mts* S. America
121 □D2 **Andilamena** Madag.
121 □D2 **Andilanatoby** Madag.
77 D2 **Andizhan** Uzbek.
121 □D2 **Andoany** Madag.
Andong China *see* **Dandong**
65 B2 **Andong** S. Korea
107 D1 **Andorra** *country* Europe
107 D1 **Andorra la Vella** Andorra
99 C3 **Andover** U.K.
154 B2 **Andradina** Brazil
89 D2 **Andreapol'** Rus. Fed.
155 D2 **Andrelândia** Brazil
139 C2 **Andrews** U.S.A.
109 C2 **Andria** Italy
121 □D3 **Androka** Madag.
146 C2 **Andros** *i.* Bahamas
111 B3 **Andros** *i.* Greece
143 E4 **Andros Town** Bahamas
73 B3 **Andrott** *i.* India
90 B1 **Andrushivka** Ukr.
92 G2 **Andselv** Norway
106 C2 **Andújar** Spain
120 A2 **Andulo** Angola
114 C3 **Anéfis** Mali
115 D3 **Aney** Niger
83 H3 **Angara** *r.* Rus. Fed.
69 C1 **Angarsk** Rus. Fed.
93 G3 **Ånge** Sweden
144 A2 **Ángel de la Guarda, Isla** *i.* Mex.
64 B1 **Angeles** Phil.
150 B1 **Angel Falls** *waterfall* Venez.
93 F4 **Ängelholm** Sweden
92 G3 **Ångermanälven** *r.* Sweden
104 B2 **Angers** France
129 E1 **Angikuni Lake** *l.* Can.
98 A2 **Anglesey** *i.* U.K.
121 C2 **Angoche** Moz.
79 C2 **Angohrān** Iran
120 A2 **Angola** *country* Africa
140 C2 **Angola** U.S.A.
128 A2 **Angoon** U.S.A.
104 C2 **Angoulême** France
77 D2 **Angren** Uzbek.
147 D3 **Anguilla** *terr.* West Indies
75 C2 **Angul** India
93 F4 **Anholt** *i.* Denmark
71 B3 **Anhua** China
70 B2 **Anhui** *prov.* China
154 B1 **Anhumas** Brazil
154 C1 **Anicuns** Brazil
66 D1 **Aniva, Mys** *c.* Rus. Fed.
65 B2 **Anjŭ** N. Korea
70 A2 **Ankang** China
80 B2 **Ankara** Turkey
70 B2 **Anlu** China
91 E1 **Anna** Rus. Fed.
115 C1 **Annaba** Alg.
101 F2 **Annaberg-Buchholtz** Ger.
78 B2 **An Nafūd** *des.* Saudi Arabia
81 C2 **An Najaf** Iraq
96 C3 **Annan** U.K.
141 D3 **Annapolis** U.S.A.
75 C2 **Annapurna I** *mt.* Jammu and Kashmir/Nepal
140 C2 **Ann Arbor** U.S.A.
150 C1 **Anna Regina** Guyana
81 C2 **An Nāşirīyah** Iraq
105 D2 **Annecy** France
78 B3 **An Nimāş** Saudi Arabia
62 B1 **Anning** China
142 C2 **Anniston** U.S.A.
105 C2 **Annonay** France
79 B2 **An Nu'ayrīyah** Saudi Arabia
121 □D2 **Anorontany, Tanjona** *hd* Madag.
111 C3 **Ano Viannos** Greece
71 B3 **Anpu** China
70 B2 **Anqing** China
102 C2 **Ansbach** Ger.
70 C1 **Anshan** China
71 A3 **Anshun** China
116 B1 **An Sirḩān, Wādī** *watercourse* Saudi Arabia
114 C3 **Ansongo** Mali
150 A3 **Antabamba** Peru
80 B2 **Antakya** Turkey
121 □E2 **Antalaha** Madag.
80 B2 **Antalya** Turkey
80 B2 **Antalya Körfezi** *g.* Turkey
121 □D2 **Antananarivo** Madag.
55 Q3 **Antarctic Peninsula** Antarctica
96 B2 **An Teallach** *mt.* U.K.
106 C2 **Antequera** Spain
138 B2 **Anthony** U.S.A.
114 B2 **Anti Atlas** *mts* Morocco
105 D3 **Antibes** France
131 D2 **Anticosti, Île d'** *i.* Can.
131 D2 **Antigonish** Can.
147 D3 **Antigua** *i.* Antigua
147 D3 **Antigua and Barbuda** *country* West Indies
145 C2 **Antiguo-Morelos** Mex.
111 B3 **Antikythira** *i.* Greece
Antioch Turkey *see* Antakya
152 A3 **Antofagasta** Chile
154 C3 **Antonina** Brazil
97 C1 **Antrim** U.K.
97 C1 **Antrim Hills** U.K.
121 □D2 **Antsalova** Madag.
121 □D2 **Antsirabe** Madag.
121 □D2 **Antsirañana** Madag.
121 □D2 **Antsohihy** Madag.
100 B2 **Antwerpen** Belgium
An Uaimh Rep. of Ireland *see* Navan
74 B2 **Anupgarh** India
73 C4 **Anuradhapura** Sri Lanka
Anvers Belgium *see* Antwerpen
68 C2 **Anxi** China
51 C3 **Anxious Bay** Austr.
70 B2 **Anyang** China
65 B2 **Anyang** S. Korea
108 B2 **Anzio** Italy
66 D2 **Aomori** Japan
Aoraki *mt.* N.Z. *see* **Cook, Mount**
108 A1 **Aosta** Italy
143 D3 **Apalachee Bay** U.S.A.
150 B2 **Apaporis** *r.* Col.
154 B2 **Aparecida do Tabuado** Brazil
64 B1 **Aparri** Phil.
86 C2 **Apatity** Rus. Fed.
144 B3 **Apatzingán** Mex.
100 B1 **Apeldoorn** Neth.
100 C1 **Apen** Ger.
49 G4 **Apia** Samoa
154 C2 **Apiaí** Brazil
64 B2 **Apo, Mount** *vol.* Phil.
101 E2 **Apolda** Ger.
52 B3 **Apollo Bay** Austr.
143 D3 **Apopka, Lake** U.S.A.
154 B1 **Aporé** Brazil
154 B1 **Aporé** *r.* Brazil
80 B2 **Apostolos Andreas, Cape** Cyprus
133 E3 **Appalachian Mountains** U.S.A.
108 A2 **Appennino** *mts* Italy
53 D2 **Appin** Austr.
140 D2 **Appleton** U.S.A.
108 B2 **Aprilia** Italy
91 D3 **Apsheronsk** Rus. Fed.
154 B2 **Apucarana** Brazil
154 B2 **Apucarana, Serra da** *hills* Brazil
78 A2 **Aqaba, Gulf of** Asia
154 A1 **Aquidauana** *r.* Brazil
75 C2 **Ara** India
117 A4 **Arab, Bahr el** *watercourse* Sudan
56 B4 **Arabian Sea** Indian Ocean
151 E3 **Aracaju** Brazil
151 E2 **Aracati** Brazil
154 B2 **Araçatuba** Brazil
155 D1 **Aracruz** Brazil
155 D1 **Araçuaí** Brazil
110 B1 **Arad** Romania
115 E3 **Arada** Chad
156 C6 **Arafura Sea** Austr./Indon.
154 B1 **Aragarças** Brazil
107 C1 **Aragon** *r.* Spain
151 D2 **Araguaia** *r.* Brazil
151 D2 **Araguaína** Brazil
154 C1 **Araguari** Brazil
67 C3 **Arai** Japan
115 C2 **Arak** Alg.
81 C2 **Arāk** Iran
62 A1 **Arakan Yoma** *mts* Myanmar
81 C1 **Arak's** *r.* Armenia/Turkey
76 B2 **Aral Sea** *salt l.* Kazakh./Uzbek.
76 C2 **Aral'sk** Kazakh.
Aral'skoye More *salt l.* Kazakh./Uzbek. *see* **Aral Sea**
106 C1 **Aranda de Duero** Spain
109 D2 **Arandelovac** Serb. and Mont.
97 B1 **Aran Island** Rep. of Ireland
97 B2 **Aran Islands** Rep. of Ireland
106 C1 **Aranjuez** Spain
122 A1 **Aranos** Namibia
139 D3 **Aransas Pass** U.S.A.

67 B4 **Arao** Japan
114 B3 **Araouane** Mali
151 E2 **Arapiraca** Brazil
154 B2 **Arapongas** Brazil
154 C3 **Araquari** Brazil
78 B1 **'Ar'ar** Saudi Arabia
154 C2 **Araraquara** Brazil
151 C2 **Araras** Brazil
154 B3 **Araras, Serra das** *mts* Brazil
52 B3 **Ararat** Austr.
80 C2 **Ararat, Mount** Turkey
155 D2 **Araruama, Lago de** *lag.* Brazil
155 E1 **Arataca** Brazil
Aratürük China *see* **Yiwu**
150 A1 **Arauca** Col.
154 C1 **Araxá** Brazil
81 C2 **Arbīl** Iraq
96 C2 **Arbroath** U.K.
74 A2 **Arbu Lut, Dasht-e** *des.* Afgh.
104 B3 **Arcachon** France
143 D3 **Arcadia** U.S.A.
134 B2 **Arcata** U.S.A.
145 B3 **Arcelia** Mex.
86 D2 **Archangel** Rus. Fed.
51 D1 **Archer** *r.* Austr.
134 D2 **Arco** U.S.A.
106 B2 **Arcos de la Frontera** Spain
127 F2 **Arctic Bay** Can.
160 **Arctic Ocean**
126 C2 **Arctic Red** *r.* Can.
81 C2 **Ardabīl** Iran
81 C1 **Ardahan** Turkey
93 E3 **Årdalstangen** Norway
100 B3 **Ardennes** *mts* Belgium
81 D2 **Ardestān** Iran
53 C2 **Ardlethan** Austr.
139 D2 **Ardmore** U.S.A.
96 A2 **Ardnamurchan, Point of** U.K.
52 A2 **Ardrossan** Austr.
96 B3 **Ardrossan** U.K.
135 B3 **Arena, Point** U.S.A.
93 E4 **Arendal** Norway
101 E1 **Arendsee (Altmark)** Ger.
150 A3 **Arequipa** Peru
151 C2 **Arere** Brazil
106 C1 **Arévalo** Spain
108 B2 **Arezzo** Italy
104 B2 **Argentan** France
153 B4 **Argentina** *country* S.America
153 A6 **Argentino, Lago** *l.* Arg.
104 C2 **Argenton-sur-Creuse** France
110 C2 **Argeș** *r.* Romania
74 A1 **Arghandab** *r.* Afgh.
111 B3 **Argolikos Kolpos** *b.* Greece
111 B3 **Argos** Greece
111 B3 **Argostoli** Greece
107 C1 **Arguís** Spain
69 E1 **Argun'** *r.* China/Rus. Fed.
50 B1 **Argyle, Lake** Austr.
93 F4 **Århus** Denmark
122 A2 **Ariamsvlei** Namibia
152 A2 **Arica** Chile
96 A2 **Arinagour** U.K.
155 C1 **Arinos** Brazil
150 C3 **Aripuanã** Brazil
150 B2 **Aripuanã** *r.* Brazil
150 B2 **Ariquemes** Brazil
154 B1 **Ariranhá** *r.* Brazil
138 A2 **Arizona** *state* U.S.A.
144 A1 **Arizpe** Mex.
78 B2 **'Arjah** Saudi Arabia
92 G2 **Arjeplog** Sweden
142 B2 **Arkadelphia** U.S.A.
77 C1 **Arkalyk** Kazakh.
142 B2 **Arkansas** *r.* U.S.A.
142 B1 **Arkansas** *state* U.S.A.
137 D3 **Arkansas City** U.S.A.
Arkhangel'sk Rus. Fed. *see* **Archangel**
97 C2 **Arklow** Rep. of Ireland
102 C1 **Arkona, Kap** *c.* Ger.
82 G1 **Arkticheskogo Instituta, Ostrova** *is* Rus. Fed.
105 C3 **Arles** France
115 C3 **Arlit** Niger
100 B3 **Arlon** Belgium
97 C1 **Armagh** U.K.
116 B2 **Armant** Egypt
81 C1 **Armavir** Rus. Fed.
81 C1 **Armenia** *country* Asia
150 A1 **Armenia** Col.
144 B3 **Armeria** Mex.
53 D2 **Armidale** Austr.
130 B1 **Armstrong** Can.
80 B1 **Armyans'k** Ukr.
80 B2 **Arnaoutis, Cape** Cyprus
100 B2 **Arnhem** Neth.
51 C1 **Arnhem, Cape** Austr.
51 C1 **Arnhem Bay** Austr.
51 C1 **Arnhem Land** *reg.* Austr.
108 B2 **Arno** *r.* Italy
52 A2 **Arno Bay** Austr.
130 C2 **Arnprior** Can.
100 D2 **Arnsberg** Ger.
101 E2 **Arnstadt** Ger.
122 A2 **Aroab** Namibia
101 D2 **Arolsen** Ger.
78 A3 **Aroma** Sudan
108 A1 **Arona** Italy
144 B2 **Aros** *r.* Mex.
81 C2 **Ar Ramādī** Iraq
96 B3 **Arran** *i.* U.K.
80 B2 **Ar Raqqah** Syria
104 C1 **Arras** France
78 B2 **Ar-Rass** Saudi Arabia
145 C3 **Arriagá** Mex.
79 C2 **Ar Rimāl** *reg.* Saudi Arabia
Ar Riyāḍ Saudi Arabia *see* **Riyadh**
145 C2 **Arroyo Seco** Mex.
79 C2 **Ar Rustāq** Oman
80 C2 **Ar Ruṭbah** Iraq
81 D3 **Arsenajān** Iran
66 B2 **Arsen'yev** Rus. Fed.
111 B3 **Arta** Greece
144 B3 **Arteaga** Mex.
66 B2 **Artem** Rus. Fed.
91 D2 **Artemivs'k** Ukr.
104 C2 **Artenay** France
138 C2 **Artesia** U.S.A.
51 E2 **Arthur Point** Austr.
54 B2 **Arthur's Pass** N.Z.
152 C4 **Artigas** Uru.
129 D1 **Artillery Lake** Can.
90 B2 **Artsyz** Ukr.
77 D3 **Artux** China
81 C1 **Artvin** Turkey
59 C3 **Aru, Kepulauan** *is* Indon.
119 D2 **Arua** Uganda
147 D3 **Aruba** *terr.* West Indies
119 D3 **Arusha** Tanz.
69 C1 **Arvayheer** Mongolia
129 E1 **Arviat** Can.
92 G2 **Arvidsjaur** Sweden
93 F4 **Arvika** Sweden
87 D3 **Arzamas** Rus. Fed.
107 C2 **Arzew** Alg.
100 C2 **Arzfeld** Ger.
101 F2 **Aš** Czech Rep.
115 C4 **Asaba** Nigeria
66 D2 **Asahi-dake** *vol.* Japan
66 D2 **Asahikawa** Japan
78 B3 **Āsalē** *l.* Eth.
75 C2 **Asansol** India
131 C2 **Asbestos** Can.
109 C2 **Ascea** Italy
152 B2 **Ascensión** Bol.
112 C4 **Ascension** *i.* S. Atlantic Ocean
101 D3 **Aschaffenburg** Ger.
100 C2 **Ascheberg** Ger.
101 E2 **Aschersleben** Ger.
108 B2 **Ascoli Piceno** Italy
92 G3 **Åsele** Sweden
110 B2 **Asenovgrad** Bulg.
50 A2 **Ashburton** *watercourse* Austr.
54 B2 **Ashburton** N.Z.
142 B2 **Ashdown** U.S.A.
143 D1 **Asheville** U.S.A.
53 D1 **Ashford** Austr.
99 D3 **Ashford** U.K.
76 B3 **Ashgabat** Turkm.
98 C1 **Ashington** U.K.
67 B4 **Ashizuri-misaki** *pt* Japan
Ashkhabad Turkm. *see* **Ashgabat**
136 D3 **Ashland** *KS* U.S.A.
140 C3 **Ashland** *KY* U.S.A.
140 C2 **Ashland** *OH* U.S.A.
134 B2 **Ashland** *OR* U.S.A.
140 A1 **Ashland** *WI* U.S.A.
88 C3 **Ashmyany** Belarus
78 B3 **Ash Sharawrah** Saudi Arabia
79 C2 **Ash Shāriqah** U.A.E.
81 C2 **Ash Sharqāṭ** Iraq
81 C2 **Ash Shaṭrah** Iraq
79 B3 **Ash Shiḥr** Yemen
79 C2 **Ash Shināṣ** Oman
78 B2 **Ash Shu'bah** Saudi Arabia
78 B2 **Ash Shumlūl** Saudi Arabia
140 C2 **Ashtabula** U.S.A.
131 D1 **Ashuanipi Lake** Can.
106 B2 **Asilah** Morocco
108 A2 **Asinara, Golfo dell'** *b.* *Sardinia* Italy
82 G3 **Asino** Rus. Fed.
88 C3 **Asipovichy** Belarus
78 B2 **'Asīr** *reg.* Saudi Arabia
93 F4 **Askim** Norway
68 C1 **Askiz** Rus. Fed.
116 B3 **Asmara** Eritrea
93 F4 **Åsnen** *l.* Sweden
116 B2 **Asoteriba, Jebel** *mt.* Sudan
103 D2 **Aspang-Markt** Austria
136 B3 **Aspen** U.S.A.
54 A2 **Aspiring, Mount** N.Z.
117 C3 **Assab** Eritrea
116 A2 **Aş Şaḥrā' al Gharbīyah** *des.* Egypt
116 B2 **Aş Şaḥrā' ash Sharqīyah** *des.* Egypt
78 B2 **As Salamiyah** Saudi Arabia
81 C2 **As Samāwah** Iraq
79 C2 **Aş Şanām** *reg.* Saudi Arabia
115 E2 **As Sarīr** *reg.* Libya
100 C1 **Assen** Neth.
100 B2 **Assesse** Belgium
115 D1 **As Sidrah** Libya
129 D3 **Assiniboia** Can.
128 C2 **Assiniboine, Mount** Can.
154 B2 **Assis** Brazil
78 B2 **Aş Şubayḥīyah** Kuwait
81 C2 **As Sulaymānīyah** Iraq
78 B2 **As Sulaymī** Saudi Arabia
78 B2 **As Sulayyil** Saudi Arabia
78 B2 **As Sūq** Saudi Arabia
80 B2 **As Suwaydā'** Syria
79 C2 **As Suwayq** Oman
As Suways Egypt *see* **Suez**
111 B3 **Astakos** Greece
77 D1 **Astana** Kazakh.
81 C2 **Āstārā** Iran
108 A2 **Asti** Italy
74 B1 **Astor** Jammu and Kashmir

106 B1 **Astorga** Spain
134 B1 **Astoria** U.S.A.
87 D4 **Astrakhan'** Rus. Fed.
88 C3 **Astravyets** Belarus
111 C3 **Astypalaia** *i.* Greece
152 C3 **Asunción** Para.
116 B2 **Aswān** Egypt
116 B2 **Asyūṭ** Egypt
152 B3 **Atacama, Desierto de** *des.* Chile
152 B3 **Atacama, Salar de** *salt flat* Chile
114 C4 **Atakpamé** Togo
111 B3 **Atalanti** Greece
150 A3 **Atalaya** Peru
78 B3 **'Ataq** Yemen
114 A2 **Atâr** Maur.
135 B3 **Atascadero** U.S.A.
77 D2 **Atasu** Kazakh.
116 B3 **Atbara** Sudan
116 B3 **Atbara** *r.* Sudan
77 C1 **Atbasar** Kazakh.
137 D3 **Atchison** U.S.A.
108 B2 **Aterno** *r.* Italy
108 B2 **Atessa** Italy
100 A2 **Ath** Belgium
128 C2 **Athabasca** Can.
129 C2 **Athabasca** *r.* Can.
129 D2 **Athabasca, Lake** Can.
111 B3 **Athens** Greece
143 D2 **Athens** *GA* U.S.A.
140 C3 **Athens** *OH* U.S.A.
143 D1 **Athens** *TN* U.S.A.
139 D2 **Athens** *TX* U.S.A.
Athina Greece *see* **Athens**
97 C2 **Athlone** Rep. of Ireland
111 B2 **Athos** *mt.* Greece
97 C2 **Athy** Rep. of Ireland
115 D3 **Ati** Chad
130 A2 **Atikokan** Can.
87 D3 **Atkarsk** Rus. Fed.
143 D2 **Atlanta** U.S.A.
137 D2 **Atlantic** U.S.A.
141 E3 **Atlantic City** U.S.A.
158 **Atlantic Ocean**
122 A3 **Atlantis** S. Africa
114 B1 **Atlas Mountains** *mts* Africa
114 C1 **Atlas Saharien** *mts* Alg.
128 A2 **Atlin** Can.
128 A2 **Atlin Lake** Can.
142 C2 **Atmore** U.S.A.
139 D2 **Atoka** U.S.A.
75 C2 **Atrai** *r.* India
78 B2 **Aṭ Ṭā'if** Saudi Arabia
63 B2 **Attapu** Laos
111 C3 **Attavyros** *mt.* Greece
130 B1 **Attawapiskat** Can.
130 B1 **Attawapiskat** *r.* Can.
130 B1 **Attawapiskat Lake** Can.
100 C2 **Attendorn** Ger.
116 B2 **Aṭ Ṭūr** Egypt
78 B3 **At Turbah** Yemen
76 B2 **Atyrau** Kazakh.
105 C3 **Aubenas** France
126 C2 **Aubry Lake** Can.
142 C2 **Auburn** *AL* U.S.A.
135 B3 **Auburn** *CA* U.S.A.
137 D2 **Auburn** *NE* U.S.A.
141 D2 **Auburn** *NY* U.S.A.
104 C2 **Aubusson** France
104 C3 **Auch** France
54 B1 **Auckland** N.Z.
49 E6 **Auckland Islands** N.Z.
101 F2 **Aue** Ger.
102 C2 **Augsburg** Ger.
109 C3 **Augusta** *Sicily* Italy
143 D2 **Augusta** *GA* U.S.A.
137 D3 **Augusta** *KS* U.S.A.
141 F2 **Augusta** *ME* U.S.A.
50 A2 **Augustus, Mount** Austr.
100 A2 **Aulnoye-Aymeries** France
122 B2 **Auob** *watercourse* Namibia/S. Africa
74 B3 **Aurangabad** India
100 C1 **Aurich** Ger.
154 B1 **Aurilândia** Brazil
104 C3 **Aurillac** France
136 C3 **Aurora** *CO* U.S.A.
140 B2 **Aurora** *IL* U.S.A.
137 D2 **Aurora** *NE* U.S.A.
122 A2 **Aus** Namibia
137 E2 **Austin** *MN* U.S.A.
135 C3 **Austin** *NV* U.S.A.
139 D2 **Austin** *TX* U.S.A.
50 B2 **Australia** *country* Oceania
159 D7 **Australian-Antarctic Basin** Indian Ocean
53 C3 **Australian Capital Territory** *admin. div.* Austr.
102 C2 **Austria** *country* Europe
144 B3 **Autlán** Mex.
105 C2 **Autun** France
105 C2 **Auxerre** France
105 D2 **Auxonne** France
105 C2 **Avallon** France
131 E2 **Avalon Peninsula** Can.
154 C2 **Avaré** Brazil
91 D2 **Avdiyivka** Ukr.
106 B1 **Aveiro** Port.
109 B2 **Avellino** Italy
100 A2 **Avesnes-sur-Helpe** France
93 G3 **Avesta** Sweden
108 B2 **Avezzano** Italy
96 C2 **Aviemore** U.K.
109 C2 **Avigliano** Italy
105 C3 **Avignon** France
106 C1 **Ávila** Spain
106 B1 **Avilés** Spain
109 C3 **Avola** *Sicily* Italy
99 C3 **Avon** *r. England* U.K.
99 B2 **Avon** *r. England* U.K.
104 B2 **Avranches** France
54 B1 **Awanui** N.Z.
117 C4 **Āwash** Eth.
117 C3 **Āwash** *r.* Eth.
115 D2 **Awbārī** Libya
117 C4 **Aw Dheegle** Somalia
96 B2 **Awe, Loch** *l.* U.K.
117 A4 **Aweil** Sudan
126 E1 **Axel Heiberg Island** Can.
114 B4 **Axim** Ghana
150 A3 **Ayacucho** Peru
77 E2 **Ayagoz** Kazakh.
68 B2 **Ayakkum Hu** *salt l.* China
106 B2 **Ayamonte** Spain
83 K3 **Ayan** Rus. Fed.
150 A3 **Ayaviri** Peru
76 A2 **Aybas** Kazakh.
91 D2 **Aydar** *r.* Ukr.
77 C2 **Aydarkul', Ozero** *l.* Uzbek.
111 C3 **Aydın** Turkey
77 C2 **Ayeat, Gora** *hill* Kazakh.
Ayers Rock *hill* Austr. *see* **Uluru**
99 C3 **Aylesbury** U.K.
106 C1 **Ayllón** Spain
129 D1 **Aylmer Lake** Can.
117 B4 **Ayod** Sudan
83 M2 **Ayon, Ostrov** *i.* Rus. Fed.
114 B3 **'Ayoûn el 'Atroûs** Maur.
51 D1 **Ayr** Austr.
96 B3 **Ayr** U.K.
98 A1 **Ayre, Point of** Isle of Man
76 C2 **Ayteke Bi** Kazakh.
110 C2 **Aytos** Bulg.
145 C3 **Ayutla** Mex.
63 B2 **Ayutthaya** Thai.
111 C3 **Ayvacık** Turkey
111 C3 **Ayvalık** Turkey
114 C3 **Azaouagh, Vallée de** *watercourse* Mali/Niger
Azbine *mts* Niger *see* **L'Aïr, Massif de**
81 C1 **Azerbaijan** *country* Asia
86 D2 **Azopol'ye** Rus. Fed.
84 A5 **Azores** *aut. reg.* N. Atlantic Ocean
91 D2 **Azov** Rus. Fed.
91 D2 **Azov, Sea of** Rus. Fed./Ukr.
Azraq, Bahr el *r.* Eth./Sudan *see* **Blue Nile**
106 B2 **Azuaga** Spain
146 B4 **Azuero, Península de** *pen.* Panama
153 C4 **Azul** Arg.
80 B2 **Az Zaqāzīq** Egypt
80 B2 **Az Zarqā'** Jordan
78 B3 **Az Zaydīyah** Yemen
114 C2 **Azzel Matti, Sebkha** *salt pan* Alg.
78 B2 **Az Zilfī** Saudi Arabia
78 B3 **Az Zuqur** *i.* Yemen

B

117 C4 **Baardheere** Somalia
77 C3 **Bābā, Kūh-e** *mts* Afgh.
110 C2 **Babadag** Romania
111 C2 **Babaeski** Turkey
117 C3 **Bāb al Mandab** *str.* Africa/Asia
61 C2 **Babana** Indon.
59 C3 **Babar** *i.* Indon.
119 D3 **Babati** Tanz.
89 E2 **Babayevo** Rus. Fed.
128 B2 **Babine** *r.* Can.
128 B2 **Babine Lake** Can.
59 C3 **Babo** Indon.
81 D2 **Bābol** Iran
122 A3 **Baboon Point** S. Africa
88 C3 **Babruysk** Belarus
64 B1 **Babuyan** *i.* Phil.
64 B1 **Babuyan Islands** Phil.
151 D2 **Bacabal** Brazil
59 C3 **Bacan** *i.* Indon.
110 C1 **Bacău** Romania
52 B3 **Bacchus Marsh** Austr.
77 D3 **Bachu** China
129 E1 **Back** *r.* Can.
109 C1 **Bačka Palanka** Serb. and Mont.
62 B1 **Bac Lac** Vietnam
63 B3 **Bac Liêu** Vietnam
64 B1 **Bacolod** Phil.
130 C1 **Bacqueville, Lac** *l.* Can.
106 B2 **Badajoz** Spain
62 A1 **Badarpur** India
101 E2 **Bad Berka** Ger.
101 D2 **Bad Berleburg** Ger.
101 E1 **Bad Bevensen** Ger.
100 C2 **Bad Ems** Ger.
103 D2 **Baden** Austria
102 B2 **Baden-Baden** Ger.
101 E2 **Bad Harzburg** Ger.
101 D2 **Bad Hersfeld** Ger.
102 C2 **Bad Hofgastein** Austria
101 D2 **Bad Homburg vor der Höhe** Ger.
74 A2 **Badin** Pak.
80 B2 **Bādiyat ash Shām** *des.* Asia
101 E2 **Bad Kissingen** Ger.
100 C3 **Bad Kreuznach** Ger.
101 E2 **Bad Lauterberg im Harz** Ger.
101 D2 **Bad Lippspringe** Ger.
101 D3 **Bad Mergentheim** Ger.
101 D2 **Bad Nauheim** Ger.

100 C2 **Bad Neuenahr-Ahrweiler** Ger.
101 E2 **Bad Neustadt an der Saale** Ger.
101 E1 **Bad Oldesloe** Ger.
101 D2 **Bad Pyrmont** Ger.
78 A2 **Badr Ḩunayn** Saudi Arabia
101 D1 **Bad Salzuflen** Ger.
101 E2 **Bad Salzungen** Ger.
102 C1 **Bad Schwartau** Ger.
101 E1 **Bad Segeberg** Ger.
73 C4 **Badulla** Sri Lanka
100 D1 **Bad Zwischenahn** Ger.
106 C2 **Baeza** Spain
114 A3 **Bafatá** Guinea-Bissau
160 O2 **Baffin Bay** *sea* Can./Greenland
127 G2 **Baffin Island** Can.
118 B2 **Bafia** Cameroon
114 A3 **Bafing** *r.* Guinea/Mali
114 A3 **Bafoulabé** Mali
118 B2 **Bafoussam** Cameroon
76 B3 **Bāfq** Iran
80 B1 **Bafra** Turkey
79 C2 **Bāft** Iran
119 C2 **Bafwasende** Dem. Rep. Congo
119 D3 **Bagamoyo** Tanz.
60 B1 **Bagan Datuk** Malaysia
120 B2 **Bagani** Namibia
60 B1 **Bagansiapiapi** Indon.
138 A2 **Bagdad** U.S.A.
152 C4 **Bagé** Brazil
81 C2 **Baghdād** Iraq
77 C3 **Baghlān** Afgh.
104 C3 **Bagnères-de-Luchon** France
88 B3 **Bagrationovsk** Rus. Fed.
Bagrax China *see* **Bohu**
64 B1 **Baguio** Phil.
115 C3 **Bagzane, Monts** *mts* Niger
146 C2 **Bahamas, The** *country* West Indies
75 C2 **Baharampur** India
60 B1 **Bahau** Malaysia
72 B2 **Bahawalnagar** Pak.
74 B2 **Bahawalpur** Pak.
153 B4 **Bahía Blanca** Arg.
144 A2 **Bahía Kino** Mex.
152 C3 **Bahía Negra** Para.
144 A2 **Bahía Tortugas** Mex.
117 B3 **Bahir Dar** Eth.
75 C2 **Bahraich** India
79 C2 **Bahrain** *country* Asia
116 A2 **Bahrīyah, Wāḩāt al** *oasis* Egypt
79 D2 **Bāhū Kālāt** Iran
110 B1 **Baia Mare** Romania
69 E1 **Baicheng** China
131 D2 **Baie-Comeau** Can.
Baie-du-Poste Can. *see* **Mistissini**
131 C2 **Baie-St-Paul** Can.
65 B1 **Baihe** China
69 D1 **Baikal, Lake** Rus. Fed.
110 B2 **Băileşti** Romania
68 C2 **Baima** China
75 C2 **Bainang** China
143 D2 **Bainbridge** U.S.A.
49 F2 **Bairiki** Kiribati
Bairin Youqi China *see* **Daban**
53 C3 **Bairnsdale** Austr.
65 B1 **Baishan** *Jilin* China
65 B1 **Baishanzhen** *Jilin* China
70 A2 **Baiyin** China
116 B3 **Baiyuda Desert** Sudan
103 D2 **Baja** Hungary
144 A1 **Baja California** *pen.* Mex.
78 B3 **Bājil** Yemen
114 A3 **Bakel** Senegal
135 C3 **Baker** *CA* U.S.A.
136 C1 **Baker** *MT* U.S.A.
134 C2 **Baker** *OR* U.S.A.
134 B1 **Baker, Mount** *vol.* U.S.A.
129 E1 **Baker Foreland** *hd* Can.
129 E1 **Baker Lake** Can.
129 E1 **Baker Lake** *l.* Can.
135 C3 **Bakersfield** U.S.A.
91 C3 **Bakhchysaray** Ukr.
76 B3 **Bakherden** Turkm.
91 C1 **Bakhmach** Ukr.
Bākhtarān Iran *see* **Kermānshāh**
Bakı Azer. *see* **Baku**
111 C2 **Bakırköy** Turkey
92 □C2 **Bakkaflói** *b.* Iceland
118 C2 **Bakouma** C.A.R.
81 C1 **Baku** Azer.
64 A2 **Balabac** Phil.
64 A2 **Balabac** *i.* Phil.
64 A2 **Balabac Strait** Malaysia/Phil.
61 C2 **Balaiberkuak** Indon.
52 A2 **Balaklava** Austr.
91 C3 **Balaklava** Ukr.
91 D2 **Balakliya** Ukr.
87 D3 **Balakovo** Rus. Fed.
76 C3 **Bālā Morghāb** Afgh.
145 C3 **Balancán** Mex.
111 C3 **Balan Dağı** *hill* Turkey
64 B1 **Balanga** Phil.
87 D3 **Balashov** Rus. Fed.
103 D2 **Balaton** *l.* Hungary
103 D2 **Balatonboglár** Hungary
150 C2 **Balbina, Represa de** *resr* Brazil
97 C2 **Balbriggan** Rep. of Ireland
52 A2 **Balcanoona** Austr.
110 C2 **Balchik** Bulg.
54 A3 **Balclutha** N.Z.
129 E2 **Baldock Lake** Can.
129 D2 **Baldy Mountain** Can.
138 B2 **Baldy Peak** U.S.A.
Baleares, Islas *is* Spain *see* **Balearic Islands**
107 D2 **Balearic Islands** *is* Spain
155 E1 **Baleia, Ponta da** *pt* Brazil
75 C2 **Baleshwar** India
61 C2 **Bali** *i.* Indon.
60 A1 **Balige** Indon.
75 C2 **Baliguda** India
111 C3 **Balıkesir** Turkey
61 C2 **Balikpapan** Indon.
59 D3 **Balimo** P.N.G.
102 B2 **Balingen** Ger.
61 C2 **Bali Sea** Indon.
110 B2 **Balkan Mountains** Bulg./Serb. and Mont.
77 D2 **Balkhash** Kazakh.
77 D2 **Balkhash, Lake** Kazakh.
Balkhash, Ozero *l.* Kazakh. *see* **Balkhash, Lake**
50 B3 **Balladonia** Austr.
97 B2 **Ballaghaderreen** Rep. of Ireland
92 G2 **Ballangen** Norway
52 B3 **Ballarat** Austr.
50 B2 **Ballard, Lake** *salt flat* Austr.
96 C2 **Ballater** U.K.
114 B3 **Ballé** Mali
53 D1 **Ballina** Austr.
97 B1 **Ballina** Rep. of Ireland
97 B2 **Ballinasloe** Rep. of Ireland
139 D2 **Ballinger** U.S.A.
97 B2 **Ballinrobe** Rep. of Ireland
97 B1 **Ballycastle** Rep. of Ireland
97 C1 **Ballycastle** U.K.
97 D1 **Ballyclare** U.K.
97 C1 **Ballymena** U.K.
97 C1 **Ballymoney** U.K.
97 D1 **Ballynahinch** U.K.
97 B1 **Ballyshannon** Rep. of Ireland
95 B2 **Ballyvoy** U.K.
51 D2 **Balonne** *r.* Austr.
74 B2 **Balotra** India
75 C2 **Balrampur** India
52 B2 **Balranald** Austr.
110 B2 **Balş** Romania
151 D2 **Balsas** Brazil
145 C3 **Balsas** Mex.
90 B2 **Balta** Ukr.
90 B2 **Bălţi** Moldova
93 G4 **Baltic Sea** *g.* Europe
80 B2 **Balţīm** Egypt
123 C1 **Baltimore** S. Africa
141 D3 **Baltimore** U.S.A.
88 A3 **Baltiysk** Rus. Fed.
62 A1 **Balu** India
88 C2 **Balvi** Latvia
77 D2 **Balykchy** Kyrg.
87 E4 **Balykshi** Kazakh.
79 C2 **Bam** Iran
51 D1 **Bamaga** Austr.
130 A1 **Bamaji Lake** Can.
114 B3 **Bamako** Mali
118 C2 **Bambari** C.A.R.
101 E3 **Bamberg** Ger.
119 C2 **Bambili** Dem. Rep. Congo
119 C2 **Bambouti** C.A.R.
155 C2 **Bambuí** Brazil
118 B2 **Bamenda** Cameroon
74 A1 **Bāmīān** Afgh.
152 B2 **Bañados del Izozog** *swamp* Bol.
119 C2 **Banalia** Dem. Rep. Congo
151 C3 **Bananal, Ilha do** *i.* Brazil
74 B2 **Banas** *r.* India
111 C3 **Banaz** Turkey
62 B2 **Ban Ban** Laos
97 C1 **Banbridge** U.K.
99 C2 **Banbury** U.K.
130 C2 **Bancroft** Can.
119 C2 **Banda** Dem. Rep. Congo
75 C2 **Banda** India
59 C3 **Banda, Kepulauan** *is* Indon.
60 A1 **Banda Aceh** Indon.
79 C2 **Bandar-e 'Abbās** Iran
81 C2 **Bandar-e Anzalī** Iran
79 C2 **Bandar-e Chārak** Iran
81 C2 **Bandar-e Emām Khomeynī** Iran
79 C2 **Bandar-e Lengeh** Iran
79 C2 **Bandar-e Maqām** Iran
60 B2 **Bandar Lampung** Indon.
61 C1 **Bandar Seri Begawan** Brunei
59 C3 **Banda Sea** Indon.
155 D2 **Bandeiras, Pico de** *mt.* Brazil
123 C1 **Bandelierkop** S. Africa
144 B2 **Banderas, Bahía de** *b.* Mex.
114 B3 **Bandiagara** Mali
111 C2 **Bandırma** Turkey
97 B3 **Bandon** Rep. of Ireland
118 B3 **Bandundu** Dem. Rep. Congo
61 B2 **Bandung** Indon.
128 C2 **Banff** Can.
96 C2 **Banff** U.K.
114 B3 **Banfora** Burkina
64 B2 **Banga** Phil.
73 B3 **Bangalore** India
118 C2 **Bangassou** C.A.R.
59 C3 **Banggai** Indon.
59 C3 **Banggai, Kepulauan** *is* Indon.
61 C1 **Banggi** *i. Sabah* Malaysia
115 E1 **Banghāzī** Libya
60 B2 **Bangka** *i.* Indon.
61 C2 **Bangkalan** Indon.
60 B1 **Bangkinang** Indon.

60 B2 **Bangko** Indon.
63 B2 **Bangkok** Thai.
75 C2 **Bangladesh** *country* Asia
97 D1 **Bangor** *Northern Ireland* U.K.
98 A2 **Bangor** *Wales* U.K.
141 F2 **Bangor** U.S.A.
63 A2 **Bang Saphan Yai** Thai.
64 B1 **Bangued** Phil.
118 B2 **Bangui** C.A.R.
121 B2 **Bangweulu, Lake** Zambia
62 B1 **Ban Houayxay** Laos
62 B2 **Ban Huai Khon** Thai
116 B2 **Banī Suwayf** Egypt
115 D1 **Banī Walīd** Libya
80 B2 **Bāniyās** Syria
109 C2 **Banja Luka** Bos.-Herz.
61 C2 **Banjarmasin** Indon.
114 A3 **Banjul** Gambia
128 A2 **Banks Island** *B.C.* Can.
126 C2 **Banks Island** *N.W.T.* Can.
129 E1 **Banks Lake** *l.* Can.
54 B2 **Banks Peninsula** N.Z.
75 C2 **Bankura** India
62 A1 **Banmauk** Myanmar
62 B2 **Ban Mouang** Laos
97 C1 **Bann** *r.* U.K.
62 B2 **Ban Napè** Laos
63 A3 **Ban Na San** Thai.
143 E4 **Bannerman Town** Bahamas
74 B1 **Bannu** Pak.
74 B2 **Banswara** India
63 A3 **Ban Tha Kham** Thai.
62 A2 **Ban Tha Song Yang** Thai.
63 B2 **Ban Tôp** Laos
97 B3 **Bantry** Rep. of Ireland
97 B3 **Bantry Bay** Rep. of Ireland
118 B2 **Banyo** Cameroon
107 D1 **Banyoles** Spain
61 C2 **Banyuwangi** Indon.
Bao'an China *see* **Shenzhen**
69 D2 **Baochang** China
70 B2 **Baoding** China
70 A2 **Baoji** China
63 B2 **Bao Lôc** Vietnam
66 B1 **Baoqing** China
62 A1 **Baoshan** China
70 B1 **Baotou** China
65 B1 **Baotou Shan** *mt.* China/N. Korea
81 C2 **Ba'qūbah** Iraq
109 C2 **Bar** Serb. and Mont.
117 C4 **Baraawe** Somalia
147 C2 **Baracoa** Cuba
53 C2 **Baradine** Austr.
147 C3 **Barahona** Dom. Rep.
116 B3 **Baraka** *watercourse* Eritrea/Sudan
61 C1 **Baram** *r. Sarawak* Malaysia
88 C3 **Baranavichy** Belarus
78 A2 **Baranīs** Egypt
90 B1 **Baranivka** Ukr.
76 B2 **Barankul** Kazakh.
128 A2 **Baranof Island** U.S.A.
59 C3 **Barat Daya, Kepulauan** *is* Indon.
155 D2 **Barbacena** Brazil
147 E3 **Barbados** *country* West Indies
107 D1 **Barbastro** Spain
104 B2 **Barbezieux-St-Hilaire** France
51 D2 **Barcaldine** Austr.
107 D1 **Barcelona** Spain
150 B1 **Barcelona** Venez.
105 D3 **Barcelonnette** France
150 B2 **Barcelos** Brazil
Barcoo Creek *watercourse* Austr. *see* **Cooper Creek**
103 D2 **Barcs** Hungary
75 C2 **Barddhaman** India
103 E2 **Bardejov** Slovakia
79 C2 **Bardsīr** Iran
75 B2 **Bareilly** India
160 B2 **Barents Sea** Arctic Ocean
78 A3 **Barentu** Eritrea
75 C2 **Barh** India
141 F2 **Bar Harbor** U.S.A.
109 C2 **Bari** Italy
74 B1 **Barikot** Afgh.
150 A1 **Barinas** Venez.
75 C2 **Baripada** India
75 D2 **Barisal** Bangl.
60 B2 **Barisan, Pegunungan** *mts* Indon.
61 C2 **Barito** *r.* Indon.
79 C2 **Barkā** Oman
88 C2 **Barkava** Latvia
51 C1 **Barkly Tableland** *reg.* Austr.
68 C2 **Barkol** China
110 C1 **Bârlad** Romania
105 D2 **Bar-le-Duc** France
50 A2 **Barlee, Lake** *salt flat* Austr.
109 C2 **Barletta** Italy
53 C2 **Barmedman** Austr.
74 B2 **Barmer** India
99 A2 **Barmouth** U.K.
101 D1 **Barmstedt** Ger.
98 C1 **Barnard Castle** U.K.
53 B2 **Barnato** Austr.
82 G3 **Barnaul** Rus. Fed.
127 G2 **Barnes Icecap** Can.
100 B1 **Barneveld** Neth.
98 C2 **Barnsley** U.K.
99 A3 **Barnstaple** U.K.
143 D2 **Barnwell** U.S.A.
Baroda India *see* **Vadodara**
150 B1 **Barquisimeto** Venez.
96 A2 **Barra** *i.* U.K.
53 D2 **Barraba** Austr.
151 D2 **Barra do Corda** Brazil
154 B1 **Barra do Garças** Brazil
150 C2 **Barra do São Manuel** Brazil
150 A3 **Barranca** *Lima* Peru
150 A2 **Barranca** *Loreto* Peru
152 C3 **Barranqueras** Arg.
150 A1 **Barranquilla** Col.
151 D3 **Barreiras** Brazil
154 C2 **Barretos** Brazil
130 C2 **Barrie** Can.
128 B2 **Barrière** Can.
52 B2 **Barrier Range** *hills* Austr.
53 D2 **Barrington, Mount** Austr.
129 D2 **Barrington Lake** Can.
53 C1 **Barringun** Austr.
97 C2 **Barrow** *r.* Rep. of Ireland
51 C2 **Barrow Creek** Austr.
98 B1 **Barrow-in-Furness** U.K.
50 A2 **Barrow Island** Austr.
126 F2 **Barrow Strait** Can.
99 B3 **Barry** U.K.
130 C2 **Barrys Bay** Can.
74 B2 **Barsalpur** India
135 C4 **Barstow** U.S.A.
105 C2 **Bar-sur-Aube** France
80 B1 **Bartın** Turkey
51 D1 **Bartle Frere, Mount** Austr.
139 D1 **Bartlesville** U.S.A.
103 E1 **Bartoszyce** Pol.
61 C2 **Barung** *i.* Indon.
69 D1 **Baruun Urt** Mongolia
91 D2 **Barvinkove** Ukr.
53 C2 **Barwon** *r.* Austr.
88 C3 **Barysaw** Belarus
110 C2 **Basarabi** Romania
105 D2 **Basel** Switz.
91 C2 **Bashtanka** Ukr.
64 B2 **Basilan** *i.* Phil.
99 D3 **Basildon** U.K.
99 C3 **Basingstoke** U.K.
81 C2 **Başkale** Turkey
130 C2 **Baskatong, Réservoir** *resr* Can.
Basle Switz. *see* **Basel**
118 C2 **Basoko** Dem. Rep. Congo
81 C2 **Basra** Iraq
128 C2 **Bassano** Can.
114 C4 **Bassar** Togo
63 A2 **Bassein** Myanmar
147 D3 **Basse-Terre** Guadeloupe
147 D3 **Basseterre** St Kitts and Nevis
114 B3 **Bassikounou** Maur.
51 D3 **Bass Strait** Austr.
79 C2 **Bastak** Iran
101 E2 **Bastheim** Ger.
75 C2 **Basti** India
105 D3 **Bastia** *Corsica* France
100 B2 **Bastogne** Belgium
142 B2 **Bastrop** U.S.A.
Basuo China *see* **Dongfang**
118 A2 **Bata** Equat. Guinea
83 J2 **Batagay** Rus. Fed.
154 B2 **Bataguaçu** Brazil
106 B2 **Batalha** Port.
71 C3 **Batan** *i.* Phil.
118 B2 **Batangafo** C.A.R.
64 B1 **Batangas** Phil.
60 B2 **Batanghari** *r.* Indon.
71 C3 **Batan Islands** Phil.
141 D2 **Batavia** U.S.A.
91 D2 **Bataysk** Rus. Fed.
130 B2 **Batchawana Mountain** Can.
50 C1 **Batchelor** Austr.
63 B2 **Bătdâmbâng** Cambodia
53 D3 **Batemans Bay** Austr.
142 B1 **Batesville** U.S.A.
89 D2 **Batetskiy** Rus. Fed.
99 B3 **Bath** U.K.
74 B1 **Bathinda** India
53 C2 **Bathurst** Austr.
131 D2 **Bathurst** Can.
126 D2 **Bathurst Inlet** Can.
126 D2 **Bathurst Inlet** *inlet* Can.
50 C1 **Bathurst Island** Austr.
126 E1 **Bathurst Island** Can.
78 B1 **Bāṭin, Wādī al** *watercourse* Asia
81 C2 **Batman** Turkey
115 C1 **Batna** Alg.
142 B2 **Baton Rouge** U.S.A.
144 B2 **Batopilas** Mex.
118 B2 **Batouri** Cameroon
154 B1 **Batovi** Brazil
92 I1 **Båtsfjord** Norway
73 C4 **Batticaloa** Sri Lanka
109 B2 **Battipaglia** Italy
129 D2 **Battle** *r.* Can.
140 B2 **Battle Creek** U.S.A.
135 C2 **Battle Mountain** U.S.A.
74 B1 **Battura Glacier** Jammu and Kashmir
117 B4 **Batu** *mt.* Eth.
60 A2 **Batu, Pulau-pulau** *is* Indon.
81 C1 **Bat'umi** Georgia
60 B1 **Batu Pahat** Malaysia
59 C3 **Baubau** Indon.
115 C3 **Bauchi** Nigeria
104 B2 **Baugé** France
105 D2 **Baume-les-Dames** France
154 C2 **Bauru** Brazil
154 B1 **Baús** Brazil
88 B2 **Bauska** Latvia
102 C1 **Bautzen** Ger.
144 B2 **Bavispe** *r.* Mex.
87 E3 **Bavly** Rus. Fed.
62 A1 **Bawdwin** Myanmar
61 C2 **Bawean** *i.* Indon.
114 B3 **Bawku** Ghana
146 C2 **Bayamo** Cuba

Bayan Gol China *see* **Dengkou**
68 C1 **Bayanhongor** Mongolia
70 A2 **Bayan Hot** China
64 B2 **Bayawan** Phil.
80 C1 **Bayburt** Turkey
140 C2 **Bay City** *MI* U.S.A.
139 D3 **Bay City** *TX* U.S.A.
86 F2 **Baydaratskaya Guba** *b.* Rus. Fed.
117 C4 **Baydhabo** Somalia
81 C2 **Bayjī** Iraq
Baykal, Ozero *l.* Rus. Fed. *see* **Baikal, Lake**
83 I3 **Baykal'skiy Khrebet** *mts* Rus. Fed.
76 C2 **Baykonyr** Kazakh.
87 E3 **Baymak** Rus. Fed.
64 B1 **Bayombong** Phil.
104 B3 **Bayonne** France
111 C3 **Bayramiç** Turkey
101 E3 **Bayreuth** Ger.
78 B3 **Bayt al Faqīh** Yemen
106 C2 **Baza** Spain
106 C2 **Baza, Sierra de** *mts* Spain
76 A2 **Bazardyuzyu, Gora** *mt.* Azer./Rus. Fed.
104 B3 **Bazas** France
74 A2 **Bazdar** Pak.
70 A2 **Bazhong** China
79 D2 **Bazmān** Iran
79 D2 **Bazmān, Kūh-e** *mt.* Iran
99 D3 **Beachy Head** *hd* U.K.
123 C3 **Beacon Bay** S. Africa
50 B1 **Beagle Gulf** Austr.
121 □D2 **Bealanana** Madag.
130 B2 **Beardmore** Can.
134 E1 **Bear Paw Mountain** U.S.A.
147 C3 **Beata, Cabo** *c.* Dom. Rep.
147 C3 **Beata, Isla** *i.* Dom. Rep.
137 D2 **Beatrice** U.S.A.
135 C3 **Beatty** U.S.A.
53 D1 **Beaudesert** Austr.
52 B3 **Beaufort** Austr.
61 C1 **Beaufort** *Sabah* Malaysia
143 D2 **Beaufort** U.S.A.
160 L2 **Beaufort Sea** Can./U.S.A.
122 B3 **Beaufort West** S. Africa
96 B2 **Beauly** *r.* U.K.
100 B2 **Beaumont** Belgium
54 A3 **Beaumont** N.Z.
139 E2 **Beaumont** U.S.A.
105 C2 **Beaune** France
100 B2 **Beauraing** Belgium
129 E2 **Beauséjour** Can.
104 C2 **Beauvais** France
129 D2 **Beauval** Can.
129 D2 **Beaver** *r.* Can.
135 D3 **Beaver** U.S.A.
126 B2 **Beaver Creek** Can.
140 B2 **Beaver Dam** U.S.A.
129 E2 **Beaver Hill Lake** Can.
140 B1 **Beaver Island** U.S.A.
128 C2 **Beaverlodge** Can.
74 B2 **Beawar** India
154 C2 **Bebedouro** Brazil
101 D2 **Bebra** Ger.
106 B1 **Becerreá** Spain
114 B1 **Béchar** Alg.
140 C3 **Beckley** U.S.A.
117 B4 **Bedelē** Eth.
99 C2 **Bedford** U.K.
140 B3 **Bedford** U.S.A.
100 C1 **Bedum** Neth.
53 D2 **Beecroft Peninsula** Austr.
101 F1 **Beelitz** Ger.
53 D1 **Beenleigh** Austr.
80 B2 **Be'ér Sheva'** Israel
139 D3 **Beeville** U.S.A.
53 C3 **Bega** Austr.
107 D1 **Begur, Cap de** *c.* Spain
81 D2 **Behshahr** Iran
69 E1 **Bei'an** China
71 A3 **Beihai** China
70 B2 **Beijing** China
100 C1 **Beilen** Neth.
96 A2 **Beinn Mhòr** *hill* U.K.
121 C2 **Beira** Moz.
80 B2 **Beirut** Lebanon
123 C1 **Beitbridge** Zimbabwe
106 B2 **Beja** Port.
115 C1 **Bejaïa** Alg.
106 B1 **Béjar** Spain
74 A2 **Beji** *r.* Pak.
76 B2 **Bekdash** Turkm.
103 E2 **Békés** Hungary
103 E2 **Békéscsaba** Hungary
121 □D3 **Bekily** Madag.
74 A2 **Bela** Pak.
123 C1 **Bela-Bela** S. Africa
118 B2 **Bélabo** Cameroon
109 D2 **Bela Crkva** Serb. and Mont.
61 C1 **Belaga** *Sarawak* Malaysia
88 C3 **Belarus** *country* Europe
Belau *country* N. Pacific Ocean *see* **Palau**
123 D2 **Bela Vista** Moz.
60 A1 **Belawan** Indon.
83 M2 **Belaya** *r.* Rus. Fed.
103 D1 **Bełchatów** Pol.
130 C1 **Belcher Islands** Can.
117 C4 **Beledweyne** Somalia
151 D2 **Belém** Brazil
138 B2 **Belen** U.S.A.
89 E3 **Belev** Rus. Fed.
97 D1 **Belfast** U.K.
141 F2 **Belfast** U.S.A.
105 D2 **Belfort** France
73 B3 **Belgaum** India
100 B2 **Belgium** *country* Europe
91 D1 **Belgorod** Rus. Fed.
134 D1 **Belgrade** U.S.A.
109 D2 **Belgrade** Serb. and Mont.
115 D4 **Beli** Nigeria
60 B2 **Belinyu** Indon.
61 B2 **Belitung** *i.* Indon.
146 B3 **Belize** Belize
146 B3 **Belize** *country* Central America
83 K1 **Bel'kovskiy, Ostrov** *i.* Rus. Fed.
128 B2 **Bella Bella** Can.
104 C2 **Bellac** France
128 B2 **Bella Coola** Can.
53 C1 **Bellata** Austr.
136 C2 **Belle Fourche** U.S.A.
136 C2 **Belle Fourche** *r.* U.S.A.
143 D3 **Belle Glade** U.S.A.
104 B2 **Belle-Île** *i.* France
131 E1 **Belle Isle** *i.* Can.
131 E1 **Belle Isle, Strait of** Can.
130 C2 **Belleville** Can.
140 B3 **Belleville** *IL* U.S.A.
137 D3 **Belleville** *KS* U.S.A.
134 B1 **Bellevue** U.S.A.
134 B1 **Bellingham** U.S.A.
55 O2 **Bellingshausen Sea** Antarctica
105 D2 **Bellinzona** Switz.
108 B1 **Belluno** Italy
122 A3 **Bellville** S. Africa
155 E1 **Belmonte** Brazil
146 B3 **Belmopan** Belize
97 B1 **Belmullet** Rep. of Ireland
69 E1 **Belogorsk** Rus. Fed.
121 □D3 **Beloha** Madag.
155 D1 **Belo Horizonte** Brazil
140 B2 **Beloit** U.S.A.
86 C2 **Belomorsk** Rus. Fed.
91 D3 **Belorechensk** Rus. Fed.
87 E3 **Beloretsk** Rus. Fed.
Belorussia *country* Europe *see* **Belarus**
86 F2 **Beloyarskiy** Rus. Fed.
86 C2 **Beloye, Ozero** *l.* Rus. Fed.
Beloye More *sea* Rus. Fed. *see* **White Sea**
86 C2 **Belozersk** Rus. Fed.
77 E2 **Belukha, Gora** *mt.* Kazakh./Rus. Fed.
86 D2 **Belush'ye** Rus. Fed.
89 D2 **Belyy** Rus. Fed.
82 F2 **Belyy, Ostrov** *i.* Rus. Fed.
101 F1 **Belzig** Ger.
137 E1 **Bemidji** U.S.A.
121 □D2 **Bé, Nosy** *i.* Madag.
118 C3 **Bena Dibele** Dem. Rep. Congo
53 C3 **Benalla** Austr.
106 B1 **Benavente** Spain
96 A2 **Benbecula** *i.* U.K.
134 B2 **Bend** U.S.A.
123 C3 **Bendearg** *mt.* S. Africa
52 B3 **Bendigo** Austr.
121 C2 **Bene** Moz.
102 C2 **Benešov** Czech Rep.
109 B2 **Benevento** Italy
159 C2 **Bengal, Bay of** *sea* Indian Ocean
70 B2 **Bengbu** China
61 B1 **Bengkayang** Indon.
60 B2 **Bengkulu** Indon.
120 A2 **Benguela** Angola
96 B1 **Ben Hope** *hill* U.K.
152 B2 **Beni** *r.* Bol.
119 C2 **Beni** Dem. Rep. Congo
114 B1 **Beni-Abbès** Alg.
107 C2 **Benidorm** Spain
114 B1 **Beni Mellal** Morocco
114 C3 **Benin** *country* Africa
114 C4 **Benin, Bight of** *g.* Africa
115 C4 **Benin City** Nigeria
153 C4 **Benito Juárez** Arg.
150 B2 **Benjamim Constant** Brazil
144 A1 **Benjamín Hill** Mex.
59 C3 **Benjina** Indon.
96 B2 **Ben Lawers** *mt.* U.K.
96 B2 **Ben Lomond** *hill* U.K.
96 C2 **Ben Macdui** *mt.* U.K.
96 A2 **Ben More** *hill* U.K.
54 B2 **Benmore, Lake** N.Z.
96 B1 **Ben More Assynt** *hill* U.K.
128 A2 **Bennett** Can.
83 K1 **Bennetta, Ostrov** *i.* Rus. Fed.
96 B2 **Ben Nevis** *mt.* U.K.
141 E2 **Bennington** U.S.A.
123 C2 **Benoni** S. Africa
101 D3 **Bensheim** Ger.
138 A2 **Benson** U.S.A.
58 C3 **Benteng** Indon.
140 B2 **Benton Harbor** U.S.A.
142 B1 **Bentonville** U.S.A.
115 C4 **Benue** *r.* Nigeria
97 B1 **Benwee Head** *hd* Rep. of Ireland
96 B2 **Ben Wyvis** *mt.* U.K.
70 C1 **Benxi** China
Beograd Serb. and Mont. *see* **Belgrade**
75 C2 **Beohari** India
67 B4 **Beppu** Japan
109 C2 **Berane** Serb. and Mont.
109 C2 **Berat** Albania
59 C3 **Berau, Teluk** *b.* Indon.
116 B3 **Berber** Sudan
117 C3 **Berbera** Somalia
118 B2 **Berbérati** C.A.R.
104 C1 **Berck** France
91 D2 **Berdyans'k** Ukr.
90 B2 **Berdychiv** Ukr.

90 A2 **Berehove** Ukr.
59 D3 **Bereina** P.N.G.
129 E2 **Berens River** Can.
90 A2 **Berezhany** Ukr.
90 C2 **Berezivka** Ukr.
90 B1 **Berezne** Ukr.
86 D2 **Bereznik** Rus. Fed.
86 E3 **Berezniki** Rus. Fed.
86 F2 **Berezovo** Rus. Fed.
107 D1 **Berga** Spain
111 C3 **Bergama** Turkey
108 A1 **Bergamo** Italy
102 C1 **Bergen** *Mecklenburg-Vorpommern* Ger.
101 D1 **Bergen** *Niedersachsen* Ger.
93 E3 **Bergen** Norway
100 B2 **Bergen op Zoom** Neth.
104 C3 **Bergerac** France
100 C2 **Bergheim (Erft)** Ger.
100 C2 **Bergisch Gladbach** Ger.
122 A1 **Bergland** Namibia
92 H2 **Bergsviken** Sweden
83 M3 **Beringa, Ostrov** *i.* Rus. Fed.
100 B2 **Beringen** Belgium
124 B1 **Bering Sea** N. Pacific Ocean
83 N2 **Bering Strait** Rus. Fed./U.S.A.
135 B3 **Berkeley** U.S.A.
100 B1 **Berkhout** Neth.
55 Q2 **Berkner Island** Antarctica
110 B2 **Berkovitsa** Bulg.
92 I1 **Berlevåg** Norway
101 F1 **Berlin** Ger.
141 E2 **Berlin** U.S.A.
101 E2 **Berlingerode** Ger.
53 D3 **Bermagui** Austr.
144 B2 **Bermejíllo** Mex.
152 B3 **Bermejo** Bol.
131 D1 **Bermen, Lac** *l.* Can.
125 F4 **Bermuda** *terr.* N. Atlantic Ocean
105 D2 **Bern** Switz.
101 E2 **Bernburg (Saale)** Ger.
127 F2 **Bernier Bay** Can.
100 C3 **Bernkastel-Kues** Ger.
121 □D3 **Beroroha** Madag.
52 B2 **Berri** Austr.
107 D2 **Berrouaghia** Alg.
146 C2 **Berry Islands** Bahamas
100 C1 **Bersenbrück** Ger.
90 B2 **Bershad'** Ukr.
131 D1 **Berté, Lac** *l.* Can.
118 B2 **Bertoua** Cameroon
150 B2 **Beruri** Brazil
98 B1 **Berwick-upon-Tweed** U.K.
91 C2 **Beryslav** Ukr.
121 □D2 **Besalampy** Madag.
105 D2 **Besançon** France
129 D2 **Besnard Lake** Can.
142 C2 **Bessemer** U.S.A.
76 B2 **Besshoky, Gora** *hill* Kazakh.
106 B1 **Betanzos** Spain
118 B2 **Bétaré Oya** Cameroon
122 A2 **Bethanie** Namibia
123 C2 **Bethlehem** S. Africa
141 D2 **Bethlehem** U.S.A.
121 □D3 **Betioky** Madag.
77 D2 **Betpak-Dala** *plain* Kazakh.
121 □D3 **Betroka** Madag.
131 D2 **Betsiamites** Can.
121 □D2 **Betsiboka** *r.* Madag.
137 E2 **Bettendorf** U.S.A.
75 C2 **Bettiah** India
75 B2 **Betul** India
75 B2 **Betwa** *r.* India
98 B2 **Betws-y-coed** U.K.
98 C2 **Beverley** U.K.
101 D2 **Beverungen** Ger.
100 B1 **Beverwijk** Neth.
99 D3 **Bexhill** U.K.
111 C2 **Beykoz** Turkey
114 B4 **Beyla** Guinea
76 B2 **Beyneu** Kazakh.
80 B1 **Beypazarı** Turkey
Beyrouth Lebanon *see* **Beirut**
80 B2 **Beyşehir** Turkey
80 B2 **Beyşehir Gölü** *l.* Turkey
91 D2 **Beysug** *r.* Rus. Fed.
88 C2 **Bezhanitsy** Rus. Fed.
89 E2 **Bezhetsk** Rus. Fed.
105 C3 **Béziers** France
75 C2 **Bhadrak** India
73 B3 **Bhadravati** India
75 C2 **Bhagalpur** India
74 A2 **Bhairi Hol** *mt.* Pak.
74 B1 **Bhakkar** Pak.
62 A1 **Bhamo** Myanmar
75 C3 **Bhanjanagar** India
74 B2 **Bharatpur** India
74 B2 **Bharuch** India
74 B2 **Bhavnagar** India
75 C3 **Bhawanipatna** India
123 D2 **Bhekuzulu** S. Africa
74 B2 **Bhilwara** India
73 B3 **Bhima** *r.* India
74 B2 **Bhiwani** India
123 C3 **Bhongweni** S. Africa
74 B2 **Bhopal** India
75 C2 **Bhubaneshwar** India
74 A2 **Bhuj** India
62 A2 **Bhumiphol Dam** Thai.
74 B2 **Bhusawal** India
75 D2 **Bhutan** *country* Asia
62 B2 **Bia, Phou** *mt.* Laos
59 D3 **Biak** Indon.
59 D3 **Biak** *i.* Indon.
103 E1 **Biała Podlaska** Pol.
103 D1 **Białogard** Pol.
103 E1 **Białystok** Pol.
109 C3 **Bianco** Italy
104 B3 **Biarritz** France
105 D2 **Biasca** Switz.
66 D2 **Bibai** Japan
120 A2 **Bibala** Angola
102 B2 **Biberach an der Riß** Ger.
115 C4 **Bida** Nigeria
141 E2 **Biddeford** U.S.A.
99 A3 **Bideford** U.K.
99 A3 **Bideford Bay** U.K.
101 D2 **Biedenkopf** Ger.
105 D2 **Biel** Switz.
101 D1 **Bielefeld** Ger.
108 A1 **Biella** Italy
103 D2 **Bielsko-Biała** Pol.
63 B2 **Biên Hoa** Vietnam
130 C1 **Bienville, Lac** *l.* Can.
100 B3 **Bièvre** Belgium
118 B3 **Bifoun** Gabon
111 C2 **Biga** Turkey
123 D2 **Big Bend** Swaziland
129 D2 **Biggar** Can.
96 C3 **Biggar** U.K.
134 D1 **Big Hole** *r.* U.S.A.
136 B1 **Bighorn** *r.* U.S.A.
136 B2 **Bighorn Mountains** U.S.A.
139 C2 **Big Lake** U.S.A.
140 B2 **Big Rapids** U.S.A.
129 D2 **Big River** Can.
129 E2 **Big Sand Lake** Can.
137 D2 **Big Sioux** *r.* U.S.A.
139 C2 **Big Spring** U.S.A.
134 E1 **Big Timber** U.S.A.
130 B1 **Big Trout Lake** Can.
130 A1 **Big Trout Lake** *l.* Can.
109 C2 **Bihać** Bos.-Herz.
75 C2 **Bihar Sharif** India
110 B1 **Bihor, Vârful** *mt.* Romania
114 A3 **Bijagós, Arquipélago dos** *is* Guinea-Bissau
81 C2 **Bījār** Iran
109 C2 **Bijeljina** Bos.-Herz.
109 C2 **Bijelo Polje** Serb. and Mont.
71 A3 **Bijie** China
74 B2 **Bikaner** India
69 E1 **Bikin** Rus. Fed.
118 B3 **Bikoro** Dem. Rep. Congo
79 C2 **Bilād Banī Bū 'Alī** Oman
75 C2 **Bilaspur** India
90 C2 **Bila Tserkva** Ukr.
63 A2 **Bilauktaung Range** *mts* Myanmar/Thai.
106 C1 **Bilbao** Spain
111 C2 **Bilecik** Turkey
103 E1 **Biłgoraj** Pol.
90 C2 **Bilhorod-Dnistrovs'kyy** Ukr.
119 C2 **Bili** Dem. Rep. Congo
83 M2 **Bilibino** Rus. Fed.
134 E1 **Billings** U.S.A.
99 B3 **Bill of Portland** *hd* U.K.
115 D3 **Bilma** Niger
51 E2 **Biloela** Austr.
91 C2 **Bilohirs'k** Ukr.
90 B1 **Bilohir"ya** Ukr.
91 C1 **Bilopillya** Ukr.
91 D2 **Bilovods'k** Ukr.
142 C2 **Biloxi** U.S.A.
51 C2 **Bilpa Morea Claypan** *salt flat* Austr.
101 E2 **Bilshausen** Ger.
115 E3 **Biltine** Chad
90 C2 **Bilyayivka** Ukr.
143 E3 **Bimini Islands** Bahamas
75 B2 **Bina-Etawa** India
59 C3 **Binaija, Gunung** *mt.* Indon.
118 B3 **Bindu** Dem. Rep. Congo
121 C2 **Bindura** Zimbabwe
107 D1 **Binefar** Spain
53 D1 **Bingara** Austr.
100 C3 **Bingen am Rhein** Ger.
141 F1 **Bingham** U.S.A.
141 D2 **Binghamton** U.S.A.
81 C2 **Bingöl** Turkey
60 A1 **Binjai** Indon.
60 B2 **Bintuhan** Indon.
61 C1 **Bintulu** *Sarawak* Malaysia
70 B2 **Binzhou** China
118 A2 **Bioco** *i.* Equat. Guinea
109 C2 **Biograd na Moru** Croatia
118 C1 **Birao** C.A.R.
75 C2 **Biratnagar** Nepal
128 C2 **Birch Mountains** Can.
100 B1 **Birdaard** Neth.
51 C2 **Birdsville** Austr.
80 B2 **Birecik** Turkey
60 A1 **Bireun** Indon.
75 C2 **Birganj** Nepal
117 B3 **Birhan** *mt.* Eth.
154 B2 **Birigüi** Brazil
76 B3 **Bīrjand** Iran
98 B2 **Birkenhead** U.K.
99 C2 **Birmingham** U.K.
142 C2 **Birmingham** U.S.A.
114 A2 **Bîr Mogreïn** Maur.
115 C3 **Birnin-Kebbi** Nigeria
115 C3 **Birnin Konni** Niger
69 E1 **Birobidzhan** Rus. Fed.
97 C2 **Birr** Rep. of Ireland
96 C1 **Birsay** U.K.
78 A2 **Bi'r Shalatayn** Egypt
88 B2 **Biržai** Lith.
75 B2 **Bisalpur** India
138 B2 **Bisbee** U.S.A.
104 A2 **Biscay, Bay of** *sea* France/Spain
102 C2 **Bischofshofen** Austria
77 D2 **Bishkek** Kyrg.
123 C3 **Bisho** S. Africa
135 C3 **Bishop** U.S.A.
69 E1 **Bishui** China
150 B1 **Bisinaca** Col.

115 C1 **Biskra** Alg.
136 C1 **Bismarck** U.S.A.
48 D3 **Bismarck Sea** P.N.G.
107 D2 **Bissa, Djebel** *mt.* Alg.
114 A3 **Bissau** Guinea-Bissau
129 E2 **Bissett** Can.
128 C2 **Bistcho Lake** Can.
110 B1 **Bistrița** Romania
110 C1 **Bistrița** *r.* Romania
100 C3 **Bitburg** Ger.
105 D2 **Bitche** France
115 D3 **Bitkine** Chad
109 D2 **Bitola** Macedonia
109 C2 **Bitonto** Italy
122 A3 **Bitterfontein** S. Africa
134 D1 **Bitterroot** *r.* U.S.A.
134 C1 **Bitterroot Range** *mts* U.S.A.
91 D1 **Bityug** *r.* Rus. Fed.
115 D3 **Biu** Nigeria
67 C3 **Biwa-ko** *l.* Japan
68 B1 **Biysk** Rus. Fed.
115 C1 **Bizerte** Tunisia
92 □A2 **Bjargtangar** *hd* Iceland
92 G3 **Bjästa** Sweden
92 G2 **Bjerkvik** Norway
Björneborg Fin. *see* **Pori**
82 C2 **Bjørnøya** *i.* Arctic Ocean
114 B3 **Bla** Mali
137 E3 **Black** *r.* U.S.A.
51 D2 **Blackall** Austr.
98 B2 **Blackburn** U.K.
134 D2 **Blackfoot** U.S.A.
Black Forest *mts* Ger. *see* Schwarzwald
136 C2 **Black Hills** U.S.A.
96 B2 **Black Isle** *pen.* U.K.
129 D2 **Black Lake** Can.
129 D2 **Black Lake** *l.* Can.
99 B3 **Black Mountains** U.K.
98 B2 **Blackpool** U.K.
Black River *r.* Vietnam *see* **Đa, Sông**
140 A2 **Black River Falls** U.S.A.
140 C3 **Blacksburg** U.S.A.
80 B1 **Black Sea** Asia/Europe
97 A1 **Blacksod Bay** Rep. of Ireland
97 C2 **Blackstairs Mountains** Rep. of Ireland
114 B4 **Black Volta** *r.* Africa
97 C2 **Blackwater** *r.* Rep. of Ireland
128 B1 **Blackwater Lake** *l.* Can.
50 A3 **Blackwood** *r.* Austr.
76 A2 **Blagodarnyy** Rus. Fed.
110 B2 **Blagoevgrad** Bulg.
69 E1 **Blagoveshchensk** Rus. Fed.
129 D2 **Blaine Lake** Can.
137 D2 **Blair** U.S.A.
96 C2 **Blair Atholl** U.K.
96 C2 **Blairgowrie** U.K.
143 D2 **Blakely** U.S.A.
153 B4 **Blanca, Bahía** *b.* Arg.
52 A1 **Blanche, Lake** *salt flat* Austr.
152 B2 **Blanco** *r.* Bol.
131 E1 **Blanc-Sablon** Can.
92 □A2 **Blanda** *r.* Iceland
99 B3 **Blandford Forum** U.K.
135 E3 **Blanding** U.S.A.
107 D1 **Blanes** Spain
60 A1 **Blangkejeren** Indon.
100 C2 **Blankenheim** Ger.
100 C2 **Blankenrath** Ger.
103 D2 **Blansko** Czech Rep.
121 C2 **Blantyre** Malawi
98 C1 **Blaydon** U.K.
53 C2 **Blayney** Austr.
54 B2 **Blenheim** N.Z.
115 C1 **Blida** Alg.
130 B2 **Blind River** Can.
123 C2 **Bloemfontein** S. Africa
123 C2 **Bloemhof** S. Africa
123 C2 **Bloemhof Dam** S. Africa
92 □A2 **Blönduós** Iceland
97 B1 **Bloody Foreland** *pt* Rep. of Ireland
138 B1 **Bloomfield** U.S.A.
140 B2 **Bloomington** *IL* U.S.A.
140 B3 **Bloomington** *IN* U.S.A.
140 C3 **Bluefield** U.S.A.
146 B3 **Bluefields** Nic.
53 C2 **Blue Mountains** Austr.
134 C1 **Blue Mountains** U.S.A.
116 B3 **Blue Nile** *r.* Eth./Sudan
126 D2 **Bluenose Lake** Can.
140 C3 **Blue Ridge** *mts* U.S.A.
97 B1 **Blue Stack Mountains** Rep. of Ireland
54 A3 **Bluff** N.Z.
135 E3 **Bluff** U.S.A.
152 D3 **Blumenau** Brazil
52 A2 **Blyth** Austr.
98 C1 **Blyth** U.K.
135 D4 **Blythe** U.S.A.
142 C1 **Blytheville** U.S.A.
114 A4 **Bo** Sierra Leone
64 B1 **Boac** Phil.
151 D2 **Boa Esperança, Açude** *resr* Brazil
150 B1 **Boa Vista** Brazil
53 C2 **Bobadah** Austr.
71 B3 **Bobai** China
121 □D2 **Bobaomby, Tanjona** *c.* Madag.
114 B3 **Bobo-Dioulasso** Burkina
89 F3 **Bobrov** Rus. Fed.
91 C1 **Bobrovytsya** Ukr.
91 C2 **Bobrynets'** Ukr.
121 □D3 **Boby** *mt.* Madag.
150 B2 **Boca do Acre** Brazil
155 D1 **Bocaiúva** Brazil
118 B2 **Bocaranga** C.A.R.
103 E2 **Bochnia** Pol.
100 C2 **Bocholt** Ger.
100 C2 **Bochum** Ger.
123 C1 **Bochum** S. Africa
101 E1 **Bockenem** Ger.
118 B2 **Boda** C.A.R.
83 I3 **Bodaybo** Rus. Fed.
115 D3 **Bodélé** *reg.* Chad
92 H2 **Boden** Sweden
99 A3 **Bodmin** U.K.
99 A3 **Bodmin Moor** *moorland* U.K.
92 F2 **Bodø** Norway
111 C3 **Bodrum** Turkey
118 C3 **Boende** Dem. Rep. Congo
142 C2 **Bogalusa** U.S.A.
114 B3 **Bogandé** Burkina
68 B2 **Bogda Shan** *mts* China
53 D1 **Boggabilla** Austr.
97 B2 **Boggeragh Mountains** Rep. of Ireland
100 B3 **Bogny-sur-Meuse** France
97 C2 **Bog of Allen** *reg.* Rep. of Ireland
53 C3 **Bogong, Mount** Austr.
60 B2 **Bogor** Indon.
89 E3 **Bogoroditsk** Rus. Fed.
150 A1 **Bogotá** Col.
82 G3 **Bogotol** Rus. Fed.
83 H3 **Boguchany** Rus. Fed.
91 E2 **Boguchar** Rus. Fed.
70 B2 **Bo Hai** *g.* China
100 A3 **Bohain-en-Vermandois** France
70 B2 **Bohai Wan** *b.* China
123 C2 **Bohlokong** S. Africa
102 C2 **Böhmer Wald** *mts* Ger.
91 D1 **Bohodukhiv** Ukr.
64 B2 **Bohol** *i.* Phil.
64 B2 **Bohol Sea** Phil.
68 B2 **Bohu** China
155 C2 **Boi, Ponta do** *pt* Brazil
154 B1 **Bois** *r.* Brazil
126 C2 **Bois, Lac des** *l.* Can.
134 C2 **Boise** U.S.A.
139 C1 **Boise City** U.S.A.
123 C2 **Boitumelong** S. Africa
101 E1 **Boizenburg** Ger.
76 B3 **Bojnūrd** Iran
118 B3 **Bokatola** Dem. Rep. Congo
114 A3 **Boké** Guinea
118 C3 **Bokele** Dem. Rep. Congo
93 E4 **Boknafjorden** *sea chan.* Norway
115 D3 **Bokoro** Chad
63 A2 **Bokpyin** Myanmar
89 D2 **Boksitogorsk** Rus. Fed.
122 B2 **Bokspits** S. Africa
114 A3 **Bolama** Guinea-Bissau
75 C2 **Bolangir** India
104 C2 **Bolbec** France
77 E2 **Bole** China
118 B3 **Boleko** Dem. Rep. Congo
114 B3 **Bolgatanga** Ghana
90 B2 **Bolhrad** Ukr.
66 B1 **Boli** China
110 C2 **Bolintin-Vale** Romania
137 E3 **Bolivar** U.S.A.
150 A1 **Bolívar, Pico** *mt.* Venez.
152 B2 **Bolivia** *country* S. America
89 E3 **Bolkhov** Rus. Fed.
105 C3 **Bollène** France
93 G3 **Bollnäs** Sweden
53 C1 **Bollon** Austr.
101 E2 **Bollstedt** Ger.
93 F4 **Bolmen** *l.* Sweden
118 B3 **Bolobo** Dem. Rep. Congo
108 B2 **Bologna** Italy
89 D2 **Bologovo** Rus. Fed.
89 D2 **Bologoye** Rus. Fed.
118 B2 **Bolomba** Dem. Rep. Congo
63 B2 **Bolovens, Phouphieng** *plat.* Laos
83 H1 **Bol'shevik, Ostrov** *i.* Rus. Fed.
86 E2 **Bol'shezemel'skaya Tundra** *lowland* Rus. Fed.
83 L2 **Bol'shoy Aluy** *r.* Rus. Fed.
66 B2 **Bol'shoy Kamen'** Rus. Fed.
Bol'shoy Kavkaz *mts* Asia/Europe *see* **Caucasus**
83 K2 **Bol'shoy Lyakhovskiy, Ostrov** *i.* Rus. Fed.
100 B1 **Bolsward** Neth.
98 B2 **Bolton** U.K.
80 B1 **Bolu** Turkey
92 □A2 **Bolungarvík** Iceland
108 B1 **Bolzano** Italy
118 B3 **Boma** Dem. Rep. Congo
53 D2 **Bomaderry** Austr.
53 C3 **Bombala** Austr.
Bombay India *see* **Mumbai**
155 C1 **Bom Despacho** Brazil
75 D2 **Bomdila** India
151 D3 **Bom Jesus da Lapa** Brazil
155 D2 **Bom Jesus do Itabapoana** Brazil
115 D1 **Bon, Cap** *c.* Tunisia
147 D3 **Bonaire** *i.* Neth. Antilles
50 B1 **Bonaparte Archipelago** *is* Austr.
131 E2 **Bonavista** Can.
131 E2 **Bonavista Bay** Can.
118 C2 **Bondo** Dem. Rep. Congo
114 B4 **Bondoukou** Côte d'Ivoire
58 C3 **Bonerate, Kepulauan** *is* Indon.
155 C1 **Bonfinópolis de Minas** Brazil
117 B4 **Bonga** Eth.

75 D2 **Bongaigaon** India
118 C2 **Bongandanga** Dem. Rep. Congo
118 C2 **Bongo, Massif des** *mts* C.A.R.
115 D3 **Bongor** Chad
114 B4 **Bongouanou** Côte d'Ivoire
63 B2 **Bông Sơn** Vietnam
139 D2 **Bonham** U.S.A.
105 D3 **Bonifacio** *Corsica* France
108 A2 **Bonifacio, Strait of** France/Italy
100 C2 **Bonn** Ger.
134 C1 **Bonners Ferry** U.S.A.
50 A3 **Bonnie Rock** Austr.
129 C2 **Bonnyville** Can.
108 A2 **Bonorva** *Sardinia* Italy
61 C1 **Bontang** Indon.
64 B1 **Bontoc** Phil.
58 B3 **Bontosunggu** Indon.
123 C3 **Bontrug** S. Africa
52 B2 **Booligal** Austr.
53 C1 **Boomi** Austr.
53 D1 **Boonah** Austr.
137 E2 **Boone** U.S.A.
142 C2 **Booneville** U.S.A.
137 E3 **Boonville** U.S.A.
53 C2 **Boorowa** Austr.
126 F2 **Boothia, Gulf of** Can.
126 E2 **Boothia Peninsula** Can.
100 C2 **Boppard** Ger.
117 B4 **Bor** Sudan
80 B2 **Bor** Turkey
109 D2 **Bor** Serb. and Mont.
121 □E2 **Boraha, Nosy** *i.* Madag.
93 F4 **Borås** Sweden
79 C2 **Borāzjān** Iran
150 C2 **Borba** Brazil
104 B3 **Bordeaux** France
127 F2 **Borden Peninsula** Can.
52 B3 **Bordertown** Austr.
107 D2 **Bordj Bou Arréridj** Alg.
107 D2 **Bordj Bounaama** Alg.
115 C1 **Bordj Messaouda** Alg.
115 C2 **Bordj Omer Driss** Alg.
94 B1 **Borðoy** *i.* Faroe Is
92 □A3 **Borgarnes** Iceland
108 A1 **Borgosesia** Italy
87 D3 **Borisoglebsk** Rus. Fed.
89 E2 **Borisoglebskiy** Rus. Fed.
91 D1 **Borisovka** Rus. Fed.
100 C2 **Borken** Ger.
92 G2 **Borkenes** Norway
100 C1 **Borkum** Ger.
100 C1 **Borkum** *i.* Ger.
93 G3 **Borlänge** Sweden
101 F2 **Borna** Ger.
61 C1 **Borneo** *i.* Asia
93 F4 **Bornholm** *i.* Denmark
111 C3 **Bornova** Turkey
90 B1 **Borodyanka** Ukr.
89 D2 **Borovichi** Rus. Fed.
89 E2 **Borovsk** Rus. Fed.
51 C1 **Borroloola** Austr.
110 B1 **Borşa** Romania
90 B2 **Borshchiv** Ukr.
69 D1 **Borshchovochnyy Khrebet** *mts* Rus. Fed.
101 E1 **Börßum** Ger.
Bortala China *see* **Bole**
81 C2 **Borūjerd** Iran
90 A2 **Boryslav** Ukr.
90 C1 **Boryspil'** Ukr.
91 C1 **Borzna** Ukr.
69 D1 **Borzya** Rus. Fed.
109 C1 **Bosanska Dubica** Bos.-Herz.
109 C1 **Bosanska Gradiška** Bos.-Herz.
109 C2 **Bosanska Krupa** Bos.-Herz.
109 C1 **Bosanski Novi** Bos.-Herz.
109 C2 **Bosansko Grahovo** Bos.-Herz.
71 A3 **Bose** China
123 C2 **Boshof** S. Africa
109 C2 **Bosnia-Herzegovina** *country* Europe
118 B2 **Bosobolo** Dem. Rep. Congo
110 C2 **Bosporus** *str.* Turkey
118 B2 **Bossangoa** C.A.R.
118 B2 **Bossembélé** C.A.R.
68 B2 **Bosten Hu** *l.* China
98 C2 **Boston** U.K.
141 E2 **Boston** U.S.A.
142 B1 **Boston Mountains** U.S.A.
53 D2 **Botany Bay** Austr.
110 B2 **Botev** *mt.* Bulg.
93 G3 **Bothnia, Gulf of** Fin./Sweden
110 C1 **Botoşani** Romania
123 C2 **Botshabelo** S. Africa
120 B3 **Botswana** *country* Africa
109 C3 **Botte Donato, Monte** *mt.* Italy
136 C1 **Bottineau** U.S.A.
100 C2 **Bottrop** Ger.
154 C2 **Botucatu** Brazil
114 B4 **Bouaké** Côte d'Ivoire
118 B2 **Bouar** C.A.R.
114 B1 **Bouârfa** Morocco
131 D2 **Bouctouche** Can.
107 E2 **Bougaa** Alg.
114 B3 **Bougouni** Mali
100 B3 **Bouillon** Belgium
107 D2 **Bouira** Alg.
114 A2 **Boujdour** Western Sahara
136 B2 **Boulder** U.S.A.
135 D3 **Boulder City** U.S.A.
51 C2 **Boulia** Austr.
104 C2 **Boulogne-Billancourt** France
99 D3 **Boulogne-sur-Mer** France
118 B3 **Boumango** Gabon
118 B2 **Boumba** *r.* Cameroon
107 D2 **Boumerdes** Alg.
114 B4 **Bouna** Côte d'Ivoire
114 B4 **Boundiali** Côte d'Ivoire
134 D2 **Bountiful** U.S.A.
114 B3 **Bourem** Mali
104 C2 **Bourganeuf** France
105 D2 **Bourg-en-Bresse** France
104 C2 **Bourges** France
53 C2 **Bourke** Austr.
99 C3 **Bournemouth** U.K.
115 C1 **Bou Saâda** Alg.
115 D3 **Bousso** Chad
114 A3 **Boutilimit** Maur.
129 C3 **Bow** *r.* Can.
51 D2 **Bowen** Austr.
129 C3 **Bow Island** Can.
140 B3 **Bowling Green** *KY* U.S.A.
140 C2 **Bowling Green** *OH* U.S.A.
136 C1 **Bowman** U.S.A.
101 D3 **Boxberg** Ger.
100 B2 **Boxtel** Neth.
80 B1 **Boyabat** Turkey
71 B3 **Boyang** China
97 B2 **Boyle** Rep. of Ireland
97 C2 **Boyne** *r.* Rep. of Ireland
136 B2 **Boysen Reservoir** U.S.A.
152 B3 **Boyuibe** Bol.
111 C3 **Bozburun** Turkey
111 C3 **Bozcaada** *i.* Turkey
111 C3 **Bozdağ** *mt.* Turkey
111 C3 **Boz Dağları** *mts* Turkey
111 C3 **Bozdoğan** Turkey
134 D1 **Bozeman** U.S.A.
118 B2 **Bozoum** C.A.R.
111 D3 **Bozüyük** Turkey
109 C2 **Brač** *i.* Croatia
130 C2 **Bracebridge** Can.
131 D2 **Brachet, Lac au** *l.* Can.
99 C3 **Bracknell** U.K.
109 C2 **Bradano** *r.* Italy
143 D3 **Bradenton** U.S.A.
98 C2 **Bradford** U.K.
141 D2 **Bradford** U.S.A.
139 D2 **Brady** U.S.A.
96 C2 **Braemar** U.K.
106 B1 **Braga** Port.
151 D2 **Bragança** Brazil
106 B1 **Bragança** Port.
155 C2 **Bragança Paulista** Brazil
89 D3 **Brahin** Belarus
73 C3 **Brahmapur** India
62 A1 **Brahmaputra** *r.* China/India
110 C1 **Brăila** Romania
137 E1 **Brainerd** U.S.A.
99 D3 **Braintree** U.K.
100 B2 **Braives** Belgium
101 D1 **Brake (Unterweser)** Ger.
100 D1 **Bramsche** Ger.
150 B2 **Branco** *r.* Brazil
101 F1 **Brandenburg** Ger.
129 E3 **Brandon** Can.
97 A2 **Brandon Mountain** Rep. of Ireland
122 B3 **Brandvlei** S. Africa
103 D1 **Braniewo** Pol.
130 B2 **Brantford** Can.
131 D2 **Bras d'Or Lake** Can.
155 D1 **Brasil, Planalto do** *plat.* Brazil
154 C1 **Brasilândia** Brazil
154 C1 **Brasília** Brazil
155 D1 **Brasília de Minas** Brazil
88 C2 **Braslaw** Belarus
110 C1 **Braşov** Romania
103 D2 **Bratislava** Slovakia
83 H3 **Bratsk** Rus. Fed.
102 C2 **Braunau am Inn** Austria
101 E1 **Braunschweig** Ger.
92 □A2 **Brautarholt** Iceland
Bravo del Norte, Río *r.* Mex./U.S.A. *see* **Rio Grande**
135 C4 **Brawley** U.S.A.
97 C2 **Bray** Rep. of Ireland
150 C2 **Brazil** *country* S. America
139 D3 **Brazos** *r.* U.S.A.
118 B3 **Brazzaville** Congo
109 C2 **Brčko** Bos.-Herz.
96 C2 **Brechin** U.K.
100 B2 **Brecht** Belgium
139 D2 **Breckenridge** U.S.A.
103 D2 **Břeclav** Czech Rep.
99 B3 **Brecon** U.K.
99 B3 **Brecon Beacons** *reg.* U.K.
100 B2 **Breda** Neth.
122 B3 **Bredasdorp** S. Africa
102 B2 **Bregenz** Austria
92 H1 **Breivikbotn** Norway
92 E3 **Brekstad** Norway
101 D1 **Bremen** Ger.
101 D1 **Bremerhaven** Ger.
134 B1 **Bremerton** U.S.A.
101 D1 **Bremervörde** Ger.
139 D2 **Brenham** U.S.A.
108 B1 **Brennero** Italy
102 C2 **Brenner Pass** Austria/Italy
99 D3 **Brentwood** U.K.
108 B1 **Brescia** Italy
108 B1 **Bressanone** Italy
96 □ **Bressay** *i.* U.K.
104 B2 **Bressuire** France
88 B3 **Brest** Belarus
104 B2 **Brest** France
142 C3 **Breton Sound** *b.* U.S.A.
151 C2 **Breves** Brazil
53 C1 **Brewarrina** Austr.
134 C1 **Brewster** U.S.A.
89 E2 **Breytovo** Rus. Fed.
109 C1 **Brezovo Polje** *hill* Croatia

118 C2 **Bria** C.A.R.
105 D3 **Briançon** France
90 B2 **Briceni** Moldova
99 B3 **Bridgend** U.K.
141 E2 **Bridgeport** *CT* U.S.A.
136 C2 **Bridgeport** *NE* U.S.A.
147 E3 **Bridgetown** Barbados
131 D2 **Bridgewater** Can.
99 B3 **Bridgwater** U.K.
98 C1 **Bridlington** U.K.
98 C1 **Bridlington Bay** U.K.
105 D2 **Brig** Switz.
134 D2 **Brigham City** U.S.A.
54 B3 **Brighton** N.Z.
99 C3 **Brighton** U.K.
105 D3 **Brignoles** France
101 D2 **Brilon** Ger.
109 C2 **Brindisi** Italy
53 D1 **Brisbane** Austr.
99 B3 **Bristol** U.K.
143 D1 **Bristol** U.S.A.
99 A3 **Bristol Channel** *est.* U.K.
128 B2 **British Columbia** *prov.* Can.
56 C6 **British Indian Ocean Territory** *terr.* Indian Ocean
123 C2 **Brits** S. Africa
122 B3 **Britstown** S. Africa
104 C2 **Brive-la-Gaillarde** France
106 C1 **Briviesca** Spain
103 D2 **Brno** Czech Rep.
143 D2 **Broad** *r.* U.S.A.
130 C1 **Broadback** *r.* Can.
96 C3 **Broad Law** *hill* U.K.
136 B1 **Broadus** U.S.A.
129 D2 **Brochet** Can.
129 D2 **Brochet, Lac** *l.* Can.
101 E1 **Bröckel** Ger.
126 D1 **Brock Island** Can.
130 C2 **Brockville** Can.
127 F2 **Brodeur Peninsula** Can.
96 B3 **Brodick** U.K.
103 D1 **Brodnica** Pol.
90 B1 **Brody** Ukr.
139 D1 **Broken Arrow** U.S.A.
137 D2 **Broken Bow** U.S.A.
52 B2 **Broken Hill** Austr.
99 B2 **Bromsgrove** U.K.
93 E4 **Brønderslev** Denmark
92 F2 **Brønnøysund** Norway
64 A2 **Brooke's Point** Phil.
142 B2 **Brookhaven** U.S.A.
134 B2 **Brookings** *OR* U.S.A.
137 D2 **Brookings** *SD* U.S.A.
129 C2 **Brooks** Can.
126 B2 **Brooks Range** *mts* U.S.A.
143 D3 **Brooksville** U.S.A.
96 B2 **Broom, Loch** *inlet* U.K.
50 B1 **Broome** Austr.
134 B2 **Brothers** U.S.A.
Broughton Island Can. *see* **Qikiqtarjuaq**
90 C1 **Brovary** Ukr.
139 C2 **Brownfield** U.S.A.
128 C3 **Browning** U.S.A.
142 C1 **Brownsville** *TN* U.S.A.
139 D3 **Brownsville** *TX* U.S.A.
139 D2 **Brownwood** U.S.A.
92 □A2 **Brú** Iceland
104 C1 **Bruay-la-Bussière** France
140 B1 **Bruce Crossing** U.S.A.
103 D2 **Bruck an der Mur** Austria
Bruges Belgium *see* **Brugge**
100 A2 **Brugge** Belgium
128 C2 **Brûlé** Can.
151 D3 **Brumado** Brazil
93 F3 **Brumunddal** Norway
61 C1 **Brunei** *country* Asia
102 C2 **Brunico** Italy
101 D1 **Brunsbüttel** Ger.
143 D2 **Brunswick** *GA* U.S.A.
141 F2 **Brunswick** *ME* U.S.A.
53 D1 **Brunswick Head** Austr.
136 C2 **Brush** U.S.A.
100 B2 **Brussels** Belgium
Bruxelles Belgium *see* **Brussels**
139 D2 **Bryan** U.S.A.
89 D3 **Bryansk** Rus. Fed.
91 D2 **Bryn'kovskaya** Rus. Fed.
91 D2 **Bryukhovetskaya** Rus. Fed.
103 D1 **Brzeg** Pol.
114 A3 **Buba** Guinea-Bissau
80 B2 **Bucak** Turkey
150 A1 **Bucaramanga** Col.
53 C3 **Buchan** Austr.
114 A4 **Buchanan** Liberia
110 C2 **Bucharest** Romania
101 D1 **Bucholz in der Nordheide** Ger.
110 C1 **Bucin, Pasul** *pass* Romania
101 D1 **Bückeburg** Ger.
138 A2 **Buckeye** U.S.A.
96 C2 **Buckhaven** U.K.
96 C2 **Buckie** U.K.
51 C1 **Buckingham Bay** Austr.
51 D2 **Buckland Tableland** *reg.* Austr.
52 A2 **Buckleboo** Austr.
141 F2 **Bucksport** U.S.A.
București Romania *see* **Bucharest**
89 D3 **Buda-Kashalyova** Belarus
103 D2 **Budapest** Hungary
75 B2 **Budaun** India
108 A2 **Buddusò** *Sardinia* Italy
99 A3 **Bude** U.K.
87 D4 **Budennovsk** Rus. Fed.
89 D2 **Budogoshch'** Rus. Fed.
108 A2 **Budoni** *Sardinia* Italy
118 A2 **Buea** Cameroon
144 B2 **Buenaventura** Mex.
106 C1 **Buendia, Embalse de** *resr* Spain
155 D1 **Buenópolis** Brazil
153 C4 **Buenos Aires** Arg.
153 A5 **Buenos Aires, Lago** *l.* Arg./Chile
141 D2 **Buffalo** *NY* U.S.A.
136 C1 **Buffalo** *SD* U.S.A.
136 B2 **Buffalo** *WY* U.S.A.
129 D2 **Buffalo Narrows** Can.
122 A2 **Buffels** *watercourse* S. Africa
110 C2 **Buftea** Romania
103 E1 **Bug** *r.* Pol.
61 C2 **Bugel, Tanjung** *pt* Indon.
109 C2 **Bugojno** Bos.-Herz.
64 A2 **Bugsuk** *i.* Phil.
87 E3 **Buguruslan** Rus. Fed.
110 C1 **Buhuși** Romania
99 B2 **Builth Wells** U.K.
69 D1 **Buir Nur** *l.* Mongolia
120 A3 **Buitepos** Namibia
109 D2 **Bujanovac** Serb. and Mont.
119 C3 **Bujumbura** Burundi
69 D1 **Bukachacha** Rus. Fed.
119 C3 **Bukavu** Dem. Rep. Congo
76 C3 **Bukhara** Uzbek.
60 B2 **Bukittinggi** Indon.
119 D3 **Bukoba** Tanz.
53 D2 **Bulahdelah** Austr.
121 B3 **Bulawayo** Zimbabwe
111 C3 **Buldan** Turkey
123 D2 **Bulembu** Swaziland
69 C1 **Bulgan** Mongolia
110 C2 **Bulgaria** *country* Europe
54 B2 **Buller** *r.* N.Z.
52 B1 **Bulloo Downs** Austr.
122 A1 **Büllsport** Namibia
58 C3 **Bulukumba** Indon.
118 B3 **Bulungu** Dem. Rep. Congo
118 C2 **Bumba** Dem. Rep. Congo
62 A1 **Bumhkang** Myanmar
118 B3 **Buna** Dem. Rep. Congo
50 A3 **Bunbury** Austr.
97 C1 **Buncrana** Rep. of Ireland
119 D3 **Bunda** Tanz.
51 E2 **Bundaberg** Austr.
53 D2 **Bundarra** Austr.
74 B2 **Bundi** India
97 B1 **Bundoran** Rep. of Ireland
53 C3 **Bungendore** Austr.
67 B4 **Bungo-suidō** *sea chan.* Japan
119 D2 **Bunia** Dem. Rep. Congo
118 C3 **Bunianga** Dem. Rep. Congo
63 B2 **Buôn Mê Thuôt** Vietnam
119 D3 **Bura** Kenya
75 C1 **Burang** China
117 C4 **Burao** Somalia
78 B2 **Buraydah** Saudi Arabia
100 D2 **Burbach** Ger.
80 B2 **Burdur** Turkey
117 B3 **Burē** Eth.
99 D2 **Bure** *r.* U.K.
110 C2 **Burgas** Bulg.
101 E1 **Burg bei Magdeburg** Ger.
101 E1 **Burgdorf** *Niedersachsen* Ger.
101 E1 **Burgdorf** *Niedersachsen* Ger.
131 E2 **Burgeo** Can.
123 D1 **Burgersfort** S. Africa
100 A2 **Burgh-Haamstede** Neth.
145 C2 **Burgos** Mex.
106 C1 **Burgos** Spain
111 C3 **Burhaniye** Turkey
74 B2 **Burhanpur** India
101 D1 **Burhave (Butjadingen)** Ger.
131 E2 **Burin** Can.
151 D2 **Buriti Bravo** Brazil
155 C1 **Buritis** Brazil
51 C1 **Burketown** Austr.
114 B3 **Burkina** *country* Africa
134 D2 **Burley** U.S.A.
136 C3 **Burlington** *CO* U.S.A.
137 E2 **Burlington** *IA* U.S.A.
143 E1 **Burlington** *NC* U.S.A.
141 E2 **Burlington** *VT* U.S.A.
Burma *country* Asia *see* **Myanmar**
134 B2 **Burney** U.S.A.
51 D4 **Burnie** Austr.
98 B2 **Burnley** U.K.
134 C2 **Burns** U.S.A.
128 B2 **Burns Lake** Can.
77 E2 **Burqin** China
52 A2 **Burra** Austr.
109 D2 **Burrel** Albania
97 B2 **Burren** *reg.* Rep. of Ireland
53 C2 **Burrendong Reservoir** Austr.
53 C2 **Burren Junction** Austr.
107 C2 **Burriana** Spain
53 C2 **Burrinjuck Reservoir** Austr.
144 B2 **Burro, Serranías del** *mts* Mex.
111 C2 **Bursa** Turkey
116 B2 **Būr Safājah** Egypt
Būr Sa'īd Egypt *see* **Port Said**
130 C1 **Burton, Lac** *l.* Can.
97 B1 **Burtonport** Rep. of Ireland
99 C2 **Burton upon Trent** U.K.
59 C3 **Buru** *i.* Indon.
119 C3 **Burundi** *country* Africa
119 C3 **Bururi** Burundi
91 C1 **Buryn'** Ukr.
76 B2 **Burynshyk** Kazakh.
99 D2 **Bury St Edmunds** U.K.
118 C3 **Busanga** Dem. Rep. Congo
79 C2 **Būshehr** Iran
119 D3 **Bushenyi** Uganda

118 C2 **Businga** Dem. Rep. Congo
50 A3 **Busselton** Austr.
139 C3 **Bustamante** Mex.
64 A1 **Busuanga** Phil.
118 C2 **Buta** Dem. Rep. Congo
119 C3 **Butare** Rwanda
123 C2 **Butha-Buthe** Lesotho
140 D2 **Butler** U.S.A.
59 C3 **Buton** *i.* Indon.
134 D1 **Butte** U.S.A.
60 B1 **Butterworth** Malaysia
96 A1 **Butt of Lewis** *hd* U.K.
129 E2 **Button Bay** Can.
64 B2 **Butuan** Phil.
91 E1 **Buturlinovka** Rus. Fed.
75 C2 **Butwal** Nepal
101 D2 **Butzbach** Ger.
117 C4 **Buulobarde** Somalia
117 C5 **Buur Gaabo** Somalia
117 C4 **Buurhabaka** Somalia
101 D1 **Buxtehude** Ger.
89 F2 **Buy** Rus. Fed.
87 D4 **Buynaksk** Rus. Fed.
111 C3 **Büyükmenderes** *r.* Turkey
110 C1 **Buzău** Romania
121 C2 **Búzi** Moz.
87 E3 **Buzuluk** Rus. Fed.
110 C2 **Byala** Bulg.
88 C3 **Byalynichy** Belarus
88 D3 **Byarezina** *r.* Belarus
88 B3 **Byaroza** Belarus
103 D1 **Bydgoszcz** Pol.
88 C3 **Byerazino** Belarus
88 C2 **Byeshankovichy** Belarus
89 D3 **Bykhaw** Belarus
127 F2 **Bylot Island** Can.
53 C2 **Byrock** Austr.
53 D1 **Byron Bay** Austr.
83 J2 **Bytantay** *r.* Rus. Fed.
103 D1 **Bytom** Pol.
103 D1 **Bytów** Pol.

C

154 B2 **Caarapó** Brazil
64 B1 **Cabanatuan** Phil.
117 C3 **Cabdul Qaadir** Somalia
106 B2 **Cabeza del Buey** Spain
152 B2 **Cabezas** Bol.
150 A1 **Cabimas** Venez.
120 A1 **Cabinda** Angola
118 B3 **Cabinda** *prov.* Angola
155 D2 **Cabo Frio** Brazil
155 D2 **Cabo Frio, Ilha do** *i.* Brazil
130 C2 **Cabonga, Réservoir** *resr* Can.
51 E2 **Caboolture** Austr.
150 A2 **Cabo Pantoja** Peru
144 A1 **Caborca** Mex.
131 D2 **Cabot Strait** Can.
155 D1 **Cabral, Serra do** *mts* Brazil
107 D2 **Cabrera** *i.* Spain
129 D2 **Cabri** Can.
107 C2 **Cabriel** *r.* Spain
152 C3 **Caçador** Brazil
109 D2 **Čačak** Serb. and Mont.
108 A2 **Caccia, Capo** *c.* *Sardinia* Italy
151 C3 **Cáceres** Brazil
106 B2 **Cáceres** Spain
128 B2 **Cache Creek** Can.
114 A3 **Cacheu** Guinea-Bissau
151 C2 **Cachimbo, Serra do** *hills* Brazil
154 B1 **Cachoeira Alta** Brazil
155 D2 **Cachoeiro de Itapemirim** Brazil
114 A3 **Cacine** Guinea-Bissau
120 A2 **Cacolo** Angola
154 B1 **Caçu** Brazil
103 D2 **Čadca** Slovakia
101 D1 **Cadenberge** Ger.
145 B2 **Cadereyta** Mex.
140 B2 **Cadillac** U.S.A.
106 B2 **Cádiz** Spain
106 B2 **Cádiz, Golfo de** *g.* Spain
128 C2 **Cadotte Lake** Can.
104 B2 **Caen** France
98 A2 **Caernarfon** U.K.
98 A2 **Caernarfon Bay** U.K.
152 B3 **Cafayate** Arg.
64 B2 **Cagayan de Oro** Phil.
108 B2 **Cagli** Italy
108 A3 **Cagliari** *Sardinia* Italy
108 A3 **Cagliari, Golfo di** *b.* *Sardinia* Italy
97 B3 **Caha Mountains** Rep. of Ireland
97 A3 **Cahermore** Rep. of Ireland
97 A3 **Cahersiveen** Rep. of Ireland
97 C2 **Cahir** Rep. of Ireland
121 C2 **Cahora Bassa, Lago de** *resr* Moz.
97 C2 **Cahore Point** Rep. of Ireland
104 C3 **Cahors** France
90 B2 **Cahul** Moldova
121 C2 **Caia** Moz.
151 C3 **Caiabis, Serra dos** *hills* Brazil
120 B2 **Caianda** Angola
154 B1 **Caiapó, Serra do** *mts* Brazil
154 B1 **Caiapônia** Brazil
147 C2 **Caicos Islands** Turks and Caicos Is
96 C2 **Cairngorm Mountains** U.K.
98 A1 **Cairnryan** U.K.
51 D1 **Cairns** Austr.
116 B1 **Cairo** Egypt
98 C2 **Caistor** U.K.
120 A2 **Caiundo** Angola
150 A2 **Cajamarca** Peru
109 C1 **Čakovec** Croatia
123 C3 **Cala** S. Africa
150 B1 **Calabozo** Venez.
110 B2 **Calafat** Romania
153 A6 **Calafate** Arg.
107 C1 **Calahorra** Spain
104 C1 **Calais** France
141 F1 **Calais** U.S.A.
152 B3 **Calama** Chile
64 A1 **Calamian Group** *is* Phil.
107 C1 **Calamocha** Spain
120 A1 **Calandula** Angola
60 A1 **Calang** Indon.
115 E1 **Calanscio Sand Sea** *des.* Libya
64 B1 **Calapan** Phil.
110 C2 **Călărași** Romania
107 C1 **Calatayud** Spain
64 B1 **Calayan** *i.* Phil.
64 B1 **Calbayog** Phil.
151 E2 **Calcanhar, Ponta do** *pt* Brazil
151 C1 **Calçoene** Brazil
Calcutta India *see* **Kolkata**
106 B2 **Caldas da Rainha** Port.
154 C1 **Caldas Novas** Brazil
152 A3 **Caldera** Chile
134 C2 **Caldwell** U.S.A.
123 C3 **Caledon** *r.* Lesotho/S. Africa
122 A3 **Caledon** S. Africa
153 B5 **Caleta Olivia** Arg.
98 A1 **Calf of Man** *i.* Isle of Man
128 C2 **Calgary** Can.
150 A1 **Cali** Col.
73 B3 **Calicut** India
135 D3 **Caliente** U.S.A.
135 B2 **California** *state* U.S.A.
144 A1 **California, Golfo de** *g.* Mex.
135 B3 **California Aqueduct** *canal* U.S.A.
122 B3 **Calitzdorp** S. Africa
145 C2 **Calkiní** Mex.
52 B1 **Callabonna, Lake** *salt flat* Austr.
96 B2 **Callander** U.K.
150 A3 **Callao** Peru
108 B3 **Caltagirone** *Sicily* Italy
108 B3 **Caltanissetta** *Sicily* Italy
120 A2 **Caluquembe** Angola
117 D3 **Caluula** Somalia
105 D3 **Calvi** *Corsica* France
107 D2 **Calvià** Spain
144 B2 **Calvillo** Mex.
122 A3 **Calvinia** S. Africa
109 C2 **Calvo, Monte** *mt.* Italy
144 B2 **Camacho** Mex.
120 A2 **Camacupa** Angola
146 C2 **Camagüey** Cuba
150 A3 **Camana** Peru
154 B1 **Camapuã** Brazil
145 C2 **Camargo** Mex.
63 B3 **Ca Mau** Vietnam
63 B2 **Cambodia** *country* Asia
99 A3 **Camborne** U.K.
105 C1 **Cambrai** France
99 B2 **Cambrian Mountains** U.K.
54 C1 **Cambridge** N.Z.
99 D2 **Cambridge** U.K.
141 E2 **Cambridge** *MA* U.S.A.
141 D3 **Cambridge** *MD* U.S.A.
137 E1 **Cambridge** *MN* U.S.A.
140 C2 **Cambridge** *OH* U.S.A.
131 D1 **Cambrien, Lac** *l.* Can.
53 D2 **Camden** Austr.
142 B2 **Camden** *AR* U.S.A.
141 F2 **Camden** *ME* U.S.A.
118 B2 **Cameroon** *country* Africa
151 D2 **Cametá** Brazil
64 B1 **Camiguin** *i.* Phil.
152 B3 **Camiri** Bol.
151 D2 **Camocim** Brazil
51 C1 **Camooweal** Austr.
63 A3 **Camorta** *i.* India
153 A5 **Campana, Isla** *i.* Chile
122 B2 **Campbell** S. Africa
54 B2 **Campbell, Cape** N.Z.
128 B2 **Campbell River** Can.
140 B3 **Campbellsville** U.S.A.
131 D2 **Campbellton** Can.
96 B3 **Campbeltown** U.K.
145 C3 **Campeche** Mex.
145 C3 **Campeche, Bahía de** *g.* Mex.
52 B3 **Camperdown** Austr.
110 C1 **Câmpina** Romania
151 E2 **Campina Grande** Brazil
154 C2 **Campinas** Brazil
154 C1 **Campina Verde** Brazil
108 B2 **Campobasso** Italy
155 C2 **Campo Belo** Brazil
154 C1 **Campo Florido** Brazil
152 B3 **Campo Gallo** Arg.
154 B2 **Campo Grande** Brazil
151 D2 **Campo Maior** Brazil
106 B2 **Campo Maior** Port.
154 B2 **Campo Mourão** Brazil
155 D2 **Campos** Brazil
155 C1 **Campos Altos** Brazil
155 C2 **Campos do Jordão** Brazil
110 C1 **Câmpulung** Romania
138 A2 **Camp Verde** U.S.A.
63 B2 **Cam Ranh** Vietnam
128 C2 **Camrose** Can.

129 D2 **Camsell Portage** Can.
111 C2 **Çan** Turkey
126 E2 **Canada** *country* N. America
139 C1 **Canadian** U.S.A.
139 D1 **Canadian** *r.* U.S.A.
111 C2 **Çanakkale** Turkey
144 A1 **Cananea** Mex.
154 C2 **Cananéia** Brazil
Canarias, Islas *terr.* N. Atlantic Ocean *see* Canary Islands
114 A2 **Canary Islands** *terr.* N. Atlantic Ocean
155 C1 **Canastra, Serra da** *mts* Brazil
144 B2 **Canatlán** Mex.
143 D3 **Canaveral, Cape** U.S.A.
155 E1 **Canavieiras** Brazil
53 C3 **Canberra** Austr.
145 D2 **Cancún** Mex.
111 C3 **Çandarlı** Turkey
145 C3 **Candelaria** Mex.
129 D2 **Candle Lake** *l.* Can.
120 A2 **Cangamba** Angola
106 B1 **Cangas del Narcea** Spain
152 C4 **Canguçu** Brazil
70 B2 **Cangzhou** China
131 D1 **Caniapiscau** Can.
131 D1 **Caniapiscau** *r.* Can.
131 C1 **Caniapiscau, Lac** *l.* Can.
108 B3 **Canicattì** *Sicily* Italy
151 E2 **Canindé** Brazil
144 B2 **Cañitas de Felipe Pescador** Mex.
80 B1 **Çankırı** Turkey
128 C2 **Canmore** Can.
96 A2 **Canna** *i.* U.K.
73 B3 **Cannanore** India
105 D3 **Cannes** France
99 B2 **Cannock** U.K.
53 C3 **Cann River** Austr.
152 C3 **Canoas** Brazil
129 D2 **Canoe Lake** *l.* Can.
154 B3 **Canoinhas** Brazil
136 B3 **Canon City** U.S.A.
129 D2 **Canora** Can.
53 C2 **Canowindra** Austr.
106 C1 **Cantábrica, Cordillera** *mts* Spain
106 B1 **Cantábrico, Mar** *sea* Spain
99 D3 **Canterbury** U.K.
54 B2 **Canterbury Bight** *b.* N.Z.
54 B2 **Canterbury Plains** N.Z.
63 B2 **Cân Thơ** Vietnam
151 D2 **Canto do Buriti** Brazil
Canton China *see* Guangzhou
142 C2 **Canton** *MS* U.S.A.
140 C2 **Canton** *OH* U.S.A.
139 C1 **Canyon** U.S.A.
134 D1 **Canyon Ferry Lake** U.S.A.
62 B1 **Cao Băng** Vietnam
154 C2 **Capão Bonito** Brazil
155 D2 **Caparaó, Serra do** *mts* Brazil
51 D4 **Cape Barren Island** Austr.
52 A3 **Cape Borda** Austr.
131 D2 **Cape Breton Island** Can.
114 B4 **Cape Coast** Ghana
141 E2 **Cape Cod Bay** U.S.A.
127 F2 **Cape Dorset** Can.
143 E2 **Cape Fear** *r.* U.S.A.
137 F3 **Cape Girardeau** U.S.A.
155 D1 **Capelinha** Brazil
100 B2 **Capelle aan de IJssel** Neth.
120 A1 **Capenda-Camulemba** Angola
122 A3 **Cape Town** S. Africa
112 B2 **Cape Verde** *country* N. Atlantic Ocean
51 D1 **Cape York Peninsula** Austr.
147 C3 **Cap-Haïtien** Haiti
151 D2 **Capim** *r.* Brazil
58 D1 **Capitol Hill** N. Mariana Is
109 C2 **Čapljina** Bos.-Herz.
109 B3 **Capo d'Orlando** *Sicily* Italy
108 A2 **Capraia, Isola di** *i.* Italy
108 A2 **Caprara, Punta** *pt Sardinia* Italy
108 B2 **Capri, Isola di** *i.* Italy
120 B2 **Caprivi Strip** *reg.* Namibia
150 B2 **Caquetá** *r.* Col.
110 B2 **Caracal** Romania
150 B1 **Caracas** Venez.
151 D2 **Caracol** Brazil
155 C2 **Caraguatatuba** Brazil
153 A4 **Carahue** Chile
155 D1 **Caraí** Brazil
155 D2 **Carangola** Brazil
110 B1 **Caransebeş** Romania
131 D2 **Caraquet** Can.
146 B3 **Caratasca, Laguna** *lag.* Hond.
155 D1 **Caratinga** Brazil
150 B2 **Carauari** Brazil
107 C2 **Caravaca de la Cruz** Spain
155 E1 **Caravelas** Brazil
129 E3 **Carberry** Can.
144 A2 **Carbó** Mex.
108 A3 **Carbonara, Capo** *c. Sardinia* Italy
136 B3 **Carbondale** *CO* U.S.A.
140 B3 **Carbondale** *IL* U.S.A.
131 E2 **Carbonear** Can.
155 D1 **Carbonita** Brazil
107 C2 **Carcaixent** Spain
104 C3 **Carcassonne** France
128 A1 **Carcross** Can.
145 C3 **Cárdenas** Mex.
99 B3 **Cardiff** U.K.
99 A2 **Cardigan** U.K.
99 A2 **Cardigan Bay** U.K.
128 C3 **Cardston** Can.
110 B1 **Carei** Romania
104 B2 **Carentan** France
50 B2 **Carey, Lake** *salt flat* Austr.
155 D2 **Cariacica** Brazil
146 B3 **Caribbean Sea** N. Atlantic Ocean
141 F1 **Caribou** U.S.A.
130 B1 **Caribou Lake** Can.
128 C2 **Caribou Mountains** Can.
144 B2 **Carichic** Mex.
100 B3 **Carignan** France
53 C2 **Carinda** Austr.
107 C1 **Cariñena** Spain
130 C2 **Carleton Place** Can.
123 C2 **Carletonville** S. Africa
97 C1 **Carlingford Lough** *inlet* Rep. of Ireland/U.K.
98 B1 **Carlisle** U.K.
141 D2 **Carlisle** U.S.A.
155 D1 **Carlos Chagas** Brazil
97 C2 **Carlow** Rep. of Ireland
135 C4 **Carlsbad** *CA* U.S.A.
138 C2 **Carlsbad** *NM* U.S.A.
129 D3 **Carlyle** Can.
128 A1 **Carmacks** Can.
129 E3 **Carman** Can.
99 A3 **Carmarthen** U.K.
99 A3 **Carmarthen Bay** U.K.
104 C3 **Carmaux** France
145 C3 **Carmelita** Guat.
144 A2 **Carmen, Isla** *i.* Mex.
104 B2 **Carnac** France
122 B3 **Carnarvon** S. Africa
97 C1 **Carndonagh** Rep. of Ireland
50 B2 **Carnegie, Lake** *salt flat* Austr.
96 B2 **Carn Eighe** *mt.* U.K.
63 A3 **Car Nicobar** *i.* India
118 B2 **Carnot** C.A.R.
52 A2 **Carnot, Cape** Austr.
97 C2 **Carnsore Point** Rep. of Ireland
151 D2 **Carolina** Brazil
59 D2 **Caroline Islands** N. Pacific Ocean
103 D2 **Carpathian Mountains** Europe
110 B1 **Carpații Meridionali** *mts* Romania
51 C1 **Carpentaria, Gulf of** Austr.
105 D3 **Carpentras** France
97 B3 **Carrantuohill** *mt.* Rep. of Ireland
105 E3 **Carrara** Italy
97 C2 **Carrickmacross** Rep. of Ireland
97 B2 **Carrick-on-Shannon** Rep. of Ireland
97 C2 **Carrick-on-Suir** Rep. of Ireland
137 D1 **Carrington** U.S.A.
139 D3 **Carrizo Springs** U.S.A.
138 B2 **Carrizozo** U.S.A.
137 E2 **Carroll** U.S.A.
143 C2 **Carrollton** U.S.A.
129 D2 **Carrot River** Can.
135 C3 **Carson City** U.S.A.
150 A1 **Cartagena** Col.
107 C2 **Cartagena** Spain
146 B4 **Cartago** Costa Rica
137 E3 **Carthage** *MO* U.S.A.
139 E2 **Carthage** *TX* U.S.A.
131 E1 **Cartwright** Can.
151 E2 **Caruarú** Brazil
114 B1 **Casablanca** Morocco
154 C2 **Casa Branca** Brazil
144 B1 **Casa de Janos** Mex.
138 A2 **Casa Grande** U.S.A.
108 A1 **Casale Monferrato** Italy
109 C2 **Casarano** Italy
134 C2 **Cascade** U.S.A.
134 B2 **Cascade Range** *mts* Can./U.S.A.
106 B2 **Cascais** Port.
154 B2 **Cascavel** Brazil
108 B2 **Caserta** Italy
117 D3 **Caseyr, Raas** *c.* Somalia
97 C2 **Cashel** Rep. of Ireland
53 D1 **Casino** Austr.
107 C1 **Caspe** Spain
136 B2 **Casper** U.S.A.
81 C1 **Caspian Sea** Asia/Europe
154 C2 **Cássia** Brazil
128 B2 **Cassiar** Can.
128 A2 **Cassiar Mountains** Can.
154 B1 **Cassilândia** Brazil
108 B2 **Cassino** Italy
96 B2 **Cassley** *r.* U.K.
151 D2 **Castanhal** Brazil
152 B4 **Castaño** *r.* Arg.
144 B2 **Castaños** Mex.
104 C3 **Casteljaloux** France
107 C2 **Castelló de la Plana** Spain
106 B2 **Castelo Branco** Port.
108 B3 **Castelvetrano** *Sicily* Italy
52 B3 **Casterton** Austr.
108 B2 **Castiglione della Pescaia** Italy
97 B2 **Castlebar** Rep. of Ireland
96 A2 **Castlebay** U.K.
97 C1 **Castleblayney** Rep. of Ireland
97 C1 **Castlederg** U.K.
96 C3 **Castle Douglas** U.K.
128 C3 **Castlegar** Can.
97 B2 **Castleisland** Rep. of Ireland
52 B3 **Castlemaine** Austr.

97 B2 **Castlerea** Rep. of Ireland
53 C2 **Castlereagh** *r.* Austr.
136 C3 **Castle Rock** U.S.A.
129 C2 **Castor** Can.
104 C3 **Castres** France
100 B1 **Castricum** Neth.
147 D3 **Castries** St Lucia
154 C2 **Castro** Brazil
153 A5 **Castro** Chile
106 B2 **Castro Verde** Port.
109 C3 **Castrovillari** Italy
150 A2 **Catacaos** Peru
155 D2 **Cataguases** Brazil
154 C1 **Catalão** Brazil
152 B3 **Catamarca** Arg.
64 B1 **Catanduanes** *i.* Phil.
154 C2 **Catanduva** Brazil
154 B3 **Catanduvas** Brazil
109 C3 **Catania** *Sicily* Italy
109 C3 **Catanzaro** Italy
64 B1 **Catarman** Phil.
64 B1 **Catbalogan** Phil.
145 C3 **Catemaco** Mex.
147 C2 **Cat Island** Bahamas
130 A1 **Cat Lake** *l.* Can.
145 D2 **Catoche, Cabo** *c.* Mex.
141 E2 **Catskill Mountains** U.S.A.
64 B2 **Cauayan** Phil.
150 A1 **Cauca** *r.* Col.
151 E2 **Caucaia** Brazil
81 C1 **Caucasus** *mts* Asia/Europe
100 A2 **Caudry** France
109 C3 **Caulonia** Italy
131 D2 **Causapscal** Can.
105 D3 **Cavaillon** France
151 D3 **Cavalcante** Brazil
97 C2 **Cavan** Rep. of Ireland
154 B3 **Cavernoso, Serra do** *mts* Brazil
151 D2 **Caxias** Brazil
152 C3 **Caxias do Sul** Brazil
120 A1 **Caxito** Angola
151 C1 **Cayenne** Fr. Guiana
146 B3 **Cayman Islands** *terr.* West Indies
117 C4 **Caynabo** Somalia
120 B2 **Cazombo** Angola
144 B2 **Ceballos** Mex.
64 B1 **Cebu** Phil.
64 B1 **Cebu** *i.* Phil.
108 B2 **Cecina** Italy
137 F2 **Cedar** *r.* U.S.A.
135 D3 **Cedar City** U.S.A.
137 E2 **Cedar Falls** U.S.A.
129 D2 **Cedar Lake** *l.* Can.
137 E2 **Cedar Rapids** U.S.A.
144 A2 **Cedros, Isla** *i.* Mex.
51 C3 **Ceduna** Austr.
117 C4 **Ceeldheere** Somalia
117 C3 **Ceerigaabo** Somalia
108 B3 **Cefalù** *Sicily* Italy
145 B2 **Celaya** Mex.
Celebes *i.* Indon. *see* **Sulawesi**
156 B5 **Celebes Sea** Indon./Phil.
145 C2 **Celestún** Mex.
101 E1 **Celle** Ger.
95 B3 **Celtic Sea** Rep. of Ireland/U.K.
59 D3 **Cenderawasih, Teluk** *b.* Indon.
150 A1 **Central, Cordillera** *mts* Col.
150 A3 **Central, Cordillera** *mts* Peru
64 B1 **Central, Cordillera** *mts* Phil.
118 C2 **Central African Republic** *country* Africa
74 A2 **Central Brahui Range** *mts* Pak.
137 D2 **Central City** U.S.A.
140 B3 **Centralia** *IL* U.S.A.
134 B1 **Centralia** *WA* U.S.A.
74 A2 **Central Makran Range** *mts* Pak.
59 D3 **Central Range** *mts* P.N.G.
Central Siberian Plateau Rus. Fed. *see* **Sredne-Sibirskoye Ploskogor'ye**
Cephalonia *i.* Greece *see* **Kefallonia**
152 B3 **Ceres** Arg.
154 C1 **Ceres** Brazil
122 A3 **Ceres** S. Africa
104 C3 **Céret** France
106 C1 **Cerezo de Abajo** Spain
109 C2 **Cerignola** Italy
110 C2 **Cernavodă** Romania
145 C2 **Cerralvo** Mex.
144 B2 **Cerralvo, Isla** *i.* Mex.
145 B2 **Cerritos** Mex.
154 C2 **Cerro Azul** Brazil
145 C2 **Cerro Azul** Mex.
150 A3 **Cerro de Pasco** Peru
105 D3 **Cervione** *Corsica* France
106 B1 **Cervo** Spain
108 B2 **Cesena** Italy
88 C2 **Cēsis** Latvia
102 C2 **České Budějovice** Czech Rep.
101 F3 **Český Les** *mts* Czech Rep./Ger.
111 C3 **Çeşme** Turkey
53 D2 **Cessnock** Austr.
109 C2 **Cetinje** Serb. and Mont.
109 C3 **Cetraro** Italy
106 B2 **Ceuta** N. Africa
105 C3 **Cévennes** *mts* France
Ceylon *country* Asia *see* **Sri Lanka**
79 D2 **Chābahār** Iran
75 C1 **Chabyêr Caka** *salt l.* China
150 A2 **Chachapoyas** Peru
89 D3 **Chachersk** Belarus
63 B2 **Chachoengsao** Thai.
115 D3 **Chad** *country* Africa
115 D3 **Chad, Lake** Africa
69 C1 **Chadaasan** Mongolia
68 C1 **Chadan** Rus. Fed.
123 C1 **Chadibe** Botswana
136 C2 **Chadron** U.S.A.
65 B2 **Chaeryŏng** N. Korea
74 A2 **Chagai** Pak.
77 C3 **Chaghcharān** Afgh.
89 E2 **Chagoda** Rus. Fed.
76 B2 **Chagyl** Turkm.
75 C2 **Chaibasa** India
63 B2 **Chainat** Thai.
63 B2 **Chalyaphum** Thai.
152 C4 **Chajarí** Arg.
131 D1 **Chakonipau, Lake** Can.
150 A3 **Chala** Peru
74 A1 **Chalap Dalan** *mts* Afgh.
131 D2 **Chaleur Bay** *inlet* Can.
74 B2 **Chalisgaon** India
111 C3 **Chalki** *i.* Greece
111 B3 **Chalkida** Greece
104 B2 **Challans** France
134 D2 **Challis** U.S.A.
105 C2 **Châlons-en-Champagne** France
105 C2 **Chalon-sur-Saône** France
138 B1 **Chama** U.S.A.
121 C2 **Chama** Zambia
74 A1 **Chaman** Pak.
74 B1 **Chamba** India
74 B2 **Chambal** *r.* India
137 D2 **Chamberlain** U.S.A.
141 D3 **Chambersburg** U.S.A.
105 D2 **Chambéry** France
121 C2 **Chambeshi** Zambia
140 B2 **Champaign** U.S.A.
141 E2 **Champlain, Lake** Can./U.S.A.
145 C3 **Champotón** Mex.
152 A3 **Chañaral** Chile
126 B2 **Chandalar** *r.* U.S.A.
142 C3 **Chandeleur Islands** U.S.A.
74 B1 **Chandigarh** India
138 A2 **Chandler** U.S.A.
75 B3 **Chandrapur** India
63 B2 **Chang, Ko** *i.* Thai.
Chang'an China *see* **Rong'an**
121 C3 **Changane** *r.* Moz.
121 C2 **Changara** Moz.
65 B1 **Changbai** China
65 B1 **Changbai Shan** *mts* China/N. Korea
69 E2 **Changchun** China
71 B3 **Changde** China
65 B2 **Ch'angdo** N. Korea
71 C3 **Changhua** Taiwan
65 B3 **Changhŭng** S. Korea
Chang Jiang *r.* China *see* **Yangtze**
65 B1 **Changjin** N. Korea
65 B1 **Changjin-gang** *r.* N. Korea
71 B3 **Changsha** China
65 B2 **Changsŏng** S. Korea
71 B3 **Changting** China
65 B2 **Ch'angwŏn** S. Korea
70 B2 **Changyuan** China
70 B2 **Changzhi** China
70 B2 **Changzhou** China
111 B3 **Chania** Greece
95 C4 **Channel Islands** Europe
135 C4 **Channel Islands** U.S.A.
131 E2 **Channel-Port-aux-Basques** Can.
63 B2 **Chanthaburi** Thai.
104 C2 **Chantilly** France
137 D3 **Chanute** U.S.A.
82 G3 **Chany, Ozero** *salt l.* Rus. Fed.
71 B3 **Chaoyang** China
Chaoyang China *see* **Huinan**
71 B3 **Chaozhou** China
144 B2 **Chapala, Laguna de** *l.* Mex.
76 B1 **Chapayev** Kazakh.
152 C3 **Chapecó** Brazil
143 E1 **Chapel Hill** U.S.A.
130 B2 **Chapleau** Can.
89 E3 **Chaplygin** Rus. Fed.
91 C2 **Chaplynka** Ukr.
145 B2 **Charcas** Mex.
99 B3 **Chard** U.K.
104 B2 **Charente** *r.* France
77 C3 **Chārīkār** Afgh.
86 E2 **Charkayuvom** Rus. Fed.
100 B2 **Charleroi** Belgium
141 D3 **Charles, Cape** U.S.A.
137 E2 **Charles City** U.S.A.
140 B3 **Charleston** *IL* U.S.A.
143 E2 **Charleston** *SC* U.S.A.
140 C3 **Charleston** *WV* U.S.A.
135 C3 **Charleston Peak** U.S.A.
51 D2 **Charleville** Austr.
105 C2 **Charleville-Mézières** France
143 D1 **Charlotte** U.S.A.
143 D3 **Charlotte Harbor** *b.* U.S.A.
141 D3 **Charlottesville** U.S.A.
131 D2 **Charlottetown** Can.
52 B3 **Charlton** Austr.
130 C1 **Charlton Island** Can.
51 D2 **Charters Towers** Austr.
104 C2 **Chartres** France
128 C2 **Chase** Can.
88 C3 **Chashniki** Belarus
54 A3 **Chaslands Mistake** *c.* N.Z.
65 B1 **Chasŏng** N. Korea
104 B2 **Chassiron, Pointe de** *pt* France

104 B2 **Châteaubriant** France
104 C2 **Château-du-Loir** France
104 C2 **Châteaudun** France
104 B2 **Châteaulin** France
105 D3 **Châteauneuf-les-Martigues** France
104 C2 **Châteauneuf-sur-Loire** France
105 C2 **Château-Thierry** France
128 C2 **Chateh** Can.
100 B2 **Châtelet** Belgium
104 C2 **Châtellerault** France
140 C2 **Chatham** *Ont.* Can.
49 F6 **Chatham Islands** N.Z.
105 C2 **Châtillon-sur-Seine** France
143 D2 **Chattahoochee** *r.* U.S.A.
143 C1 **Chattanooga** U.S.A.
63 B2 **Châu Đốc** Vietnam
62 A1 **Chauk** Myanmar
105 D2 **Chaumont** France
105 C2 **Chauny** France
151 D2 **Chaves** Brazil
106 B1 **Chaves** Port.
130 C1 **Chavigny, Lac** *l.* Can.
89 D3 **Chavusy** Belarus
89 E2 **Chayevo** Rus. Fed.
86 E3 **Chaykovskiy** Rus. Fed.
102 C1 **Cheb** Czech Rep.
87 D3 **Cheboksary** Rus. Fed.
140 C1 **Cheboygan** U.S.A.
65 B2 **Chech'ŏn** S. Korea
62 A2 **Cheduba Island** Myanmar
114 B2 **Chegga** Maur.
134 B1 **Chehalis** U.S.A.
65 B3 **Cheju** S. Korea
65 B3 **Cheju-do** *i.* S. Korea
65 B3 **Cheju-haehyŏp** *sea chan.* S. Korea
89 E2 **Chekhov** Rus. Fed.
134 B1 **Chelan, Lake** U.S.A.
81 D2 **Cheleken** Turkm.
107 D2 **Chélif, Oued** *r.* Alg.
103 E1 **Chełm** Pol.
99 D3 **Chelmer** *r.* U.K.
103 D1 **Chełmno** Pol.
99 D3 **Chelmsford** U.K.
99 B3 **Cheltenham** U.K.
87 F3 **Chelyabinsk** Rus. Fed.
101 F2 **Chemnitz** Ger.
114 B2 **Chenachane** Alg.
70 B1 **Chengde** China
70 A2 **Chengdu** China
71 B4 **Chengmai** China
Chengshou China *see* Yingshan
70 A2 **Chengxian** China
Chengyang China *see* **Juxian**
73 C3 **Chennai** India
71 B3 **Chenzhou** China
99 B3 **Chepstow** U.K.
104 B2 **Cherbourg** France
89 E3 **Cheremisinovo** Rus. Fed.
69 C1 **Cheremkhovo** Rus. Fed.
89 E2 **Cherepovets** Rus. Fed.
91 C2 **Cherkasy** Ukr.
87 D4 **Cherkessk** Rus. Fed.
91 C1 **Chernihiv** Ukr.
91 D2 **Cherninivka** Ukr.
90 B2 **Chernivtsi** Ukr.
90 B1 **Chernyakhiv** Ukr.
88 B3 **Chernyakhovsk** Rus. Fed.
89 E3 **Chernyanka** Rus. Fed.
83 I2 **Chernyshevskiy** Rus. Fed.
137 D2 **Cherokee** U.S.A.
83 K2 **Cherskogo, Khrebet** *mts* Rus. Fed.
91 E2 **Chertkovo** Rus. Fed.
90 A1 **Chervonohrad** Ukr.
88 C3 **Chervyen'** Belarus
89 D3 **Cherykaw** Belarus
141 D3 **Chesapeake Bay** U.S.A.
86 D2 **Cheshskaya Guba** *b.* Rus. Fed.
98 B2 **Chester** U.K.
140 B3 **Chester** *IL* U.S.A.
143 D2 **Chester** *SC* U.S.A.
98 C2 **Chesterfield** U.K.
129 E1 **Chesterfield Inlet** Can.
129 E1 **Chesterfield Inlet** *inlet* Can.
141 F1 **Chesuncook Lake** U.S.A.
131 D2 **Chéticamp** Can.
145 D3 **Chetumal** Mex.
128 B2 **Chetwynd** Can.
98 B1 **Cheviot Hills** U.K.
136 C2 **Cheyenne** U.S.A.
136 C2 **Cheyenne** *r.* U.S.A.
136 C3 **Cheyenne Wells** U.S.A.
75 C2 **Chhapra** India
75 B2 **Chhatarpur** India
71 C3 **Chiai** Taiwan
62 A2 **Chiang Dao** Thai.
62 A2 **Chiang Mai** Thai.
62 A2 **Chiang Rai** Thai.
108 A1 **Chiavenno** Italy
70 B3 **Chibi** China
121 C3 **Chiboma** Moz.
130 C2 **Chibougamau** Can.
123 D1 **Chibuto** Moz.
75 D1 **Chibuzhang Hu** *l.* China
140 B2 **Chicago** U.S.A.
128 A2 **Chichagof Island** U.S.A.
99 C3 **Chichester** U.K.
50 A2 **Chichester Range** *mts* Austr.
139 D1 **Chickasha** U.S.A.
150 A2 **Chiclayo** Peru
153 B5 **Chico** *r.* Arg.
135 B3 **Chico** U.S.A.
131 C2 **Chicoutimi** Can.
108 B2 **Chieti** Italy
145 C3 **Chietla** Mex.
69 D2 **Chifeng** China
155 D1 **Chifre, Serra do** *mts* Brazil
77 D2 **Chiganak** Kazakh.
145 C3 **Chignahuapán** Mex.
121 C3 **Chigubo** Moz.
144 B2 **Chihuahua** Mex.
88 C2 **Chikhachevo** Rus. Fed.
67 C3 **Chikuma-gawa** *r.* Japan
128 B2 **Chilanko** *r.* Can.
74 B1 **Chilas** Jammu and Kashmir
139 C2 **Childress** U.S.A.
153 A4 **Chile** *country* S. America
152 B3 **Chilecito** Arg.
75 C3 **Chilika Lake** India
121 B2 **Chililabombwe** Zambia
128 B2 **Chilko** *r.* Can.
128 B2 **Chilko Lake** Can.
153 A4 **Chillán** Chile
137 E3 **Chillicothe** *MO* U.S.A.
140 C3 **Chillicothe** *OH* U.S.A.
128 B3 **Chilliwack** Can.
153 A5 **Chiloé, Isla de** *i.* Chile
145 C3 **Chilpancingo** Mex.
53 C3 **Chiltern** Austr.
71 C3 **Chilung** Taiwan
119 D3 **Chimala** Tanz.
152 B4 **Chimbas** Arg.
87 E4 **Chimbay** Uzbek.
150 A2 **Chimborazo** *mt.* Ecuador
150 A2 **Chimbote** Peru
Chimkent Kazakh. *see* Shymkent
121 C2 **Chimoio** Moz.
77 C3 **Chimtargha, Qullai** *mt.* Tajik.
68 C2 **China** *country* Asia
145 C2 **China** Mex.
150 A3 **Chincha Alta** Peru
128 C2 **Chinchaga** *r.* Can.
145 D3 **Chinchorro, Banco** *sea feature* Mex.
121 C2 **Chinde** Moz.
65 B3 **Chindo** S. Korea
65 B3 **Chin-do** *i.* S. Korea
68 C2 **Chindu** China
62 A1 **Chindwin** *r.* Myanmar
65 B2 **Chinghwa** N. Korea
120 B2 **Chingola** Zambia
120 A2 **Chinguar** Angola
65 B2 **Chinhae** S. Korea
121 C2 **Chinhoyi** Zimbabwe
74 B1 **Chiniot** Pak.
144 B2 **Chinipas** Mex.
65 B2 **Chinju** S. Korea
118 C2 **Chinko** *r.* C.A.R.
138 B1 **Chinle** U.S.A.
71 B3 **Chinmen** Taiwan
67 C3 **Chino** Japan
104 C2 **Chinon** France
138 A2 **Chino Valley** U.S.A.
121 C2 **Chinsali** Zambia
108 B1 **Chioggia** Italy
111 C3 **Chios** Greece
111 C3 **Chios** *i.* Greece
121 C2 **Chipata** Zambia
120 A2 **Chipindo** Angola
121 C3 **Chipinge** Zimbabwe
73 B3 **Chiplun** India
99 B3 **Chippenham** U.K.
99 C3 **Chipping Norton** U.K.
77 C2 **Chirchik** Uzbek.
121 C3 **Chiredzi** Zimbabwe
138 B2 **Chiricahua Peak** U.S.A.
146 B4 **Chiriquí, Golfo de** *b.* Panama
65 B2 **Chiri-san** *mt.* S. Korea
146 B4 **Chirripo** *mt.* Costa Rica
121 B2 **Chirundu** Zimbabwe
130 C1 **Chisasibi** Can.
137 E1 **Chisholm** U.S.A.
90 B2 **Chişinău** Moldova
87 E3 **Chistopol'** Rus. Fed.
69 D1 **Chita** Rus. Fed.
120 A2 **Chitado** Angola
121 C2 **Chitambo** Zambia
120 B1 **Chitato** Angola
121 C1 **Chitipa** Malawi
73 B3 **Chitradurga** India
74 B1 **Chitral** Pak.
146 B4 **Chitré** Panama
75 D2 **Chittagong** Bangl.
74 B2 **Chittaurgarh** India
121 C2 **Chitungwiza** Zimbabwe
120 B2 **Chiume** Angola
121 C2 **Chivhu** Zimbabwe
153 B4 **Choele Choel** Arg.
144 B2 **Choix** Mex.
103 D1 **Chojnice** Pol.
117 B3 **Ch'ok'ē Mountains** Eth.
83 K2 **Chokurdakh** Rus. Fed.
121 C3 **Chókwé** Moz.
104 B2 **Cholet** France
102 C1 **Chomutov** Czech Rep.
83 I2 **Chona** *r.* Rus. Fed.
65 B2 **Ch'ŏnan** S. Korea
150 A2 **Chone** Ecuador
65 B1 **Ch'ŏngjin** N. Korea
65 B2 **Chŏngju** N. Korea
65 B2 **Chŏngp'yŏng** N. Korea
70 A3 **Chongqing** China
70 A2 **Chongqing** *mun.* China
65 B2 **Chŏngŭp** S. Korea
71 A3 **Chongzuo** China
65 B2 **Chŏnju** S. Korea
154 B3 **Chopimzinho** Brazil
98 B2 **Chorley** U.K.
91 C2 **Chornomors'ke** Ukr.
90 B2 **Chortkiv** Ukr.
65 B2 **Ch'ŏrwŏn** S. Korea

65 B1 **Ch'osan** N. Korea
67 D3 **Chōshi** Japan
103 D1 **Choszczno** Pol.
114 A2 **Choûm** Maur.
69 D1 **Choybalsan** Mongolia
69 D1 **Choyr** Mongolia
54 B2 **Christchurch** N.Z.
99 C3 **Christchurch** U.K.
127 G2 **Christian, Cape** Can.
123 C2 **Christiana** S. Africa
54 A2 **Christina, Mount** N.Z.
48 B4 **Christmas Island** *terr.* Indian Ocean
111 C3 **Chrysi** *i.* Greece
153 B5 **Chubut** *r.* Arg.
90 B1 **Chudniv** Ukr.
89 D2 **Chudovo** Rus. Fed.
Chudskoye Ozero *l.* Estonia/Rus. Fed. *see* Peipus, Lake
126 B2 **Chugach Mountains** U.S.A.
67 B4 **Chūgoku-sanchi** *mts* Japan
66 B2 **Chuguyevka** Rus. Fed.
91 D2 **Chuhuyiv** Ukr.
160 J3 **Chukchi Sea** Rus. Fed./U.S.A.
83 N2 **Chukotskiy Poluostrov** *pen.* Rus. Fed.
135 C4 **Chula Vista** U.S.A.
82 G3 **Chulym** Rus. Fed.
152 B3 **Chumbicha** Arg.
83 K3 **Chumikan** Rus. Fed.
63 A2 **Chumphon** Thai.
65 B2 **Ch'unch'ŏn** S. Korea
Chungking China *see* Chongqing
83 H2 **Chunya** *r.* Rus. Fed.
150 A3 **Chuquibamba** Peru
152 B3 **Chuquicamata** Chile
105 D2 **Chur** Switz.
62 A1 **Churachandpur** India
129 E2 **Churchill** Can.
129 E2 **Churchill** *r. Man.* Can.
131 D1 **Churchill** *r. Nfld.* Can.
129 E2 **Churchill, Cape** Can.
131 D1 **Churchill Falls** Can.
129 D2 **Churchill Lake** Can.
74 B2 **Churu** India
131 C2 **Chute-des-Passes** Can.
62 B1 **Chuxiong** China
90 B2 **Ciadîr-Lunga** Moldova
61 B2 **Ciamis** Indon.
60 B2 **Cianjur** Indon.
154 B2 **Cianorte** Brazil
103 E1 **Ciechanów** Pol.
146 C2 **Ciego de Avila** Cuba
146 B2 **Cienfuegos** Cuba
107 C2 **Cieza** Spain
106 C2 **Cigüela** *r.* Spain
80 B2 **Cihanbeyli** Turkey
144 B3 **Cihuatlán** Mex.
106 C2 **Cíjara, Embalse de** *resr* Spain
61 B2 **Cilacap** Indon.
139 C1 **Cimarron** *r.* U.S.A.
90 B2 **Cimişlia** Moldova
108 B2 **Cimone, Monte** *mt.* Italy
140 C3 **Cincinnati** U.S.A.
111 C3 **Çine** Turkey
100 B2 **Ciney** Belgium
145 C3 **Cintalapa** Mex.
126 B2 **Circle** *AK* U.S.A.
136 B1 **Circle** *MT* U.S.A.
58 B3 **Cirebon** Indon.
99 C3 **Cirencester** U.K.
108 A1 **Ciriè** Italy
109 C3 **Cirò Marina** Italy
109 C2 **Čitluk** Bos.-Herz.
122 A3 **Citrusdal** S. Africa
145 B2 **Ciudad Acuña** Mex.
145 B3 **Ciudad Altamirano** Mex.
150 B1 **Ciudad Bolívar** Venez.
144 B2 **Ciudad Camargo** Mex.
144 A2 **Ciudad Constitución** Mex.
145 C3 **Ciudad del Carmen** Mex.
144 B2 **Ciudad Delicias** Mex.
145 C2 **Ciudad de Valles** Mex.
150 B1 **Ciudad Guayana** Venez.
138 B3 **Ciudad Guerrero** Mex.
144 B3 **Ciudad Guzmán** Mex.
145 C3 **Ciudad Hidalgo** Mex.
145 C3 **Ciudad Ixtepec** Mex.
144 B1 **Ciudad Juárez** Mex.
145 C2 **Ciudad Mante** Mex.
145 C2 **Ciudad Mier** Mex.
144 B2 **Ciudad Obregón** Mex.
106 C2 **Ciudad Real** Spain
145 C2 **Ciudad Río Bravo** Mex.
106 B1 **Ciudad Rodrigo** Spain
145 C2 **Ciudad Victoria** Mex.
107 D1 **Ciutadella de Menorca** Spain
108 B1 **Cividale del Friuli** Italy
108 B2 **Civitanova Marche** Italy
108 B2 **Civitavecchia** Italy
104 C2 **Civray** France
111 C3 **Çivril** Turkey
70 C2 **Cixi** China
99 D3 **Clacton-on-Sea** U.K.
128 C2 **Claire, Lake** Can.
105 C2 **Clamecy** France
122 A3 **Clanwilliam** S. Africa
52 A2 **Clare** Austr.
97 A2 **Clare Island** Rep. of Ireland
141 E2 **Claremont** U.S.A.
97 B2 **Claremorris** Rep. of Ireland
54 B2 **Clarence** N.Z.
131 E2 **Clarenville** Can.
128 C2 **Claresholm** Can.
137 D2 **Clarinda** U.S.A.
123 C3 **Clarkebury** S. Africa
134 C1 **Clark Fork** *r.* U.S.A.
143 D2 **Clark Hill Reservoir** U.S.A.
140 C3 **Clarksburg** U.S.A.
142 B2 **Clarksdale** U.S.A.
142 B1 **Clarksville** *AR* U.S.A.
142 C1 **Clarksville** *TN* U.S.A.
154 B1 **Claro** *r.* Brazil
139 C1 **Clayton** U.S.A.
97 B3 **Clear, Cape** Rep. of Ireland
137 E2 **Clear Lake** U.S.A.
135 B3 **Clear Lake** *l.* U.S.A.
128 C2 **Clearwater** Can.
129 C2 **Clearwater** *r.* Can.
143 D3 **Clearwater** U.S.A.
134 C1 **Clearwater** *r.* U.S.A.
139 D2 **Cleburne** U.S.A.
51 D2 **Clermont** Austr.
105 C2 **Clermont-Ferrand** France
52 A2 **Cleve** Austr.
142 B2 **Cleveland** *MS* U.S.A.
140 C2 **Cleveland** *OH* U.S.A.
143 D1 **Cleveland** *TN* U.S.A.
134 D1 **Cleveland, Mount** U.S.A.
143 D3 **Clewiston** U.S.A.
97 A2 **Clifden** Rep. of Ireland
53 D1 **Clifton** Austr.
138 B2 **Clifton** U.S.A.
128 B2 **Clinton** Can.
137 E2 **Clinton** *IA* U.S.A.
137 E3 **Clinton** *MO* U.S.A.
139 D1 **Clinton** *OK* U.S.A.
96 A2 **Clishham** *hill* U.K.
98 B2 **Clitheroe** U.K.
97 B3 **Clonakilty** Rep. of Ireland
51 D2 **Cloncurry** Austr.
97 C1 **Clones** Rep. of Ireland
97 C2 **Clonmel** Rep. of Ireland
100 D1 **Cloppenburg** Ger.
136 B2 **Cloud Peak** U.S.A.
139 C2 **Clovis** U.S.A.
129 D2 **Cluff Lake Mine** Can.
110 B1 **Cluj-Napoca** Romania
51 C2 **Cluny** Austr.
105 D2 **Cluses** France
54 A3 **Clutha** *r.* N.Z.
96 B3 **Clyde** *r.* U.K.
96 B3 **Clyde, Firth of** *est.* U.K.
96 B3 **Clydebank** U.K.
127 G2 **Clyde River** Can.
144 B3 **Coalcomán** Mex.
135 C3 **Coaldale** U.S.A.
128 B2 **Coal River** Can.
150 B2 **Coari** Brazil
150 B2 **Coari** *r.* Brazil
142 B2 **Coastal Plain** U.S.A.
128 B2 **Coast Mountains** Can.
135 B2 **Coast Ranges** *mts* U.S.A.
96 B3 **Coatbridge** U.K.
127 F2 **Coats Island** Can.
55 R2 **Coats Land** *reg.* Antarctica
145 C3 **Coatzacoalcos** Mex.
146 A3 **Cobán** Guat.
53 C2 **Cobar** Austr.
97 B3 **Cóbh** Rep. of Ireland
152 B2 **Cobija** Bol.
141 D2 **Cobourg** Can.
50 C1 **Cobourg Peninsula** Austr.
53 C3 **Cobram** Austr.
101 E2 **Coburg** Ger.
152 B2 **Cochabamba** Bol.
100 C2 **Cochem** Ger.
73 B4 **Cochin** India
128 C2 **Cochrane** *Alta* Can.
130 B2 **Cochrane** *Ont.* Can.
153 A5 **Cochrane** Chile
52 B2 **Cockburn** Austr.
Cockburn Town Turks and Caicos Is *see* Grand Turk
98 B1 **Cockermouth** U.K.
122 B3 **Cockscomb** *mt.* S. Africa
146 B3 **Coco** *r.* Hond./Nic.
48 A4 **Cocos Islands** *terr.* Indian Ocean
144 B2 **Cocula** Mex.
150 A1 **Cocuy, Sierra Nevada del** *mt.* Col.
141 E2 **Cod, Cape** U.S.A.
108 B2 **Codigoro** Italy
131 D1 **Cod Island** Can.
151 D2 **Codó** Brazil
136 B2 **Cody** U.S.A.
51 D1 **Coen** Austr.
100 C2 **Coesfeld** Ger.
134 C1 **Coeur d'Alene** U.S.A.
123 C3 **Coffee Bay** S. Africa
137 D3 **Coffeyville** U.S.A.
53 D2 **Coffs Harbour** Austr.
104 B2 **Cognac** France
118 A2 **Cogo** Equat. Guinea
52 B3 **Cohuna** Austr.
146 B4 **Coiba, Isla** *i.* Panama
153 A5 **Coihaique** Chile
73 B3 **Coimbatore** India
106 B1 **Coimbra** Port.
52 B3 **Colac** Austr.
155 D1 **Colatina** Brazil
136 C3 **Colby** U.S.A.
99 D3 **Colchester** U.K.
129 C2 **Cold Lake** *l.* Can.
96 C3 **Coldstream** U.K.
139 D2 **Coleman** U.S.A.
52 B3 **Coleraine** Austr.
97 C1 **Coleraine** U.K.
123 C3 **Colesberg** S. Africa
144 B3 **Colima** Mex.
144 B3 **Colima, Nevado de** *vol.* Mex.
96 A2 **Coll** *i.* U.K.
53 C1 **Collarenebri** Austr.

50 B1 **Collier Bay** Austr.
54 B2 **Collingwood** N.Z.
97 B1 **Collooney** Rep. of Ireland
105 D2 **Colmar** France
100 C2 **Cologne** Ger.
154 C2 **Colômbia** Brazil
150 A1 **Colombia** *country* S. America
73 B4 **Colombo** Sri Lanka
104 C3 **Colomiers** France
152 C4 **Colón** Arg.
146 C4 **Colón** Panama
109 C3 **Colonna, Capo** *c.* Italy
96 A2 **Colonsay** *i.* U.K.
153 B4 **Colorado** *r.* Arg.
138 A2 **Colorado** *r.* Mex./U.S.A.
139 D3 **Colorado** *r.* U.S.A.
136 B3 **Colorado** *state* U.S.A.
135 E3 **Colorado Plateau** U.S.A.
136 C3 **Colorado Springs** U.S.A.
144 B2 **Colotlán** Mex.
136 B1 **Colstrip** U.S.A.
137 E3 **Columbia** *MO* U.S.A.
143 D2 **Columbia** *SC* U.S.A.
142 C1 **Columbia** *TN* U.S.A.
134 B1 **Columbia** *r.* U.S.A.
128 C2 **Columbia, Mount** Can.
134 D1 **Columbia Falls** U.S.A.
128 B2 **Columbia Mountains** Can.
134 C1 **Columbia Plateau** U.S.A.
143 D2 **Columbus** *GA* U.S.A.
140 B3 **Columbus** *IN* U.S.A.
142 C2 **Columbus** *MS* U.S.A.
137 D2 **Columbus** *NE* U.S.A.
138 B2 **Columbus** *NM* U.S.A.
140 C3 **Columbus** *OH* U.S.A.
134 C1 **Colville** U.S.A.
126 A2 **Colville** *r.* U.S.A.
126 C2 **Colville Lake** Can.
98 B2 **Colwyn Bay** U.K.
108 B2 **Comacchio** Italy
145 C3 **Comalcalco** Mex.
110 C1 **Comănești** Romania
130 C1 **Comencho, Lac** *l.* Can.
97 C2 **Comeragh Mountains** Rep. of Ireland
75 D2 **Comilla** Bangl.
108 A2 **Comino, Capo** *c. Sardinia* Italy
145 C3 **Comitán de Domínguez** Mex.
104 C2 **Commentry** France
139 D2 **Commerce** U.S.A.
127 F2 **Committee Bay** Can.
108 A1 **Como** Italy
108 A1 **Como, Lago di** *l.* Italy
153 B5 **Comodoro Rivadavia** Arg.
121 D2 **Comoros** *country* Africa
104 C2 **Compiègne** France
144 B2 **Compostela** Mex.
90 B2 **Comrat** Moldova
114 A4 **Conakry** Guinea
155 E1 **Conceição da Barra** Brazil
151 D2 **Conceição do Araguaia** Brazil
155 D1 **Conceição do Mato Dentro** Brazil
152 B3 **Concepción** Arg.
153 A4 **Concepción** Chile
144 B2 **Concepción** Mex.
146 B4 **Concepción** Panama
135 B4 **Conception, Point** U.S.A.
154 C2 **Conchas** Brazil
138 C1 **Conchas Lake** U.S.A.
144 B2 **Conchos** *r. Chihuahua* Mex.
145 C2 **Conchos** *r. Nuevo León/ Tamaulipas* Mex.
135 B3 **Concord** *CA* U.S.A.
141 E2 **Concord** *NH* U.S.A.
152 C4 **Concordia** Arg.
122 A2 **Concordia** S. Africa
137 D3 **Concordia** U.S.A.
53 C2 **Condobolin** Austr.
104 C3 **Condom** France
134 B1 **Condon** U.S.A.
108 B1 **Conegliano** Italy
104 C2 **Confolens** France
118 B3 **Congo** *country* Africa
118 B3 **Congo** *r.* Congo/Dem. Rep. Congo
118 C3 **Congo, Democratic Republic of** *country* Africa
129 C2 **Conklin** Can.
97 B1 **Conn, Lough** *l.* Rep. of Ireland
97 B2 **Connaught** *reg.* Rep. of Ireland
141 E2 **Connecticut** *r.* U.S.A.
141 E2 **Connecticut** *state* U.S.A.
97 B2 **Connemara** *reg.* Rep. of Ireland
134 D1 **Conrad** U.S.A.
139 D2 **Conroe** U.S.A.
155 D2 **Conselheiro Lafaiete** Brazil
155 D1 **Conselheiro Pena** Brazil
98 C1 **Consett** U.K.
63 B3 **Côn Sơn** *i.* Vietnam
110 C2 **Constanța** Romania
106 B2 **Constantina** Spain
115 C1 **Constantine** Alg.
134 D2 **Contact** U.S.A.
150 A2 **Contamana** Peru
153 A6 **Contreras, Isla** *i.* Chile
126 D2 **Contwoyto Lake** Can.
142 B1 **Conway** *AR* U.S.A.
141 E2 **Conway** *NH* U.S.A.
51 C2 **Coober Pedy** Austr.
54 B2 **Cook, Mount** *mt.* N.Z.
143 C1 **Cookeville** U.S.A.
49 G4 **Cook Islands** S. Pacific Ocean
131 E1 **Cook's Harbour** Can.
97 C1 **Cookstown** U.K.
54 B2 **Cook Strait** N.Z.
51 D1 **Cooktown** Austr.
53 C2 **Coolabah** Austr.
53 C2 **Coolamon** Austr.
53 D1 **Coolangatta** Austr.
50 B3 **Coolgardie** Austr.
53 C3 **Cooma** Austr.
52 B2 **Coombah** Austr.
53 C2 **Coonabarabran** Austr.
52 A3 **Coonalpyn** Austr.
53 C2 **Coonamble** Austr.
52 A1 **Cooper Creek** *watercourse* Austr.
134 B2 **Coos Bay** U.S.A.
53 C2 **Cootamundra** Austr.
145 C3 **Copainalá** Mex.
145 C3 **Copala** Mex.
93 F4 **Copenhagen** Denmark
109 C2 **Copertino** Italy
152 A3 **Copiapó** Chile
140 B1 **Copper Harbor** U.S.A.
Coppermine Can. *see* **Kugluktuk**
126 D2 **Coppermine** *r.* Can.
122 B2 **Copperton** S. Africa
152 A3 **Coquimbo** Chile
110 B2 **Corabia** Romania
155 D1 **Coração de Jesus** Brazil
150 A3 **Coracora** Peru
53 D1 **Coraki** Austr.
50 A2 **Coral Bay** Austr.
127 F2 **Coral Harbour** Can.
156 D7 **Coral Sea** S. Pacific Ocean
52 B3 **Corangamite, Lake** Austr.
99 C2 **Corby** U.K.
153 A5 **Corcovado, Golfo de** *sea chan.* Chile
143 D2 **Cordele** U.S.A.
64 B1 **Cordilleras Range** *mts* Phil.
152 B4 **Córdoba** Arg.
145 C3 **Córdoba** Mex.
106 C2 **Córdoba** Spain
153 B4 **Córdoba, Sierras de** *mts* Arg.
111 A3 **Corfu** *i.* Greece
106 B2 **Coria** Spain
142 C2 **Corinth** U.S.A.
155 D1 **Corinto** Brazil
97 B3 **Cork** Rep. of Ireland
111 C2 **Çorlu** Turkey
154 B2 **Cornélio Procópio** Brazil
131 E2 **Corner Brook** Can.
53 C3 **Corner Inlet** *b.* Austr.
135 B3 **Corning** *CA* U.S.A.
141 D2 **Corning** *NY* U.S.A.
Corn Islands *is* Nic. *see* **Maíz, Islas del**
108 B2 **Corno, Monte** *mt.* Italy
130 C2 **Cornwall** Can.
126 E1 **Cornwallis Island** Can.
150 B1 **Coro** Venez.
154 C1 **Coromandel** Brazil
54 C1 **Coromandel Peninsula** N.Z.
129 C2 **Coronation** Can.
126 D2 **Coronation Gulf** Can.
152 C3 **Coronel Oviedo** Para.
153 B4 **Coronel Suárez** Arg.
109 D2 **Çorovodë** Albania
139 D3 **Corpus Christi** U.S.A.
152 B2 **Corque** Bol.
151 D3 **Corrente** Brazil
154 B1 **Correntes** Brazil
151 D3 **Correntina** Brazil
97 B2 **Corrib, Lough** *l.* Rep. of Ireland
152 C3 **Corrientes** Arg.
144 B2 **Corrientes, Cabo** *c.* Mex.
53 C3 **Corryong** Austr.
Corse *i.* France *see* **Corsica**
105 D3 **Corse, Cap** *c. Corsica* France
105 D3 **Corsica** *i.* France
139 D2 **Corsicana** U.S.A.
105 D3 **Corte** *Corsica* France
106 B2 **Cortegana** Spain
136 B3 **Cortez** U.S.A.
108 B1 **Cortina d'Ampezzo** Italy
141 D2 **Cortland** U.S.A.
108 B2 **Cortona** Italy
106 B2 **Coruche** Port.
Çoruh Turkey *see* **Artvin**
80 B1 **Çorum** Turkey
152 C2 **Corumbá** Brazil
154 C1 **Corumbá** *r.* Brazil
134 B2 **Corvallis** U.S.A.
98 B2 **Corwen** U.K.
144 B2 **Cosalá** Mex.
145 C3 **Cosamaloapan** Mex.
109 C3 **Cosenza** Italy
105 C2 **Cosne-Cours-sur-Loire** France
107 C2 **Costa Blanca** *coastal area* Spain
107 D1 **Costa Brava** *coastal area* Spain
106 B2 **Costa del Sol** *coastal area* Spain
146 B3 **Costa de Mosquitos** *coastal area* Nic.
154 B1 **Costa Rica** Brazil
146 B3 **Costa Rica** *country* Central America
144 B2 **Costa Rica** Mex.
110 B2 **Costești** Romania
64 B2 **Cotabato** Phil.
114 B4 **Côte d'Ivoire** *country* Africa
150 A2 **Cotopaxi, Volcán** *vol.* Ecuador
99 B3 **Cotswold Hills** U.K.

134 B2 **Cottage Grove** U.S.A.
102 C1 **Cottbus** Ger.
52 A3 **Coüedic, Cape de** Austr.
137 D2 **Council Bluffs** U.S.A.
88 B2 **Courland Lagoon** *b.* Lith./Rus. Fed.
128 B3 **Courtenay** Can.
104 B2 **Coutances** France
104 B2 **Coutras** France
100 B2 **Couvin** Belgium
99 C2 **Coventry** U.K.
140 C3 **Covington** U.S.A.
50 B3 **Cowan, Lake** *salt flat* Austr.
96 C2 **Cowdenbeath** U.K.
53 C3 **Cowes** Austr.
134 B1 **Cowlitz** *r.* U.S.A.
53 C2 **Cowra** Austr.
154 B1 **Coxim** Brazil
75 D2 **Cox's Bazar** Bangl.
145 B3 **Coyuca de Benitez** Mex.
145 D2 **Cozumel** Mex.
145 D2 **Cozumel, Isla de** *i.* Mex.
123 C3 **Cradock** S. Africa
136 B2 **Craig** U.S.A.
102 C2 **Crailsheim** Ger.
110 B2 **Craiova** Romania
129 D2 **Cranberry Portage** Can.
53 C3 **Cranbourne** Austr.
128 C3 **Cranbrook** Can.
151 D2 **Crateús** Brazil
151 E2 **Crato** Brazil
136 C2 **Crawford** U.S.A.
140 B2 **Crawfordsville** U.S.A.
99 C3 **Crawley** U.K.
134 D1 **Crazy Mountains** U.S.A.
129 D2 **Cree** *r.* Can.
144 B2 **Creel** Mex.
129 D2 **Cree Lake** Can.
100 B1 **Creil** Neth.
105 D2 **Crema** Italy
108 B1 **Cremona** Italy
108 B2 **Cres** *i.* Croatia
134 B2 **Crescent City** U.S.A.
128 C3 **Creston** Can.
137 E2 **Creston** U.S.A.
142 C2 **Crestview** U.S.A.
111 B3 **Crete** *i.* Greece
107 D1 **Creus, Cap de** *c.* Spain
98 B2 **Crewe** U.K.
96 B2 **Crianlarich** U.K.
152 D3 **Criciúma** Brazil
96 C2 **Crieff** U.K.
108 B1 **Crikvenica** Croatia
91 C2 **Crimea** *pen.* Ukr.
101 F2 **Crimmitschau** Ger.
154 C1 **Cristalina** Brazil
101 E1 **Crivitz** Ger.
109 C2 **Crna Gora** *aut. rep.* Serb. and Mont.
109 C1 **Črnomelj** Slovenia
97 B2 **Croagh Patrick** *hill* Rep. of Ireland
109 C1 **Croatia** *country* Europe
61 C1 **Crocker, Banjaran** *mts* Malaysia
139 D2 **Crockett** U.S.A.
59 C3 **Croker Island** Austr.
99 D2 **Cromer** U.K.
54 A3 **Cromwell** N.Z.
137 D1 **Crookston** U.S.A.
53 C2 **Crookwell** Austr.
136 C1 **Crosby** U.S.A.
143 D3 **Cross City** U.S.A.
142 B2 **Crossett** U.S.A.
98 B1 **Cross Fell** *hill* U.K.
129 E2 **Cross Lake** *l.* Can.
143 C1 **Crossville** U.S.A.
109 C3 **Crotone** Italy
99 D3 **Crowborough** U.K.
142 B2 **Crowley** U.S.A.
128 C3 **Crowsnest Pass** Can.
146 C3 **Cruz, Cabo** *c.* Cuba
152 C3 **Cruz Alta** Brazil
152 B4 **Cruz del Eje** Arg.
155 D2 **Cruzeiro** Brazil
150 A2 **Cruzeiro do Sul** Brazil
52 A2 **Crystal Brook** Austr.
139 D3 **Crystal City** U.S.A.
140 B1 **Crystal Falls** U.S.A.
103 E2 **Csongrád** Hungary
120 B2 **Cuando** *r.* Angola/Zambia
120 A2 **Cuangar** Angola
118 B3 **Cuango** *r.* Angola/Dem. Rep. Congo
120 A1 **Cuanza** *r.* Angola
139 C3 **Cuatro Ciénegas** Mex.
144 B2 **Cuauhtémoc** Mex.
145 C3 **Cuautla** Mex.
146 B2 **Cuba** *country* West Indies
120 A2 **Cubal** Angola
120 B2 **Cubango** *r.* Angola/Namibia
150 A1 **Cúcuta** Col.
73 B3 **Cuddalore** India
73 B3 **Cuddapah** India
106 C1 **Cuéllar** Spain
120 A2 **Cuemba** Angola
150 A2 **Cuenca** Ecuador
107 C1 **Cuenca** Spain
107 C1 **Cuenca, Serrania de** *mts* Spain
145 C3 **Cuernavaca** Mex.
139 D3 **Cuero** U.S.A.
151 C3 **Cuiabá** Brazil
151 C3 **Cuiabá** *r.* Brazil
96 A2 **Cuillin Sound** *sea chan.* U.K.
120 A1 **Cuilo** Angola
120 B2 **Cuito** *r.* Angola
120 A2 **Cuito Cuanavale** Angola
60 B1 **Cukai** Malaysia
53 C3 **Culcairn** Austr.
53 C1 **Culgoa** Austr.
144 B2 **Culiacán** Mex.
64 A1 **Culion** *i.* Phil.
107 C2 **Cullera** Spain
142 C2 **Cullman** U.S.A.
97 C1 **Cullybackey** U.K.
151 C3 **Culuene** *r.* Brazil
150 B1 **Cumaná** Venez.
141 D3 **Cumberland** U.S.A.
140 B3 **Cumberland** *r.* U.S.A.
129 D2 **Cumberland Lake** Can.
127 G2 **Cumberland Peninsula** Can.
142 C1 **Cumberland Plateau** U.S.A.
127 G2 **Cumberland Sound** *sea chan.* Can.
96 C3 **Cumbernauld** U.K.
135 B3 **Cummings** U.S.A.
96 B3 **Cumnock** U.K.
144 B1 **Cumpas** Mex.
145 C3 **Cunduacán** Mex.
120 A2 **Cunene** *r.* Angola
108 A2 **Cuneo** Italy
53 C1 **Cunnamulla** Austr.
108 A1 **Cuorgnè** Italy
96 C2 **Cupar** U.K.
147 D3 **Curaçao** *i.* Neth. Antilles
150 A2 **Curaray** *r.* Ecuador
153 A4 **Curicó** Chile
154 C3 **Curitiba** Brazil
52 A2 **Curnamona** Austr.
51 D3 **Currie** Austr.
51 E2 **Curtis Island** Austr.
151 C2 **Curuá** *r.* Brazil
60 B2 **Curup** Indon.
151 D2 **Cururupu** Brazil
155 D1 **Curvelo** Brazil
150 A3 **Cusco** Peru
139 D1 **Cushing** U.S.A.
134 D1 **Cut Bank** U.S.A.
75 C2 **Cuttack** India
101 D1 **Cuxhaven** Ger.
64 B1 **Cuyo Islands** Phil.
Cuzco Peru *see* **Cusco**
119 C3 **Cyangugu** Rwanda
111 B3 **Cyclades** *is* Greece
129 C3 **Cypress Hills** Can.
80 B2 **Cyprus** *country* Asia
102 C2 **Czech Republic** *country* Europe
103 D1 **Czersk** Pol.
103 D1 **Częstochowa** Pol.

D

62 B1 **Đa, Sông** *r.* Vietnam
69 D2 **Daban** China
114 A3 **Dabola** Guinea
Dacca Bangl. *see* **Dhaka**
102 C2 **Dachau** Ger.
74 A2 **Dadu** Pak.
64 B1 **Daet** Phil.
114 A3 **Dagana** Senegal
64 B1 **Dagupan** Phil.
74 B3 **Dahanu** India
69 D2 **Da Hinggan Ling** *mts* China
116 C3 **Dahlak Archipelago** *is* Eritrea
100 C2 **Dahlem** Ger.
60 B2 **Daik** Indon.
106 C2 **Daimiel** Spain
51 C2 **Dajarra** Austr.
114 A3 **Dakar** Senegal
116 A2 **Dākhilah, Wāḥāt ad** *oasis* Egypt
63 A3 **Dakoank** India
88 C3 **Dakol'ka** *r.* Belarus
109 D2 **Đakovica** Serb. and Mont.
109 C1 **Đakovo** Croatia
120 B2 **Dala** Angola
68 C2 **Dalain Hob** China
93 G3 **Dalälven** *r.* Sweden
111 C3 **Dalaman** Turkey
111 C3 **Dalaman** *r.* Turkey
69 C2 **Dalandzadgad** Mongolia
63 B2 **Đa Lat** Vietnam
74 A2 **Dalbandin** Pak.
96 C3 **Dalbeattie** U.K.
51 E2 **Dalby** Austr.
143 C1 **Dale Hollow Lake** U.S.A.
53 C3 **Dalgety** Austr.
139 C1 **Dalhart** U.S.A.
131 D2 **Dalhousie** Can.
62 B1 **Dali** China
70 C2 **Dalian** China
96 C3 **Dalkeith** U.K.
139 D2 **Dallas** U.S.A.
128 A2 **Dall Island** U.S.A.
109 C2 **Dalmacija** *reg.* Croatia
66 C2 **Dal'negorsk** Rus. Fed.
66 B1 **Dal'nerechensk** Rus. Fed.
114 B4 **Daloa** Côte d'Ivoire
51 D2 **Dalrymple, Mount** Austr.
92 □A3 **Dalsmynni** Iceland
75 C2 **Daltenganj** India
143 D2 **Dalton** U.S.A.
60 B1 **Daludalu** Indon.
92 □B2 **Dalvík** Iceland
50 C1 **Daly** *r.* Austr.
51 C1 **Daly Waters** Austr.
74 B2 **Daman** India
80 B2 **Damanhūr** Egypt
59 C3 **Damar** *i.* Indon.
80 B2 **Damascus** Syria
115 D3 **Damaturu** Nigeria
76 B3 **Damāvand, Qolleh-ye** *mt.* Iran
81 D2 **Damghan** Iran

101 D1 **Damme** Ger.
75 B2 **Damoh** India
114 B4 **Damongo** Ghana
59 C3 **Dampir, Selat** *sea chan.* Indon.
75 D1 **Damxung** China
114 B4 **Danané** Côte d'Ivoire
63 B2 **Đa Năng** Vietnam
141 E2 **Danbury** U.S.A.
65 A1 **Dandong** China
146 B3 **Dangriga** Belize
70 B2 **Dangshan** China
89 F2 **Danilov** Rus. Fed.
89 E2 **Danilovskaya Vozvyshennost'** *hills* Rus. Fed.
70 B2 **Danjiangkou** China
89 E3 **Dankov** Rus. Fed.
146 B3 **Danlí** Hond.
101 E1 **Dannenberg (Elbe)** Ger.
54 C2 **Dannevirke** N.Z.
62 B2 **Dan Sai** Thai.
70 B2 **Dantu** China
110 A1 **Danube** *r.* Europe
140 B2 **Danville** *IL* U.S.A.
140 C3 **Danville** *KY* U.S.A.
141 D3 **Danville** *VA* U.S.A.
71 A4 **Danzhou** China
71 B3 **Daoxian** China
114 C3 **Dapaong** Togo
68 C2 **Da Qaidam Zhen** China
69 E1 **Daqing** China
80 B2 **Dar'ā** Syria
79 C2 **Dārāb** Iran
115 D1 **Daraj** Libya
81 D2 **Dārān** Iran
63 B2 **Đa Răng, Sông** *r.* Vietnam
75 C2 **Darbhanga** India
119 D3 **Dar es Salaam** Tanz.
74 B1 **Dargai** Pak.
54 B1 **Dargaville** N.Z.
53 C3 **Dargo** Austr.
69 D1 **Darhan** Mongolia
150 A1 **Darién, Golfo del** *g.* Col.
75 C2 **Darjiling** India
68 C2 **Darlag** China
52 B2 **Darling** *r.* Austr.
53 C1 **Darling Downs** *hills* Austr.
50 A3 **Darling Range** *hills* Austr.
98 C1 **Darlington** U.K.
53 C2 **Darlington Point** Austr.
103 D1 **Darłowo** Pol.
101 D3 **Darmstadt** Ger.
115 E1 **Darnah** Libya
52 B2 **Darnick** Austr.
107 C1 **Daroca** Spain
99 D3 **Dartford** U.K.
99 A3 **Dartmoor** *hills* U.K.
131 D2 **Dartmouth** Can.
99 B3 **Dartmouth** U.K.
59 D3 **Daru** P.N.G.
50 C1 **Darwin** Austr.
76 B2 **Dashoguz** Turkm.
74 A2 **Dasht** *r.* Pak.
61 C1 **Datadian** Indon.
111 C3 **Datça** Turkey
70 B1 **Datong** China
64 B2 **Datu Piang** Phil.
74 B1 **Daud Khel** Pak.
88 B2 **Daugava** *r.* Latvia
88 C2 **Daugavpils** Latvia
100 C2 **Daun** Ger.
129 D2 **Dauphin** Can.
129 E2 **Dauphin Lake** Can.
73 B3 **Davangere** India
64 B2 **Davao** Phil.
64 B2 **Davao Gulf** Phil.
137 E2 **Davenport** U.S.A.
99 C2 **Daventry** U.K.
123 C2 **Daveyton** S. Africa
146 B4 **David** Panama
129 D2 **Davidson** Can.
126 E3 **Davidson Lake** Can.
135 B3 **Davis** U.S.A.
131 D1 **Davis Inlet** Can.
159 F3 **Davis Sea** Antarctica
160 P3 **Davis Strait** Can./Greenland
105 D2 **Davos** Switz.
79 C3 **Dawqah** Oman
126 B2 **Dawson** Can.
143 D2 **Dawson** U.S.A.
128 B2 **Dawson Creek** Can.
128 B2 **Dawsons Landing** Can.
68 C2 **Dawu** China
Dawukou China *see* Shizuishan
104 B3 **Dax** France
68 C2 **Da Xueshan** *mts* China
80 C2 **Dayr az Zawr** Syria
140 C3 **Dayton** U.S.A.
143 D3 **Daytona Beach** U.S.A.
70 B2 **Da Yunhe** *canal* China
70 A2 **Dazhou** China
122 B3 **De Aar** S. Africa
80 B2 **Dead Sea** *salt l.* Asia
71 B3 **De'an** China
152 B4 **Deán Funes** Arg.
128 B2 **Dease Lake** Can.
126 D2 **Dease Strait** Can.
135 C3 **Death Valley** *depr.* U.S.A.
104 C2 **Deauville** France
61 C1 **Debak** *Sarawak* Malaysia
109 D2 **Debar** Macedonia
103 E2 **Debrecen** Hungary
117 B3 **Debre Markos** Eth.
117 B3 **Debre Tabor** Eth.
117 B4 **Debre Zeyit** Eth.
142 C2 **Decatur** *AL* U.S.A.
140 B3 **Decatur** *IL* U.S.A.
73 B3 **Deccan** *plat.* India
102 C1 **Děčín** Czech Rep.
137 E2 **Decorah** U.S.A.
88 C2 **Dedovichi** Rus. Fed.
121 C2 **Dedza** Malawi
98 B2 **Dee** *r. England/Wales* U.K.
96 C2 **Dee** *r. Scotland* U.K.
53 D1 **Deepwater** Austr.
131 E2 **Deer Lake** Can.
134 D1 **Deer Lodge** U.S.A.
140 C2 **Defiance** U.S.A.
68 C2 **Dêgê** China
117 C4 **Degeh Bur** Eth.
102 C2 **Deggendorf** Ger.
91 E2 **Degtevo** Rus. Fed.
75 B1 **Dehra Dun** India
75 C2 **Dehri** India
69 E2 **Dehui** China
100 A2 **Deinze** Belgium
110 B1 **Dej** Romania
140 B2 **De Kalb** U.S.A.
78 A3 **Dekemhare** Eritrea
118 C3 **Dekese** Dem. Rep. Congo
135 C3 **Delano** U.S.A.
135 D3 **Delano Peak** U.S.A.
49 F2 **Delap-Uliga-Djarrit** Marshall Islands
74 A1 **Delārām** Afgh.
123 C2 **Delareyville** S. Africa
129 D2 **Delaronde Lake** Can.
140 C2 **Delaware** U.S.A.
141 D3 **Delaware** *r.* U.S.A.
141 D3 **Delaware** *state* U.S.A.
141 D3 **Delaware Bay** U.S.A.
53 C3 **Delegate** Austr.
105 D2 **Delémont** Switz.
100 B1 **Delft** Neth.
100 C1 **Delfzijl** Neth.
121 D2 **Delgado, Cabo** *c.* Moz.
75 B2 **Delhi** India
60 B2 **Deli** *i.* Indon.
126 C2 **Déline** Can.
101 F2 **Delitzsch** Ger.
107 D2 **Dellys** Alg.
101 D1 **Delmenhorst** Ger.
109 B1 **Delnice** Croatia
83 L1 **De-Longa, Ostrova** *is* Rus. Fed.
129 D3 **Deloraine** Can.
111 B3 **Delphi** Greece
139 C3 **Del Rio** U.S.A.
136 B3 **Delta** *CO* U.S.A.
135 D3 **Delta** *UT* U.S.A.
126 B2 **Delta Junction** U.S.A.
109 D3 **Delvinë** Albania
118 C3 **Demba** Dem. Rep. Congo
117 B4 **Dembī Dolo** Eth.
89 D2 **Demidov** Rus. Fed.
138 B2 **Deming** U.S.A.
111 C3 **Demirci** Turkey
110 C2 **Demirköy** Turkey
102 C1 **Demmin** Ger.
142 C2 **Demopolis** U.S.A.
60 B2 **Dempo, Gunung** *vol.* Indon.
89 D2 **Demyansk** Rus. Fed.
122 B3 **De Naawte** S. Africa
117 C3 **Denakil** *reg.* Eritrea/Eth.
100 B1 **Den Burg** Neth.
100 B2 **Dendermonde** Belgium
70 A1 **Dengkou** China
70 B2 **Dengzhou** China
Den Haag Neth. *see* The Hague
50 A2 **Denham** Austr.
100 B1 **Den Helder** Neth.
52 B3 **Deniliquin** Austr.
134 C2 **Denio** U.S.A.
137 D2 **Denison** *IA* U.S.A.
139 D2 **Denison** *TX* U.S.A.
111 C3 **Denizli** Turkey
53 D2 **Denman** Austr.
50 A3 **Denmark** Austr.
93 E4 **Denmark** *country* Europe
160 Q3 **Denmark Strait** Greenland/Iceland
61 C2 **Denpasar** Indon.
139 D2 **Denton** U.S.A.
50 A3 **D'Entrecasteaux, Point** Austr.
136 B3 **Denver** U.S.A.
75 C2 **Deogarh** *Orissa* India
74 B2 **Deogarh** *Rajasthan* India
75 C2 **Deoghar** India
83 K2 **Deputatskiy** Rus. Fed.
68 C3 **Dêqên** China
142 B2 **De Queen** U.S.A.
74 A2 **Dera Bugti** Pak.
74 B1 **Dera Ghazi Khan** Pak.
74 B1 **Dera Ismail Khan** Pak.
87 D4 **Derbent** Rus. Fed.
50 B1 **Derby** Austr.
99 C2 **Derby** U.K.
97 B2 **Derg, Lough** *l.* Rep. of Ireland
91 D1 **Derhachi** Ukr.
142 B2 **De Ridder** U.S.A.
91 D2 **Derkul** *r.* Rus. Fed./Ukr.
116 B3 **Derudeb** Sudan
122 B3 **De Rust** S. Africa
109 C2 **Derventa** Bos.-Herz.
98 C2 **Derwent** *r.* U.K.
98 B1 **Derwent Water** *l.* U.K.
77 C1 **Derzhavinsk** Kazakh.
152 B2 **Desaguadero** *r.* Bol.
129 D2 **Deschambault Lake** Can.
134 B1 **Deschutes** *r.* U.S.A.
117 B3 **Desē** Eth.
153 B5 **Deseado** Arg.
153 B5 **Deseado** *r.* Arg.
137 E2 **Des Moines** U.S.A.
137 E2 **Des Moines** *r.* U.S.A.

91 C1 **Desna** *r.* Rus. Fed./Ukr.
89 D3 **Desnogorsk** Rus. Fed.
101 F2 **Dessau** Ger.
126 B2 **Destruction Bay** Can.
128 C1 **Detah** Can.
101 D2 **Detmold** Ger.
140 C2 **Detroit** U.S.A.
137 D1 **Detroit Lakes** U.S.A.
100 B2 **Deurne** Neth.
110 B1 **Deva** Romania
100 C1 **Deventer** Neth.
96 C2 **Deveron** *r.* U.K.
103 D2 **Devét Skal** *hill* Czech Rep.
137 D1 **Devil's Lake** U.S.A.
128 A2 **Devil's Paw** *mt.* U.S.A.
99 C3 **Devizes** U.K.
74 B2 **Devli** India
110 C2 **Devnya** Bulg.
128 C2 **Devon** Can.
126 E1 **Devon Island** Can.
51 D4 **Devonport** Austr.
74 B2 **Dewas** India
137 F3 **Dexter** U.S.A.
70 A2 **Deyang** China
59 D3 **Deyong, Tanjung** *pt* Indon.
81 C2 **Dezfūl** Iran
70 B2 **Dezhou** China
79 C2 **Dhahran** Saudi Arabia
75 D2 **Dhaka** Bangl.
78 B3 **Dhamār** Yemen
75 C2 **Dhamtari** India
75 C2 **Dhanbad** India
75 C2 **Dhankuta** Nepal
62 A1 **Dharmanagar** India
75 C2 **Dharmjaygarh** India
73 B3 **Dharwad** India
74 B2 **Dhasa** India
78 B3 **Dhubāb** Yemen
74 B2 **Dhule** India
144 A1 **Diablo, Picacho del** *mt.* Mex.
51 C2 **Diamantina** *watercourse* Austr.
155 D1 **Diamantina** Brazil
151 D3 **Diamantina, Chapada** *plat.* Brazil
151 C3 **Diamantino** Brazil
71 B3 **Dianbai** China
151 D3 **Dianópolis** Brazil
114 B4 **Dianra** Côte d'Ivoire
114 C3 **Diapaga** Burkina
79 C2 **Dibā al Ḥiṣn** U.A.E.
118 C3 **Dibaya** Dem. Rep. Congo
62 A1 **Dibrugarh** India
136 C1 **Dickinson** U.S.A.
142 C1 **Dickson** U.S.A.
Dicle *r.* Turkey *see* **Tigris**
105 D3 **Die** France
129 D2 **Diefenbaker, Lake** Can.
114 B3 **Diéma** Mali
62 B2 **Diên Châu** Vietnam
101 D1 **Diepholz** Ger.
104 C2 **Dieppe** France
115 D3 **Diffa** Niger
131 D2 **Digby** Can.
105 D3 **Digne-les-Bains** France
105 C2 **Digoin** France
64 B2 **Digos** Phil.
59 D3 **Digul** *r.* Indon.
Dihang *r.* China/India *see* **Brahmaputra**
105 D2 **Dijon** France
117 C3 **Dikhil** Djibouti
111 C3 **Dikili** Turkey
100 A2 **Diksmuide** Belgium
115 D3 **Dikwa** Nigeria
117 B4 **Dīla** Eth.
59 C3 **Dili** East Timor
101 D2 **Dillenburg** Ger.
134 D1 **Dillon** U.S.A.
118 C4 **Dilolo** Dem. Rep. Congo
62 A1 **Dimapur** India
Dimashq Syria *see* **Damascus**
52 B3 **Dimboola** Austr.
110 C2 **Dimitrovgrad** Bulg.
87 D3 **Dimitrovgrad** Rus. Fed.
64 B1 **Dinagat** *i.* Phil.
104 B2 **Dinan** France
100 B2 **Dinant** Belgium
111 D3 **Dinar** Turkey
81 D2 **Dīnār, Kūh-e** *mt.* Iran
73 B3 **Dindigul** India
123 D1 **Dindiza** Moz.
101 E2 **Dingelstädt** Ger.
97 A2 **Dingle** Rep. of Ireland
97 A2 **Dingle Bay** Rep. of Ireland
96 B2 **Dingwall** U.K.
70 A2 **Dingxi** China
75 C2 **Dinngyê** China
154 B3 **Dionísio Cerqueira** Brazil
114 A3 **Diourbel** Senegal
64 B2 **Dipolog** Phil.
74 B1 **Dir** Pak.
51 D1 **Direction, Cape** Austr.
117 C4 **Dirē Dawa** Eth.
120 B2 **Dirico** Angola
50 A2 **Dirk Hartog Island** Austr.
53 C1 **Dirranbandi** Austr.
78 B3 **Ḍirs** Saudi Arabia
50 B2 **Disappointment, Lake** *salt flat* Austr.
52 B3 **Discovery Bay** *b.* Austr.
143 E1 **Dismal Swamp** U.S.A.
99 D2 **Diss** U.K.
108 B3 **Dittaino** *r. Sicily* Italy
74 B2 **Diu** India
155 D2 **Divinópolis** Brazil
87 D4 **Divnoye** Rus. Fed.
114 B4 **Divo** Côte d'Ivoire
80 B2 **Divriği** Turkey
140 B2 **Dixon** U.S.A.
128 A2 **Dixon Entrance** *sea chan.* Can./U.S.A.
80 C2 **Diyarbakır** Turkey
74 A2 **Diz** Pak.
115 D2 **Djado** Niger
115 D2 **Djado, Plateau du** Niger
118 B3 **Djambala** Congo
115 C2 **Djanet** Alg.
115 C1 **Djelfa** Alg.
119 C2 **Djéma** C.A.R.
114 B3 **Djenné** Mali
114 B3 **Djibo** Burkina
117 C3 **Djibouti** *country* Africa
117 C3 **Djibouti** Djibouti
114 C4 **Djougou** Benin
92 □C3 **Djúpivogur** Iceland
91 E1 **Dmitriyevka** Rus. Fed.
89 E3 **Dmitriyev-L'govskiy** Rus. Fed.
89 E2 **Dmitrov** Rus. Fed.
Dnepr *r.* Rus. Fed. *see* **Dnieper**
91 C2 **Dnieper** *r.* Europe
Dnipro *r.* Ukr. *see* **Dnieper**
91 C2 **Dniprodzerzhyns'k** Ukr.
91 D2 **Dnipropetrovs'k** Ukr.
91 C2 **Dniprorudne** Ukr.
90 B2 **Dnister** *r.* Ukr.
88 C2 **Dno** Rus. Fed.
115 D4 **Doba** Chad
88 B2 **Dobele** Latvia
101 F2 **Döbeln** Ger.
59 C3 **Doberai, Jazirah** *pen.* Indon.
59 C3 **Dobo** Indon.
109 C2 **Doboj** Bos.-Herz.
110 C2 **Dobrich** Bulg.
89 F3 **Dobrinka** Rus. Fed.
89 E3 **Dobroye** Rus. Fed.
89 D3 **Dobrush** Belarus
155 E1 **Doce** *r.* Brazil
145 B2 **Doctor Arroyo** Mex.
144 B2 **Doctor Belisario Domínguez** Mex.
111 C3 **Dodecanese** *is* Greece
Dodekanisos *is* Greece *see* Dodecanese
136 C3 **Dodge City** U.S.A.
119 D3 **Dodoma** Tanz.
100 C2 **Doetinchem** Neth.
59 C3 **Dofa** Indon.
75 C1 **Dogai Coring** *salt l.* China
128 B2 **Dog Creek** Can.
67 B3 **Dōgo** *i.* Japan
115 C3 **Dogondoutchi** Niger
81 C2 **Doğubeyazıt** Turkey
79 C2 **Doha** Qatar
62 A2 **Doi Saket** Thai.
100 B1 **Dokkum** Neth.
88 C3 **Dokshytsy** Belarus
91 D2 **Dokuchayevs'k** Ukr.
59 D3 **Dolak, Pulau** *i.* Indon.
131 C2 **Dolbeau** Can.
104 B2 **Dol-de-Bretagne** France
105 D2 **Dole** France
99 B2 **Dolgellau** U.K.
89 E3 **Dolgorukovo** Rus. Fed.
89 E3 **Dolgoye** Rus. Fed.
Dolisie Congo *see* **Loubomo**
108 B1 **Dolomiti** *mts* Italy
117 C4 **Dolo Odo** Eth.
126 D2 **Dolphin and Union Strait** Can.
90 A2 **Dolyna** Ukr.
102 C2 **Domažlice** Czech Rep.
93 E3 **Dombås** Norway
103 D2 **Dombóvár** Hungary
128 B2 **Dome Creek** Can.
147 D3 **Dominica** *country* West Indies
147 C3 **Dominican Republic** *country* West Indies
89 E2 **Domodedovo** Rus. Fed.
111 B3 **Domokos** Greece
61 C2 **Dompu** Indon.
89 E3 **Don** *r.* Rus. Fed.
96 C2 **Don** *r.* U.K.
97 D1 **Donaghadee** U.K.
52 B3 **Donald** Austr.
Donau *r.* Austria/Ger. *see* **Danube**
102 C2 **Donauwörth** Ger.
106 B2 **Don Benito** Spain
98 C2 **Doncaster** U.K.
120 A1 **Dondo** Angola
121 C2 **Dondo** Moz.
73 C4 **Dondra Head** *hd* Sri Lanka
97 B1 **Donegal** Rep. of Ireland
97 B1 **Donegal Bay** Rep. of Ireland
91 D2 **Donets'k** Ukr.
91 D2 **Donets'kyy Kryazh** *hills* Rus. Fed./Ukr.
50 A2 **Dongara** Austr.
62 B1 **Dongchuan** China
71 A4 **Dongfang** China
66 B1 **Dongfanghong** China
58 B3 **Donggala** Indon.
65 A2 **Donggang** China
62 B2 **Đông Ha** Vietnam
Dong Hai *sea* N. Pacific Ocean *see* **East China Sea**
62 B2 **Đông Hôi** Vietnam
118 B2 **Dongou** Congo
71 B3 **Dongshan** China
70 B2 **Dongsheng** China
70 C2 **Dongtai** China
71 B3 **Dongting Hu** *l.* China
Dong Ujimqin Qi China *see* **Uliastai**
70 B2 **Dongying** China
54 B1 **Donnellys Crossing** N.Z.

107 C1 **Donostia - San Sebastián** Spain
117 C4 **Dooxo Nugaaleed** *val.* Somalia
99 B3 **Dorchester** U.K.
122 A1 **Dordabis** Namibia
104 B2 **Dordogne** *r.* France
100 B2 **Dordrecht** Neth.
123 C3 **Dordrecht** S. Africa
129 D2 **Doré Lake** *l.* Can.
101 D1 **Dorfmark** Ger.
114 B3 **Dori** Burkina
122 A3 **Doring** *r.* S. Africa
96 B2 **Dornoch** U.K.
96 B2 **Dornoch Firth** *est.* U.K.
89 D3 **Dorogobuzh** Rus. Fed.
90 B2 **Dorohoi** Romania
68 C1 **Döröö Nuur** *salt l.* Mongolia
92 G3 **Dorotea** Sweden
50 A2 **Dorre Island** Austr.
53 D2 **Dorrigo** Austr.
118 B2 **Dorsale Camerounaise** *slope* Cameroon/Nigeria
100 C2 **Dortmund** Ger.
100 C2 **Dortmund-Ems-Kanal** *canal* Ger.
153 B5 **Dos Bahías, Cabo** *c.* Arg.
101 F1 **Dosse** *r.* Ger.
114 C3 **Dosso** Niger
143 C2 **Dothan** U.S.A.
101 D1 **Dötlingen** Ger.
105 C1 **Douai** France
118 A2 **Douala** Cameroon
104 B2 **Douarnenez** France
114 B3 **Douentza** Mali
98 A1 **Douglas** Isle of Man
122 B2 **Douglas** S. Africa
128 A2 **Douglas** *AK* U.S.A.
138 B2 **Douglas** *AZ* U.S.A.
143 D2 **Douglas** *GA* U.S.A.
136 B2 **Douglas** *WY* U.S.A.
104 C1 **Doullens** France
154 B1 **Dourada, Serra** *hills* Brazil
154 B2 **Dourados** Brazil
154 B2 **Dourados, Serra dos** *hills* Brazil
106 B1 **Douro** *r.* Port.
99 D3 **Dover** U.K.
141 D3 **Dover** U.S.A.
95 D3 **Dover, Strait of** France/U.K.
141 F1 **Dover-Foxcroft** U.S.A.
79 C2 **Dowlatābād** *Būshehr* Iran
79 C2 **Dowlatābād** *Kermān* Iran
97 D1 **Downpatrick** U.K.
77 C3 **Dowshī** Afgh.
67 B3 **Dōzen** *is* Japan
130 C2 **Dozois, Réservoir** *resr* Can.
154 B2 **Dracena** Brazil
100 C1 **Drachten** Neth.
110 B2 **Drăgănești-Olt** Romania
110 B2 **Drăgășani** Romania
88 C3 **Drahichyn** Belarus
123 C2 **Drakensberg** *mts* Lesotho/S. Africa
123 C2 **Drakensberg** *mts* S. Africa
158 B8 **Drake Passage** S. Atlantic Ocean
111 B2 **Drama** Greece
93 F4 **Drammen** Norway
109 C1 **Drava** *r.* Europe
128 C2 **Drayton Valley** Can.
101 D2 **Dreieich** Ger.
111 B3 **Drepano, Akra** *pt* Greece
102 C1 **Dresden** Ger.
104 C2 **Dreux** France
100 B1 **Driemond** Neth.
109 C2 **Drina** *r.* Bos.-Herz./Serb. and Mont.
109 C2 **Drniš** Croatia
110 B2 **Drobeta-Turnu Severin** Romania
101 D1 **Drochtersen** Ger.
97 C2 **Drogheda** Rep. of Ireland
90 A2 **Drohobych** Ukr.
97 C1 **Dromore** U.K.
74 B1 **Drosh** Pak.
53 C3 **Drouin** Austr.
128 C2 **Drumheller** Can.
140 C1 **Drummond Island** U.S.A.
131 C2 **Drummondville** Can.
88 B3 **Druskininkai** Lith.
91 D2 **Druzhkivka** Ukr.
88 D2 **Druzhnaya Gorka** Rus. Fed.
130 A2 **Dryden** Can.
50 B1 **Drysdale** *r.* Austr.
78 A2 **Ḍubā** Saudi Arabia
79 C2 **Dubai** U.A.E.
129 D1 **Dubawnt Lake** Can.
Dubayy U.A.E. *see* **Dubai**
78 A2 **Dubbagh, Jabal ad** *mt.* Saudi Arabia
53 C2 **Dubbo** Austr.
97 C2 **Dublin** Rep. of Ireland
143 D2 **Dublin** U.S.A.
90 B1 **Dubno** Ukr.
141 D2 **Du Bois** U.S.A.
114 A4 **Dubréka** Guinea
109 C2 **Dubrovnik** Croatia
90 B1 **Dubrovytsya** Ukr.
89 D3 **Dubrowna** Belarus
137 E2 **Dubuque** U.S.A.
129 D2 **Duck Bay** Can.
63 B2 **Đức Trọng** Vietnam
101 E2 **Duderstadt** Ger.
82 G2 **Dudinka** Rus. Fed.
99 B2 **Dudley** U.K.
106 B1 **Duero** *r.* Spain
131 C1 **Duffreboy, Lac** *l.* Can.
96 C2 **Dufftown** U.K.
109 C2 **Dugi Rat** Croatia
100 C2 **Duisburg** Ger.
123 D1 **Duiwelskloof** S. Africa
123 C3 **Dukathole** S. Africa
79 C2 **Dukhān** Qatar
89 D2 **Dukhovshchina** Rus. Fed.
Dukou China *see* **Panzhihua**
88 C2 **Dūkštas** Lith.
68 C2 **Dulan** China
152 B4 **Dulce** *r.* Arg.
100 C2 **Dülmen** Ger.
110 C2 **Dulovo** Bulg.
137 E1 **Duluth** U.S.A.
64 B2 **Dumaguete** Phil.
60 B1 **Dumai** Indon.
64 B1 **Dumaran** *i.* Phil.
142 B2 **Dumas** *AR* U.S.A.
139 C1 **Dumas** *TX* U.S.A.
96 B3 **Dumbarton** U.K.
103 D2 **Ďumbier** *mt.* Slovakia
96 C3 **Dumfries** U.K.
55 J3 **Dumont d'Urville Sea** Antarctica
116 B1 **Dumyāṭ** Egypt
Duna *r.* Hungary *see* **Danube**
Dunaj *r.* Slovakia *see* **Danube**
103 D2 **Dunakeszi** Hungary
Dunărea *r.* Romania *see* **Danube**
110 C1 **Dunării, Delta** Romania
103 D2 **Dunaújváros** Hungary
Dunav *r.* Serb. and Mont. *see* **Danube**
90 B2 **Dunayivtsi** Ukr.
96 C2 **Dunbar** U.K.
96 C1 **Dunbeath** U.K.
128 B3 **Duncan** Can.
139 D2 **Duncan** U.S.A.
96 C1 **Duncansby Head** *hd* U.K.
97 C1 **Dundalk** Rep. of Ireland
97 C2 **Dundalk Bay** Rep. of Ireland
Dundas Greenland *see* **Uummannaq**
123 D2 **Dundee** S. Africa
96 C2 **Dundee** U.K.
97 D1 **Dundrum Bay** U.K.
54 B3 **Dunedin** N.Z.
96 C2 **Dunfermline** U.K.
97 C1 **Dungannon** U.K.
74 B2 **Dungarpur** India
97 C2 **Dungarvan** Rep. of Ireland
99 D3 **Dungeness** *hd* U.K.
97 C1 **Dungiven** U.K.
53 D2 **Dungog** Austr.
119 C2 **Dungu** Dem. Rep. Congo
60 B1 **Dungun** Malaysia
116 B2 **Dungunab** Sudan
69 E2 **Dunhua** China
68 C2 **Dunhuang** China
Dunkerque France *see* Dunkirk
104 C1 **Dunkirk** France
141 D2 **Dunkirk** U.S.A.
97 C2 **Dún Laoghaire** Rep. of Ireland
97 D1 **Dunmurry** U.K.
96 C1 **Dunnet Head** *hd* U.K.
96 C3 **Duns** U.K.
99 C3 **Dunstable** U.K.
110 B2 **Dupnitsa** Bulg.
136 C1 **Dupree** U.S.A.
50 B1 **Durack** *r.* Austr.
144 B2 **Durango** Mex.
106 C1 **Durango** Spain
136 B3 **Durango** U.S.A.
139 D2 **Durant** U.S.A.
153 C4 **Durazno** Uru.
123 D2 **Durban** S. Africa
104 C3 **Durban-Corbières** France
122 A3 **Durbanville** S. Africa
100 B2 **Durbuy** Belgium
100 C2 **Düren** Ger.
98 C1 **Durham** U.K.
143 E1 **Durham** U.S.A.
60 B1 **Duri** Indon.
109 C2 **Durmitor** *mt.* Serb. and Mont.
96 B1 **Durness** U.K.
109 C2 **Durrës** Albania
97 A3 **Dursey Island** Rep. of Ireland
111 C3 **Dursunbey** Turkey
59 D3 **D'Urville, Tanjung** *pt* Indon.
54 B2 **D'Urville Island** N.Z.
71 A3 **Dushan** China
77 C3 **Dushanbe** Tajik.
100 C2 **Düsseldorf** Ger.
71 A3 **Duyun** China
91 D2 **Dvorichna** Ukr.
74 A2 **Dwarka** India
123 C1 **Dwarsberg** S. Africa
134 C1 **Dworshak Reservoir** U.S.A.
89 D3 **Dyat'kovo** Rus. Fed.
96 C2 **Dyce** U.K.
127 G2 **Dyer, Cape** Can.
142 C1 **Dyersburg** U.S.A.
103 D2 **Dyje** *r.* Austria/Czech Rep.
103 D1 **Dylewska Góra** *hill* Pol.
91 D2 **Dymytrov** Ukr.
123 C3 **Dyoki** S. Africa
87 E3 **Dyurtyuli** Rus. Fed.
69 D2 **Dzamïn Üüd** Mongolia
Dzhambul Kazakh. *see* **Taraz**
81 D1 **Dzhanga** Turkm.
76 B2 **Dzhangala** Kazakh.
91 C2 **Dzhankoy** Ukr.
77 C2 **Dzhizak** Uzbek.
91 D3 **Dzhubga** Rus. Fed.
83 K3 **Dzhugdzhur, Khrebet** *mts* Rus. Fed.
77 D2 **Dzhungarskiy Alatau, Khrebet** *mts* China/Kazakh.
76 C2 **Dzhusaly** Kazakh.
103 E1 **Działdowo** Pol.

69 D1 **Dzuunmod** Mongolia
88 C3 **Dzyarzhynsk** Belarus
88 C3 **Dzyatlavichy** Belarus

E

131 E1 **Eagle** *r.* Can.
134 C1 **Eagle Cap** *mt.* U.S.A.
130 A2 **Eagle Lake** *l.* Can.
134 B2 **Eagle Lake** *l.* U.S.A.
139 C3 **Eagle Pass** U.S.A.
126 B2 **Eagle Plain** Can.
130 A1 **Ear Falls** Can.
99 D3 **Eastbourne** U.K.
156 C3 **East China Sea** N. Pacific Ocean
54 B1 **East Coast Bays** N.Z.
99 D2 **East Dereham** U.K.
129 D3 **Eastend** Can.
148 B4 **Easter Island** *i.* S. Pacific Ocean
123 C3 **Eastern Cape** *prov.* S. Africa
Eastern Desert *des.* Egypt *see* **Aş Şaḩrā' ash Sharqīyah**
73 B3 **Eastern Ghats** *mts* India
129 E2 **Easterville** Can.
153 C6 **East Falkland** *i.* Falkland Is
100 C1 **East Frisian Islands** *is* Ger.
96 B3 **East Kilbride** U.K.
99 C3 **Eastleigh** U.K.
140 C2 **East Liverpool** U.S.A.
123 C3 **East London** S. Africa
130 C1 **Eastmain** Can.
130 C1 **Eastmain** *r.* Can.
143 D2 **Eastman** U.S.A.
140 A3 **East St Louis** U.S.A.
East Sea N. Pacific Ocean *see* **Japan, Sea of**
83 K2 **East Siberian Sea** Rus. Fed.
59 C3 **East Timor** *country* Asia
140 A2 **Eau Claire** U.S.A.
59 D2 **Eauripik** *atoll* Micronesia
145 C2 **Ebano** Mex.
99 B3 **Ebbw Vale** U.K.
102 C1 **Eberswalde-Finow** Ger.
109 C2 **Eboli** Italy
118 B2 **Ebolowa** Cameroon
107 D1 **Ebro** *r.* Spain
114 C1 **Ech Chélif** Alg.
144 A2 **Echeverria, Pico** *mt.* Mex.
129 E2 **Echoing** *r.* Can.
100 C3 **Echternach** Lux.
52 B3 **Echuca** Austr.
106 B2 **Écija** Spain
102 B1 **Eckernförde** Ger.
127 F2 **Eclipse Sound** *sea chan.* Can.
150 A2 **Ecuador** *country* S. America
116 C3 **Ed** Eritrea
117 A3 **Ed Da'ein** Sudan
117 B3 **Ed Damazin** Sudan
116 B3 **Ed Damer** Sudan
116 B3 **Ed Debba** Sudan
116 B3 **Ed Dueim** Sudan
51 D4 **Eddystone Point** Austr.
100 B1 **Ede** Neth.
118 B2 **Edéa** Cameroon
154 C1 **Edéia** Brazil
53 C3 **Eden** Austr.
98 B1 **Eden** *r.* U.K.
123 C2 **Edenburg** S. Africa
97 C2 **Edenderry** Rep. of Ireland
52 B3 **Edenhope** Austr.
111 B2 **Edessa** Greece
82 C1 **Edgeøya** *i.* Svalbard
139 D3 **Edinburg** U.S.A.
96 C3 **Edinburgh** U.K.
110 C2 **Edirne** Turkey
128 C2 **Edmonton** Can.
131 D2 **Edmundston** Can.
111 C3 **Edremit** Turkey
111 C3 **Edremit Körfezi** *b.* Turkey
128 C2 **Edson** Can.
119 C3 **Edward, Lake** Dem. Rep. Congo/Uganda
139 C2 **Edwards Plateau** *TX* U.S.A.
100 C1 **Eenrum** Neth.
140 B3 **Effingham** U.S.A.
135 C3 **Egan Range** *mts* U.S.A.
103 E2 **Eger** Hungary
93 E4 **Egersund** Norway
92 □C2 **Egilsstaðir** Iceland
80 B2 **Eğirdir** Turkey
80 B2 **Eğirdir Gölü** *l.* Turkey
104 C2 **Égletons** France
Egmont, Mt *vol.* N.Z. *see* **Taranaki, Mount**
83 M2 **Egvekinot** Rus. Fed.
116 A2 **Egypt** *country* Africa
68 C2 **Ehen Hudag** China
100 C1 **Eibergen** Neth.
100 C2 **Eifel** *hills* Ger.
96 A2 **Eigg** *i.* U.K.
73 B4 **Eight Degree Channel** India/Maldives
50 B1 **Eighty Mile Beach** Austr.
101 F2 **Eilenburg** Ger.
101 D2 **Einbeck** Ger.
100 B2 **Eindhoven** Neth.
150 B2 **Eirunepé** Brazil
120 B2 **Eiseb** *watercourse* Namibia
101 E2 **Eisenach** Ger.
102 C1 **Eisenhüttenstadt** Ger.
103 D2 **Eisenstadt** Austria
101 E2 **Eisleben Lutherstadt** Ger.
107 D2 **Eivissa** Spain
Eivissa *i.* Spain *see* **Ibiza**
107 C1 **Ejea de los Caballeros** Spain
121 □D3 **Ejeda** Madag.
Ejin Qi China *see* **Dalain Hob**
93 H4 **Ekenäs** Fin.
77 D1 **Ekibastuz** Kazakh.
92 J2 **Ekostrovskaya Imandra, Ozero** *l.* Rus. Fed.
93 F4 **Eksjö** Sweden
122 A2 **Eksteenfontein** S. Africa
130 B1 **Ekwan** *r.* Can.
62 A2 **Ela** Myanmar
123 C2 **Elandsdoorn** S. Africa
111 B3 **Elassona** Greece
80 B3 **Elat** Israel
80 B2 **Elazığ** Turkey
108 B2 **Elba, Isola d'** *i.* Italy
150 A1 **El Banco** Col.
109 D2 **Elbasan** Albania
150 B1 **El Baúl** Venez.
114 C1 **El Bayadh** Alg.
101 D1 **Elbe** *r.* Ger.
136 B3 **Elbert, Mount** U.S.A.
143 D2 **Elberton** U.S.A.
104 C2 **Elbeuf** France
80 B2 **Elbistan** Turkey
103 D1 **Elbląg** Pol.
87 D4 **El'brus** *mt.* Rus. Fed.
Elburz Mountains Iran *see* **Alborz, Reshteh-ye**
150 B1 **El Callao** Venez.
139 D3 **El Campo** U.S.A.
135 C4 **El Centro** U.S.A.
152 B2 **El Cerro** Bol.
107 C2 **Elche-Elx** Spain
107 C2 **Elda** Spain
137 E3 **Eldon** U.S.A.
144 B2 **El Dorado** Mex.
142 B2 **El Dorado** *AR* U.S.A.
137 D3 **El Dorado** *KS* U.S.A.
114 B2 **El Eglab** *plat.* Alg.
106 C2 **El Ejido** Spain
89 E2 **Elektrostal'** Rus. Fed.
150 A2 **El Encanto** Col.
146 C2 **Eleuthera** *i.* Bahamas
117 A3 **El Fasher** Sudan
144 B2 **El Fuerte** Mex.
117 A3 **El Geneina** Sudan
116 B3 **El Geteina** Sudan
96 C2 **Elgin** U.K.
140 B2 **Elgin** U.S.A.
115 C1 **El Goléa** Alg.
144 A1 **El Golfo de Santa Clara** Mex.
119 D2 **Elgon, Mount** Uganda
114 A2 **El Ḥammâmi** *reg.* Maur.
114 A2 **El Hierro** *i.* Canary Is
145 C2 **El Higo** Mex.
114 C2 **El Homr** Alg.
87 D4 **Elista** Rus. Fed.
141 E2 **Elizabeth** U.S.A.
143 E1 **Elizabeth City** U.S.A.
140 B3 **Elizabethtown** U.S.A.
114 B1 **El Jadida** Morocco
103 E1 **Ełk** Pol.
139 D1 **Elk City** U.S.A.
128 C2 **Elkford** Can.
140 B2 **Elkhart** U.S.A.
El Khartum Sudan *see* **Khartoum**
110 C2 **Elkhovo** Bulg.
140 D3 **Elkins** U.S.A.
128 C3 **Elko** Can.
134 C2 **Elko** U.S.A.
129 C2 **Elk Point** Can.
126 E1 **Ellef Ringnes Island** Can.
137 D1 **Ellendale** U.S.A.
134 B1 **Ellensburg** U.S.A.
54 B2 **Ellesmere, Lake** N.Z.
127 F1 **Ellesmere Island** Can.
98 B2 **Ellesmere Port** U.K.
126 E2 **Ellice** *r.* Can.
Ellice Islands *country* S. Pacific Ocean *see* **Tuvalu**
123 C3 **Elliotdale** S. Africa
123 C1 **Ellisras** S. Africa
96 C2 **Ellon** U.K.
141 F2 **Ellsworth** U.S.A.
55 O2 **Ellsworth Mountains** Antarctica
111 C3 **Elmalı** Turkey
115 C1 **El Meghaïer** Alg.
141 D2 **Elmira** U.S.A.
107 C2 **El Moral** Spain
101 D1 **Elmshorn** Ger.
117 A3 **El Muglad** Sudan
64 A1 **El Nido** Phil.
117 B3 **El Obeid** Sudan
144 B2 **El Oro** Mex.
115 C1 **El Oued** Alg.
138 A2 **Eloy** U.S.A.
138 B2 **El Paso** U.S.A.
144 B1 **El Porvenír** Mex.
107 D1 **El Prat de Llobregat** Spain
139 D1 **El Reno** U.S.A.
145 B2 **El Salado** Mex.
144 B2 **El Salto** Mex.
146 B3 **El Salvador** *country* Central America
145 B2 **El Salvador** Mex.
138 B3 **El Sauz** Mex.
144 A1 **El Socorro** Mex.
145 C2 **El Temascal** Mex.
150 B1 **El Tigre** Venez.
147 D4 **El Tocuyo** Venez.
88 C2 **Elva** Estonia
106 B2 **Elvas** Port.
93 F3 **Elverum** Norway
119 E2 **El Wak** Kenya

99 D2 **Ely** U.K.
137 E1 **Ely** *MN* U.S.A.
135 D3 **Ely** *NV* U.S.A.
81 D2 **Emāmrūd** Iran
93 G4 **Emån** *r.* Sweden
76 B2 **Emba** Kazakh.
76 B2 **Emba** *r.* Kazakh.
123 C2 **Embalenhle** S. Africa
154 C1 **Emborcação, Represa de** *resr* Brazil
119 D3 **Embu** Kenya
100 C1 **Emden** Ger.
51 D2 **Emerald** Austr.
129 E3 **Emerson** Can.
111 C3 **Emet** Turkey
123 D2 **eMgwenya** S. Africa
123 D2 **eMijindini** S. Africa
115 D3 **Emi Koussi** *mt.* Chad
110 C2 **Emine, Nos** *pt* Bulg.
80 B2 **Emirdağ** Turkey
88 B2 **Emmaste** Estonia
100 B1 **Emmeloord** Neth.
100 C2 **Emmelshausen** Ger.
100 C1 **Emmen** Neth.
139 C3 **Emory Peak** U.S.A.
144 A2 **Empalme** Mex.
123 D2 **Empangeni** S. Africa
108 B2 **Empoli** Italy
137 D3 **Emporia** *KS* U.S.A.
141 D3 **Emporia** *VA* U.S.A.
100 C1 **Ems** *r.* Ger.
100 C1 **Emsdetten** Ger.
123 C2 **Emzinoni** S. Africa
59 D3 **Enarotali** Indon.
144 B2 **Encarnación** Mex.
152 C3 **Encarnación** Para.
155 D1 **Encruzilhada** Brazil
58 C3 **Endeh** Indon.
126 A2 **Endicott Mountains** U.S.A.
91 C2 **Enerhodar** Ukr.
87 D3 **Engel's** Rus. Fed.
60 B2 **Enggano** *i.* Indon.
98 C2 **England** *admin. div.* U.K.
130 A1 **English** *r.* Can.
95 C4 **English Channel** France/U.K.
139 D1 **Enid** U.S.A.
100 B1 **Enkhuizen** Neth.
93 G4 **Enköping** Sweden
108 B3 **Enna** *Sicily* Italy
129 D1 **Ennadai Lake** Can.
117 A3 **En Nahud** Sudan
115 E3 **Ennedi, Massif** *mts* Chad
53 C1 **Enngonia** Austr.
97 B2 **Ennis** Rep. of Ireland
139 D2 **Ennis** U.S.A.
97 C2 **Enniscorthy** Rep. of Ireland
97 C1 **Enniskillen** U.K.
97 B2 **Ennistymon** Rep. of Ireland
102 C2 **Enns** *r.* Austria
92 H2 **Enontekiö** Fin.
53 C3 **Ensay** Austr.
100 C1 **Enschede** Neth.
144 A1 **Ensenada** Mex.
70 A2 **Enshi** China
128 C1 **Enterprise** Can.
142 C2 **Enterprise** *AL* U.S.A.
134 C1 **Enterprise** *OR* U.S.A.
152 B3 **Entre Ríos** Bol.
106 B2 **Entroncamento** Port.
115 C4 **Enugu** Nigeria
150 A2 **Envira** Brazil
135 D3 **Ephraim** U.S.A.
134 C1 **Ephrata** U.S.A.
105 D2 **Épinal** France
99 C3 **Epsom** U.K.
118 A2 **Equatorial Guinea** *country* Africa
101 F3 **Erbendorf** Ger.
100 C3 **Erbeskopf** *hill* Ger.
81 C2 **Erciş** Turkey
65 B1 **Erdao Jiang** *r.* China
111 C2 **Erdek** Turkey
80 B2 **Erdemli** Turkey
152 C3 **Erechim** Brazil
69 D1 **Ereentsav** Mongolia
80 B2 **Ereğli** *Konya* Turkey
80 B1 **Ereğli** *Zonguldak* Turkey
69 D2 **Erenhot** China
Erevan Armenia *see* **Yerevan**
101 E2 **Erfurt** Ger.
80 B2 **Ergani** Turkey
114 B2 **'Erg Chech** *des.* Alg./Mali
115 D3 **Erg du Ténéré** *des.* Niger
111 C2 **Ergene** *r.* Turkey
140 C2 **Erie** U.S.A.
140 C2 **Erie, Lake** Can./U.S.A.
66 D2 **Erimo-misaki** *c.* Japan
116 B3 **Eritrea** *country* Africa
101 E3 **Erlangen** Ger.
50 C2 **Erldunda** Austr.
123 C2 **Ermelo** S. Africa
80 B2 **Ermenek** Turkey
111 B3 **Ermoupoli** Greece
73 B4 **Ernakulam** India
73 B3 **Erode** India
100 B2 **Erp** Neth.
114 B1 **Er Rachidia** Morocco
117 B3 **Er Rahad** Sudan
97 B1 **Errigal** *hill* Rep. of Ireland
97 A1 **Erris Head** *hd* Rep. of Ireland
109 D2 **Ersekë** Albania
91 E1 **Ertil'** Rus. Fed.
101 D2 **Erwitte** Ger.
102 C1 **Erzgebirge** *mts* Czech Rep./Ger.
80 B2 **Erzincan** Turkey
81 C2 **Erzurum** Turkey
93 E4 **Esbjerg** Denmark
135 D3 **Escalante** U.S.A.
144 B2 **Escalón** Mex.
140 B1 **Escanaba** U.S.A.
145 C3 **Escárcega** Mex.
107 C1 **Escatrón** Spain
100 A2 **Escaut** *r.* Belgium
101 E1 **Eschede** Ger.
100 B3 **Esch-sur-Alzette** Lux.
101 E2 **Eschwege** Ger.
100 C2 **Eschweiler** Ger.
135 C4 **Escondido** U.S.A.
144 B2 **Escuinapa** Mex.
111 C3 **Eşen** Turkey
81 D2 **Eşfahān** Iran
123 D2 **Esikhawini** S. Africa
98 B1 **Esk** *r.* U.K.
131 D1 **Esker** Can.
92 C2 **Eskifjörður** Iceland
93 G4 **Eskilstuna** Sweden
Eskimo Point Can. *see* **Arviat**
80 B2 **Eskişehir** Turkey
81 C2 **Eslāmābād-e Gharb** Iran
111 C3 **Esler Dağı** *mt.* Turkey
111 C3 **Eşme** Turkey
150 A1 **Esmeraldas** Ecuador
79 D2 **Espakeh** Iran
104 C3 **Espalion** France
130 B2 **Espanola** Can.
138 B1 **Espanola** U.S.A.
50 B3 **Esperance** Austr.
144 B2 **Esperanza** Mex.
106 B2 **Espichel, Cabo** *c.* Port.
155 D1 **Espinhaço, Serra do** *mts* Brazil
151 D3 **Espinosa** Brazil
144 A2 **Espíritu Santo, Isla** *i.* Mex.
93 H3 **Espoo** Fin.
153 A5 **Esquel** Arg.
114 B1 **Essaouira** Morocco
114 A2 **Es Semara** Western Sahara
100 C2 **Essen** Ger.
150 C1 **Essequibo** *r.* Guyana
83 L3 **Esso** Rus. Fed.
79 C2 **Eşţahbān** Iran
151 E3 **Estância** Brazil
123 C2 **Estcourt** S. Africa
107 C1 **Estella** Spain
106 B2 **Estepona** Spain
106 C1 **Esteras de Medinaceli** Spain
129 D2 **Esterhazy** Can.
152 B3 **Esteros** Para.
136 B2 **Estes Park** U.S.A.
129 D3 **Estevan** Can.
137 E2 **Estherville** U.S.A.
129 D2 **Eston** Can.
88 C2 **Estonia** *country* Europe
106 B1 **Estrela, Serra da** *mts* Port.
106 B2 **Estremoz** Port.
52 A1 **Etadunna** Austr.
104 C2 **Étampes** France
104 C1 **Étaples** France
75 B2 **Etawah** India
123 D2 **eThandakukhanya** S. Africa
117 B4 **Ethiopia** *country* Africa
109 C3 **Etna, Monte** *vol. Sicily* Italy
128 A2 **Etolin Island** *i.* U.S.A.
120 A2 **Etosha Pan** *salt pan* Namibia
100 C3 **Ettelbruck** Lux.
100 B2 **Etten-Leur** Neth.
107 C1 **Etxarri-Aranatz** Spain
99 D3 **Eu** France
53 C2 **Euabalong** Austr.
Euboea *i.* Greece *see* **Evvoia**
50 B3 **Eucla** Austr.
143 C2 **Eufaula** U.S.A.
139 D1 **Eufaula Lake** *resr* U.S.A.
134 B2 **Eugene** U.S.A.
144 A2 **Eugenia, Punta** *pt* Mex.
53 C1 **Eulo** Austr.
53 C2 **Eumungerie** Austr.
139 C2 **Eunice** U.S.A.
80 C2 **Euphrates** *r.* Asia
134 B2 **Eureka** *CA* U.S.A.
134 C1 **Eureka** *MT* U.S.A.
135 C3 **Eureka** *NV* U.S.A.
52 B2 **Euriowie** Austr.
53 C3 **Euroa** Austr.
106 B2 **Europa Point** Gibraltar
128 B2 **Eutsuk Lake** Can.
130 C1 **Evans, Lac** *l.* Can.
53 D1 **Evans Head** Austr.
127 F2 **Evans Strait** Can.
136 A2 **Evanston** U.S.A.
140 B3 **Evansville** U.S.A.
123 C2 **Evaton** S. Africa
79 C2 **Evaz** Iran
83 L2 **Evensk** Rus. Fed.
50 C2 **Everard Range** *hills* Austr.
75 C2 **Everest, Mount** China/Nepal
134 B1 **Everett** U.S.A.
100 A2 **Evergem** Belgium
143 D3 **Everglades** *swamp* U.S.A.
118 B2 **Evinayong** Equat. Guinea
93 E4 **Evje** Norway
106 B2 **Évora** Port.
104 C2 **Évreux** France
111 C2 **Evros** *r.* Greece/Turkey
111 B3 **Evrotas** *r.* Greece
80 B2 **Evrychou** Cyprus
111 B3 **Evvoia** *i.* Greece
119 E2 **Ewaso Ngiro** *r.* Kenya
152 B2 **Exaltación** Bol.
99 B3 **Exe** *r.* U.K.
99 B3 **Exeter** U.K.
99 B3 **Exmoor** *hills* U.K.
99 B3 **Exmouth** U.K.
50 A2 **Exmouth Gulf** Austr.
146 C2 **Exuma Cays** *is* Bahamas
91 D2 **Eya** *r.* Rus. Fed.

117 C4 **Eyl** Somalia
52 A1 **Eyre, Lake** *salt flat* Austr.
51 C3 **Eyre Peninsula** Austr.
94 B1 **Eysturoy** *i.* Faroe Is
123 D2 **Ezakheni** S. Africa
123 C2 **Ezenzeleni** S. Africa
70 B2 **Ezhou** China
86 E2 **Ezhva** Rus. Fed.
111 C3 **Ezine** Turkey

F

138 B2 **Fabens** U.S.A.
108 B2 **Fabriano** Italy
115 D3 **Fachi** Niger
114 C3 **Fada-N'Gourma** Burkina
108 B2 **Faenza** Italy
59 C3 **Fafanlap** Indon.
110 B1 **Făgăraş** Romania
49 G4 **Fagatogo** American Samoa
93 E3 **Fagernes** Norway
93 G4 **Fagersta** Sweden
153 B6 **Fagnano, Lago** *l.* Arg./Chile
114 B3 **Faguibine, Lac** *l.* Mali
92 □B3 **Fagurhólsmýri** Iceland
126 B2 **Fairbanks** U.S.A.
137 D2 **Fairbury** U.S.A.
135 B3 **Fairfield** U.S.A.
96 □ **Fair Isle** *i.* U.K.
137 E2 **Fairmont** *MN* U.S.A.
140 C3 **Fairmont** *WV* U.S.A.
128 C2 **Fairview** Can.
59 D2 **Fais** *i.* Micronesia
74 B1 **Faisalabad** Pak.
136 C1 **Faith** U.S.A.
75 C2 **Faizabad** India
59 C3 **Fakfak** Indon.
65 A1 **Faku** China
114 A4 **Falaba** Sierra Leone
139 D3 **Falcon Lake** *l.* Mex./U.S.A.
139 D3 **Falfurrias** U.S.A.
128 C2 **Falher** Can.
101 F2 **Falkenberg** Ger.
93 F4 **Falkenberg** Sweden
101 F1 **Falkensee** Ger.
96 C3 **Falkirk** U.K.
153 C6 **Falkland Islands** *terr.* S. Atlantic Ocean
93 F4 **Falköping** Sweden
135 C3 **Fallon** U.S.A.
141 E2 **Fall River** U.S.A.
137 D2 **Falls City** U.S.A.
99 A3 **Falmouth** U.K.
122 A3 **False Bay** S. Africa
93 F4 **Falster** *i.* Denmark
110 C1 **Fălticeni** Romania
93 G3 **Falun** Sweden
71 A3 **Fangchenggang** China
71 C3 **Fangshan** Taiwan
69 E1 **Fangzheng** China
108 B2 **Fano** Italy
62 B1 **Fan Si Pan** *mt.* Vietnam
119 C2 **Faradje** Dem. Rep. Congo
121 □D3 **Farafangana** Madag.
116 A2 **Farāfirah, Wāḩāt al** *oasis* Egypt
76 C3 **Farāh** Afgh.
114 A3 **Faranah** Guinea
78 B3 **Farasān, Jazā'ir** *is* Saudi Arabia
54 B2 **Farewell, Cape** N.Z.
137 D1 **Fargo** U.S.A.
137 E2 **Faribault** U.S.A.
141 E2 **Farmington** *ME* U.S.A.
138 B1 **Farmington** *NM* U.S.A.
141 D3 **Farmville** U.S.A.
99 C3 **Farnborough** U.K.
128 C2 **Farnham, Mount** Can.
128 A1 **Faro** Can.
106 B2 **Faro** Port.
88 A2 **Fårö** *i.* Sweden
94 B1 **Faroe Islands** *terr.* N. Atlantic Ocean
79 C2 **Farrāshband** Iran
Farvel, Kap *c.* Greenland *see* **Nunap Isua**
139 C2 **Farwell** U.S.A.
79 C2 **Fāryāb** Iran
79 C2 **Fasā** Iran
109 C2 **Fasano** Italy
90 B1 **Fastiv** Ukr.
75 B2 **Fatehgarh** India
75 C2 **Fatehpur** India
92 G2 **Fauske** Norway
92 □A3 **Faxaflói** *b.* Iceland
92 G3 **Faxälven** *r.* Sweden
115 D3 **Faya** Chad
142 B1 **Fayetteville** *AR* U.S.A.
143 E1 **Fayetteville** *NC* U.S.A.
142 C1 **Fayetteville** *TN* U.S.A.
74 B1 **Fazilka** India
114 A2 **Fdérik** Maur.
143 E2 **Fear, Cape** U.S.A.
54 C2 **Featherston** N.Z.
104 C2 **Fécamp** France
102 C1 **Fehmarn** *i.* Ger.
101 F1 **Fehrbellin** Ger.
155 D2 **Feia, Lagoa** *lag.* Brazil
150 A2 **Feijó** Brazil
54 C2 **Feilding** N.Z.
151 E3 **Feira de Santana** Brazil
107 D2 **Felanitx** Spain
145 D3 **Felipe C. Puerto** Mex.
155 D1 **Felixlândia** Brazil
99 D3 **Felixstowe** U.K.
101 D2 **Felsberg** Ger.
108 B1 **Feltre** Italy
93 F3 **Femunden** *l.* Norway
71 B3 **Fengcheng** *Jiangxi* China
65 A1 **Fengcheng** *Liaoning* China
62 A1 **Fengqing** China
70 B2 **Fengxian** China
Fengxiang China *see* **Lincang**
71 C3 **Fengyüan** Taiwan
70 B1 **Fengzhen** China
105 D3 **Feno, Capo di** *c. Corsica* France
121 □D2 **Fenoarivo Atsinanana** Madag.
91 D2 **Feodosiya** Ukr.
108 A3 **Fer, Cap de** *c.* Alg.
77 D2 **Fergana** Uzbek.
137 D1 **Fergus Falls** U.S.A.
114 B4 **Ferkessédougou** Côte d'Ivoire
108 B2 **Fermo** Italy
131 D1 **Fermont** Can.
106 B1 **Fermoselle** Spain
97 B2 **Fermoy** Rep. of Ireland
143 D2 **Fernandina Beach** U.S.A.
154 B2 **Fernandópolis** Brazil
128 C3 **Fernie** Can.
108 B2 **Ferrara** Italy
154 B2 **Ferreiros** Brazil
108 A2 **Ferro, Capo** *c. Sardinia* Italy
106 B1 **Ferrol** Spain
100 B1 **Ferwerd** Neth.
114 B1 **Fès** Morocco
118 B3 **Feshi** Dem. Rep. Congo
137 E3 **Festus** U.S.A.
111 C3 **Fethiye** Turkey
96 □ **Fetlar** *i.* U.K.
130 C1 **Feuilles, Rivière aux** *r.* Can.
77 D3 **Feyzābād** Afgh.
Fez Morocco *see* **Fès**
121 □D3 **Fianarantsoa** Madag.
117 B4 **Fichē** Eth.
109 C2 **Fier** Albania
96 C2 **Fife Ness** *pt* U.K.
104 C3 **Figeac** France
106 B1 **Figueira da Foz** Port.
107 D1 **Figueres** Spain
114 B1 **Figuig** Morocco
49 F4 **Fiji** *country* S. Pacific Ocean
152 B3 **Filadelfia** Para.
55 O2 **Filchner Ice Shelf** Antarctica
98 C1 **Filey** U.K.
111 B3 **Filippiada** Greece
93 F4 **Filipstad** Sweden
96 C2 **Findhorn** *r.* U.K.
140 C2 **Findlay** U.S.A.
51 D4 **Fingal** Austr.
141 D2 **Finger Lakes** U.S.A.
92 I3 **Finland** *country* Europe
93 H4 **Finland, Gulf of** Europe
128 B2 **Finlay** *r.* Can.
53 C3 **Finley** Austr.
101 E2 **Finne** *ridge* Ger.
92 H2 **Finnmarksvidda** *reg.* Norway
92 G2 **Finnsnes** Norway
93 G4 **Finspång** Sweden
96 A2 **Fionnphort** U.K.
Fırat *r.* Turkey *see* **Euphrates**
Firenze Italy *see* **Florence**
105 C2 **Firminy** France
75 B2 **Firozabad** India
74 B1 **Firozpur** India
79 C2 **Fīrūzābād** Iran
122 A2 **Fish** *watercourse* Namibia
122 B3 **Fish** *r.* S. Africa
99 A3 **Fishguard** U.K.
105 C2 **Fismes** France
106 B1 **Fisterra, Cabo** *c.* Spain
141 E2 **Fitchburg** U.S.A.
129 C2 **Fitzgerald** Can.
50 B1 **Fitzroy Crossing** Austr.
108 B2 **Fivizzano** Italy
119 C3 **Fizi** Dem. Rep. Congo
92 G3 **Fjällsjöälven** *r.* Sweden
123 C3 **Flagstaff** S. Africa
138 A1 **Flagstaff** U.S.A.
130 C1 **Flaherty Island** Can.
98 C1 **Flamborough Head** *hd* U.K.
101 F1 **Fläming** *hills* Ger.
136 B2 **Flaming Gorge Reservoir** U.S.A.
134 D1 **Flathead** *r.* U.S.A.
134 D1 **Flathead Lake** U.S.A.
51 D1 **Flattery, Cape** Austr.
134 B1 **Flattery, Cape** U.S.A.
98 B2 **Fleetwood** U.K.
93 E4 **Flekkefjord** Norway
102 B1 **Flensburg** Ger.
104 B2 **Flers** France
51 D1 **Flinders** *r.* Austr.
50 A3 **Flinders Bay** Austr.
51 D3 **Flinders Island** Austr.
52 A2 **Flinders Ranges** *mts* Austr.
129 D2 **Flin Flon** Can.
140 C2 **Flint** U.S.A.
107 D1 **Florac** France
108 B2 **Florence** Italy
142 C2 **Florence** *AL* U.S.A.
138 A2 **Florence** *AZ* U.S.A.
134 B2 **Florence** *OR* U.S.A.
143 E2 **Florence** *SC* U.S.A.
150 A1 **Florencia** Col.
146 B3 **Flores** Guat.
58 C3 **Flores** *i.* Indon.
58 B3 **Flores Sea** Indon.
151 E2 **Floresta** Brazil
139 D3 **Floresville** U.S.A.
151 D2 **Floriano** Brazil
152 D3 **Florianópolis** Brazil
153 C4 **Florida** Uru.
143 D2 **Florida** *state* U.S.A.

143 D4 Florida, Straits of Bahamas/U.S.A.
143 D4 Florida Keys is U.S.A.
111 B2 Florina Greece
93 E3 Florø Norway
129 D2 Foam Lake Can.
109 C2 Foča Bos.-Herz.
110 C1 Focşani Romania
71 B3 Fogang China
109 C2 Foggia Italy
131 E2 Fogo Island Can.
104 C3 Foix France
89 D3 Fokino Rus. Fed.
130 B2 Foleyet Can.
108 B2 Foligno Italy
99 D3 Folkestone U.K.
143 D2 Folkston U.S.A.
108 B2 Follonica Italy
129 D2 Fond-du-Lac Can.
129 D2 Fond du Lac r. Can.
140 B2 Fond du Lac U.S.A.
106 B1 Fondevila Spain
108 B2 Fondi Italy
146 B3 Fonseca, Golfo do b. Central America
150 B2 Fonte Boa Brazil
104 B2 Fontenay-le-Comte France
92 □C2 Fontur pt Iceland
53 C2 Forbes Austr.
101 E3 Forchheim Ger.
93 E3 Førde Norway
53 C1 Fords Bridge Austr.
142 B2 Fordyce U.S.A.
142 C2 Forest U.S.A.
53 C3 Forest Hill Austr.
131 D2 Forestville Can.
96 C2 Forfar U.K.
134 B1 Forks U.S.A.
108 B2 Forlì Italy
107 D2 Formentera i. Spain
107 D2 Formentor, Cap de c. Spain
155 C2 Formiga Brazil
152 C3 Formosa Arg.
Formosa country Asia see Taiwan
154 C1 Formosa Brazil
96 C2 Forres U.K.
50 B3 Forrest Austr.
142 B1 Forrest City U.S.A.
51 D1 Forsayth Austr.
93 H3 Forssa Fin.
53 D2 Forster Austr.
136 B1 Forsyth U.S.A.
74 B2 Fort Abbas Pak.
130 B1 Fort Albany Can.
151 E2 Fortaleza Brazil
128 C2 Fort Assiniboine Can.
96 B2 Fort Augustus U.K.
134 D1 Fort Benton U.S.A.
135 B3 Fort Bragg U.S.A.
Fort Chimo Can. see Kuujjuaq
129 C2 Fort Chipewyan Can.
136 B2 Fort Collins U.S.A.
147 D3 Fort-de-France Martinique
137 E2 Fort Dodge U.S.A.
130 A2 Fort Frances Can.
Fort Franklin Can. see Délįne
Fort George Can. see Chisasibi
126 C2 Fort Good Hope Can.
96 C2 Forth r. U.K.
96 C2 Forth, Firth of est. U.K.
152 C3 Fortín Madrejón Para.
143 D3 Fort Lauderdale U.S.A.
128 B1 Fort Liard Can.
129 C2 Fort Mackay Can.
129 C2 Fort McMurray Can.
126 C2 Fort McPherson Can.
136 C2 Fort Morgan U.S.A.
143 D3 Fort Myers U.S.A.
128 B2 Fort Nelson Can.
128 B2 Fort Nelson r. Can.
142 C2 Fort Payne U.S.A.
136 B1 Fort Peck U.S.A.
136 B1 Fort Peck Reservoir U.S.A.
143 D3 Fort Pierce U.S.A.
128 C1 Fort Providence Can.
129 D2 Fort Qu'Appelle Can.
128 C1 Fort Resolution Can.
Fort Rupert Can. see Waskaganish
128 B2 Fort St James Can.
128 B2 Fort St John Can.
128 C2 Fort Saskatchewan Can.
137 E3 Fort Scott U.S.A.
130 B1 Fort Severn Can.
76 B2 Fort-Shevchenko Kazakh.
128 B1 Fort Simpson Can.
129 C1 Fort Smith Can.
142 B1 Fort Smith U.S.A.
139 C2 Fort Stockton U.S.A.
138 C2 Fort Sumner U.S.A.
128 C2 Fort Vermilion Can.
142 C2 Fort Walton Beach U.S.A.
140 B2 Fort Wayne U.S.A.
96 B2 Fort William U.K.
139 D2 Fort Worth U.S.A.
126 B2 Fort Yukon U.S.A.
71 B3 Foshan China
92 F3 Fosna pen. Norway
93 E3 Fosnavåg Norway
92 □B3 Foss Iceland
92 □A2 Fossá Iceland
108 A2 Fossano Italy
53 C3 Foster Austr.
104 B2 Fougères France
96 □ Foula i. U.K.
111 C3 Fournoi i. Greece
114 A3 Fouta Djallon reg. Guinea
54 A3 Foveaux Strait N.Z.
136 C3 Fowler U.S.A.
50 C3 Fowlers Bay Austr.
128 C2 Fox Creek Can.
127 F2 Foxe Basin g. Can.
127 F2 Foxe Channel Can.
127 F2 Foxe Peninsula Can.
54 B2 Fox Glacier N.Z.
128 C2 Fox Lake Can.
128 A1 Fox Mountain Can.
54 C2 Foxton N.Z.
129 D2 Fox Valley Can.
97 C1 Foyle, Lough b. Rep. of Ireland/U.K.
154 B3 Foz de Areia, Represa de resr Brazil
120 A2 Foz do Cunene Angola
154 B3 Foz do Iguaçu Brazil
107 D1 Fraga Spain
154 C2 Franca Brazil
109 C2 Francavilla Fontana Italy
104 C2 France country Europe
118 B3 Franceville Gabon
137 D2 Francis Case, Lake U.S.A.
155 D1 Francisco Sá Brazil
120 B3 Francistown Botswana
128 B2 François Lake Can.
101 D2 Frankenberg (Eder) Ger.
101 D3 Frankenthal (Pfalz) Ger.
101 E2 Frankenwald mts Ger.
140 C3 Frankfort U.S.A.
101 D2 Frankfurt am Main Ger.
102 C1 Frankfurt an der Oder Ger.
102 C2 Fränkische Alb mts Ger.
101 E3 Fränkische Schweiz reg. Ger.
141 D2 Franklin U.S.A.
126 C2 Franklin Bay Can.
134 C1 Franklin D. Roosevelt Lake U.S.A.
128 B1 Franklin Mountains Can.
126 E2 Franklin Strait Can.
82 E1 Frantsa-Iosifa, Zemlya is Rus. Fed.
54 B2 Franz Josef Glacier N.Z.
Franz Josef Land is Rus. Fed. see Frantsa-Iosifa, Zemlya
108 A3 Frasca, Capo della c. Sardinia Italy
128 B3 Fraser r. B.C. Can.
131 D1 Fraser r. Nfld. Can.
122 B3 Fraserburg S. Africa
96 C2 Fraserburgh U.K.
130 B2 Fraserdale Can.
51 E2 Fraser Island Austr.
128 B2 Fraser Lake Can.
153 C4 Fray Bentos Uru.
93 E4 Fredericia Denmark
139 D2 Frederick U.S.A.
139 D2 Fredericksburg TX U.S.A.
141 D3 Fredericksburg VA U.S.A.
128 A2 Frederick Sound sea chan. U.S.A.
131 D2 Fredericton Can.
93 F4 Frederikshavn Denmark
Fredrikshamn Fin. see Hamina
93 F4 Fredrikstad Norway
140 B2 Freeport IL U.S.A.
139 D3 Freeport TX U.S.A.
146 C2 Freeport City Bahamas
139 D3 Freer U.S.A.
123 C2 Free State prov. S. Africa
114 A4 Freetown Sierra Leone
106 B2 Fregenal de la Sierra Spain
104 B2 Fréhel, Cap c. France
102 B2 Freiburg im Breisgau Ger.
102 C2 Freising Ger.
102 C2 Freistadt Austria
105 D3 Fréjus France
50 A3 Fremantle Austr.
137 D2 Fremont NE U.S.A.
140 C2 Fremont OH U.S.A.
151 C1 French Guiana terr. S. America
134 E1 Frenchman r. U.S.A.
49 H5 French Polynesia terr. S. Pacific Ocean
144 B2 Fresnillo Mex.
135 C3 Fresno U.S.A.
107 D2 Freu, Cap des c. Spain
105 D2 Freyming-Merlebach France
114 A3 Fria Guinea
152 B3 Frias Arg.
102 B2 Friedrichshafen Ger.
101 F1 Friesack Ger.
100 C1 Friesoythe Ger.
Frobisher Bay Can. see Iqaluit
127 G2 Frobisher Bay b. Can.
101 F2 Frohburg Ger.
87 D4 Frolovo Rus. Fed.
52 A2 Frome, Lake salt flat Austr.
52 A2 Frome Downs Austr.
100 C2 Fröndenberg Ger.
145 C3 Frontera Mex.
144 B1 Fronteras Mex.
108 B2 Frosinone Italy
92 E3 Frøya i. Norway
Frunze Kyrg. see Bishkek
105 D2 Frutigen Switz.
103 D2 Frýdek-Místek Czech Rep.
71 B3 Fu'an China
106 C1 Fuenlabrada Spain
152 C3 Fuerte Olimpo Para.
114 A2 Fuerteventura i. Canary Is
64 B1 Fuga i. Phil.
67 C3 Fuji Japan
71 B3 Fujian prov. China
67 C3 Fujinomiya Japan
67 C3 Fuji-san vol. Japan
67 C3 Fukui Japan
67 B4 Fukuoka Japan

67 D3 **Fukushima** Japan
101 D2 **Fulda** Ger.
101 D2 **Fulda** *r.* Ger.
70 A3 **Fuling** China
137 E3 **Fulton** U.S.A.
105 C2 **Fumay** France
49 F3 **Funafuti** *atoll* Tuvalu
114 A1 **Funchal** Madeira
106 B1 **Fundão** Port.
131 D2 **Fundy, Bay of** *g.* Can.
70 B2 **Funing** *Jiangsu* China
71 A3 **Funing** *Yunnan* China
115 C3 **Funtua** Nigeria
79 C2 **Fürgun, Kūh-e** *mt.* Iran
89 F2 **Furmanov** Rus. Fed.
155 C2 **Furnas, Represa** *resr* Brazil
51 D4 **Furneaux Group** *is* Austr.
100 C1 **Fürstenau** Ger.
101 E3 **Fürth** Ger.
66 D3 **Furukawa** Japan
127 F2 **Fury and Hecla Strait** Can.
65 A1 **Fushun** China
65 B1 **Fusong** China
79 C2 **Fuwayriţ** Qatar
70 B2 **Fuyang** China
69 E1 **Fuyu** China
68 B1 **Fuyun** China
71 B3 **Fuzhou** China
Fuzhou China *see* **Linchuan**
93 F4 **Fyn** *i.* Denmark
F.Y.R.O.M. *country* Europe *see* **Macedonia**

G

117 C4 **Gaalkacyo** Somalia
120 A2 **Gabela** Angola
115 D1 **Gabès** Tunisia
115 D1 **Gabès, Golfe de** *g.* Tunisia
118 B3 **Gabon** *country* Africa
123 C1 **Gaborone** Botswana
110 C2 **Gabrovo** Bulg.
114 A3 **Gabú** Guinea-Bissau
73 B3 **Gadag** India
75 C2 **Gadchiroli** India
101 E1 **Gadebusch** Ger.
142 C2 **Gadsden** U.S.A.
110 C2 **Găeşti** Romania
108 B2 **Gaeta** Italy
143 D1 **Gaffney** U.S.A.
115 C1 **Gafsa** Tunisia
89 E2 **Gagarin** Rus. Fed.
114 B4 **Gagnoa** Côte d'Ivoire
131 D1 **Gagnon** Can.
81 C1 **Gagra** Georgia
122 A2 **Gaiab** *watercourse* Namibia
104 C3 **Gaillac** France
143 D3 **Gainesville** *FL* U.S.A.
143 D2 **Gainesville** *GA* U.S.A.
139 D2 **Gainesville** *TX* U.S.A.
98 C2 **Gainsborough** U.K.
52 A2 **Gairdner, Lake** *salt flat* Austr.
96 B2 **Gairloch** U.K.
119 E3 **Galana** *r.* Kenya
103 D2 **Galanta** Slovakia
148 C2 **Galapagos Islands** *is* Pacific Ocean
96 C3 **Galashiels** U.K.
110 C1 **Galaţi** Romania
93 E3 **Galdhøpiggen** *mt.* Norway
145 B2 **Galeana** Mex.
128 C2 **Galena Bay** Can.
140 A2 **Galesburg** U.S.A.
122 B2 **Galeshewe** S. Africa
86 D3 **Galich** Rus. Fed.
116 B1 **Galilee, Sea of** Israel
142 C1 **Gallatin** U.S.A.
73 C4 **Galle** Sri Lanka
150 A1 **Gallinas, Punta** *pt* Col.
109 C2 **Gallipoli** Italy
Gallipoli Turkey *see* **Gelibolu**
92 H2 **Gällivare** Sweden
138 B1 **Gallup** U.S.A.
114 A2 **Galtat Zemmour** Western Sahara
97 B2 **Galtymore** *hill* Rep. of Ireland
139 E3 **Galveston** U.S.A.
139 E3 **Galveston Bay** U.S.A.
97 B2 **Galway** Rep. of Ireland
97 B2 **Galway Bay** Rep. of Ireland
154 C1 **Gamá** Brazil
123 D3 **Gamalakhe** S. Africa
Gambia, The *country* Africa *see* **The Gambia**
52 A3 **Gambier Islands** Austr.
131 E2 **Gambo** Can.
118 B3 **Gamboma** Congo
138 B1 **Ganado** U.S.A.
81 D3 **Ganāveh** Iran
81 C1 **Gäncä** Azer.
Gand Belgium *see* **Gent**
61 C2 **Gandadiwata, Bukit** *mt.* Indon.
118 C3 **Gandajika** Dem. Rep. Congo
131 E2 **Gander** Can.
131 E2 **Gander** *r.* Can.
101 D1 **Ganderkesee** Ger.
107 D1 **Gandesa** Spain
74 B2 **Gandhidham** India
74 B2 **Gandhinagar** India
74 B2 **Gandhi Sagar** *resr* India
107 C2 **Gandía** Spain
Ganga *r.* Bangl./India *see* **Ganges**
153 B5 **Gangán** Arg.
74 B2 **Ganganagar** India
68 C2 **Gangca** China
75 C1 **Gangdisê Shan** *mts* China
75 D2 **Ganges** *r.* Bangl./India
105 C3 **Ganges** France
75 C2 **Ganges, Mouths of the** Bangl./India
75 C2 **Gangtok** India
105 C2 **Gannat** France
136 B2 **Gannett Peak** U.S.A.
122 A3 **Gansbaai** S. Africa
70 A1 **Gansu** *prov.* China
71 B3 **Ganzhou** China
114 B3 **Gao** Mali
114 A3 **Gaoual** Guinea
70 B2 **Gaoyou** China
70 B2 **Gaoyou Hu** *l.* China
105 D3 **Gap** France
107 C2 **Gap Carbon** *hd* Alg.
75 C1 **Gar** China
53 C1 **Garah** Austr.
151 E2 **Garanhuns** Brazil
135 B2 **Garberville** U.S.A.
101 D1 **Garbsen** Ger.
154 C2 **Garça** Brazil
108 B1 **Garda, Lago di** *l.* Italy
101 E1 **Gardelegen** Ger.
136 C3 **Garden City** U.S.A.
129 E2 **Garden Hill** Can.
77 C3 **Gardīz** Afgh.
88 B2 **Gargždai** Lith.
123 C3 **Gariep Dam** *resr* S. Africa
122 A3 **Garies** S. Africa
119 D3 **Garissa** Kenya
102 C2 **Garmisch-Partenkirchen** Ger.
52 B2 **Garnpung Lake** *imp. l.* Austr.
104 B3 **Garonne** *r.* France
117 C4 **Garoowe** Somalia
74 B2 **Garoth** India
118 B2 **Garoua** Cameroon
96 B2 **Garry** *r.* U.K.
126 E2 **Garry Lake** Can.
119 E3 **Garsen** Kenya
61 B2 **Garut** Indon.
140 B2 **Gary** U.S.A.
145 B2 **Garza García** Mex.
68 C2 **Garzê** China
104 B2 **Gascony, Gulf of** *g.* France/Spain
50 A2 **Gascoyne** *r.* Austr.
115 D3 **Gashua** Nigeria
131 D2 **Gaspé** Can.
131 D2 **Gaspé, Péninsule de** Can.
143 E1 **Gaston, Lake** U.S.A.
143 D1 **Gastonia** U.S.A.
107 C2 **Gata, Cabo de** *c.* Spain
88 D2 **Gatchina** Rus. Fed.
98 C1 **Gateshead** U.K.
139 D2 **Gatesville** U.S.A.
130 C2 **Gatineau** *r.* Can.
53 D1 **Gatton** Austr.
129 E2 **Gauer Lake** Can.
93 E4 **Gausta** *mt.* Norway
123 C2 **Gauteng** *prov.* S. Africa
79 C2 **Gāvbandī** Iran
111 B3 **Gavdos** *i.* Greece
93 G3 **Gävle** Sweden
89 F2 **Gavrilov Posad** Rus. Fed.
89 E2 **Gavrilov-Yam** Rus. Fed.
62 A1 **Gawai** Myanmar
52 A2 **Gawler** Austr.
52 A2 **Gawler Ranges** *hills* Austr.
75 C2 **Gaya** India
114 C3 **Gaya** Niger
140 C1 **Gaylord** U.S.A.
86 E2 **Gayny** Rus. Fed.
80 B2 **Gaza** *terr.* Asia
76 C2 **Gaz-Achak** Turkm.
76 B3 **Gazandzhyk** Turkm.
80 B2 **Gaziantep** Turkey
114 B4 **Gbarnga** Liberia
103 D1 **Gdańsk** Pol.
88 A3 **Gdańsk, Gulf of** Pol./Rus. Fed.
88 C2 **Gdov** Rus. Fed.
103 D1 **Gdynia** Pol.
116 B3 **Gedaref** Sudan
101 D2 **Gedern** Ger.
111 C3 **Gediz** *r.* Turkey
102 C1 **Gedser** Denmark
100 B2 **Geel** Belgium
52 B3 **Geelong** Austr.
101 E1 **Geesthacht** Ger.
75 C1 **Gê'gyai** China
129 D2 **Geikie** *r.* Can.
93 E3 **Geilo** Norway
62 B1 **Gejiu** China
108 B3 **Gela** *Sicily* Italy
91 D3 **Gelendzhik** Rus. Fed.
111 C2 **Gelibolu** Turkey
100 C2 **Gelsenkirchen** Ger.
118 B2 **Gemena** Dem. Rep. Congo
111 C2 **Gemlik** Turkey
117 C4 **Genalē Wenz** *r.* Eth.
153 B4 **General Acha** Arg.
153 B4 **General Alvear** Arg.
153 C4 **General Belgrano** Arg.
144 B2 **General Cepeda** Mex.
153 B4 **General Pico** Arg.
153 B4 **General Roca** Arg.
64 B2 **General Santos** Phil.
141 D2 **Genesee** *r.* U.S.A.
141 D2 **Geneseo** U.S.A.
Geneva Switz. *see* **Genève**
141 D2 **Geneva** U.S.A.
Geneva, Lake France/Switz. *see* **Léman, Lac**
105 D2 **Genève** Switz.
106 B2 **Genil** *r.* Spain
100 B2 **Genk** Belgium
108 A2 **Genoa** Italy
Genova Italy *see* **Genoa**

100 A2 **Gent** Belgium
101 F1 **Genthin** Ger.
50 A3 **Geographe Bay** Austr.
131 D1 **George** *r.* Can.
122 B3 **George** S. Africa
143 D3 **George, Lake** *FL* U.S.A.
141 E2 **George, Lake** *NY* U.S.A.
114 A3 **Georgetown** Gambia
151 C1 **Georgetown** Guyana
60 B1 **Georgetown** Malaysia
143 E2 **Georgetown** *SC* U.S.A.
139 D2 **Georgetown** *TX* U.S.A.
55 I2 **George V Land** *reg.* Antarctica
81 C1 **Georgia** *country* Asia
143 D2 **Georgia** *state* U.S.A.
130 B2 **Georgian Bay** Can.
51 C2 **Georgina** *watercourse* Austr.
77 E2 **Georgiyevka** Kazakh.
87 D4 **Georgiyevsk** Rus. Fed.
101 F2 **Gera** Ger.
151 D3 **Geral de Goiás, Serra** *hills* Brazil
54 B2 **Geraldine** N.Z.
50 A2 **Geraldton** Austr.
80 B1 **Gerede** Turkey
74 A1 **Gereshk** Afgh.
135 C2 **Gerlach** U.S.A
103 E2 **Gerlachovský štít** *mt.* Slovakia
102 C1 **Germany** *country* Europe
100 C2 **Gerolstein** Ger.
101 E3 **Gerolzhofen** Ger.
101 D2 **Gersfeld (Rhön)** Ger.
75 C1 **Gêrzê** China
141 D3 **Gettysburg** *PA* U.S.A.
136 D1 **Gettysburg** *SD* U.S.A.
109 D2 **Gevgelija** Macedonia
111 C3 **Geyikli** Turkey
122 B2 **Ghaap Plateau** S. Africa
115 C1 **Ghadāmis** Libya
75 C2 **Ghaghara** *r.* India
114 B4 **Ghana** *country* Africa
120 B3 **Ghanzi** Botswana
115 C1 **Ghardaïa** Alg.
115 D1 **Gharyān** Libya
75 C2 **Ghatal** India
75 C2 **Ghazipur** India
77 C3 **Ghaznī** Afgh.
110 B1 **Gherla** Romania
105 D3 **Ghisonaccia** *Corsica* France
74 B2 **Ghotaru** India
74 A2 **Ghotki** Pak.
79 C3 **Ghubbat al Qamar** *b.* Yemen
91 E3 **Giaginskaya** Rus. Fed.
97 C1 **Giant's Causeway** *lava field* U.K.
61 C2 **Gianyar** Indon.
109 C3 **Giarre** *Sicily* Italy
108 A1 **Giaveno** Italy
122 A2 **Gibeon** Namibia
106 B2 **Gibraltar** *terr.* Europe
106 B2 **Gibraltar, Strait of** Morocco/Spain
50 B2 **Gibson Desert** Austr.
68 C1 **Gichgeniyn Nuruu** *mts* Mongolia
117 B4 **Gīdolē** Eth.
104 C2 **Gien** France
101 D2 **Gießen** Ger.
101 E1 **Gifhorn** Ger.
128 C2 **Gift Lake** Can.
67 C3 **Gifu** Japan
96 B3 **Gigha** *i.* U.K.
106 B1 **Gijón-Xixón** Spain
138 A2 **Gila** *r.* U.S.A.
138 A2 **Gila Bend** U.S.A.
51 D1 **Gilbert** *r.* Austr.
49 F2 **Gilbert Islands** Kiribati
134 D1 **Gildford** U.S.A.
53 C2 **Gilgandra** Austr.
74 B1 **Gilgit** Jammu and Kashmir
74 B1 **Gilgit** *r.* Jammu and Kashmir
53 C2 **Gilgunnia** Austr.
129 E2 **Gillam** Can.
136 B2 **Gillette** U.S.A.
99 D3 **Gillingham** U.K.
129 E2 **Gimli** Can.
117 C4 **Gīnīr** Eth.
109 C2 **Ginosa** Italy
53 C3 **Gippsland** *reg.* Austr.
74 A2 **Girdar Dhor** *r.* Pak.
80 B1 **Giresun** Turkey
107 D1 **Girona** Spain
96 B3 **Girvan** U.K.
54 C1 **Gisborne** N.Z.
93 F4 **Gislaved** Sweden
119 C3 **Gitarama** Rwanda
108 B2 **Giulianova** Italy
110 C2 **Giurgiu** Romania
110 C1 **Giuvala, Pasul** *pass* Romania
105 C2 **Givors** France
123 D1 **Giyani** S. Africa
109 D2 **Gjirokastër** Albania
126 E2 **Gjoa Haven** Can.
93 F3 **Gjøvik** Norway
131 E2 **Glace Bay** Can.
134 B1 **Glacier Peak** *vol.* U.S.A.
51 E2 **Gladstone** Austr.
92 □A2 **Gláma** *mts* Iceland
109 C2 **Glamoč** Bos.-Herz.
100 C3 **Glan** *r.* Ger.
97 B2 **Glanaruddery Mountains** Rep. of Ireland
96 B3 **Glasgow** U.K.
140 B3 **Glasgow** *KY* U.S.A.
136 B1 **Glasgow** *MT* U.S.A.
99 B3 **Glastonbury** U.K.
101 F2 **Glauchau** Ger.
86 E3 **Glazov** Rus. Fed.
89 E3 **Glazunovka** Rus. Fed.
96 B2 **Glen Coe** *val.* U.K.
138 A2 **Glendale** U.S.A.
53 D2 **Glen Davis** Austr.
136 C1 **Glendive** U.S.A.
52 B3 **Glenelg** *r.* Austr.
53 D1 **Glen Innes** Austr.
126 B2 **Glennallen** U.S.A.
96 C2 **Glenrothes** U.K.
141 E2 **Glens Falls** U.S.A.
96 C2 **Glen Shee** *val.* U.K.
97 B1 **Glenties** Rep. of Ireland
138 B2 **Glenwood** U.S.A.
136 B3 **Glenwood Springs** U.S.A.
103 D1 **Gliwice** Pol.
138 A2 **Globe** U.S.A.
103 D1 **Głogów** Pol.
92 F2 **Glomfjord** Norway
93 F4 **Glomma** *r.* Norway
53 D2 **Gloucester** Austr.
99 B3 **Gloucester** U.K.
101 F1 **Glöwen** Ger.
77 E1 **Glubokoye** Kazakh.
101 D1 **Glückstadt** Ger.
103 C2 **Gmünd** Austria
102 C2 **Gmunden** Austria
101 D1 **Gnarrenburg** Ger.
103 D1 **Gniezno** Pol.
109 D2 **Gnjilane** Serb. and Mont.
75 D2 **Goalpara** India
96 B3 **Goat Fell** *hill* U.K.
117 C4 **Goba** Eth.
120 A3 **Gobabis** Namibia
153 A5 **Gobernador Gregores** Arg.
69 D2 **Gobi** *des.* China/Mongolia
100 C2 **Goch** Ger.
122 A1 **Gochas** Namibia
74 B3 **Godavari** *r.* India
73 C3 **Godavari, Mouths of the** India
130 B2 **Goderich** Can.
74 B2 **Godhra** India
129 E2 **Gods** *r.* Can.
129 E2 **Gods Lake** *l.* Can.
Godthåb Greenland *see* **Nuuk**
Godwin-Austen, Mount China/Jammu and Kashmir *see* **K2**
130 C2 **Goéland, Lac au** *l.* Can.
131 D1 **Goélands, Lac aux** *l.* Can.
100 A2 **Goes** Neth.
154 C1 **Goiandira** Brazil
154 C1 **Goiânia** Brazil
154 B1 **Goiás** Brazil
154 B2 **Goio-Erê** Brazil
111 C2 **Gökçeada** *i.* Turkey
111 C3 **Gökçedağ** Turkey
121 B2 **Gokwe** Zimbabwe
93 E3 **Gol** Norway
62 A1 **Golaghat** India
111 C2 **Gölcük** Turkey
103 E1 **Gołdap** Pol.
101 F1 **Goldberg** Ger.
53 D1 **Gold Coast** Austr.
114 B4 **Gold Coast** *coastal area* Ghana
128 C2 **Golden** Can.
54 B2 **Golden Bay** N.Z.
128 B3 **Golden Hinde** *mt.* Can.
97 B2 **Golden Vale** *lowland* Rep. of Ireland
135 C3 **Goldfield** U.S.A.
128 B3 **Gold River** Can.
143 E1 **Goldsboro** U.S.A.
135 C4 **Goleta** U.S.A.
68 C2 **Golmud** China
81 D2 **Golpāyegān** Iran
96 C2 **Golspie** U.K.
119 C3 **Goma** Dem. Rep. Congo
75 C2 **Gomati** *r.* India
115 D3 **Gombe** Nigeria
115 D3 **Gombi** Nigeria
Gomel' Belarus *see* **Homyel'**
144 B2 **Gómez Palacio** Mex.
147 C3 **Gonaïves** Haiti
81 D2 **Gonbad-e Kavus** Iran
117 B3 **Gonder** Eth.
75 C2 **Gondia** India
111 C2 **Gönen** Turkey
115 D4 **Gongola** *r.* Nigeria
53 C2 **Gongolgon** Austr.
145 C2 **Gonzáles** Mex.
139 D3 **Gonzales** U.S.A.
122 A3 **Good Hope, Cape of** S. Africa
134 D2 **Gooding** U.S.A.
136 C3 **Goodland** U.S.A.
53 C1 **Goodooga** Austr.
98 C2 **Goole** U.K.
53 C2 **Goolgowi** Austr.
52 A3 **Goolwa** Austr.
53 D1 **Goondiwindi** Austr.
134 B2 **Goose Lake** U.S.A.
102 B2 **Göppingen** Ger.
75 C2 **Gorakhpur** India
109 C2 **Goražde** Bos.-Herz.
111 C3 **Gördes** Turkey
89 D3 **Gordeyevka** Rus. Fed.
51 D4 **Gordon, Lake** Austr.
115 D4 **Goré** Chad
117 B4 **Gorē** Eth.
54 A3 **Gore** N.Z.
97 C2 **Gorey** Rep. of Ireland
81 D2 **Gorgān** Iran
81 C1 **Gori** Georgia
108 B1 **Gorizia** Italy
Gor'kiy Rus. Fed. *see* **Nizhniy Novgorod**

103 E2 **Gorlice** Pol.
103 C1 **Görlitz** Ger.
109 D2 **Gornji Milanovac** Serb. and Mont.
109 C2 **Gornji Vakuf** Bos.-Herz.
77 E1 **Gorno-Altaysk** Rus. Fed.
110 C2 **Gornotrakiyska Nizina** *lowland* Bulg.
77 E1 **Gornyak** Rus. Fed.
59 D3 **Goroka** P.N.G.
114 B3 **Gorom Gorom** Burkina
59 C2 **Gorontalo** Indon.
89 E3 **Gorshechnoye** Rus. Fed.
97 B2 **Gorumna Island** Rep. of Ireland
91 D3 **Goryachiy Klyuch** Rus. Fed.
103 D1 **Gorzów Wielkopolski** Pol.
53 D2 **Gosford** Austr.
66 D2 **Goshogawara** Japan
101 E2 **Goslar** Ger.
109 C2 **Gospić** Croatia
99 C3 **Gosport** U.K.
109 D2 **Gostivar** Macedonia
Göteborg Sweden *see* **Gothenburg**
101 E2 **Gotha** Ger.
93 F4 **Gothenburg** Sweden
136 C2 **Gothenburg** U.S.A.
93 G4 **Gotland** *i.* Sweden
111 B2 **Gotse Delchev** Bulg.
93 G4 **Gotska Sandön** *i.* Sweden
67 B4 **Gōtsu** Japan
101 D2 **Göttingen** Ger.
128 B2 **Gott Peak** Can.
100 B1 **Gouda** Neth.
114 A3 **Goudiri** Senegal
115 D3 **Goudoumaria** Niger
130 C2 **Gouin, Réservoir** *resr* Can.
53 C2 **Goulburn** Austr.
53 B3 **Goulburn** *r. N.S.W.* Austr.
53 B3 **Goulburn** *r. Vic.* Austr.
114 B3 **Goundam** Mali
107 D2 **Gouraya** Alg.
104 C3 **Gourdon** France
115 D3 **Gouré** Niger
122 B3 **Gourits** *r.* S. Africa
114 B3 **Gourma-Rharous** Mali
53 C3 **Gourock Range** *mts* Austr.
155 D1 **Governador Valadares** Brazil
143 E3 **Governor's Harbour** Bahamas
68 C2 **Govĭ Altayn Nuruu** *mts* Mongolia
75 C2 **Govind Ballash Pant Sagar** *resr* India
99 A3 **Gower** *pen.* U.K.
152 C3 **Goya** Arg.
81 C1 **Göyçay** Azer.
75 C1 **Gozha Co** *salt l.* China
122 B3 **Graaf-Reinet** S. Africa
101 E1 **Grabow** Ger.
109 C2 **Gračac** Croatia
87 E3 **Grachevka** Rus. Fed.
101 F2 **Gräfenhainichen** Ger.
53 D1 **Grafton** Austr.
137 D1 **Grafton** U.S.A.
139 D2 **Graham** U.S.A.
128 A2 **Graham Island** Can.
55 P3 **Graham Land** *reg.* Antarctica
123 C3 **Grahamstown** S. Africa
151 D2 **Grajaú** Brazil
111 B2 **Grammos** *mt.* Greece
96 B2 **Grampian Mountains** U.K.
146 B3 **Granada** Nic.
106 C2 **Granada** Spain
141 E1 **Granby** Can.
114 A2 **Gran Canaria** *i.* Canary Is
152 B3 **Gran Chaco** *reg.* Arg./Para.
136 C1 **Grand** *r.* U.S.A.
146 C2 **Grand Bahama** *i.* Bahamas
131 E2 **Grand Bank** Can.
158 C2 **Grand Banks of Newfoundland** *sea feature* N. Atlantic Ocean
Grand Canal China *see* **Da Yunhe**
138 A1 **Grand Canyon** U.S.A.
138 A1 **Grand Canyon** *gorge* U.S.A.
146 B3 **Grand Cayman** *i.* Cayman Is
129 C2 **Grand Centre** Can.
134 C1 **Grand Coulee** U.S.A.
152 B2 **Grande** *r.* Bol.
154 B2 **Grande** *r.* Brazil
153 B6 **Grande, Bahía** *b.* Arg.
155 D2 **Grande, Ilha** *i.* Brazil
128 C2 **Grande Cache** Can.
121 D2 **Grande Comore** *i.* Comoros
128 C2 **Grande Prairie** Can.
115 D3 **Grand Erg de Bilma** *des.* Niger
114 B1 **Grand Erg Occidental** *des.* Alg.
115 C2 **Grand Erg Oriental** *des.* Alg.
131 D2 **Grande-Rivière** Can.
152 B4 **Grandes, Salinas** *salt marsh* Arg.
131 D2 **Grand Falls** *N.B.* Can.
131 E2 **Grand Falls** *Nfld.* Can.
128 C3 **Grand Forks** Can.
137 D1 **Grand Forks** U.S.A.
128 C1 **Grandin, Lac** *l.* Can.
137 D2 **Grand Island** U.S.A.
142 B3 **Grand Isle** U.S.A.
136 B3 **Grand Junction** U.S.A.
114 B4 **Grand-Lahou** Côte d'Ivoire
131 D2 **Grand Lake** *l. N.B.* Can.
131 E2 **Grand Lake** *l. Nfld.* Can.
137 E1 **Grand Marais** U.S.A.
106 B2 **Grândola** Port.
129 E2 **Grand Rapids** Can.
140 B2 **Grand Rapids** *MI* U.S.A.
137 E1 **Grand Rapids** *MN* U.S.A.
136 A2 **Grand Teton** *mt.* U.S.A.
147 C2 **Grand Turk** Turks and Caicos Is
134 C1 **Grangeville** U.S.A.
128 B2 **Granisle** Can.
134 E1 **Granite Peak** U.S.A.
108 B3 **Granitola, Capo** *c. Sicily* Italy
93 F4 **Gränna** Sweden
101 F1 **Gransee** Ger.
99 C2 **Grantham** U.K.
96 C2 **Grantown-on-Spey** U.K.
138 B1 **Grants** U.S.A.
134 B2 **Grants Pass** U.S.A.
104 B2 **Granville** France
129 D2 **Granville Lake** Can.
155 D1 **Grão Mogol** Brazil
123 D1 **Graskop** S. Africa
105 D3 **Grasse** France
107 D1 **Graus** Spain
92 F2 **Gravdal** Norway
104 B2 **Grave, Pointe de** *pt* France
129 D3 **Gravelbourg** Can.
130 C2 **Gravenhurst** Can.
53 D1 **Gravesend** Austr.
99 D3 **Gravesend** U.K.
105 D2 **Gray** France
103 D2 **Graz** Austria
146 C2 **Great Abaco** *i.* Bahamas
50 B3 **Great Australian Bight** *g.* Austr.
54 C1 **Great Barrier Island** N.Z.
51 D1 **Great Barrier Reef** Austr.
135 C3 **Great Basin** U.S.A.
126 D2 **Great Bear Lake** Can.
137 D3 **Great Bend** U.S.A.
63 A2 **Great Coco Island** Cocos Is
53 B3 **Great Dividing Range** *mts* Austr.
146 B2 **Greater Antilles** *is* Caribbean Sea
134 D1 **Great Falls** U.S.A.
123 C3 **Great Fish** *r.* S. Africa
123 C3 **Great Fish Point** S. Africa
147 C2 **Great Inagua** *i.* Bahamas
122 B3 **Great Karoo** *plat.* S. Africa
123 C3 **Great Kei** *r.* S. Africa
99 B2 **Great Malvern** U.K.
122 A2 **Great Namaqualand** *reg.* Namibia
63 A3 **Great Nicobar** *i.* India
99 D2 **Great Ouse** *r.* U.K.
119 D3 **Great Rift Valley** Africa
119 D3 **Great Ruaha** *r.* Tanz.
134 D2 **Great Salt Lake** U.S.A.
135 D2 **Great Salt Lake Desert** U.S.A.
116 A2 **Great Sand Sea** *des.* Egypt/Libya
50 B2 **Great Sandy Desert** Austr.
128 C1 **Great Slave Lake** Can.
143 D1 **Great Smoky Mountains** U.S.A.
50 B2 **Great Victoria Desert** Austr.
70 B1 **Great Wall** China
99 D2 **Great Yarmouth** U.K.
106 B1 **Gredos, Sierra de** *mts* Spain
111 B3 **Greece** *country* Europe
136 C2 **Greeley** U.S.A.
82 F1 **Greem-Bell, Ostrov** *i.* Rus. Fed.
140 B3 **Green** *r. KY* U.S.A.
136 B3 **Green** *r. WY* U.S.A.
140 B2 **Green Bay** U.S.A.
140 B1 **Green Bay** *b.* U.S.A.
140 C3 **Greenbrier** *r.* U.S.A.
140 B3 **Greencastle** U.S.A.
143 D1 **Greeneville** U.S.A.
141 E2 **Greenfield** U.S.A.
129 D2 **Green Lake** Can.
127 I2 **Greenland** *terr.* N. America
160 R2 **Greenland Sea** Greenland/Svalbard
96 B3 **Greenock** U.K.
135 D3 **Green River** *UT* U.S.A.
136 B2 **Green River** *WY* U.S.A.
140 D3 **Greensburg** *IN* U.S.A.
141 D2 **Greensburg** *PA* U.S.A.
143 E2 **Green Swamp** U.S.A.
138 A2 **Green Valley** U.S.A.
114 B4 **Greenville** Liberia
142 C2 **Greenville** *AL* U.S.A.
142 B2 **Greenville** *MS* U.S.A.
143 E1 **Greenville** *NC* U.S.A.
143 D2 **Greenville** *SC* U.S.A.
139 D2 **Greenville** *TX* U.S.A.
53 D2 **Greenwell Point** Austr.
143 D2 **Greenwood** U.S.A.
50 B2 **Gregory, Lake** *salt flat* Austr.
51 D1 **Gregory Range** *hills* Austr.
102 C1 **Greifswald** Ger.
101 F2 **Greiz** Ger.
93 F4 **Grenå** Denmark
142 C2 **Grenada** U.S.A.
147 D3 **Grenada** *country* West Indies
104 C3 **Grenade** France
53 C2 **Grenfell** Austr.
129 D2 **Grenfell** Can.
105 D2 **Grenoble** France
51 D1 **Grenville, Cape** Austr.
134 B1 **Gresham** U.S.A.
100 C1 **Greven** Ger.
111 B2 **Grevena** Greece
100 C2 **Grevenbroich** Ger.
101 E1 **Grevesmühlen** Ger.
136 B2 **Greybull** U.S.A.
128 A1 **Grey Hunter Peak** Can.
131 F1 **Grey Islands** Can.
54 B2 **Greymouth** N.Z.

52 B1 **Grey Range** *hills* Austr.
97 C2 **Greystones** Rep. of Ireland
143 D2 **Griffin** U.S.A.
53 C2 **Griffith** Austr.
101 F2 **Grimma** Ger.
102 C1 **Grimmen** Ger.
98 C2 **Grimsby** U.K.
128 C2 **Grimshaw** Can.
92 □B2 **Grímsstaðir** Iceland
93 E4 **Grimstad** Norway
137 E2 **Grinnell** U.S.A.
123 C3 **Griqualand East** *reg.* S. Africa
122 B2 **Griqualand West** *reg.* S. Africa
127 F1 **Grise Fiord** Can.
96 C1 **Gritley** U.K.
123 C2 **Groblersdal** S. Africa
122 B2 **Groblershoop** S. Africa
Grodno Belarus *see* **Hrodna**
104 B2 **Groix, Île de** *i.* France
100 C1 **Gronau (Westfalen)** Ger.
92 F3 **Grong** Norway
100 C1 **Groningen** Neth.
122 B2 **Grootdrink** S. Africa
51 C1 **Groote Eylandt** *i.* Austr.
120 A2 **Grootfontein** Namibia
122 A2 **Groot Karas Berg** *plat.* Namibia
122 B3 **Groot Swartberge** *mts* S. Africa
123 C3 **Groot Winterberg** *mt.* S. Africa
101 D2 **Großenlüder** Ger.
102 C2 **Großer Rachel** *mt.* Ger.
103 C2 **Grosser Speikkogel** *mt.* Austria
108 B2 **Grosseto** Italy
101 D3 **Groß-Gerau** Ger.
102 C2 **Großglockner** *mt.* Austria
100 C1 **Groß-Hesepe** Ger.
101 E2 **Großlohra** Ger.
122 A1 **Gross Ums** Namibia
131 E1 **Groswater Bay** Can.
130 B2 **Groundhog** *r.* Can.
135 B3 **Grover Beach** U.S.A.
141 E2 **Groveton** U.S.A.
87 D4 **Groznyy** Rus. Fed.
109 C1 **Grubišno Polje** Croatia
103 D1 **Grudziądz** Pol.
122 A2 **Grünau** Namibia
92 □A3 **Grundarfjörður** Iceland
89 E3 **Gryazi** Rus. Fed.
89 F2 **Gryazovets** Rus. Fed.
103 D1 **Gryfice** Pol.
102 C1 **Gryfino** Pol.
146 C2 **Guacanayabo, Golfo de** *b.* Cuba
144 B2 **Guadalajara** Mex.
49 E3 **Guadalcanal** *i.* Solomon Islands
107 C1 **Guadalope** *r.* Spain
106 B2 **Guadalquivir** *r.* Spain
132 B4 **Guadalupe** *i.* Mex.
106 B2 **Guadalupe, Sierra de** *mts* Spain
138 C2 **Guadalupe Peak** U.S.A.
144 B2 **Guadalupe Victoria** Mex.
144 B2 **Guadalupe y Calvo** Mex.
106 C1 **Guadarrama, Sierra de** *mts* Spain
147 D3 **Guadeloupe** *terr.* West Indies
106 B2 **Guadiana** *r.* Port./Spain
106 C2 **Guadix** Spain
154 B2 **Guaíra** Brazil
150 A2 **Gualaceo** Ecuador
59 D2 **Guam** *terr.* N. Pacific Ocean
144 B2 **Guamúchil** Mex.
144 B2 **Guanacevi** Mex.
151 D3 **Guanambi** Brazil
150 B1 **Guanare** Venez.
146 B2 **Guane** Cuba
70 A2 **Guang'an** China
71 B3 **Guangchang** China
71 B3 **Guangdong** *prov.* China
71 A3 **Guangxi Zhuangzu Zizhiqu** *aut. reg.* China
70 A2 **Guangyuan** China
71 B3 **Guangzhou** China
155 D1 **Guanhães** Brazil
147 D4 **Guanipa** *r.* Venez.
71 A3 **Guanling** China
65 A1 **Guanshui** China
Guansuo China *see* **Guanling**
147 C2 **Guantánamo** Cuba
150 B3 **Guaporé** *r.* Bol./Brazil
154 B3 **Guarapuava** Brazil
154 C3 **Guaraqueçaba** Brazil
155 C2 **Guaratinguetá** Brazil
106 B1 **Guarda** Port.
154 C1 **Guarda Mor** Brazil
106 C1 **Guardo** Spain
155 C2 **Guarujá** Brazil
144 B2 **Guasave** Mex.
146 A3 **Guatemala** *country* Central America
146 A3 **Guatemala City** Guat.
150 B1 **Guaviare** *r.* Col.
155 C2 **Guaxupé** Brazil
150 A2 **Guayaquil** Ecuador
150 B3 **Guayaramerín** Bol.
144 A2 **Guaymas** Mex.
117 B3 **Guba** Eth.
86 E1 **Guba Dolgaya** Rus. Fed.
89 E3 **Gubkin** Rus. Fed.
115 C1 **Guelma** Alg.
114 A2 **Guelmine** Morocco
130 B2 **Guelph** Can.
145 C2 **Guémez** Mex.
104 C2 **Guéret** France
95 C4 **Guernsey** *terr.* Channel Is
144 A2 **Guerrero Negro** Mex.
131 D1 **Guers, Lac** *l.* Can.
70 B2 **Guichi** China
118 B2 **Guider** Cameroon
108 B2 **Guidonia-Montecelio** Italy
71 A3 **Guigang** China
100 A3 **Guignicourt** France
123 D1 **Guija** Moz.
99 C3 **Guildford** U.K.
71 B3 **Guilin** China
130 C1 **Guillaume-Delisle, Lac** *l.* Can.
106 B1 **Guimarães** Port.
114 A3 **Guinea** *country* Africa
112 D3 **Guinea, Gulf of** Africa
114 A3 **Guinea-Bissau** *country* Africa
104 B2 **Guingamp** France
104 B2 **Guipavas** France
154 B1 **Guiratinga** Brazil
150 B1 **Güiria** Venez.
100 A3 **Guise** France
64 B1 **Guiuan** Phil.
71 A3 **Guiyang** China
71 A3 **Guizhou** *prov.* China
74 B1 **Gujranwala** Pak.
74 B1 **Gujrat** Pak.
91 D2 **Gukovo** Rus. Fed.
76 B2 **Gulabie** Uzbek.
53 C2 **Gulargambone** Austr.
73 B3 **Gulbarga** India
88 C2 **Gulbene** Latvia
142 C2 **Gulfport** U.S.A.
79 C2 **Gulf, The** Asia
69 E1 **Gulian** China
77 C2 **Gulistan** Uzbek.
Gulja China *see* **Yining**
129 D2 **Gull Lake** Can.
111 C3 **Güllük** Turkey
119 D2 **Gulu** Uganda
120 B2 **Gumare** Botswana
76 B3 **Gumdag** Turkm.
75 C2 **Gumla** India
100 C2 **Gummersbach** Ger.
74 B2 **Guna** India
53 C3 **Gundagai** Austr.
111 C3 **Güney** Turkey
118 B3 **Gungu** Dem. Rep. Congo
129 E2 **Gunisao** *r.* Can.
53 D2 **Gunnedah** Austr.
136 B3 **Gunnison** *CO* U.S.A.
135 D3 **Gunnison** *UT* U.S.A.
136 B3 **Gunnison** *r.* U.S.A.
73 B3 **Guntakal** India
60 A1 **Gunungsitoli** Indon.
60 A1 **Gunungtua** Indon.
102 C2 **Günzburg** Ger.
102 C2 **Gunzenhausen** Ger.
70 B2 **Guojiaba** China
74 B2 **Gurgaon** India
151 D2 **Gurgueia** *r.* Brazil
150 B1 **Guri, Embalse de** *resr* Venez.
154 C1 **Gurinhatã** Brazil
151 D2 **Gurupi** *r.* Brazil
74 B2 **Guru Sikhar** *mt.* India
Gur'yev Kazakh. *see* **Atyrau**
115 C3 **Gusau** Nigeria
65 A2 **Gushan** China
74 A1 **Gushgy** Turkm.
70 B2 **Gushi** China
83 I3 **Gusinoozersk** Rus. Fed.
89 F2 **Gus'-Khrustal'nyy** Rus. Fed.
108 A3 **Guspini** *Sardinia* Italy
128 A2 **Gustavus** U.S.A.
101 F1 **Güstrow** Ger.
101 D2 **Gütersloh** Ger.
121 C2 **Gutu** Zimbabwe
75 D2 **Guwahati** India
150 C1 **Guyana** *country* S. America
Guyi China *see* **Sanjiang**
139 C1 **Guymon** U.S.A.
53 D2 **Guyra** Austr.
70 A2 **Guyuan** China
144 B1 **Guzmán** Mex.
144 B1 **Guzmán, Lago de** *l.* Mex.
74 A2 **Gwadar** Pak.
75 B2 **Gwalior** India
121 B3 **Gwanda** Zimbabwe
97 B1 **Gweebarra Bay** Rep. of Ireland
97 B1 **Gweedore** Rep. of Ireland
121 B2 **Gweru** Zimbabwe
115 D3 **Gwoza** Nigeria
53 D2 **Gwydir** *r.* Austr.
75 C2 **Gyangzê** China
75 C1 **Gyaring Co** *l.* China
68 C2 **Gyaring Hu** *l.* China
86 G1 **Gydanskiy Poluostrov** *pen.* Rus. Fed.
Gyêgu China *see* **Yushu**
51 E2 **Gympie** Austr.
103 D2 **Gyöngyös** Hungary
103 D2 **Győr** Hungary
129 E2 **Gypsumville** Can.
103 E2 **Gyula** Hungary
81 C1 **Gyumri** Armenia
76 B3 **Gyzylarbat** Turkm.

88 B2 **Haapsalu** Estonia
100 B1 **Haarlem** Neth.
101 C2 **Haarstrang** *ridge* Ger.
54 A2 **Haast** N.Z.
78 B3 **Habbān** Yemen

81 C2 **Ḥabbānīyah, Hawr al** *l.* Iraq
67 C4 **Hachijō-jima** *i.* Japan
66 D2 **Hachinohe** Japan
121 C3 **Hacufera** Moz.
79 C2 **Ḥadd, Ra's al** *pt* Oman
96 C3 **Haddington** U.K.
115 D3 **Hadejia** Nigeria
93 E4 **Haderslev** Denmark
91 C1 **Hadyach** Ukr.
65 B2 **Haeju** N. Korea
65 B2 **Haeju-man** *b.* N. Korea
65 B3 **Haenam** S. Korea
78 B2 **Ḥafar al Bāṭin** Saudi Arabia
62 A1 **Haflong** India
92 □A3 **Hafnarfjörður** Iceland
78 A3 **Hagar Nish Plateau** Eritrea
48 D2 **Hagåtña** Guam
100 C2 **Hagen** Ger.
101 E1 **Hagenow** Ger.
128 B2 **Hagensborg** Can.
141 D3 **Hagerstown** U.S.A.
93 F3 **Hagfors** Sweden
67 B4 **Hagi** Japan
62 B1 **Ha Giang** Vietnam
97 B2 **Hag's Head** *hd* Rep. of Ireland
119 D3 **Hai** Tanz.
62 B1 **Hai Dương** Vietnam
71 B3 **Haifeng** China
71 B3 **Haikou** China
78 B2 **Ḥā'īl** Saudi Arabia
69 D1 **Hailar** China
92 H2 **Hailuoto** *i.* Fin.
69 D3 **Hainan** *i.* China
71 A4 **Hainan** *prov.* China
128 A2 **Haines** U.S.A.
128 A1 **Haines Junction** Can.
101 E2 **Hainich** *ridge* Ger.
101 E2 **Hainleite** *ridge* Ger.
62 B1 **Hai Phong** Vietnam
147 C3 **Haiti** *country* West Indies
116 B3 **Haiya** Sudan
103 E2 **Hajdúböszörmény** Hungary
78 B3 **Ḥajjah** Yemen
79 C2 **Ḥājjīābād** Iran
62 A1 **Haka** Myanmar
81 C2 **Hakkârı** Turkey
66 D2 **Hakodate** Japan
Ḥalab Syria *see* **Aleppo**
78 B2 **Ḥalabān** Saudi Arabia
81 C2 **Halabja** Iraq
116 B2 **Halaib** Sudan
78 A2 **Halaib Triangle** *terr.* Egypt/Sudan
79 C3 **Ḥalāniyāt, Juzur al** *is* Oman
78 A2 **Ḥālat 'Ammār** Saudi Arabia
68 C1 **Halban** Mongolia
101 E2 **Halberstadt** Ger.
64 B1 **Halcon, Mount** Phil.
93 F4 **Halden** Norway
101 E1 **Haldensleben** Ger.
75 D2 **Haldwani** India
79 C2 **Hāleh** Iran
54 A3 **Halfmoon Bay** N.Z.
131 D2 **Halifax** Can.
98 C2 **Halifax** U.K.
141 D3 **Halifax** U.S.A.
65 B3 **Halla-san** *mt.* S. Korea
127 F2 **Hall Beach** Can.
100 B2 **Halle** Belgium
102 C2 **Hallein** Austria
101 E2 **Halle (Saale)** Ger.
137 D1 **Hallock** U.S.A.
127 G2 **Hall Peninsula** Can.
50 B1 **Halls Creek** Austr.
59 C2 **Halmahera** *i.* Indon.
93 F4 **Halmstad** Sweden
67 B4 **Hamada** Japan
81 C2 **Hamadān** Iran
80 B2 **Ḥamāh** Syria
67 C4 **Hamamatsu** Japan
93 F3 **Hamar** Norway
116 B2 **Ḥamāṭah, Jabal** *mt.* Egypt
73 C4 **Hambantota** Sri Lanka
101 D1 **Hamburg** Ger.
78 A2 **Ḥamḍ, Wādī al** *watercourse* Saudi Arabia
78 B3 **Ḥamḍah** Saudi Arabia
93 H3 **Hämeenlinna** Fin.
101 D1 **Hameln** Ger.
50 A2 **Hamersley Range** *mts* Austr.
65 B2 **Hamhŭng** N. Korea
68 C2 **Hami** China
116 B2 **Hamid** Sudan
52 B3 **Hamilton** Austr.
130 C2 **Hamilton** Can.
54 C1 **Hamilton** N.Z.
96 B3 **Hamilton** U.K.
142 C2 **Hamilton** *AL* U.S.A.
134 D1 **Hamilton** *MT* U.S.A.
140 C3 **Hamilton** *OH* U.S.A.
93 I3 **Hamina** Fin.
100 C2 **Hamm** Ger.
114 B2 **Hammada du Drâa** *plat.* Alg.
81 C2 **Ḥammār, Hawr al** *imp. l.* Iraq
101 D2 **Hammelburg** Ger.
92 G3 **Hammerdal** Sweden
92 H1 **Hammerfest** Norway
142 B2 **Hammond** U.S.A.
141 E3 **Hammonton** U.S.A.
79 C2 **Hāmūn-e Jaz Mūrīān** *salt marsh* Iran
74 A2 **Hamun-i-Lora** *dry lake* Pak.
74 A2 **Hamun-i-Mashkel** *salt flat* Pak.
78 A2 **Ḥanak** Saudi Arabia
66 D3 **Hanamaki** Japan
101 D2 **Hanau** Ger.
70 B2 **Hancheng** China
140 B1 **Hancock** U.S.A.
70 B2 **Handan** China
135 C3 **Hanford** U.S.A.
68 C1 **Hangayn Nuruu** *mts* Mongolia
Hanggin Houqi China *see* **Xamba**
Hangö Fin. *see* **Hanko**
70 C2 **Hangzhou** China
70 C2 **Hangzhou Wan** *b.* China
Hanjia China *see* **Pengshui**
70 B2 **Hanjiang** China
93 H4 **Hanko** Fin.
135 D3 **Hanksville** U.S.A.
54 B2 **Hanmer Springs** N.Z.
129 C2 **Hanna** Can.
137 E3 **Hannibal** U.S.A.
101 D1 **Hannover** Ger.
101 D2 **Hannoversch Münden** Ger.
93 F4 **Hanöbukten** *b.* Sweden
62 B1 **Ha Nôi** Vietnam
Hanoi Vietnam *see* **Ha Nôi**
130 B2 **Hanover** Can.
122 B3 **Hanover** S. Africa
93 E4 **Hanstholm** Denmark
88 C3 **Hantsavichy** Belarus
75 C2 **Hanumana** India
74 B2 **Hanumangarh** India
70 A2 **Hanzhong** China
92 H2 **Haparanda** Sweden
100 B2 **Hapert** Neth.
131 D1 **Happy Valley-Goose Bay** Can.
78 A2 **Ḥaql** Saudi Arabia
79 B2 **Ḥaraḍh** Saudi Arabia
88 C2 **Haradok** Belarus
78 B3 **Ḥarajā** Saudi Arabia
121 C2 **Harare** Zimbabwe
79 C3 **Ḥarāsīs, Jiddat al** *des.* Oman
69 D1 **Har-Ayrag** Mongolia
69 E1 **Harbin** China
131 E2 **Harbour Breton** Can.
74 B2 **Harda** India
100 C1 **Hardenberg** Neth.
100 B1 **Harderwijk** Neth.
122 A3 **Hardeveld** *mts* S. Africa
134 E1 **Hardin** U.S.A.
128 C1 **Hardisty Lake** Can.
100 C1 **Haren (Ems)** Ger.
117 C4 **Hārer** Eth.
117 C4 **Hargeysa** Somalia
110 C1 **Harghita-Mădăraș, Vârful** *mt.* Romania
68 C2 **Har Hu** *l.* China
74 B1 **Haripur** Pak.
74 A1 **Harī Rūd** *r.* Afgh./Iran
100 B1 **Harlingen** Neth.
139 D3 **Harlingen** U.S.A.
99 D3 **Harlow** U.K.
134 E1 **Harlowton** U.S.A.
134 C2 **Harney Basin** U.S.A.
134 C2 **Harney Lake** U.S.A.
93 G3 **Härnösand** Sweden
69 E1 **Har Nur** China
68 C1 **Har Nuur** *l.* Mongolia
114 B4 **Harper** Liberia
101 D1 **Harpstedt** Ger.
130 C1 **Harricanaw** *r.* Can.
53 D2 **Harrington** Austr.
131 E1 **Harrington Harbour** Can.
96 A2 **Harris** *pen.* U.K.
96 A2 **Harris, Sound of** *sea chan.* U.K.
140 B3 **Harrisburg** *IL* U.S.A.
141 D2 **Harrisburg** *PA* U.S.A.
123 C2 **Harrismith** S. Africa
142 B1 **Harrison** U.S.A.
131 E1 **Harrison, Cape** Can.
126 A2 **Harrison Bay** U.S.A.
141 D3 **Harrisonburg** U.S.A.
137 E3 **Harrisonville** U.S.A.
98 C2 **Harrogate** U.K.
110 C2 **Hârșova** Romania
92 G2 **Harstad** Norway
122 B2 **Hartbees** *watercourse* S. Africa
103 D2 **Hartberg** Austria
141 E2 **Hartford** U.S.A.
99 A3 **Hartland Point** U.K.
98 C1 **Hartlepool** U.K.
128 B2 **Hartley Bay** Can.
123 B2 **Harts** *r.* S. Africa
143 D2 **Hartwell Reservoir** U.S.A.
68 C1 **Har Us Nuur** *l.* Mongolia
136 C1 **Harvey** U.S.A.
99 D3 **Harwich** U.K.
101 E2 **Harz** *hills* Ger.
73 B3 **Hassan** India
100 B2 **Hasselt** Belgium
115 C1 **Hassi Messaoud** Alg.
93 F4 **Hässleholm** Sweden
100 B2 **Hastière-Lavaux** Belgium
53 C3 **Hastings** Austr.
54 C1 **Hastings** N.Z.
99 D3 **Hastings** U.K.
137 E2 **Hastings** *MN* U.S.A.
137 D2 **Hastings** *NE* U.S.A.
Hatay Turkey *see* **Antakya**
129 D2 **Hatchet Lake** Can.
52 B2 **Hatfield** Austr.
68 C1 **Hatgal** Mongolia
62 B2 **Ha Tinh** Vietnam
143 E1 **Hatteras, Cape** U.S.A.
142 C2 **Hattiesburg** U.S.A.
100 C2 **Hattingen** Ger.
63 B3 **Hat Yai** Thai.
117 C4 **Haud** *reg.* Eth.
93 E4 **Haugesund** Norway
93 E4 **Haukeligrend** Norway
92 I2 **Haukipudas** Fin.
54 C1 **Hauraki Gulf** N.Z.

114 B1 **Haut Atlas** *mts* Morocco
131 D2 **Hauterive** Can.
114 B1 **Hauts Plateaux** *plat.* Alg.
146 B2 **Havana** Cuba
99 C3 **Havant** U.K.
101 E1 **Havel** *r.* Ger.
101 F1 **Havelberg** Ger.
54 B2 **Havelock** N.Z.
54 C1 **Havelock North** N.Z.
99 A3 **Haverfordwest** U.K.
103 D2 **Havlíčkův Brod** Czech Rep.
92 H1 **Havøysund** Norway
111 C3 **Havran** Turkey
134 E1 **Havre** U.S.A.
131 D2 **Havre Aubert** Can.
131 D1 **Havre-St-Pierre** Can.
124 A5 **Hawaii** *is.* N. Pacific Ocean
98 B2 **Hawarden** U.K.
54 A2 **Hawea, Lake** N.Z.
54 B1 **Hawera** N.Z.
98 B1 **Hawes** U.K.
96 C3 **Hawick** U.K.
54 C1 **Hawke Bay** N.Z.
52 A2 **Hawker** Austr.
52 B1 **Hawkers Gate** Austr.
135 C3 **Hawthorne** U.S.A.
52 B2 **Hay** Austr.
128 C1 **Hay** *r.* Can.
134 C1 **Hayden** U.S.A.
129 E2 **Hayes** *r. Man.* Can.
126 E2 **Hayes** *r. Nunavut* Can.
79 C3 **Haymā'** Oman
111 C2 **Hayrabolu** Turkey
128 C1 **Hay River** Can.
137 D3 **Hays** U.S.A.
78 B3 **Ḩays** Yemen
90 B2 **Haysyn** Ukr.
99 C3 **Haywards Heath** U.K.
74 A1 **Hazarajat** *reg.* Afgh.
140 C3 **Hazard** U.S.A.
75 C2 **Hazaribagh** India
75 C2 **Hazaribagh Range** *mts* India
128 B2 **Hazelton** Can.
141 D2 **Hazleton** U.S.A.
53 C3 **Healesville** Austr.
130 B2 **Hearst** Can.
70 B2 **Hebei** *prov.* China
53 C1 **Hebel** Austr.
142 B1 **Heber Springs** U.S.A.
70 B2 **Hebi** China
131 D1 **Hebron** Can.
128 A2 **Hecate Strait** Can.
71 A3 **Hechi** China
93 F3 **Hede** Sweden
100 B1 **Heerenveen** Neth.
100 B1 **Heerhugowaard** Neth.
100 B2 **Heerlen** Neth.
80 B2 **Ḩefa** Israel
70 B2 **Hefei** China
70 B3 **Hefeng** China
69 E1 **Hegang** China
102 B1 **Heide** Ger.
122 A1 **Heide** Namibia
102 B2 **Heidelberg** Ger.
122 B3 **Heidelberg** S. Africa
102 B2 **Heilbronn** Ger.
69 E1 **Heilong Jiang** *r.* China/Rus. Fed.
93 I3 **Heinola** Fin.
92 F3 **Helagsfjället** *mt.* Sweden
142 B2 **Helena** *AR* U.S.A.
134 D1 **Helena** *MT* U.S.A.
96 B2 **Helensburgh** U.K.
102 B1 **Helgoland** *i.* Ger.
102 B1 **Helgoländer Bucht** *b.* Ger.
Helixi China *see* **Ningguo**
92 □A3 **Hella** Iceland
100 B2 **Hellevoetsluis** Neth.
107 C2 **Hellín** Spain
76 C3 **Helmand** *r.* Afgh.
101 E2 **Helmbrechts** Ger.
122 A2 **Helmeringhausen** Namibia
100 B2 **Helmond** Neth.
96 C1 **Helmsdale** U.K.
96 C1 **Helmsdale** *r.* U.K.
101 E1 **Helmstedt** Ger.
65 B1 **Helong** China
93 F4 **Helsingborg** Sweden
Helsingfors Fin. *see* Helsinki
93 F4 **Helsingør** Denmark
93 H3 **Helsinki** Fin.
97 C2 **Helvick Head** *hd* Rep. of Ireland
99 C3 **Hemel Hempstead** U.K.
101 D1 **Hemmoor** Ger.
92 F2 **Hemnesberget** Norway
70 B2 **Henan** *prov.* China
140 B3 **Henderson** *KY* U.S.A.
143 E1 **Henderson** *NC* U.S.A.
135 D3 **Henderson** *NV* U.S.A.
139 E2 **Henderson** *TX* U.S.A.
143 D1 **Hendersonville** U.S.A.
99 C3 **Hendon** U.K.
62 A1 **Hengduan Shan** *mts* China
100 C1 **Hengelo** Neth.
Hengnan China *see* Hengyang
70 B2 **Hengshui** China
71 A3 **Hengxian** China
71 B3 **Hengyang** China
Hengzhou China *see* Hengxian
91 C2 **Heniches'k** Ukr.
100 C2 **Hennef (Sieg)** Ger.
130 B1 **Henrietta Maria, Cape** Can.
139 D1 **Henryetta** U.S.A.
127 G2 **Henry Kater, Cape** Can.
101 D1 **Henstedt-Ulzburg** Ger.
120 A3 **Hentiesbaai** Namibia
62 A2 **Henzada** Myanmar
71 A3 **Hepu** China
76 C3 **Herāt** Afgh.
129 D2 **Herbert** Can.
101 D2 **Herbstein** Ger.
99 B2 **Hereford** U.K.
139 C2 **Hereford** U.S.A.
101 D1 **Herford** Ger.
100 C2 **Herkenbosch** Neth.
96 □ **Herma Ness** *hd* U.K.
122 A3 **Hermanus** S. Africa
53 C2 **Hermidale** Austr.
134 C1 **Hermiston** U.S.A.
59 D3 **Hermit Islands** P.N.G.
144 A2 **Hermosillo** Mex.
154 B3 **Hernandarias** Para.
100 C2 **Herne** Ger.
93 E4 **Herning** Denmark
99 C3 **Hertford** U.K.
123 C2 **Hertzogville** S. Africa
51 E2 **Hervey Bay** *b.* Austr.
101 F2 **Herzberg** Ger.
101 E3 **Herzogenaurach** Ger.
71 A3 **Heshan** China
128 A1 **Hess** *r.* Can.
101 D2 **Hessisch Lichtenau** Ger.
136 C1 **Hettinger** U.S.A.
101 E2 **Hettstedt** Ger.
98 B1 **Hexham** U.K.
71 B3 **Heyuan** China
52 B3 **Heywood** Austr.
70 B2 **Heze** China
71 B3 **Hezhou** China
137 D3 **Hiawatha** U.S.A.
137 E1 **Hibbing** U.S.A.
54 C1 **Hicks Bay** N.Z.
66 D2 **Hidaka-sanmyaku** *mts* Japan
145 C2 **Hidalgo** Mex.
144 B2 **Hidalgo del Parral** Mex.
154 C1 **Hidrolândia** Brazil
High Atlas *mts* Morocco *see* Haut Atlas
134 B2 **High Desert** U.S.A.
128 C2 **High Level** Can.
143 E1 **High Point** U.S.A.
128 C2 **High Prairie** Can.
128 C2 **High River** Can.
129 D2 **Highrock Lake** Can.
99 C3 **High Wycombe** U.K.
88 B2 **Hiiumaa** *i.* Estonia
78 A2 **Hijaz** *reg.* Saudi Arabia
54 C1 **Hikurangi** *mt.* N.Z.
101 E2 **Hildburghausen** Ger.
101 E2 **Hilders** Ger.
101 D1 **Hildesheim** Ger.
100 C2 **Hillesheim** Ger.
140 C3 **Hillsboro** *OH* U.S.A.
139 D2 **Hillsboro** *TX* U.S.A.
53 C2 **Hillston** Austr.
143 D2 **Hilton Head Island** U.S.A.
100 B1 **Hilversum** Neth.
72 B1 **Himalaya** *mts* Asia
67 B4 **Himeji** Japan
123 C2 **Himeville** S. Africa
80 B2 **Ḩimş** Syria
51 D1 **Hinchinbrook Island** Austr.
74 A1 **Hindu Kush** *mts* Afgh./Pak.
143 D2 **Hinesville** U.S.A.
75 B2 **Hinganghat** India
81 C2 **Hınıs** Turkey
92 G2 **Hinnøya** *i.* Norway
106 B2 **Hinojosa del Duque** Spain
128 C2 **Hinton** Can.
75 C2 **Hirakud Reservoir** India
66 D2 **Hirosaki** Japan
67 B4 **Hiroshima** Japan
101 E3 **Hirschaid** Ger.
101 E2 **Hirschberg** Ger.
105 C2 **Hirson** France
93 E4 **Hirtshals** Denmark
74 B2 **Hisar** India
147 C2 **Hispaniola** *i.* Caribbean Sea
81 C2 **Hīt** Iraq
67 D3 **Hitachi** Japan
67 D3 **Hitachinaka** Japan
92 E3 **Hitra** *i.* Norway
93 G4 **Hjälmaren** *l.* Sweden
129 D1 **Hjalmar Lake** Can.
93 F4 **Hjørring** Denmark
123 D2 **Hlabisa** S. Africa
92 □B2 **Hlíð** Iceland
91 C2 **Hlobyne** Ukr.
123 C2 **Hlohlowane** S. Africa
123 C2 **Hlotse** Lesotho
91 C1 **Hlukhiv** Ukr.
88 C2 **Hlybokaye** Belarus
114 C4 **Ho** Ghana
122 A1 **Hoachanas** Namibia
51 D4 **Hobart** Austr.
139 D1 **Hobart** U.S.A.
139 C2 **Hobbs** U.S.A.
93 E4 **Hobro** Denmark
117 C4 **Hobyo** Somalia
63 B2 **Hô Chi Minh City** Vietnam
114 B3 **Ḥôḍ** *reg.* Maur.
103 E2 **Hódmezővásárhely** Hungary
100 B2 **Hoek van Holland** Neth.
65 B2 **Hoeyang** N. Korea
101 E2 **Hof** Ger.
101 E2 **Hofheim in Unterfranken** Ger.
92 □B3 **Höfn** *Austurland* Iceland
92 □A2 **Höfn** *Vestfirðir* Iceland
92 □B3 **Hofsjökull** *ice cap* Iceland
67 B4 **Hōfu** Japan
115 C2 **Hoggar** *plat.* Alg.
93 G4 **Högsby** Sweden

93 E3 **Høgste Breakulen** *mt.* Norway
101 D2 **Hohe Rhön** *mts* Ger.
100 C2 **Hohe Venn** *moorland* Belgium
70 B1 **Hohhot** China
75 C1 **Hoh Xil Shan** *mts* China
63 B2 **Hôi An** Vietnam
62 A1 **Hojai** India
54 B2 **Hokitika** N.Z.
66 D2 **Hokkaidō** *i.* Japan
128 B2 **Holberg** Can.
138 A2 **Holbrook** U.S.A.
137 D2 **Holdrege** U.S.A.
146 C2 **Holguín** Cuba
92 □B2 **Hóll** Iceland
Holland *country* Europe *see* **Netherlands**
140 B2 **Holland** U.S.A.
100 B1 **Hollum** Neth.
142 C2 **Holly Springs** U.S.A.
143 D3 **Hollywood** U.S.A.
92 F2 **Holm** Norway
126 D2 **Holman** Can.
92 H3 **Holmsund** Sweden
122 A2 **Holoog** Namibia
93 E4 **Holstebro** Denmark
143 D1 **Holston** *r.* U.S.A.
98 A2 **Holyhead** U.K.
98 C1 **Holy Island** *England* U.K.
98 A2 **Holy Island** *Wales* U.K.
136 C2 **Holyoke** U.S.A.
101 D2 **Holzminden** Ger.
62 A1 **Homalin** Myanmar
101 D2 **Homberg (Efze)** Ger.
114 B3 **Hombori** Mali
127 G2 **Home Bay** Can.
143 D3 **Homestead** U.S.A.
92 F3 **Hommelvik** Norway
89 D3 **Homyel'** Belarus
122 A3 **Hondeklipbaai** S. Africa
145 D3 **Hondo** *r.* Belize/Mex.
139 D3 **Hondo** U.S.A.
146 B3 **Honduras** *country* Central America
93 F3 **Hønefoss** Norway
135 B2 **Honey Lake** U.S.A.
104 C2 **Honfleur** France
62 B1 **Hông Gai** Vietnam
70 B3 **Honghu** China
71 A3 **Hongjiang** China
69 D3 **Hong Kong** China
71 B3 **Hong Kong** *special admin. reg.* China
65 B1 **Hongwŏn** N. Korea
70 B2 **Hongze Hu** *l.* China
49 E3 **Honiara** Solomon Islands
66 D3 **Honjō** Japan
92 I1 **Honningsvåg** Norway
67 B3 **Honshū** *i.* Japan
134 B1 **Hood, Mount** *vol.* U.S.A.
50 A3 **Hood Point** Austr.
134 B1 **Hood River** U.S.A.
100 C1 **Hoogeveen** Neth.
100 C1 **Hoogezand-Sappemeer** Neth.
100 C2 **Hoog-Keppel** Neth.
Hook of Holland Neth. *see* Hoek van Holland
128 A2 **Hoonah** U.S.A.
100 B1 **Hoorn** Neth.
128 B3 **Hope** Can.
142 B2 **Hope** U.S.A.
83 N2 **Hope, Point** U.S.A.
131 D1 **Hopedale** Can.
131 D1 **Hope Mountains** Can.
52 B3 **Hopetoun** Austr.
122 B2 **Hopetown** S. Africa
141 D3 **Hopewell** U.S.A.
130 C1 **Hopewell Islands** Can.
50 B2 **Hopkins, Lake** *salt flat* Austr.
140 B3 **Hopkinsville** U.S.A.
134 B1 **Hoquiam** U.S.A.
81 C1 **Horasan** Turkey
93 F4 **Hörby** Sweden
89 D3 **Horki** Belarus
91 D2 **Horlivka** Ukr.
79 D2 **Hormak** Iran
79 C2 **Hormuz, Strait of** Iran/Oman
103 D2 **Horn** Austria
92 □A2 **Horn** *c.* Iceland
153 B6 **Horn, Cape** *c.* Chile
141 D2 **Hornell** U.S.A.
130 B2 **Hornepayne** Can.
98 C2 **Hornsea** U.K.
90 B2 **Horodenka** Ukr.
91 C1 **Horodnya** Ukr.
90 B2 **Horodok** *Khmel'nyts'ka Oblast'* Ukr.
90 A2 **Horodok** *L'vivs'ka Oblast'* Ukr.
90 A1 **Horokhiv** Ukr.
Horqin Youyi Qianqi China *see* **Ulanhot**
131 E1 **Horse Islands** Can.
52 B3 **Horsham** Austr.
126 C2 **Horton** *r.* Can.
117 B4 **Hosa'ina** Eth.
74 A2 **Hoshab** Pak.
74 B1 **Hoshiarpur** India
77 E3 **Hotan** China
122 B2 **Hotazel** S. Africa
142 B2 **Hot Springs** *AR* U.S.A.
136 C2 **Hot Springs** *SD* U.S.A.
128 C1 **Hottah Lake** Can.
100 B2 **Houffalize** Belgium
70 B2 **Houma** China
142 B3 **Houma** U.S.A.
128 B2 **Houston** Can.
139 D3 **Houston** U.S.A.
122 B3 **Houwater** S. Africa
68 C1 **Hovd** Mongolia
99 C3 **Hove** U.K.
68 C1 **Hövsgöl Nuur** *l.* Mongolia
68 C2 **Hövüün** Mongolia
116 A3 **Howar, Wadi** *watercourse* Sudan
53 C3 **Howe, Cape** Austr.
53 C3 **Howlong** Austr.
101 D2 **Höxter** Ger.
96 C1 **Hoy** *i.* U.K.
93 E3 **Høyanger** Norway
102 C1 **Hoyerswerda** Ger.
103 D1 **Hradec Králové** Czech Rep.
109 C2 **Hrasnica** Bos.-Herz.
91 C1 **Hrebinka** Ukr.
88 B3 **Hrodna** Belarus
62 A1 **Hsi-hseng** Myanmar
71 C3 **Hsinchu** Taiwan
71 C3 **Hsinying** Taiwan
62 A1 **Hsipaw** Myanmar
70 A2 **Huachi** China
150 A3 **Huacho** Peru
69 D2 **Huade** China
65 B1 **Huadian** China
70 B2 **Huaibei** China
71 A3 **Huaihua** China
70 B2 **Huainan** China
70 B2 **Huaiyang** China
70 B2 **Huaiyin** China
145 C3 **Huajuápan de León** Mex.
59 C3 **Huaki** Indon.
71 C3 **Hualien** Taiwan
150 A2 **Huallaga** *r.* Peru
120 A2 **Huambo** Angola
150 A3 **Huancayo** Peru
Huangcaoba China *see* **Xingyi**
70 B2 **Huangchuan** China
Huang Hai *sea* N. Pacific Ocean *see* **Yellow Sea**
70 B2 **Huang He** *r.* China
71 A4 **Huangliu** China
70 B3 **Huangshan** China
70 B2 **Huangshi** China
70 A2 **Huangtu Gaoyuan** *plat.* China
71 C3 **Huangyan** China
65 B1 **Huanren** China
150 A2 **Huánuco** Peru
152 B2 **Huanuni** Bol.
150 A2 **Huaráz** Peru
150 A3 **Huarmey** Peru
152 A3 **Huasco** Chile
152 A3 **Huasco** *r.* Chile
144 B2 **Huatabampo** Mex.
145 C3 **Huatusco** Mex.
71 A3 **Huayuan** China
70 B2 **Hubei** *prov.* China
73 B3 **Hubli** India
100 C2 **Hückelhoven** Ger.
98 C2 **Hucknall** U.K.
98 C2 **Huddersfield** U.K.
93 G3 **Hudiksvall** Sweden
141 E2 **Hudson** *r.* U.S.A.
129 D2 **Hudson Bay** Can.
127 F3 **Hudson Bay** *sea* Can.
128 B2 **Hudson's Hope** Can.
127 G2 **Hudson Strait** Can.
63 B2 **Huê** Vietnam
146 A3 **Huehuetenango** Guat.
144 B2 **Huehueto, Cerro** *mt.* Mex.
145 C2 **Huejutla** Mex.
106 B2 **Huelva** Spain
107 C2 **Huércal-Overa** Spain
107 C1 **Huesca** Spain
106 C2 **Huéscar** Spain
50 B3 **Hughes** Austr.
139 D2 **Hugo** U.S.A.
122 B2 **Huhudi** S. Africa
122 A2 **Huib-Hoch Plateau** Namibia
71 B3 **Huichang** China
65 B1 **Huich'ŏn** N. Korea
71 B3 **Huilai** China
120 A2 **Huíla Plateau** Angola
62 B1 **Huili** China
65 B1 **Huinan** China
93 H3 **Huittinen** Fin.
145 C3 **Huixtla** Mex.
Huiyang China *see* **Huizhou**
62 B1 **Huize** China
71 B3 **Huizhou** China
69 C1 **Hujirt** Mongolia
78 B2 **Hujr** Saudi Arabia
122 B1 **Hukuntsi** Botswana
78 B2 **Ḩulayfah** Saudi Arabia
66 B1 **Hulin** China
130 C2 **Hull** Can.
Hulun China *see* **Hailar**
69 D1 **Hulun Nur** *l.* China
91 D2 **Hulyaypole** Ukr.
69 E1 **Huma** China
150 B2 **Humaitá** Brazil
122 B3 **Humansdorp** S. Africa
98 C2 **Humber** *est.* U.K.
126 D3 **Humboldt** Can.
142 C1 **Humboldt** U.S.A.
135 C2 **Humboldt** *r.* U.S.A.
103 E2 **Humenné** Slovakia
53 C3 **Hume Reservoir** Austr.
138 A1 **Humphreys Peak** U.S.A.
92 □A2 **Húnaflói** *b.* Iceland
71 B3 **Hunan** *prov.* China
65 C1 **Hunchun** China
110 B1 **Hunedoara** Romania
101 D2 **Hünfeld** Ger.

103 D2 **Hungary** *country* Europe
52 B1 **Hungerford** Austr.
65 B2 **Hŭngnam** N. Korea
65 A1 **Hun He** *r.* China
99 D2 **Hunstanton** U.K.
101 D1 **Hunte** *r.* Ger.
51 D4 **Hunter Islands** Austr.
99 C2 **Huntingdon** U.K.
140 B2 **Huntington** *IN* U.S.A.
140 C3 **Huntington** *WV* U.S.A.
54 C1 **Huntly** N.Z.
96 C2 **Huntly** U.K.
130 C2 **Huntsville** Can.
142 C2 **Huntsville** *AL* U.S.A.
139 D2 **Huntsville** *TX* U.S.A.
59 D3 **Huon Peninsula** P.N.G.
70 B2 **Huozhou** China
137 D2 **Huron** U.S.A.
140 C2 **Huron, Lake** Can./U.S.A.
135 D3 **Hurricane** U.S.A.
92 □B2 **Húsavík** Iceland
110 C1 **Huşi** Romania
126 A2 **Huslia** U.S.A.
78 B3 **Ḩuşn Āl 'Abr** Yemen
102 B1 **Husum** Ger.
69 C1 **Hutag** Mongolia
60 A1 **Hutanopan** Indon.
137 D3 **Hutchinson** U.S.A.
70 C2 **Huzhou** China
92 □C3 **Hvalnes** Iceland
92 □B3 **Hvannadalshnúkur** *vol.* Iceland
109 C2 **Hvar** *i.* Croatia
120 B2 **Hwange** Zimbabwe
136 C2 **Hyannis** U.S.A.
68 C1 **Hyargas Nuur** *salt l.* Mongolia
50 A3 **Hyden** Austr.
73 B3 **Hyderabad** India
74 A2 **Hyderabad** Pak.
105 D3 **Hyères** France
105 D3 **Hyères, Îles d'** *is* France
65 B1 **Hyesan** N. Korea
128 B2 **Hyland Post** Can.
67 B3 **Hyōno-sen** *mt.* Japan
99 D3 **Hythe** U.K.
93 H3 **Hyvinkää** Fin.

I

150 B2 **Iaco** *r.* Brazil
110 C2 **Ialomiţa** *r.* Romania
110 C1 **Ianca** Romania
110 C1 **Iaşi** Romania
64 A1 **Iba** Phil.
115 C4 **Ibadan** Nigeria
150 A1 **Ibagué** Col.
150 A1 **Ibarra** Ecuador
78 B3 **Ibb** Yemen
100 C1 **Ibbenbüren** Ger.
115 C4 **Ibi** Nigeria
155 C1 **Ibiá** Brazil
155 D1 **Ibiraçu** Brazil
107 D2 **Ibiza** *i.* Spain
151 D3 **Ibotirama** Brazil
79 C2 **Ibrā'** Oman
79 C2 **Ibrī** Oman
150 A3 **Ica** Peru
80 B2 **İçel** Turkey
92 □B2 **Iceland** *country* Europe
66 D3 **Ichinoseki** Japan
91 C1 **Ichnya** Ukr.
65 B2 **Ich'ŏn** N. Korea
139 E2 **Idabel** U.S.A.
134 D2 **Idaho** *state* U.S.A.
134 D2 **Idaho Falls** U.S.A.
100 C3 **Idar-Oberstein** Ger.
116 B2 **Idfū** Egypt
115 D2 **Idhān Awbārī** *des.* Libya
115 D2 **Idhān Murzūq** *des.* Libya
118 B3 **Idiofa** Dem. Rep. Congo
80 B2 **Idlib** Syria
154 B2 **Iepê** Brazil
100 A2 **Ieper** Belgium
119 D3 **Ifakara** Tanz.
121 □D3 **Ifanadiana** Madag.
115 C4 **Ife** Nigeria
114 C3 **Ifôghas, Adrar des** *hills* Mali
61 C1 **Igan** *Sarawak* Malaysia
154 C2 **Igarapava** Brazil
82 G2 **Igarka** Rus. Fed.
74 B3 **Igatpuri** India
81 C2 **Iğdır** Turkey
108 A3 **Iglesias** *Sardinia* Italy
127 F2 **Igloolik** Can.
Igluligaarjuk Can. *see* **Chesterfield Inlet**
130 A2 **Ignace** Can.
88 C2 **Ignalina** Lith.
110 C2 **İğneada** Turkey
111 B3 **Igoumenitsa** Greece
86 E3 **Igra** Rus. Fed.
86 F2 **Igrim** Rus. Fed.
154 B3 **Iguaçu** *r.* Brazil
154 B3 **Iguaçu Falls** Arg./Brazil
145 C3 **Iguala** Mex.
107 D1 **Igualada** Spain
154 C2 **Iguape** Brazil
154 B2 **Iguatemi** Brazil
154 B2 **Iguatemi** *r.* Brazil
151 E2 **Iguatu** Brazil
118 A3 **Iguéla** Gabon
119 D3 **Igunga** Tanz.
69 D2 **Ihbulag** Mongolia
121 □D3 **Ihosy** Madag.
92 I3 **Iisalmi** Fin.
115 C4 **Ijebu-Ode** Nigeria
100 B1 **IJmuiden** Neth.
100 B1 **IJssel** *r.* Neth.
100 B1 **IJsselmeer** *l.* Neth.
123 C2 **Ikageng** S. Africa
111 C3 **Ikaria** *i.* Greece
118 C3 **Ikela** Dem. Rep. Congo
110 B2 **Ikhtiman** Bulg.
67 A4 **Iki** *i.* Japan
121 □D3 **Ikongo** Madag.
65 B2 **Iksan** S. Korea
64 B1 **Ilagan** Phil.
81 C2 **Īlām** Iran
75 C2 **Ilam** Nepal
103 D1 **Iława** Pol.
79 C2 **Ilazārān, Kūh-e** *mt.* Iran
129 D2 **Île-à-la-Crosse** Can.
129 D2 **Île-à-la-Crosse, Lac** *l.* Can.
118 C3 **Ilebo** Dem. Rep. Congo
119 D2 **Ileret** Kenya
99 D3 **Ilford** U.K.
99 A3 **Ilfracombe** U.K.
155 D2 **Ilha Grande, Baía da** *b.* Brazil
154 B2 **Ilha Grande, Represa** *resr* Brazil
154 B2 **Ilha Solteíra, Represa** *resr* Brazil
106 B1 **Ílhavo** Port.
151 E3 **Ilhéus** Brazil
64 B2 **Iligan** Phil.
152 A4 **Illapel** Chile
90 C2 **Illichivs'k** Ukr.
140 A3 **Illinois** *r.* U.S.A.
140 B3 **Illinois** *state* U.S.A.
90 B2 **Illintsi** Ukr.
115 C2 **Illizi** Alg.
89 D2 **Il'men', Ozero** *l.* Rus. Fed.
101 E2 **Ilmenau** Ger.
150 A3 **Ilo** Peru
64 B1 **Iloilo** Phil.
92 J3 **Ilomantsi** Fin.
115 C4 **Ilorin** Nigeria
53 D1 **Iluka** Austr.
127 H2 **Ilulissat** Greenland
67 A4 **Imari** Japan
117 C4 **Īmī** Eth.
108 B2 **Imola** Italy
151 D2 **Imperatriz** Brazil
136 C2 **Imperial** U.S.A.
118 B2 **Impfondo** Congo
62 A1 **Imphal** India
111 C2 **İmroz** Turkey
150 B3 **Inambari** *r.* Peru
115 C2 **In Aménas** Alg.
59 C3 **Inanwatan** Indon.
92 I2 **Inari** Fin.
92 I2 **Inarijärvi** *l.* Fin.
67 D3 **Inawashiro-ko** *l.* Japan
80 B1 **İnce Burun** *pt* Turkey
65 B2 **Inch'ŏn** S. Korea
123 D2 **Incomati** *r.* Moz.
78 A3 **Inda Silasē** Eth.
144 B2 **Indé** Mex.
135 C3 **Independence** *CA* U.S.A.
137 E2 **Independence** *IA* U.S.A.
137 D3 **Independence** *KS* U.S.A.
137 E3 **Independence** *MO* U.S.A.
134 C2 **Independence Mountains** U.S.A.
76 B2 **Inderborskiy** Kazakh.
72 B2 **India** *country* Asia
141 D2 **Indiana** U.S.A.
140 B2 **Indiana** *state* U.S.A.
140 B3 **Indianapolis** U.S.A.
129 D2 **Indian Head** Can.
159 **Indian Ocean**
137 E2 **Indianola** *IA* U.S.A.
142 B2 **Indianola** *MS* U.S.A.
135 C3 **Indian Springs** U.S.A.
86 D2 **Indiga** Rus. Fed.
83 K2 **Indigirka** *r.* Rus. Fed.
109 D1 **Inđija** Serb. and Mont.
135 C4 **Indio** U.S.A.
58 B3 **Indonesia** *country* Asia
74 B2 **Indore** India
61 B2 **Indramayu, Tanjung** *pt* Indon.
104 C2 **Indre** *r.* France
74 A2 **Indus** *r.* China/Pak.
74 A2 **Indus, Mouths of the** Pak.
80 B1 **İnebolu** Turkey
111 C2 **İnegöl** Turkey
144 B3 **Infiernillo, Presa** *resr* Mex.
53 D1 **Inglewood** Austr.
102 C2 **Ingolstadt** Ger.
75 C2 **Ingraj Bazar** India
123 D2 **Inhaca** Moz.
121 C3 **Inhambane** Moz.
97 A2 **Inishbofin** *i.* Rep. of Ireland
97 B2 **Inishmore** *i.* Rep. of Ireland
97 C1 **Inishowen** *pen.* Rep. of Ireland
54 B2 **Inland Kaikoura Range** *mts* N.Z.
102 C2 **Inn** *r.* Europe
127 G1 **Innaanganeq** *c.* Greenland
69 D2 **Inner Mongolia** *reg.* China
96 B2 **Inner Sound** *sea chan.* U.K.
51 D1 **Innisfail** Austr.
102 C2 **Innsbruck** Austria
154 B1 **Inocência** Brazil
118 B3 **Inongo** Dem. Rep. Congo
103 D1 **Inowrocław** Pol.
114 C2 **In Salah** Alg.
62 A2 **Insein** Myanmar
86 F2 **Inta** Rus. Fed.
137 E1 **International Falls** U.S.A.

130 C1 **Inukjuak** Can.
126 C2 **Inuvik** Can.
96 B2 **Inveraray** U.K.
54 A3 **Invercargill** N.Z.
53 D1 **Inverell** Austr.
96 B2 **Invergordon** U.K.
128 C2 **Invermere** Can.
131 D2 **Inverness** Can.
96 B2 **Inverness** U.K.
96 C2 **Inverurie** U.K.
52 A3 **Investigator Strait** Austr.
77 E1 **Inya** Rus. Fed.
119 D3 **Inyonga** Tanz.
87 D3 **Inza** Rus. Fed.
111 B3 **Ioannina** Greece
137 D3 **Iola** U.S.A.
96 A2 **Iona** *i.* U.K.
111 B3 **Ionian Islands** Greece
109 C3 **Ionian Sea** Greece/Italy
Ionioi Nisoi *is* Greece *see* Ionian Islands
111 C3 **Ios** *i.* Greece
137 E2 **Iowa** *state* U.S.A.
137 E2 **Iowa City** U.S.A.
154 C1 **Ipameri** Brazil
155 D1 **Ipatinga** Brazil
81 C1 **Ipatovo** Rus. Fed.
123 C2 **Ipelegeng** S. Africa
150 A1 **Ipiales** Col.
154 B3 **Ipiranga** Brazil
60 B1 **Ipoh** Malaysia
154 B1 **Iporá** Brazil
118 C2 **Ippy** C.A.R.
111 C2 **İpsala** Turkey
53 D1 **Ipswich** Austr.
99 D2 **Ipswich** U.K.
127 G2 **Iqaluit** Can.
152 A3 **Iquique** Chile
150 A2 **Iquitos** Peru
111 C3 **Irakleio** Greece
Iraklion Greece *see* **Irakleio**
76 B3 **Iran** *country* Asia
61 C1 **Iran, Pegunungan** *mts* Indon.
79 D2 **Īrānshahr** Iran
144 B2 **Irapuato** Mex.
81 C2 **Iraq** *country* Asia
154 B3 **Irati** Brazil
80 B2 **Irbid** Jordan
86 F3 **Irbit** Rus. Fed.
151 D3 **Irecê** Brazil
97 C2 **Ireland, Republic of** *country* Europe
118 C3 **Irema** Dem. Rep. Congo
76 C2 **Irgiz** Kazakh.
114 B3 **Irîgui** *reg.* Mali/Maur.
119 D3 **Iringa** Tanz.
151 C2 **Iriri** *r.* Brazil
95 B3 **Irish Sea** Rep. of Ireland/U.K.
69 C1 **Irkutsk** Rus. Fed.
52 A2 **Iron Knob** Austr.
140 B1 **Iron Mountain** U.S.A.
140 A1 **Ironwood** U.S.A.
64 B1 **Irosin** Phil.
67 C4 **Irō-zaki** *pt* Japan
90 C1 **Irpin'** Ukr.
62 A2 **Irrawaddy** *r.* Myanmar
63 A2 **Irrawaddy, Mouths of the** Myanmar
86 F2 **Irtysh** *r.* Kazakh./Rus. Fed.
107 C1 **Irún** Spain
96 B3 **Irvine** U.K.
64 B2 **Isabela** Phil.
146 B3 **Isabelia, Cordillera** *mts* Nic.
92 □A2 **Ísafjörður** Iceland
67 B4 **Isahaya** Japan
105 E2 **Isar** *r.* Ger.
96 □ **Isbister** U.K.
108 B2 **Ischia, Isola d'** *i.* Italy
67 C4 **Ise** Japan
118 C2 **Isengi** Dem. Rep. Congo
100 C2 **Iserlohn** Ger.
101 D1 **Isernhagen** Ger.
67 C4 **Ise-wan** *b.* Japan
114 C4 **Iseyin** Nigeria
Isfahan Iran *see* **Eşfahān**
66 D2 **Ishikari-wan** *b.* Japan
77 D1 **Ishim** *r.* Kazakh./Rus. Fed.
66 D3 **Ishinomaki** Japan
67 D3 **Ishioka** Japan
140 B1 **Ishpeming** U.S.A.
111 C2 **Işıklar Dağı** *mts* Turkey
111 C3 **Işıklı** Turkey
123 D2 **Isipingo** S. Africa
119 C2 **Isiro** Dem. Rep. Congo
80 B2 **İskenderun** Turkey
82 G3 **Iskitim** Rus. Fed.
110 B2 **Iskŭr** *r.* Bulg.
128 A2 **Iskut** *r.* Can.
74 B1 **Islamabad** Pak.
52 A2 **Island Lagoon** *salt flat* Austr.
129 E2 **Island Lake** *l.* Can.
54 B1 **Islands, Bay of** N.Z.
96 A3 **Islay** *i.* U.K.
98 A1 **Isle of Man** *i.* Irish Sea
77 D3 **Ismoili Somonī, Qullai** *mt.* Tajik.
109 C3 **Isola di Capo Rizzuto** Italy
110 C2 **Isperikh** Bulg.
80 B2 **Israel** *country* Asia
105 C2 **Issoire** France
111 C2 **İstanbul** Turkey
İstanbul Boğazı *str.* Turkey *see* **Bosporus**
111 B3 **Istiaia** Greece
108 B1 **Istra** *pen.* Croatia
105 C3 **Istres** France
151 D3 **Itaberaba** Brazil
155 D1 **Itabira** Brazil
155 D2 **Itabirito** Brazil
151 E3 **Itabuna** Brazil
150 C2 **Itacoatiara** Brazil
154 B2 **Itaguajé** Brazil
154 C2 **Itaí** Brazil
154 B3 **Itaipu, Represa de** *resr* Brazil
151 C2 **Itaituba** Brazil
152 D3 **Itajaí** Brazil
155 C2 **Itajubá** Brazil
108 B2 **Italy** *country* Europe
155 D1 **Itamarandiba** Brazil
155 D1 **Itambacuri** Brazil
155 D1 **Itambé, Pico de** *mt.* Brazil
62 A1 **Itanagar** India
154 C2 **Itanhaém** Brazil
155 D1 **Itanhém** Brazil
155 D1 **Itaobím** Brazil
154 C1 **Itapajipe** Brazil
155 E1 **Itapebi** Brazil
155 D2 **Itapemirim** Brazil
155 D2 **Itaperuna** Brazil
155 D1 **Itapetinga** Brazil
154 C2 **Itapetininga** Brazil
154 C2 **Itapeva** Brazil
151 E3 **Itapicuru** *r.* Brazil
151 D2 **Itapicuru Mirim** Brazil
154 C1 **Itapuranga** Brazil
154 C2 **Itararé** Brazil
75 B2 **Itarsi** India
154 B1 **Itarumã** Brazil
155 D2 **Itaúna** Brazil
71 C3 **Itbayat** *i.* Phil.
141 D2 **Ithaca** U.S.A.
101 D1 **Ith Hils** *ridge* Ger.
118 C2 **Itimbiri** *r.* Dem. Rep. Congo
155 D1 **Itinga** Brazil
154 B1 **Itiquira** Brazil
154 A1 **Itiquira** *r.* Brazil
67 C4 **Itō** Japan
154 C2 **Itu** Brazil
150 A2 **Ituí** *r.* Brazil
154 C1 **Ituiutaba** Brazil
119 C3 **Itula** Dem. Rep. Congo
154 C1 **Itumbiara** Brazil
154 B1 **Iturama** Brazil
101 D1 **Itzehoe** Ger.
83 N2 **Iul'tin** Rus. Fed.
154 B2 **Ivaí** *r.* Brazil
92 I2 **Ivalo** Fin.
88 C3 **Ivanava** Belarus
52 B2 **Ivanhoe** Austr.
90 B1 **Ivankiv** Ukr.
90 A2 **Ivano-Frankivs'k** Ukr.
89 F2 **Ivanovo** Rus. Fed.
88 C3 **Ivatsevichy** Belarus
111 C2 **Ivaylovgrad** Bulg.
86 F2 **Ivdel'** Rus. Fed.
154 B2 **Ivinheima** Brazil
154 B2 **Ivinheima** *r.* Brazil
127 H2 **Ivittuut** Greenland
Ivory Coast *country* Africa *see* **Côte d'Ivoire**
108 A1 **Ivrea** Italy
111 C3 **İvrindi** Turkey
127 F2 **Ivujivik** Can.
67 D3 **Iwaki** Japan
67 B4 **Iwakuni** Japan
66 D2 **Iwamizawa** Japan
66 D2 **Iwanai** Japan
88 C3 **Iwye** Belarus
123 D3 **Ixopo** S. Africa
144 B2 **Ixtlán** Mex.
145 D2 **Izamal** Mex.
81 C1 **Izberbash** Rus. Fed.
86 E3 **Izhevsk** Rus. Fed.
86 E2 **Izhma** Rus. Fed.
89 E3 **Izmalkovo** Rus. Fed.
90 B2 **Izmayil** Ukr.
111 C3 **İzmir** Turkey
111 C2 **İznik Gölü** *l.* Turkey
67 B3 **Izumo** Japan
90 B1 **Izyaslav** Ukr.
91 D2 **Izyum** Ukr.

J

Jabal, Bahr el *r.* Sudan/Uganda *see* **White Nile**
106 C2 **Jabalón** *r.* Spain
75 B2 **Jabalpur** India
50 C1 **Jabiru** Austr.
109 C2 **Jablanica** Bos.-Herz.
151 E2 **Jaboatão** Brazil
154 C2 **Jaboticabal** Brazil
107 C1 **Jaca** Spain
145 C2 **Jacala** Mex.
151 C2 **Jacareacanga** Brazil
155 C2 **Jacareí** Brazil
155 D1 **Jacinto** Brazil
141 E1 **Jackman** U.S.A.
142 C2 **Jackson** *AL* U.S.A.
140 C2 **Jackson** *MI* U.S.A.
142 B2 **Jackson** *MS* U.S.A.
142 C1 **Jackson** *TN* U.S.A.
136 A2 **Jackson** *WY* U.S.A.
54 A2 **Jackson Head** *hd* N.Z.
142 B2 **Jacksonville** *AR* U.S.A.
143 D2 **Jacksonville** *FL* U.S.A.
140 A3 **Jacksonville** *IL* U.S.A.
143 E2 **Jacksonville** *NC* U.S.A.
139 D2 **Jacksonville** *TX* U.S.A.
147 C3 **Jacmel** Haiti
74 A2 **Jacobabad** Pak.
151 D3 **Jacobina** Brazil

131 D2 **Jacques Cartier, Mont** *mt.* Can.
151 D2 **Jacunda** Brazil
154 C2 **Jacupiranga** Brazil
109 C2 **Jadovnik** *mt.* Bos.-Herz.
150 A2 **Jaén** Peru
106 C2 **Jaén** Spain
52 A3 **Jaffa, Cape** Austr.
73 B4 **Jaffna** Sri Lanka
73 C3 **Jagdalpur** India
123 C2 **Jagersfontein** S. Africa
79 C2 **Jaghīn** Iran
154 C2 **Jaguariaíva** Brazil
79 C2 **Jahrom** Iran
74 B2 **Jaipur** India
74 B2 **Jaisalmer** India
75 C2 **Jajarkot** Nepal
109 C2 **Jajce** Bos.-Herz.
60 B2 **Jakarta** Indon.
128 A1 **Jakes Corner** Can.
92 G2 **Jäkkvik** Sweden
92 H3 **Jakobstad** Fin.
77 D3 **Jalālābād** Afgh.
77 D2 **Jalal-Abad** Kyrg.
74 B1 **Jalandhar** India
145 C3 **Jalapa** Mex.
154 B2 **Jales** Brazil
74 B2 **Jalgaon** India
115 D4 **Jalingo** Nigeria
74 B3 **Jalna** India
144 B2 **Jalpa** Mex.
75 C2 **Jalpaiguri** India
145 C2 **Jalpan** Mex.
115 E2 **Jālū** Libya
146 C3 **Jamaica** *country* West Indies
146 C3 **Jamaica Channel** Haiti/Jamaica
75 C2 **Jamalpur** Bangl.
60 B2 **Jambi** Indon.
137 D2 **James** *r. ND/SD* U.S.A.
141 D3 **James** *r. VA* U.S.A.
130 B1 **James Bay** Can.
52 A2 **Jamestown** Austr.
137 D1 **Jamestown** *ND* U.S.A.
141 D2 **Jamestown** *NY* U.S.A.
74 B1 **Jammu** Jammu and Kashmir
74 B1 **Jammu and Kashmir** *terr.* Asia
74 B2 **Jamnagar** India
93 I3 **Jämsä** Fin.
75 C2 **Jamshedpur** India
75 C2 **Jamuna** *r.* Bangl.
75 C2 **Janakpur** Nepal
155 D1 **Janaúba** Brazil
81 D2 **Jandaq** Iran
140 B2 **Janesville** U.S.A.
84 C2 **Jan Mayen** *i.* Arctic Ocean
122 B3 **Jansenville** S. Africa
155 D1 **Januária** Brazil
74 B2 **Jaora** India
67 C3 **Japan** *country* Asia
156 C3 **Japan, Sea of** N. Pacific Ocean
150 B2 **Japurá** *r.* Brazil
154 C1 **Jaraguá** Brazil
154 B2 **Jaraguari** Brazil
152 C3 **Jardim** Brazil
69 D1 **Jargalant** Mongolia
103 D1 **Jarocin** Pol.
103 E1 **Jarosław** Pol.
92 F3 **Järpen** Sweden
70 A2 **Jartai** China
150 B3 **Jarú** Brazil
Jarud China *see* **Lubei**
79 C2 **Jāsk** Iran
103 E2 **Jasło** Pol.
128 C2 **Jasper** Can.
140 B3 **Jasper** *IN* U.S.A.
139 E2 **Jasper** *TX* U.S.A.
103 D2 **Jastrzębie-Zdrój** Pol.
103 D2 **Jászberény** Hungary
154 B1 **Jataí** Brazil
74 A2 **Jati** Pak.
154 C2 **Jaú** Brazil
150 B2 **Jaú** *r.* Brazil
145 C2 **Jaumave** Mex.
75 C2 **Jaunpur** India
154 B1 **Jauru** Brazil
61 B2 **Java** *i.* Indon.
69 D1 **Javarthushuu** Mongolia
159 D4 **Java Sea** Indon.
Jawa *i.* Indon. *see* **Java**
117 C4 **Jawhar** Somalia
103 D1 **Jawor** Pol.
103 D1 **Jaworzno** Pol.
59 D3 **Jaya, Puncak** *mt.* Indon.
59 D3 **Jayapura** Indon.
128 B1 **Jean Marie River** Can.
131 D1 **Jeannin, Lac** *l.* Can.
116 A3 **Jebel Abyad Plateau** Sudan
96 C3 **Jedburgh** U.K.
78 A2 **Jeddah** Saudi Arabia
101 E1 **Jeetze** *r.* Ger.
135 C3 **Jefferson, Mount** U.S.A.
137 E3 **Jefferson City** U.S.A.
88 C2 **Jēkabpils** Latvia
103 D1 **Jelenia Góra** Pol.
88 B2 **Jelgava** Latvia
61 C2 **Jember** Indon.
101 E2 **Jena** Ger.
Jengish Chokusu *mt.* China/Kyrg. *see* **Pobeda Peak**
80 B2 **Jenīn** West Bank
142 B2 **Jennings** U.S.A.
151 D3 **Jequié** Brazil
155 D1 **Jequitaí** Brazil
155 D1 **Jequitinhonha** Brazil
155 E1 **Jequitinhonha** *r.* Brazil
147 C3 **Jérémie** Haiti
144 B2 **Jerez** Mex.
106 B2 **Jerez de la Frontera** Spain
109 D3 **Jergucat** Albania
115 C1 **Jerid, Chott el** *salt l.* Tunisia
134 D2 **Jerome** U.S.A.
95 C4 **Jersey** *terr.* Channel Is
151 D2 **Jerumenha** Brazil
80 B2 **Jerusalem** Israel/West Bank
53 D3 **Jervis Bay Territory** *admin. div.* Austr.
108 B1 **Jesenice** Slovenia
108 B2 **Jesi** Italy
101 F2 **Jessen** Ger.
75 C2 **Jessore** Bangl.
143 D2 **Jesup** U.S.A.
145 C3 **Jesús Carranza** Mex.
74 B2 **Jhalawar** India
74 B1 **Jhang** Pak.
75 B2 **Jhansi** India
75 C2 **Jharsuguda** India
74 B1 **Jhelum** Pak.
70 C2 **Jiading** China
69 E1 **Jiamusi** China
71 B3 **Ji'an** *Jiangxi* China
65 B1 **Ji'an** *Jilin* China
62 A1 **Jianchuan** China
Jiandaoyu China *see* **Zigui**
70 B2 **Jiangsu** *prov.* China
71 B3 **Jiangxi** *prov.* China
70 A2 **Jiangyou** China
70 B3 **Jianli** China
70 B2 **Jianqiao** China
71 B3 **Jianyang** *Fujian* China
70 A2 **Jianyang** *Sichuan* China
70 C2 **Jiaozhou** China
70 B2 **Jiaozuo** China
70 C2 **Jiaxing** China
68 C2 **Jiayuguan** China
Jiddah Saudi Arabia *see* **Jeddah**
92 G2 **Jiehkkevarri** *mt.* Norway
70 B2 **Jiexiu** China
68 C2 **Jigzhi** China
103 D2 **Jihlava** Czech Rep.
117 C4 **Jijiga** Eth.
116 A2 **Jilf al Kabīr, Haḍabat al** *plat.* Egypt
117 C4 **Jilib** Somalia
69 E2 **Jilin** China
65 B1 **Jilin** *prov.* China
65 A1 **Jilin Hada Ling** *mts* China
117 B4 **Jīma** Eth.
144 B2 **Jiménez** *Chihuahua* Mex.
145 C2 **Jiménez** *Tamaulipas* Mex.
70 B2 **Jinan** China
70 B2 **Jincheng** China
53 C3 **Jindabyne** Austr.
103 D2 **Jindřichův Hradec** Czech Rep.
71 B3 **Jingdezhen** China
71 B3 **Jinggangshan** China
62 B1 **Jinghong** China
70 B2 **Jingmen** China
70 A2 **Jingning** China
70 A2 **Jingtai** China
71 A3 **Jingxi** China
65 B1 **Jingyu** China
70 A2 **Jingyuan** China
70 B2 **Jingzhou** China
70 B2 **Jingzhou** China
71 B3 **Jinhua** China
70 B1 **Jining** *Nei Mongol* China
70 B2 **Jining** *Shandong* China
119 D2 **Jinja** Uganda
117 B4 **Jinka** Eth.
146 B3 **Jinotepe** Nic.
71 A3 **Jinping** China
Jinsha Jiang *r.* China *see* **Yangtze**
70 B3 **Jinshi** China
70 B2 **Jinzhong** China
70 C1 **Jinzhou** China
150 B2 **Jiparaná** *r.* Brazil
79 C2 **Jīroft** Iran
71 A3 **Jishou** China
110 B2 **Jiu** *r.* Romania
70 A2 **Jiuding Shan** *mt.* China
70 B3 **Jiujiang** China
66 B1 **Jixi** China
78 B3 **Jīzān** Saudi Arabia
151 E2 **João Pessoa** Brazil
155 C1 **João Pinheiro** Brazil
74 B2 **Jodhpur** India
92 I3 **Joensuu** Fin.
67 C3 **Jōetsu** Japan
121 C3 **Jofane** Moz.
88 C2 **Jõgeva** Estonia
123 C2 **Johannesburg** S. Africa
134 C2 **John Day** U.S.A.
134 B1 **John Day** *r.* U.S.A.
128 C2 **John d'Or Prairie** Can.
143 E1 **John H. Kerr Reservoir** U.S.A.
96 C1 **John o'Groats** U.K.
143 D1 **Johnson City** U.S.A.
128 A1 **Johnson's Crossing** Can.
49 G2 **Johnston Atoll** N. Pacific Ocean
96 B3 **Johnstone** U.K.
141 D2 **Johnstown** U.S.A.
60 B1 **Johor Bahru** Malaysia
88 C2 **Jõhvi** Estonia
154 C3 **Joinville** Brazil
105 D2 **Joinville** France
92 G2 **Jokkmokk** Sweden
92 □B2 **Jökulsá á Fjöllum** *r.* Iceland
140 B2 **Joliet** U.S.A.
130 C2 **Joliette** Can.
64 B2 **Jolo** Phil.
64 B2 **Jolo** *i.* Phil.
61 C2 **Jombang** Indon.

75 C2 **Jomsom** Nepal
88 B2 **Jonava** Lith.
142 B1 **Jonesboro** *AR* U.S.A.
142 B2 **Jonesboro** *LA* U.S.A.
127 F1 **Jones Sound** *sea chan.* Can.
93 F4 **Jönköping** Sweden
131 C2 **Jonquière** Can.
145 C3 **Jonuta** Mex.
137 E3 **Joplin** U.S.A.
80 B2 **Jordan** *country* Asia
80 B2 **Jordan** *r.* Asia
136 B1 **Jordan** U.S.A.
134 C2 **Jordan Valley** U.S.A.
62 A1 **Jorhat** India
93 E4 **Jørpeland** Norway
115 C4 **Jos** Nigeria
145 C3 **José Cardel** Mex.
131 D1 **Joseph, Lac** *l.* Can.
50 B1 **Joseph Bonaparte Gulf** Austr.
115 C4 **Jos Plateau** Nigeria
93 E3 **Jotunheimen** *mts* Norway
122 B3 **Joubertina** S. Africa
123 C2 **Jouberton** S. Africa
93 I3 **Joutseno** Fin.
134 B1 **Juan de Fuca Strait** Can./U.S.A.
Juanshui China *see* **Tongcheng**
145 B2 **Juaréz** Mex.
151 D2 **Juàzeiro** Brazil
151 E2 **Juàzeiro do Norte** Brazil
117 B4 **Juba** Sudan
117 C5 **Jubba** *r.* Somalia
78 B2 **Jubbah** Saudi Arabia
107 C2 **Júcar** *r.* Spain
145 C3 **Juchitán** Mex.
102 C2 **Judenburg** Austria
101 D2 **Jühnde** Ger.
146 B3 **Juigalpa** Nic.
100 C1 **Juist** *i.* Ger.
155 D2 **Juiz de Fora** Brazil
150 A3 **Juliaca** Peru
75 C2 **Jumla** Nepal
74 B2 **Junagadh** India
139 D2 **Junction** U.S.A.
137 D3 **Junction City** U.S.A.
154 C2 **Jundiaí** Brazil
128 A2 **Juneau** U.S.A.
53 C2 **Junee** Austr.
105 D2 **Jungfrau** *mt.* Switz.
141 D2 **Juniata** *r.* U.S.A.
92 G3 **Junsele** Sweden
134 C2 **Juntura** U.S.A.
154 C2 **Juquiá** Brazil
117 A4 **Jur** *r.* Sudan
105 D2 **Jura** *mts* France/Switz.
96 B2 **Jura** *i.* U.K.
96 B3 **Jura, Sound of** *sea chan.* U.K.
88 B2 **Jurbarkas** Lith.
88 B2 **Jūrmala** Latvia
150 B2 **Juruá** *r.* Brazil
150 C2 **Juruena** *r.* Brazil
150 B2 **Jutaí** *r.* Brazil
101 F2 **Jüterbog** Ger.
70 B2 **Juxian** China
79 C2 **Jūyom** Iran
122 B1 **Jwaneng** Botswana
93 I3 **Jyväskylä** Fin.

K

74 B1 **K2** *mt.* China/ Jammu and Kashmir
119 C3 **Kabalo** Dem. Rep. Congo
119 C3 **Kabare** Dem. Rep. Congo
130 B2 **Kabinakagami Lake** Can.
118 C3 **Kabinda** Dem. Rep. Congo
118 B2 **Kabo** C.A.R.
120 B2 **Kabompo** Zambia
119 C3 **Kabongo** Dem. Rep. Congo
77 C3 **Kābul** Afgh.
64 B2 **Kaburuang** *i.* Indon.
121 B2 **Kabwe** Zambia
74 A2 **Kachchh, Gulf of** India
74 B2 **Kachchh, Rann of** *marsh* India
83 I3 **Kachug** Rus. Fed.
81 C1 **Kaçkar Dağı** *mt.* Turkey
111 C2 **Kadıköy** Turkey
114 B3 **Kadiolo** Mali
73 B3 **Kadmat** *i.* India
121 B2 **Kadoma** Zimbabwe
63 A2 **Kadonkani** Myanmar
117 A3 **Kadugli** Sudan
115 C3 **Kaduna** Nigeria
89 E2 **Kaduy** Rus. Fed.
86 E2 **Kadzherom** Rus. Fed.
114 A3 **Kaédi** Maur.
118 B1 **Kaélé** Cameroon
65 B2 **Kaesŏng** N. Korea
114 A3 **Kaffrine** Senegal
111 B3 **Kafireas, Akra** *pt* Greece
121 B2 **Kafue** Zambia
120 B2 **Kafue** *r.* Zambia
118 B2 **Kaga Bandoro** C.A.R.
91 E2 **Kagal'nitskaya** Rus. Fed.
67 B4 **Kagoshima** Japan
90 C2 **Kaharlyk** Ukr.
61 C2 **Kahayan** *r.* Indon.
118 B3 **Kahemba** Dem. Rep. Congo
101 E2 **Kahla** Ger.
79 C2 **Kahnūj** Iran
92 H2 **Kahperusvaarat** *mts* Fin.
80 B2 **Kahramanmaraş** Turkey
79 C2 **Kahūrak** Iran
59 C3 **Kai, Kepulauan** *is* Indon.
115 C4 **Kaiama** Nigeria
54 B2 **Kaiapoi** N.Z.
59 C3 **Kai Besar** *i.* Indon.
70 B2 **Kaifeng** China
Kaihua China *see* **Wenshan**
122 B2 **Kaiingveld** *reg.* S. Africa
59 C3 **Kai Kecil** *i.* Indon.
54 B2 **Kaikoura** N.Z.
114 A4 **Kailahun** Sierra Leone
71 A3 **Kaili** China
59 C3 **Kaimana** Indon.
54 C1 **Kaimanawa Mountains** N.Z.
67 C4 **Kainan** Japan
115 C3 **Kainji Reservoir** Nigeria
54 B1 **Kaipara Harbour** N.Z.
74 B2 **Kairana** India
115 D1 **Kairouan** Tunisia
54 B1 **Kaitaia** N.Z.
54 C1 **Kaitawa** N.Z.
Kaitong China *see* **Tongyu**
59 C3 **Kaiwatu** Indon.
65 A1 **Kaiyuan** *Liaoning* China
62 B1 **Kaiyuan** *Yunnan* China
92 I3 **Kajaani** Fin.
51 D2 **Kajabbi** Austr.
122 B2 **Kakamas** S. Africa
119 D2 **Kakamega** Kenya
91 C2 **Kakhovka** Ukr.
91 C2 **Kakhovs'ke Vodoskhovyshche** *resr* Ukr.
73 C3 **Kakinada** India
128 C1 **Kakisa** Can.
119 C3 **Kakoswa** Dem. Rep. Congo
126 B2 **Kaktovik** U.S.A.
Kalaallit Nunaat *terr.* N. America *see* **Greenland**
59 C3 **Kalabahi** Indon.
120 B2 **Kalabo** Zambia
91 E1 **Kalach** Rus. Fed.
119 D2 **Kalacha Dida** Kenya
62 A1 **Kaladan** *r.* India/Myanmar
120 B3 **Kalahari Desert** Africa
92 H3 **Kalajoki** Fin.
111 B2 **Kalamaria** Greece
111 B3 **Kalamata** Greece
140 B2 **Kalamazoo** U.S.A.
111 B3 **Kalampaka** Greece
91 C2 **Kalanchak** Ukr.
63 B2 **Kalasin** Thai.
79 C2 **Kalāt** Iran
74 A2 **Kalat** Pak.
50 A2 **Kalbarri** Austr.
111 C3 **Kale** Turkey
80 B1 **Kalecik** Turkey
118 C3 **Kalema** Dem. Rep. Congo
119 C3 **Kalemie** Dem. Rep. Congo
62 A1 **Kalemyo** Myanmar
Kalgan China *see* **Zhangjiakou**
50 B3 **Kalgoorlie** Austr.
109 C2 **Kali** Croatia
110 C2 **Kaliakra, Nos** *pt* Bulg.
119 C3 **Kalima** Dem. Rep. Congo
61 C2 **Kalimantan** *reg.* Indon.
88 B3 **Kaliningrad** Rus. Fed.
91 D2 **Kalininskaya** Rus. Fed.
88 C3 **Kalinkavichy** Belarus
134 D1 **Kalispell** U.S.A.
103 D1 **Kalisz** Pol.
91 E2 **Kalitva** *r.* Rus. Fed.
92 H2 **Kalix** Sweden
92 H2 **Kalixälven** *r.* Sweden
111 C3 **Kalkan** Turkey
120 A3 **Kalkfeld** Namibia
92 I3 **Kallavesi** *l.* Fin.
92 F3 **Kallsjön** *l.* Sweden
93 G4 **Kalmar** Sweden
93 G4 **Kalmarsund** *sea chan.* Sweden
120 B2 **Kalomo** Zambia
128 B2 **Kalone Peak** Can.
75 B1 **Kalpa** India
70 D3 **Kalpeni** *i.* India
75 B2 **Kalpi** India
101 D1 **Kaltenkirchen** Ger.
89 E3 **Kaluga** Rus. Fed.
93 F4 **Kalundborg** Denmark
90 A2 **Kalush** Ukr.
89 E2 **Kalyazin** Rus. Fed.
111 C3 **Kalymnos** *i.* Greece
119 C3 **Kama** Dem. Rep. Congo
62 A2 **Kama** Myanmar
86 E3 **Kama** *r.* Rus. Fed.
66 D3 **Kamaishi** Japan
80 B2 **Kaman** Turkey
120 A2 **Kamanjab** Namibia
78 B3 **Kamarān** *i.* Yemen
74 A2 **Kamarod** Pak.
50 B3 **Kambalda** Austr.
119 C4 **Kambove** Dem. Rep. Congo
110 C2 **Kamchiya** *r.* Bulg.
108 B2 **Kamenjak, Rt** *pt* Croatia
76 B1 **Kamenka** Kazakh.
91 D1 **Kamenka** Rus. Fed.
91 E2 **Kamenolomni** Rus. Fed.
83 M2 **Kamenskoye** Rus. Fed.
91 E2 **Kamensk-Shakhtinskiy** Rus. Fed.
86 F3 **Kamensk-Ural'skiy** Rus. Fed.
122 A3 **Kamiesberge** *mts* S. Africa
122 A3 **Kamieskroon** S. Africa
129 D1 **Kamilukuak Lake** *l.* Can.
119 C3 **Kamina** Dem. Rep. Congo
129 E1 **Kaminak Lake** Can.
90 A1 **Kamin'-Kashyrs'kyy** Ukr.
128 B2 **Kamloops** Can.
118 C3 **Kamonia** Dem. Rep. Congo
119 D2 **Kampala** Uganda

60 B1 **Kampar** *r.* Indon.
60 B1 **Kampar** Malaysia
100 B1 **Kampen** Neth.
119 C3 **Kampene** Dem. Rep. Congo
63 A2 **Kamphaeng Phet** Thai.
63 B2 **Kâmpóng Cham** Cambodia
63 B2 **Kâmpóng Chhnăng** Cambodia
Kâmpóng Saôm Cambodia *see* **Sihanoukville**
63 B2 **Kâmpóng Spœ** Cambodia
63 B2 **Kâmpôt** Cambodia
129 D2 **Kamsack** Can.
86 E3 **Kamskoye Vodokhranilishche** *resr* Rus. Fed.
117 C4 **Kamsuuma** Somalia
90 B2 **Kam"yanets'-Podil's'kyy** Ukr.
90 A1 **Kam"yanka-Buz'ka** Ukr.
88 B3 **Kamyanyets** Belarus
91 D2 **Kamyshevatskaya** Rus. Fed.
87 D3 **Kamyshin** Rus. Fed.
135 D3 **Kanab** U.S.A.
118 C3 **Kananga** Dem. Rep. Congo
87 D3 **Kanash** Rus. Fed.
140 C3 **Kanawha** *r.* U.S.A.
67 C3 **Kanazawa** Japan
62 A1 **Kanbalu** Myanmar
63 A2 **Kanchanaburi** Thai.
73 B3 **Kanchipuram** India
77 C3 **Kandahār** Afgh.
86 C2 **Kandalaksha** Rus. Fed.
61 C2 **Kandangan** Indon.
74 A2 **Kandhkot** Pak.
114 C3 **Kandi** Benin
74 B2 **Kandla** India
53 C2 **Kandos** Austr.
121 □D2 **Kandreho** Madag.
73 C4 **Kandy** Sri Lanka
76 B2 **Kandyagash** Kazakh.
127 G1 **Kane Bassin** *b.* Greenland
91 D2 **Kanevskaya** Rus. Fed.
122 B1 **Kang** Botswana
127 H2 **Kangaatsiaq** Greenland
114 B3 **Kangaba** Mali
80 B2 **Kangal** Turkey
79 C2 **Kangān** Iran
60 B1 **Kangar** Malaysia
52 A3 **Kangaroo Island** Austr.
75 C2 **Kangchenjunga** *mt.* India/Nepal
65 B2 **Kangdong** N. Korea
61 C2 **Kangean, Kepulauan** *is* Indon.
127 I2 **Kangeq** *c.* Greenland
127 I2 **Kangerlussuaq** *inlet* Greenland
127 H2 **Kangerlussuaq** *inlet* Greenland
127 H2 **Kangersuatsiaq** Greenland
65 B1 **Kanggye** N. Korea
131 D1 **Kangiqsualujjuaq** Can.
127 G2 **Kangiqsujuaq** Can.
127 G2 **Kangirsuk** Can.
75 C2 **Kangmar** China
65 B2 **Kangnŭng** S. Korea
65 A1 **Kangping** China
72 D2 **Kangto** *mt.* China/India
62 A1 **Kani** Myanmar
86 D2 **Kanin, Poluostrov** *pen.* Rus. Fed.
86 D2 **Kanin Nos** Rus. Fed.
91 C2 **Kaniv** Ukr.
93 H3 **Kankaanpää** Fin.
140 B2 **Kankakee** U.S.A.
114 B3 **Kankan** Guinea
75 C2 **Kanker** India
Kannur India *see* **Cannanore**
115 C3 **Kano** Nigeria
122 B3 **Kanonpunt** *pt* S. Africa
67 B4 **Kanoya** Japan
75 C2 **Kanpur** India
136 C3 **Kansas** *r.* U.S.A.
137 D3 **Kansas** *state* U.S.A.
137 E3 **Kansas City** U.S.A.
83 H3 **Kansk** Rus. Fed.
114 C3 **Kantchari** Burkina
91 D2 **Kantemirovka** Rus. Fed.
97 B2 **Kanturk** Rep. of Ireland
123 D2 **KaNyamazane** S. Africa
123 C1 **Kanye** Botswana
71 C3 **Kaohsiung** Taiwan
120 A2 **Kaokoveld** *plat.* Namibia
114 A3 **Kaolack** Senegal
120 B2 **Kaoma** Zambia
118 C3 **Kapanga** Dem. Rep. Congo
77 D2 **Kapchagay** Kazakh.
77 D2 **Kapchagayskoye Vodokhranilishche** *resr* Kazakh.
100 B2 **Kapellen** Belgium
121 B2 **Kapiri Mposhi** Zambia
127 H2 **Kapisillit** Greenland
130 B1 **Kapiskau** *r.* Can.
61 C1 **Kapit** *Sarawak* Malaysia
63 A3 **Kapoe** Thai.
117 B4 **Kapoeta** Sudan
103 D2 **Kaposvár** Hungary
61 B2 **Kapuas** *r.* Indon.
52 A2 **Kapunda** Austr.
130 B2 **Kapuskasing** Can.
103 D2 **Kapuvár** Hungary
88 C3 **Kapyl'** Belarus
114 C4 **Kara** Togo
111 C3 **Kara Ada** *i.* Turkey
76 C1 **Karabalyk** Kazakh.
76 B2 **Kara-Bogaz-Gol, Zaliv** *b.* Turkm.
76 B2 **Karabogazkel'** Turkm.
80 B1 **Karabük** Turkey
76 C2 **Karabutak** Kazakh.
110 C2 **Karacaköy** Turkey
89 D3 **Karachev** Rus. Fed.
74 A2 **Karachi** Pak.
Kara Deniz *sea* Asia/Europe *see* **Black Sea**
77 D2 **Karaganda** Kazakh.
77 D2 **Karagayly** Kazakh.
83 L3 **Karaginskiy Zaliv** *b.* Rus. Fed.
81 D2 **Karaj** Iran
76 B2 **Karakalpakiya** Kazakh.
64 B2 **Karakelong** *i.* Indon.
77 D2 **Kara-Köl** Kyrg.
77 D2 **Karakol** Kyrg.
74 B1 **Karakoram** *mts* Asia
76 B2 **Karakum, Peski** *des.* Kazakh.
Karakum Desert Turkm. *see* **Karakumy, Peski**
76 C3 **Karakumy, Peski** *des.* Turkm.
80 B2 **Karaman** Turkey
77 E2 **Karamay** China
54 B2 **Karamea** N.Z.
54 B2 **Karamea Bight** *b.* N.Z.
80 B2 **Karapınar** Turkey
122 A2 **Karasburg** Namibia
86 F1 **Kara Sea** *sea* Rus. Fed.
92 I2 **Kárášjohka** Norway
82 G3 **Karasuk** Rus. Fed.
77 D2 **Karatau** Kazakh.
77 C2 **Karatau, Khrebet** *mts* Kazakh.
86 F2 **Karatayka** Rus. Fed.
67 A4 **Karatsu** Japan
60 B2 **Karawang** Indon.
81 C2 **Karbalā'** Iraq
103 E2 **Karcag** Hungary
111 B3 **Karditsa** Greece
88 B2 **Kärdla** Estonia
122 B3 **Kareeberge** *mts* S. Africa
75 B2 **Kareli** India
74 B1 **Kargil** Jammu and Kashmir
121 B2 **Kariba** Zimbabwe
121 B2 **Kariba, Lake** *resr* Zambia/Zimbabwe
61 B2 **Karimata, Pulau-pulau** *is* Indon.
61 B2 **Karimata, Selat** *str.* Indon.
73 B3 **Karimnagar** India
61 C2 **Karimunjawa, Pulau-pulau** *is* Indon.
91 C2 **Karkinits'ka Zatoka** *g.* Ukr.
91 D2 **Karlivka** Ukr.
109 C1 **Karlovac** Croatia
102 C1 **Karlovy Vary** Czech Rep.
93 F4 **Karlshamn** Sweden
93 G4 **Karlskrona** Sweden
102 B2 **Karlsruhe** Ger.
93 F4 **Karlstad** Sweden
101 D3 **Karlstadt** Ger.
89 D3 **Karma** Belarus
93 E4 **Karmøy** *i.* Norway
75 D2 **Karnafuli Reservoir** Bangl.
74 B2 **Karnal** India
110 C2 **Karnobat** Bulg.
74 A2 **Karodi** Pak.
121 B2 **Karoi** Zimbabwe
121 C1 **Karonga** Malawi
116 B3 **Karora** Eritrea
111 C3 **Karpathos** *i.* Greece
111 B3 **Karpenisi** Greece
86 D2 **Karpogory** Rus. Fed.
50 A2 **Karratha** Austr.
81 C1 **Kars** Turkey
88 C2 **Kārsava** Latvia
77 C3 **Karshi** Uzbek.
86 E2 **Karskiye Vorota, Proliv** *str.* Rus. Fed.
Karskoye More *sea* Rus. Fed. *see* **Kara Sea**
101 E1 **Karstädt** Ger.
111 C2 **Kartal** Turkey
87 F3 **Kartaly** Rus. Fed.
73 B3 **Karwar** India
83 I3 **Karymskoye** Rus. Fed.
111 B3 **Karystos** Greece
80 A2 **Kaş** Turkey
130 B1 **Kasabonika Lake** Can.
118 C4 **Kasaji** Dem. Rep. Congo
121 C2 **Kasama** Zambia
120 B2 **Kasane** Botswana
118 B3 **Kasangulu** Dem. Rep. Congo
73 B3 **Kasaragod** India
129 D1 **Kasba Lake** Can.
120 B2 **Kasempa** Zambia
119 C4 **Kasenga** Dem. Rep. Congo
119 C3 **Kasese** Dem. Rep. Congo
119 D2 **Kasese** Uganda
81 D2 **Kāshān** Iran
Kashgar China *see* **Kashi**
77 D3 **Kashi** China
67 D3 **Kashima-nada** *b.* Japan
89 E2 **Kashin** Rus. Fed.
89 E3 **Kashira** Rus. Fed.
89 E3 **Kashirskoye** Rus. Fed.
67 C3 **Kashiwazaki** Japan
76 B3 **Kāshmar** Iran
74 A2 **Kashmor** Pak.
119 C3 **Kashyukulu** Dem. Rep. Congo
87 D3 **Kasimov** Rus. Fed.
93 H3 **Kaskinen** Fin.
119 C3 **Kasongo** Dem. Rep. Congo
118 B3 **Kasongo-Lunda** Dem. Rep. Congo
111 C3 **Kasos** *i.* Greece
Kaspiyskoye More *sea* Asia/Europe *see* **Caspian Sea**
116 B3 **Kassala** Sudan
101 D2 **Kassel** Ger.

80 B1 **Kastamonu** Turkey
111 B3 **Kastelli** Greece
111 B2 **Kastoria** Greece
89 D3 **Kastsyukovichy** Belarus
119 D3 **Kasulu** Tanz.
121 C2 **Kasungu** Malawi
141 F1 **Katahdin, Mount** U.S.A.
118 C3 **Katako-Kombe** Dem. Rep. Congo
50 A3 **Katanning** Austr.
63 A3 **Katchall** *i.* India
111 B2 **Katerini** Greece
128 A2 **Kate's Needle** *mt.* Can./U.S.A.
121 C2 **Katete** Zambia
62 A1 **Katha** Myanmar
50 C1 **Katherine** *r.* Austr.
74 B2 **Kathiawar** *pen.* India
123 C2 **Kathlehong** S. Africa
75 C2 **Kathmandu** Nepal
122 B2 **Kathu** S. Africa
74 B1 **Kathua** Jammu and Kashmir
114 B3 **Kati** Mali
75 C2 **Katihar** India
54 C1 **Katikati** N.Z.
123 C3 **Kati-Kati** S. Africa
120 B2 **Katima Mulilo** Namibia
111 B3 **Kato Achaïa** Greece
53 D2 **Katoomba** Austr.
103 D1 **Katowice** Pol.
78 A2 **Kātrīnā, Jabal** *mt.* Egypt
93 G4 **Katrineholm** Sweden
115 C3 **Katsina** Nigeria
115 C4 **Katsina-Ala** Nigeria
77 C3 **Kattakurgan** Uzbek.
93 F4 **Kattegat** *str.* Denmark/Sweden
100 B1 **Katwijk aan Zee** Neth.
93 H3 **Kauhajoki** Fin.
88 B3 **Kaunas** Lith.
115 C3 **Kaura-Namoda** Nigeria
92 H2 **Kautokeino** Norway
111 B2 **Kavala** Greece
66 C2 **Kavalerovo** Rus. Fed.
73 C3 **Kavali** India
73 B3 **Kavaratti** *i.* India
110 C2 **Kavarna** Bulg.
81 D2 **Kavīr, Dasht-e** *des.* Iran
67 C3 **Kawagoe** Japan
54 B1 **Kawakawa** N.Z.
67 C3 **Kawanishi** Japan
130 C2 **Kawartha Lakes** Can.
67 C3 **Kawasaki** Japan
54 C1 **Kawerau** N.Z.
63 A2 **Kawkareik** Myanmar
62 A1 **Kawlin** Myanmar
63 A2 **Kawmapyin** Myanmar
63 A2 **Kawthaung** Myanmar
77 D3 **Kaxgar He** *r.* China
114 B3 **Kaya** Burkina
61 C1 **Kayan** *r.* Indon.
136 B2 **Kaycee** U.S.A.
138 A1 **Kayenta** U.S.A.
114 A3 **Kayes** Mali
77 D2 **Kaynar** Kazakh.
80 B2 **Kayseri** Turkey
77 D1 **Kazakhskiy Melkosopochnik** *plain* Kazakh.
81 D1 **Kazakhskiy Zaliv** *b.* Kazakh.
76 C2 **Kazakhstan** *country* Asia
87 D3 **Kazan'** Rus. Fed.
80 A1 **Kazanlŭk** Bulg.
76 A2 **Kazbek** *mt.* Georgia/Rus. Fed.
81 D3 **Kāzerūn** Iran
103 E2 **Kazincbarcika** Hungary
86 F2 **Kazymskiy Mys** Rus. Fed.
111 B3 **Kea** *i.* Greece
97 C1 **Keady** U.K.
137 D2 **Kearney** U.S.A.
138 A2 **Kearny** U.S.A.
116 A3 **Kebkabiya** Sudan
92 G2 **Kebnekaise** *mt.* Sweden
117 C4 **K'ebrī Dehar** Eth.
61 B2 **Kebumen** Indon.
128 B2 **Kechika** *r.* Can.
103 D2 **Kecskemét** Hungary
88 B2 **Kėdainiai** Lith.
114 A3 **Kédougou** Senegal
103 D1 **Kędzierzyn-Koźle** Pol.
128 B1 **Keele** *r.* Can.
128 A1 **Keele Peak** Can.
Keeling Taiwan *see* **Chilung**
141 E2 **Keene** U.S.A.
122 A2 **Keetmanshoop** Namibia
129 E3 **Keewatin** Can.
111 B3 **Kefallonia** *i.* Greece
59 C3 **Kefamenanu** Indon.
92 □A3 **Keflavík** Iceland
77 D2 **Kegen** Kazakh.
128 C2 **Keg River** Can.
62 A1 **Kehsi Mansam** Myanmar
98 C2 **Keighley** U.K.
88 B2 **Keila** Estonia
122 B2 **Keimoes** S. Africa
92 I3 **Keitele** *l.* Fin.
52 B3 **Keith** Austr.
103 E2 **Kékes** *mt.* Hungary
60 B1 **Kelang** Malaysia
92 J2 **Keles-Uayv, Gora** *hill* Rus. Fed.
102 C2 **Kelheim** Ger.
80 B1 **Kelkit** *r.* Turkey
128 B1 **Keller Lake** *l.* Can.
134 C1 **Kellogg** U.S.A.
92 I2 **Kelloselkä** Fin.
97 C2 **Kells** Rep. of Ireland
88 B2 **Kelmė** Lith.
115 D4 **Kelo** Chad
128 C3 **Kelowna** Can.
96 C3 **Kelso** U.K.
134 B1 **Kelso** U.S.A.
60 B1 **Keluang** Malaysia
129 D2 **Kelvington** Can.
86 C2 **Kem'** Rus. Fed.
128 B2 **Kemano** Can.
111 C3 **Kemer** Turkey
82 G3 **Kemerovo** Rus. Fed.
92 H2 **Kemi** Fin.
92 I2 **Kemijärvi** Fin.
92 I2 **Kemijoki** *r.* Fin.
136 A2 **Kemmerer** U.S.A.
92 I3 **Kempele** Fin.
53 D2 **Kempsey** Austr.
130 C2 **Kempt, Lac** *l.* Can.
102 C2 **Kempten (Allgäu)** Ger.
123 C2 **Kempton Park** S. Africa
61 C2 **Kemujan** *l.* Indon.
129 D2 **Kenaston** Can.
98 B1 **Kendal** U.K.
59 C3 **Kendari** Indon.
61 C2 **Kendawangan** Indon.
115 D3 **Kendégué** Chad
114 A4 **Kenema** Sierra Leone
118 B3 **Kenge** Dem. Rep. Congo
62 A1 **Kengtung** Myanmar
122 B2 **Kenhardt** S. Africa
114 B1 **Kénitra** Morocco
97 B3 **Kenmare** Rep. of Ireland
136 C1 **Kenmare** U.S.A.
97 A3 **Kenmare River** *inlet* Rep. of Ireland
100 C3 **Kenn** Ger.
137 E3 **Kennett** U.S.A.
134 C1 **Kennewick** U.S.A.
129 E3 **Kenora** Can.
140 B2 **Kenosha** U.S.A.
138 C2 **Kent** U.S.A.
77 C2 **Kentau** Kazakh.
140 B3 **Kentucky** *r.* U.S.A.
140 C3 **Kentucky** *state* U.S.A.
140 B3 **Kentucky Lake** U.S.A.
119 D2 **Kenya** *country* Africa
Kenya, Mount Kenya *see* Kirinyaga
137 E2 **Keokuk** U.S.A.
75 C2 **Keonjhar** India
111 C3 **Kepsut** Turkey
52 B3 **Kerang** Austr.
91 D2 **Kerch** Ukr.
59 D3 **Kerema** P.N.G.
128 C3 **Keremeos** Can.
116 B3 **Keren** Eritrea
81 C2 **Kerend** Iran
159 C7 **Kerguelen Plateau** *sea feature* Indian Ocean
119 D3 **Kericho** Kenya
54 B1 **Kerikeri** N.Z.
60 B2 **Kerinci, Gunung** *vol.* Indon.
77 C3 **Kerki** Turkm.
111 A3 **Kerkyra** Greece
Kerkyra *i.* Greece *see* **Corfu**
116 B3 **Kerma** Sudan
49 F5 **Kermadec Islands** S. Pacific Ocean
79 C1 **Kermān** Iran
81 C2 **Kermānshāh** Iran
139 C2 **Kermit** U.S.A.
135 C3 **Kern** *r.* U.S.A.
100 C2 **Kerpen** Ger.
129 D2 **Kerrobert** Can.
139 D2 **Kerrville** U.S.A.
80 B2 **Keryneia** Cyprus
130 B1 **Kesagami Lake** Can.
111 C2 **Keşan** Turkey
66 D3 **Kesennuma** Japan
74 B2 **Keshod** India
100 C2 **Kessel** Neth.
98 B1 **Keswick** U.K.
103 D2 **Keszthely** Hungary
82 G3 **Ket'** *r.* Rus. Fed.
61 C2 **Ketapang** Indon.
128 A2 **Ketchikan** U.S.A.
134 D2 **Ketchum** U.S.A.
99 C2 **Kettering** U.K.
93 H3 **Keuruu** Fin.
100 C2 **Kevelaer** Ger.
140 B2 **Kewanee** U.S.A.
140 B1 **Keweenaw Bay** *b.* U.S.A.
140 B1 **Keweenaw Peninsula** U.S.A.
143 D3 **Key Largo** U.S.A.
141 D3 **Keyser** U.S.A.
143 D4 **Key West** U.S.A.
123 C2 **Kgotsong** S. Africa
69 E1 **Khabarovsk** Rus. Fed.
80 B1 **Khadyzhensk** Rus. Fed.
62 A1 **Khagrachari** Bangl.
74 A2 **Khairpur** Pak.
122 B1 **Khakhea** Botswana
68 C1 **Khamar-Daban, Khrebet** *mts* Rus. Fed.
74 B2 **Khambhat** India
73 B3 **Khambhat, Gulf of** India
74 B2 **Khamgaon** India
78 B3 **Khamir** Yemen
78 B3 **Khamis Mushayţ** Saudi Arabia
77 C3 **Khānābād** Afgh.
74 B2 **Khandwa** India
83 K2 **Khandyga** Rus. Fed.
74 B1 **Khanewal** Pak.
66 B2 **Khanka, Lake** China/Rus. Fed.
74 B2 **Khanpur** Pak.
77 D2 **Khantau** Kazakh.
83 H2 **Khantayskoye, Ozero** *l.* Rus. Fed.
86 F2 **Khanty-Mansiysk** Rus. Fed.
63 A3 **Khao Chum Thong** Thai.

63 A2 Khao Laem Reservoir Thai.
87 D4 Kharabali Rus. Fed.
75 C2 Kharagpur India
79 C2 Khārān *r.* Iran
116 B2 Khārijah, Wāḥāt al *oasis* Egypt
91 D2 Kharkiv Ukr.
Khar'kov Ukr. *see* Kharkiv
110 C2 Kharmanli Bulg.
86 D3 Kharovsk Rus. Fed.
116 B3 Khartoum Sudan
87 D4 Khasav'yurt Rus. Fed.
79 D2 Khāsh Iran
78 A3 Khashm el Girba Sudan
78 A3 Khashm el Girba Dam Sudan
74 D2 Khasi Hills India
110 C2 Khaskovo Bulg.
123 C3 Khayamnandi S. Africa
77 C2 Khayatbashi, Gora *mt.* Uzbek.
78 A2 Khaybar Saudi Arabia
122 A3 Khayelitsha S. Africa
62 B2 Khê Bo Vietnam
107 D2 Khemis Miliana Alg.
63 B2 Khemmarat Thai.
115 C1 Khenchela Alg.
81 D3 Kherāmeh Iran
91 C2 Kherson Ukr.
83 H2 Kheta *r.* Rus. Fed.
69 D1 Khilok Rus. Fed.
89 E2 Khimki Rus. Fed.
89 E3 Khlevnoye Rus. Fed.
90 B2 Khmel'nyts'kyy Ukr.
76 B1 Khobda Kazakh.
76 B2 Khodzheyli Uzbek.
89 E3 Khokhol'skiy Rus. Fed.
74 B2 Khokhropar Pak.
89 D2 Kholm Rus. Fed.
89 D2 Kholm-Zhirkovskiy Rus. Fed.
79 C2 Khonj Iran
63 B2 Khon Kaen Thai.
62 A1 Khonsa India
83 K2 Khonuu Rus. Fed.
86 E2 Khoreyver Rus. Fed.
69 D1 Khorinsk Rus. Fed.
91 C2 Khorol Ukr.
81 C2 Khorramābād Iran
81 C2 Khorramshahr Iran
77 D3 Khorugh Tajik.
74 A1 Khowst Afgh.
62 A1 Khreum Myanmar
76 B1 Khromtau Kazakh.
90 B2 Khrystynivka Ukr.
77 C2 Khŭjand Tajik.
63 B2 Khu Khan Thai.
78 A2 Khulays Saudi Arabia
75 C2 Khulna Bangl.
81 D2 Khunsar Iran
79 B2 Khurayṣ Saudi Arabia
74 B1 Khushab Pak.
90 A2 Khust Ukr.
123 C2 Khutsong S. Africa
74 A2 Khuzdar Pak.
79 C2 Khvormūj Iran
81 C2 Khvoy Iran
89 D2 Khvoynaya Rus. Fed.
77 D3 Khyber Pass Afgh./Pak.
53 D2 Kiama Austr.
119 C3 Kiambi Dem. Rep. Congo
119 D3 Kibiti Tanz.
109 D2 Kičevo Macedonia
114 C3 Kidal Mali
99 B2 Kidderminster U.K.
114 A3 Kidira Senegal
54 C1 Kidnappers, Cape N.Z.
102 C1 Kiel Ger.
103 E1 Kielce Pol.
98 B1 Kielder Water *resr* U.K.
90 C1 Kiev Ukr.
114 A3 Kiffa Maur.
119 D3 Kigali Rwanda
119 C3 Kigoma Tanz.
88 B2 Kihnu *i.* Estonia
92 I2 Kiiminki Fin.
67 B4 Kii-suidō *sea chan.* Japan
109 D1 Kikinda Serb. and Mont.
119 C3 Kikondja Dem. Rep. Congo
59 D3 Kikori P.N.G.
59 D3 Kikori *r.* P.N.G.
118 B3 Kikwit Dem. Rep. Congo
65 B1 Kilchu N. Korea
118 B3 Kilembe Dem. Rep. Congo
139 E2 Kilgore U.S.A.
119 D3 Kilimanjaro *vol.* Tanz.
80 B2 Kılıs Turkey
90 B2 Kiliya Ukr.
97 B2 Kilkee Rep. of Ireland
97 D1 Kilkeel U.K.
97 C2 Kilkenny Rep. of Ireland
111 B2 Kilkis Greece
97 B1 Killala Bay Rep. of Ireland
97 B2 Killaloe Rep. of Ireland
129 C2 Killam Can.
97 B2 Killarney Rep. of Ireland
139 D2 Killeen U.S.A.
96 B2 Killin U.K.
97 B1 Killybegs Rep. of Ireland
96 B3 Kilmarnock U.K.
53 B3 Kilmore Austr.
119 D3 Kilosa Tanz.
97 B2 Kilrush Rep. of Ireland
119 C3 Kilwa Dem. Rep. Congo
119 D3 Kilwa Masoko Tanz.
119 D3 Kimambi Tanz.
52 A2 Kimba Austr.
136 C2 Kimball U.S.A.
128 C3 Kimberley Can.
122 B2 Kimberley S. Africa
50 B1 Kimberley Plateau Austr.
65 B1 Kimch'aek N. Korea
65 B2 Kimch'ŏn S. Korea
127 G2 Kimmirut Can.
89 E3 Kimovsk Rus. Fed.
118 B3 Kimpese Dem. Rep. Congo
89 E2 Kimry Rus. Fed.
61 C1 Kinabalu, Gunung *mt.* *Sabah* Malaysia
128 C2 Kinbasket Lake Can.
130 B2 Kincardine Can.
62 A1 Kinchang Myanmar
119 C3 Kinda Dem. Rep. Congo
98 C2 Kinder Scout *hill* U.K.
129 D2 Kindersley Can.
114 A3 Kindia Guinea
119 C3 Kindu Dem. Rep. Congo
86 D3 Kineshma Rus. Fed.
51 E2 Kingaroy Austr.
135 B3 King City U.S.A.
130 C1 King George Islands Can.
88 C2 Kingisepp Rus. Fed.
51 D3 King Island Austr.
50 B1 King Leopold Ranges *hills* Austr.
138 A1 Kingman U.S.A.
135 B3 Kings *r.* U.S.A.
52 A3 Kingscote Austr.
99 D2 King's Lynn U.K.
49 F3 Kingsmill Group *is.* Kiribati
50 B1 King Sound *b.* Austr.
134 D2 Kings Peak U.S.A.
143 D1 Kingsport U.S.A.
130 C2 Kingston Can.
146 C3 Kingston Jamaica
141 E2 Kingston U.S.A.
52 A3 Kingston South East Austr.
98 C2 Kingston upon Hull U.K.
147 D3 Kingstown St Vincent
139 D3 Kingsville U.S.A.
99 B3 Kingswood U.K.
96 B2 Kingussie U.K.
126 E2 King William Island Can.
123 C3 King William's Town S. Africa
67 D3 Kinka-san *i.* Japan
93 F4 Kinna Sweden
97 B3 Kinsale Rep. of Ireland
118 B3 Kinshasa Dem. Rep. Congo
143 E1 Kinston U.S.A.
88 B2 Kintai Lith.
114 B4 Kintampo Ghana
96 B3 Kintyre *pen.* U.K.
130 C2 Kipawa, Lac *l.* Can.
83 I3 Kirensk Rus. Fed.
89 E3 Kireyevsk Rus. Fed.
Kirghizia *country* Asia *see* Kyrgyzstan
49 G3 Kiribati *country* Pacific Ocean
80 B2 Kırıkkale Turkey
89 E2 Kirillov Rus. Fed.
Kirin China *see* Jilin
119 D3 Kirinyaga *mt.* Kenya
89 D2 Kirishi Rus. Fed.
111 C3 Kırkağaç Turkey
96 C2 Kirkcaldy U.K.
96 B3 Kirkcudbright U.K.
92 J2 Kirkenes Norway
130 B2 Kirkland Lake Can.
137 E2 Kirksville U.S.A.
81 C2 Kirkūk Iraq
96 C1 Kirkwall U.K.
89 D3 Kirov *Kaluzhskaya Oblast'* Rus. Fed.
86 D3 Kirov Rus. Fed.
Kirovabad Azer. *see* Gäncä
86 E3 Kirovo-Chepetsk Rus. Fed.
91 C2 Kirovohrad Ukr.
86 C2 Kirovsk Rus. Fed.
91 D2 Kirovs'ke Ukr.
96 C2 Kirriemuir U.K.
86 E3 Kirs Rus. Fed.
74 A2 Kirthar Range *mts* Pak.
92 H2 Kiruna Sweden
67 C3 Kiryū Japan
89 E2 Kirzhach Rus. Fed.
119 C2 Kisangani Dem. Rep. Congo
118 B3 Kisantu Dem. Rep. Congo
60 A1 Kisaran Indon.
82 G3 Kiselevsk Rus. Fed.
75 C2 Kishanganj India
115 C4 Kishi Nigeria
Kishinev Moldova *see* Chișinău
77 D1 Kishkenekol' Kazakh.
74 B1 Kishtwar Jammu and Kashmir
119 D3 Kisii Kenya
103 D2 Kiskunfélegyháza Hungary
103 D2 Kiskunhalas Hungary
87 D4 Kislovodsk Rus. Fed.
117 C5 Kismaayo Somalia
119 C3 Kisoro Uganda
114 A4 Kissidougou Guinea
143 D3 Kissimmee U.S.A.
143 D3 Kissimmee, Lake U.S.A.
129 D2 Kississing Lake Can.
119 D3 Kisumu Kenya
114 B3 Kita Mali
66 D3 Kitakami Japan
66 D3 Kitakami-gawa *r.* Japan
67 B4 Kita-Kyūshū Japan
119 D2 Kitale Kenya
66 D2 Kitami Japan
130 B2 Kitchener Can.
93 J3 Kitee Fin.
119 D2 Kitgum Uganda
128 B2 Kitimat Can.
118 B3 Kitona Dem. Rep. Congo

119 D3 **Kitunda** Tanz.
128 B2 **Kitwanga** Can.
121 B2 **Kitwe** Zambia
101 E3 **Kitzingen** Ger.
92 I3 **Kiuruvesi** Fin.
119 C3 **Kivu, Lake** Dem. Rep. Congo/Rwanda
110 C2 **Kıyıköy** Turkey
86 E3 **Kizel** Rus. Fed.
111 C3 **Kızılca Dağ** *mt.* Turkey
87 D4 **Kizlyar** Rus. Fed.
92 I1 **Kjøllefjord** Norway
92 G2 **Kjøpsvik** Norway
102 C1 **Kladno** Czech Rep.
102 C2 **Klagenfurt** Austria
88 B2 **Klaipėda** Lith.
94 B1 **Klaksvík** Faroe Is
134 B2 **Klamath** *r.* U.S.A.
134 B2 **Klamath Falls** U.S.A.
134 B2 **Klamath Mountains** U.S.A.
102 C2 **Klatovy** Czech Rep.
122 A3 **Klawer** S. Africa
128 A2 **Klawock** U.S.A.
128 B2 **Kleena Kleene** Can.
122 B2 **Kleinbegin** S. Africa
122 A2 **Kleinsee** S. Africa
123 C2 **Klerksdorp** S. Africa
89 D3 **Kletnya** Rus. Fed.
100 C2 **Kleve** Ger.
89 D3 **Klimavichy** Belarus
89 D3 **Klimovo** Rus. Fed.
89 E2 **Klimovsk** Rus. Fed.
89 E2 **Klin** Rus. Fed.
101 F2 **Klínovec** *mt.* Czech Rep.
93 G4 **Klintehamn** Sweden
89 D3 **Klintsy** Rus. Fed.
109 C2 **Ključ** Bos.-Herz.
103 D1 **Kłodzko** Pol.
100 C1 **Kloosterhaar** Neth.
103 D2 **Klosterneuburg** Austria
101 E1 **Klötze (Altmark)** Ger.
103 D1 **Kluczbork** Pol.
128 A2 **Klukwan** U.S.A.
74 A2 **Klupro** Pak.
88 C3 **Klyetsk** Belarus
98 C1 **Knaresborough** U.K.
93 F3 **Knästen** *hill* Sweden
129 E2 **Knee Lake** Can.
101 E1 **Knesebeck** Ger.
101 E3 **Knetzgau** Ger.
109 C2 **Knin** Croatia
103 C2 **Knittelfeld** Austria
109 D2 **Knjaževac** Serb. and Mont.
100 A2 **Knokke-Heist** Belgium
143 D1 **Knoxville** U.S.A.
122 B3 **Knysna** S. Africa
67 C4 **Kōbe** Japan
København Denmark *see* **Copenhagen**
100 C2 **Koblenz** Ger.
59 C3 **Kobroör** *i.* Indon.
88 B3 **Kobryn** Belarus
109 D2 **Kočani** Macedonia
111 C2 **Kocasu** *r.* Turkey
75 C2 **Koch Bihar** India
Kochi India *see* **Cochin**
67 B4 **Kōchi** Japan
87 D4 **Kochubey** Rus. Fed.
75 C2 **Kodarma** India
117 B4 **Kodok** Sudan
90 B2 **Kodyma** Ukr.
111 C2 **Kodzhaele** *mt.* Bulg./Greece
122 A2 **Koës** Namibia
122 C2 **Koffiefontein** S. Africa
114 B4 **Koforidua** Ghana
67 C3 **Kōfu** Japan
131 D1 **Kogaluk** *r.* Can.
74 B1 **Kohat** Pak.
62 A1 **Kohima** India
88 C2 **Kohtla-Järve** Estonia
77 D2 **Kokand** Uzbek.
92 H3 **Kokkola** Fin.
140 B2 **Kokomo** U.S.A.
77 E2 **Kokpekti** Kazakh.
77 C1 **Kokshetau** Kazakh.
131 D1 **Koksoak** *r.* Can.
123 C3 **Kokstad** S. Africa
Koktokay China *see* **Fuyun**
58 C3 **Kolaka** Indon.
86 C2 **Kola Peninsula** *pen.* Rus. Fed.
92 H2 **Kolari** Fin.
114 A3 **Kolda** Senegal
93 E4 **Kolding** Denmark
107 D2 **Koléa** Alg.
86 D2 **Kolguyev, Ostrov** *i.* Rus. Fed.
73 B3 **Kolhapur** India
88 B2 **Kolkasrags** *pt* Latvia
75 C2 **Kolkata** India
Kollam India *see* **Quilon**
Köln Ger. *see* **Cologne**
103 D1 **Kołobrzeg** Pol.
114 B3 **Kolokani** Mali
89 E2 **Kolomna** Rus. Fed.
90 B2 **Kolomyya** Ukr.
122 B2 **Kolonkwane** Botswana
82 G3 **Kolpashevo** Rus. Fed.
89 E3 **Kolpny** Rus. Fed.
Kol'skiy Poluostrov *pen.* Rus. Fed. *see* **Kola Peninsula**
78 B3 **Koluli** Eritrea
119 C4 **Kolwezi** Dem. Rep. Congo
83 L2 **Kolyma** *r.* Rus. Fed.
83 L2 **Kolymskaya Nizmennost'** *lowland* Rus. Fed.
83 M2 **Kolymskiy, Khrebet** *mts* Rus. Fed.
67 C3 **Komaki** Japan
83 M3 **Komandorskiye Ostrova** *is* Rus. Fed.
103 D2 **Komárno** Slovakia
123 D2 **Komati** *r.* Swaziland
67 C3 **Komatsu** Japan
119 C3 **Kombe** Dem. Rep. Congo
90 C2 **Kominternivs'ke** Ukr.
109 C2 **Komiža** Croatia
103 D2 **Komló** Hungary
118 B3 **Komono** Congo
111 C2 **Komotini** Greece
122 B3 **Komsberg** *mts* S. Africa
83 H1 **Komsomolets, Ostrov** *i.* Rus. Fed.
89 F2 **Komsomol'sk** Rus. Fed.
91 C2 **Komsomol's'k** Ukr.
87 D4 **Komsomol'skiy** Rus. Fed.
69 E1 **Komsomol'sk-na-Amure** Rus. Fed.
89 E2 **Konakovo** Rus. Fed.
75 C3 **Kondagaon** India
86 F2 **Kondinskoye** Rus. Fed.
119 D3 **Kondoa** Tanz.
86 C2 **Kondopoga** Rus. Fed.
89 E3 **Kondrovo** Rus. Fed.
127 I2 **Kong Christian IX Land** *reg.* Greenland
127 I2 **Kong Frederik VI Kyst** *coastal area* Greenland
65 B2 **Kongju** S. Korea
119 C3 **Kongolo** Dem. Rep. Congo
93 E4 **Kongsberg** Norway
93 F3 **Kongsvinger** Norway
77 D3 **Kongur Shan** *mt.* China
100 C2 **Königswinter** Ger.
103 D1 **Konin** Pol.
109 C2 **Konjic** Bos.-Herz.
122 A2 **Konkiep** *watercourse* Namibia
91 C1 **Konotop** Ukr.
102 B2 **Konstanz** Ger.
115 C3 **Kontagora** Nigeria
63 B2 **Kon Tum** Vietnam
63 B2 **Kontum, Plateau du** Vietnam
80 B2 **Konya** Turkey
100 C3 **Konz** Ger.
86 E3 **Konzhakovskiy Kamen', Gora** *mt.* Rus. Fed.
134 C1 **Kooskia** U.S.A.
128 C3 **Kootenay Lake** Can.
122 B3 **Kootjieskolk** S. Africa
92 □B2 **Kópasker** Iceland
108 B1 **Koper** Slovenia
93 G4 **Kopparberg** Sweden
109 C1 **Koprivnica** Croatia
89 F3 **Korablino** Rus. Fed.
73 C3 **Koraput** India
101 D2 **Korbach** Ger.
109 D2 **Korçë** Albania
109 C2 **Korčula** Croatia
109 C2 **Korčula** *i.* Croatia
65 B1 **Korea, North** *country* Asia
65 B2 **Korea, South** *country* Asia
70 C2 **Korea Bay** *g.* China/N. Korea
65 B3 **Korea Strait** Japan/S. Korea
91 D2 **Korenovsk** Rus. Fed.
90 B1 **Korets'** Ukr.
111 C2 **Körfez** Turkey
114 B4 **Korhogo** Côte d'Ivoire
111 B3 **Korinthiakos Kolpos** *sea chan.* Greece
111 B3 **Korinthos** Greece
103 D2 **Kőris-hegy** *hill* Hungary
109 D2 **Koritnik** *mt.* Albania
67 D3 **Kōriyama** Japan
80 B2 **Korkuteli** Turkey
68 B2 **Korla** China
103 D2 **Körmend** Hungary
114 B3 **Koro** Mali
131 D1 **Koroc** *r.* Can.
91 D1 **Korocha** Rus. Fed.
119 D3 **Korogwe** Tanz.
59 C2 **Koror** Palau
90 B1 **Korosten'** Ukr.
90 B1 **Korostyshiv** Ukr.
115 D3 **Koro Toro** Chad
91 C2 **Korsun'-Shevchenkivs'kyy** Ukr.
103 E1 **Korsze** Pol.
100 A2 **Kortrijk** Belgium
83 L3 **Koryakskaya, Sopka** *vol.* Rus. Fed.
83 M2 **Koryakskiy Khrebet** *mts* Rus. Fed.
86 D2 **Koryazhma** Rus. Fed.
65 B2 **Koryŏng** S. Korea
91 C1 **Koryukivka** Ukr.
111 C3 **Kos** Greece
111 C3 **Kos** *i.* Greece
65 B2 **Kosan** N. Korea
103 D1 **Kościan** Pol.
53 C3 **Kosciuszko, Mount** Austr.
68 B1 **Kosh-Agach** Rus. Fed.
103 E2 **Košice** Slovakia
92 H2 **Koskullskulle** Sweden
65 B2 **Kosŏng** N. Korea
109 D2 **Kosovo** *prov.* Serb. and Mont.
109 D2 **Kosovska Mitrovica** Serb. and Mont.
114 B4 **Kossou, Lac de** *l.* Côte d'Ivoire
76 C1 **Kostanay** Kazakh.
110 B2 **Kostenets** Bulg.
123 C2 **Koster** S. Africa
117 B3 **Kosti** Sudan
86 C2 **Kostomuksha** Rus. Fed.
90 B1 **Kostopil'** Ukr.
89 F2 **Kostroma** Rus. Fed.
89 F2 **Kostroma** *r.* Rus. Fed.
102 C1 **Kostrzyn** Pol.

103 D1 **Koszalin** Pol.
103 D2 **Kőszeg** Hungary
74 B2 **Kota** India
60 B2 **Kotaagung** Indon.
61 C2 **Kotabaru** Indon.
61 C1 **Kota Belud** *Sabah* Malaysia
60 B1 **Kota Bharu** Malaysia
60 B2 **Kotabumi** Indon.
61 C1 **Kota Kinabalu** *Sabah* Malaysia
61 C1 **Kota Samarahan** *Sarawak* Malaysia
86 D3 **Kotel'nich** Rus. Fed.
87 D4 **Kotel'nikovo** Rus. Fed.
83 K1 **Kotel'nyy, Ostrov** *i.* Rus. Fed.
101 E2 **Köthen (Anhalt)** Ger.
93 I3 **Kotka** Fin.
86 D2 **Kotlas** Rus. Fed.
109 C2 **Kotor Varoš** Bos.-Herz.
87 D3 **Kotovo** Rus. Fed.
91 E1 **Kotovsk** Rus. Fed.
90 B2 **Kotovs'k** Ukr.
83 H2 **Kotuy** *r.* Rus. Fed.
100 A2 **Koudekerke** Neth.
114 B3 **Koudougou** Burkina
122 B3 **Kougaberge** *mts* S. Africa
118 B3 **Koulamoutou** Gabon
114 B3 **Koulikoro** Mali
114 A3 **Koundâra** Guinea
151 C1 **Kourou** Fr. Guiana
114 B3 **Kouroussa** Guinea
115 D3 **Kousséri** Cameroon
114 B3 **Koutiala** Mali
93 I3 **Kouvola** Fin.
92 J2 **Kovdor** Rus. Fed.
90 A1 **Kovel'** Ukr.
89 F2 **Kovrov** Rus. Fed.
54 B2 **Kowhitirangi** N.Z.
111 C3 **Köyceğiz** Turkey
86 D2 **Koyda** Rus. Fed.
126 A2 **Koyukuk** *r.* U.S.A.
111 B2 **Kozani** Greece
90 C1 **Kozelets'** Ukr.
89 E3 **Kozel'sk** Rus. Fed.
Kozhikode India *see* **Calicut**
90 B2 **Kozyatyn** Ukr.
63 A3 **Krabi** Thai.
63 A2 **Kra Buri** Thai.
63 B2 **Krâchéh** Cambodia
93 E4 **Kragerø** Norway
100 B1 **Kraggenburg** Neth.
109 D2 **Kragujevac** Serb. and Mont.
60 B2 **Krakatau** *i.* Indon.
103 D1 **Kraków** Pol.
91 D2 **Kramators'k** Ukr.
93 G3 **Kramfors** Sweden
111 B3 **Kranidi** Greece
86 E1 **Krasino** Rus. Fed.
88 C2 **Krāslava** Latvia
101 F2 **Kraslice** Czech Rep.
89 D3 **Krasnapollye** Belarus
89 D3 **Krasnaya Gora** Rus. Fed.
87 D3 **Krasnoarmeysk** Rus. Fed.
91 D2 **Krasnoarmiys'k** Ukr.
86 D2 **Krasnoborsk** Rus. Fed.
91 D2 **Krasnodar** Rus. Fed.
91 D2 **Krasnodon** Ukr.
88 C2 **Krasnogorodskoye** Rus. Fed.
91 D1 **Krasnogvardeyskoye** Rus. Fed.
91 D2 **Krasnohrad** Ukr.
91 C2 **Krasnohvardiys'ke** Ukr.
86 E3 **Krasnokamsk** Rus. Fed.
89 D2 **Krasnomayskiy** Rus. Fed.
91 C2 **Krasnoperekops'k** Ukr.
87 D3 **Krasnoslobodsk** Rus. Fed.
86 E3 **Krasnoufimsk** Rus. Fed.
83 H3 **Krasnoyarsk** Rus. Fed.
89 F2 **Krasnoye-na-Volge** Rus. Fed.
89 D3 **Krasnyy** Rus. Fed.
89 E2 **Krasnyy Kholm** Rus. Fed.
87 C4 **Krasnyy Luch** Ukr.
91 E2 **Krasnyy Sulin** Rus. Fed.
90 B2 **Krasyliv** Ukr.
100 C2 **Krefeld** Ger.
91 C2 **Kremenchuk** Ukr.
91 C2 **Kremenchuts'ka Vodoskhovyshche** *resr* Ukr.
103 D2 **Křemešník** *hill* Czech Rep.
91 D2 **Kreminna** Ukr.
103 D2 **Krems an der Donau** Austria
89 D2 **Kresttsy** Rus. Fed.
88 B2 **Kretinga** Lith.
100 C2 **Kreuzau** Ger.
100 C2 **Kreuztal** Ger.
118 A2 **Kribi** Cameroon
111 B3 **Krikellos** Greece
66 D1 **Kril'on, Mys** *c.* Rus. Fed.
73 C3 **Krishna** *r.* India
73 C3 **Krishna, Mouths of the** India
75 C2 **Krishnanagar** India
93 E4 **Kristiansand** Norway
93 F4 **Kristianstad** Sweden
92 E3 **Kristiansund** Norway
93 F4 **Kristinehamn** Sweden
Kriti *i.* Greece *see* **Crete**
Krivoy Rog Ukr. *see* **Kryvyy Rih**
109 C1 **Križevci** Croatia
108 B1 **Krk** *i.* Croatia
92 F3 **Krokom** Sweden
91 C1 **Krolevets'** Ukr.
101 E2 **Kronach** Ger.
63 B2 **Krŏng Kaôh Kŏng** Cambodia
127 I2 **Kronprins Frederik Bjerge** *nunataks* Greenland
123 C2 **Kroonstad** S. Africa
87 D4 **Kropotkin** Rus. Fed.
103 E2 **Krosno** Pol.
103 D1 **Krotoszyn** Pol.
60 B2 **Krui** Indon.
109 C2 **Krujë** Albania
111 C2 **Krumovgrad** Bulg.
Krung Thep Thai. *see* **Bangkok**
88 C3 **Krupki** Belarus
109 D2 **Kruševac** Serb. and Mont.
101 E2 **Krušné Hory** *mts* Czech Rep.
128 A2 **Kruzof Island** U.S.A.
89 D3 **Krychaw** Belarus
91 D3 **Krymsk** Rus. Fed.
111 C3 **Krytiko Pelagos** *sea* Greece
91 C2 **Kryvyy Rih** Ukr.
114 B2 **Ksabi** Alg.
107 D2 **Ksar el Boukhari** Alg.
114 B1 **Ksar el Kebir** Morocco
89 E3 **Kshenskiy** Rus. Fed.
78 B2 **Kū', Jabal al** *hill* Saudi Arabia
61 C1 **Kuala Belait** Brunei
60 B1 **Kuala Kerai** Malaysia
60 B1 **Kuala Lipis** Malaysia
60 B1 **Kuala Lumpur** Malaysia
61 C2 **Kualapembuang** Indon.
60 B1 **Kuala Terengganu** Malaysia
60 B2 **Kualatungal** Indon.
61 C1 **Kuamut** *Sabah* Malaysia
65 A1 **Kuandian** China
60 B1 **Kuantan** Malaysia
91 D2 **Kuban'** *r.* Rus. Fed.
89 E2 **Kubenskoye, Ozero** *l.* Rus. Fed.
110 C2 **Kubrat** Bulg.
61 C1 **Kubuang** Indon.
61 C1 **Kuching** *Sarawak* Malaysia
109 C2 **Kuçovë** Albania
61 C1 **Kudat** *Sabah* Malaysia
61 C2 **Kudus** Indon.
102 C2 **Kufstein** Austria
127 F2 **Kugaaruk** Can.
126 D2 **Kugluktuk** Can.
92 I3 **Kuhmo** Fin.
79 C2 **Kūhrān, Kūh-e** *mt.* Iran
Kuitin China *see* **Kuytun**
120 A2 **Kuito** Angola
92 I2 **Kuivaniemi** Fin.
65 B2 **Kujang** N. Korea
109 D2 **Kukës** Albania
111 C3 **Kula** Turkey
75 D2 **Kula Kangri** *mt.* Bhutan
76 B2 **Kulandy** Kazakh.
88 B2 **Kuldīga** Latvia
122 B1 **Kule** Botswana
101 E2 **Kulmbach** Ger.
77 C3 **Kŭlob** Tajik.
76 B2 **Kul'sary** Kazakh.
77 D1 **Kulunda** Rus. Fed.
127 I2 **Kulusuk** Greenland
67 C3 **Kumagaya** Japan
67 B4 **Kumamoto** Japan
109 D2 **Kumanovo** Macedonia
114 B4 **Kumasi** Ghana
118 A2 **Kumba** Cameroon
78 B2 **Kumdah** Saudi Arabia
87 E3 **Kumertau** Rus. Fed.
65 B2 **Kumi** S. Korea
93 G4 **Kumla** Sweden
115 D3 **Kumo** Nigeria
62 A1 **Kumon Range** *mts* Myanmar
62 B2 **Kumphawapi** Thai.
Kumul China *see* **Hami**
66 D2 **Kunashir, Ostrov** *i.* Rus. Fed.
77 D2 **Kungei Alatau** *mts* Kazakh./Kyrg.
76 B2 **Kungrad** Uzbek.
93 F4 **Kungsbacka** Sweden
118 B2 **Kungu** Dem. Rep. Congo
86 E3 **Kungur** Rus. Fed.
62 A1 **Kunhing** Myanmar
77 D3 **Kunlun Shan** *mts* China
62 B1 **Kunming** China
65 B2 **Kunsan** S. Korea
50 B1 **Kununurra** Austr.
92 I3 **Kuopio** Fin.
109 C1 **Kupa** *r.* Croatia/Slovenia
59 C3 **Kupang** Indon.
88 B2 **Kupiškis** Lith.
111 C2 **Küplü** Turkey
128 A2 **Kupreanof Island** U.S.A.
91 D2 **Kup"yans'k** Ukr.
77 E2 **Kuqa** China
67 B4 **Kurashiki** Japan
67 B3 **Kurayoshi** Japan
89 E3 **Kurchatov** Rus. Fed.
110 C2 **Kŭrdzhali** Bulg.
67 B4 **Kure** Japan
88 B2 **Kuressaare** Estonia
86 F3 **Kurgan** Rus. Fed.
93 H3 **Kurikka** Fin.
156 C3 **Kuril Trench** *sea feature* N. Pacific Ocean
89 E3 **Kurkino** Rus. Fed.
117 B3 **Kurmuk** Sudan
73 B3 **Kurnool** India
67 D3 **Kuroiso** Japan
53 D2 **Kurri Kurri** Austr.
89 E3 **Kursk** Rus. Fed.
122 B2 **Kuruman** S. Africa
122 B2 **Kuruman** *watercourse* S. Africa
67 B4 **Kurume** Japan
83 I3 **Kurumkan** Rus. Fed.
73 C4 **Kurunegala** Sri Lanka
111 C3 **Kuşadası** Turkey

111 C3 **Kuşadası Körfezi** *b.* Turkey
111 C2 **Kuş Gölü** *l.* Turkey
91 D2 **Kushchevskaya** Rus. Fed.
66 D2 **Kushiro** Japan
76 C1 **Kushmurun** Kazakh.
75 C2 **Kushtia** Bangl.
66 D2 **Kussharo-ko** *l.* Japan
111 C3 **Kütahya** Turkey
81 C1 **K'ut'aisi** Georgia
109 C1 **Kutjevo** Croatia
103 D1 **Kutno** Pol.
118 B3 **Kutu** Dem. Rep. Congo
126 D2 **Kuujjua** *r.* Can.
131 D1 **Kuujjuaq** Can.
130 C1 **Kuujjuarapik** Can.
92 I2 **Kuusamo** Fin.
120 A2 **Kuvango** Angola
89 D2 **Kuvshinovo** Rus. Fed.
78 B2 **Kuwait** *country* Asia
79 B2 **Kuwait** Kuwait
Kuybyshev Rus. Fed. *see* Samara
91 D2 **Kuybysheve** Ukr.
87 D3 **Kuybyshevskoye Vodokhranilishche** *resr* Rus. Fed.
77 E2 **Kuytun** China
111 C3 **Kuyucak** Turkey
87 D3 **Kuznetsk** Rus. Fed.
90 B1 **Kuznetsovs'k** Ukr.
92 H1 **Kvalsund** Norway
123 D2 **KwaMashu** S. Africa
65 B2 **Kwangju** S. Korea
65 B1 **Kwanmo-bong** *mt.* N. Korea
123 C3 **Kwanobuhle** S. Africa
122 B3 **Kwanonzame** S. Africa
123 C3 **Kwatinidubu** S. Africa
123 C2 **KwaZamokhule** S. Africa
123 D2 **Kwazulu-Natal** *prov.* S. Africa
121 B2 **Kwekwe** Zimbabwe
118 B3 **Kwenge** *r.* Dem. Rep. Congo
103 D1 **Kwidzyn** Pol.
118 B3 **Kwilu** *r.* Angola/ Dem. Rep. Congo
59 C3 **Kwoka** *mt.* Indon.
53 C3 **Kyabram** Austr.
62 A2 **Kyaikto** Myanmar
69 D1 **Kyakhta** Rus. Fed.
52 A2 **Kyancutta** Austr.
62 A1 **Kyaukpadaung** Myanmar
62 A2 **Kyaukpyu** Myanmar
88 B3 **Kybartai** Lith.
62 A2 **Kyebogyi** Myanmar
62 A2 **Kyeintali** Myanmar
74 B1 **Kyelang** India
Kyiv Ukr. *see* **Kiev**
Kyklades *is* Greece *see* **Cyclades**
129 D2 **Kyle** Can.
96 B2 **Kyle of Lochalsh** U.K.
100 C3 **Kyll** *r.* Ger.
111 B3 **Kyllini** *mt.* Greece
111 B3 **Kymi** Greece
52 B3 **Kyneton** Austr.
119 D2 **Kyoga, Lake** Uganda
53 D1 **Kyogle** Austr.
65 B2 **Kyŏnggi-man** *b.* N. Korea
65 B2 **Kyŏngju** S. Korea
67 C4 **Kyōto** Japan
111 B3 **Kyparissia** Greece
111 B3 **Kyra Panagia** *i.* Greece
77 D2 **Kyrgyzstan** *country* Asia
101 F1 **Kyritz** Ger.
92 H3 **Kyrönjoki** *r.* Fin.
86 E2 **Kyrta** Rus. Fed.
86 D2 **Kyssa** Rus. Fed.
111 B3 **Kythira** *i.* Greece
111 B3 **Kythnos** *i.* Greece
128 B2 **Kyuquot** Can.
67 B4 **Kyūshū** *i.* Japan
110 B2 **Kyustendil** Bulg.
90 C1 **Kyyivs'ke Vodoskhovyshche** *resr* Ukr.
92 H3 **Kyyjärvi** Fin.
68 C1 **Kyzyl** Rus. Fed.
76 C2 **Kyzylkum Desert** Kazakh./Uzbek.
77 C2 **Kyzylorda** Kazakh.

L

145 C3 **La Angostura, Presa de** *resr* Mex.
117 C4 **Laascaanood** Somalia
145 D3 **La Ascensión, Bahía de** *b.* Mex.
150 B1 **La Asunción** Venez.
114 A2 **Laâyoune** Western Sahara
87 D4 **Laba** *r.* Rus. Fed.
144 B2 **La Babia** Mex.
146 B3 **La Bahía, Islas de** *is* Hond.
130 C1 **La Baleine, Grande Rivière de** *r.* Can.
131 D1 **La Baleine, Rivière à** *r.* Can.
152 B3 **La Banda** Arg.
104 B2 **La Baule-Escoublac** France
114 A3 **Labé** Guinea
128 A1 **Laberge, Lake** Can.
129 C2 **La Biche, Lac** *l.* Can.
87 D4 **Labinsk** Rus. Fed.
64 B1 **Labo** Phil.
144 B2 **La Boquilla, Presa de** *resr* Mex.
104 B3 **Labouheyre** France
131 D1 **Labrador** *reg.* Can.
131 D1 **Labrador City** Can.
158 C1 **Labrador Sea** Can./Greenland
150 B2 **Lábrea** Brazil
61 C1 **Labuan** Malaysia
60 B1 **Labuhanbilik** Indon.
59 C3 **Labuna** Indon.
63 A2 **Labutta** Myanmar
86 F2 **Labytnangi** Rus. Fed.
109 C2 **Laç** Albania
106 B1 **La Cabrera, Sierra de** *mts* Spain
105 C2 **La Capelle** France
73 B3 **Laccadive Islands** India
129 E2 **Lac du Bonnet** Can.
146 B3 **La Ceiba** Hond.
53 B2 **Lachlan** *r.* Austr.
141 E1 **Lachute** Can.
105 D3 **La Ciotat** France
129 C2 **Lac La Biche** Can.
Lac la Martre Can. *see* **Wha Ti**
141 E1 **Lac-Mégantic** Can.
128 C2 **Lacombe** Can.
145 C3 **La Concordia** Mex.
108 A3 **Laconi** *Sardinia* Italy
141 E2 **Laconia** U.S.A.
104 B2 **La Coubre, Pointe de** *pt* France
128 C2 **La Crete** Can.
140 A2 **La Crosse** U.S.A.
144 B2 **La Cruz** Mex.
144 B2 **La Cuesta** Mex.
75 B1 **Ladakh Range** *mts* India
106 C1 **La Demanda, Sierra de** *mts* Spain
122 B3 **Ladismith** S. Africa
79 D2 **Lādīz** Iran
86 C2 **Ladoga, Lake** Rus. Fed.
Ladozhskoye Ozero *l.* Rus. Fed. *see* **Ladoga, Lake**
128 B3 **Ladysmith** Can.
123 C2 **Ladysmith** S. Africa
59 D3 **Lae** P.N.G.
152 B3 **La Esmeralda** Bol.
93 F4 **Læsø** *i.* Denmark
143 C2 **La Fayette** U.S.A.
140 B2 **Lafayette** *IN* U.S.A.
142 B2 **Lafayette** *LA* U.S.A.
115 C4 **Lafia** Nigeria
104 B2 **La Flèche** France
143 D1 **La Follette** U.S.A.
131 C1 **Laforge** Can.
79 C2 **Lāft** Iran
108 A3 **La Galite** *i.* Tunisia
81 C1 **Lagan'** Rus. Fed.
118 B2 **Lagdo, Lac de** *l.* Cameroon
115 C1 **Laghouat** Alg.
155 D1 **Lagoa Santa** Brazil
114 A2 **La Gomera** *i.* Canary Is
147 C3 **La Gonâve, Île de** *i.* Haiti
114 C4 **Lagos** Nigeria
106 B2 **Lagos** Port.
134 C1 **La Grande** U.S.A.
130 C1 **La Grande 2, Réservoir** *resr* Can.
131 C1 **La Grande 3, Réservoir** *resr* Can.
130 C1 **La Grande 4, Réservoir** *resr* Can.
50 B1 **Lagrange** Austr.
143 C2 **La Grange** U.S.A.
150 B1 **La Gran Sabana** *plat.* Venez.
147 C3 **La Guajira, Península de** *pen.* Col.
152 D3 **Laguna** Brazil
150 A2 **Lagunas** Peru
La Habana Cuba *see* **Havana**
61 C1 **Lahad Datu** *Sabah* Malaysia
104 B2 **La Hague, Cap de** *c.* France
60 B2 **Lahat** Indon.
78 B3 **Laḩij** Yemen
81 C2 **Lāhījān** Iran
100 C2 **Lahnstein** Ger.
74 B1 **Lahore** Pak.
74 A2 **Lahri** Pak.
93 I3 **Lahti** Fin.
115 D4 **Laï** Chad
53 D1 **Laidley** Austr.
104 C2 **L'Aigle** France
122 B3 **Laingsburg** S. Africa
92 H2 **Lainioälven** *r.* Sweden
115 C3 **L'Aïr, Massif de** *mts* Niger
96 B1 **Lairg** U.K.
108 B1 **Laives** Italy
70 B2 **Laiwu** China
70 C2 **Laiyang** China
70 B2 **Laizhou** China
70 B2 **Laizhou Wan** *b.* China
50 C1 **Lajamanu** Austr.
152 C3 **Lajes** Brazil
144 B2 **La Junta** Mex.
136 C3 **La Junta** U.S.A.
146 B2 **La Juventud, Isla de** *i.* Cuba
53 C2 **Lake Cargelligo** Austr.
53 D2 **Lake Cathie** Austr.
142 B2 **Lake Charles** U.S.A.
143 D2 **Lake City** *FL* U.S.A.
143 E2 **Lake City** *SC* U.S.A.
128 B3 **Lake Cowichan** Can.
138 A2 **Lake Havasu City** U.S.A.
143 D3 **Lakeland** U.S.A.
128 C2 **Lake Louise** Can.
134 B1 **Lake Oswego** U.S.A.
54 A2 **Lake Paringa** N.Z.
142 B2 **Lake Providence** U.S.A.
54 B2 **Lake Pukaki** N.Z.
53 C3 **Lakes Entrance** Austr.
134 B2 **Lakeview** U.S.A.
136 B3 **Lakewood** *CO* U.S.A.
141 E2 **Lakewood** *NJ* U.S.A.
143 D3 **Lake Worth** U.S.A.

74 A2 **Lakhpat** India
74 B1 **Lakki** Pak.
111 B3 **Lakonikos Kolpos** *b.* Greece
92 H1 **Lakselv** Norway
144 A2 **La Laguna, Picacho de** *mt.* Mex.
145 C3 **La Libertad** Guat.
106 B1 **Lalín** Spain
75 B2 **Lalitpur** India
129 D2 **La Loche** Can.
100 B2 **La Louvière** Belgium
108 A2 **La Maddalena** *Sardinia* Italy
131 D2 **La Madeleine, Îles de** *is* Can.
61 C1 **Lamag** *Sabah* Malaysia
La Manche *str.* France/U.K. *see* **English Channel**
136 C3 **Lamar** U.S.A.
79 C2 **Lamard** Iran
108 A3 **La Marmora, Punta** *mt.* *Sardinia* Italy
128 C1 **La Martre, Lac** *l.* Can.
118 B3 **Lambaréné** Gabon
122 A3 **Lambert's Bay** S. Africa
92 □A2 **Lambeyri** Iceland
106 B1 **Lamego** Port.
150 A3 **La Merced** Peru
52 B3 **Lameroo** Austr.
139 C2 **Lamesa** U.S.A.
111 B3 **Lamia** Greece
137 E2 **Lamoni** U.S.A.
62 A2 **Lampang** Thai.
139 D2 **Lampasas** U.S.A.
145 B2 **Lampazos** Mex.
99 A2 **Lampeter** U.K.
62 A2 **Lamphun** Thai.
119 E3 **Lamu** Kenya
107 D2 **La Nao, Cabo de** *c.* Spain
96 C3 **Lanark** U.K.
63 A2 **Lanbi Kyun** *i.* Myanmar
Lancang Jiang *r.* China *see* **Mekong**
98 B1 **Lancaster** U.K.
135 C4 **Lancaster** *CA* U.S.A.
140 C3 **Lancaster** *OH* U.S.A.
141 D2 **Lancaster** *PA* U.S.A.
143 D2 **Lancaster** *SC* U.S.A.
127 F2 **Lancaster Sound** *str.* Can.
Lanchow China *see* **Lanzhou**
102 C2 **Landeck** Austria
136 B2 **Lander** U.S.A.
99 A3 **Land's End** *pt* U.K.
102 C2 **Landshut** Ger.
93 F4 **Landskrona** Sweden
143 C2 **Lanett** U.S.A.
122 B2 **Langberg** *mts* S. Africa
137 D1 **Langdon** U.S.A.
93 F4 **Langeland** *i.* Denmark
101 D1 **Langen** Ger.
100 C1 **Langeoog** Ger.
100 C1 **Langeoog** *i.* Ger.
101 D2 **Langgöns** Ger.
92 □A3 **Langjökull** *ice cap* Iceland
105 C3 **Langogne** France
104 B3 **Langon** France
105 D2 **Langres** France
60 A1 **Langsa** Indon.
62 B1 **Lang Sơn** Vietnam
101 D1 **Langwedel** Ger.
129 D2 **Lanigan** Can.
153 A4 **Lanín, Volcán** *vol.* Arg./Chile
81 C2 **Länkäran** Azer.
104 B2 **Lannion** France
140 C2 **Lansing** U.S.A.
71 B3 **Lanxi** China
117 B4 **Lanya** Sudan
114 A2 **Lanzarote** *i.* Canary Is
70 A2 **Lanzhou** China
64 B1 **Laoag** Phil.
62 B1 **Lao Cai** Vietnam
70 B2 **Laohekou** China
Laojunmiao China *see* Yumen
65 B1 **Laoling** China
65 B1 **Lao Ling** *mts* China
105 C2 **Laon** France
62 B2 **Laos** *country* Asia
65 B1 **Laotougou** China
154 C3 **Lapa** Brazil
114 A2 **La Palma** *i.* Canary Is
146 C4 **La Palma** Panama
150 B1 **La Paragua** Venez.
152 B2 **La Paz** Bol.
144 A2 **La Paz** Mex.
150 B2 **La Pedrera** Col.
66 D1 **La Pérouse Strait** Japan/Rus. Fed.
145 C2 **La Pesca** Mex.
144 B2 **La Piedad** Mex.
153 C4 **La Plata** Arg.
153 C4 **La Plata, Río de** *sea chan.* Arg./Uru.
93 I3 **Lappeenranta** Fin.
92 G2 **Lappland** *reg.* Europe
111 C2 **Lâpseki** Turkey
83 J1 **Laptev Sea** Rus. Fed.
Laptevykh, More *sea* Rus. Fed. *see* **Laptev Sea**
92 H3 **Lapua** Fin.
152 B3 **La Quiaca** Arg.
79 C2 **Lār** Iran
114 B1 **Larache** Morocco
136 B2 **Laramie** U.S.A.
136 B2 **Laramie Mountains** U.S.A.
154 B3 **Laranjeiras do Sul** Brazil
59 C3 **Larantuka** Indon.
59 C3 **Larat** *i.* Indon.
107 D2 **Larba** Alg.
106 C1 **Laredo** Spain
139 D3 **Laredo** U.S.A.
96 B3 **Largs** U.K.
152 B3 **La Rioja** Arg.
111 B3 **Larisa** Greece
74 A2 **Larkana** Pak.
80 B2 **Larnaka** Cyprus
97 D1 **Larne** U.K.
100 B2 **La Roche-en-Ardenne** Belgium
104 B2 **La Rochelle** France
104 B2 **La Roche-sur-Yon** France
107 C2 **La Roda** Spain
147 D3 **La Romana** Dom. Rep.
129 D2 **La Ronge** Can.
129 D2 **La Ronge, Lac** *l.* Can.
50 C1 **Larrimah** Austr.
55 P3 **Larsen Ice Shelf** Antarctica
93 F4 **Larvik** Norway
130 C2 **La Sarre** Can.
138 B2 **Las Cruces** U.S.A.
153 C4 **Las Flores** Arg.
153 B4 **Las Heras** Arg.
62 A1 **Lashio** Myanmar
109 C3 **La Sila** *reg.* Italy
152 B3 **Las Lomitas** Arg.
144 B2 **Las Nieves** Mex.
114 A2 **Las Palmas de Gran Canaria** Canary Is
108 A2 **La Spezia** Italy
150 B3 **Las Piedras, Río de** *r.* Peru
153 B5 **Las Plumas** Arg.
129 D2 **Last Mountain Lake** Can.
152 B3 **Las Tórtolas, Cerro** *mt.* Chile
118 B3 **Lastoursville** Gabon
109 C2 **Lastovo** *i.* Croatia
144 A2 **Las Tres Vírgenes, Volcán** *vol.* Mex.
146 C2 **Las Tunas** Cuba
144 B2 **Las Varas** *Chihuahua* Mex.
144 B2 **Las Varas** *Nayarit* Mex.
138 B1 **Las Vegas** *NM* U.S.A.
135 C3 **Las Vegas** *NV* U.S.A.
131 E1 **La Tabatière** Can.
104 B3 **La Teste** France
108 B2 **Latina** Italy
147 D3 **La Tortuga, Isla** *i.* Venez.
64 B1 **La Trinidad** Phil.
89 E2 **Latskoye** Rus. Fed.
131 C2 **La Tuque** Can.
88 B2 **Latvia** *country* Europe
102 C1 **Lauchhammer** Ger.
101 E3 **Lauf an der Pegnitz** Ger.
105 D2 **Laufen** Switz.
51 D4 **Launceston** Austr.
99 A3 **Launceston** U.K.
62 A1 **Launggyaung** Myanmar
51 D1 **Laura** Austr.
142 C2 **Laurel** *MS* U.S.A.
134 E1 **Laurel** *MT* U.S.A.
109 C2 **Lauria** Italy
143 E2 **Laurinburg** U.S.A.
105 D2 **Lausanne** Switz.
61 C2 **Laut** *i.* Indon.
101 D2 **Lautersbach (Hessen)** Ger.
61 C2 **Laut Kecil, Kepulauan** *is* Indon.
100 C1 **Lauwersmeer** *l.* Neth.
104 B2 **Laval** France
50 B2 **Laverton** Austr.
155 D2 **Lavras** Brazil
123 D2 **Lavumisa** Swaziland
61 C1 **Lawas** *Sarawak* Malaysia
62 A1 **Lawksawk** Myanmar
114 B3 **Lawra** Ghana
137 D3 **Lawrence** U.S.A.
142 C1 **Lawrenceburg** U.S.A.
139 D2 **Lawton** U.S.A.
78 A2 **Lawz, Jabal al** *mt.* Saudi Arabia
93 F4 **Laxå** Sweden
109 D2 **Lazarevac** Serb. and Mont.
144 A1 **Lázaro Cárdenas** *Baja California Norte* Mex.
144 B3 **Lázaro Cárdenas** *Michoacán* Mex.
88 B3 **Lazdijai** Lith.
136 C2 **Lead** U.S.A.
129 D2 **Leader** Can.
136 B3 **Leadville** U.S.A.
Leaf Bay Can. *see* **Tasiujaq**
129 D2 **Leaf Rapids** Can.
97 B2 **Leane, Lough** *l.* Rep. of Ireland
130 C1 **L'Eau Claire, Lac à** *l.* Can.
137 E3 **Leavenworth** U.S.A.
80 B2 **Lebanon** *country* Asia
137 E3 **Lebanon** *MO* U.S.A.
141 E2 **Lebanon** *NH* U.S.A.
134 B2 **Lebanon** *OR* U.S.A.
141 D2 **Lebanon** *PA* U.S.A.
89 E3 **Lebedyan'** Rus. Fed.
91 C1 **Lebedyn** Ukr.
104 C2 **Le Blanc** France
103 D1 **Lębork** Pol.
123 C1 **Lebowakgomo** S. Africa
106 B2 **Lebrija** Spain
153 A4 **Lebu** Chile
104 C3 **Le Bugue** France
109 C2 **Lecce** Italy
108 A1 **Lecco** Italy
102 C2 **Lech** *r.* Austria/Ger.
111 B3 **Lechaina** Greece
71 B3 **Lechang** China
102 B1 **Leck** Ger.
104 C3 **Lectoure** France
106 B1 **Ledesma** Spain
104 C2 **Le Dorat** France
128 C2 **Leduc** Can.
137 E1 **Leech Lake** U.S.A.
98 C2 **Leeds** U.K.

98 B2 **Leek** U.K.
100 C1 **Leer (Ostfriesland)** Ger.
143 D3 **Leesburg** U.S.A.
142 B2 **Leesville** U.S.A.
53 C2 **Leeton** Austr.
122 B3 **Leeu-Gamka** S. Africa
100 B1 **Leeuwarden** Neth.
50 A3 **Leeuwin, Cape** Austr.
147 D3 **Leeward Islands** Caribbean Sea
111 B3 **Lefkada** Greece
111 B3 **Lefkada** *i.* Greece
Lefkosia Cyprus *see* **Nicosia**
64 B1 **Legaspi** Phil.
108 B1 **Legnago** Italy
103 D1 **Legnica** Pol.
75 B1 **Leh** Jammu and Kashmir
104 C2 **Le Havre** France
122 B1 **Lehututu** Botswana
74 B1 **Leiah** Pak.
103 D2 **Leibnitz** Austria
99 C2 **Leicester** U.K.
51 C1 **Leichhardt** *r.* Austr.
100 B1 **Leiden** Neth.
100 A2 **Leie** *r.* Belgium
52 A2 **Leigh Creek** Austr.
93 E3 **Leikanger** Norway
101 D1 **Leine** *r.* Ger.
97 C2 **Leinster** *reg.* Rep. of Ireland
101 F2 **Leipzig** Ger.
92 F2 **Leiranger** Norway
106 B2 **Leiria** Port.
93 E4 **Leirvik** Norway
97 C2 **Leixlip** Rep. of Ireland
71 B3 **Leiyang** China
71 B3 **Leizhou** China
71 A3 **Leizhou Bandao** *pen.* China
118 B3 **Lékana** Congo
100 B1 **Lelystad** Neth.
153 B6 **Le Maire, Estrecho de** *sea chan.* Arg.
105 D2 **Léman, Lac** *l.* France/Switz.
104 C2 **Le Mans** France
137 D2 **Le Mars** U.S.A.
154 C2 **Leme** Brazil
80 B2 **Lemesos** Cyprus
101 D1 **Lemförde** Ger.
127 G2 **Lemieux Islands** Can.
136 C1 **Lemmon** U.S.A.
135 C3 **Lemoore** U.S.A.
131 D1 **Le Moyne, Lac** *l.* Can.
62 A1 **Lemro** *r.* Myanmar
109 C2 **Le Murge** *hills* Italy
83 J2 **Lena** *r.* Rus. Fed.
100 C1 **Lengerich** Ger.
71 B3 **Lengshuijiang** China
71 B3 **Lengshuitan** China
91 D2 **Lenine** Ukr.
Leningrad Rus. Fed. *see* **St Petersburg**
91 D2 **Leningradskaya** Rus. Fed.
77 D3 **Lenin Peak** Kyrg./Tajik.
Leninsk Kazakh. *see* **Baykonur**
89 E3 **Leninskiy** Rus. Fed.
100 A2 **Lens** Belgium
104 C1 **Lens** France
83 I2 **Lensk** Rus. Fed.
103 D2 **Lenti** Hungary
109 C3 **Lentini** *Sicily* Italy
114 B3 **Léo** Burkina
103 D2 **Leoben** Austria
99 B2 **Leominster** U.K.
144 B2 **León** Mex.
146 B3 **León** Nic.
106 B1 **León** Spain
122 A1 **Leonardville** Namibia
50 B2 **Leonora** Austr.
155 D2 **Leopoldina** Brazil
123 C1 **Lephepe** Botswana
123 C3 **Lephoi** S. Africa
71 B3 **Leping** China
105 C2 **Le-Puy-en-Velay** France
150 A2 **Lérida** Col.
106 C1 **Lerma** Spain
111 C3 **Leros** *i.* Greece
130 C1 **Le Roy, Lac** *l.* Can.
93 F4 **Lerum** Sweden
96 □ **Lerwick** U.K.
111 C3 **Lesbos** *i.* Greece
147 C3 **Les Cayes** Haiti
69 C3 **Leshan** China
86 D2 **Leshukonskoye** Rus. Fed.
109 D2 **Leskovac** Serb. and Mont.
104 B2 **Lesneven** France
89 E2 **Lesnoye** Rus. Fed.
83 H3 **Lesosibirsk** Rus. Fed.
123 C2 **Lesotho** *country* Africa
66 B1 **Lesozavodsk** Rus. Fed.
104 B2 **Les Sables-d'Olonne** France
147 D3 **Lesser Antilles** *is* Caribbean Sea
81 C1 **Lesser Caucasus** *mts* Asia
128 C2 **Lesser Slave Lake** Can.
105 C3 **Les Vans** France
Lesvos *i.* Greece *see* **Lesbos**
103 D1 **Leszno** Pol.
99 C3 **Letchworth** U.K.
128 C3 **Lethbridge** Can.
150 C1 **Lethem** Guyana
59 C3 **Leti, Kepulauan** *is* Indon.
150 B2 **Leticia** Col.
123 C1 **Letlhakeng** Botswana
104 C1 **Le Touquet-Paris-Plage** France
99 D3 **Le Tréport** France
63 A2 **Letsok-aw Kyun** *i.* Myanmar
123 C2 **Letsopa** S. Africa
97 C1 **Letterkenny** Rep. of Ireland
105 C3 **Leucate, Étang de** *l.* France
60 A1 **Leuser, Gunung** *mt.* Indon.
100 B2 **Leuven** Belgium
111 B3 **Levadeia** Greece
92 F3 **Levanger** Norway
139 C2 **Levelland** U.S.A.
50 B1 **Lévêque, Cape** Austr.
100 C2 **Leverkusen** Ger.
103 D2 **Levice** Slovakia
54 C2 **Levin** N.Z.
131 C2 **Lévis** Can.
89 E3 **Lev Tolstoy** Rus. Fed.
99 D3 **Lewes** U.K.
96 A1 **Lewis, Isle of** *i.* U.K.
140 C3 **Lewisburg** U.S.A.
134 D1 **Lewis Range** *mts* U.S.A.
134 C1 **Lewiston** *ID* U.S.A.
141 E2 **Lewiston** *ME* U.S.A.
134 E1 **Lewistown** U.S.A.
140 C3 **Lexington** *KY* U.S.A.
136 D2 **Lexington** *NE* U.S.A.
141 D3 **Lexington** *VA* U.S.A.
64 B1 **Leyte** *i.* Phil.
109 C2 **Lezhë** Albania
89 F2 **Lezhnevo** Rus. Fed.
89 E3 **L'gov** Rus. Fed.
75 C2 **Lhagoi Kangri** *mt.* China
75 D2 **Lhasa** China
75 C2 **Lhazê** China
60 A1 **Lhokseumawe** Indon.
67 B3 **Liancourt Rocks** *i.* N. Pacific Ocean
71 B3 **Lianhua** China
71 B3 **Lianjiang** China
70 C1 **Lianshan** China
70 B2 **Lianyungang** China
71 B3 **Lianzhou** China
70 B2 **Liaocheng** China
70 C1 **Liaodong Bandao** *pen.* China
70 C1 **Liaodong Wan** *b.* China
65 A1 **Liao He** *r.* China
70 C1 **Liaoning** *prov.* China
65 A1 **Liaoyang** China
65 B1 **Liaoyuan** China
128 B1 **Liard** *r.* Can.
134 C1 **Libby** U.S.A.
118 B2 **Libenge** Dem. Rep. Congo
136 C3 **Liberal** U.S.A.
103 D1 **Liberec** Czech Rep.
114 B4 **Liberia** *country* Africa
146 B3 **Liberia** Costa Rica
150 B1 **Libertad** Venez.
100 B3 **Libin** Belgium
104 B3 **Libourne** France
118 A2 **Libreville** Gabon
115 D2 **Libya** *country* Africa
115 E2 **Libyan Desert** Egypt/Libya
116 A1 **Libyan Plateau** Egypt
108 B3 **Licata** *Sicily* Italy
Licheng China *see* **Lipu**
121 C2 **Lichinga** Moz.
101 E2 **Lichte** Ger.
123 C2 **Lichtenburg** S. Africa
101 E2 **Lichtenfels** Ger.
88 C3 **Lida** Belarus
93 F4 **Lidköping** Sweden
50 C2 **Liebig, Mount** Austr.
105 D2 **Liechtenstein** *country* Europe
100 B2 **Liège** Belgium
92 J3 **Lieksa** Fin.
119 C2 **Lienart** Dem. Rep. Congo
102 C2 **Lienz** Austria
88 B2 **Liepāja** Latvia
102 C2 **Liezen** Austria
97 C2 **Liffey** *r.* Rep. of Ireland
97 C1 **Lifford** Rep. of Ireland
53 C1 **Lightning Ridge** Austr.
121 C2 **Ligonha** *r.* Moz.
105 D3 **Ligurian Sea** France/Italy
119 C4 **Likasi** Dem. Rep. Congo
128 B2 **Likely** Can.
89 E2 **Likhoslavl'** Rus. Fed.
61 B1 **Liku** Indon.
105 D3 **L'Île-Rousse** *Corsica* France
71 B3 **Liling** China
93 F4 **Lilla Edet** Sweden
100 B2 **Lille** Belgium
105 C1 **Lille** France
93 E4 **Lille Bælt** *sea chan.* Denmark
93 F3 **Lillehammer** Norway
93 F4 **Lillestrøm** Norway
128 B2 **Lillooet** Can.
121 C2 **Lilongwe** Malawi
64 B2 **Liloy** Phil.
150 A3 **Lima** Peru
140 C2 **Lima** U.S.A.
97 C1 **Limavady** U.K.
153 B4 **Limay** *r.* Arg.
101 F2 **Limbach-Oberfrohna** Ger.
88 B2 **Limbaži** Latvia
118 A2 **Limbe** Cameroon
100 D2 **Limburg an der Lahn** Ger.
122 B2 **Lime Acres** S. Africa
154 C2 **Limeira** Brazil
97 B2 **Limerick** Rep. of Ireland
93 E4 **Limfjorden** *sea chan.* Denmark
111 C3 **Limnos** *i.* Greece
104 C2 **Limoges** France
146 B3 **Limón** Costa Rica
136 C3 **Limon** U.S.A.
104 C3 **Limoux** France
123 C1 **Limpopo** *prov.* S. Africa
121 C3 **Limpopo** *r.* S. Africa/Zimbabwe
64 A1 **Linapacan** *i.* Phil.
153 A4 **Linares** Chile

145 C2 **Linares** Mex.
106 C2 **Linares** Spain
62 B1 **Lincang** China
71 B3 **Linchuan** China
98 C2 **Lincoln** U.K.
140 B2 **Lincoln** *IL* U.S.A.
141 F1 **Lincoln** *ME* U.S.A.
137 D2 **Lincoln** *NE* U.S.A.
151 C1 **Linden** Guyana
142 C1 **Linden** U.S.A.
119 C2 **Lindi** *r.* Dem. Rep. Congo
119 D3 **Lindi** Tanz.
Lindisfarne *i.* U.K. *see* Holy Island
80 A2 **Lindos** Greece
141 D2 **Lindsay** Can.
49 H3 **Line Islands** Kiribati
70 B2 **Linfen** China
64 B1 **Lingayen** Phil.
70 B2 **Lingbao** China
123 C3 **Lingelethu** S. Africa
123 C3 **Lingelihle** S. Africa
100 C1 **Lingen (Ems)** Ger.
60 B2 **Lingga, Kepulauan** *is* Indon.
71 A3 **Lingshan** China
71 A4 **Lingshui** China
114 A3 **Linguère** Senegal
155 D1 **Linhares** Brazil
70 A1 **Linhe** China
93 G4 **Linköping** Sweden
66 B1 **Linkou** China
70 B2 **Linqing** China
154 C2 **Lins** Brazil
136 C1 **Linton** U.S.A.
69 D2 **Linxi** China
69 C2 **Linxia** China
70 B2 **Linyi** *Shandong* China
70 B2 **Linyi** *Shandong* China
70 B2 **Linying** China
102 C2 **Linz** Austria
105 C3 **Lion, Golfe du** *g.* France
109 B3 **Lipari** Italy
108 B3 **Lipari, Isole** *is* Italy
89 E3 **Lipetsk** Rus. Fed.
110 B1 **Lipova** Romania
101 D2 **Lippstadt** Ger.
71 B3 **Lipu** China
76 C1 **Lisakovsk** Kazakh.
118 C2 **Lisala** Dem. Rep. Congo
Lisboa Port. *see* **Lisbon**
106 B2 **Lisbon** Port.
97 C1 **Lisburn** U.K.
97 B2 **Liscannor Bay** Rep. of Ireland
104 C2 **Lisieux** France
99 A3 **Liskeard** U.K.
89 E3 **Liski** Rus. Fed.
53 D1 **Lismore** Austr.
97 C1 **Lisnaskea** U.K.
97 B2 **Listowel** Rep. of Ireland
71 A3 **Litang** *Guangxi* China
68 C2 **Litang** *Sichuan* China
140 B3 **Litchfield** *IL* U.S.A.
137 E1 **Litchfield** *MN* U.S.A.
53 D2 **Lithgow** Austr.
111 B3 **Lithino, Akra** *pt* Greece
88 B2 **Lithuania** *country* Europe
102 C1 **Litoměřice** Czech Rep.
146 C2 **Little Abaco** *i.* Bahamas
73 D3 **Little Andaman** *i.* India
137 E1 **Little Falls** U.S.A.
139 C2 **Littlefield** U.S.A.
99 C3 **Littlehampton** U.K.
122 A2 **Little Karas Berg** *plat.* Namibia
122 B3 **Little Karoo** *plat.* S. Africa
96 A2 **Little Minch** *sea chan.* U.K.
136 C1 **Little Missouri** *r.* U.S.A.
63 A3 **Little Nicobar** *i.* India
142 B2 **Little Rock** U.S.A.
141 E2 **Littleton** U.S.A.
70 B2 **Liujiachang** China
71 A3 **Liuzhou** China
88 C2 **Līvāni** Latvia
50 B1 **Liveringa** Austr.
138 C2 **Livermore, Mount** U.S.A.
131 D2 **Liverpool** Can.
98 B2 **Liverpool** U.K.
127 F2 **Liverpool, Cape** Can.
53 C2 **Liverpool Range** *mts* Austr.
134 D1 **Livingston** *MT* U.S.A.
139 E2 **Livingston** *TX* U.S.A.
139 D2 **Livingston, Lake** U.S.A.
120 B2 **Livingstone** Zambia
109 C2 **Livno** Bos.-Herz.
89 E3 **Livny** Rus. Fed.
140 C2 **Livonia** U.S.A.
108 B2 **Livorno** Italy
119 D3 **Liwale** Tanz.
70 B2 **Liyang** China
99 A4 **Lizard Point** U.K.
108 B1 **Ljubljana** Slovenia
93 G3 **Ljungan** *r.* Sweden
93 F4 **Ljungby** Sweden
93 G3 **Ljusdal** Sweden
93 G3 **Ljusnan** *r.* Sweden
99 B3 **Llandeilo** U.K.
99 B3 **Llandovery** U.K.
99 B2 **Llandrindod Wells** U.K.
98 B2 **Llandudno** U.K.
99 A3 **Llanelli** U.K.
98 A2 **Llangefni** U.K.
139 C2 **Llano Estacado** *plain* U.S.A.
150 B1 **Llanos** *reg.* Col./Venez.
107 D1 **Lleida** Spain
99 A2 **Lleyn Peninsula** U.K.
107 C2 **Lliria** Spain
106 C1 **Llodio** Spain
128 B2 **Lloyd George, Mount** Can.
129 D2 **Lloyd Lake** Can.
129 C2 **Lloydminster** Can.
152 B3 **Llullaillaco, Volcán** *vol.* Chile
123 C2 **Lobatse** Botswana
120 A2 **Lobito** Angola
101 F1 **Loburg** Ger.
96 B2 **Lochaber** *mts* U.K.
104 C2 **Loches** France
96 B2 **Lochgilphead** U.K.
96 B1 **Lochinver** U.K.
96 A2 **Lochmaddy** U.K.
96 C2 **Lochnagar** *mt.* U.K.
52 A2 **Lock** Austr.
96 C3 **Lockerbie** U.K.
139 D3 **Lockhart** U.S.A.
141 D2 **Lock Haven** U.S.A.
141 D2 **Lockport** U.S.A.
63 B2 **Lôc Ninh** Vietnam
105 C3 **Lodève** France
86 C2 **Lodeynoye Pole** Rus. Fed.
92 F2 **Løding** Norway
119 D2 **Lodwar** Kenya
103 D1 **Łódź** Pol.
62 B2 **Loei** Thai.
122 A3 **Loeriesfontein** S. Africa
92 F2 **Lofoten** *is* Norway
134 D2 **Logan** U.S.A.
126 B2 **Logan, Mount** Can.
140 B2 **Logansport** U.S.A.
108 B1 **Logatec** Slovenia
106 C1 **Logroño** Spain
101 D1 **Löhne** Ger.
101 D1 **Lohne (Oldenburg)** Ger.
62 A2 **Loikaw** Myanmar
62 A2 **Loi Lan** *mt.* Myanmar/Thai.
104 B2 **Loire** *r.* France
150 A2 **Loja** Ecuador
106 C2 **Loja** Spain
92 I2 **Lokan tekojärvi** *l.* Fin.
100 B2 **Lokeren** Belgium
122 B1 **Lokgwabe** Botswana
119 D2 **Lokichar** Kenya
119 D2 **Lokichokio** Kenya
89 D2 **Loknya** Rus. Fed.
115 C4 **Lokoja** Nigeria
89 D3 **Lokot'** Rus. Fed.
88 C2 **Loksa** Estonia
127 G2 **Loks Land** *i.* Can.
93 F4 **Lolland** *i.* Denmark
119 D3 **Lollondo** Tanz.
122 B2 **Lolwane** S. Africa
110 B2 **Lom** Bulg.
93 E3 **Lom** Norway
119 C2 **Lomami** *r.* Dem. Rep. Congo
153 C4 **Lomas de Zamora** Arg.
61 C2 **Lombok** *i.* Indon.
61 C2 **Lombok, Selat** *sea chan.* Indon.
114 C4 **Lomé** Togo
118 C3 **Lomela** *r.* Dem. Rep. Congo
100 B2 **Lommel** Belgium
96 B2 **Lomond, Loch** *l.* U.K.
88 C2 **Lomonosov** Rus. Fed.
135 B4 **Lompoc** U.S.A.
63 B2 **Lom Sak** Thai.
103 E1 **Łomża** Pol.
130 B2 **London** Can.
99 C3 **London** U.K.
140 C3 **London** U.S.A.
97 C1 **Londonderry** U.K.
50 B1 **Londonderry, Cape** Austr.
154 B2 **Londrina** Brazil
83 M2 **Longa, Proliv** *sea chan.* Rus. Fed.
61 C1 **Long Akah** *Sarawak* Malaysia
143 E2 **Long Bay** *b.* U.S.A.
135 C4 **Long Beach** U.S.A.
97 C2 **Longford** Rep. of Ireland
61 C2 **Longiram** Indon.
147 C2 **Long Island** Bahamas
130 C1 **Long Island** Can.
59 D3 **Long Island** P.N.G.
141 E2 **Long Island** U.S.A.
130 B2 **Longlac** Can.
130 B2 **Long Lake** *l.* Can.
136 B2 **Longmont** U.S.A.
140 C2 **Long Point** *pt* Can.
71 B3 **Longquan** China
131 E2 **Long Range Mountains** Can.
51 D2 **Longreach** Austr.
99 D2 **Long Stratton** U.K.
98 B1 **Longtown** U.K.
105 D2 **Longuyon** France
139 E2 **Longview** *TX* U.S.A.
134 B1 **Longview** *WA* U.S.A.
70 A2 **Longxi** China
71 B3 **Longxi Shan** *mt.* China
63 B2 **Long Xuyên** Vietnam
71 B3 **Longyan** China
82 C1 **Longyearbyen** Svalbard
102 B2 **Lons-le-Saunier** France
143 E2 **Lookout, Cape** U.S.A.
97 B2 **Loop Head** *hd* Rep. of Ireland
63 B2 **Lop Buri** Thai.
64 B1 **Lopez** Phil.
68 C2 **Lop Nur** *salt l.* China
118 B2 **Lopori** *r.* Dem. Rep. Congo
106 B2 **Lora del Río** Spain
140 C2 **Lorain** U.S.A.
74 A1 **Loralai** Pak.
107 C2 **Lorca** Spain
138 B2 **Lordsburg** U.S.A.
155 C2 **Lorena** Brazil
152 B2 **Loreto** Bol.
144 A2 **Loreto** Mex.
104 B2 **Lorient** France
96 B2 **Lorn, Firth of** *est.* U.K.
52 B3 **Lorne** Austr.
138 B1 **Los Alamos** U.S.A.

139 D3 **Los Aldamas** Mex.
153 A4 **Los Ángeles** Chile
135 C4 **Los Angeles** U.S.A.
135 B3 **Los Banos** U.S.A.
152 B3 **Los Blancos** Arg.
153 A5 **Los Chonos, Archipiélago de** *is* Chile
91 E1 **Losevo** Rus. Fed.
108 B2 **Lošinj** *i.* Croatia
144 B2 **Los Mochis** Mex.
146 B4 **Los Mosquitos, Golfo de** *b.* Panama
118 B2 **Losombo** Dem. Rep. Congo
147 D3 **Los Roques, Islas** *is* Venez.
96 C2 **Lossiemouth** U.K.
150 B1 **Los Teques** Venez.
152 A4 **Los Vilos** Chile
104 C3 **Lot** *r.* France
96 C1 **Loth** U.K.
119 D2 **Lotikipi Plain** Kenya
118 C3 **Loto** Dem. Rep. Congo
89 E2 **Lotoshino** Rus. Fed.
62 B1 **Louang Namtha** Laos
62 B2 **Louangphrabang** Laos
118 B3 **Loubomo** Congo
104 B2 **Loudéac** France
71 B3 **Loudi** China
118 B3 **Loudima** Congo
114 A3 **Louga** Senegal
99 C2 **Loughborough** U.K.
97 B2 **Loughrea** Rep. of Ireland
105 D2 **Louhans** France
97 B2 **Louisburgh** Rep. of Ireland
142 B2 **Louisiana** *state* U.S.A.
123 C1 **Louis Trichardt** S. Africa
140 B3 **Louisville** *KY* U.S.A.
142 C2 **Louisville** *MS* U.S.A.
86 C2 **Loukhi** Rus. Fed.
130 C1 **Loups Marins, Lacs des** *lakes* Can.
104 B3 **Lourdes** France
151 C1 **Lourenço** Brazil
106 B1 **Lousã** Port.
53 C2 **Louth** Austr.
98 C2 **Louth** U.K.
Louvain Belgium *see* **Leuven**
89 D2 **Lovat'** *r.* Rus. Fed.
110 B2 **Lovech** Bulg.
136 B2 **Loveland** U.S.A.
135 C2 **Lovelock** U.S.A.
139 C2 **Lovington** U.S.A.
119 C3 **Lowa** Dem. Rep. Congo
141 E2 **Lowell** U.S.A.
128 C3 **Lower Arrow Lake** Can.
54 B2 **Lower Hutt** N.Z.
97 C1 **Lower Lough Erne** *l.* U.K.
128 B2 **Lower Post** Can.
99 D2 **Lowestoft** U.K.
103 D1 **Łowicz** Pol.
141 D2 **Lowville** U.S.A.
52 B2 **Loxton** Austr.
Loyang China *see* **Luoyang**
49 E4 **Loyauté, Îles** New Caledonia
89 D3 **Loyew** Belarus
92 F2 **Løypskardtinden** *mt.* Norway
109 C2 **Loznica** Serb. and Mont.
91 D2 **Lozova** Ukr.
120 B2 **Luacano** Angola
70 B2 **Lu'an** China
120 A1 **Luanda** Angola
121 C2 **Luangwa** *r.* Zambia
121 B2 **Luanshya** Zambia
106 B1 **Luarca** Spain
120 B2 **Luau** Angola
103 E1 **Lubaczów** Pol.
120 A2 **Lubango** Angola
119 C3 **Lubao** Dem. Rep. Congo
103 E1 **Lubartów** Pol.
101 D1 **Lübbecke** Ger.
139 C2 **Lubbock** U.S.A.
101 E1 **Lübeck** Ger.
69 E2 **Lubei** China
87 E3 **Lubenka** Kazakh.
103 D1 **Lubin** Pol.
103 E1 **Lublin** Pol.
91 C1 **Lubny** Ukr.
61 C1 **Lubok Antu** *Sarawak* Malaysia
101 E1 **Lübow** Ger.
101 E1 **Lübtheen** Ger.
119 C3 **Lubudi** Dem. Rep. Congo
60 B2 **Lubuklinggau** Indon.
119 C4 **Lubumbashi** Dem. Rep. Congo
120 B2 **Lubungu** Zambia
119 C3 **Lubutu** Dem. Rep. Congo
120 A1 **Lucala** Angola
97 C2 **Lucan** Rep. of Ireland
120 B1 **Lucapa** Angola
96 B3 **Luce Bay** U.K.
154 B2 **Lucélia** Brazil
64 B1 **Lucena** Phil.
106 C2 **Lucena** Spain
103 D2 **Lučenec** Slovakia
109 C2 **Lucera** Italy
Lucerne Switz. *see* **Luzern**
101 E1 **Lüchow** Ger.
120 A2 **Lucira** Angola
101 F1 **Luckenwalde** Ger.
122 B2 **Luckhoff** S. Africa
75 C2 **Lucknow** India
120 B2 **Lucusse** Angola
Lüda China *see* **Dalian**
100 C2 **Lüdenscheid** Ger.
101 E1 **Lüder** Ger.
120 A3 **Lüderitz** Namibia
74 B1 **Ludhiana** India
140 B2 **Ludington** U.S.A.
99 B2 **Ludlow** U.K.
135 C4 **Ludlow** U.S.A.
110 C2 **Ludogorie** *reg.* Bulg.
93 G3 **Ludvika** Sweden
102 D2 **Ludwigsburg** Ger.
101 F1 **Ludwigsfelde** Ger.
101 D3 **Ludwigshafen am Rhein** Ger.
101 E1 **Ludwigslust** Ger.
88 C2 **Ludza** Latvia
118 C3 **Luebo** Dem. Rep. Congo
120 A2 **Luena** Angola
70 A2 **Lüeyang** China
71 B3 **Lufeng** China
139 E2 **Lufkin** U.S.A.
88 C2 **Luga** Rus. Fed.
88 C2 **Luga** *r.* Rus. Fed.
105 D2 **Lugano** Switz.
121 C2 **Lugenda** *r.* Moz.
106 B1 **Lugo** Spain
110 B1 **Lugoj** Romania
91 D2 **Luhans'k** Ukr.
119 D3 **Luhombero** Tanz.
90 B1 **Luhyny** Ukr.
120 B2 **Luiana** Angola
118 C3 **Luilaka** *r.* Dem. Rep. Congo
105 D2 **Luino** Italy
92 I2 **Luiro** *r.* Fin.
118 C3 **Luiza** Dem. Rep. Congo
70 B2 **Lujiang** China
109 C2 **Lukavac** Bos.-Herz.
118 B3 **Lukenie** *r.* Dem. Rep. Congo
138 A2 **Lukeville** U.S.A.
89 E3 **Lukhovitsy** Rus. Fed.
103 E1 **Łuków** Pol.
120 B2 **Lukulu** Zambia
92 H2 **Luleå** Sweden
92 H2 **Luleälven** *r.* Sweden
110 C2 **Lüleburgaz** Turkey
70 B2 **Lüliang Shan** *mts* China
61 C2 **Lumajang** Indon.
75 C1 **Lumajangdong Co** *salt l.* China
120 B2 **Lumbala Kaquengue** Angola
120 B2 **Lumbala N'guimbo** Angola
143 E2 **Lumberton** U.S.A.
61 C1 **Lumbis** Indon.
106 B1 **Lumbrales** Spain
63 B2 **Lumphăt** Cambodia
129 D2 **Lumsden** Can.
54 A3 **Lumsden** N.Z.
93 F4 **Lund** Sweden
121 C2 **Lundazi** Zambia
99 A3 **Lundy Island** U.K.
101 E1 **Lüneburg** Ger.
101 E1 **Lüneburger Heide** *reg.* Ger.
100 C2 **Lünen** Ger.
105 D2 **Lunéville** France
120 B2 **Lunga** *r.* Zambia
114 A4 **Lungi** Sierra Leone
62 A1 **Lunglei** India
97 C2 **Lungnaquilla Mountain** Rep. of Ireland
120 B2 **Lungwebungu** *r.* Zambia
74 B2 **Luni** *r.* India
88 C3 **Luninyets** Belarus
114 A4 **Lunsar** Sierra Leone
77 E2 **Luntai** China
71 A3 **Luodian** China
71 B3 **Luoding** China
70 B2 **Luohe** China
70 B2 **Luoyang** China
121 B2 **Lupane** Zimbabwe
71 A3 **Lupanshui** China
110 B1 **Lupeni** Romania
121 C2 **Lupilichi** Moz.
101 F2 **Luppa** Ger.
121 D2 **Lúrio** Moz.
121 D2 **Lurio** *r.* Moz.
121 B2 **Lusaka** Zambia
118 C3 **Lusambo** Dem. Rep. Congo
109 C2 **Lushnjë** Albania
136 C2 **Lusk** U.S.A.
76 B3 **Lut, Dasht-e** *des.* Iran
101 F2 **Lutherstadt Wittenberg** Ger.
99 C3 **Luton** U.K.
61 C1 **Lutong** *Sarawak* Malaysia
129 C1 **Łutselk'e** Can.
90 B1 **Luts'k** Ukr.
122 B2 **Lutzputs** S. Africa
122 A3 **Lutzville** S. Africa
117 C4 **Luuq** Somalia
137 D2 **Luverne** U.S.A.
119 C3 **Luvua** *r.* Dem. Rep. Congo
123 D1 **Luvuvhu** *r.* S. Africa
119 D2 **Luwero** Uganda
59 C3 **Luwuk** Indon.
100 C3 **Luxembourg** *country* Europe
100 C3 **Luxembourg** Lux.
105 D2 **Luxeuil-les-Bains** France
123 C3 **Luxolweni** S. Africa
116 B2 **Luxor** Egypt
100 B2 **Luyksgestel** Neth.
86 D2 **Luza** Rus. Fed.
105 D2 **Luzern** Switz.
71 A3 **Luzhou** China
154 C1 **Luziânia** Brazil
151 D2 **Luzilândia** Brazil
64 B1 **Luzon** *i.* Phil.
71 C3 **Luzon Strait** Phil.
90 A2 **L'viv** Ukr.
L'vov Ukr. *see* **L'viv**
88 C3 **Lyakhavichy** Belarus
92 G3 **Lycksele** Sweden
123 D2 **Lydenburg** S. Africa
88 C3 **Lyel'chytsy** Belarus
88 C3 **Lyepyel'** Belarus
99 B3 **Lyme Bay** U.K.
141 D3 **Lynchburg** U.S.A.
129 D2 **Lynn Lake** Can.
129 D1 **Lynx Lake** Can.

105 C2 **Lyon** France
89 D2 **Lyozna** Belarus
86 E3 **Lys'va** Rus. Fed.
91 D2 **Lysychans'k** Ukr.
98 B2 **Lytham St Anne's** U.K.
88 C3 **Lyuban'** Belarus
89 E2 **Lyubertsy** Rus. Fed.
90 B1 **Lyubeshiv** Ukr.
89 F2 **Lyubim** Rus. Fed.
91 D2 **Lyubotyn** Ukr.
89 D2 **Lyubytino** Rus. Fed.
89 D3 **Lyudinovo** Rus. Fed.

M

80 B2 **Ma'ān** Jordan
88 C2 **Maardu** Estonia
100 B2 **Maas** *r.* Neth.
100 B2 **Maaseik** Belgium
64 B1 **Maasin** Phil.
100 B2 **Maastricht** Neth.
121 C3 **Mabalane** Moz.
150 C1 **Mabaruma** Guyana
121 C3 **Mabote** Moz.
122 B2 **Mabule** Botswana
122 B1 **Mabutsane** Botswana
155 D2 **Macaé** Brazil
121 C2 **Macaloge** Moz.
126 E2 **MacAlpine Lake** Can.
151 C1 **Macapá** Brazil
150 A2 **Macará** Ecuador
155 D1 **Macarani** Brazil
61 C2 **Macassar Strait** Indon.
151 E2 **Macau** Brazil
71 B3 **Macau** *special admin. reg.* China
123 D1 **Maccaretane** Moz.
98 B2 **Macclesfield** U.K.
50 B2 **Macdonald, Lake** *salt flat* Austr.
50 C2 **Macdonnell Ranges** *mts* Austr.
130 A1 **MacDowell Lake** Can.
106 B1 **Macedo de Cavaleiros** Port.
52 B3 **Macedon** *mt.* Austr.
109 D2 **Macedonia** *country* Europe
151 E2 **Maceió** Brazil
108 B2 **Macerata** Italy
52 A2 **Macfarlane, Lake** *salt flat* Austr.
97 B3 **Macgillycuddy's Reeks** *mts* Rep. of Ireland
74 A2 **Mach** Pak.
155 C2 **Machado** Brazil
121 C3 **Machaila** Moz.
119 D3 **Machakos** Kenya
150 A2 **Machala** Ecuador
121 C3 **Machanga** Moz.
70 B2 **Macheng** China
141 F2 **Machias** U.S.A.
150 A1 **Machiques** Venez.
150 A3 **Machupicchu** Peru
123 D2 **Macia** Moz.
110 C1 **Măcin** Romania
53 D1 **Macintyre** *r.* Austr.
51 D2 **Mackay** Austr.
50 B2 **Mackay, Lake** *salt flat* Austr.
129 C1 **MacKay Lake** Can.
128 B2 **Mackenzie** Can.
128 A1 **Mackenzie** *r.* Can.
126 B2 **Mackenzie Bay** Can.
126 D1 **Mackenzie King Island** Can.
128 A1 **Mackenzie Mountains** Can.
129 D2 **Macklin** Can.
53 D2 **Macksville** Austr.
53 D1 **Maclean** Austr.
50 A2 **MacLeod, Lake** *imp. l.* Austr.
140 A2 **Macomb** U.S.A.
108 A2 **Macomer** *Sardinia* Italy
105 C2 **Mâcon** France
143 D2 **Macon** *GA* U.S.A.
137 E3 **Macon** *MO* U.S.A.
53 C2 **Macquarie** *r.* Austr.
53 C2 **Macquarie Marshes** Austr.
97 B3 **Macroom** Rep. of Ireland
52 A1 **Macumba** *watercourse* Austr.
145 C3 **Macuspana** Mex.
144 B2 **Macuzari, Presa** *resr* Mex.
123 D2 **Madadeni** S. Africa
121 □D3 **Madagascar** *country* Africa
115 D2 **Madama** Niger
111 B2 **Madan** Bulg.
59 D3 **Madang** P.N.G.
150 C2 **Madeira** *r.* Brazil
114 A1 **Madeira** *terr.* N. Atlantic Ocean
144 B2 **Madera** Mex.
135 B3 **Madera** U.S.A.
73 B3 **Madgaon** India
118 B3 **Madingou** Congo
140 B3 **Madison** *IN* U.S.A.
137 D2 **Madison** *SD* U.S.A.
140 B2 **Madison** *WI* U.S.A.
140 C3 **Madison** *WV* U.S.A.
134 D1 **Madison** *r.* U.S.A.
140 B3 **Madisonville** U.S.A.
61 C2 **Madiun** Indon.
119 D2 **Mado Gashi** Kenya
68 C2 **Madoi** China
88 C2 **Madona** Latvia
78 A2 **Madrakah** Saudi Arabia
Madras India *see* **Chennai**
134 B2 **Madras** U.S.A.
145 C2 **Madre, Laguna** *lag.* Mex.
145 B3 **Madre del Sur, Sierra** *mts* Mex.
144 B2 **Madre Occidental, Sierra** *mts* Mex.
145 B2 **Madre Oriental, Sierra** *mts* Mex.
106 C1 **Madrid** Spain
106 C2 **Madridejos** Spain
61 C2 **Madura** *i.* Indon.
61 C2 **Madura, Selat** *sea chan.* Indon.
73 B4 **Madurai** India
67 C3 **Maebashi** Japan
62 A2 **Mae Hong Son** Thai.
62 A1 **Mae Sai** Thai.
62 A2 **Mae Sariang** Thai.
62 A2 **Mae Suai** Thai.
123 C2 **Mafeteng** Lesotho
119 D3 **Mafia Island** Tanz.
123 C2 **Mafikeng** S. Africa
119 D3 **Mafinga** Tanz.
154 C3 **Mafra** Brazil
83 L3 **Magadan** Rus. Fed.
153 A6 **Magallanes, Estrecho de** *sea chan.* Chile
147 C4 **Magangue** Col.
144 A1 **Magdalena** Mex.
138 B2 **Magdalena** U.S.A.
144 A2 **Magdalena, Bahía** *b.* Mex.
101 E1 **Magdeburg** Ger.
97 C1 **Magherafelt** U.K.
87 E3 **Magnitogorsk** Rus. Fed.
142 B2 **Magnolia** U.S.A.
131 D1 **Magpie, Lac** *l.* Can.
114 A3 **Magṭa' Laḥjar** Maur.
151 D2 **Maguarinho, Cabo** *c.* Brazil
123 D2 **Magude** Moz.
62 A1 **Magwe** Myanmar
81 C2 **Mahābād** Iran
74 B2 **Mahajan** India
121 □D2 **Mahajanga** Madag.
61 C2 **Mahakam** *r.* Indon.
123 C1 **Mahalapye** Botswana
121 □D2 **Mahalevona** Madag.
75 C2 **Mahanadi** *r.* India
121 □D2 **Mahanoro** Madag.
63 B2 **Maha Sarakham** Thai.
121 □D2 **Mahavavy** *r.* Madag.
78 B2 **Mahd adh Dhahab** Saudi Arabia
150 C1 **Mahdia** Guyana
113 H4 **Mahé** *i.* Seychelles
74 B2 **Mahesana** India
74 B2 **Mahi** *r.* India
54 C1 **Mahia Peninsula** N.Z.
89 D3 **Mahilyow** Belarus
107 D2 **Mahón** Spain
74 B2 **Mahuva** India
110 C2 **Mahya Dağı** *mt.* Turkey
129 D2 **Maidstone** Can.
99 D3 **Maidstone** U.K.
115 D3 **Maiduguri** Nigeria
75 C2 **Mailani** India
101 D2 **Main** *r.* Ger.
118 B3 **Mai-Ndombe, Lac** *l.* Dem. Rep. Congo
101 E3 **Main-Donau-Kanal** *canal* Ger.
141 F1 **Maine** *state* U.S.A.
62 A1 **Maingkwan** Myanmar
96 C1 **Mainland** *i. Scotland* U.K.
96 □ **Mainland** *i. Scotland* U.K.
121 □D2 **Maintirano** Madag.
101 D2 **Mainz** Ger.
150 B1 **Maiquetía** Venez.
53 D2 **Maitland** *N.S.W.* Austr.
52 A2 **Maitland** *S.A.* Austr.
146 B3 **Maíz, Islas del** *is* Nic.
67 C3 **Maizuru** Japan
109 C2 **Maja Jezercë** *mt.* Albania
61 C2 **Majene** Indon.
Majorca *i.* Spain *see* Mallorca
123 C2 **Majwemasweu** S. Africa
118 B3 **Makabana** Congo
58 B3 **Makale** Indon.
77 E2 **Makanchi** Kazakh.
109 C2 **Makarska** Croatia
58 B3 **Makassar** Indon.
76 B2 **Makat** Kazakh.
123 D2 **Makatini Flats** *lowland* S. Africa
114 A4 **Makeni** Sierra Leone
120 B3 **Makgadikgadi** *salt pan* Botswana
87 D4 **Makhachkala** Rus. Fed.
76 B2 **Makhambet** Kazakh.
119 D3 **Makindu** Kenya
77 D1 **Makinsk** Kazakh.
91 D2 **Makiyivka** Ukr.
Makkah Saudi Arabia *see* Mecca
131 E1 **Makkovik** Can.
103 E2 **Makó** Hungary
118 B2 **Makokou** Gabon
119 D3 **Makongolosi** Tanz.
122 B2 **Makopong** Botswana
79 D2 **Makran** *reg.* Iran/Pak.
89 E2 **Maksatikha** Rus. Fed.
81 C2 **Mākū** Iran
62 A1 **Makum** India
67 B4 **Makurazaki** Japan
115 C4 **Makurdi** Nigeria
92 G2 **Malå** Sweden
146 B4 **Mala, Punta** *pt* Panama
118 A2 **Malabo** Equat. Guinea
60 A1 **Malacca, Strait of** Indon./Malaysia
134 D2 **Malad City** U.S.A.
88 C3 **Maladzyechna** Belarus
106 C2 **Málaga** Spain
117 B4 **Malakal** Sudan

61 C2 **Malang** Indon.
120 A1 **Malanje** Angola
93 G4 **Mälaren** *l.* Sweden
153 B4 **Malargüe** Arg.
80 B2 **Malatya** Turkey
121 C2 **Malawi** *country* Africa
Malawi, Lake Africa *see* Nyasa, Lake
89 D2 **Malaya Vishera** Rus. Fed.
64 B2 **Malaybalay** Phil.
81 C2 **Malāyer** Iran
60 B1 **Malaysia** *country* Asia
81 C2 **Malazgirt** Turkey
103 D1 **Malbork** Pol.
101 F1 **Malchin** Ger.
100 A2 **Maldegem** Belgium
56 C5 **Maldives** *country* Indian Ocean
153 C4 **Maldonado** Uru.
56 C5 **Male** Maldives
111 B3 **Maleas, Akra** *pt* Greece
103 D2 **Malé Karpaty** *hills* Slovakia
134 C2 **Malheur Lake** U.S.A.
114 B3 **Mali** *country* Africa
114 A3 **Mali** Guinea
58 C3 **Malili** Indon.
119 E3 **Malindi** Kenya
97 C1 **Malin Head** *hd* Rep. of Ireland
97 B1 **Malin More** Rep. of Ireland
111 C2 **Malkara** Turkey
88 C3 **Mal'kavichy** Belarus
110 C2 **Malko Tŭrnovo** Bulg.
53 C3 **Mallacoota** Austr.
53 C3 **Mallacoota Inlet** *b.* Austr.
96 B2 **Mallaig** U.K.
129 E1 **Mallery Lake** Can.
107 D2 **Mallorca** *i.* Spain
97 B2 **Mallow** Rep. of Ireland
92 H2 **Malmberget** Sweden
100 C2 **Malmédy** Belgium
122 A3 **Malmesbury** S. Africa
93 F4 **Malmö** Sweden
62 B1 **Malong** China
118 C4 **Malonga** Dem. Rep. Congo
93 E3 **Måløy** Norway
89 E2 **Maloyaroslavets** Rus. Fed.
89 E2 **Maloye Borisovo** Rus. Fed.
85 E6 **Malta** *country* Europe
88 C2 **Malta** Latvia
134 E1 **Malta** U.S.A.
122 A1 **Maltahöhe** Namibia
98 C1 **Malton** U.K.
59 C3 **Maluku** *is* Indon.
93 F3 **Malung** Sweden
123 C2 **Maluti Mountains** Lesotho
73 B3 **Malvan** India
142 B2 **Malvern** U.S.A.
90 B1 **Malyn** Ukr.
83 L2 **Malyy Anyuy** *r.* Rus. Fed.
83 K2 **Malyy Lyakhovskiy, Ostrov** *i.* Rus. Fed.
123 C2 **Mamafubedu** S. Africa
119 C2 **Mambasa** Dem. Rep. Congo
118 B2 **Mambéré** *r.* C.A.R.
123 C2 **Mamelodi** S. Africa
150 B3 **Mamoré** *r.* Bol./Brazil
114 A3 **Mamou** Guinea
61 C2 **Mamuju** Indon.
114 B4 **Man** Côte d'Ivoire
150 B2 **Manacapuru** Brazil
107 D2 **Manacor** Spain
59 C2 **Manado** Indon.
146 B3 **Managua** Nic.
121 □D3 **Manakara** Madag.
78 B3 **Manākhah** Yemen
79 C2 **Manama** Bahrain
59 D3 **Manam Island** P.N.G.
121 □D3 **Mananara** *r.* Madag.
121 □D2 **Mananara Avaratra** Madag.
121 □D3 **Mananjary** Madag.
114 A3 **Manantali, Lac de** *l.* Mali
77 E2 **Manas Hu** *l.* China
59 C3 **Manatuto** East Timor
150 B2 **Manaus** Brazil
80 B2 **Manavgat** Turkey
98 B2 **Manchester** U.K.
141 E2 **Manchester** U.S.A.
121 □D3 **Mandabe** Madag.
93 E4 **Mandal** Norway
59 D3 **Mandala, Puncak** *mt.* Indon.
62 A1 **Mandalay** Myanmar
69 D1 **Mandalgovĭ** Mongolia
136 C1 **Mandan** U.S.A.
118 B1 **Mandara Mountains** Cameroon/Nigeria
108 A3 **Mandas** *Sardinia* Italy
100 C2 **Manderscheid** Ger.
74 B1 **Mandi** India
114 B3 **Mandiana** Guinea
74 B1 **Mandi Burewala** Pak.
75 C2 **Mandla** India
121 □D2 **Mandritsara** Madag.
74 B2 **Mandsaur** India
50 A3 **Mandurah** Austr.
73 B3 **Mandya** India
108 B1 **Manerbio** Italy
90 B1 **Manevychi** Ukr.
109 C2 **Manfredonia** Italy
114 B3 **Manga** Burkina
118 B3 **Mangai** Dem. Rep. Congo
54 C1 **Mangakino** N.Z.
110 C2 **Mangalia** Romania
73 B3 **Mangalore** India
123 C2 **Mangaung** S. Africa
61 B2 **Manggar** Indon.
68 C2 **Mangnai** China
121 C2 **Mangochi** Malawi
59 C3 **Mangole** *i.* Indon.
154 B3 **Mangueirinha** Brazil
69 E1 **Mangui** China
76 B2 **Mangystau** Kazakh.
137 D3 **Manhattan** U.S.A.
121 C3 **Manhica** Moz.
155 D2 **Manhuaçu** Brazil
121 □D2 **Mania** *r.* Madag.
108 B1 **Maniago** Italy
150 B2 **Manicoré** Brazil
131 D2 **Manicouagan** *r.* Can.
131 D1 **Manicouagan, Réservoir** *resr* Can.
79 B2 **Manīfah** Saudi Arabia
64 B1 **Manila** Phil.
53 D2 **Manilla** Austr.
111 C3 **Manisa** Turkey
140 B2 **Manistee** U.S.A.
129 E2 **Manitoba** *prov.* Can.
129 E2 **Manitoba, Lake** Can.
140 B1 **Manitou Islands** U.S.A.
130 B2 **Manitoulin Island** Can.
140 B2 **Manitowoc** U.S.A.
130 C2 **Maniwaki** Can.
150 A1 **Manizales** Col.
137 E2 **Mankato** U.S.A.
114 B4 **Mankono** Côte d'Ivoire
129 D3 **Mankota** Can.
73 C4 **Mankulam** Sri Lanka
74 B2 **Manmad** India
73 B4 **Mannar, Gulf of** India/Sri Lanka
101 D3 **Mannheim** Ger.
128 C2 **Manning** Can.
52 A2 **Mannum** Austr.
129 C2 **Mannville** Can.
59 C3 **Manokwari** Indon.
119 C3 **Manono** Dem. Rep. Congo
63 A2 **Manoron** Myanmar
105 D3 **Manosque** France
131 C1 **Manouane, Lac** *l.* Can.
107 D1 **Manresa** Spain
121 B2 **Mansa** Zambia
127 F2 **Mansel Island** Can.
92 I2 **Mansel'kya** *ridge* Fin./Rus. Fed.
53 C3 **Mansfield** Austr.
98 C2 **Mansfield** U.K.
142 B2 **Mansfield** *LA* U.S.A.
140 C2 **Mansfield** *OH* U.S.A.
141 D2 **Mansfield** *PA* U.S.A.
150 A2 **Manta** Ecuador
143 E1 **Manteo** U.S.A.
104 C2 **Mantes-la-Jolie** France
155 C2 **Mantiqueira, Serra da** *mts* Brazil
108 B1 **Mantova** Italy
Mantua Italy *see* **Mantova**
151 C2 **Manuelzinho** Brazil
59 C3 **Manui** *i.* Indon.
54 B1 **Manukau** N.Z.
142 B2 **Many** U.S.A.
87 D4 **Manych-Gudilo, Ozero** *l.* Rus. Fed.
119 D3 **Manyoni** Tanz.
106 C2 **Manzanares** Spain
144 B3 **Manzanillo** Mex.
69 D1 **Manzhouli** China
123 D2 **Manzini** Swaziland
115 D3 **Mao** Chad
59 D3 **Maoke, Pegunungan** *mts* Indon.
123 C2 **Maokeng** S. Africa
65 A1 **Maokui Shan** *mt.* China
71 B3 **Maoming** China
121 C3 **Mapai** Moz.
75 C1 **Mapam Yumco** *l.* China
145 C3 **Mapastepec** Mex.
144 B2 **Mapimí** Mex.
144 B2 **Mapimí, Bolsón de** *des.* Mex.
64 A2 **Mapin** *i.* Phil.
121 C3 **Mapinhane** Moz.
129 D3 **Maple Creek** Can.
121 C3 **Maputo** Moz.
123 D2 **Maputo** *r.* Moz./S. Africa
75 C2 **Maquan He** *r.* China
120 A1 **Maquela do Zombo** Angola
153 B5 **Maquinchao** Arg.
137 E2 **Maquoketa** U.S.A.
150 B2 **Maraã** Brazil
151 D2 **Maraba** Brazil
151 C1 **Maracá, Ilha de** *i.* Brazil
150 A1 **Maracaibo** Venez.
150 A1 **Maracaibo, Lago de** *l.* Venez.
154 A2 **Maracajú, Serra de** *hills* Brazil
150 B1 **Maracay** Venez.
115 D2 **Marādah** Libya
115 C3 **Maradi** Niger
81 C2 **Marāgheh** Iran
151 D2 **Marajó, Baía de** *est.* Brazil
151 C2 **Marajó, Ilha de** *i.* Brazil
79 C2 **Marākī** Iran
119 D2 **Maralal** Kenya
50 C3 **Maralinga** Austr.
81 C2 **Marand** Iran
150 A2 **Marañón** *r.* Peru
130 B2 **Marathon** Can.
143 D4 **Marathon** U.S.A.
106 C2 **Marbella** Spain
50 A2 **Marble Bar** Austr.
123 C1 **Marble Hall** S. Africa
123 D3 **Marburg** S. Africa
101 D2 **Marburg an der Lahn** Ger.
99 D2 **March** U.K.
100 B2 **Marche-en-Famenne** Belgium
106 B2 **Marchena** Spain
152 B4 **Mar Chiquita, Lago** *l.* Arg.

141 E2 **Marcy, Mount** U.S.A.
74 B1 **Mardan** Pak.
153 C4 **Mar del Plata** Arg.
81 C2 **Mardın** Turkey
96 B2 **Maree, Loch** *l.* U.K.
108 B3 **Marettimo, Isola** *i. Sicily* Italy
89 D2 **Marevo** Rus. Fed.
138 C2 **Marfa** U.S.A.
50 A3 **Margaret River** Austr.
147 D3 **Margarita, Isla de** *i.* Venez.
123 D3 **Margate** S. Africa
99 D3 **Margate** U.K.
119 C2 **Margherita Peak** Dem. Rep. Congo/Uganda
76 C3 **Margo, Dasht-i** *des.* Afgh.
91 C2 **Marhanets'** Ukr.
62 A1 **Mari** Myanmar
152 B3 **María Elena** Chile
156 C5 **Mariana Trench** *sea feature* N. Pacific Ocean
142 B2 **Marianna** *AR* U.S.A.
143 C2 **Marianna** *FL* U.S.A.
102 C2 **Mariánské Lázně** Czech Rep.
144 B2 **Marías, Islas** *is* Mex.
78 B3 **Ma'rib** Yemen
109 C1 **Maribor** Slovenia
117 A4 **Maridi** *watercourse* Sudan
55 M2 **Marie Byrd Land** *reg.* Antarctica
147 D3 **Marie-Galante** *i.* Guadeloupe
93 G3 **Mariehamn** Fin.
122 A1 **Mariental** Namibia
93 F4 **Mariestad** Sweden
143 D2 **Marietta** *GA* U.S.A.
140 C3 **Marietta** *OH* U.S.A.
105 D3 **Marignane** France
83 K3 **Marii, Mys** *pt* Rus. Fed.
88 B3 **Marijampolė** Lith.
154 C2 **Marília** Brazil
106 B1 **Marín** Spain
109 C3 **Marina di Gioiosa Ionica** Italy
88 C3 **Mar"ina Horka** Belarus
140 B1 **Marinette** U.S.A.
154 B2 **Maringá** Brazil
106 B2 **Marinha Grande** Port.
140 B2 **Marion** *IN* U.S.A.
140 C2 **Marion** *OH* U.S.A.
143 E2 **Marion** *SC* U.S.A.
140 C3 **Marion** *VA* U.S.A.
143 D2 **Marion, Lake** U.S.A.
52 A3 **Marion Bay** Austr.
152 B3 **Mariscal Estigarribia** Para.
110 C2 **Maritsa** *r.* Bulg.
91 D2 **Mariupol'** Ukr.
117 C4 **Marka** Somalia
123 C1 **Marken** S. Africa
100 B1 **Markermeer** *l.* Neth.
83 I2 **Markha** *r.* Rus. Fed.
91 D2 **Markivka** Ukr.
142 B2 **Marksville** U.S.A.
101 D3 **Marktheidenfeld** Ger.
101 F2 **Marktredwitz** Ger.
100 C2 **Marl** Ger.
100 A3 **Marle** France
139 D2 **Marlin** U.S.A.
104 C3 **Marmande** France
111 C2 **Marmara Denizi** *g.* Turkey
111 C3 **Marmaris** Turkey
104 C2 **Marne-la-Vallée** France
121 □D2 **Maroantsetra** Madag.
101 E2 **Maroldsweisach** Ger.
121 □D2 **Maromokotro** *mt.* Madag.
121 C2 **Marondera** Zimbabwe
151 C1 **Maroni** *r.* Fr. Guiana
118 B1 **Maroua** Cameroon
121 □D2 **Marovoay** Madag.
49 H4 **Marquesas Islands** French Polynesia
140 B1 **Marquette** U.S.A.
117 A3 **Marra, Jebel** *mt.* Sudan
123 D2 **Marracuene** Moz.
114 B1 **Marrakech** Morocco
117 A3 **Marra Plateau** Sudan
52 A1 **Marree** Austr.
86 F2 **Marresale** Rus. Fed.
121 C2 **Marromeu** Moz.
121 C2 **Marrupa** Moz.
116 B2 **Marsá al 'Alam** Egypt
115 D1 **Marsa al Burayqah** Libya
119 D2 **Marsabit** Kenya
108 B3 **Marsala** *Sicily* Italy
116 A1 **Marsá Maṭrūh** Egypt
101 D2 **Marsberg** Ger.
108 B2 **Marsciano** Italy
53 C2 **Marsden** Austr.
105 D3 **Marseille** France
137 D2 **Marshall** *MN* U.S.A.
137 E3 **Marshall** *MO* U.S.A.
139 E2 **Marshall** *TX* U.S.A.
49 E2 **Marshall Islands** *country* N. Pacific Ocean
137 E2 **Marshalltown** U.S.A.
140 A2 **Marshfield** U.S.A.
143 E3 **Marsh Harbour** Bahamas
142 B3 **Marsh Island** U.S.A.
88 A2 **Märsta** Sweden
63 A2 **Martaban, Gulf of** Myanmar
61 C2 **Martapura** *Kalimantan Selatan* Indon.
60 B2 **Martapura** *Sumatera* Indon.
141 E2 **Martha's Vineyard** *i.* U.S.A.
105 D2 **Martigny** Switz.
103 D2 **Martin** Slovakia
136 C2 **Martin** U.S.A.
145 C2 **Martínez** Mex.
147 D3 **Martinique** *terr.* West Indies
141 D3 **Martinsburg** U.S.A.
140 D3 **Martinsville** U.S.A.
54 C2 **Marton** N.Z.
107 D1 **Martorell** Spain
106 C2 **Martos** Spain
76 B1 **Martuk** Kazakh.
105 C3 **Marvejols** France
76 C3 **Mary** Turkm.
51 E2 **Maryborough** Austr.
122 B2 **Marydale** S. Africa
141 D3 **Maryland** *state* U.S.A.
137 D3 **Marysville** U.S.A.
137 E2 **Maryville** *MO* U.S.A.
143 D1 **Maryville** *TN* U.S.A.
119 D3 **Masai Steppe** *plain* Tanz.
119 D3 **Masaka** Uganda
65 B2 **Masan** S. Korea
119 D4 **Masasi** Tanz.
64 B1 **Masbate** Phil.
64 B1 **Masbate** *i.* Phil.
123 C2 **Maseru** Lesotho
76 B3 **Mashhad** Iran
123 C3 **Masibambane** S. Africa
79 C3 **Masīlah, Wādī al** *watercourse* Yemen
123 C2 **Masilo** S. Africa
119 D2 **Masindi** Uganda
79 C2 **Masīrah** *i.* Oman
79 C3 **Maṣīrah, Khalīj** *b.* Oman
81 C2 **Masjed Soleymān** Iran
97 B2 **Mask, Lough** *l.* Rep. of Ireland
121 □E2 **Masoala, Tanjona** *c.* Madag.
137 E2 **Mason City** U.S.A.
Masqaṭ Oman *see* **Muscat**
108 B2 **Massa** Italy
141 E2 **Massachusetts** *state* U.S.A.
141 E2 **Massachusetts Bay** U.S.A.
121 C3 **Massangena** Moz.
120 A1 **Massango** Angola
116 B3 **Massawa** Eritrea
141 E2 **Massena** U.S.A.
128 A2 **Masset** Can.
105 C2 **Massif Central** *mts* France
140 C2 **Massillon** U.S.A.
114 B3 **Massina** Mali
121 C3 **Massinga** Moz.
123 D1 **Massingir** Moz.
78 A2 **Mastābah** Saudi Arabia
54 C2 **Masterton** N.Z.
74 A2 **Mastung** Pak.
78 A2 **Mastūrah** Saudi Arabia
88 B3 **Masty** Belarus
67 B4 **Masuda** Japan
Masuku Gabon *see* **Franceville**
121 C3 **Masvingo** Zimbabwe
118 B3 **Matadi** Dem. Rep. Congo
146 B3 **Matagalpa** Nic.
130 C2 **Matagami** Can.
130 C2 **Matagami, Lac** *l.* Can.
139 D3 **Matagorda Island** U.S.A.
120 A2 **Matala** Angola
114 A3 **Matam** Senegal
144 B2 **Matamoros** *Coahuila* Mex.
145 C2 **Matamoros** *Tamaulipas* Mex.
119 D3 **Matandu** *r.* Tanz.
131 D2 **Matane** Can.
146 B2 **Matanzas** Cuba
73 C4 **Matara** Sri Lanka
61 C2 **Mataram** Indon.
50 C1 **Mataranka** Austr.
107 D1 **Mataró** Spain
123 C3 **Matatiele** S. Africa
54 A3 **Mataura** N.Z.
49 F4 **Matā'utu** Wallis and Futuna Is
54 C1 **Matawai** N.Z.
152 B2 **Mategua** Bol.
145 B2 **Matehuala** Mex.
109 C2 **Matera** Italy
139 D3 **Mathis** U.S.A.
75 B2 **Mathura** India
64 B2 **Mati** Phil.
98 C2 **Matlock** U.K.
150 C3 **Mato Grosso** Brazil
154 B1 **Mato Grosso, Planalto do** *plat.* Brazil
123 D2 **Matola** Moz.
Matou China *see* **Pingguo**
67 B3 **Matsue** Japan
66 D2 **Matsumae** Japan
67 C4 **Matsusaka** Japan
71 C3 **Matsu Tao** *i.* Taiwan
67 B4 **Matsuyama** Japan
130 B1 **Mattagami** *r.* Can.
105 D2 **Matterhorn** *mt.* Italy/Switz.
134 C2 **Matterhorn** *mt.* U.S.A.
140 B3 **Mattoon** U.S.A.
150 B1 **Maturín** Venez.
123 C2 **Matwabeng** S. Africa
100 A2 **Maubeuge** France
104 C3 **Maubourguet** France
140 C2 **Maumee** *r.* U.S.A.
120 B2 **Maun** Botswana
62 A1 **Maungdaw** Myanmar
50 C2 **Maurice, Lake** *salt flat* Austr.
114 A3 **Mauritania** *country* Africa
113 H6 **Mauritius** *country* Indian Ocean
78 B2 **Māwān, Khashm** *hill* Saudi Arabia
118 B3 **Mawanga** Dem. Rep. Congo
71 B3 **Mawei** China
62 A1 **Mawkmai** Myanmar
62 A1 **Mawlaik** Myanmar
78 B2 **Mawqaq** Saudi Arabia
78 B3 **Mawza** Yemen
108 A3 **Maxia, Punta** *mt. Sardinia* Italy
83 J2 **Maya** *r.* Rus. Fed.

147 C2 **Mayaguana** *i.* Bahamas
96 B3 **Maybole** U.K.
104 B2 **Mayenne** France
104 B2 **Mayenne** *r.* France
128 C2 **Mayerthorpe** Can.
140 B3 **Mayfield** U.S.A.
87 D4 **Maykop** Rus. Fed.
126 B2 **Mayo** Can.
118 B3 **Mayoko** Congo
121 D2 **Mayotte** *terr.* Africa
83 J3 **Mayskiy** Rus. Fed.
140 C3 **Maysville** U.S.A.
118 B3 **Mayumba** Gabon
137 D1 **Mayville** U.S.A.
151 C2 **Mazagão** Brazil
104 C3 **Mazamet** France
77 D3 **Mazar** China
108 B3 **Mazara del Vallo** *Sicily* Italy
77 C3 **Mazār-e Sharīf** Afgh.
144 A2 **Mazatán** Mex.
146 A3 **Mazatenango** Guat.
144 B2 **Mazatlán** Mex.
88 B2 **Mažeikiai** Lith.
88 B2 **Mazirbe** Latvia
121 B3 **Mazunga** Zimbabwe
88 C3 **Mazyr** Belarus
123 D2 **Mbabane** Swaziland
118 B2 **Mbaïki** C.A.R.
121 C1 **Mbala** Zambia
119 D2 **Mbale** Uganda
118 B2 **Mbalmayo** Cameroon
118 B3 **Mbandaka** Dem. Rep. Congo
118 A2 **Mbanga** Cameroon
120 A1 **M'banza Congo** Angola
119 D3 **Mbeya** Tanz.
119 D4 **Mbinga** Tanz.
118 B2 **Mbomo** Congo
118 B2 **Mbouda** Cameroon
114 A3 **Mbour** Senegal
114 A3 **Mbout** Maur.
118 C3 **Mbuji-Mayi** Dem. Rep. Congo
119 D3 **Mbuyuni** Tanz.
139 D2 **McAlester** U.S.A.
139 D3 **McAllen** U.S.A.
128 B2 **McBride** Can.
134 C2 **McCall** U.S.A.
126 E2 **McClintock Channel** Can.
126 D2 **McClure Strait** Can.
142 B2 **McComb** U.S.A.
136 C2 **McConaughy, Lake** U.S.A.
136 C2 **McCook** U.S.A.
134 C2 **McDermitt** U.S.A.
134 D1 **McDonald Peak** U.S.A.
134 D1 **McGuire, Mount** U.S.A.
128 C2 **McLennan** Can.
128 B2 **McLeod Lake** Can.
134 B1 **McMinnville** *OR* U.S.A.
142 C1 **McMinnville** *TN* U.S.A.
137 D3 **McPherson** U.S.A.
123 C3 **Mdantsane** S. Africa
135 D3 **Mead, Lake** *resr* U.S.A.
129 D2 **Meadow Lake** Can.
140 C2 **Meadville** U.S.A.
66 D2 **Meaken-dake** *vol.* Japan
106 B1 **Mealhada** Port.
131 E1 **Mealy Mountains** Can.
128 C2 **Meander River** Can.
78 A2 **Mecca** Saudi Arabia
100 B2 **Mechelen** Belgium
100 B2 **Mechelen** Neth.
100 C2 **Mechernich** Ger.
100 C2 **Meckenheim** Ger.
106 B1 **Meda** Port.
60 A1 **Medan** Indon.
153 B5 **Medanosa, Punta** *pt* Arg.
73 C4 **Medawachchiya** Sri Lanka
107 D2 **Médéa** Alg.
150 A1 **Medellín** Col.
115 D1 **Medenine** Tunisia
134 B2 **Medford** U.S.A.
110 C2 **Medgidia** Romania
110 B1 **Mediaş** Romania
136 B2 **Medicine Bow Mountains** U.S.A.
136 B2 **Medicine Bow Peak** U.S.A.
129 C2 **Medicine Hat** Can.
137 D3 **Medicine Lodge** U.S.A.
155 D1 **Medina** Brazil
78 A2 **Medina** Saudi Arabia
106 C1 **Medinaceli** Spain
106 C1 **Medina del Campo** Spain
106 B1 **Medina de Rioseco** Spain
84 D6 **Mediterranean Sea**
129 C2 **Medley** Can.
87 E3 **Mednogorsk** Rus. Fed.
83 L2 **Medvezh'i, Ostrova** *is* Rus. Fed.
86 C2 **Medvezh'yegorsk** Rus. Fed.
50 A2 **Meekatharra** Austr.
136 B2 **Meeker** U.S.A.
75 B2 **Meerut** India
100 A2 **Meetkerke** Belgium
111 B3 **Megalopoli** Greece
75 C2 **Meghasani** *mt.* India
80 A2 **Megisti** *i.* Greece
92 I1 **Mehamn** Norway
50 A2 **Meharry, Mount** Austr.
79 C2 **Mehrān** *watercourse* Iran
154 C1 **Meia Ponte** *r.* Brazil
118 B2 **Meiganga** Cameroon
65 B1 **Meihekou** China
Meijiang China *see* **Ningdu**
62 A1 **Meiktila** Myanmar
101 E2 **Meiningen** Ger.
102 C1 **Meißen** Ger.
71 B3 **Meizhou** China
152 B3 **Mejicana** *mt.* Arg.
152 A3 **Mejillones** Chile
117 B3 **Mek'elē** Eth.
114 C2 **Mekerrhane, Sebkha** *salt pan* Alg.
114 B1 **Meknès** Morocco
63 B2 **Mekong** *r.* Asia
63 B3 **Mekong, Mouths of the** Vietnam
60 B1 **Melaka** Malaysia
53 B3 **Melbourne** Austr.
143 D3 **Melbourne** U.S.A.
108 A2 **Mele, Capo** *c.* Italy
131 C1 **Mélèzes, Rivière aux** *r.* Can.
115 D3 **Mélfi** Chad
109 C2 **Melfi** Italy
129 D2 **Melfort** Can.
92 F3 **Melhus** Norway
106 B1 **Melide** Spain
114 B1 **Melilla** N. Africa
91 D2 **Melitopol'** Ukr.
101 D1 **Melle** Ger.
93 F4 **Mellerud** Sweden
101 E2 **Mellrichstadt** Ger.
100 D1 **Mellum** *i.* Ger.
152 C4 **Melo** Uru.
115 C1 **Melrhir, Chott** *salt l.* Alg.
99 C2 **Melton Mowbray** U.K.
104 C2 **Melun** France
129 D2 **Melville** Can.
51 D1 **Melville, Cape** Austr.
131 E1 **Melville, Lake** Can.
50 C1 **Melville Island** Austr.
126 D1 **Melville Island** Can.
127 F2 **Melville Peninsula** Can.
102 C2 **Memmingen** Ger.
61 B1 **Mempawah** Indon.
80 B3 **Memphis** Egypt
142 B1 **Memphis** *TN* U.S.A.
139 C2 **Memphis** *TX* U.S.A.
91 C1 **Mena** Ukr.
142 B2 **Mena** U.S.A.
114 C3 **Ménaka** Mali
Mènam Khong *r.* Laos/Thai. *see* **Mekong**
105 C3 **Mende** France
116 B3 **Mendefera** Eritrea
145 C2 **Méndez** Mex.
119 D2 **Mendī** Eth.
59 D3 **Mendi** P.N.G.
99 B3 **Mendip Hills** U.K.
153 B4 **Mendoza** Arg.
111 C3 **Menemen** Turkey
60 B2 **Menggala** Indon.
62 B1 **Mengzi** China
131 D1 **Menihek** Can.
52 B2 **Menindee** Austr.
52 B2 **Menindee Lake** Austr.
52 A3 **Meningie** Austr.
104 C2 **Mennecy** France
140 B1 **Menominee** U.S.A.
120 A2 **Menongue** Angola
107 D1 **Menorca** *i.* Spain
60 A2 **Mentawai, Kepulauan** *is* Indon.
60 B2 **Mentok** Indon.
50 B2 **Menzies** Austr.
100 C1 **Meppel** Neth.
100 C1 **Meppen** Ger.
123 D1 **Mepuze** Moz.
123 C2 **Meqheleng** S. Africa
108 B1 **Merano** Italy
59 D3 **Merauke** Indon.
52 B2 **Merbein** Austr.
135 B3 **Merced** U.S.A.
152 C3 **Mercedes** Arg.
127 G2 **Mercy, Cape** Can.
139 C1 **Meredith, Lake** U.S.A.
91 D2 **Merefa** Ukr.
116 A3 **Merga Oasis** Sudan
63 A2 **Mergui** Myanmar
63 A2 **Mergui Archipelago** *is* Myanmar
110 C2 **Meriç** *r.* Greece/Turkey
145 D2 **Mérida** Mex.
106 B2 **Mérida** Spain
150 A1 **Mérida** Venez.
142 C2 **Meridian** U.S.A.
53 C3 **Merimbula** Austr.
116 B3 **Merowe** Sudan
50 A3 **Merredin** Austr.
96 B3 **Merrick** *hill* U.K.
140 B1 **Merrill** U.S.A.
140 B2 **Merrillville** U.S.A.
128 B2 **Merritt** Can.
53 C2 **Merrygoen** Austr.
116 C3 **Mersa Fatma** Eritrea
100 C3 **Mersch** Lux.
101 E2 **Merseburg (Saale)** Ger.
98 B2 **Mersey** *r.* U.K.
60 B1 **Mersing** Malaysia
99 D3 **Mers-les-Bains** France
74 B2 **Merta** India
99 B3 **Merthyr Tydfil** U.K.
106 B2 **Mértola** Port.
119 D3 **Meru** *vol.* Tanz.
100 C3 **Merzig** Ger.
138 A2 **Mesa** U.S.A.
109 C2 **Mesagne** Italy
101 D2 **Meschede** Ger.
89 E3 **Meshchovsk** Rus. Fed.
91 E2 **Meshkovskaya** Rus. Fed.
111 B2 **Mesimeri** Greece
111 B3 **Mesolongi** Greece
121 D2 **Messalo** *r.* Moz.
109 C3 **Messina** *Sicily* Italy
123 D1 **Messina** S. Africa
109 C3 **Messina, Stretta di** *str.* Italy
111 B3 **Messiniakos Kolpos** *b.* Greece
110 B2 **Mesta** *r.* Bulg.
150 B1 **Meta** *r.* Col./Venez.

127 G2 **Meta Incognita Peninsula** Can.
152 B3 **Metán** Arg.
111 B3 **Methoni** Greece
109 C2 **Metković** Croatia
60 B2 **Metro** Indon.
117 B4 **Metu** Eth.
105 D2 **Metz** France
100 B2 **Meuse** *r.* Belgium/France
139 D2 **Mexia** U.S.A.
144 A1 **Mexicali** Mex.
144 B2 **Mexico** *country* Central America
145 C3 **Mexico City** Mex.
137 E3 **Mexico** U.S.A.
125 E5 **Mexico, Gulf of** Mex./U.S.A.
101 F1 **Meyenburg** Ger.
76 C3 **Meymaneh** Afgh.
86 D2 **Mezen'** Rus. Fed.
86 D2 **Mezen'** *r.* Rus. Fed.
86 E1 **Mezhdusharskiy, Ostrov** *i.* Rus. Fed.
103 E2 **Mezőtúr** Hungary
144 B2 **Mezquitic** Mex.
88 C2 **Mežvidi** Latvia
121 C2 **Mfuwe** Zambia
123 D2 **Mhlume** Swaziland
74 B2 **Mhow** India
145 C3 **Miahuatlán** Mex.
106 B2 **Miajadas** Spain
143 D3 **Miami** *FL* U.S.A.
139 E1 **Miami** *OK* U.S.A.
143 D3 **Miami Beach** U.S.A.
81 C2 **Miandowāb** Iran
121 □D2 **Miandrivazo** Madag.
81 C2 **Mīāneh** Iran
74 B1 **Mianwali** Pak.
70 A2 **Mianyang** China
121 □D2 **Miarinarivo** Madag.
87 F3 **Miass** Rus. Fed.
128 C2 **Mica Creek** Can.
103 E2 **Michalovce** Slovakia
140 B1 **Michigan** *state* U.S.A.
140 B2 **Michigan, Lake** U.S.A.
140 B2 **Michigan City** U.S.A.
130 B2 **Michipicoten Island** Can.
130 B2 **Michipicoten River** Can.
89 F3 **Michurinsk** Rus. Fed.
48 D2 **Micronesia, Federated States of** *country* N. Pacific Ocean
100 A2 **Middelburg** Neth.
123 C3 **Middelburg** *E. Cape* S. Africa
123 C2 **Middelburg** *Mpumalanga* S. Africa
100 B2 **Middelharnis** Neth.
134 B2 **Middle Alkali Lake** U.S.A.
73 D3 **Middle Andaman** *i.* India
136 D2 **Middle Loup** *r.* U.S.A.
140 C3 **Middlesboro** U.S.A.
98 C1 **Middlesbrough** U.K.
141 E2 **Middletown** *NY* U.S.A.
140 C3 **Middletown** *OH* U.S.A.
78 B3 **Mīdī** Yemen
130 C2 **Midland** Can.
140 C2 **Midland** *MI* U.S.A.
139 C2 **Midland** *TX* U.S.A.
97 B3 **Midleton** Rep. of Ireland
94 B1 **Miðvágur** Faroe Is
49 F1 **Midway Islands** N. Pacific Ocean
109 D2 **Midzhur** *mt.* Bulg./Serb. and Mont.
103 E1 **Mielec** Pol.
110 C1 **Miercurea-Ciuc** Romania
106 B1 **Mieres** Spain
101 E1 **Mieste** Ger.
145 C3 **Miguel Alemán, Presa** *resr* Mex.
144 B2 **Miguel Auza** Mex.
144 B2 **Miguel Hidalgo, Presa** *resr* Mex.
63 A2 **Migyaunglaung** Myanmar
89 E3 **Mikhaylov** Rus. Fed.
Mikhaylovgrad Bulg. *see* **Montana**
66 B2 **Mikhaylovka** Rus. Fed.
77 D1 **Mikhaylovskiy** Rus. Fed.
93 I3 **Mikkeli** Fin.
86 E2 **Mikun'** Rus. Fed.
67 C3 **Mikuni-sanmyaku** *mts* Japan
108 A1 **Milan** Italy
121 C2 **Milange** Moz.
Milano Italy *see* **Milan**
111 C3 **Milas** Turkey
137 D1 **Milbank** U.S.A.
99 D2 **Mildenhall** U.K.
52 B2 **Mildura** Austr.
62 B1 **Mile** China
136 B1 **Miles City** U.S.A.
141 D3 **Milford** *DE* U.S.A.
135 D3 **Milford** *UT* U.S.A.
99 A3 **Milford Haven** U.K.
54 A2 **Milford Sound** N.Z.
107 D2 **Miliana** Alg.
116 B3 **Milk, Wadi el** *watercourse* Sudan
83 L3 **Mil'kovo** Rus. Fed.
129 C3 **Milk River** Can.
105 C3 **Millau** France
143 D2 **Milledgeville** U.S.A.
137 E1 **Mille Lacs** *lakes* U.S.A.
130 A2 **Mille Lacs, Lac des** *l.* Can.
137 D2 **Miller** U.S.A.
91 E2 **Millerovo** Rus. Fed.
52 A2 **Millers Creek** Austr.
52 B3 **Millicent** Austr.
141 F1 **Millinocket** U.S.A.
53 D1 **Millmerran** Austr.
98 B1 **Millom** U.K.
128 C1 **Mills Lake** *l.* Can.
111 B3 **Milos** *i.* Greece
89 E3 **Miloslavskoye** Rus. Fed.
91 E2 **Milove** Ukr.
52 B1 **Milparinka** Austr.
54 A3 **Milton** N.Z.
99 C2 **Milton Keynes** U.K.
140 B2 **Milwaukee** U.S.A.
104 B3 **Mimizan** France
118 B3 **Mimongo** Gabon
79 C2 **Mīnāb** Iran
58 C2 **Minahasa, Semenanjung** *pen.* Indon.
79 C2 **Mina Jebel Ali** U.A.E.
60 B1 **Minas** Indon.
153 C4 **Minas** Uru.
155 D1 **Minas Novas** Brazil
145 C3 **Minatitlán** Mex.
62 A1 **Minbu** Myanmar
64 B2 **Mindanao** *i.* Phil.
101 D1 **Minden** Ger.
142 B2 **Minden** *LA* U.S.A.
137 D2 **Minden** *NE* U.S.A.
64 B1 **Mindoro** *i.* Phil.
64 A1 **Mindoro Strait** Phil.
118 B3 **Mindouli** Congo
99 B3 **Minehead** U.K.
154 B1 **Mineiros** Brazil
139 D2 **Mineral Wells** U.S.A.
77 E3 **Minfeng** China
119 C4 **Minga** Dem. Rep. Congo
81 C1 **Mingäçevir** Azer.
131 D1 **Mingan** Can.
52 B2 **Mingary** Austr.
70 B2 **Mingguang** China
62 A1 **Mingin** Myanmar
107 C2 **Minglanilla** Spain
119 D4 **Mingoyo** Tanz.
69 E1 **Mingshui** China
71 B3 **Mingxi** China
73 B4 **Minicoy** *i.* India
50 A2 **Minilya** Austr.
131 D1 **Minipi Lake** Can.
130 A1 **Miniss Lake** Can.
115 C4 **Minna** Nigeria
137 E2 **Minneapolis** U.S.A.
129 E2 **Minnedosa** Can.
137 E2 **Minnesota** *r.* U.S.A.
137 E1 **Minnesota** *state* U.S.A.
106 B1 **Miño** *r.* Port./Spain
Minorca *i.* Spain *see* **Menorca**
136 C1 **Minot** U.S.A.
88 C3 **Minsk** Belarus
103 E1 **Mińsk Mazowiecki** Pol.
131 D2 **Minto** Can.
130 C1 **Minto, Lac** *l.* Can.
70 A2 **Minxian** China
155 D1 **Mirabela** Brazil
155 D1 **Miralta** Brazil
131 D2 **Miramichi** Can.
111 C3 **Mirampelou, Kolpos** *b.* Greece
152 C3 **Miranda** Brazil
152 C2 **Miranda** *r.* Brazil
106 C1 **Miranda de Ebro** Spain
106 B1 **Mirandela** Port.
154 B2 **Mirandópolis** Brazil
79 C3 **Mirbāṭ** Oman
61 C1 **Miri** *Sarawak* Malaysia
153 C4 **Mirim, Lagoa** *l.* Brazil
79 D2 **Mīrjāveh** Iran
83 I2 **Mirnyy** Rus. Fed.
101 F1 **Mirow** Ger.
74 A2 **Mirpur Khas** Pak.
111 B3 **Mirtoö Pelagos** *sea* Greece
65 B2 **Miryang** S. Korea
75 C2 **Mirzapur** India
66 B1 **Mishan** China
146 B3 **Miskitos, Cayos** *is* Nic.
103 E2 **Miskolc** Hungary
59 C3 **Misoöl** *i.* Indon.
115 D1 **Miṣrātah** Libya
130 B1 **Missinaibi** *r.* Can.
130 B2 **Missinaibi Lake** Can.
128 B3 **Mission** Can.
130 B1 **Missisa Lake** Can.
142 C3 **Mississippi** *r.* U.S.A.
142 C2 **Mississippi** *state* U.S.A.
142 C3 **Mississippi Delta** U.S.A.
134 D1 **Missoula** U.S.A.
137 E3 **Missouri** *r.* U.S.A.
137 E3 **Missouri** *state* U.S.A.
131 C2 **Mistassibi** *r.* Can.
130 C1 **Mistassini, Lac** *l.* Can.
131 D1 **Mistastin Lake** Can.
103 D2 **Mistelbach** Austria
131 D1 **Mistinibi, Lac** *l.* Can.
130 C1 **Mistissini** Can.
51 D2 **Mitchell** Austr.
51 D1 **Mitchell** *r.* Austr.
137 D2 **Mitchell** U.S.A.
97 B2 **Mitchelstown** Rep. of Ireland
74 A2 **Mithi** Pak.
67 D3 **Mito** Japan
119 D3 **Mitole** Tanz.
53 D2 **Mittagong** Austr.
101 E2 **Mittelhausen** Ger.
101 D1 **Mittellandkanal** *canal* Ger.
101 F3 **Mitterteich** Ger.
150 A1 **Mitú** Col.
119 C4 **Mitumba, Chaîne des** *mts* Dem. Rep. Congo
119 C3 **Mitumba, Monts** *mts* Dem. Rep. Congo
118 B2 **Mitzic** Gabon
78 B2 **Miyah, Wādī al** *watercourse* Saudi Arabia
67 C4 **Miyake-jima** *i.* Japan
66 D3 **Miyako** Japan

76 B4 **Miyakonojō** Japan
87 B2 **Miyaly** Kazakh.
Miyang China *see* **Mile**
67 B4 **Miyazaki** Japan
115 D1 **Mizdah** Libya
97 B3 **Mizen Head** *hd* Rep. of Ireland
90 A2 **Mizhhir"ya** Ukr.
93 G4 **Mjölby** Sweden
93 F3 **Mjøsa** *l.* Norway
119 D3 **Mkomazi** Tanz.
103 C1 **Mladá Boleslav** Czech Rep.
109 D2 **Mladenovac** Serb. and Mont.
103 E1 **Mława** Pol.
123 C3 **Mlungisi** S. Africa
90 B1 **Mlyniv** Ukr.
123 C2 **Mmabatho** S. Africa
123 C2 **Mmathethe** Botswana
135 E3 **Moab** U.S.A.
123 D2 **Moamba** Moz.
119 C3 **Moba** Dem. Rep. Congo
118 C2 **Mobayi-Mbongo** Dem. Rep. Congo
137 E3 **Moberly** U.S.A.
142 C2 **Mobile** U.S.A.
142 C2 **Mobile Bay** U.S.A.
136 C1 **Mobridge** U.S.A.
121 D2 **Moçambique** Moz.
62 B1 **Môc Châu** Vietnam
123 C1 **Mochudi** Botswana
121 D2 **Mocimboa da Praia** Moz.
150 A1 **Mocoa** Col.
154 C2 **Mococa** Brazil
144 B2 **Mocorito** Mex.
144 B1 **Moctezuma** *Chihuahua* Mex.
145 B2 **Moctezuma** *San Luis Potosí* Mex.
144 B2 **Moctezuma** *Sonora* Mex.
121 C2 **Mocuba** Moz.
105 D2 **Modane** France
122 B2 **Modder** *r.* S. Africa
108 B2 **Modena** Italy
135 B3 **Modesto** U.S.A.
53 C3 **Moe** Austr.
100 C2 **Moers** Ger.
96 C3 **Moffat** U.K.
Mogadishu Somalia *see* **Muqdisho**
123 C1 **Mogalakwena** *r.* S. Africa
62 A1 **Mogaung** Myanmar
Mogilev Belarus *see* **Mahilyow**
154 C2 **Mogi-Mirim** Brazil
83 I3 **Mogocha** Rus. Fed.
62 A1 **Mogok** Myanmar
103 D2 **Mohács** Hungary
123 C3 **Mohale's Hoek** Lesotho
107 D2 **Mohammadia** Alg.
141 E2 **Mohawk** *r.* U.S.A.
119 D3 **Mohoro** Tanz.
90 B2 **Mohyliv Podil's'kyy** Ukr.
110 C1 **Moinești** Romania
92 F2 **Mo i Rana** Norway
104 C3 **Moissac** France
135 C3 **Mojave** U.S.A.
135 C3 **Mojave Desert** U.S.A.
62 B1 **Mojiang** China
155 C2 **Moji das Cruzes** Brazil
154 C2 **Moji-Guaçu** *r.* Brazil
54 B1 **Mokau** N.Z.
123 C2 **Mokhotlong** Lesotho
65 B3 **Mokp'o** S. Korea
145 C2 **Molango** Mex.
Moldavia *country* Europe *see* **Moldova**
92 E3 **Molde** Norway
90 B2 **Moldova** *country* Europe
110 B1 **Moldoveanu, Vârful** *mt.* Romania
90 B2 **Moldovei Centrale, Podișul** *plat.* Moldova
123 C1 **Molepolole** Botswana
88 C2 **Molėtai** Lith.
109 C2 **Molfetta** Italy
107 C1 **Molina de Aragón** Spain
150 A3 **Mollendo** Peru
53 C2 **Molong** Austr.
122 B2 **Molopo** *watercourse* Botswana/S. Africa
118 B2 **Moloundou** Cameroon
Moluccas *is* Indon. *see* **Maluku**
59 C3 **Molucca Sea** Indon.
52 B2 **Momba** Austr.
119 D3 **Mombasa** Kenya
154 B1 **Mombuca, Serra da** *hills* Brazil
93 F4 **Møn** *i.* Denmark
105 D3 **Monaco** *country* Europe
96 B2 **Monadhliath Mountains** U.K.
97 C1 **Monaghan** Rep. of Ireland
89 D3 **Monastyrshchina** Rus. Fed.
90 B2 **Monastyryshche** Ukr.
66 D2 **Monbetsu** Japan
108 A1 **Moncalieri** Italy
86 C2 **Monchegorsk** Rus. Fed.
100 C2 **Mönchengladbach** Ger.
144 B2 **Monclova** Mex.
131 D2 **Moncton** Can.
106 B1 **Mondego** *r.* Port.
123 D2 **Mondlo** S. Africa
108 A2 **Mondovì** Italy
111 B3 **Monemvasia** Greece
66 D1 **Moneron, Ostrov** *i.* Rus. Fed.
137 E3 **Monett** U.S.A.
108 B1 **Monfalcone** Italy
106 B1 **Monforte** Spain
62 B1 **Mông Cai** Vietnam
62 B1 **Mong Lin** Myanmar
68 C1 **Mongolia** *country* Asia
62 A1 **Mong Pawk** Myanmar
62 A1 **Mong Ping** Myanmar
120 B2 **Mongu** Zambia
135 C3 **Monitor Range** *mts* U.S.A.
114 C4 **Mono** *r.* Togo
135 C3 **Mono Lake** U.S.A.
109 C2 **Monopoli** Italy
107 C1 **Monreal del Campo** Spain
142 B2 **Monroe** *LA* U.S.A.
140 B2 **Monroe** *WI* U.S.A.
142 C2 **Monroeville** U.S.A.
114 A4 **Monrovia** Liberia
100 A2 **Mons** Belgium
122 B3 **Montagu** S. Africa
109 C3 **Montalto** *mt.* Italy
110 B2 **Montana** Bulg.
134 E1 **Montana** *state* U.S.A.
104 C2 **Montargis** France
104 C3 **Montauban** France
141 E2 **Montauk Point** U.S.A.
123 C2 **Mont-aux-Sources** *mt.* Lesotho
105 C2 **Montbard** France
105 D2 **Mont Blanc** *mt.* France/Italy
105 C2 **Montbrison** France
100 B3 **Montcornet** France
104 B3 **Mont-de-Marsan** France
104 C2 **Montdidier** France
151 C2 **Monte Alegre** Brazil
105 D3 **Monte-Carlo** Monaco
152 C4 **Monte Caseros** Arg.
146 C3 **Montego Bay** Jamaica
105 C3 **Montélimar** France
109 C2 **Montella** Italy
145 C2 **Montemorelos** Mex.
104 B2 **Montendre** France
Montenegro *aut. rep.* Serb. and Mont. *see* **Crna Gora**
121 C2 **Montepuez** Moz.
108 B2 **Montepulciano** Italy
135 B3 **Monterey** U.S.A.
135 B3 **Monterey Bay** U.S.A.
150 A1 **Montería** Col.
152 B2 **Montero** Bol.
145 B2 **Monterrey** Mex.
109 C2 **Montesano sulla Marcellana** Italy
109 C2 **Monte Sant'Angelo** Italy
151 E3 **Monte Santo** Brazil
108 A2 **Monte Santu, Capo di** *c.* *Sardinia* Italy
155 D1 **Montes Claros** Brazil
153 C4 **Montevideo** Uru.
137 D2 **Montevideo** U.S.A.
136 B3 **Monte Vista** U.S.A.
142 C2 **Montgomery** U.S.A.
105 D2 **Monthey** Switz.
142 B2 **Monticello** *AR* U.S.A.
135 E3 **Monticello** *UT* U.S.A.
104 C2 **Montignac** France
106 C2 **Montilla** Spain
131 D2 **Mont-Joli** Can.
130 C2 **Mont-Laurier** Can.
104 C2 **Montluçon** France
131 C2 **Montmagny** Can.
104 C2 **Montmorillon** France
51 E2 **Monto** Austr.
134 D2 **Montpelier** *ID* U.S.A.
141 E2 **Montpelier** *VT* U.S.A.
105 C3 **Montpellier** France
130 C2 **Montréal** Can.
129 D2 **Montreal Lake** Can.
129 D2 **Montreal Lake** *l.* Can.
99 D3 **Montreuil** France
105 D2 **Montreux** Switz.
96 C2 **Montrose** U.K.
136 B3 **Montrose** U.S.A.
147 D3 **Montserrat** *terr.* West Indies
62 A1 **Monywa** Myanmar
108 A1 **Monza** Italy
107 D1 **Monzón** Spain
123 C1 **Mookane** Botswana
53 D1 **Moonie** Austr.
53 C1 **Moonie** *r.* Austr.
52 A2 **Moonta** Austr.
50 A2 **Moore, Lake** *salt flat* Austr.
137 D1 **Moorhead** U.S.A.
53 C3 **Mooroopna** Austr.
122 A3 **Moorreesburg** S. Africa
130 B1 **Moose** *r.* Can.
130 B1 **Moose Factory** Can.
141 F1 **Moosehead Lake** U.S.A.
129 D2 **Moose Jaw** Can.
137 E1 **Moose Lake** U.S.A.
129 D2 **Moosomin** Can.
130 B1 **Moosonee** Can.
52 B2 **Mootwingee** Austr.
123 C1 **Mopane** S. Africa
114 B3 **Mopti** Mali
150 A3 **Moquegua** Peru
93 F3 **Mora** Sweden
137 E1 **Mora** U.S.A.
75 B2 **Moradabad** India
121 □D2 **Moramanga** Madag.
103 D2 **Morava** *r.* Europe
96 B2 **Moray Firth** *b.* U.K.
100 C3 **Morbach** Ger.
74 B2 **Morbi** India
104 B3 **Morcenx** France
69 E1 **Mordaga** China
129 E3 **Morden** Can.
91 E1 **Mordovo** Rus. Fed.
98 B1 **Morecambe** U.K.
98 B1 **Morecambe Bay** U.K.
53 C1 **Moree** Austr.
59 D3 **Morehead** P.N.G.
140 C3 **Morehead** U.S.A.
143 E2 **Morehead City** U.S.A.

145 B3 Morelia Mex.
107 C1 Morella Spain
106 B2 Morena, Sierra *mts* Spain
110 C2 Moreni Romania
128 A2 Moresby, Mount Can.
128 A2 Moresby Island Can.
142 B3 Morgan City U.S.A.
143 D1 Morganton U.S.A.
140 D3 Morgantown U.S.A.
105 D2 Morges Switz.
66 D2 Mori Japan
128 B2 Morice Lake Can.
66 D3 Morioka Japan
53 D2 Morisset Austr.
104 B2 Morlaix France
51 C1 Mornington Island Austr.
59 D3 Morobe P.N.G.
114 B1 Morocco *country* Africa
119 D3 Morogoro Tanz.
64 B2 Moro Gulf Phil.
122 B2 Morokweng S. Africa
121 □D3 Morombe Madag.
68 C1 Mörön Mongolia
121 □D3 Morondava Madag.
121 D2 Moroni Comoros
59 C2 Morotai *i.* Indon.
119 D2 Moroto Uganda
98 C1 Morpeth U.K.
154 C1 Morrinhos Brazil
129 E3 Morris Can.
137 D1 Morris U.S.A.
143 D1 Morristown U.S.A.
87 D3 Morshanka Rus. Fed.
154 B1 Mortes, Rio das *r.* Brazil
52 B3 Mortlake Austr.
53 D3 Moruya Austr.
96 B2 Morvern *reg.* U.K.
53 C3 Morwell Austr.
102 B2 Mosbach Ger.
89 E2 Moscow Rus. Fed.
134 C1 Moscow U.S.A.
100 C2 Mosel *r.* Ger.
105 D2 Moselle *r.* France
134 C1 Moses Lake U.S.A.
92 □A3 Mosfellsbær Iceland
54 B3 Mosgiel N.Z.
89 D2 Moshenskoye Rus. Fed.
119 D3 Moshi Tanz.
92 F2 Mosjøen Norway
Moskva Rus. Fed. *see* Moscow
103 D2 Mosonmagyaróvár Hungary
93 F4 Moss Norway
122 B3 Mossel Bay S. Africa
122 B3 Mossel Bay *b.* S. Africa
118 B3 Mossendjo Congo
52 B2 Mossgiel Austr.
51 D1 Mossman Austr.
151 E2 Mossoró Brazil
53 D2 Moss Vale Austr.
102 C1 Most Czech Rep.
114 C1 Mostaganem Alg.
109 C2 Mostar Bos.-Herz.
152 C4 Mostardas Brazil
93 G4 Motala Sweden
96 C3 Motherwell U.K.
107 C2 Motilla del Palancar Spain
122 B1 Motokwe Botswana
106 C2 Motril Spain
110 B2 Motru Romania
145 D2 Motul Mex.
111 C3 Moudros Greece
118 B3 Mouila Gabon
52 B3 Moulamein Austr.
105 C2 Moulins France
63 A2 Moulmein Myanmar
143 D2 Moultrie U.S.A.
143 E2 Moultrie, Lake U.S.A.
140 B3 Mound City U.S.A.
115 D4 Moundou Chad
137 E3 Mountain Grove U.S.A.
142 B1 Mountain Home *AR* U.S.A.
134 C2 Mountain Home *ID* U.S.A.
143 D1 Mount Airy U.S.A.
52 A3 Mount Barker Austr.
53 C3 Mount Beauty Austr.
121 C2 Mount Darwin Zimbabwe
141 F2 Mount Desert Island U.S.A.
123 C3 Mount Fletcher S. Africa
123 C3 Mount Frere S. Africa
52 B3 Mount Gambier Austr.
59 D3 Mount Hagen P.N.G.
53 C2 Mount Hope Austr.
51 C2 Mount Isa Austr.
50 A2 Mount Magnet Austr.
52 B2 Mount Manara Austr.
54 C1 Mount Maunganui N.Z.
137 E2 Mount Pleasant *IA* U.S.A.
140 C2 Mount Pleasant *MI* U.S.A.
139 E2 Mount Pleasant *TX* U.S.A.
99 A3 Mount's Bay U.K.
134 B2 Mount Shasta U.S.A.
140 B3 Mount Vernon *IL* U.S.A.
140 C2 Mount Vernon *OH* U.S.A.
134 B1 Mount Vernon *WA* U.S.A.
51 D2 Moura Austr.
115 E3 Mourdi, Dépression du *depr.* Chad
97 C1 Mourne Mountains U.K.
100 A2 Mouscron Belgium
115 D3 Moussoro Chad
58 C2 Moutong Indon.
115 C2 Mouydir, Monts du *plat.* Alg.
100 B3 Mouzon France
97 B1 Moy *r.* Rep. of Ireland
117 B4 Moyale Eth.
123 C3 Moyeni Lesotho
77 D2 Moyynty Kazakh.
121 C3 Mozambique *country* Africa
113 G5 Mozambique Channel Africa
89 E2 Mozhaysk Rus. Fed.
119 D3 Mpanda Tanz.
121 C2 Mpika Zambia
121 C1 Mporokoso Zambia
123 C2 Mpumalanga *prov.* S. Africa
88 C2 Mshinskaya Rus. Fed.
107 D2 M'Sila Alg.
89 D2 Msta *r.* Rus. Fed.
89 D2 Mstinskiy Most Rus. Fed.
89 D3 Mstsislaw Belarus
89 E3 Mtsensk Rus. Fed.
119 E4 Mtwara Tanz.
118 B3 Muanda Dem. Rep. Congo
62 B2 Muang Khammouan Laos
63 B2 Muang Không Laos
62 B1 Muang Ngoy Laos
62 B2 Muang Pakbeng Laos
62 B2 Muang Pakxan Laos
62 B1 Muang Sing Laos
62 B2 Muang Vangviang Laos
62 B2 Muang Xaignabouri Laos
60 B1 Muar Malaysia
60 B2 Muarabungo Indon.
60 B2 Muaradua Indon.
61 C2 Muaralaung Indon.
60 A2 Muarasiberut Indon.
60 B2 Muaratembesi Indon.
61 C2 Muarateweh Indon.
119 D2 Mubende Uganda
115 D3 Mubi Nigeria
120 B2 Muconda Angola
155 E1 Mucuri Brazil
155 E1 Mucuri *r.* Brazil
66 A2 Mudanjiang China
66 A1 Mudan Jiang *r.* China
111 C2 Mudanya Turkey
101 E1 Müden (Örtze) Ger.
53 C2 Mudgee Austr.
63 A2 Mudon Myanmar
80 B1 Mudurnu Turkey
121 C2 Mueda Moz.
121 B2 Mufulira Zambia
120 B2 Mufumbwe Zambia
111 C3 Muğla Turkey
116 B2 Muhammad Qol Sudan
101 F2 Mühlberg Ger.
101 E2 Mühlhausen (Thüringen) Ger.
63 B3 Mui Ca Mau *c.* Vietnam
97 C2 Muine Bheag Rep. of Ireland
121 C2 Muite Moz.
65 B2 Muju S. Korea
90 A2 Mukacheve Ukr.
61 C1 Mukah *Sarawak* Malaysia
63 B2 Mukdahan Thai.
50 A3 Mukinbudin Austr.
60 B2 Mukomuko Indon.
121 C2 Mulanje, Mount Malawi
101 F2 Mulde *r.* Ger.
144 A2 Mulegé Mex.
139 C2 Muleshoe U.S.A.
106 C2 Mulhacén *mt.* Spain
100 C2 Mülheim an der Ruhr Ger.
105 D2 Mulhouse France
66 B2 Muling China
66 B1 Muling He *r.* China
96 B2 Mull *i.* U.K.
53 C2 Mullaley Austr.
136 C2 Mullen U.S.A.
61 C1 Muller, Pegunungan *mts* Indon.
50 A2 Mullewa Austr.
97 C2 Mullingar Rep. of Ireland
96 B3 Mull of Galloway *c.* U.K.
96 B3 Mull of Kintyre *hd* U.K.
96 A3 Mull of Oa *hd* U.K.
120 B2 Mulobezi Zambia
74 B1 Multan Pak.
73 B3 Mumbai India
120 B2 Mumbwa Zambia
145 D2 Muna Mex.
101 E2 Münchberg Ger.
München Ger. *see* Munich
140 B2 Muncie U.S.A.
50 B3 Mundrabilla Austr.
119 C2 Mungbere Dem. Rep. Congo
75 C2 Munger India
52 A1 Mungeranie Austr.
53 C1 Mungindi Austr.
102 C2 Munich Ger.
155 D2 Muniz Freire Brazil
101 E1 Münster *Niedersachsen* Ger.
100 C2 Münster *Nordrhein-Westfalen* Ger.
97 B2 Munster *reg.* Rep. of Ireland
100 C2 Münsterland *reg.* Ger.
62 B1 Mương Nhie Vietnam
92 H2 Muonio Fin.
92 H2 Muonioälven *r.* Fin./Sweden
117 C4 Muqdisho Somalia
103 D2 Mur *r.* Austria
119 C3 Muramvya Burundi
119 D3 Muranga Kenya
81 B2 Murat *r.* Turkey
111 C2 Muratlı Turkey
50 A2 Murchison *watercourse* Austr.
107 C2 Murcia Spain
111 C2 Mürefte Turkey
110 B1 Mureşul *r.* Romania
104 C3 Muret France
142 C1 Murfreesboro U.S.A.
77 C3 Murghab *r.* Afgh.
77 D3 Murghob Tajik.
155 D2 Muriaé Brazil
120 B1 Muriege Angola
101 F1 Müritz *l.* Ger.
86 C2 Murmansk Rus. Fed.
87 D3 Murom Rus. Fed.

66 D2 **Muroran** Japan
106 B1 **Muros** Spain
67 B4 **Muroto** Japan
67 B4 **Muroto-zaki** *pt* Japan
143 D1 **Murphy** U.S.A.
53 C1 **Murra Murra** Austr.
52 A3 **Murray** *r.* Austr.
128 B2 **Murray** *r.* Can.
140 B3 **Murray** U.S.A.
143 D2 **Murray, Lake** U.S.A.
52 A3 **Murray Bridge** Austr.
122 B3 **Murraysburg** S. Africa
52 B3 **Murrayville** Austr.
52 B2 **Murrumbidgee** *r.* Austr.
121 C2 **Murrupula** Moz.
53 D2 **Murrurundi** Austr.
109 C1 **Murska Sobota** Slovenia
54 C1 **Murupara** N.Z.
75 C2 **Murwara** India
53 D1 **Murwillumbah** Austr.
115 D2 **Murzūq** Libya
81 C2 **Muş** Turkey
110 B2 **Musala** *mt.* Bulg.
65 B1 **Musan** N. Korea
78 B3 **Musaymir** Yemen
79 C2 **Muscat** Oman
137 E2 **Muscatine** U.S.A.
50 C2 **Musgrave Ranges** *mts* Austr.
118 B3 **Mushie** Dem. Rep. Congo
60 B2 **Musi** *r.* Indon.
140 B2 **Muskegon** U.S.A.
139 D1 **Muskogee** U.S.A.
128 B2 **Muskwa** *r.* Can.
74 A1 **Muslimbagh** Pak.
78 A3 **Musmar** Sudan
119 D3 **Musoma** Tanz.
96 C3 **Musselburgh** U.K.
88 B2 **Mustjala** Estonia
53 D2 **Muswellbrook** Austr.
116 A2 **Mūţ** Egypt
121 C2 **Mutare** Zimbabwe
66 D2 **Mutsu** Japan
121 C2 **Mutuali** Moz.
92 I2 **Muurola** Fin.
70 A2 **Mu Us Shamo** *des.* China
120 A1 **Muxaluando** Angola
86 C2 **Muyezerskiy** Rus. Fed.
119 D3 **Muyinga** Burundi
76 B2 **Muynak** Uzbek.
74 B1 **Muzaffargarh** Pak.
75 C2 **Muzaffarpur** India
144 B2 **Múzquiz** Mex.
75 C1 **Muztag** *mt.* China
119 C3 **Mwanza** Dem. Rep. Congo
119 D3 **Mwanza** Tanz.
118 C3 **Mweka** Dem. Rep. Congo
121 B2 **Mwenda** Zambia
118 C3 **Mwene-Ditu** Dem. Rep. Congo
121 C3 **Mwenezi** Zimbabwe
119 C3 **Mweru, Lake** Dem. Rep. Congo/Zambia
118 C3 **Mwimba** Dem. Rep. Congo
120 B2 **Mwinilunga** Zambia
88 C3 **Myadzyel** Belarus
62 A2 **Myanaung** Myanmar
62 A1 **Myanmar** *country* Asia
63 A2 **Myaungmya** Myanmar
62 A2 **Myede** Myanmar
62 A1 **Myingyan** Myanmar
62 A1 **Myitkyina** Myanmar
91 C2 **Mykolayiv** Ukr.
111 C3 **Mykonos** Greece
111 C3 **Mykonos** *i.* Greece
86 E2 **Myla** Rus. Fed.
75 D2 **Mymensingh** Bangl.
62 A1 **Myohaung** Myanmar
65 B1 **Myŏnggan** N. Korea
88 C2 **Myory** Belarus
92 □B3 **Mýrdalsjökull** *ice cap* Iceland
91 C2 **Myrhorod** Ukr.
90 C2 **Myronivka** Ukr.
143 E2 **Myrtle Beach** U.S.A.
53 C3 **Myrtleford** Austr.
134 B2 **Myrtle Point** U.S.A.
89 E2 **Myshkin** Rus. Fed.
103 C1 **Myślibórz** Pol.
73 B3 **Mysore** India
83 N2 **Mys Shmidta** Rus. Fed.
63 B2 **My Tho** Vietnam
111 C3 **Mytilini** Greece
89 E3 **Mytishchi** Rus. Fed.
123 C3 **Mzamomhle** S. Africa
121 C2 **Mzimba** Malawi
121 C2 **Mzuzu** Malawi

N

97 C2 **Naas** Rep. of Ireland
122 A2 **Nababeep** S. Africa
87 E3 **Naberezhnyye Chelny** Rus. Fed.
59 D3 **Nabire** Indon.
80 B2 **Nāblus** West Bank
123 C1 **Naboomspruit** S. Africa
121 D2 **Nacala** Moz.
63 A2 **Nachuge** India
139 E2 **Nacogdoches** U.S.A.
144 B1 **Nacozari de García** Mex.
74 B2 **Nadiad** India
90 A2 **Nadvirna** Ukr.
86 C2 **Nadvoitsy** Rus. Fed.
86 G2 **Nadym** Rus. Fed.
93 F4 **Næstved** Denmark
111 B3 **Nafpaktos** Greece
111 B3 **Nafplio** Greece
115 D1 **Nafūsah, Jabal** *hills* Libya
78 B2 **Nafy** Saudi Arabia
64 B1 **Naga** Phil.
130 B1 **Nagagami** *r.* Can.
67 C3 **Nagano** Japan
67 C3 **Nagaoka** Japan
75 D2 **Nagaon** India
74 B1 **Nagar** India
74 B2 **Nagar Parkar** Pak.
67 A4 **Nagasaki** Japan
67 B4 **Nagato** Japan
74 B2 **Nagaur** India
73 B4 **Nagercoil** India
74 A2 **Nagha Kalat** Pak.
75 B2 **Nagina** India
67 C3 **Nagoya** Japan
75 B2 **Nagpur** India
68 C2 **Nagqu** China
103 D2 **Nagyatád** Hungary
103 D2 **Nagykanizsa** Hungary
128 B1 **Nahanni Butte** Can.
76 A3 **Nahāvand** Iran
101 E1 **Nahrendorf** Ger.
153 A5 **Nahuel Huapí, Lago** *l.* Arg.
131 D1 **Nain** Can.
81 D2 **Nā'īn** Iran
96 C2 **Nairn** U.K.
119 D3 **Nairobi** Kenya
119 D3 **Naivasha** Kenya
81 D2 **Najafābād** Iran
78 B2 **Najd** *reg.* Saudi Arabia
106 C1 **Nájera** Spain
65 C1 **Najin** N. Korea
78 B3 **Najrān** Saudi Arabia
Nakambé *watercourse* Burkina/Ghana *see* **White Volta**
67 C3 **Nakatsugawa** Japan
78 A3 **Nakfa** Eritrea
66 B2 **Nakhodka** Rus. Fed.
63 B2 **Nakhon Pathom** Thai.
63 B2 **Nakhon Ratchasima** Thai.
63 B2 **Nakhon Sawan** Thai.
63 A3 **Nakhon Si Thammarat** Thai.
130 B1 **Nakina** Can.
121 C1 **Nakonde** Zambia
93 F4 **Nakskov** Denmark
119 D3 **Nakuru** Kenya
128 C2 **Nakusp** Can.
75 D2 **Nalbari** India
87 D4 **Nal'chik** Rus. Fed.
115 D1 **Nālūt** Libya
123 C2 **Namahadi** S. Africa
77 D2 **Namangan** Uzbek.
122 A2 **Namaqualand** *reg.* S. Africa
51 E2 **Nambour** Austr.
53 D2 **Nambucca Heads** Austr.
65 B2 **Namch'ŏn** N. Korea
75 D1 **Nam Co** *salt l.* China
62 B1 **Nam Định** Vietnam
120 A3 **Namib Desert** Namibia
120 A2 **Namibe** Angola
120 A3 **Namibia** *country* Africa
72 D2 **Namjagbarwa Feng** *mt.* China
59 C3 **Namlea** Indon.
53 C2 **Namoi** *r.* Austr.
134 C2 **Nampa** U.S.A.
114 B3 **Nampala** Mali
65 B2 **Namp'o** N. Korea
121 C2 **Nampula** Moz.
62 A1 **Namrup** India
62 A1 **Namsang** Myanmar
92 F3 **Namsos** Norway
63 A2 **Nam Tok** Thai.
83 J2 **Namtsy** Rus. Fed.
62 A1 **Namtu** Myanmar
100 B2 **Namur** Belgium
120 B2 **Namwala** Zambia
65 B2 **Namwŏn** S. Korea
62 A1 **Namya Ra** Myanmar
62 B2 **Nan** Thai.
128 B3 **Nanaimo** Can.
71 B3 **Nan'an** China
122 A1 **Nananib Plateau** Namibia
67 C3 **Nanao** Japan
71 B3 **Nanchang** *Jiangxi* China
71 B3 **Nanchang** *Jiangxi* China
70 A2 **Nanchong** China
63 A3 **Nancowry** *i.* India
105 D2 **Nancy** France
75 C1 **Nanda Devi** *mt.* India
71 A3 **Nandan** China
73 B3 **Nanded** India
74 B2 **Nandurbar** India
73 B3 **Nandyal** India
71 B3 **Nanfeng** China
118 B2 **Nanga Eboko** Cameroon
61 C2 **Nangahpinoh** Indon.
77 D3 **Nanga Parbat** *mt.* Jammu and Kashmir
61 C2 **Nangatayap** Indon.
70 B2 **Nangong** China
119 D3 **Nangulangwa** Tanz.
70 C2 **Nanhui** China
70 B2 **Nanjing** China
Nanking China *see* **Nanjing**
120 A2 **Nankova** Angola
71 B3 **Nan Ling** *mts* China
71 A3 **Nanning** China
127 H2 **Nanortalik** Greenland
71 A3 **Nanpan Jiang** *r.* China
75 C2 **Nanpara** India
71 B3 **Nanping** China
69 E3 **Nansei-shotō** *is* Japan
104 B2 **Nantes** France
70 C2 **Nantong** China
141 F2 **Nantucket Island** U.S.A.
155 D1 **Nanuque** Brazil
64 B2 **Nanusa, Kepulauan** *is* Indon.

71 B3 **Nanxiong** China
70 B2 **Nanyang** China
70 B2 **Nanzhang** China
131 C1 **Naococane, Lac** *l.* Can.
74 A2 **Naokot** Pak.
135 B3 **Napa** U.S.A.
126 D2 **Napaktulik Lake** Can.
127 H2 **Napasoq** Greenland
54 C1 **Napier** N.Z.
108 B2 **Naples** Italy
143 D3 **Naples** U.S.A.
150 A2 **Napo** *r.* Ecuador
Napoli Italy *see* **Naples**
114 B3 **Nara** Mali
93 I4 **Narach** Belarus
52 B3 **Naracoorte** Austr.
145 C2 **Naranjos** Mex.
63 B3 **Narathiwat** Thai.
105 C3 **Narbonne** France
63 A2 **Narcondam Island** India
127 G1 **Nares Strait** Can./Greenland
122 A1 **Narib** Namibia
87 D4 **Narimanov** Rus. Fed.
67 D3 **Narita** Japan
74 B2 **Narmada** *r.* India
74 B2 **Narnaul** India
108 B2 **Narni** Italy
90 B1 **Narodychi** Ukr.
89 E2 **Naro-Fominsk** Rus. Fed.
53 D3 **Narooma** Austr.
88 C3 **Narowlya** Belarus
53 C2 **Narrabri** Austr.
53 C2 **Narrandera** Austr.
53 C2 **Narromine** Austr.
88 C2 **Narva** Estonia
88 C2 **Narva Bay** Estonia/Rus. Fed.
88 C2 **Narva Reservoir** *resr* Estonia/Rus. Fed.
92 G2 **Narvik** Norway
86 E2 **Nar'yan-Mar** Rus. Fed.
77 D2 **Naryn** Kyrg.
74 B2 **Nashik** India
141 E2 **Nashua** U.S.A.
142 C1 **Nashville** U.S.A.
117 B4 **Nasir** Sudan
128 B2 **Nass** *r.* Can.
146 C2 **Nassau** Bahamas
116 B2 **Nasser, Lake** *resr* Egypt
93 F4 **Nässjö** Sweden
130 C1 **Nastapoca** *r.* Can.
130 C1 **Nastapoka Islands** Can.
120 B3 **Nata** Botswana
151 E2 **Natal** Brazil
131 D1 **Natashquan** Can.
131 D1 **Natashquan** *r.* Can.
142 B2 **Natchez** U.S.A.
142 B2 **Natchitoches** U.S.A.
53 C3 **Nathalia** Austr.
107 D1 **Nati, Punta** *pt* Spain
114 C3 **Natitingou** Benin
151 D3 **Natividade** Brazil
67 D3 **Natori** Japan
61 B1 **Natuna, Kepulauan** *is* Indon.
61 B1 **Natuna Besar** *i.* Indon.
120 A3 **Nauchas** Namibia
101 F1 **Nauen** Ger.
88 B2 **Naujoji Akmenė** Lith.
101 E2 **Naumburg (Saale)** Ger.
49 E3 **Nauru** *country* S. Pacific Ocean
145 C2 **Nautla** Mex.
88 C3 **Navahrudak** Belarus
106 B2 **Navalmoral de la Mata** Spain
106 B2 **Navalvillar de Pela** Spain
97 C2 **Navan** Rep. of Ireland
88 C2 **Navapolatsk** Belarus
83 M2 **Navarin, Mys** *c.* Rus. Fed.
153 B6 **Navarino, Isla** *i.* Chile
96 B1 **Naver** *r.* U.K.
89 D3 **Navlya** Rus. Fed.
110 C2 **Năvodari** Romania
77 C2 **Navoi** Uzbek.
144 B2 **Navojoa** Mex.
144 B2 **Navolato** Mex.
74 A2 **Nawabshah** Pak.
62 A1 **Nawnghkio** Myanmar
62 A1 **Nawngleng** Myanmar
81 C2 **Naxçıvan** Azer.
111 C3 **Naxos** *i.* Greece
144 B2 **Nayar** Mex.
66 D2 **Nayoro** Japan
80 B2 **Nazareth** Israel
144 B2 **Nazas** Mex.
144 B2 **Nazas** *r.* Mex.
150 A3 **Nazca** Peru
111 C3 **Nazilli** Turkey
117 B4 **Nazrēt** Eth.
79 C2 **Nazwá** Oman
121 B1 **Nchelenge** Zambia
122 B1 **Ncojane** Botswana
120 A1 **N'dalatando** Angola
118 C2 **Ndélé** C.A.R.
118 B3 **Ndendé** Gabon
115 D3 **Ndjamena** Chad
121 B2 **Ndola** Zambia
97 C1 **Neagh, Lough** *l.* U.K.
50 C2 **Neale, Lake** *salt flat* Austr.
111 B2 **Nea Roda** Greece
99 B3 **Neath** U.K.
53 C1 **Nebine Creek** *r.* Austr.
76 B3 **Nebitdag** Turkm.
150 B1 **Neblina, Pico da** *mt.* Brazil
89 D2 **Nebolchi** Rus. Fed.
136 C2 **Nebraska** *state* U.S.A.
137 D2 **Nebraska City** U.S.A.
108 B3 **Nebrodi, Monti** *mts* *Sicily* Italy
153 C4 **Necochea** Arg.
131 C1 **Nedlouc, Lac** *l.* Can.
135 D4 **Needles** U.S.A.
74 B2 **Neemuch** India
129 E2 **Neepawa** Can.
87 E3 **Neftekamsk** Rus. Fed.
82 F2 **Nefteyugansk** Rus. Fed.
120 A1 **Negage** Angola
117 B4 **Negēlē** Eth.
150 A2 **Negra, Punta** *pt* Peru
63 A2 **Negrais, Cape** Myanmar
153 B5 **Negro** *r.* Arg.
150 C2 **Negro** *r.* S. America
152 C4 **Negro** *r.* Uru.
106 B2 **Negro, Cabo** *c.* Morocco
64 B2 **Negros** *i.* Phil.
69 E1 **Nehe** China
70 A3 **Neijiang** China
129 D2 **Neilburg** Can.
150 A1 **Neiva** Col.
129 E2 **Nejanilini Lake** Can.
117 B4 **Nek'emtē** Eth.
89 F2 **Nekrasovskoye** Rus. Fed.
89 D2 **Nelidovo** Rus. Fed.
73 B3 **Nellore** India
128 C3 **Nelson** Can.
129 E2 **Nelson** *r.* Can.
54 B2 **Nelson** N.Z.
52 B3 **Nelson, Cape** Austr.
53 D2 **Nelson Bay** Austr.
129 E2 **Nelson House** Can.
134 E1 **Nelson Reservoir** U.S.A.
123 D2 **Nelspruit** S. Africa
114 B3 **Néma** Maur.
88 B2 **Neman** Rus. Fed.
104 C2 **Nemours** France
66 D2 **Nemuro** Japan
90 B2 **Nemyriv** Ukr.
97 B2 **Nenagh** Rep. of Ireland
99 D2 **Nene** *r.* U.K.
69 E1 **Nenjiang** China
137 E3 **Neosho** U.S.A.
75 C2 **Nepal** *country* Asia
75 C2 **Nepalganj** Nepal
135 D3 **Nephi** U.S.A.
97 B1 **Nephin** *hill* Rep. of Ireland
97 B1 **Nephin Beg Range** *hills* Rep. of Ireland
131 D2 **Nepisiguit** *r.* Can.
119 C2 **Nepoko** *r.* Dem. Rep. Congo
104 C3 **Nérac** France
53 D1 **Nerang** Austr.
69 D1 **Nerchinsk** Rus. Fed.
89 F2 **Nerekhta** Rus. Fed.
109 C2 **Neretva** *r.* Bos.-Herz./Croatia
120 B2 **Neriquinha** Angola
88 B3 **Neris** *r.* Lith.
89 E2 **Nerl'** *r.* Rus. Fed.
86 F2 **Nerokhi** Rus. Fed.
154 C1 **Nerópolis** Brazil
83 J3 **Neryungri** Rus. Fed.
92 □C2 **Neskaupstaður** Iceland
96 B2 **Ness, Loch** *l.* U.K.
136 D3 **Ness City** U.S.A.
111 B2 **Nestos** *r.* Greece
100 B1 **Netherlands** *country* Europe
147 D3 **Netherlands Antilles** *terr.* West Indies
127 G2 **Nettilling Lake** Can.
101 F1 **Neubrandenburg** Ger.
105 D2 **Neuchâtel** Switz.
100 C2 **Neuerburg** Ger.
100 B3 **Neufchâteau** Belgium
105 D2 **Neufchâteau** France
104 C2 **Neufchâtel-en-Bray** France
101 D2 **Neuhof** Ger.
102 B1 **Neumünster** Ger.
102 B2 **Neunkirchen** Ger.
153 B4 **Neuquén** Arg.
153 B4 **Neuquén** *r.* Arg.
101 F1 **Neuruppin** Ger.
100 C2 **Neuss** Ger.
101 D1 **Neustadt am Rübenberge** Ger.
101 E3 **Neustadt an der Aisch** Ger.
101 F1 **Neustrelitz** Ger.
100 C2 **Neuwied** Ger.
137 E3 **Nevada** U.S.A.
135 C3 **Nevada** *state* U.S.A.
106 C2 **Nevada, Sierra** *mts* Spain
135 B2 **Nevada, Sierra** *mts* U.S.A.
88 C2 **Nevel'** Rus. Fed.
105 C2 **Nevers** France
53 C2 **Nevertire** Austr.
109 C2 **Nevesinje** Bos.-Herz.
87 D4 **Nevinnomyssk** Rus. Fed.
128 B2 **New Aiyansh** Can.
140 B3 **New Albany** U.S.A.
151 C1 **New Amsterdam** Guyana
141 E2 **Newark** *NJ* U.S.A.
140 C2 **Newark** *OH* U.S.A.
98 C2 **Newark-on-Trent** U.K.
141 E2 **New Bedford** U.S.A.
143 E1 **New Bern** U.S.A.
143 D2 **Newberry** U.S.A.
139 E2 **New Boston** U.S.A.
139 D3 **New Braunfels** U.S.A.
97 C2 **Newbridge** Rep. of Ireland
48 D3 **New Britain** *i.* P.N.G.
131 D2 **New Brunswick** *prov.* Can.
99 C3 **Newbury** U.K.
49 E4 **New Caledonia** *terr.* S. Pacific Ocean
53 D2 **Newcastle** Austr.
123 C2 **Newcastle** S. Africa
97 D1 **Newcastle** U.K.
140 C2 **New Castle** U.S.A.
136 C2 **Newcastle** U.S.A.
98 B2 **Newcastle-under-Lyme** U.K.
98 C1 **Newcastle upon Tyne** U.K.
97 B2 **Newcastle West** Rep. of Ireland
74 B2 **New Delhi** India

128 C3 **New Denver** Can.
53 D2 **New England Range** *mts* Austr.
131 E2 **Newfoundland** *i.* Can.
131 E1 **Newfoundland and Labrador** *prov.* Can.
131 D2 **New Glasgow** Can.
59 D3 **New Guinea** *i.* Indon./P.N.G.
141 E2 **New Hampshire** *state* U.S.A.
141 E2 **New Haven** U.S.A.
128 B2 **New Hazelton** Can.
New Hebrides *country* S. Pacific Ocean *see* **Vanuatu**
142 B2 **New Iberia** U.S.A.
48 D3 **New Ireland** *i.* P.N.G.
141 E3 **New Jersey** *state* U.S.A.
130 C2 **New Liskeard** Can.
50 A2 **Newman** Austr.
138 B2 **New Mexico** *state* U.S.A.
142 B3 **New Orleans** U.S.A.
140 C2 **New Philadelphia** U.S.A.
54 B1 **New Plymouth** N.Z.
99 C3 **Newport** *England* U.K.
99 B3 **Newport** *Wales* U.K.
142 B1 **Newport** *AR* U.S.A.
134 B2 **Newport** *OR* U.S.A.
141 E2 **Newport** *RI* U.S.A.
141 E2 **Newport** *VT* U.S.A.
134 C1 **Newport** *WA* U.S.A.
141 D3 **Newport News** U.S.A.
143 E3 **New Providence** *i.* Bahamas
99 A3 **Newquay** U.K.
142 B2 **New Roads** U.S.A.
97 C2 **New Ross** Rep. of Ireland
97 C1 **Newry** U.K.
New Siberia Islands Rus. Fed. *see* **Novosibirskiye Ostrova**
52 B2 **New South Wales** *state* Austr.
137 E2 **Newton** *IA* U.S.A.
137 D3 **Newton** *KS* U.S.A.
99 B3 **Newton Abbot** U.K.
96 B3 **Newton Stewart** U.K.
97 B2 **Newtown** Rep. of Ireland
99 B2 **Newtown** U.K.
136 C1 **New Town** U.S.A.
97 D1 **Newtownabbey** U.K.
97 D1 **Newtownards** U.K.
96 C3 **Newtown St Boswells** U.K.
97 C1 **Newtownstewart** U.K.
137 E2 **New Ulm** U.S.A.
141 E2 **New York** U.S.A.
141 D2 **New York** *state* U.S.A.
54 B2 **New Zealand** *country* Oceania
79 C2 **Neyrīz** Iran
76 B3 **Neyshābūr** Iran
145 C3 **Nezahualcóyotl, Presa** *resr* Mex.
61 B1 **Ngabang** Indon.
75 C2 **Ngamring** China
75 C1 **Ngangla Ringco** *salt l.* China
77 E3 **Nganglong Kangri** *mt.* China
75 C1 **Nganglong Kangri** *mts* China
75 C1 **Ngangzê Co** *salt l.* China
62 A2 **Ngao** Thai.
118 B2 **Ngaoundéré** Cameroon
54 C1 **Ngaruawahia** N.Z.
62 A2 **Ngathainggyaung** Myanmar
118 B3 **Ngo** Congo
63 B2 **Ngoc Linh** *mt.* Vietnam
115 D4 **Ngol Bembo** Nigeria
68 C2 **Ngoring Hu** *l.* China
115 D3 **Ngourti** Niger
115 D3 **Nguigmi** Niger
59 D2 **Ngulu** *atoll* Micronesia
115 D3 **Nguru** Nigeria
123 D2 **Ngwelezana** S. Africa
121 C2 **Nhamalabué** Moz.
63 B2 **Nha Trang** Vietnam
52 B3 **Nhill** Austr.
123 D2 **Nhlangano** Swaziland
51 C1 **Nhulunbuy** Austr.
141 D2 **Niagara Falls** Can.
114 C3 **Niamey** Niger
119 C2 **Niangara** Dem. Rep. Congo
114 B3 **Niangay, Lac** *l.* Mali
60 A1 **Nias** *i.* Indon.
146 B3 **Nicaragua** *country* Central America
146 B3 **Nicaragua, Lago de** *l.* Nic.
105 D3 **Nice** France
73 D4 **Nicobar Islands** India
80 B2 **Nicosia** Cyprus
146 B4 **Nicoya, Golfo de** *b.* Costa Rica
88 B2 **Nida** Lith.
103 E1 **Nidzica** Pol.
102 B1 **Niebüll** Ger.
101 D2 **Niederaula** Ger.
118 B2 **Niefang** Equat. Guinea
101 F1 **Niemegk** Ger.
101 D1 **Nienburg (Weser)** Ger.
100 B1 **Nieuwe-Niedorp** Neth.
151 C1 **Nieuw Nickerie** Suriname
122 A3 **Nieuwoudtville** S. Africa
100 A2 **Nieuwpoort** Belgium
80 B2 **Niğde** Turkey
115 C3 **Niger** *country* Africa
115 C4 **Niger** *r.* Africa
115 C4 **Niger, Mouths of the** Nigeria
115 C4 **Nigeria** *country* Africa
130 B2 **Nighthawk Lake** Can.
111 B2 **Nigrita** Greece
67 C3 **Niigata** Japan
67 B4 **Niihama** Japan
67 C4 **Nii-jima** *i.* Japan
67 C3 **Niitsu** Japan
100 B2 **Nijmegen** Neth.
100 C1 **Nijverdal** Neth.
92 J2 **Nikel'** Rus. Fed.
83 M3 **Nikol'skoye** Rus. Fed.
91 C2 **Nikopol'** Ukr.
80 B1 **Niksar** Turkey
79 D2 **Nīkshahr** Iran
109 C2 **Nikšić** Serb. and Mont.
116 B1 **Nile** *r.* Africa
140 B2 **Niles** U.S.A.
105 C3 **Nîmes** France
53 C3 **Nimmitabel** Austr.
117 B4 **Nimule** Sudan
53 C1 **Nindigully** Austr.
73 B4 **Nine Degree Channel** India
53 C3 **Ninety Mile Beach** Austr.
54 B1 **Ninety Mile Beach** N.Z.
70 C3 **Ningbo** China
71 B3 **Ningde** China
71 B3 **Ningdu** China
70 B2 **Ningguo** China
71 C3 **Ninghai** China
Ningjiang China *see* Songyuan
68 C2 **Ningjing Shan** *mts* China
70 A2 **Ningxia Huizu Zizhiqu** *aut. reg.* China
70 B2 **Ningyang** China
62 B1 **Ninh Binh** Vietnam
63 B2 **Ninh Hoa** Vietnam
66 D2 **Ninohe** Japan
137 D2 **Niobrara** *r.* U.S.A.
114 B3 **Niono** Mali
114 B3 **Nioro** Mali
104 B2 **Niort** France
129 D2 **Nipawin** Can.
130 B2 **Nipigon** Can.
130 B2 **Nipigon, Lake** Can.
131 D1 **Nipishish Lake** Can.
130 C2 **Nipissing, Lake** Can.
135 C3 **Nipton** U.S.A.
151 D3 **Niquelândia** Brazil
73 B3 **Nirmal** India
109 D2 **Niš** Serb. and Mont.
109 D2 **Nišava** *r.* Serb. and Mont.
108 B3 **Niscemi** *Sicily* Italy
67 B4 **Nishino-omote** Japan
155 D2 **Niterói** Brazil
96 C3 **Nith** *r.* U.K.
103 D2 **Nitra** Slovakia
49 G4 **Niue** *terr.* S. Pacific Ocean
92 H3 **Nivala** Fin.
100 B2 **Nivelles** Belgium
73 B3 **Nizamabad** India
87 E3 **Nizhnekamsk** Rus. Fed.
83 H3 **Nizhneudinsk** Rus. Fed.
82 G2 **Nizhnevartovsk** Rus. Fed.
89 F3 **Nizhniy Kislyay** Rus. Fed.
87 D3 **Nizhniy Lomov** Rus. Fed.
87 D3 **Nizhniy Novgorod** Rus. Fed.
86 E2 **Nizhniy Odes** Rus. Fed.
86 E3 **Nizhniy Tagil** Rus. Fed.
83 G2 **Nizhnyaya Tunguska** *r.* Rus. Fed.
91 C1 **Nizhyn** Ukr.
119 D3 **Njinjo** Tanz.
119 D3 **Njombe** Tanz.
121 C2 **Nkhotakota** Malawi
118 A2 **Nkongsamba** Cameroon
123 C3 **Nkululeko** S. Africa
123 C3 **Nkwenkwezi** S. Africa
67 B4 **Nobeoka** Japan
52 B1 **Noccundra** Austr.
144 A1 **Nogales** Mex.
138 A2 **Nogales** U.S.A.
104 C2 **Nogent-le-Rotrou** France
89 E2 **Noginsk** Rus. Fed.
74 B2 **Nohar** India
100 C3 **Nohfelden** Ger.
104 B2 **Noirmoutier, Île de** *i.* France
104 B2 **Noirmoutier-en-l'Île** France
67 C4 **Nojima-zaki** *c.* Japan
74 B2 **Nokha** India
93 H3 **Nokia** Fin.
74 A2 **Nok Kundi** Pak.
118 B2 **Nola** C.A.R.
86 D3 **Nolinsk** Rus. Fed.
123 C3 **Nomonde** S. Africa
123 D2 **Nondweni** S. Africa
62 B2 **Nong Khai** Thai.
52 A2 **Nonning** Austr.
144 B2 **Nonoava** Mex.
65 B2 **Nonsan** S. Korea
63 B2 **Nonthaburi** Thai.
122 B3 **Nonzwakazi** S. Africa
77 C3 **Norak** Tajik.
130 C2 **Noranda** Can.
82 C1 **Nordaustlandet** *i.* Svalbard
128 C2 **Nordegg** Can.
100 C1 **Norden** Ger.
83 H1 **Nordenshel'da, Arkhipelag** *is* Rus. Fed.
100 C1 **Norderney** Ger.
100 C1 **Norderney** *i.* Ger.
101 E1 **Norderstedt** Ger.
93 E3 **Nordfjordeid** Norway
101 E2 **Nordhausen** Ger.
101 D1 **Nordholz** Ger.
100 C1 **Nordhorn** Ger.
92 I1 **Nordkapp** *c.* Norway
92 F3 **Nordli** Norway
102 C2 **Nördlingen** Ger.
92 G3 **Nordmaling** Sweden
94 B1 **Norðoyar** *i.* Faroe Is
97 C2 **Nore** *r.* Rep. of Ireland
137 D2 **Norfolk** *NE* U.S.A.
141 D3 **Norfolk** *VA* U.S.A.
49 E4 **Norfolk Island** *terr.* S. Pacific Ocean

93 E3 **Norheimsund** Norway
82 G2 **Noril'sk** Rus. Fed.
139 D1 **Norman** U.S.A.
Normandes, Îles *is* Europe *see* **Channel Islands**
51 D1 **Normanton** Austr.
93 G4 **Norrköping** Sweden
93 G4 **Norrtälje** Sweden
50 B3 **Norseman** Austr.
92 G3 **Norsjö** Sweden
98 C1 **Northallerton** U.K.
50 A2 **Northampton** Austr.
99 C2 **Northampton** U.K.
73 D3 **North Andaman** *i.* India
129 D2 **North Battleford** Can.
130 C2 **North Bay** Can.
130 C1 **North Belcher Islands** Can.
96 C2 **North Berwick** U.K.
North Cape Norway *see* Nordkapp
54 B1 **North Cape** *c.* N.Z.
130 A1 **North Caribou Lake** Can.
143 E1 **North Carolina** *state* U.S.A.
130 B2 **North Channel** *lake channel* Can.
96 A3 **North Channel** U.K.
128 B3 **North Cowichan** Can.
136 C1 **North Dakota** *state* U.S.A.
99 C3 **North Downs** *hills* U.K.
143 E3 **Northeast Providence Channel** Bahamas
101 D2 **Northeim** Ger.
122 A2 **Northern Cape** *prov.* S. Africa
129 E2 **Northern Indian Lake** Can.
97 C1 **Northern Ireland** *prov.* U.K.
48 D2 **Northern Mariana Islands** *terr.* N. Pacific Ocean
50 C1 **Northern Territory** *admin. div.* Austr.
96 C2 **North Esk** *r.* U.K.
137 E2 **Northfield** U.S.A.
99 D3 **North Foreland** *c.* U.K.
54 B1 **North Island** N.Z.
129 E2 **North Knife Lake** Can.
65 B1 **North Korea** *country* Asia
62 A1 **North Lakhimpur** India
136 C2 **North Platte** U.S.A.
136 C2 **North Platte** *r.* U.S.A.
96 C1 **North Ronaldsay** *i.* U.K.
94 D2 **North Sea** *sea* Europe
130 A1 **North Spirit Lake** *l.* Can.
53 D1 **North Stradbroke Island** Austr.
54 B1 **North Taranaki Bight** *b.* N.Z.
130 C1 **North Twin Island** Can.
98 B1 **North Tyne** *r.* U.K.
96 A2 **North Uist** *i.* U.K.
131 D2 **Northumberland Strait** Can.
122 C2 **North West** *prov.* S. Africa
50 A2 **North West Cape** Austr.
143 E3 **Northwest Providence Channel** Bahamas
131 E1 **North West River** Can.
128 B1 **Northwest Territories** *admin. div.* Can.
98 C1 **North York Moors** *moorland* U.K.
140 C3 **Norton** U.S.A.
121 C2 **Norton** Zimbabwe
140 C2 **Norwalk** U.S.A.
93 F3 **Norway** *country* Europe
129 E2 **Norway House** Can.
160 A3 **Norwegian Sea** N. Atlantic Ocean
99 D2 **Norwich** U.K.
141 E2 **Norwich** *CT* U.S.A.
141 D2 **Norwich** *NY* U.S.A.
66 D2 **Noshiro** Japan
91 C1 **Nosivka** Ukr.
122 B2 **Nosop** *watercourse* Africa
86 E2 **Nosovaya** Rus. Fed.
79 C2 **Noşratābād** Iran
Nossob *watercourse* Africa *see* **Nosop**
103 D1 **Noteć** *r.* Pol.
93 E4 **Notodden** Norway
67 C3 **Noto-hantō** *pen.* Japan
131 D2 **Notre Dame, Monts** *mts* Can.
131 E2 **Notre Dame Bay** Can.
130 C1 **Nottaway** *r.* Can.
99 C2 **Nottingham** U.K.
114 A2 **Nouâdhibou** Maur.
114 A3 **Nouakchott** Maur.
114 A3 **Nouâmghâr** Maur.
49 E4 **Nouméa** New Caledonia
114 B3 **Nouna** Burkina
154 B2 **Nova Esperança** Brazil
155 D2 **Nova Friburgo** Brazil
109 C1 **Nova Gradiška** Croatia
154 C2 **Nova Granada** Brazil
155 D2 **Nova Iguaçu** Brazil
91 C2 **Nova Kakhovka** Ukr.
155 D1 **Nova Lima** Brazil
154 B2 **Nova Londrina** Brazil
91 C2 **Nova Odesa** Ukr.
150 B1 **Nova Paraiso** Brazil
131 D2 **Nova Scotia** *prov.* Can.
155 D1 **Nova Venécia** Brazil
83 K1 **Novaya Sibir', Ostrov** *i.* Rus. Fed.
86 E1 **Novaya Zemlya** *is* Rus. Fed.
103 D2 **Nové Zámky** Slovakia
91 C1 **Novhorod-Sivers'kyy** Ukr.
110 B2 **Novi Iskŭr** Bulg.
108 A2 **Novi Ligure** Italy
109 D2 **Novi Pazar** Serb. and Mont.
109 C1 **Novi Sad** Serb. and Mont.
87 D3 **Novoanninskiy** Rus. Fed.
150 B2 **Novo Aripuanã** Brazil
91 D2 **Novoazovs'k** Ukr.
91 E2 **Novocherkassk** Rus. Fed.
86 D2 **Novodvinsk** Rus. Fed.
152 C3 **Novo Hamburgo** Brazil
154 C2 **Novo Horizonte** Brazil
90 B1 **Novohrad-Volyns'kyy** Ukr.
103 D2 **Novo Mesto** Slovenia
91 D3 **Novomikhaylovskiy** Rus. Fed.
89 E3 **Novomoskovsk** Rus. Fed.
91 D2 **Novomoskovs'k** Ukr.
91 C2 **Novomyrhorod** Ukr.
91 C2 **Novooleksiyivka** Ukr.
91 D2 **Novopskov** Ukr.
91 D3 **Novorossiysk** Rus. Fed.
88 C2 **Novorzhev** Rus. Fed.
87 E3 **Novosergiyevka** Rus. Fed.
91 D2 **Novoshakhtinsk** Rus. Fed.
82 G3 **Novosibirsk** Rus. Fed.
83 K1 **Novosibirskiye Ostrova** *is* Rus. Fed.
89 E3 **Novosil'** Rus. Fed.
89 D2 **Novosokol'niki** Rus. Fed.
91 C2 **Novotroyits'ke** Ukr.
91 C2 **Novoukrayinka** Ukr.
90 A1 **Novovolyns'k** Ukr.
89 D3 **Novozybkov** Rus. Fed.
103 D2 **Nový Jičín** Czech Rep.
86 E2 **Novyy Bor** Rus. Fed.
91 D1 **Novyy Oskol** Rus. Fed.
86 G2 **Novyy Port** Rus. Fed.
82 G2 **Novyy Urengoy** Rus. Fed.
69 E1 **Novyy Urgal** Rus. Fed.
103 D1 **Nowogard** Pol.
53 D2 **Nowra** Austr.
81 D2 **Now Shahr** Iran
74 B1 **Nowshera** Pak.
103 E2 **Nowy Sącz** Pol.
103 E2 **Nowy Targ** Pol.
87 G2 **Noyabr'sk** Rus. Fed.
105 C2 **Noyon** France
121 C2 **Nsanje** Malawi
118 B3 **Ntandembele** Dem. Rep. Congo
119 D3 **Ntungamo** Uganda
79 C2 **Nu'aym** *reg.* Oman
116 B2 **Nubian Desert** Sudan
150 A3 **Nudo Coropuna** *mt.* Peru
129 E1 **Nueltin Lake** Can.
153 A5 **Nueva Lubecka** Arg.
145 B2 **Nueva Rosita** Mex.
144 B1 **Nuevo Casas Grandes** Mex.
144 B2 **Nuevo Ideal** Mex.
145 C2 **Nuevo Laredo** Mex.
117 C4 **Nugaal** *watercourse* Somalia
105 C2 **Nuits-St-Georges** France
62 A1 **Nu Jiang** *r.* China
49 F4 **Nuku'alofa** Tonga
76 B2 **Nukus** Uzbek.
50 B2 **Nullagine** Austr.
50 B3 **Nullarbor Plain** Austr.
115 D4 **Numan** Nigeria
67 C3 **Numazu** Japan
93 E3 **Numedal** *val.* Norway
59 C3 **Numfoor** *i.* Indon.
53 C3 **Numurkah** Austr.
127 J3 **Nunap Isua** *c.* Greenland
127 F3 **Nunavik** *reg.* Can.
129 E1 **Nunavut** *admin. div.* Can.
99 C2 **Nuneaton** U.K.
106 B1 **Nuñomoral** Spain
108 A2 **Nuoro** *Sardinia* Italy
78 B2 **Nuqrah** Saudi Arabia
52 A2 **Nuriootpa** Austr.
92 I3 **Nurmes** Fin.
101 E3 **Nürnberg** Ger.
62 A1 **Nu Shan** *mts* China
74 A2 **Nushki** Pak.
127 H2 **Nuuk** Greenland
127 H2 **Nuussuaq** Greenland
127 H2 **Nuussuaq** *pen.* Greenland
78 A2 **Nuwaybi' al Muzayyinah** Egypt
122 B3 **Nuweveldberge** *mts* S. Africa
86 F2 **Nyagan'** Rus. Fed.
75 D1 **Nyainqêntanglha Feng** *mt.* China
75 D2 **Nyainqêntanglha Shan** *mts* China
117 A3 **Nyala** Sudan
75 C2 **Nyalam** China
86 D2 **Nyandoma** Rus. Fed.
118 B3 **Nyanga** *r.* Gabon
121 C2 **Nyanga** Zimbabwe
121 C1 **Nyasa, Lake** Africa
93 F4 **Nyborg** Denmark
92 I1 **Nyborg** Norway
93 G4 **Nybro** Sweden
119 D3 **Nyeri** Kenya
75 C1 **Nyima** China
68 C3 **Nyingchi** China
103 E2 **Nyíregyháza** Hungary
93 F4 **Nykøbing** Denmark
93 G4 **Nyköping** Sweden
123 C1 **Nylstroom** S. Africa
53 C2 **Nymagee** Austr.
93 G4 **Nynäshamn** Sweden
53 C2 **Nyngan** Austr.
88 B3 **Nyoman** *r.* Belarus/Lith.
105 D3 **Nyons** France
86 E2 **Nyrob** Rus. Fed.
134 C2 **Nyssa** U.S.A.
119 C3 **Nyunzu** Dem. Rep. Congo
91 C2 **Nyzhn'ohirs'kyy** Ukr.
119 D3 **Nzega** Tanz.
114 B4 **Nzérékoré** Guinea
120 A1 **N'zeto** Angola

O

136 C2 **Oahe, Lake** U.S.A.
52 B2 **Oakbank** Austr.
142 B2 **Oakdale** U.S.A.
53 D1 **Oakey** Austr.
134 B1 **Oak Harbor** U.S.A.
140 C3 **Oak Hill** U.S.A.
135 B3 **Oakland** U.S.A.
50 B2 **Oakover** *r.* Austr.
134 B2 **Oakridge** U.S.A.
143 D1 **Oak Ridge** U.S.A.
54 B3 **Oamaru** N.Z.
64 B1 **Oas** Phil.
145 C3 **Oaxaca** Mex.
86 F2 **Ob'** *r.* Rus. Fed.
118 B2 **Obala** Cameroon
96 B2 **Oban** U.K.
106 B1 **O Barco** Spain
53 C2 **Oberon** Austr.
101 F3 **Oberpfälzer Wald** *mts* Ger.
101 F3 **Oberviechtach** Ger.
59 C3 **Obi** *i.* Indon.
151 C2 **Óbidos** Brazil
66 D2 **Obihiro** Japan
69 E1 **Obluch'ye** Rus. Fed.
89 E2 **Obninsk** Rus. Fed.
119 C2 **Obo** C.A.R.
117 C3 **Obock** Djibouti
118 B3 **Obouya** Congo
89 E3 **Oboyan'** Rus. Fed.
144 B2 **Obregón, Presa** *resr* Mex.
109 D2 **Obrenovac** Serb. and Mont.
87 E3 **Obshchiy Syrt** *hills* Rus. Fed.
86 G2 **Obskaya Guba** *sea chan.* Rus. Fed.
114 B4 **Obuasi** Ghana
90 C1 **Obukhiv** Ukr.
86 D2 **Ob"yachevo** Rus. Fed.
143 D3 **Ocala** U.S.A.
144 B2 **Ocampo** Mex.
106 C2 **Ocaña** Spain
150 A1 **Occidental, Cordillera** *mts* Col.
150 A3 **Occidental, Cordillera** *mts* Peru
141 D3 **Ocean City** U.S.A.
128 B2 **Ocean Falls** Can.
135 C4 **Oceanside** U.S.A.
91 C2 **Ochakiv** Ukr.
86 E3 **Ocher** Rus. Fed.
101 E3 **Ochsenfurt** Ger.
143 D2 **Oconee** *r.* U.S.A.
145 C3 **Ocosingo** Mex.
58 C3 **Ocussi** *enclave* East Timor
116 B2 **Oda, Jebel** *mt.* Sudan
66 D2 **Ōdate** Japan
67 C3 **Odawara** Japan
93 E3 **Odda** Norway
106 B2 **Odemira** Port.
111 C3 **Ödemiş** Turkey
93 F4 **Odense** Denmark
101 D3 **Odenwald** *reg.* Ger.
102 C1 **Oderbucht** *b.* Ger.
90 C2 **Odesa** Ukr.
139 C2 **Odessa** U.S.A.
114 B4 **Odienné** Côte d'Ivoire
103 D2 **Odra** *r.* Ger./Pol.
151 D2 **Oeiras** Brazil
100 D2 **Oelde** Ger.
136 C2 **Oelrichs** U.S.A.
101 F2 **Oelsnitz** Ger.
100 B1 **Oenkerk** Neth.
109 C2 **Ofanto** *r.* Italy
101 D2 **Offenbach am Main** Ger.
102 B2 **Offenburg** Ger.
117 C4 **Ogadēn** *reg.* Eth.
66 C3 **Oga-hantō** *pen.* Japan
67 C3 **Ōgaki** Japan
136 C2 **Ogallala** U.S.A.
115 C4 **Ogbomosho** Nigeria
134 D2 **Ogden** U.S.A.
141 D2 **Ogdensburg** U.S.A.
126 B2 **Ogilvie** *r.* Can.
126 B2 **Ogilvie Mountains** Can.
143 D2 **Oglethorpe, Mount** U.S.A.
130 B1 **Ogoki** *r.* Can.
130 B1 **Ogoki Reservoir** Can.
88 B2 **Ogre** Latvia
109 C1 **Ogulin** Croatia
140 B3 **Ohio** *r.* U.S.A.
140 C2 **Ohio** *state* U.S.A.
101 E2 **Ohrdruf** Ger.
109 D2 **Ohrid** Macedonia
151 C1 **Oiapoque** Brazil
141 D2 **Oil City** U.S.A.
100 A3 **Oise** *r.* France
67 B4 **Ōita** Japan
144 B2 **Ojinaga** Mex.
152 B3 **Ojos del Salado, Nevado** *mt.* Arg./Chile
89 F2 **Oka** *r.* Rus. Fed.
120 A3 **Okahandja** Namibia
120 A3 **Okakarara** Namibia
128 C3 **Okanagan Falls** Can.
128 C3 **Okanagan Lake** Can.
134 C1 **Okanogan** U.S.A.
134 C1 **Okanogan** *r.* U.S.A.
74 B1 **Okara** Pak.
120 B2 **Okavango** *r.* Botswana/Namibia
120 B2 **Okavango Delta** *swamp* Botswana
67 C3 **Okaya** Japan
67 B4 **Okayama** Japan
67 C4 **Okazaki** Japan
143 D3 **Okeechobee, Lake** U.S.A.
143 D2 **Okefenokee Swamp** U.S.A.
99 A3 **Okehampton** U.K.
74 A2 **Okha** India
83 K3 **Okha** Rus. Fed.
75 C2 **Okhaldhunga** Nepal
83 K3 **Okhotka** *r.* Rus. Fed.
83 K3 **Okhotsk** Rus. Fed.
156 C2 **Okhotsk, Sea of** Japan/Rus. Fed.
91 C1 **Okhtyrka** Ukr.
69 E3 **Okinawa** *i.* Japan
67 B3 **Oki-shotō** *is* Japan
139 D1 **Oklahoma** *state* U.S.A.
139 D1 **Oklahoma City** U.S.A.
139 D1 **Okmulgee** U.S.A.
78 A2 **Oko, Wadi** *watercourse* Sudan
118 B3 **Okondja** Gabon
128 C2 **Okotoks** Can.
89 D3 **Okovskiy Les** *for.* Rus. Fed.
118 B3 **Okoyo** Congo
92 H1 **Øksfjord** Norway
62 A2 **Oktwin** Myanmar
86 D2 **Oktyabr'skiy** *Arkhangel'skaya Oblast'* Rus. Fed.
83 L3 **Oktyabr'skiy** *Kamchatskaya Oblast'* Rus. Fed.
87 E3 **Oktyabr'skiy** *Respublika Bashkortostan* Rus. Fed.
86 F2 **Oktyabr'skoye** Rus. Fed.
83 H1 **Oktyabr'skoy Revolyutsii, Ostrov** *i.* Rus. Fed.
89 D2 **Okulovka** Rus. Fed.
66 C2 **Okushiri-tō** *i.* Japan
92 □A3 **Ólafsvík** Iceland
93 G4 **Öland** *i.* Sweden
52 B2 **Olary** Austr.
153 B4 **Olavarría** Arg.
103 D1 **Oława** Pol.
108 A2 **Olbia** *Sardinia* Italy
126 B2 **Old Crow** Can.
101 D1 **Oldenburg** Ger.
102 C1 **Oldenburg in Holstein** Ger.
100 C1 **Oldenzaal** Neth.
97 B3 **Old Head of Kinsale** *hd* Rep. of Ireland
128 C2 **Olds** Can.
129 D2 **Old Wives Lake** Can.
141 D2 **Olean** U.S.A.
103 E1 **Olecko** Pol.
83 J2 **Olekminsk** Rus. Fed.
91 C2 **Oleksandriya** Ukr.
86 C2 **Olenegorsk** Rus. Fed.
83 I2 **Olenek** Rus. Fed.
83 I2 **Olenek** *r.* Rus. Fed.
89 D2 **Olenino** Rus. Fed.
90 B1 **Olevs'k** Ukr.
106 B2 **Olhão** Port.
122 A2 **Olifants** *watercourse* Namibia
123 D1 **Olifants** S. Africa
123 D1 **Olifants** *r. Northern* S. Africa
122 A3 **Olifants** *r. W. Cape* S. Africa
122 B2 **Olifantshoek** S. Africa
154 C2 **Olímpia** Brazil
151 E2 **Olinda** Brazil
123 C1 **Oliphants Drift** S. Africa
107 C2 **Oliva** Spain
155 D2 **Oliveira** Brazil
106 B2 **Olivenza** Spain
152 B3 **Ollagüe** Chile
150 A2 **Olmos** Peru
140 B3 **Olney** U.S.A.
103 D2 **Olomouc** Czech Rep.
64 B1 **Olongapo** Phil.
104 B3 **Oloron-Ste-Marie** France
107 D1 **Olot** Spain
69 D1 **Olovyannaya** Rus. Fed.
100 C2 **Olpe** Ger.
103 E1 **Olsztyn** Pol.
110 B2 **Olt** *r.* Romania
81 C1 **Oltu** Turkey
111 B3 **Olympia** Greece
134 B1 **Olympia** U.S.A.
111 B2 **Olympos** *mt.* Greece
134 B1 **Olympus, Mount** U.S.A.
83 M3 **Olyutorskiy, Mys** *c.* Rus. Fed.
97 C1 **Omagh** U.K.
137 D2 **Omaha** U.S.A.
79 C2 **Oman** *country* Asia
79 C2 **Oman, Gulf of** Asia
120 A3 **Omaruru** Namibia
120 B2 **Omatako** *watercourse* Namibia
116 B3 **Omdurman** Sudan
53 C3 **Omeo** Austr.
145 C3 **Ometepec** Mex.
78 A3 **Om Hajēr** Eritrea
128 B2 **Omineca Mountains** Can.
67 C3 **Ōmiya** Japan
100 C1 **Ommen** Neth.
83 L2 **Omolon** *r.* Rus. Fed.
100 B3 **Omont** France
82 F3 **Omsk** Rus. Fed.
83 L2 **Omsukchan** Rus. Fed.
110 C1 **Omu, Vârful** *mt.* Romania
67 A4 **Ōmura** Japan
141 D3 **Onancock** U.S.A.
140 C1 **Onaping Lake** Can.
131 C2 **Onatchiway, Lac** *l.* Can.
120 A2 **Oncócua** Angola
122 B3 **Onderstedorings** S. Africa
120 A2 **Ondjiva** Angola
86 C2 **Onega** Rus. Fed.
86 C2 **Onega** *r.* Rus. Fed.
86 C2 **Onega, Lake** *l.* Rus. Fed.
128 B2 **100 Mile House** Can.
141 D2 **Oneida Lake** U.S.A.

137 D2 **O'Neill** U.S.A.
141 D2 **Oneonta** U.S.A.
110 C1 **Oneşti** Romania
Onezhskoye, Ozero *l.* Rus. Fed. *see* **Onega, Lake**
122 B2 **Ongers** *watercourse* S. Africa
65 B2 **Ongjin** N. Korea
73 C3 **Ongole** India
121 □D3 **Onilahy** *r.* Madag.
115 C4 **Onitsha** Nigeria
122 A2 **Onseepkans** S. Africa
50 A2 **Onslow** Austr.
143 E2 **Onslow Bay** U.S.A.
130 A1 **Ontario** *prov.* Can.
134 C2 **Ontario** U.S.A.
141 D2 **Ontario, Lake** Can./U.S.A.
51 C2 **Oodnadatta** Austr.
Oostende Belgium *see* **Ostend**
100 B2 **Oosterhout** Neth.
100 A2 **Oosterschelde** *est.* Neth.
100 B1 **Oost-Vlieland** Neth.
128 B2 **Ootsa Lake** Can.
128 B2 **Ootsa Lake** *l.* Can.
118 C3 **Opala** Dem. Rep. Congo
130 C1 **Opataca, Lac** *l.* Can.
103 D2 **Opava** Czech Rep.
143 C2 **Opelika** U.S.A.
142 B2 **Opelousas** U.S.A.
130 C1 **Opinaca, Réservoir** *resr* Can.
131 D1 **Opiscotéo, Lac** *l.* Can.
88 C2 **Opochka** Rus. Fed.
144 A2 **Opodepe** Mex.
103 D1 **Opole** Pol.
106 B1 **Oporto** Port.
54 C1 **Opotiki** N.Z.
93 E3 **Oppdal** Norway
54 B1 **Opunake** N.Z.
120 A2 **Opuwo** Namibia
110 B1 **Oradea** Romania
109 D2 **Orahovac** Serb. and Mont.
114 B1 **Oran** Alg.
152 B3 **Orán** Arg.
65 B1 **Ŏrang** N. Korea
53 C2 **Orange** Austr.
105 C3 **Orange** France
122 A2 **Orange** *r.* Namibia/S. Africa
139 E2 **Orange** U.S.A.
143 D2 **Orangeburg** U.S.A.
140 C2 **Orangeville** Can.
101 F1 **Oranienburg** Ger.
122 A2 **Oranjemund** Namibia
120 B3 **Orapa** Botswana
110 B1 **Orăştie** Romania
108 B2 **Orbetello** Italy
53 C3 **Orbost** Austr.
50 B1 **Ord, Mount** Austr.
106 B1 **Ordes** Spain
80 B1 **Ordu** Turkey
Ordzhonikidze Rus. Fed. *see* **Vladikavkaz**
91 C2 **Ordzhonikidze** Ukr.
93 G4 **Örebro** Sweden
134 B2 **Oregon** *state* U.S.A.
134 B1 **Oregon City** U.S.A.
87 C3 **Orekhovo-Zuyevo** Rus. Fed.
89 E3 **Orel** Rus. Fed.
83 K3 **Orel', Ozero** *l.* Rus. Fed.
135 D2 **Orem** U.S.A.
111 C3 **Ören** Turkey
87 E3 **Orenburg** Rus. Fed.
54 A3 **Orepuki** N.Z.
93 F4 **Öresund** *str.* Denmark/Sweden
99 D2 **Orford Ness** *hd* U.K.
111 C3 **Orhaneli** Turkey
111 C2 **Orhangazi** Turkey
83 I3 **Orhon Gol** *r.* Mongolia
152 B2 **Oriental, Cordillera** *mts* Bol.
150 A1 **Oriental, Cordillera** *mts* Col.
150 A3 **Oriental, Cordillera** *mts* Peru
107 C2 **Orihuela** Spain
91 D2 **Orikhiv** Ukr.
130 C2 **Orillia** Can.
150 B1 **Orinoco** *r.* Col./Venez.
150 B1 **Orinoco Delta** Venez.
93 H4 **Orissaare** Estonia
108 A3 **Oristano** *Sardinia* Italy
93 I3 **Orivesi** *l.* Fin.
151 C2 **Oriximiná** Brazil
145 C3 **Orizaba** Mex.
145 C3 **Orizaba, Pico de** *vol.* Mex.
92 E3 **Orkanger** Norway
93 F4 **Örkelljunga** Sweden
92 E3 **Orkla** *r.* Norway
96 C1 **Orkney Islands** *is* U.K.
154 C2 **Orlândia** Brazil
143 D3 **Orlando** U.S.A.
104 C2 **Orléans** France
74 A2 **Ormara** Pak.
64 B1 **Ormoc** Phil.
98 B2 **Ormskirk** U.K.
92 G3 **Örnsköldsvik** Sweden
114 B3 **Orodara** Burkina
134 C1 **Orofino** U.S.A.
Oroqen Zizhiqi China *see* **Alihe**
64 B2 **Oroquieta** Phil.
108 A2 **Orosei** *Sardinia* Italy
108 A2 **Orosei, Golfo di** *b. Sardinia* Italy
103 E2 **Orosháza** Hungary
135 B3 **Oroville** U.S.A.
52 A2 **Orroroo** Austr.
89 D3 **Orsha** Belarus
87 E3 **Orsk** Rus. Fed.
93 E3 **Ørsta** Norway
106 B1 **Ortegal, Cabo** *c.* Spain
104 B3 **Orthez** France
106 B1 **Ortigueira** Spain
137 D1 **Ortonville** U.S.A.
83 J2 **Orulgan, Khrebet** *mts* Rus. Fed.
81 C2 **Orūmīyeh, Daryācheh-ye** *salt l.* Iran
152 B2 **Oruro** Bol.
108 B2 **Orvieto** Italy
146 B4 **Osa, Península de** *pen.* Costa Rica
137 E3 **Osage** *r.* U.S.A.
67 C4 **Ōsaka** Japan
101 E1 **Oschersleben (Bode)** Ger.
108 A2 **Oschiri** *Sardinia* Italy
89 E3 **Osetr** *r.* Rus. Fed.
77 D2 **Osh** Kyrg.
120 A2 **Oshakati** Namibia
130 C2 **Oshawa** Can.
66 C2 **Ō-shima** *i.* Japan
67 C4 **Ō-shima** *i.* Japan
140 B2 **Oshkosh** U.S.A.
81 C2 **Oshnovīyeh** Iran
115 C4 **Oshogbo** Nigeria
118 B3 **Oshwe** Dem. Rep. Congo
109 C1 **Osijek** Croatia
128 B2 **Osilinka** *r.* Can.
108 B2 **Osimo** Italy
123 D2 **Osizweni** S. Africa
137 E2 **Oskaloosa** U.S.A.
93 G4 **Oskarshamn** Sweden
89 E3 **Oskol** *r.* Rus. Fed.
93 F4 **Oslo** Norway
93 F4 **Oslofjorden** *sea chan.* Norway
80 B1 **Osmancık** Turkey
111 C2 **Osmaneli** Turkey
80 B2 **Osmaniye** Turkey
88 C2 **Os'mino** Rus. Fed.
100 D1 **Osnabrück** Ger.
153 A5 **Osorno** Chile
106 C1 **Osorno** Spain
128 C3 **Osoyoos** Can.
100 B2 **Oss** Neth.
51 D4 **Ossa, Mount** Austr.
83 L3 **Ossora** Rus. Fed.
89 D2 **Ostashkov** Rus. Fed.
101 D1 **Oste** *r.* Ger.
100 A2 **Ostend** Belgium
101 E1 **Osterburg (Altmark)** Ger.
93 F3 **Österdalälven** *l.* Sweden
101 D1 **Osterholz-Scharmbeck** Ger.
101 E2 **Osterode am Harz** Ger.
92 F3 **Östersund** Sweden
Ostfriesische Inseln *is* Ger. *see* **East Frisian Islands**
100 C1 **Ostfriesland** *reg.* Ger.
93 G3 **Östhammar** Sweden
103 D2 **Ostrava** Czech Rep.
103 D1 **Ostróda** Pol.
89 E3 **Ostrogozhsk** Rus. Fed.
103 E1 **Ostrołęka** Pol.
101 F2 **Ostrov** Czech Rep.
88 C2 **Ostrov** Rus. Fed.
103 E1 **Ostrowiec Świętokrzyski** Pol.
103 E1 **Ostrów Mazowiecka** Pol.
103 D1 **Ostrów Wielkopolski** Pol.
110 B2 **Osŭm** *r.* Bulg.
67 B4 **Ōsumi-kaikyō** *sea chan.* Japan
67 B4 **Ōsumi-shotō** *is* Japan
106 B2 **Osuna** Spain
141 D2 **Oswego** U.S.A.
99 B2 **Oswestry** U.K.
67 C3 **Ōta** Japan
54 B3 **Otago Peninsula** N.Z.
54 C2 **Otaki** N.Z.
66 D2 **Otaru** Japan
120 A2 **Otavi** Namibia
134 C1 **Othello** U.S.A.
120 A3 **Otjiwarongo** Namibia
117 B3 **Otoro, Jebel** *mt.* Sudan
93 E4 **Otra** *r.* Norway
109 C2 **Otranto, Strait of** Albania/Italy
67 C3 **Ōtsu** Japan
93 E3 **Otta** Norway
130 C2 **Ottawa** Can.
130 C2 **Ottawa** *r.* Can.
140 B2 **Ottawa** *IL* U.S.A.
137 D3 **Ottawa** *KS* U.S.A.
130 B1 **Otter Rapids** Can.
100 B2 **Ottignies** Belgium
137 E2 **Ottumwa** U.S.A.
150 A2 **Otuzco** Peru
52 B3 **Otway, Cape** Austr.
142 B2 **Ouachita** *r.* U.S.A.
142 B2 **Ouachita, Lake** U.S.A.
142 B2 **Ouachita Mountains** U.S.A.
118 C2 **Ouadda** C.A.R.
115 D3 **Ouaddaï** *reg.* Chad
114 B3 **Ouagadougou** Burkina
114 B3 **Ouahigouya** Burkina
114 B3 **Oualâta** Maur.
118 C2 **Ouanda-Djailé** C.A.R.
114 B2 **Ouarâne** *reg.* Maur.
115 C1 **Ouargla** Alg.
114 B1 **Ouarzazate** Morocco
100 A2 **Oudenaarde** Belgium
122 B3 **Oudtshoorn** S. Africa
107 C2 **Oued Tlélat** Alg.
104 A2 **Ouessant, Île d'** *i.* France
118 B2 **Ouesso** Congo
114 B1 **Oujda** Morocco
107 D2 **Ouled Farès** Alg.
92 I2 **Oulu** Fin.
92 I3 **Oulujärvi** *l.* Fin.

108 A1 **Oulx** Italy
115 E3 **Oum-Chalouba** Chad
115 D3 **Oum-Hadjer** Chad
115 E3 **Ounianga Kébir** Chad
100 B2 **Oupeye** Belgium
100 C3 **Our** *r.* Ger./Lux.
106 B1 **Ourense** Spain
154 C2 **Ourinhos** Brazil
155 D2 **Ouro Preto** Brazil
100 B2 **Ourthe** *r.* Belgium
98 C2 **Ouse** *r.* U.K.
131 D2 **Outardes** *r.* Can.
131 D1 **Outardes Quatre, Réservoir** *resr* Can.
96 A2 **Outer Hebrides** *is* U.K.
120 A3 **Outjo** Namibia
129 D2 **Outlook** Can.
92 I3 **Outokumpu** Fin.
52 B3 **Ouyen** Austr.
106 B1 **Ovar** Port.
92 H2 **Överkalix** Sweden
135 D3 **Overton** U.S.A.
92 H2 **Övertorneå** Sweden
106 B1 **Oviedo** Spain
93 E3 **Øvre Årdal** Norway
93 F3 **Øvre Rendal** Norway
90 B1 **Ovruch** Ukr.
118 B3 **Owando** Congo
67 C4 **Owase** Japan
137 E2 **Owatonna** U.S.A.
140 B3 **Owensboro** U.S.A.
135 C3 **Owens Lake** U.S.A.
130 B2 **Owen Sound** Can.
115 C4 **Owerri** Nigeria
140 C2 **Owosso** U.S.A.
134 C2 **Owyhee** U.S.A.
134 C2 **Owyhee** *r.* U.S.A.
54 B2 **Oxford** N.Z.
99 C3 **Oxford** U.K.
142 C2 **Oxford** U.S.A.
129 E2 **Oxford Lake** Can.
52 B2 **Oxley** Austr.
Ox Mountains Rep. of Ireland *see* **Slieve Gamph**
135 C4 **Oxnard** U.S.A.
67 C3 **Oyama** Japan
118 B2 **Oyem** Gabon
129 C2 **Oyen** Can.
105 D2 **Oyonnax** France
64 B2 **Ozamiz** Phil.
142 C2 **Ozark** U.S.A.
137 E3 **Ozark Plateau** U.S.A.
137 E3 **Ozarks, Lake of the** U.S.A.
83 L3 **Ozernovskiy** Rus. Fed.
88 B3 **Ozersk** Rus. Fed.
89 E3 **Ozery** Rus. Fed.
87 D3 **Ozinki** Rus. Fed.

P

127 H2 **Paamiut** Greenland
122 A3 **Paarl** S. Africa
103 D1 **Pabianice** Pol.
75 C2 **Pabna** Bangl.
74 A2 **Pab Range** *mts* Pak.
109 C3 **Pachino** *Sicily* Italy
145 C2 **Pachuca** Mex.
156 **Pacific Ocean**
103 D1 **Paczków** Pol.
60 B2 **Padang** Indon.
60 B1 **Padang Endau** Malaysia
60 B2 **Padangpanjang** Indon.
60 A1 **Padangsidimpuan** Indon.
101 D2 **Paderborn** Ger.
Padova Italy *see* **Padua**
139 D3 **Padre Island** U.S.A.
52 B3 **Padthaway** Austr.
108 B1 **Padua** Italy
140 B3 **Paducah** *KY* U.S.A.
139 C2 **Paducah** *TX* U.S.A.
65 B1 **Paegam** N. Korea
65 A2 **Paengnyŏng-do** *i.* S. Korea
54 C1 **Paeroa** N.Z.
80 B2 **Pafos** Cyprus
109 C2 **Pag** Croatia
64 B2 **Pagadian** Phil.
60 B2 **Pagai Selatan** *i.* Indon.
60 B2 **Pagai Utara** *i.* Indon.
59 D1 **Pagan** *i.* N. Mariana Is
61 C2 **Pagatan** Indon.
138 A1 **Page** U.S.A.
88 B2 **Pagėgiai** Lith.
136 B3 **Pagosa Springs** U.S.A.
88 C2 **Paide** Estonia
93 I3 **Päijänne** *l.* Fin.
75 C2 **Paikü Co** *l.* China
138 A1 **Painted Desert** U.S.A.
96 B3 **Paisley** U.K.
92 H2 **Pajala** Sweden
150 B1 **Pakaraima Mountains** Brazil
150 C1 **Pakaraima Mountains** Guyana
74 A2 **Pakistan** *country* Asia
62 A1 **Pakokku** Myanmar
88 B2 **Pakruojis** Lith.
103 D2 **Paks** Hungary
130 A1 **Pakwash Lake** Can.
63 B2 **Pakxé** Laos
115 D4 **Pala** Chad
60 B2 **Palabuhanratu, Teluk** *b.* Indon.
111 C3 **Palaikastro** Greece
111 B3 **Palaiochora** Greece
122 B1 **Palamakoloi** Botswana
107 D1 **Palamós** Spain
83 L3 **Palana** Rus. Fed.
64 B1 **Palanan** Phil.
61 C2 **Palangkaraya** Indon.
74 B2 **Palanpur** India
120 B3 **Palapye** Botswana
83 L2 **Palatka** Rus. Fed.
143 D3 **Palatka** U.S.A.
59 C2 **Palau** *country* N. Pacific Ocean
63 A2 **Palaw** Myanmar
64 A2 **Palawan** *i.* Phil.
93 H4 **Paldiski** Estonia
60 B2 **Palembang** Indon.
106 C1 **Palencia** Spain
145 C3 **Palenque** Mex.
108 B3 **Palermo** *Sicily* Italy
139 D2 **Palestine** U.S.A.
62 A1 **Paletwa** Myanmar
74 B2 **Pali** India
109 C2 **Palinuro, Capo** *c.* Italy
111 B3 **Paliouri, Akra** *pt* Greece
100 B3 **Paliseul** Belgium
92 I3 **Paljakka** *hill* Fin.
88 C2 **Palkino** Rus. Fed.
73 B4 **Palk Strait** India/Sri Lanka
54 C2 **Palliser, Cape** N.Z.
106 B2 **Palma del Río** Spain
107 D2 **Palma de Mallorca** Spain
151 D3 **Palmas** Brazil
154 B3 **Palmas** Brazil
114 B4 **Palmas, Cape** Liberia
154 C3 **Palmeira** Brazil
151 D2 **Palmeirais** Brazil
55 P2 **Palmer Land** *reg.* Antarctica
54 C2 **Palmerston North** N.Z.
109 C3 **Palmi** Italy
145 C2 **Palmillas** Mex.
150 A1 **Palmira** Col.
135 C4 **Palm Springs** U.S.A.
49 G3 **Palmyra Atoll** N. Pacific Ocean
117 B3 **Paloich** Sudan
145 C3 **Palomares** Mex.
107 C2 **Palos, Cabo de** *c.* Spain
92 I3 **Paltamo** Fin.
58 B3 **Palu** Indon.
83 M2 **Palyavaam** *r.* Rus. Fed.
104 C3 **Pamiers** France
77 D3 **Pamir** *mts* Asia
143 E1 **Pamlico Sound** *sea chan.* U.S.A.
152 B2 **Pampa Grande** Bol.
153 B4 **Pampas** *reg.* Arg.
150 A1 **Pamplona** Col.
107 C1 **Pamplona** Spain
111 D2 **Pamukova** Turkey
60 B2 **Panaitan** *i.* Indon.
73 B3 **Panaji** India
146 B4 **Panama** *country* Central America
146 C4 **Panamá, Golfo de** *g.* Panama
146 C4 **Panama Canal** Panama
146 C4 **Panama City** Panama
142 C2 **Panama City** U.S.A.
135 C3 **Panamint Range** *mts* U.S.A.
61 B1 **Panarik** Indon.
64 B1 **Panay** *i.* Phil.
109 D2 **Pančevo** Serb. and Mont.
64 B1 **Pandan** Phil.
75 C2 **Pandaria** India
73 B3 **Pandharpur** India
88 B2 **Panevėžys** Lith.
61 C2 **Pangkalanbuun** Indon.
60 A1 **Pangkalansusu** Indon.
60 B2 **Pangkalpinang** Indon.
127 G2 **Pangnirtung** Can.
86 G2 **Pangody** Rus. Fed.
89 F3 **Panino** Rus. Fed.
74 B2 **Panipat** India
74 A2 **Panjgur** Pak.
65 C1 **Pan Ling** *mts* China
75 C2 **Panna** India
50 A2 **Pannawonica** Austr.
154 B2 **Panorama** Brazil
65 B1 **Panshi** China
145 C2 **Pánuco** Mex.
71 A3 **Panxian** China
62 B1 **Panzhihua** China
109 C3 **Paola** Italy
63 B2 **Paôy Pêt** Cambodia
103 D2 **Pápa** Hungary
54 B1 **Papakura** N.Z.
145 C2 **Papantla** Mex.
49 H5 **Papeete** French Polynesia
100 C1 **Papenburg** Ger.
59 D3 **Papua, Gulf of** P.N.G.
59 D3 **Papua New Guinea** *country* Oceania
62 A2 **Papun** Myanmar
50 A2 **Paraburdoo** Austr.
154 C1 **Paracatu** Brazil
155 C1 **Paracatu** *r.* Brazil
52 A2 **Parachilna** Austr.
109 D2 **Paraćin** Serb. and Mont.
155 D1 **Pará de Minas** Brazil
135 B3 **Paradise** U.S.A.
142 B1 **Paragould** U.S.A.
151 C3 **Paraguai** *r.* Brazil
152 C3 **Paraguay** *r.* Arg./Para.
152 C3 **Paraguay** *country* S. America
155 D2 **Paraíba do Sul** *r.* Brazil
154 B1 **Paraíso** Brazil
145 C3 **Paraíso** Mex.
114 C4 **Parakou** Benin
151 C1 **Paramaribo** Suriname
83 L3 **Paramushir, Ostrov** *i.* Rus. Fed.

152 B4 **Paraná** Arg.
154 A3 **Paraná** *r.* S. America
154 C3 **Paranaguá** Brazil
154 B1 **Paranaíba** Brazil
154 B2 **Paranaíba** *r.* Brazil
154 B2 **Paranapanema** *r.* Brazil
154 B2 **Paranapiacaba, Serra** *mts* Brazil
154 B2 **Paranavaí** Brazil
54 B2 **Paraparaumu** N.Z.
155 D2 **Parati** Brazil
154 B1 **Paraúna** Brazil
105 C2 **Paray-le-Monial** France
73 B3 **Parbhani** India
101 E1 **Parchim** Ger.
155 E1 **Pardo** *r. Bahia* Brazil
154 B2 **Pardo** *r. Mato Grosso do Sul* Brazil
154 C2 **Pardo** *r. São Paulo* Brazil
103 D1 **Pardubice** Czech Rep.
150 B3 **Parecis, Serra dos** *hills* Brazil
130 C2 **Parent, Lac** *l.* Can.
58 B3 **Parepare** Indon.
89 D2 **Parfino** Rus. Fed.
111 B3 **Parga** Greece
109 C3 **Parghelia** Italy
147 D3 **Paria, Gulf of** Trin. and Tob./Venez.
150 B1 **Parima, Serra** *mts* Brazil
151 C2 **Parintins** Brazil
104 C2 **Paris** France
142 C1 **Paris** *TN* U.S.A.
139 D2 **Paris** *TX* U.S.A.
93 H3 **Parkano** Fin.
138 A2 **Parker** U.S.A.
140 C3 **Parkersburg** U.S.A.
53 C2 **Parkes** Austr.
140 A1 **Park Falls** U.S.A.
137 D1 **Park Rapids** U.S.A.
108 B2 **Parma** Italy
151 D2 **Parnaíba** Brazil
151 D2 **Parnaíba** *r.* Brazil
111 B3 **Parnassos** *mt.* Greece
54 B2 **Parnassus** N.Z.
111 B3 **Parnon** *mts* Greece
88 B2 **Pärnu** Estonia
65 B2 **P'aro-ho** *l.* S. Korea
52 B2 **Paroo** *watercourse* Austr.
76 C3 **Paropamisus** *mts* Afgh.
111 C3 **Paros** *i.* Greece
144 B2 **Parras** Mex.
126 C2 **Parry, Cape** Can.
126 D1 **Parry Islands** Can.
130 B2 **Parry Sound** Can.
137 D3 **Parsons** U.S.A.
101 D2 **Partenstein** Ger.
104 B2 **Parthenay** France
97 B2 **Partry Mountains** Rep. of Ireland
151 C2 **Paru** *r.* Brazil
135 C4 **Pasadena** U.S.A.
62 A2 **Pasawng** Myanmar
142 C2 **Pascagoula** U.S.A.
110 C1 **Paşcani** Romania
134 C1 **Pasco** U.S.A.
102 C1 **Pasewalk** Ger.
129 D2 **Pasfield Lake** Can.
60 B1 **Pasir Putih** Malaysia
74 A2 **Pasni** Pak.
153 A5 **Paso Río Mayo** Arg.
135 B3 **Paso Robles** U.S.A.
155 D2 **Passa Tempo** Brazil
102 C2 **Passau** Ger.
152 C3 **Passo Fundo** Brazil
155 C2 **Passos** Brazil
88 C2 **Pastavy** Belarus
150 A2 **Pastaza** *r.* Peru
150 A1 **Pasto** Col.
61 C2 **Pasuruan** Indon.
88 B2 **Pasvalys** Lith.
153 A6 **Patagonia** *reg.* Arg.
75 C2 **Patan** Nepal
54 B1 **Patea** N.Z.
141 E2 **Paterson** U.S.A.
Pathein Myanmar *see* Bassein
136 B2 **Pathfinder Reservoir** U.S.A.
61 C2 **Pati** Indon.
62 A1 **Patkai Bum** *mts* India/Myanmar
111 C3 **Patmos** *i.* Greece
75 C2 **Patna** India
81 C2 **Patnos** Turkey
154 B3 **Pato Branco** Brazil
152 C4 **Patos, Lagoa dos** *l.* Brazil
155 C1 **Patos de Minas** Brazil
152 B4 **Patquía** Arg.
111 B3 **Patra** Greece
75 C2 **Patratu** India
154 C1 **Patrocínio** Brazil
63 B3 **Pattani** Thai.
63 B2 **Pattaya** Thai.
128 B2 **Pattullo, Mount** Can.
129 D2 **Patuanak** Can.
144 B3 **Pátzcuaro** Mex.
104 B3 **Pau** France
104 B2 **Pauillac** France
62 A1 **Pauk** Myanmar
151 D2 **Paulistana** Brazil
151 E2 **Paulo Afonso** Brazil
123 D2 **Paulpietersburg** S. Africa
139 D2 **Pauls Valley** U.S.A.
62 A2 **Paungde** Myanmar
155 D1 **Pavão** Brazil
108 A1 **Pavia** Italy
88 B2 **Pāvilosta** Latvia
110 C2 **Pavlikeni** Bulg.
77 D1 **Pavlodar** Kazakh.
91 D2 **Pavlohrad** Ukr.
91 E1 **Pavlovsk** Rus. Fed.
91 D2 **Pavlovskaya** Rus. Fed.
60 B2 **Payakumbuh** Indon.
134 C2 **Payette** U.S.A.
134 C2 **Payette** *r.* U.S.A.
86 F2 **Pay-Khoy, Khrebet** *hills* Rus. Fed.
152 C4 **Paysandú** Uru.
81 C1 **Pazar** Turkey
110 B2 **Pazardzhik** Bulg.
111 C3 **Pazarköy** Turkey
108 B1 **Pazin** Croatia
63 A2 **Pe** Myanmar
128 C2 **Peace** *r.* Can.
128 C2 **Peace River** Can.
135 E3 **Peale, Mount** U.S.A.
142 C2 **Pearl** *r.* U.S.A.
139 D3 **Pearsall** U.S.A.
121 C2 **Pebane** Moz.
109 D2 **Peć** Serb. and Mont.
155 D1 **Peçanha** Brazil
86 E2 **Pechora** Rus. Fed.
86 E2 **Pechora** *r.* Rus. Fed.
88 C2 **Pechory** Rus. Fed.
139 C2 **Pecos** U.S.A.
139 C3 **Pecos** *r.* U.S.A.
103 D2 **Pécs** Hungary
155 D1 **Pedra Azul** Brazil
154 C2 **Pedregulho** Brazil
151 D2 **Pedreiras** Brazil
73 C4 **Pedro, Point** Sri Lanka
151 D2 **Pedro Afonso** Brazil
154 B1 **Pedro Gomes** Brazil
152 C3 **Pedro Juan Caballero** Para.
96 C3 **Peebles** U.K.
143 E2 **Pee Dee** *r.* U.S.A.
126 C2 **Peel** *r.* Can.
98 A1 **Peel** Isle of Man
128 C2 **Peerless Lake** Can.
54 B2 **Pegasus Bay** N.Z.
101 E3 **Pegnitz** Ger.
62 A2 **Pegu** Myanmar
62 A2 **Pegu Yoma** *mts* Myanmar
153 B4 **Pehuajó** Arg.
101 E1 **Peine** Ger.
88 C2 **Peipus, Lake** Estonia/Rus. Fed.
111 B3 **Peiraias** Greece
154 B2 **Peixe** *r.* Brazil
61 B2 **Pekalongan** Indon.
60 B1 **Pekan** Malaysia
60 B1 **Pekanbaru** Indon.
Peking China *see* **Beijing**
130 B2 **Pelee Island** Can.
59 C3 **Peleng** *i.* Indon.
92 I2 **Pelkosenniemi** Fin.
122 A2 **Pella** S. Africa
59 D3 **Pelleluhu Islands** P.N.G.
92 H2 **Pello** Fin.
128 A1 **Pelly** *r.* Can.
128 A1 **Pelly Mountains** Can.
152 C4 **Pelotas** Brazil
152 C3 **Pelotas, Rio das** *r.* Brazil
141 F1 **Pemadumcook Lake** U.S.A.
61 B1 **Pemangkat** Indon.
60 A1 **Pematangsiantar** Indon.
121 D2 **Pemba** Moz.
120 B2 **Pemba** Zambia
119 D3 **Pemba Island** Tanz.
128 B2 **Pemberton** Can.
137 D1 **Pembina** *r.* U.S.A.
130 C2 **Pembroke** Can.
99 A3 **Pembroke** U.K.
145 C2 **Peña Nevada, Cerro** *mt.* Mex.
154 B2 **Penápolis** Brazil
106 B1 **Peñaranda de Bracamonte** Spain
107 C1 **Peñarroya** *mt.* Spain
106 B2 **Peñarroya-Pueblonuevo** Spain
106 B1 **Peñas, Cabo de** *c.* Spain
153 A5 **Penas, Golfo de** *g.* Chile
106 B1 **Peña Ubiña** *mt.* Spain
134 C1 **Pendleton** U.S.A.
128 B2 **Pendleton Bay** Can.
134 C1 **Pend Oreille Lake** U.S.A.
74 B3 **Penganga** *r.* India
123 D1 **Penge** S. Africa
70 C2 **Penglai** China
71 A3 **Pengshui** China
106 B2 **Peniche** Port.
98 B1 **Penicuik** U.K.
108 B2 **Penne** Italy
98 B1 **Pennines** *hills* U.K.
141 D2 **Pennsylvania** *state* U.S.A.
127 G2 **Penny Icecap** Can.
141 F2 **Penobscot** *r.* U.S.A.
52 B3 **Penola** Austr.
50 C3 **Penong** Austr.
98 B1 **Penrith** U.K.
142 C2 **Pensacola** U.S.A.
55 Q1 **Pensacola Mountains** Antarctica
61 C1 **Pensiangan** *Sabah* Malaysia
128 C3 **Penticton** Can.
96 C1 **Pentland Firth** *sea chan.* U.K.
99 B2 **Penygadair** *hill* U.K.
87 D3 **Penza** Rus. Fed.
99 A3 **Penzance** U.K.
140 B2 **Peoria** U.S.A.
107 C1 **Perales del Alfambra** Spain
51 E2 **Percy Isles** Austr.
86 F2 **Peregrebnoye** Rus. Fed.
150 A1 **Pereira** Col.
154 B2 **Pereira Barreto** Brazil
90 A2 **Peremyshlyany** Ukr.
89 E2 **Pereslavl'-Zalesskiy** Rus. Fed.

91 C1 **Pereyaslav-Khmel'nyts'kyy** Ukr.
153 B4 **Pergamino** Arg.
92 H3 **Perhonjoki** *r.* Fin.
131 C1 **Péribonca, Lac** *l.* Can.
152 B3 **Perico** Arg.
144 B2 **Pericos** Mex.
104 C2 **Périgueux** France
147 C4 **Perija, Sierra de** *mts* Venez.
153 A5 **Perito Moreno** Arg.
101 E1 **Perleberg** Ger.
86 E3 **Perm'** Rus. Fed.
52 A2 **Pernatty Lagoon** *salt flat* Austr.
105 C2 **Péronne** France
145 C3 **Perote** Mex.
104 C3 **Perpignan** France
99 A3 **Perranporth** U.K.
143 D2 **Perry** *FL* U.S.A.
143 D2 **Perry** *GA* U.S.A.
137 E2 **Perry** *IA* U.S.A.
139 C1 **Perryton** U.S.A.
137 F3 **Perryville** U.S.A.
99 B2 **Pershore** U.K.
91 D2 **Pershotravens'k** Ukr.
Persian Gulf Asia *see* **Gulf, The**
50 A3 **Perth** Austr.
96 C2 **Perth** U.K.
105 D3 **Pertuis** France
108 A2 **Pertusato, Capo** *c. Corsica* France
150 A2 **Peru** *country* S. America
157 H4 **Peru-Chile Trench** *sea feature* S. Pacific Ocean
108 B2 **Perugia** Italy
154 C2 **Peruíbe** Brazil
100 A2 **Péruwelz** Belgium
90 C2 **Pervomays'k** Ukr.
91 C2 **Pervomays'ke** Ukr.
89 F3 **Pervomayskiy** Rus. Fed.
91 D2 **Pervomays'kyy** Ukr.
108 B2 **Pesaro** Italy
108 B2 **Pescara** Italy
108 B2 **Pescara** *r.* Italy
74 B1 **Peshawar** Pak.
109 D2 **Peshkopi** Albania
109 C1 **Pesnica** Slovenia
89 E2 **Pestovo** Rus. Fed.
144 B3 **Petatlán** Mex.
140 B2 **Petenwell Lake** U.S.A.
52 A2 **Peterborough** Austr.
130 C2 **Peterborough** Can.
99 C2 **Peterborough** U.K.
96 D2 **Peterhead** U.K.
50 B2 **Petermann Ranges** *mts* Austr.
129 D2 **Peter Pond Lake** Can.
128 A2 **Petersburg** *AK* U.S.A.
141 D3 **Petersburg** *VA* U.S.A.
101 D1 **Petershagen** Ger.
131 D1 **Petit Lac Manicouagan** *l.* Can.
131 E1 **Petit Mécatina** *r.* Can.
145 D2 **Peto** Mex.
140 C1 **Petoskey** U.S.A.
80 B2 **Petra** Jordan
66 B2 **Petra Velikogo, Zaliv** *b.* Rus. Fed.
111 B2 **Petrich** Bulg.
151 D2 **Petrolina** Brazil
77 C1 **Petropavlovsk** Kazakh.
83 L3 **Petropavlovsk-Kamchatskiy** Rus. Fed.
110 B1 **Petroşani** Romania
89 F3 **Petrovskoye** Rus. Fed.
86 C2 **Petrozavodsk** Rus. Fed.
123 C2 **Petrusburg** S. Africa
123 C2 **Petrus Steyn** S. Africa
122 B3 **Petrusville** S. Africa
89 E2 **Petushki** Rus. Fed.
60 A1 **Peureula** Indon.
83 M2 **Pevek** Rus. Fed.
102 B2 **Pforzheim** Ger.
102 C2 **Pfunds** Austria
101 D3 **Pfungstadt** Ger.
123 C2 **Phahameng** S. Africa
123 D1 **Phalaborwa** S. Africa
74 B2 **Phalodi** India
63 B2 **Phang Hoei, San Khao** *mts* Thai.
63 A3 **Phangnga** Thai.
63 B2 **Phan Rang** Vietnam
63 B2 **Phan Thiêt** Vietnam
63 B3 **Phatthalung** Thai.
62 A2 **Phayao** Thai.
129 D2 **Phelps Lake** Can.
143 C2 **Phenix City** U.S.A.
63 A2 **Phet Buri** Thai.
63 B2 **Phichit** Thai.
141 D3 **Philadelphia** U.S.A.
136 C2 **Philip** U.S.A.
100 B2 **Philippeville** Belgium
100 A2 **Philippine** Neth.
64 B1 **Philippines** *country* Asia
64 B1 **Philippine Sea** N. Pacific Ocean
126 B2 **Philip Smith Mountains** U.S.A.
122 B3 **Philipstown** S. Africa
53 C3 **Phillip Island** Austr.
137 D3 **Phillipsburg** U.S.A.
123 C2 **Phiritona** S. Africa
63 B2 **Phitsanulok** Thai.
Phnom Penh Cambodia *see* **Phnum Pénh**
63 B2 **Phnum Pénh** Cambodia
138 A2 **Phoenix** U.S.A.
49 G3 **Phoenix Islands** Kiribati
63 B2 **Phon** Thai.
62 B1 **Phôngsali** Laos
62 B2 **Phrae** Thai.
63 A3 **Phuket** Thai.
63 B2 **Phumĭ Sâmraông** Cambodia
123 C2 **Phuthaditjhaba** S. Africa
108 A1 **Piacenza** Italy
110 C1 **Piatra Neamţ** Romania
151 D2 **Piauí** *r.* Brazil
108 B1 **Piave** *r.* Italy
117 B4 **Pibor** *r.* Sudan
117 B4 **Pibor Post** Sudan
142 C2 **Picayune** U.S.A.
152 B3 **Pichanal** Arg.
144 A2 **Pichilingue** Mex.
98 C1 **Pickering** U.K.
130 A1 **Pickle Lake** Can.
151 D2 **Picos** Brazil
153 B5 **Pico Truncado** Arg.
53 D2 **Picton** Austr.
145 C3 **Piedras Negras** Guat.
145 B2 **Piedras Negras** Mex.
93 I3 **Pieksämäki** Fin.
92 I3 **Pielinen** *l.* Fin.
136 C2 **Pierre** U.S.A.
105 C3 **Pierrelatte** France
123 D2 **Pietermaritzburg** S. Africa
123 C1 **Pietersburg** S. Africa
110 B1 **Pietrosa** *mt.* Romania
128 C2 **Pigeon Lake** Can.
153 B4 **Pigüé** Arg.
92 I3 **Pihtipudas** Fin.
145 C3 **Pijijiapan** Mex.
136 C3 **Pikes Peak** U.S.A.
122 A3 **Piketberg** S. Africa
140 C3 **Pikeville** U.S.A.
103 D1 **Piła** Pol.
153 C4 **Pilar** Arg.
152 C3 **Pilar** Para.
53 C2 **Pilliga** Austr.
154 C1 **Pilões, Serra dos** *mts* Brazil
150 B3 **Pimenta Bueno** Brazil
153 C4 **Pinamar** Arg.
80 B2 **Pınarbaşı** Turkey
146 B2 **Pinar del Río** Cuba
103 E1 **Pińczów** Pol.
151 D2 **Pindaré** *r.* Brazil
111 B2 **Pindos** *mts* Greece
142 B2 **Pine Bluff** U.S.A.
50 C1 **Pine Creek** Austr.
136 B2 **Pinedale** U.S.A.
86 D2 **Pinega** Rus. Fed.
129 D2 **Pinehouse Lake** Can.
111 B3 **Pineios** *r.* Greece
128 C1 **Pine Point** Can.
136 C2 **Pine Ridge** U.S.A.
123 D2 **Pinetown** S. Africa
70 B2 **Pingdingshan** China
71 A3 **Pingguo** China
71 B3 **Pingjiang** China
70 A2 **Pingliang** China
71 C3 **P'ingtung** Taiwan
71 A3 **Pingxiang** *Guangxi* China
71 B3 **Pingxiang** *Jiangxi* China
70 B2 **Pingyin** China
151 D2 **Pinheiro** Brazil
101 D1 **Pinneberg** Ger.
145 C3 **Pinotepa Nacional** Mex.
88 C3 **Pinsk** Belarus
135 D3 **Pioche** U.S.A.
119 C3 **Piodi** Dem. Rep. Congo
103 E1 **Pionki** Pol.
103 D1 **Piotrków Trybunalski** Pol.
137 D2 **Pipestone** U.S.A.
131 C2 **Pipmuacan, Réservoir** *resr* Can.
154 B2 **Piquiri** *r.* Brazil
154 C1 **Piracanjuba** Brazil
154 C2 **Piracicaba** Brazil
155 D1 **Piracicaba** *r.* Brazil
154 C2 **Piraçununga** Brazil
154 C2 **Piraí do Sul** Brazil
154 C2 **Pirajuí** Brazil
154 B1 **Piranhas** Brazil
151 E2 **Piranhas** *r.* Brazil
155 D1 **Pirapora** Brazil
154 C1 **Pires do Rio** Brazil
151 D2 **Piripiri** Brazil
59 C3 **Piru** Indon.
108 B2 **Pisa** Italy
152 A2 **Pisagua** Chile
150 A3 **Pisco** Peru
102 C2 **Písek** Czech Rep.
79 D2 **Pīshīn** Iran
145 D2 **Pisté** Mex.
109 C2 **Pisticci** Italy
108 B2 **Pistoia** Italy
106 C1 **Pisuerga** *r.* Spain
134 B2 **Pit** *r.* U.S.A.
154 B2 **Pitanga** Brazil
155 D1 **Pitangui** Brazil
49 H6 **Pitcairn Island** Pitcairn Islands
49 H6 **Pitcairn Islands** *terr.* S. Pacific Ocean
92 H2 **Piteå** Sweden
92 H2 **Piteälven** *r.* Sweden
110 B2 **Piteşti** Romania
75 C2 **Pithoragarh** India
96 C2 **Pitlochry** U.K.
128 B2 **Pitt Island** Can.
137 E3 **Pittsburg** U.S.A.
141 D2 **Pittsburgh** U.S.A.
141 E2 **Pittsfield** U.S.A.
53 D1 **Pittsworth** Austr.
155 C2 **Piumhí** Brazil
150 A2 **Piura** Peru
90 C2 **Pivdennyy Buh** *r.* Ukr.
131 E2 **Placentia** Can.
135 B3 **Placerville** U.S.A.
146 C2 **Placetas** Cuba

139 C2 **Plainview** U.S.A.
154 C1 **Planaltina** Brazil
142 B2 **Plaquemine** U.S.A.
106 B1 **Plasencia** Spain
147 C4 **Plato** Col.
137 D2 **Platte** *r.* U.S.A.
141 E2 **Plattsburgh** U.S.A.
101 F1 **Plau** Ger.
101 F2 **Plauen** Ger.
101 F1 **Plauer See** *l.* Ger.
89 E3 **Plavsk** Rus. Fed.
63 B2 **Plây Cu** Vietnam
129 E2 **Playgreen Lake** Can.
153 B4 **Plaza Huincul** Arg.
139 D3 **Pleasanton** U.S.A.
54 B2 **Pleasant Point** N.Z.
104 C2 **Pleaux** France
130 B1 **Pledger Lake** Can.
54 C1 **Plenty, Bay of** *g.* N.Z.
136 C1 **Plentywood** U.S.A.
86 D2 **Plesetsk** Rus. Fed.
131 C1 **Pletipi, Lac** *l.* Can.
100 C2 **Plettenberg** Ger.
122 B3 **Plettenberg Bay** S. Africa
110 B2 **Pleven** Bulg.
109 C2 **Pljevlja** Serb. and Mont.
109 C2 **Ploče** Croatia
103 D1 **Płock** Pol.
109 C2 **Pločno** *mt.* Bos.-Herz.
104 B2 **Ploemeur** France
110 C2 **Ploiești** Romania
89 F2 **Ploskoye** Rus. Fed.
104 B2 **Plouzané** France
110 B2 **Plovdiv** Bulg.
88 B2 **Plungė** Lith.
88 C3 **Plyeshchanitsy** Belarus
147 D3 **Plymouth** Montserrat
99 A3 **Plymouth** U.K.
140 B2 **Plymouth** U.S.A.
88 C2 **Plyussa** Rus. Fed.
102 C2 **Plzeň** Czech Rep.
114 B3 **Pô** Burkina
108 B1 **Po** *r.* Italy
77 E2 **Pobeda Peak** *mt.* China/Kyrg.
142 B1 **Pocahontas** U.S.A.
134 D2 **Pocatello** U.S.A.
90 B1 **Pochayiv** Ukr.
89 D3 **Pochep** Rus. Fed.
89 D3 **Pochinok** Rus. Fed.
145 C3 **Pochutla** Mex.
141 D3 **Pocomoke City** U.S.A.
155 C2 **Poços de Caldas** Brazil
89 D2 **Poddor'ye** Rus. Fed.
91 D1 **Podgorenskiy** Rus. Fed.
109 C2 **Podgorica** Serb. and Mont.
82 G3 **Podgornoye** Rus. Fed.
83 H2 **Podkamennaya Tunguska** *r.* Rus. Fed.
89 E2 **Podol'sk** Rus. Fed.
109 D2 **Podujevo** Serb. and Mont.
122 A2 **Pofadder** S. Africa
89 D3 **Pogar** Rus. Fed.
109 D2 **Pogradec** Albania
65 B2 **P'ohang** S. Korea
110 B2 **Poiana Mare** Romania
118 C3 **Poie** Dem. Rep. Congo
118 B3 **Pointe-Noire** Congo
126 D2 **Point Lake** Can.
140 C3 **Point Pleasant** U.S.A.
104 C2 **Poitiers** France
74 B2 **Pokaran** India
75 C2 **Pokhara** Nepal
83 J2 **Pokrovsk** Rus. Fed.
91 D2 **Pokrovskoye** Rus. Fed.
138 A1 **Polacca** U.S.A.
106 B1 **Pola de Lena** Spain
103 D1 **Poland** *country* Europe
88 C2 **Polatsk** Belarus
77 C3 **Pol-e Khomrī** Afgh.
61 C2 **Polewali** Indon.
118 B2 **Poli** Cameroon
102 C1 **Police** Pol.
109 C2 **Policoro** Italy
105 D2 **Poligny** France
64 B1 **Polillo Islands** Phil.
90 B1 **Polis'ke** Ukr.
103 D1 **Polkowice** Pol.
109 C3 **Pollino, Monte** *mt.* Italy
91 D2 **Polohy** Ukr.
90 B1 **Polonne** Ukr.
134 D1 **Polson** U.S.A.
91 C2 **Poltava** Ukr.
66 B2 **Poltavka** Rus. Fed.
91 D2 **Poltavskaya** Rus. Fed.
88 C2 **Põlva** Estonia
111 B2 **Polygyros** Greece
106 B2 **Pombal** Port.
108 B2 **Pomezia** Italy
92 I2 **Pomokaira** *reg.* Fin.
110 C2 **Pomorie** Bulg.
102 C1 **Pomorska, Zatoka** *b.* Pol.
155 D1 **Pompéu** Brazil
139 D1 **Ponca City** U.S.A.
147 D3 **Ponce** Puerto Rico
73 B3 **Pondicherry** India
127 F2 **Pond Inlet** Can.
106 B1 **Ponferrada** Spain
117 A4 **Pongo** *watercourse* Sudan
123 D2 **Pongola** *r.* S. Africa
128 C2 **Ponoka** Can.
84 A6 **Ponta Delgada** Azores
154 B3 **Ponta Grossa** Brazil
154 C1 **Pontalina** Brazil
105 D2 **Pont-à-Mousson** France
105 D2 **Pontarlier** France
102 B2 **Pontcharra** France
142 B2 **Pontchartrain, Lake** U.S.A.
106 B2 **Ponte de Sor** Port.
129 D3 **Ponteix** Can.
150 C3 **Pontes-e-Lacerda** Brazil
106 B1 **Pontevedra** Spain
140 B2 **Pontiac** *IL* U.S.A.
140 C2 **Pontiac** *MI* U.S.A.
61 B2 **Pontianak** Indon.
104 B2 **Pontivy** France
151 C1 **Pontoetoe** Suriname
129 E2 **Ponton** Can.
99 B3 **Pontypool** U.K.
108 B2 **Ponziane, Isole** *is* Italy
99 C3 **Poole** U.K.
Poona India *see* **Pune**
52 B2 **Pooncarie** Austr.
152 B2 **Poopó, Lago de** *l.* Bol.
150 A1 **Popayán** Col.
83 I2 **Popigay** *r.* Rus. Fed.
52 B2 **Popiltah** Austr.
129 E2 **Poplar** *r.* Can.
137 E3 **Poplar Bluff** U.S.A.
118 B3 **Popokabaka** Dem. Rep. Congo
110 C2 **Popovo** Bulg.
103 E2 **Poprad** Slovakia
151 D3 **Porangatu** Brazil
74 A2 **Porbandar** India
126 B2 **Porcupine** *r.* Can./U.S.A.
108 B1 **Poreč** Croatia
54 B2 **Porirua** N.Z.
88 C2 **Porkhov** Rus. Fed.
104 B2 **Pornic** France
83 K3 **Poronaysk** Rus. Fed.
111 B3 **Poros** Greece
93 E4 **Porsgrunn** Norway
97 C1 **Portadown** U.K.
97 D1 **Portaferry** U.K.
140 B2 **Portage** U.S.A.
129 E3 **Portage la Prairie** Can.
128 B3 **Port Alberni** Can.
106 B2 **Portalegre** Port.
139 C2 **Portales** U.S.A.
128 A2 **Port Alexander** U.S.A.
128 B2 **Port Alice** Can.
134 B1 **Port Angeles** U.S.A.
51 D4 **Port Arthur** Austr.
139 E3 **Port Arthur** U.S.A.
96 A3 **Port Askaig** U.K.
52 A2 **Port Augusta** Austr.
147 C3 **Port-au-Prince** Haiti
131 E1 **Port aux Choix** Can.
73 D3 **Port Blair** India
52 B3 **Port Campbell** Austr.
54 B3 **Port Chalmers** N.Z.
143 D3 **Port Charlotte** U.S.A.
147 C3 **Port-de-Paix** Haiti
128 A2 **Port Edward** Can.
155 D1 **Porteirinha** Brazil
151 C2 **Portel** Brazil
130 B2 **Port Elgin** Can.
123 C3 **Port Elizabeth** S. Africa
96 A3 **Port Ellen** U.K.
98 A1 **Port Erin** Isle of Man
122 A3 **Porterville** S. Africa
135 C3 **Porterville** U.S.A.
52 B3 **Port Fairy** Austr.
54 C1 **Port Fitzroy** N.Z.
118 A3 **Port-Gentil** Gabon
115 C4 **Port Harcourt** Nigeria
128 B2 **Port Hardy** Can.
Port Harrison Can. *see* **Inukjuak**
131 D2 **Port Hawkesbury** Can.
50 A2 **Port Hedland** Austr.
99 A2 **Porthmadog** U.K.
131 E1 **Port Hope Simpson** Can.
140 C2 **Port Huron** U.S.A.
106 B2 **Portimão** Port.
53 C2 **Portland** *N.S.W.* Austr.
52 B3 **Portland** *Vic.* Austr.
141 E2 **Portland** *ME* U.S.A.
134 B1 **Portland** *OR* U.S.A.
128 A2 **Portland Canal** *inlet* Can.
97 C2 **Portlaoise** Rep. of Ireland
139 D3 **Port Lavaca** U.S.A.
52 A2 **Port Lincoln** Austr.
114 A4 **Port Loko** Sierra Leone
113 H6 **Port Louis** Mauritius
53 D2 **Port Macquarie** Austr.
128 B2 **Port McNeill** Can.
131 D2 **Port-Menier** Can.
59 D3 **Port Moresby** P.N.G.
96 A1 **Port Ness** U.K.
122 A2 **Port Nolloth** S. Africa
Port-Nouveau-Québec Can. *see* **Kangiqsualujjuaq**
Porto Port. *see* **Oporto**
150 B2 **Porto Acre** Brazil
152 C4 **Porto Alegre** Brazil
151 C3 **Porto Artur** Brazil
151 C3 **Porto dos Gaúchos Óbidos** Brazil
150 C3 **Porto Esperidião** Brazil
108 B2 **Portoferraio** Italy
151 D2 **Porto Franco** Brazil
147 D3 **Port of Spain** Trin. and Tob.
108 B1 **Portogruaro** Italy
108 B2 **Portomaggiore** Italy
154 B2 **Porto Mendes** Brazil
152 C3 **Porto Murtinho** Brazil
151 D3 **Porto Nacional** Brazil
114 C4 **Porto-Novo** Benin
154 B2 **Porto Primavera, Represa** *resr* Brazil
151 C2 **Porto Santana** Brazil
155 E1 **Porto Seguro** Brazil
108 B2 **Porto Tolle** Italy
108 A2 **Porto Torres** *Sardinia* Italy
105 D3 **Porto-Vecchio** *Corsica* France
150 B2 **Porto Velho** Brazil

150 A2 **Portoviejo** Ecuador
52 B3 **Port Phillip Bay** Austr.
52 A2 **Port Pirie** Austr.
96 A2 **Portree** U.K.
128 B3 **Port Renfrew** Can.
97 C1 **Portrush** U.K.
116 B1 **Port Said** Egypt
143 C3 **Port St Joe** U.S.A.
123 C3 **Port St Johns** S. Africa
123 D3 **Port Shepstone** S. Africa
99 C3 **Portsmouth** U.K.
141 E2 **Portsmouth** *NH* U.S.A.
140 C3 **Portsmouth** *OH* U.S.A.
141 D3 **Portsmouth** *VA* U.S.A.
97 C1 **Portstewart** U.K.
116 B3 **Port Sudan** Sudan
142 C3 **Port Sulphur** U.S.A.
99 B3 **Port Talbot** U.K.
106 B2 **Portugal** *country* Europe
97 B2 **Portumna** Rep. of Ireland
105 C3 **Port-Vendres** France
49 E4 **Port Vila** Vanuatu
93 I3 **Porvoo** Fin.
65 B2 **Poryŏng** S. Korea
152 C3 **Posadas** Arg.
89 E2 **Poshekhon'ye** Rus. Fed.
92 I2 **Posio** Fin.
58 C3 **Poso** Indon.
151 D3 **Posse** Brazil
101 E2 **Pößneck** Ger.
139 C2 **Post** U.S.A.
Poste-de-la-Baleine Can. *see* **Kuujjuarapik**
122 B2 **Postmasburg** S. Africa
109 C2 **Posušje** Bos.-Herz.
139 E1 **Poteau** U.S.A.
109 C2 **Potenza** Italy
123 C1 **Potgietersrus** S. Africa
151 D2 **Poti** *r.* Brazil
81 C1 **P'ot'i** Georgia
115 D3 **Potiskum** Nigeria
141 D3 **Potomac, South Branch** *r.* U.S.A.
152 B2 **Potosí** Bol.
64 B1 **Pototan** Phil.
138 C3 **Potrero del Llano** Mex.
101 F1 **Potsdam** Ger.
141 E2 **Potsdam** U.S.A.
141 D2 **Pottstown** U.S.A.
141 D2 **Pottsville** U.S.A.
131 E2 **Pouch Cove** Can.
141 E2 **Poughkeepsie** U.S.A.
98 B2 **Poulton-le-Fylde** U.K.
155 C2 **Pouso Alegre** Brazil
63 B2 **Poŭthĭsăt** Cambodia
103 D2 **Považská Bystrica** Slovakia
109 C2 **Povlen** *mt.* Serb. and Mont.
106 B1 **Póvoa de Varzim** Port.
136 B2 **Powell** U.S.A.
135 D3 **Powell, Lake** *resr* U.S.A.
128 B3 **Powell River** Can.
154 B1 **Poxoréu** Brazil
Poyang China *see* **Boyang**
71 B3 **Poyang Hu** *l.* China
109 D2 **Požarevac** Serb. and Mont.
145 C2 **Poza Rica** Mex.
109 C1 **Požega** Croatia
109 D2 **Požega** Serb. and Mont.
79 D2 **Pozm Tīāb** Iran
103 D1 **Poznań** Pol.
106 C2 **Pozoblanco** Spain
108 B2 **Pozzuoli** Italy
60 B2 **Prabumulih** Indon.
102 C2 **Prachatice** Czech Rep.
63 A2 **Prachuap Khiri Khan** Thai.
155 E1 **Prado** Brazil
102 C1 **Prague** Czech Rep.
Praha Czech Rep. *see* **Prague**
112 B2 **Praia** Cape Verde
139 C2 **Prairie Dog Town Fork** *r.* U.S.A.
140 A2 **Prairie du Chien** U.S.A.
60 A1 **Prapat** Indon.
154 C1 **Prata** Brazil
105 E3 **Prato** Italy
137 D3 **Pratt** U.S.A.
61 C2 **Praya** Indon.
63 B2 **Preăh Vihear** Cambodia
89 F2 **Prechistoye** Rus. Fed.
129 D2 **Preeceville** Can.
88 C2 **Preiļi** Latvia
53 C2 **Premer** Austr.
105 C2 **Prémery** France
101 F1 **Premnitz** Ger.
102 C1 **Prenzlau** Ger.
63 A2 **Preparis Island** Cocos Is
63 A2 **Preparis North Channel** Cocos Is
63 A2 **Preparis South Channel** Cocos Is
103 D2 **Přerov** Czech Rep.
138 A2 **Prescott** U.S.A.
109 D2 **Preševo** Serb. and Mont.
152 B3 **Presidencia Roque Sáenz Peña** Arg.
151 D2 **Presidente Dutra** Brazil
154 B2 **Presidente Epitácio** Brazil
154 B2 **Presidente Prudente** Brazil
138 C3 **Presidio** U.S.A.
103 E2 **Prešov** Slovakia
141 F1 **Presque Isle** U.S.A.
101 F2 **Pressel** Ger.
98 B2 **Preston** U.K.
134 D2 **Preston** U.S.A.
96 B3 **Prestwick** U.K.
155 C1 **Preto** *r.* Brazil
123 C2 **Pretoria** S. Africa
111 B3 **Preveza** Greece
63 B2 **Prey Vêng** Cambodia
109 C2 **Priboj** Serb. and Mont.
135 D3 **Price** U.S.A.
88 B3 **Prienai** Lith.
122 B2 **Prieska** S. Africa
103 D2 **Prievidza** Slovakia
109 C2 **Prijedor** Bos.-Herz.
76 A2 **Prikaspiyskaya Nizmennost'** *lowland* Kazakh./Rus. Fed.
109 D2 **Prilep** Macedonia
91 D2 **Primorsko-Akhtarsk** Rus. Fed.
129 D2 **Primrose Lake** Can.
129 D2 **Prince Albert** Can.
122 B3 **Prince Albert** S. Africa
126 D2 **Prince Albert Peninsula** Can.
122 B3 **Prince Albert Road** S. Africa
126 C2 **Prince Alfred, Cape** Can.
122 A3 **Prince Alfred Hamlet** S. Africa
127 F2 **Prince Charles Island** Can.
55 E2 **Prince Charles Mountains** Antarctica
131 D2 **Prince Edward Island** *prov.* Can.
128 B2 **Prince George** Can.
126 E2 **Prince of Wales Island** Can.
128 A2 **Prince of Wales Island** U.S.A.
126 D2 **Prince of Wales Strait** Can.
126 D1 **Prince Patrick Island** Can.
126 E2 **Prince Regent Inlet** *sea chan.* Can.
128 A2 **Prince Rupert** Can.
51 D1 **Princess Charlotte Bay** Austr.
128 B2 **Princess Royal Island** Can.
128 B3 **Princeton** Can.
134 B2 **Prineville** U.S.A.
90 B1 **Pripet** *r.* Belarus/Ukr.
90 A1 **Pripet Marshes** Belarus/Ukr.
109 D2 **Priština** Serb. and Mont.
101 F1 **Pritzwalk** Ger.
109 C2 **Privlaka** Croatia
89 F2 **Privolzhsk** Rus. Fed.
109 D2 **Prizren** Serb. and Mont.
151 C1 **Professor van Blommestein Meer** *resr* Suriname
145 D2 **Progreso** Mex.
81 C1 **Prokhladnyy** Rus. Fed.
109 D2 **Prokuplje** Serb. and Mont.
126 C3 **Prophet** *r.* Can.
128 B2 **Prophet River** Can.
51 D2 **Proserpine** Austr.
89 E3 **Protvino** Rus. Fed.
110 C2 **Provadiya** Bulg.
141 E2 **Providence** U.S.A.
146 B3 **Providencia, Isla de** *i.* Caribbean Sea
83 N2 **Provideniya** Rus. Fed.
135 D2 **Provo** U.S.A.
129 C2 **Provost** Can.
154 B3 **Prudentópolis** Brazil
126 B2 **Prudhoe Bay** U.S.A.
100 C2 **Prüm** Ger.
105 D3 **Prunelli-di-Fiumorbo** *Corsica* France
103 E1 **Pruszków** Pol.
110 C1 **Prut** *r.* Europe
91 C1 **Pryluky** Ukr.
91 D2 **Prymors'k** Ukr.
139 D1 **Pryor** U.S.A.
Prypyats' *r.* Belarus *see* **Pripet**
103 E2 **Przemyśl** Pol.
111 C3 **Psara** *i.* Greece
81 C1 **Psebay** Rus. Fed.
91 D3 **Pshekha** *r.* Rus. Fed.
88 C2 **Pskov** Rus. Fed.
88 C2 **Pskov, Lake** Estonia/Rus. Fed.
111 B2 **Ptolemaïda** Greece
109 C1 **Ptuj** Slovenia
150 A2 **Pucallpa** Peru
71 B3 **Pucheng** China
65 B2 **Puch'ŏn** S. Korea
103 D1 **Puck** Pol.
92 I2 **Pudasjärvi** Fin.
86 C2 **Pudozh** Rus. Fed.
Puducheri India *see* Pondicherry
145 C3 **Puebla** Mex.
136 C3 **Pueblo** U.S.A.
153 B4 **Puelén** Arg.
106 C2 **Puente-Genil** Spain
153 A5 **Puerto Aisén** Chile
152 B2 **Puerto Alegre** Bol.
145 C3 **Puerto Ángel** Mex.
146 B4 **Puerto Armuelles** Panama
150 B1 **Puerto Ayacucho** Venez.
146 B3 **Puerto Cabezas** Nic.
153 A5 **Puerto Cisnes** Chile
144 A2 **Puerto Cortés** Mex.
145 C3 **Puerto Escondido** Mex.
152 B2 **Puerto Frey** Bol.
150 B1 **Puerto Inírida** Col.
152 C2 **Puerto Isabel** Bol.
150 A2 **Puerto Leguizamo** Col.
144 A2 **Puerto Libertad** Mex.
106 C2 **Puertollano** Spain
153 B5 **Puerto Madryn** Arg.
150 B3 **Puerto Maldonado** Peru
153 A5 **Puerto Montt** Chile
153 A6 **Puerto Natales** Chile
150 B1 **Puerto Nuevo** Col.
150 B1 **Puerto Páez** Col.
144 A1 **Puerto Peñasco** Mex.
152 C3 **Puerto Pinasco** Para.
147 C3 **Puerto Plata** Dom. Rep.
150 A2 **Puerto Portillo** Peru

64 A2 Puerto Princesa Phil.
147 D3 Puerto Rico *terr.* West Indies
158 B3 Puerto Rico Trench *sea feature* Caribbean Sea
146 A3 Puerto San José Guatemala
153 B6 Puerto Santa Cruz Arg.
144 B2 Puerto Vallarta Mex.
87 D3 Pugachev Rus. Fed.
74 B2 Pugal India
129 D2 Pukatawagan Can.
65 B1 Pukchin N. Korea
65 B1 Pukch'ŏng N. Korea
54 B1 Pukekohe N.Z.
65 B1 Puksubaek-san *mt.* N. Korea
108 B2 Pula Croatia
108 A3 Pula *Sardinia* Italy
152 B3 Pulacayo Bol.
92 I3 Pulkkila Fin.
134 C1 Pullman U.S.A.
64 B1 Pulog, Mount Phil.
150 A2 Puná, Isla *i.* Ecuador
54 B2 Punakaiki N.Z.
123 D1 Punda Maria S. Africa
73 B3 Pune India
65 B1 P'ungsan N. Korea
121 C2 Púnguè *r.* Moz.
153 B4 Punta Alta Arg.
153 A6 Punta Arenas Chile
108 A2 Punta Balestrieri *mt.* *Sardinia* Italy
146 B3 Puntarenas Costa Rica
150 A1 Punto Fijo Venez.
92 I3 Puolanka Fin.
82 G2 Pur *r.* Rus. Fed.
75 C3 Puri India
100 B1 Purmerend Neth.
75 C2 Purnia India
75 C2 Puruliya India
150 B2 Purus *r.* Peru
61 B2 Purwakarta Indon.
65 B1 Puryŏng N. Korea
65 B2 Pusan S. Korea
88 C2 Pushkinskiye Gory Rus. Fed.
88 C2 Pustoshka Rus. Fed.
62 A1 Putao Myanmar
71 B3 Putian China
Puting China *see* De'an
61 C2 Puting, Tanjung *pt* Indon.
101 F1 Putlitz Ger.
58 A2 Putrajaya Malaysia
102 C1 Puttgarden Ger.
150 A2 Putumayo *r.* Col.
61 C1 Putusibau Indon.
91 C1 Putyvl' Ukr.
127 F2 Puvurnituq Can.
70 B2 Puyang China
104 C3 Puylaurens France
99 A2 Pwllheli U.K.
63 A2 Pyapon Myanmar
82 G2 Pyasina *r.* Rus. Fed.
87 D4 Pyatigorsk Rus. Fed.
91 C2 P"yatykhatky Ukr.
62 A2 Pyè Myanmar
88 C3 Pyetrykaw Belarus
93 H3 Pyhäjärvi *l.* Fin.
92 H3 Pyhäjoki *r.* Fin.
92 I3 Pyhäsalmi Fin.
62 A2 Pyinmana Myanmar
65 B2 Pyŏksŏng N. Korea
65 B2 P'yŏnggang N. Korea
65 B2 P'yŏngyang N. Korea
135 C2 Pyramid Lake U.S.A.
80 B3 Pyramids of Giza Egypt
107 D1 Pyrenees *mts* Europe
111 B3 Pyrgos Greece
91 C1 Pyryatyn Ukr.
103 C1 Pyrzyce Pol.
88 C2 Pytalovo Rus. Fed.
62 A2 Pyu Myanmar
111 B3 Pyxaria *mt.* Greece

Q

127 G1 Qaanaaq Greenland
123 C3 Qacha's Nek Lesotho
69 D2 Qagan Nur China
68 C2 Qaidam Pendi *basin* China
74 A1 Qalāt Afgh.
78 B2 Qal'at Bīshah Saudi Arabia
129 E1 Qamanirjuaq Lake *l.* Can.
Qamanittuaq Can. *see* Baker Lake
78 B3 Qam Hadīl Saudi Arabia
78 B2 Qaryat al Ulyā Saudi Arabia
127 H2 Qasigiannguit Greenland
79 D2 Qaşr-e Qand Iran
81 C2 Qaşr-e Shīrīn Iran
127 H2 Qassimiut Greenland
78 B3 Qa'tabah Yemen
79 C2 Qatar *country* Asia
116 A2 Qattara Depression Egypt
81 C1 Qazax Azer.
81 C1 Qazımämmäd Azer.
81 C2 Qazvīn Iran
127 H2 Qeqertarsuaq *i.* Greenland
127 H2 Qeqertarsuatsiaat Greenland
127 H2 Qeqertarsuup Tunua *b.* Greenland
79 C2 Qeshm Iran
70 A3 Qianjiang *Chongqing* China
70 B2 Qianjiang *Hubei* China
65 A1 Qian Shan *mts* China
70 C2 Qidong China
68 B2 Qiemo China
71 A3 Qijiang China
68 C2 Qijiaojing China
127 G2 Qikiqtarjuaq Can.
74 A2 Qila Ladgasht Pak.
68 C2 Qilian Shan *mts* China
127 I2 Qillak *i.* Greenland
70 B3 Qimen China
127 G1 Qimusseriarsuaq *b.* Greenland
116 B2 Qinā Egypt
70 C2 Qingdao China
75 D1 Qinghai *prov.* China
68 C2 Qinghai Hu *salt l.* China
68 C2 Qinghai Nanshan *mts* China
71 B3 Qingyuan *Guangdong* China
65 A1 Qingyuan *Liaoning* China
68 B2 Qingzang Gaoyuan *plat.* China
70 B2 Qinhuangdao China
70 A2 Qin Ling *mts* China
Qinting China *see* Lianhua
70 B2 Qinyang China
71 A3 Qinzhou China
71 B4 Qionghai China
68 C2 Qionglai Shan *mts* China
71 B4 Qiongshan China
69 E1 Qiqihar China
79 C2 Qīr Iran
66 B1 Qitaihe China
70 B2 Qixian China
Qogir Feng *mt.* China/Jammu and Kashmir *see* K2
81 D2 Qom Iran
Qomolangma Feng *mt.* China/Nepal *see* Everest, Mount
Qoqek China *see* Tacheng
100 C1 Quakenbrück Ger.
63 B2 Quang Ngai Vietnam
63 B2 Quang Tri Vietnam
71 B3 Quanzhou *Fujian* China
71 B3 Quanzhou *Guangxi* China
108 A3 Quartu Sant'Elena *Sardinia* Italy
138 A2 Quartzsite U.S.A.
81 C1 Quba Azer.
53 C3 Queanbeyan Austr.
131 C2 Québec Can.
130 C1 Québec *prov.* Can.
101 E2 Quedlinburg Ger.
128 A2 Queen Charlotte Can.
128 A2 Queen Charlotte Islands Can.
128 B2 Queen Charlotte Sound *sea chan.* Can.
128 B2 Queen Charlotte Strait Can.
126 D1 Queen Elizabeth Islands Can.
126 E2 Queen Maud Gulf Can.
55 B2 Queen Maud Land *reg.* Antarctica
55 N1 Queen Maud Mountains Antactica
52 B1 Queensland *state* Austr.
51 D4 Queenstown Austr.
54 A3 Queenstown N.Z.
123 C3 Queenstown S. Africa
121 C2 Quelimane Moz.
138 B2 Quemado U.S.A.
154 B2 Querência do Norte Brazil
145 B2 Querétaro Mex.
101 E2 Querfurt Ger.
128 B2 Quesnel Can.
128 B2 Quesnel Lake Can.
74 A1 Quetta Pak.
64 A2 Quezon Phil.
64 B1 Quezon City Phil.
120 A2 Quibala Angola
150 A1 Quibdó Col.
104 B2 Quiberon France
104 C3 Quillan France
153 C4 Quilmes Arg.
73 B4 Quilon India
51 D2 Quilpie Austr.
153 A4 Quilpué Chile
120 A1 Quimbele Angola
152 B3 Quimilí Arg.
104 B2 Quimper France
104 B2 Quimperlé France
137 E3 Quincy *IL* U.S.A.
141 E2 Quincy *MA* U.S.A.
63 B2 Qui Nhon Vietnam
107 C1 Quinto Spain
121 D2 Quionga Moz.
53 D2 Quirindi Austr.
121 C3 Quissico Moz.
120 A2 Quitapa Angola
150 A2 Quito Ecuador
151 E2 Quixadá Brazil
71 A3 Qujing China
52 A2 Quorn Austr.
79 C2 Qurayat Oman
77 C3 Qŭrghonteppa Tajik.
71 B3 Quzhou China

103 D2 Raab *r.* Austria
92 H3 Raahe Fin.
100 C1 Raalte Neth.
61 C2 Raas *i.* Indon.
61 C2 Raba Indon.
114 B1 Rabat Morocco
48 D3 Rabaul P.N.G.
78 A2 Rābigh Saudi Arabia
131 E2 Race, Cape Can.
142 B3 Raceland U.S.A.
63 B3 Rach Gia Vietnam
140 B2 Racine U.S.A.

78 B3 **Radā'** Yemen
110 C1 **Rădăuţi** Romania
140 B3 **Radcliff** U.S.A.
74 B2 **Radhanpur** India
130 C1 **Radisson** Can.
103 E1 **Radom** Pol.
103 D1 **Radomsko** Pol.
90 B1 **Radomyshl'** Ukr.
109 D2 **Radoviš** Macedonia
88 B2 **Radviliškis** Lith.
78 A2 **Raḍwá, Jabal** *mt.* Saudi Arabia
90 B1 **Radyvyliv** Ukr.
75 C2 **Rae Bareli** India
128 C1 **Rae-Edzo** Can.
128 C1 **Rae Lakes** Can.
100 C2 **Raeren** Belgium
54 C1 **Raetihi** N.Z.
152 B4 **Rafaela** Arg.
118 C2 **Rafaï** C.A.R.
78 B2 **Rafḩā'** Saudi Arabia
79 C1 **Rafsanjān** Iran
64 B2 **Ragang, Mount** *vol.* Phil.
109 B3 **Ragusa** *Sicily* Italy
59 C3 **Raha** Indon.
88 D3 **Rahachow** Belarus
74 B2 **Rahimyar Khan** Pak.
73 B3 **Raichur** India
75 C2 **Raigarh** India
128 C2 **Rainbow Lake** Can.
134 B1 **Rainier, Mount** *vol.* U.S.A.
130 A2 **Rainy Lake** Can.
129 E3 **Rainy River** Can.
75 C2 **Raipur** India
93 H3 **Raisio** Fin.
73 C3 **Rajahmundry** India
61 C1 **Rajang** *r.* *Sarawak* Malaysia
74 B2 **Rajanpur** Pak.
73 B4 **Rajapalaiyam** India
74 B2 **Rajasthan Canal** India
74 B2 **Rajgarh** India
74 B2 **Rajkot** India
74 B2 **Rajpur** India
75 C2 **Rajshahi** Bangl.
54 B2 **Rakaia** *r.* N.Z.
90 A2 **Rakhiv** Ukr.
91 D1 **Rakitnoye** Rus. Fed.
88 C2 **Rakke** Estonia
88 C2 **Rakvere** Estonia
143 E1 **Raleigh** U.S.A.
49 E2 **Ralik Chain** *is.* Marshall Islands
74 B2 **Ramgarh** India
81 C2 **Rāmhormoz** Iran
78 B3 **Ramlat Dahm** *des.* Saudi Arabia/Yemen
Ramlat Rabyānah *des.* Libya *see* **Rebiana Sand Sea**
110 C1 **Râmnicu Sărat** Romania
110 B1 **Râmnicu Vâlcea** Romania
89 E3 **Ramon'** Rus. Fed.
123 C1 **Ramotswa** Botswana
75 B2 **Rampur** India
62 A2 **Ramree Island** Myanmar
98 A1 **Ramsey** Isle of Man
130 B2 **Ramsey Lake** Can.
99 D3 **Ramsgate** U.K.
75 C2 **Ranaghat** India
61 C1 **Ranau** *Sabah* Malaysia
153 A4 **Rancagua** Chile
75 C2 **Ranchi** India
93 F4 **Randers** Denmark
54 B2 **Rangiora** N.Z.
54 C1 **Rangitaiki** *r.* N.Z.
62 A2 **Rangoon** Myanmar
75 C2 **Rangpur** Bangl.
129 E1 **Rankin Inlet** Can.
53 C2 **Rankin's Springs** Austr.
96 B2 **Rannoch Moor** *moorland* U.K.
63 A3 **Ranong** Thai.
59 C3 **Ransiki** Indon.
61 C2 **Rantaupanjang** Indon.
60 A1 **Rantauprapat** Indon.
92 I2 **Ranua** Fin.
78 B2 **Ranyah, Wādī** *watercourse* Saudi Arabia
136 C2 **Rapid City** U.S.A.
88 B2 **Rapla** Estonia
74 A2 **Rapur** India
153 B5 **Rasa, Punta** *pt* Arg.
79 C2 **Ra's al Khaymah** U.A.E.
117 B3 **Ras Dashen** *mt.* Eth.
88 B2 **Raseiniai** Lith.
81 C2 **Rasht** Iran
74 A2 **Ras Koh** *mt.* Pak.
88 C2 **Rasony** Belarus
87 D3 **Rasskazovo** Rus. Fed.
79 C2 **Ras Tannūrah** Saudi Arabia
101 D1 **Rastede** Ger.
49 F2 **Ratak Chain** *is.* Marshall Islands
93 F3 **Rätan** Sweden
74 B2 **Ratangarh** India
63 A2 **Rat Buri** Thai.
62 A1 **Rathedaung** Myanmar
101 F1 **Rathenow** Ger.
97 C1 **Rathlin Island** U.K.
74 B2 **Ratlam** India
73 B3 **Ratnagiri** India
73 C4 **Ratnapura** Sri Lanka
90 A1 **Ratne** Ukr.
138 C1 **Raton** U.S.A.
96 D2 **Rattray Head** *hd* U.K.
101 E1 **Ratzeburg** Ger.
92 □B2 **Raufarhöfn** Iceland
54 C1 **Raukumara Range** *mts* N.Z.
93 H3 **Rauma** Fin.
61 C2 **Raung, Gunung** *vol.* Indon.
75 C2 **Raurkela** India
134 D1 **Ravalli** U.S.A.
81 C2 **Ravānsar** Iran
108 B2 **Ravenna** Italy
102 B2 **Ravensburg** Ger.
74 B1 **Ravi** *r.* Pak.
74 B1 **Rawalpindi** Pak.
103 D1 **Rawicz** Pol.
50 B3 **Rawlinna** Austr.
136 B2 **Rawlins** U.S.A.
153 B5 **Rawson** Arg.
73 C3 **Rayagada** India
69 E1 **Raychikhinsk** Rus. Fed.
78 B3 **Raydah** Yemen
87 E3 **Rayevskiy** Rus. Fed.
134 B1 **Raymond** U.S.A.
53 D2 **Raymond Terrace** Austr.
139 D3 **Raymondville** U.S.A.
145 C2 **Rayón** Mex.
63 B2 **Rayong** Thai.
78 A2 **Rayyis** Saudi Arabia
104 B2 **Raz, Pointe du** *pt* France
81 C2 **Razāzah, Buḩayrat ar** *l.* Iraq
110 C2 **Razgrad** Bulg.
110 C2 **Razim, Lacul** *lag.* Romania
110 B2 **Razlog** Bulg.
104 B2 **Ré, Île de** *i.* France
99 C3 **Reading** U.K.
141 D2 **Reading** U.S.A.
115 E2 **Rebiana Sand Sea** *des.* Libya
66 D1 **Rebun-tō** *i.* Japan
50 B3 **Recherche, Archipelago of the** *is* Austr.
89 D3 **Rechytsa** Belarus
151 E2 **Recife** Brazil
123 C3 **Recife, Cape** S. Africa
100 C2 **Recklinghausen** Ger.
152 C3 **Reconquista** Arg.
142 B2 **Red** *r.* U.S.A.
131 E1 **Red Bay** Can.
135 B2 **Red Bluff** U.S.A.
98 C1 **Redcar** U.K.
129 C2 **Redcliff** Can.
52 B2 **Red Cliffs** Austr.
128 C2 **Red Deer** Can.
126 D3 **Red Deer** *r.* Can.
129 D2 **Red Deer Lake** Can.
134 B2 **Redding** U.S.A.
99 C2 **Redditch** U.K.
137 D2 **Redfield** U.S.A.
130 A1 **Red Lake** Can.
137 E1 **Red Lakes** U.S.A.
134 E1 **Red Lodge** U.S.A.
134 B2 **Redmond** U.S.A.
137 D2 **Red Oak** U.S.A.
106 B2 **Redondo** Port.
78 A2 **Red Sea** Africa/Asia
128 B1 **Redstone** *r.* Can.
137 E2 **Red Wing** U.S.A.
137 D2 **Redwood Falls** U.S.A.
97 C2 **Ree, Lough** *l.* Rep. of Ireland
134 B2 **Reedsport** U.S.A.
54 B2 **Reefton** N.Z.
102 C2 **Regen** Ger.
155 E1 **Regência** Brazil
102 C2 **Regensburg** Ger.
114 C2 **Reggane** Alg.
109 C3 **Reggio di Calabria** Italy
108 B2 **Reggio nell'Emilia** Italy
110 B1 **Reghin** Romania
129 D2 **Regina** Can.
122 A1 **Rehoboth** Namibia
101 F2 **Reichenbach** Ger.
143 E1 **Reidsville** U.S.A.
99 C3 **Reigate** U.K.
105 C2 **Reims** France
101 E1 **Reinbek** Ger.
129 D2 **Reindeer** *r.* Can.
129 E2 **Reindeer Island** Can.
129 D2 **Reindeer Lake** Can.
92 F2 **Reine** Norway
100 C3 **Reinsfeld** Ger.
123 C2 **Reitz** S. Africa
122 B2 **Reivilo** S. Africa
129 D1 **Reliance** Can.
107 D2 **Relizane** Alg.
79 C2 **Remeshk** Iran
105 D2 **Remiremont** France
100 C2 **Remscheid** Ger.
102 B1 **Rendsburg** Ger.
141 D1 **Renfrew** Can.
60 B2 **Rengat** Indon.
90 B2 **Reni** Ukr.
52 B2 **Renmark** Austr.
100 D2 **Rennerod** Ger.
104 B2 **Rennes** France
129 D1 **Rennie Lake** Can.
108 B2 **Reno** *r.* Italy
135 C3 **Reno** U.S.A.
70 A3 **Renshou** China
140 B2 **Rensselaer** U.S.A.
75 C2 **Renukut** India
54 B2 **Renwick** N.Z.
58 C3 **Reo** Indon.
136 D3 **Republican** *r.* U.S.A.
127 F2 **Repulse Bay** Can.
150 A2 **Requena** Peru
107 C2 **Requena** Spain
154 B2 **Reserva** Brazil
152 C3 **Resistencia** Arg.
110 B1 **Reşiţa** Romania
126 E2 **Resolute Bay** Can.
127 G2 **Resolution Island** Can.
105 C2 **Rethel** France
111 B3 **Rethymno** Greece
113 H6 **Réunion** *terr.* Indian Ocean
107 D1 **Reus** Spain
102 B2 **Reutlingen** Ger.
128 C2 **Revelstoke** Can.
144 A3 **Revillagigedo, Islas** *is* Mex.

128 A2 **Revillagigedo Island** U.S.A.
75 C2 **Rewa** India
134 D2 **Rexburg** U.S.A.
92 □A3 **Reykjanestá** *pt* Iceland
92 □A3 **Reykjavík** Iceland
145 C2 **Reynosa** Mex.
88 C2 **Rēzekne** Latvia
Rhein *r.* Ger. *see* **Rhine**
100 C1 **Rheine** Ger.
101 F1 **Rheinsberg** Ger.
Rhin *r.* France *see* **Rhine**
100 C2 **Rhine** *r.* Europe
140 B1 **Rhinelander** U.S.A.
101 F1 **Rhinluch** *marsh* Ger.
101 F1 **Rhinow** Ger.
141 E2 **Rhode Island** *state* U.S.A.
111 C3 **Rhodes** Greece
111 C3 **Rhodes** *i.* Greece
110 B2 **Rhodope Mountains** Bulg./Greece
105 C3 **Rhône** *r.* France/Switz.
Rhuthun U.K. *see* **Ruthin**
98 B2 **Rhyl** U.K.
154 C1 **Rianópolis** Brazil
60 B1 **Riau, Kepulauan** *is* Indon.
106 B1 **Ribadeo** Spain
106 B1 **Ribadesella** Spain
154 B2 **Ribas do Rio Pardo** Brazil
121 C2 **Ribáuè** Moz.
98 B2 **Ribble** *r.* U.K.
154 C2 **Ribeira** *r.* Brazil
154 C2 **Ribeirão Preto** Brazil
104 C2 **Ribérac** France
152 B2 **Riberalta** Bol.
90 B2 **Rîbnița** Moldova
102 C1 **Ribnitz-Damgarten** Ger.
140 A1 **Rice Lake** U.S.A.
123 D2 **Richards Bay** S. Africa
126 B2 **Richardson Mountains** Can.
135 D3 **Richfield** U.S.A.
134 C1 **Richland** U.S.A.
140 A2 **Richland Center** U.S.A.
53 D2 **Richmond** *N.S.W.* Austr.
51 D2 **Richmond** *Qld* Austr.
54 B2 **Richmond** N.Z.
122 B3 **Richmond** S. Africa
98 C1 **Richmond** U.K.
140 C3 **Richmond** *IN* U.S.A.
140 C3 **Richmond** *KY* U.S.A.
141 D3 **Richmond** *VA* U.S.A.
130 C2 **Rideau Lakes** Can.
135 C3 **Ridgecrest** U.S.A.
102 C1 **Riesa** Ger.
100 D1 **Rieste** Ger.
123 B2 **Riet** *r.* S. Africa
101 D2 **Rietberg** Ger.
108 B2 **Rieti** Italy
136 B3 **Rifle** U.S.A.
88 B2 **Rīga** Latvia
88 B2 **Riga, Gulf of** Estonia/Latvia
79 C2 **Rīgān** Iran
134 D2 **Rigby** U.S.A.
131 E1 **Rigolet** Can.
93 H3 **Riihimäki** Fin.
108 B1 **Rijeka** Croatia
134 C2 **Riley** U.S.A.
78 B2 **Rimah, Wādī al** *watercourse* Saudi Arabia
103 E2 **Rimavská Sobota** Slovakia
128 C2 **Rimbey** Can.
108 B2 **Rimini** Italy
131 D2 **Rimouski** Can.
93 F3 **Ringebu** Norway
93 E4 **Ringkøbing** Denmark
92 G2 **Ringvassøy** *i.* Norway
101 D1 **Rinteln** Ger.
150 A2 **Riobamba** Ecuador
150 B3 **Rio Branco** Brazil
154 C3 **Rio Branco do Sul** Brazil
154 B2 **Rio Brilhante** Brazil
154 C2 **Rio Claro** Brazil
153 B4 **Río Colorado** Arg.
153 B4 **Río Cuarto** Arg.
155 D2 **Rio de Janeiro** Brazil
153 B6 **Río Gallegos** Arg.
153 B6 **Río Grande** Arg.
152 C4 **Rio Grande** Brazil
144 B2 **Río Grande** Mex.
139 D3 **Rio Grande** *r.* Mex./U.S.A.
139 D3 **Rio Grande City** U.S.A.
150 A1 **Ríohacha** Col.
150 A2 **Rioja** Peru
145 D2 **Río Lagartos** Mex.
105 C2 **Riom** France
152 B2 **Río Mulatos** Bol.
154 C3 **Rio Negro** Brazil
155 D1 **Rio Pardo de Minas** Brazil
138 B1 **Rio Rancho** U.S.A.
150 A2 **Río Tigre** Ecuador
154 B1 **Rio Verde** Brazil
145 C2 **Río Verde** Mex.
154 B1 **Rio Verde de Mato Grosso** Brazil
90 C1 **Ripky** Ukr.
98 C2 **Ripley** U.K.
107 D1 **Ripoll** Spain
98 C1 **Ripon** U.K.
66 D1 **Rishiri-tō** *i.* Japan
93 E4 **Risør** Norway
122 B2 **Ritchie** S. Africa
63 A2 **Ritchie's Archipelago** *is* India
134 C1 **Ritzville** U.S.A.
152 B3 **Rivadavia** Arg.
108 B1 **Riva del Garda** Italy
146 B3 **Rivas** Nic.
152 C4 **Rivera** Uru.
129 D2 **Riverhurst** Can.
52 B2 **Riverina** *reg.* Austr.
122 B3 **Riversdale** S. Africa
135 C4 **Riverside** U.S.A.
136 B2 **Riverton** U.S.A.
131 D2 **Riverview** Can.
104 C3 **Rivesaltes** France
131 D2 **Rivière-du-Loup** Can.
90 B1 **Rivne** Ukr.
54 B2 **Riwaka** N.Z.
78 B2 **Riyadh** Saudi Arabia
81 C1 **Rize** Turkey
70 B2 **Rizhao** China
105 C2 **Roanne** France
141 D3 **Roanoke** U.S.A.
143 E1 **Roanoke** *r.* U.S.A.
143 E1 **Roanoke Rapids** U.S.A.
52 A3 **Robe** Austr.
101 F1 **Röbel** Ger.
92 H3 **Robertsfors** Sweden
122 A3 **Robertson** S. Africa
114 A4 **Robertsport** Liberia
131 C2 **Roberval** Can.
50 A2 **Robinson Range** *hills* Austr.
52 B2 **Robinvale** Austr.
129 D2 **Roblin** Can.
128 C2 **Robson, Mount** Can.
108 B3 **Rocca Busambra** *mt. Sicily* Italy
153 C4 **Rocha** Uru.
98 B2 **Rochdale** U.K.
154 B1 **Rochedo** Brazil
100 B2 **Rochefort** Belgium
104 B2 **Rochefort** France
137 E2 **Rochester** *MN* U.S.A.
141 E2 **Rochester** *NH* U.S.A.
141 D2 **Rochester** *NY* U.S.A.
140 B2 **Rockford** U.S.A.
51 E2 **Rockhampton** Austr.
143 D2 **Rock Hill** U.S.A.
50 A3 **Rockingham** Austr.
140 A2 **Rock Island** U.S.A.
136 B1 **Rock Springs** *MT* U.S.A.
139 C3 **Rocksprings** U.S.A.
136 B2 **Rock Springs** *WY* U.S.A.
136 C3 **Rocky Ford** U.S.A.
143 E1 **Rocky Mount** U.S.A.
128 C2 **Rocky Mountain House** Can.
126 D3 **Rocky Mountains** Can./U.S.A.
100 B3 **Rocroi** France
102 C1 **Rødbyhavn** Denmark
131 E1 **Roddickton** Can.
104 C3 **Rodez** France
89 F2 **Rodniki** Rus. Fed.
Rodos Greece *see* **Rhodes**
Rodos *i.* Greece *see* **Rhodes**
50 A2 **Roebourne** Austr.
50 B1 **Roebuck Bay** Austr.
123 C1 **Roedtan** S. Africa
100 B2 **Roermond** Neth.
100 A2 **Roeselare** Belgium
127 F2 **Roes Welcome Sound** *sea chan.* Can.
142 B1 **Rogers** U.S.A.
122 B3 **Roggeveldberge** *esc.* S. Africa
92 G2 **Rognan** Norway
134 B2 **Rogue** *r.* U.S.A.
88 B2 **Roja** Latvia
60 B1 **Rokan** *r.* Indon.
88 C2 **Rokiškis** Lith.
90 B1 **Rokytne** Ukr.
154 B2 **Rolândia** Brazil
137 E3 **Rolla** U.S.A.
51 D2 **Roma** Austr.
59 C3 **Roma** *i.* Indon.
Roma Italy *see* **Rome**
123 C2 **Roma** Lesotho
139 D3 **Roma** U.S.A.
143 E2 **Romain, Cape** U.S.A.
110 C1 **Roman** Romania
110 B1 **Romania** *country* Europe
91 C3 **Roman-Kosh** *mt.* Ukr.
69 D1 **Romanovka** Rus. Fed.
105 D2 **Rombas** France
64 B1 **Romblon** Phil.
108 B2 **Rome** Italy
143 C2 **Rome** *GA* U.S.A.
141 D2 **Rome** *NY* U.S.A.
99 D3 **Romford** U.K.
105 C2 **Romilly-sur-Seine** France
91 C1 **Romny** Ukr.
104 C2 **Romorantin-Lanthenay** France
99 C3 **Romsey** U.K.
96 □ **Ronas Hill** *hill* U.K.
151 C3 **Roncador, Serra do** *hills* Brazil
106 B2 **Ronda** Spain
154 B2 **Rondon** Brazil
154 B1 **Rondonópolis** Brazil
74 B1 **Rondu** Jammu and Kashmir
71 A3 **Rong'an** China
71 A3 **Rongjiang** China
62 A1 **Rongklang Range** *mts* Myanmar
Rongmei China *see* **Hefeng**
93 F4 **Rønne** Denmark
55 P2 **Ronne Ice Shelf** Antarctica
101 D1 **Ronnenberg** Ger.
100 A2 **Ronse** Belgium
100 B1 **Roordahuizum** Neth.
75 B2 **Roorkee** India
100 B2 **Roosendaal** Neth.
135 E2 **Roosevelt** U.S.A.
55 K2 **Roosevelt Island** Antarctica
128 B2 **Roosevelt, Mount** Can.
104 B3 **Roquefort** France
150 B1 **Roraima, Mount** Guyana
93 F3 **Røros** Norway
153 B4 **Rosario** Arg.
144 A1 **Rosario** *Baja California Norte* Mex.

144 B2 **Rosario** *Sinaloa* Mex.
144 B2 **Rosario** *Sonora* Mex.
151 C3 **Rosário Oeste** Brazil
144 A2 **Rosarito** Mex.
109 C3 **Rosarno** Italy
104 B2 **Roscoff** France
97 B2 **Roscommon** Rep. of Ireland
97 C2 **Roscrea** Rep. of Ireland
147 D3 **Roseau** Dominica
137 D1 **Roseau** U.S.A.
134 B2 **Roseburg** U.S.A.
139 D3 **Rosenberg** U.S.A.
101 D1 **Rosengarten** Ger.
102 C2 **Rosenheim** Ger.
129 D2 **Rosetown** Can.
122 A2 **Rosh Pinah** Namibia
110 C2 **Roșiori de Vede** Romania
93 F4 **Roskilde** Denmark
89 D3 **Roslavl'** Rus. Fed.
109 C3 **Rossano** Italy
97 B1 **Rossan Point** Rep. of Ireland
55 K1 **Ross Ice Shelf** Antarctica
131 D2 **Rossignol, Lake** Can.
128 C3 **Rossland** Can.
97 C2 **Rosslare** Rep. of Ireland
114 A3 **Rosso** Maur.
105 D3 **Rosso, Capo** *c.* *Corsica* France
99 B3 **Ross-on-Wye** U.K.
91 D1 **Rossosh'** Rus. Fed.
128 A1 **Ross River** Can.
55 K2 **Ross Sea** Antarctica
92 F2 **Røssvatnet** *l.* Norway
79 C2 **Rostāq** Iran
129 D2 **Rosthern** Can.
102 C1 **Rostock** Ger.
89 E2 **Rostov** Rus. Fed.
91 D2 **Rostov-na-Donu** Rus. Fed.
92 H2 **Rosvik** Sweden
138 C2 **Roswell** U.S.A.
59 D2 **Rota** *i.* N. Mariana Is
59 C3 **Rote** *i.* Indon.
101 D1 **Rotenburg (Wümme)** Ger.
102 C2 **Roth** Ger.
98 C1 **Rothbury** U.K.
98 C2 **Rotherham** U.K.
96 B3 **Rothesay** U.K.
53 C2 **Roto** Austr.
105 D3 **Rotondo, Monte** *mt.* *Corsica* France
54 C1 **Rotorua** N.Z.
54 C1 **Rotorua, Lake** N.Z.
101 E2 **Rottenbach** Ger.
102 C2 **Rottenmann** Austria
100 B2 **Rotterdam** Neth.
102 B2 **Rottweil** Ger.
105 C1 **Roubaix** France
104 C2 **Rouen** France
Roulers Belgium *see* Roeselare
53 D2 **Round Mountain** *mt.* Austr.
131 E2 **Round Pond** *l.* Can.
139 D2 **Round Rock** U.S.A.
134 E1 **Roundup** U.S.A.
96 C1 **Rousay** *i.* U.K.
130 C2 **Rouyn** Can.
92 I2 **Rovaniemi** Fin.
91 D2 **Roven'ki** Rus. Fed.
91 D2 **Roven'ky** Ukr.
108 B1 **Rovereto** Italy
63 B2 **Rôviĕng Tbong** Cambodia
108 B1 **Rovigo** Italy
108 B1 **Rovinj** Croatia
53 C1 **Rowena** Austr.
64 B2 **Roxas** *Mindanao* Phil.
64 B1 **Roxas** *Mindoro* Phil.
64 A1 **Roxas** *Palawan* Phil.
64 B1 **Roxas** *Panay* Phil.
52 A2 **Roxby Downs** Austr.
138 C1 **Roy** U.S.A.
140 B1 **Royale, Isle** *i.* U.S.A.
104 B2 **Royan** France
99 C2 **Royston** U.K.
90 C2 **Rozdil'na** Ukr.
91 C2 **Rozdol'ne** Ukr.
100 B3 **Rozoy-sur-Serre** France
87 D3 **Rtishchevo** Rus. Fed.
54 C1 **Ruapehu, Mount** *vol.* N.Z.
54 A3 **Ruapuke Island** N.Z.
78 B3 **Rub' al Khālī** *des.* Saudi Arabia
91 D2 **Rubizhne** Ukr.
77 E1 **Rubtsovsk** Rus. Fed.
135 C2 **Ruby Mountains** U.S.A.
66 C2 **Rudnaya Pristan'** Rus. Fed.
89 D3 **Rudnya** Rus. Fed.
76 C1 **Rudnyy** Kazakh.
82 E1 **Rudol'fa, Ostrov** *i.* Rus. Fed.
101 E2 **Rudolstadt** Ger.
119 D3 **Rufiji** *r.* Tanz.
153 B4 **Rufino** Arg.
121 B2 **Rufunsa** Zambia
70 C2 **Rugao** China
99 C2 **Rugby** U.K.
136 C1 **Rugby** U.S.A.
102 C1 **Rügen** *i.* Ger.
101 E2 **Ruhla** Ger.
88 B2 **Ruhnu** *i.* Estonia
100 C2 **Ruhr** *r.* Ger.
71 C3 **Rui'an** China
138 B2 **Ruidoso** U.S.A.
144 B2 **Ruiz** Mex.
119 D3 **Rukwa, Lake** Tanz.
96 A2 **Rum** *i.* U.K.
109 C1 **Ruma** Serb. and Mont.
78 B2 **Rumāh** Saudi Arabia
117 A4 **Rumbek** Sudan
105 D2 **Rumilly** France
50 C1 **Rum Jungle** Austr.
54 B2 **Runanga** N.Z.
98 B2 **Runcorn** U.K.
120 A2 **Rundu** Namibia
68 B2 **Ruoqiang** China
130 C1 **Rupert** *r.* Can.
130 C1 **Rupert Bay** Can.
121 C2 **Rusape** Zimbabwe
110 C2 **Ruse** Bulg.
77 D3 **Rushon** Tajik.
136 C2 **Rushville** U.S.A.
53 C3 **Rushworth** Austr.
129 D2 **Russell** Can.
54 B1 **Russell** N.Z.
142 C2 **Russellville** *AL* U.S.A.
142 B1 **Russellville** *AR* U.S.A.
140 B3 **Russellville** *KY* U.S.A.
101 D2 **Rüsselsheim** Ger.
82 F2 **Russian Federation** *country* Asia/Europe
123 C2 **Rustenburg** S. Africa
142 B2 **Ruston** U.S.A.
98 B2 **Ruthin** U.K.
141 E2 **Rutland** U.S.A.
75 B1 **Rutög** China
119 E4 **Ruvuma** *r.* Moz./Tanz.
79 C2 **Ruweis** U.A.E.
77 C1 **Ruzayevka** Kazakh.
87 D3 **Ruzayevka** Rus. Fed.
119 C3 **Rwanda** *country* Africa
89 E3 **Ryazan'** Rus. Fed.
89 F3 **Ryazhsk** Rus. Fed.
86 C2 **Rybachiy, Poluostrov** *pen.* Rus. Fed.
89 E2 **Rybinsk** Rus. Fed.
89 E2 **Rybinskoye Vodokhranilishche** *resr* Rus. Fed.
103 D1 **Rybnik** Pol.
89 E3 **Rybnoye** Rus. Fed.
99 D3 **Rye** U.K.
89 D3 **Ryl'sk** Rus. Fed.
67 C3 **Ryōtsu** Japan
Ryukyu Islands Japan *see* Nansei-shotō
103 E1 **Rzeszów** Pol.
89 D2 **Rzhev** Rus. Fed.

S

79 C2 **Sa'ādatābād** Iran
101 E2 **Saale** *r.* Ger.
101 E2 **Saalfeld** Ger.
102 B2 **Saarbrücken** Ger.
88 B2 **Saaremaa** *i.* Estonia
92 I2 **Saarenkylä** Fin.
93 I3 **Saarijärvi** Fin.
102 B2 **Saarlouis** Ger.
80 B2 **Sab' Ābār** Syria
107 D1 **Sabadell** Spain
61 C1 **Sabah** *state* Malaysia
61 C2 **Sabalana** *i.* Indon.
155 D1 **Sabará** Brazil
108 B2 **Sabaudia** Italy
115 D2 **Sabhā** Libya
123 D2 **Sabie** *r.* Moz./S. Africa
145 B2 **Sabinas** Mex.
145 B2 **Sabinas Hidalgo** Mex.
131 D2 **Sable, Cape** Can.
143 D3 **Sable, Cape** U.S.A.
131 E2 **Sable Island** Can.
106 B1 **Sabugal** Port.
78 B3 **Ṣabyā** Saudi Arabia
76 B3 **Sabzevār** Iran
120 A2 **Sachanga** Angola
130 A1 **Sachigo Lake** *l.* Can.
65 B3 **Sach'on** S. Korea
126 C2 **Sachs Harbour** Can.
135 B3 **Sacramento** U.S.A.
138 B2 **Sacramento Mountains** U.S.A.
135 B2 **Sacramento Valley** U.S.A.
123 C3 **Sada** S. Africa
107 C1 **Sádaba** Spain
78 B3 **Ṣa'dah** Yemen
62 A1 **Sadiya** India
67 C3 **Sadoga-shima** *i.* Japan
107 D2 **Sa Dragonera** *i.* Spain
93 F4 **Säffle** Sweden
138 B2 **Safford** U.S.A.
99 D2 **Saffron Walden** U.K.
114 B1 **Safi** Morocco
86 D2 **Safonovo** *Arkhangel'skaya Oblast'* Rus. Fed.
89 D2 **Safonovo** *Smolenskaya Oblast'* Rus. Fed.
78 B2 **Safrā' as Sark** *esc.* Saudi Arabia
75 C2 **Saga** China
67 B4 **Saga** Japan
62 A1 **Sagaing** Myanmar
67 C3 **Sagamihara** Japan
75 B2 **Sagar** India
140 C2 **Saginaw** U.S.A.
140 C2 **Saginaw Bay** U.S.A.
106 B2 **Sagres** Port.
146 B2 **Sagua la Grande** Cuba
141 F1 **Saguenay** *r.* Can.
107 C2 **Sagunto** Spain
76 B2 **Sagyndyk, Mys** *pt* Kazakh.
106 B1 **Sahagún** Spain
114 C2 **Sahara** *des.* Africa
Saharan Atlas *mts* Alg. *see* Atlas Saharien
75 B2 **Saharanpur** India
75 C2 **Saharsa** India
114 B3 **Sahel** *reg.* Africa

144 B2 **Sahuayo** Mex.
78 B2 **Şāḩūq** *reg.* Saudi Arabia
80 B2 **Saïda** Lebanon
75 C2 **Saidpur** Bangl.
Saigon Vietnam *see* **Hô Chi Minh City**
62 A1 **Saiha** India
69 D2 **Saihan Tal** China
67 B4 **Saiki** Japan
93 I3 **Saimaa** *l.* Fin.
144 B2 **Sain Alto** Mex.
96 C3 **St Abb's Head** *hd* U.K.
99 C3 **St Albans** U.K.
99 B3 **St Alban's Head** *hd* U.K.
96 C2 **St Andrews** U.K.
100 B2 **St Anthonis** Neth.
131 E1 **St Anthony** Can.
134 D2 **St Anthony** U.S.A.
52 B3 **St Arnaud** Austr.
131 E1 **St-Augustin** Can.
131 E1 **St Augustin** *r.* Can.
143 D3 **St Augustine** U.S.A.
99 A3 **St Austell** U.K.
104 C2 **St-Avertin** France
98 B1 **St Bees Head** *hd* U.K.
105 D3 **St-Bonnet-en-Champsaur** France
99 A3 **St Bride's Bay** U.K.
104 B2 **St-Brieuc** France
130 C2 **St Catharines** Can.
99 C3 **St Catherine's Point** U.K.
137 E3 **St Charles** U.S.A.
140 C2 **St Clair, Lake** Can./U.S.A.
105 D2 **St-Claude** France
137 E1 **St Cloud** U.S.A.
140 A1 **St Croix** *r.* U.S.A.
147 D3 **St Croix** *i.* Virgin Is (U.S.A.)
105 C2 **St-Dizier** France
131 D2 **Ste-Anne-des-Monts** Can.
105 D2 **St-Égrève** France
126 B2 **St Elias Mountains** Can.
131 D1 **Ste-Marguerite** *r.* Can.
129 E2 **Sainte Rose du Lac** Can.
104 B2 **Saintes** France
105 C2 **St-Étienne** France
108 A2 **St-Florent** *Corsica* France
105 C2 **St-Flour** France
136 C3 **St Francis** U.S.A.
105 D2 **St Gallen** Switz.
104 C3 **St-Gaudens** France
53 C1 **St George** Austr.
135 D3 **St George** U.S.A.
143 D3 **St George Island** U.S.A.
131 C2 **St-Georges** Can.
147 D3 **St George's** Grenada
97 C3 **St George's Channel** Rep. of Ireland/U.K.
112 C5 **St Helena** *terr.* S. Atlantic Ocean
122 A3 **St Helena Bay** S. Africa
122 A3 **St Helena Bay** *b.* S. Africa
98 B2 **St Helens** U.K.
134 B1 **St Helens, Mount** *vol.* U.S.A.
95 C4 **St Helier** Channel Is
100 B2 **St-Hubert** Belgium
141 E1 **St-Hyacinthe** Can.
140 C1 **St Ignace** U.S.A.
130 B2 **St Ignace Island** Can.
99 A3 **St Ives** U.K.
128 A2 **St James, Cape** Can.
131 C2 **St-Jean, Lac** *l.* Can.
104 B2 **St-Jean-d'Angély** France
104 B2 **St-Jean-de-Monts** France
130 C2 **St-Jean-sur-Richelieu** Can.
141 E1 **St-Jérôme** Can.
134 C1 **St Joe** *r.* U.S.A.
131 D2 **Saint John** Can.
141 F1 **St John** *r.* U.S.A.
147 D3 **St John's** Antigua
131 E2 **St John's** Can.
138 B2 **St Johns** U.S.A.
141 E2 **St Johnsbury** U.S.A.
137 E3 **St Joseph** U.S.A.
130 A1 **St Joseph, Lake** Can.
130 B2 **St Joseph Island** Can.
104 C2 **St-Junien** France
94 B2 **St Kilda** *i.* U.K.
147 D3 **St Kitts and Nevis** *country* West Indies
100 A2 **St-Laureins** Belgium
St-Laurent, Golfe du Can. *see* **St Lawrence, Gulf of**
151 C1 **St-Laurent-du-Maroni** Fr. Guiana
131 D2 **St Lawrence** *inlet* Can.
131 D2 **St Lawrence, Gulf of** Can.
83 N2 **St Lawrence Island** U.S.A.
104 B2 **St-Lô** France
114 A3 **St-Louis** Senegal
137 E3 **St Louis** U.S.A.
137 E1 **St Louis** *r.* U.S.A.
147 D3 **St Lucia** *country* West Indies
123 D2 **St Lucia Estuary** S. Africa
147 D3 **St Maarten** *i.* West Indies
104 B2 **St-Malo** France
104 B2 **St-Malo, Golfe de** *g.* France
122 A3 **St Martin, Cape** S. Africa
141 D2 **St Marys** U.S.A.
130 C2 **St Maurice** *r.* Can.
105 D2 **St Moritz** Switz.
104 B2 **St-Nazaire** France
100 B2 **St-Niklaas** Belgium
104 C1 **St-Omer** France
129 C2 **St Paul** Can.
137 E2 **St Paul** U.S.A.
137 E2 **St Peter** U.S.A.
95 C4 **St Peter Port** Channel Is
89 D2 **St Petersburg** Rus. Fed.
143 D3 **St Petersburg** U.S.A.
131 E2 **St-Pierre** St Pierre and Miquelon
131 E2 **St Pierre and Miquelon** *terr.* N. America
104 B2 **St-Pierre-d'Oléron** France
105 C2 **St-Pourçain-sur-Sioule** France
131 D2 **St Quentin** Can.
105 C2 **St-Quentin** France
131 D2 **St Siméon** Can.
129 E2 **St Theresa Point** Can.
130 B2 **St Thomas** Can.
105 D3 **St-Tropez** France
105 D3 **St-Tropez, Cap de** *c.* France
102 C2 **St Veit an der Glan** Austria
52 A3 **St Vincent, Gulf** Austr.
147 D3 **St Vincent and the Grenadines** *country* West Indies
100 C2 **St-Vith** Belgium
129 D2 **St Walburg** Can.
100 C3 **St Wendel** Ger.
104 C2 **St-Yrieix-la-Perche** France
59 D1 **Saipan** *i.* N. Mariana Is
152 B2 **Sajama, Nevado** *mt.* Bol.
122 B2 **Sak** *watercourse* S. Africa
67 C4 **Sakai** Japan
67 B4 **Sakaide** Japan
78 B2 **Sakākah** Saudi Arabia
136 C1 **Sakakawea, Lake** U.S.A.
111 D2 **Sakarya** Turkey
111 D2 **Sakarya** *r.* Turkey
66 C3 **Sakata** Japan
65 B1 **Sakchu** N. Korea
83 K3 **Sakhalin** *i.* Rus. Fed.
123 C2 **Sakhile** S. Africa
81 C1 **Şäki** Azer.
88 B3 **Šakiai** Lith.
69 E3 **Sakishima-shotō** *is* Japan
62 B2 **Sakon Nakhon** Thai.
122 B3 **Sakrivier** S. Africa
67 D3 **Sakura** Japan
91 C2 **Saky** Ukr.
93 G4 **Sala** Sweden
130 C2 **Salaberry-de-Valleyfield** Can.
88 B2 **Salacgrīva** Latvia
109 C2 **Sala Consilina** Italy
135 C4 **Salada, Laguna** *salt l.* Mex.
152 B4 **Salado** *r.* Arg.
145 C2 **Salado** *r.* Mex.
114 B4 **Salaga** Ghana
122 B1 **Salajwe** Botswana
115 D3 **Salal** Chad
78 A2 **Salâla** Sudan
79 C3 **Şalālah** Oman
145 B2 **Salamanca** Mex.
106 B1 **Salamanca** Spain
106 B1 **Salas** Spain
59 C3 **Salawati** *i.* Indon.
58 C3 **Salayar** *i.* Indon.
148 B4 **Sala y Gómez, Isla** *i.* S. Pacific Ocean
104 C2 **Salbris** France
88 C3 **Šalčininkai** Lith.
106 C1 **Saldaña** Spain
122 A3 **Saldanha** S. Africa
88 B2 **Saldus** Latvia
53 C3 **Sale** Austr.
86 F2 **Salekhard** Rus. Fed.
73 B3 **Salem** India
137 E3 **Salem** *MO* U.S.A.
134 B2 **Salem** *OR* U.S.A.
96 B2 **Salen** U.K.
109 B2 **Salerno** Italy
98 B2 **Salford** U.K.
151 E2 **Salgado** *r.* Brazil
103 D2 **Salgótarján** Hungary
151 E2 **Salgueiro** Brazil
136 B3 **Salida** U.S.A.
111 C3 **Salihli** Turkey
88 C3 **Salihorsk** Belarus
121 C2 **Salima** Malawi
121 C2 **Salimo** Moz.
137 D3 **Salina** U.S.A.
108 B3 **Salina, Isola** *i.* Italy
145 C3 **Salina Cruz** Mex.
155 D1 **Salinas** Brazil
144 B2 **Salinas** Mex.
135 B3 **Salinas** U.S.A.
151 D2 **Salinópolis** Brazil
99 C3 **Salisbury** U.K.
141 D3 **Salisbury** *MD* U.S.A.
143 D1 **Salisbury** *NC* U.S.A.
99 B3 **Salisbury Plain** U.K.
151 D2 **Salitre** *r.* Brazil
92 I2 **Salla** Fin.
127 F2 **Salluit** Can.
75 C2 **Sallyana** Nepal
81 C2 **Salmās** Iran
134 D1 **Salmon** U.S.A.
134 C1 **Salmon** *r.* U.S.A.
128 C2 **Salmon Arm** Can.
134 C2 **Salmon River Mountains** U.S.A.
100 C3 **Salmtal** Ger.
93 H3 **Salo** Fin.
87 D4 **Sal'sk** Rus. Fed.
122 B3 **Salt** *watercourse* S. Africa
138 A2 **Salt** *r.* U.S.A.
152 B3 **Salta** Arg.
145 B2 **Saltillo** Mex.
134 D2 **Salt Lake City** U.S.A.
154 C2 **Salto** Brazil
152 C4 **Salto** Uru.
155 E1 **Salto da Divisa** Brazil
154 B2 **Salto del Guairá** Para.
135 C4 **Salton Sea** *salt l.* U.S.A.
143 D2 **Saluda** U.S.A.
108 A2 **Saluzzo** Italy
151 E3 **Salvador** Brazil

79 C2 **Salwah** Saudi Arabia
62 A2 **Salween** *r.* Myanmar
81 C2 **Salyan** Azer.
102 C2 **Salzburg** Austria
101 E1 **Salzgitter** Ger.
101 D2 **Salzkotten** Ger.
101 E1 **Salzwedel** Ger.
144 B1 **Samalayuca** Mex.
66 D2 **Samani** Japan
64 B1 **Samar** *i.* Phil.
87 E3 **Samara** Rus. Fed.
61 C2 **Samarinda** Indon.
77 C3 **Samarkand** Uzbek.
81 C2 **Sāmarrā'** Iraq
81 C1 **Şamaxı** Azer.
119 C3 **Samba** Dem. Rep. Congo
61 C1 **Sambaliung** *mts* Indon.
75 C2 **Sambalpur** India
61 C2 **Sambar, Tanjung** *pt* Indon.
61 B1 **Sambas** Indon.
121 □E2 **Sambava** Madag.
90 A2 **Sambir** Ukr.
153 C4 **Samborombón, Bahía** *b.* Arg.
65 B2 **Samch'ŏk** S. Korea
81 C2 **Samdi Dag** *mt.* Turkey
119 D3 **Same** Tanz.
78 B2 **Samīrah** Saudi Arabia
65 B1 **Samjiyŏn** N. Korea
49 G4 **Samoa** *country* S. Pacific Ocean
109 C1 **Samobor** Croatia
111 C3 **Samos** *i.* Greece
111 C2 **Samothraki** Greece
111 C2 **Samothraki** *i.* Greece
61 C2 **Sampit** Indon.
119 C3 **Sampwe** Dem. Rep. Congo
139 E2 **Sam Rayburn Reservoir** U.S.A.
80 B1 **Samsun** Turkey
81 C1 **Samtredia** Georgia
63 B3 **Samui, Ko** *i.* Thai.
63 B2 **Samut Songkhram** Thai.
114 B3 **San** Mali
78 B3 **Şan'ā'** Yemen
118 A2 **Sanaga** *r.* Cameroon
81 C2 **Sanandaj** Iran
146 B3 **San Andrés, Isla de** *i.* Caribbean Sea
138 B2 **San Andres Mountains** U.S.A.
145 C3 **San Andrés Tuxtla** Mex.
139 C2 **San Angelo** U.S.A.
139 D3 **San Antonio** U.S.A.
135 C4 **San Antonio, Mount** U.S.A.
107 D2 **San Antonio Abad** Spain
152 B3 **San Antonio de los Cobres** Arg.
153 B5 **San Antonio Oeste** Arg.
108 B2 **San Benedetto del Tronto** Italy
144 A3 **San Benedicto, Isla** *i.* Mex.
135 C4 **San Bernardino** U.S.A.
135 C4 **San Bernardino Mountains** U.S.A.
143 C3 **San Blas, Cape** U.S.A.
152 B2 **San Borja** Bol.
144 B2 **San Buenaventura** Mex.
64 B1 **San Carlos** Phil.
147 D4 **San Carlos** Venez.
153 A5 **San Carlos de Bariloche** Arg.
147 C4 **San Carlos del Zulia** Venez.
135 C4 **San Clemente Island** U.S.A.
104 C2 **Sancoins** France
150 A1 **San Cristóbal** Venez.
145 C3 **San Cristóbal de las Casas** Mex.
146 C2 **Sancti Spíritus** Cuba
123 D1 **Sand** *r.* S. Africa
61 C1 **Sandakan** *Sabah* Malaysia
93 E3 **Sandane** Norway
111 B2 **Sandanski** Bulg.
96 C1 **Sanday** *i.* U.K.
139 C2 **Sanderson** U.S.A.
150 B3 **Sandia** Peru
135 C4 **San Diego** U.S.A.
80 B2 **Sandıklı** Turkey
93 E4 **Sandnes** Norway
92 F2 **Sandnessjøen** Norway
118 C3 **Sandoa** Dem. Rep. Congo
103 E1 **Sandomierz** Pol.
89 E2 **Sandovo** Rus. Fed.
62 A2 **Sandoway** Myanmar
94 B1 **Sandoy** *i.* Faroe Is
134 C1 **Sandpoint** U.S.A.
71 B3 **Sandu** China
94 B1 **Sandur** Faroe Is
140 C2 **Sandusky** U.S.A.
122 A3 **Sandveld** *mts* S. Africa
93 F4 **Sandvika** Norway
93 G3 **Sandviken** Sweden
131 E1 **Sandwich Bay** Can.
129 D2 **Sandy Bay** Can.
51 E2 **Sandy Cape** Austr.
130 A1 **Sandy Lake** Can.
130 A1 **Sandy Lake** *l.* Can.
144 A1 **San Felipe** *Baja California Norte* Mex.
145 B2 **San Felipe** *Guanajuato* Mex.
150 B1 **San Felipe** Venez.
144 A2 **San Fernando** *Baja California Norte* Mex.
145 C2 **San Fernando** *Tamaulipas* Mex.
64 B1 **San Fernando** *Luzon* Phil.
64 B1 **San Fernando** *Luzon* Phil.
106 B2 **San Fernando** Spain
147 D3 **San Fernando** Trin. and Tob.
150 D1 **San Fernando de Apure** Venez.
143 D3 **Sanford** *FL* U.S.A.
141 E2 **Sanford** *ME* U.S.A.
152 B4 **San Francisco** Arg.
135 B3 **San Francisco** U.S.A.
107 D2 **San Francisco Javier** Spain
74 B3 **Sangamner** India
83 J2 **Sangar** Rus. Fed.
108 A3 **San Gavino Monreale** *Sardinia* Italy
101 E2 **Sangerhausen** Ger.
61 C1 **Sanggau** Indon.
118 B3 **Sangha** *r.* Congo
109 C3 **San Giovanni in Fiore** Italy
64 B2 **Sangir** *i.* Indon.
59 C2 **Sangir, Kepulauan** *is* Indon.
65 B2 **Sangju** S. Korea
61 C1 **Sangkulirang** Indon.
73 B3 **Sangli** India
118 B2 **Sangmélima** Cameroon
121 C3 **Sango** Zimbabwe
105 D2 **San Gottardo, Passo del** *pass* Switz.
136 B3 **Sangre de Cristo Range** *mts* U.S.A.
75 C2 **Sangsang** China
144 A2 **San Hipólito, Punta** *pt* Mex.
144 A2 **San Ignacio** Mex.
130 C1 **Sanikiluaq** Can.
71 A3 **Sanjiang** China
135 B3 **San Joaquin** *r.* U.S.A.
153 B5 **San Jorge, Golfo de** *g.* Arg.
146 B4 **San José** Costa Rica
64 B1 **San Jose** *Luzon* Phil.
64 B1 **San Jose** *Mindoro* Phil.
135 B3 **San Jose** U.S.A.
144 A2 **San José, Isla** *i.* Mex.
144 B2 **San José de Bavicora** Mex.
64 B1 **San Jose de Buenavista** Phil.
144 A2 **San José de Comondú** Mex.
144 B2 **San José del Cabo** Mex.
150 A1 **San José del Guaviare** Col.
152 B4 **San Juan** Arg.
146 B3 **San Juan** *r.* Costa Rica/Nic.
147 D3 **San Juan** Puerto Rico
135 D3 **San Juan** *r.* U.S.A.
107 D2 **San Juan Bautista** Spain
145 C3 **San Juan Bautista Tuxtepec** Mex.
134 B1 **San Juan Islands** U.S.A.
144 B2 **San Juanito** Mex.
136 B3 **San Juan Mountains** U.S.A.
153 B5 **San Julián** Arg.
75 C2 **Sankh** *r.* India
Sankt-Peterburg Rus. Fed. *see* **St Petersburg**
80 B2 **Şanlıurfa** Turkey
138 B3 **San Lorenzo** Mex.
106 B2 **Sanlúcar de Barrameda** Spain
144 B2 **San Lucas** Mex.
153 B4 **San Luis** Arg.
145 B2 **San Luis de la Paz** Mex.
138 A2 **San Luisito** Mex.
135 B3 **San Luis Obispo** U.S.A.
145 B2 **San Luis Potosí** Mex.
144 A1 **San Luis Río Colorado** Mex.
139 D3 **San Marcos** U.S.A.
108 B2 **San Marino** *country* Europe
108 B2 **San Marino** San Marino
144 B2 **San Martin de Bolaños** Mex.
153 A5 **San Martín de los Andes** Arg.
153 B5 **San Matías, Golfo** *g.* Arg.
70 B2 **Sanmenxia** China
146 B3 **San Miguel** El Salvador
152 B3 **San Miguel de Tucumán** Arg.
145 C3 **San Miguel Sola de Vega** Mex.
71 B3 **Sanming** China
153 B4 **San Nicolás de los Arroyos** Arg.
135 C4 **San Nicolas Island** U.S.A.
123 C2 **Sannieshof** S. Africa
103 E2 **Sanok** Pol.
64 B1 **San Pablo** Phil.
144 B2 **San Pablo Balleza** Mex.
152 B3 **San Pedro** Arg.
152 B2 **San Pedro** Bol.
114 B4 **San-Pédro** Côte d'Ivoire
144 A2 **San Pedro** Mex.
138 A2 **San Pedro** *watercourse* U.S.A.
106 B2 **San Pedro, Sierra de** *mts* Spain
144 B2 **San Pedro de las Colonias** Mex.
146 B3 **San Pedro Sula** Hond.
108 A3 **San Pietro, Isola di** *i.* *Sardinia* Italy
144 A1 **San Quintín, Cabo** *c.* Mex.
153 B4 **San Rafael** Arg.
108 A2 **San Remo** Italy
146 B3 **San Salvador** El Salvador
152 B3 **San Salvador de Jujuy** Arg.
109 C2 **San Severo** Italy
109 C2 **Sanski Most** Bos.-Herz.
152 B2 **Santa Ana** Bol.
146 B3 **Santa Ana** El Salvador
144 A1 **Santa Ana** Mex.
135 C4 **Santa Ana** U.S.A.
144 B2 **Santa Bárbara** Mex.
135 C4 **Santa Barbara** U.S.A.
154 B2 **Santa Bárbara, Serra de** *hills* Brazil
152 B3 **Santa Catalina** Chile
150 B2 **Santa Clara** Col.

146 C2 **Santa Clara** Cuba
135 C4 **Santa Clarita** U.S.A.
109 C3 **Santa Croce, Capo** *c.* *Sicily* Italy
153 B6 **Santa Cruz** *r.* Arg.
152 B2 **Santa Cruz** Bol.
64 B1 **Santa Cruz** Phil.
135 B3 **Santa Cruz** U.S.A.
145 C3 **Santa Cruz Barillas** Guat.
155 E1 **Santa Cruz Cabrália** Brazil
107 C2 **Santa Cruz de Moya** Spain
114 A2 **Santa Cruz de Tenerife** Canary Is
135 C4 **Santa Cruz Island** U.S.A.
49 E3 **Santa Cruz Islands** Solomon Islands
152 B4 **Santa Fé** Arg.
138 B1 **Santa Fe** U.S.A.
154 B1 **Santa Helena de Goiás** Brazil
153 B4 **Santa Isabel** Arg.
154 B1 **Santa Luisa, Serra de** *hills* Brazil
152 C3 **Santa Maria** Brazil
144 B1 **Santa María** *r.* Mex.
135 B4 **Santa Maria** U.S.A.
123 D2 **Santa Maria, Cabo de** *c.* Moz.
106 B2 **Santa Maria, Cabo de** *c.* Port.
151 D2 **Santa Maria das Barreiras** Brazil
109 C3 **Santa Maria di Leuca, Capo** *c.* Italy
150 A1 **Santa Marta** Col.
135 C4 **Santa Monica** U.S.A.
151 D3 **Santana** Brazil
106 C1 **Santander** Spain
108 A3 **Sant'Antioco** *Sardinia* Italy
108 A3 **Sant'Antioco, Isola di** *i.* *Sardinia* Italy
151 C2 **Santarém** Brazil
106 B2 **Santarém** Port.
154 B1 **Santa Rita do Araguaia** Brazil
153 B4 **Santa Rosa** Arg.
152 C3 **Santa Rosa** Brazil
135 B3 **Santa Rosa** *CA* U.S.A.
138 C2 **Santa Rosa** *NM* U.S.A.
146 B3 **Santa Rosa de Copán** Hond.
135 B4 **Santa Rosa Island** U.S.A.
144 A2 **Santa Rosalía** Mex.
152 C3 **Santiago** Brazil
153 A4 **Santiago** Chile
147 C3 **Santiago** Dom. Rep.
144 B2 **Santiago** Mex.
146 B4 **Santiago** Panama
64 B1 **Santiago** Phil.
106 B1 **Santiago de Compostela** Spain
144 B2 **Santiago Ixcuintla** Mex.
144 B2 **Santiago Papasquiaro** Mex.
107 D1 **Sant Jordi, Golf de** *g.* Spain
155 D2 **Santo Amaro de Campos** Brazil
155 C2 **Santo André** Brazil
152 C3 **Santo Angelo** Brazil
154 B2 **Santo Antônio da Platina** Brazil
151 E3 **Santo Antônio de Jesus** Brazil
150 B2 **Santo Antônio do Içá** Brazil
155 C2 **Santo Antônio do Monte** Brazil
147 D3 **Santo Domingo** Dom. Rep.
138 B1 **Santo Domingo Pueblo** U.S.A.
Santorini *i.* Greece *see* **Thira**
155 C2 **Santos** Brazil
152 C3 **Santo Tomé** Arg.
153 A5 **San Valentín, Cerro** *mt.* Chile
146 B3 **San Vicente** El Salvador
144 A1 **San Vicente** Mex.
150 A3 **San Vicente de Cañete** Peru
108 B2 **San Vincenzo** Italy
108 B3 **San Vito, Capo** *c.* *Sicily* Italy
71 A4 **Sanya** China
155 C2 **São Bernardo do Campo** Brazil
152 C3 **São Borja** Brazil
154 C2 **São Carlos** Brazil
151 C3 **São Félix** *Mato Grosso* Brazil
151 C2 **São Félix** *Pará* Brazil
155 D2 **São Fidélis** Brazil
155 D1 **São Francisco** Brazil
151 E3 **São Francisco** *r.* Brazil
154 C3 **São Francisco, Ilha de** *i.* Brazil
154 C3 **São Francisco do Sul** Brazil
152 C4 **São Gabriel** Brazil
155 D2 **São Gonçalo** Brazil
155 C1 **São Gotardo** Brazil
155 D2 **São João da Barra** Brazil
155 C2 **São João da Boa Vista** Brazil
106 B1 **São João da Madeira** Port.
155 D1 **São João do Paraíso** Brazil
155 D2 **São João Nepomuceno** Brazil
154 C2 **São Joaquim da Barra** Brazil
154 C2 **São José do Rio Preto** Brazil
155 C2 **São José dos Campos** Brazil
154 C3 **São José dos Pinhais** Brazil
155 C2 **São Lourenço** Brazil
151 D2 **São Luís** Brazil
154 C2 **São Manuel** Brazil
154 C1 **São Marcos** *r.* Brazil
151 D2 **São Marcos, Baía de** *b.* Brazil
155 E1 **São Mateus** Brazil
155 C2 **São Paulo** Brazil
151 D2 **São Raimundo Nonato** Brazil
155 C1 **São Romão** Brazil
155 C2 **São Sebastião, Ilha do** *i.* Brazil
154 C2 **São Sebastião do Paraíso** Brazil
154 B1 **São Simão** Brazil
154 B1 **São Simão, Barragem de** *resr* Brazil
59 C2 **Sao-Siu** Indon.
155 D2 **São Tomé, Cabo de** *c.* Brazil
112 D3 **São Tomé and Príncipe** *country* Africa
112 D3 **São Tomé** São Tomé and Príncipe
155 C2 **São Vicente** Brazil
106 B2 **São Vicente, Cabo de** *c.*Port.
59 C3 **Saparua** Indon.
89 F3 **Sapozhok** Rus. Fed.
66 D2 **Sapporo** Japan
109 C2 **Sapri** Italy
81 C2 **Saqqez** Iran
81 C2 **Sarāb** Iran
63 B2 **Sara Buri** Thai.
109 C2 **Sarajevo** Bos.-Herz.
76 B1 **Saraktash** Rus. Fed.
141 E2 **Saranac Lake** U.S.A.
109 D3 **Sarandë** Albania
64 B2 **Sarangani Islands** Phil.
87 D3 **Saransk** Rus. Fed.
87 E3 **Sarapul** Rus. Fed.
143 D3 **Sarasota** U.S.A.
90 B2 **Sarata** Ukr.
136 B2 **Saratoga** U.S.A.
141 E2 **Saratoga Springs** U.S.A.
61 C1 **Saratok** *Sarawak* Malaysia
87 D3 **Saratov** Rus. Fed.
79 D2 **Saravan** Iran
63 B2 **Saravan** Laos
61 C1 **Sarawak** *state* Malaysia
110 C2 **Saray** Turkey
111 C3 **Sarayköy** Turkey
79 D2 **Sarbāz** Iran
74 B2 **Sardarshahr** India
Sardegna *i.* Italy *see* **Sardinia**
108 A2 **Sardinia** *i.* Italy
92 G2 **Sarektjåkkå** *mt.* Sweden
77 C3 **Sar-e Pol** Afgh.
158 B3 **Sargasso Sea** Atlantic Ocean
74 B1 **Sargodha** Pak.
115 D4 **Sarh** Chad
79 D2 **Sarhad** *reg.* Iran
81 D2 **Sārī** Iran
111 C3 **Sarıgöl** Turkey
81 C1 **Sarıkamış** Turkey
61 C1 **Sarikei** *Sarawak* Malaysia
51 D2 **Sarina** Austr.
115 D2 **Sarīr Tibesti** *des.* Libya
65 B2 **Sariwŏn** N. Korea
111 C2 **Sarıyer** Turkey
77 D2 **Sarkand** Kazakh.
111 C2 **Şarköy** Turkey
59 D3 **Sarmi** Indon.
140 C2 **Sarnia** Can.
90 B1 **Sarny** Ukr.
60 B2 **Sarolangun** Indon.
111 B3 **Saronikos Kolpos** *g.* Greece
111 C2 **Saros Körfezi** *b.* Turkey
87 D3 **Sarova** Rus. Fed.
105 D2 **Sarrebourg** France
106 B1 **Sarria** Spain
107 C1 **Sarrión** Spain
105 D3 **Sartène** *Corsica* France
103 D2 **Sárvár** Hungary
76 B2 **Sarykamyshskoye Ozero** *salt l.* Turkm./Uzbek.
77 D2 **Saryozek** Kazakh.
77 D2 **Saryshagan** Kazakh.
82 F3 **Sarysu** *watercourse* Kazakh.
77 D3 **Sary-Tash** Kyrg.
75 C2 **Sasaram** India
67 A4 **Sasebo** Japan
129 D2 **Saskatchewan** *prov.* Can.
129 D2 **Saskatchewan** *r.* Can.
129 D2 **Saskatoon** Can.
83 I2 **Saskylakh** Rus. Fed.
123 C2 **Sasolburg** S. Africa
87 D3 **Sasovo** Rus. Fed.
114 B4 **Sassandra** Côte d'Ivoire
108 A2 **Sassari** *Sardinia* Italy
102 C1 **Sassnitz** Ger.
114 A3 **Satadougou** Mali
123 D1 **Satara** S. Africa
75 C2 **Satna** India
74 B2 **Satpura Range** *mts* India
63 B2 **Sattahip** Thai.
110 B1 **Satu Mare** Romania
63 B3 **Satun** Thai.
144 B2 **Saucillo** Mex.
93 E4 **Sauda** Norway
92 □B2 **Sauðárkrókur** Iceland
78 B2 **Saudi Arabia** *country* Asia
105 C3 **Saugues** France
105 C2 **Saulieu** France
130 B2 **Sault Sainte Marie** Can.
140 C1 **Sault Sainte Marie** U.S.A.
77 C1 **Saumalkol'** Kazakh.
59 C3 **Saumlakki** Indon.
104 B2 **Saumur** France
120 B1 **Saurimo** Angola
109 D2 **Sava** *r.* Europe
91 E1 **Savala** *r.* Rus. Fed.
143 D2 **Savannah** *GA* U.S.A.

142 C1 **Savannah** *TN* U.S.A.
143 D2 **Savannah** *r.* U.S.A.
63 B2 **Savannakhét** Laos
130 A1 **Savant Lake** *l.* Can.
111 C3 **Savaştepe** Turkey
89 F2 **Savino** Rus. Fed.
86 D2 **Savinskiy** Rus. Fed.
108 A2 **Savona** Italy
93 I3 **Savonlinna** Fin.
92 I2 **Savukoski** Fin.
74 B2 **Sawai Madhopur** India
62 A2 **Sawankhalok** Thai.
136 B3 **Sawatch Range** *mts* U.S.A.
116 B2 **Sawhāj** Egypt
53 D2 **Sawtell** Austr.
59 C3 **Sawu Sea** Indon.
79 C3 **Sayḩūt** Yemen
69 D2 **Saynshand** Mongolia
141 D2 **Sayre** U.S.A.
144 B3 **Sayula** *Jalisco* Mex.
145 C3 **Sayula** *Veracruz* Mex.
128 B2 **Sayward** Can.
89 E2 **Sazonovo** Rus. Fed.
114 B2 **Sbaa** Alg.
98 B1 **Scafell Pike** *hill* U.K.
109 C3 **Scalea** Italy
96 C1 **Scapa Flow** *inlet* U.K.
130 C2 **Scarborough** Can.
147 D3 **Scarborough** Trin. and Tob.
98 C1 **Scarborough** U.K.
64 A1 **Scarborough Shoal** *sea feature* Phil.
96 A2 **Scarinish** U.K.
Scarpanto *i.* Greece *see* **Karpathos**
105 D2 **Schaffhausen** Switz.
100 B1 **Schagen** Neth.
102 C2 **Schärding** Austria
100 A2 **Scharendijke** Neth.
101 D1 **Scharhörn** *sea feature* Ger.
101 D1 **Scheeßel** Ger.
131 D1 **Schefferville** Can.
135 D3 **Schell Creek Range** *mts* U.S.A.
141 E2 **Schenectady** U.S.A.
101 E3 **Scheßlitz** Ger.
100 C1 **Schiermonnikoog** *i.* Neth.
108 B1 **Schio** Italy
101 F2 **Schkeuditz** Ger.
101 E1 **Schladen** Ger.
101 E2 **Schleiz** Ger.
102 B1 **Schleswig** Ger.
101 D2 **Schloss Holte-Stukenbrock** Ger.
101 D2 **Schlüchtern** Ger.
101 E3 **Schlüsselfeld** Ger.
101 D2 **Schmallenberg** Ger.
101 D1 **Schneverdingen** Ger.
101 E1 **Schönebeck (Elbe)** Ger.
101 E1 **Schöningen** Ger.
100 B2 **Schoonhoven** Neth.
59 D3 **Schouten Islands** P.N.G.
102 B2 **Schwabische Alb** *mts* Ger.
102 C2 **Schwandorf** Ger.
61 C2 **Schwaner, Pegunungan** *mts* Indon.
101 E1 **Schwarzenbek** Ger.
101 F2 **Schwarzenberg** Ger.
122 A2 **Schwarzrand** *mts* Namibia
102 B2 **Schwarzwald** *mts* Ger.
102 C2 **Schwaz** Austria
102 C1 **Schwedt an der Oder** Ger.
101 E2 **Schweinfurt** Ger.
101 E1 **Schwerin** Ger.
101 E1 **Schweriner See** *l.* Ger.
105 D2 **Schwyz** Switz.
108 B3 **Sciacca** *Sicily* Italy
95 B4 **Scilly, Isles of** U.K.
140 C3 **Scioto** *r.* U.S.A.
136 B1 **Scobey** U.S.A.
53 D2 **Scone** Austr.
55 R3 **Scotia Ridge** *sea feature* S. Atlantic Ocean
158 C8 **Scotia Sea** S. Atlantic Ocean
96 C2 **Scotland** *admin. div.* U.K.
128 B2 **Scott, Cape** Can.
123 D3 **Scottburgh** S. Africa
136 C3 **Scott City** U.S.A.
136 C2 **Scottsbluff** U.S.A.
142 C2 **Scottsboro** U.S.A.
96 B1 **Scourie** U.K.
141 D2 **Scranton** U.S.A.
98 C2 **Scunthorpe** U.K.
105 E2 **Scuol** Switz.
129 E2 **Seal** *r.* Can.
122 B3 **Seal, Cape** S. Africa
52 B3 **Sea Lake** Austr.
139 D3 **Sealy** U.S.A.
142 B1 **Searcy** U.S.A.
98 B1 **Seascale** U.K.
134 B1 **Seattle** U.S.A.
141 E2 **Sebago Lake** U.S.A.
144 A2 **Sebastián Vizcaíno, Bahía** *b.* Mex.
110 B1 **Sebeş** Romania
60 B2 **Sebesi** *i.* Indon.
88 C2 **Sebezh** Rus. Fed.
80 B1 **Şebinkarahisar** Turkey
143 D3 **Sebring** U.S.A.
128 B3 **Sechelt** Can.
150 A2 **Sechura** Peru
73 B3 **Secunderabad** India
137 E3 **Sedalia** U.S.A.
105 C2 **Sedan** France
54 B2 **Seddon** N.Z.
138 A2 **Sedona** U.S.A.
101 E2 **Seeburg** Ger.
101 E1 **Seehausen (Altmark)** Ger.
122 A2 **Seeheim** Namibia
104 C2 **Sées** France
101 E2 **Seesen** Ger.
101 E1 **Seevetal** Ger.
114 A4 **Sefadu** Sierra Leone
123 C1 **Sefare** Botswana
60 B1 **Segamat** Malaysia
86 C2 **Segezha** Rus. Fed.
114 B3 **Ségou** Mali
106 C1 **Segovia** Spain
115 D2 **Séguédine** Niger
114 B4 **Séguéla** Côte d'Ivoire
139 D3 **Seguin** U.S.A.
107 C2 **Segura** *r.* Spain
106 C2 **Segura, Sierra de** *mts* Spain
120 B3 **Sehithwa** Botswana
93 H3 **Seinäjoki** Fin.
104 C2 **Seine** *r.* France
104 B2 **Seine, Baie de** *b.* France
103 E1 **Sejny** Pol.
60 B2 **Sekayu** Indon.
114 B4 **Sekondi** Ghana
59 C3 **Selaru** *i.* Indon.
61 C2 **Selatan, Tanjung** *pt* Indon.
126 A2 **Selawik** U.S.A.
98 C2 **Selby** U.K.
120 B3 **Selebi-Phikwe** Botswana
105 D2 **Sélestat** France
92 □A3 **Selfoss** Iceland
114 A3 **Sélibabi** Maur.
138 A1 **Seligman** U.S.A.
116 A2 **Selîma Oasis** Sudan
111 C3 **Selimiye** Turkey
114 B3 **Sélingué, Lac de** *l.* Mali
89 D2 **Selizharovo** Rus. Fed.
93 E4 **Seljord** Norway
129 E2 **Selkirk** Can.
96 C3 **Selkirk** U.K.
128 C2 **Selkirk Mountains** Can.
142 C2 **Selma** *AL* U.S.A.
135 C3 **Selma** *CA* U.S.A.
89 D3 **Sel'tso** Rus. Fed.
150 A2 **Selvas** *reg.* Brazil
134 C1 **Selway** *r.* U.S.A.
129 D1 **Selwyn Lake** Can.
128 A1 **Selwyn Mountains** Can.
51 C2 **Selwyn Range** *hills* Austr.
60 B2 **Semangka, Teluk** *b.* Indon.
61 C2 **Semarang** Indon.
61 B1 **Sematan** *Sarawak* Malaysia
118 B2 **Sembé** Congo
81 C2 **Şemdinli** Turkey
91 C1 **Semenivka** Ukr.
86 D3 **Semenov** Rus. Fed.
61 C2 **Semeru, Gunung** *vol.* Indon.
89 E3 **Semiluki** Rus. Fed.
136 B2 **Seminoe Reservoir** U.S.A.
139 C2 **Seminole** U.S.A.
143 D2 **Seminole, Lake** U.S.A.
77 E1 **Semipalatinsk** Kazakh.
61 C1 **Semitau** Indon.
81 D2 **Semnān** Iran
61 C1 **Semporna** *Sabah* Malaysia
105 C2 **Semur-en-Auxois** France
150 B2 **Sena Madureira** Brazil
120 B2 **Senanga** Zambia
67 B4 **Sendai** *Kagoshima* Japan
67 D3 **Sendai** *Miyagi* Japan
114 A3 **Senegal** *country* Africa
114 A3 **Sénégal** *r.* Maur./Senegal
102 C1 **Senftenberg** Ger.
119 D3 **Sengerema** Tanz.
151 D3 **Senhor do Bonfim** Brazil
108 B2 **Senigallia** Italy
109 B2 **Senj** Croatia
92 G2 **Senja** *i.* Norway
122 B2 **Senlac** S. Africa
104 C2 **Senlis** France
63 B2 **Senmonorom** Cambodia
117 B3 **Sennar** Sudan
130 C2 **Senneterre** Can.
123 C3 **Senqu** *r.* Lesotho
105 C2 **Sens** France
109 D1 **Senta** Serb. and Mont.
128 B2 **Sentinel Peak** Can.
75 B2 **Seoni** India
65 B2 **Seoul** S. Korea
155 D2 **Sepetiba, Baía de** *b.* Brazil
59 D3 **Sepik** *r.* P.N.G.
61 C1 **Sepinang** Indon.
131 D1 **Sept-Îles** Can.
59 C3 **Seram** *i.* Indon.
59 C3 **Seram Sea** Indon.
60 B2 **Serang** Indon.
Serbia *aut. rep.* Serb. and Mont. *see* **Srbija**
109 D2 **Serbia and Montenegro** *country* Europe
89 E3 **Serebryanyye Prudy** Rus. Fed.
60 B1 **Seremban** Malaysia
119 D3 **Serengeti Plain** Tanz.
87 D3 **Sergach** Rus. Fed.
89 E2 **Sergiyev Posad** Rus. Fed.
61 C1 **Seria** Brunei
61 C1 **Serian** *Sarawak* Malaysia
111 B3 **Serifos** *i.* Greece
80 B2 **Serik** Turkey
59 C3 **Sermata, Kepulauan** *is* Indon.
86 F3 **Serov** Rus. Fed.
120 B3 **Serowe** Botswana
106 B2 **Serpa** Port.
89 E3 **Serpukhov** Rus. Fed.
154 B1 **Serranópolis** Brazil
151 D3 **Serra da Mesa, Represa** *resr* Brazil
100 A3 **Serre** *r.* France
111 B2 **Serres** Greece
151 E3 **Serrinha** Brazil
155 D1 **Sêrro** Brazil
154 C2 **Sertãozinho** Brazil
61 C2 **Seruyan** *r.* Indon.

68 C2 **Sêrxü** China
120 A2 **Sesfontein** Namibia
108 B2 **Sessa Aurunca** Italy
107 D2 **Ses Salines, Cap de** *c.* Spain
108 A2 **Sestri Levante** Italy
105 C3 **Sète** France
155 D1 **Sete Lagoas** Brazil
92 G2 **Setermoen** Norway
93 E4 **Setesdal** *val.* Norway
115 C1 **Sétif** Alg.
67 B4 **Seto-naikai** *sea* Japan
114 B1 **Settat** Morocco
98 B1 **Settle** U.K.
106 B2 **Setúbal** Port.
106 B2 **Setúbal, Baía de** *b.* Port.
130 A1 **Seul, Lac** *l.* Can.
76 A2 **Sevan, Lake** Armenia
Sevana Lich *l.* Armenia *see* Sevan, Lake
91 C3 **Sevastopol'** Ukr.
105 C3 **Sévérac-le-Château** France
130 B1 **Severn** *r.* Can.
122 B2 **Severn** S. Africa
99 B3 **Severn** *r.* U.K.
86 D2 **Severnaya Dvina** *r.* Rus. Fed.
83 H1 **Severnaya Zemlya** *is* Rus. Fed.
86 D2 **Severnyy** *Nenetskiy Avtonomnyy Okrug* Rus. Fed.
86 F2 **Severnyy** *Respublika Komi* Rus. Fed.
86 C2 **Severodvinsk** Rus. Fed.
86 C2 **Severomorsk** Rus. Fed.
91 D3 **Severskaya** Rus. Fed.
135 D3 **Sevier** *r.* U.S.A.
135 D3 **Sevier Lake** U.S.A.
Sevilla Spain *see* **Seville**
106 B2 **Seville** Spain
128 A2 **Sewell Inlet** Can.
128 C2 **Sexsmith** Can.
144 B2 **Sextín** *r.* Mex.
86 G1 **Seyakha** Rus. Fed.
113 H4 **Seychelles** *country* Indian Ocean
92 □C2 **Seyðisfjörður** Iceland
91 C1 **Seym** *r.* Rus. Fed./Ukr.
83 L2 **Seymchan** Rus. Fed.
53 C3 **Seymour** Austr.
140 B3 **Seymour** *IN* U.S.A.
139 D2 **Seymour** *TX* U.S.A.
105 C2 **Sézanne** France
111 B3 **Sfakia** Greece
110 C1 **Sfântu Gheorghe** Romania
115 D1 **Sfax** Tunisia
's-Gravenhage Neth. *see* **The Hague**
96 A2 **Sgurr Alasdair** *hill* U.K.
70 A2 **Shaanxi** *prov.* China
91 D2 **Shabel'sk** Rus. Fed.
77 D3 **Shache** China
55 R1 **Shackleton Range** Antarctica
99 B3 **Shaftesbury** U.K.
75 C2 **Shahdol** India
77 C3 **Shah Fuladi** *mt.* Afgh.
75 B2 **Shahjahanpur** India
81 D2 **Shahr-e Kord** Iran
81 D2 **Shahrezā** Iran
89 E2 **Shakhovskaya** Rus. Fed.
77 C3 **Shakhrisabz** Uzbek.
91 E2 **Shakhty** Rus. Fed.
86 D3 **Shakhun'ya** Rus. Fed.
66 D2 **Shakotan-misaki** *c.* Japan
76 B2 **Shalkar** Kazakh.
68 C2 **Shaluli Shan** *mts* China
129 E2 **Shamattawa** Can.
139 C1 **Shamrock** U.S.A.
68 C2 **Shandan** China
70 B2 **Shandong** *prov.* China
70 C2 **Shandong Bandao** *pen.* China
121 B2 **Shangani** *r.* Zimbabwe
70 C2 **Shanghai** China
70 C2 **Shanghai** *mun.* China
71 B3 **Shanghang** China
71 B3 **Shangrao** China
70 B2 **Shangshui** China
70 C2 **Shangyu** China
69 E1 **Shangzhi** China
70 A2 **Shangzhou** China
97 B2 **Shannon** *r.* Rep. of Ireland
97 B2 **Shannon, Mouth of the** Rep. of Ireland
71 B3 **Shantou** China
70 B2 **Shanxi** *prov.* China
71 B3 **Shaoguan** China
71 B3 **Shaowu** China
70 C2 **Shaoxing** China
71 B3 **Shaoyang** China
116 C2 **Shaqrā'** Saudi Arabia
90 B2 **Sharhorod** Ukr.
88 C2 **Sharkawshchyna** Belarus
50 A2 **Shark Bay** Austr.
78 A2 **Sharm ash Shaykh** Egypt
140 C2 **Sharon** U.S.A.
86 D3 **Shar'ya** Rus. Fed.
121 B3 **Shashe** *r.* Botswana/Zimbabwe
117 B4 **Shashemenē** Eth.
134 B2 **Shasta, Mount** *vol.* U.S.A.
134 B2 **Shasta Lake** U.S.A.
89 E2 **Shatura** Rus. Fed.
129 D3 **Shaunavon** Can.
140 B2 **Shawano** U.S.A.
131 C2 **Shawinigan** Can.
139 D1 **Shawnee** U.S.A.
50 B2 **Shay Gap** Austr.
89 E3 **Shchekino** Rus. Fed.
89 E2 **Shchelkovo** Rus. Fed.
89 E3 **Shchigry** Rus. Fed.
91 C1 **Shchors** Ukr.
88 B3 **Shchuchyn** Belarus
91 D1 **Shebekino** Rus. Fed.
77 C3 **Sheberghān** Afgh.
140 B2 **Sheboygan** U.S.A.
91 D3 **Shebsh** *r.* Rus. Fed.
97 C2 **Sheelin, Lough** *l.* Rep. of Ireland
98 C2 **Sheffield** U.K.
89 E2 **Sheksna** Rus. Fed.
89 E2 **Sheksninskoye Vodokhranilishche** *resr* Rus. Fed.
83 M2 **Shelagskiy, Mys** *pt* Rus. Fed.
131 D2 **Shelburne** Can.
134 D1 **Shelby** U.S.A.
140 B3 **Shelbyville** *IN* U.S.A.
142 C1 **Shelbyville** *TN* U.S.A.
83 L2 **Shelikhova, Zaliv** *g.* Rus. Fed.
129 D2 **Shellbrook** Can.
134 B1 **Shelton** U.S.A.
137 D2 **Shenandoah** U.S.A.
141 D3 **Shenandoah** *r.* U.S.A.
141 D3 **Shenandoah Mountains** U.S.A.
118 A2 **Shendam** Nigeria
86 D2 **Shenkursk** Rus. Fed.
65 A1 **Shenyang** China
71 B3 **Shenzhen** China
90 B1 **Shepetivka** Ukr.
53 C3 **Shepparton** Austr.
99 D3 **Sheppey, Isle of** *i.* U.K.
131 D2 **Sherbrooke** *N.S.* Can.
131 C2 **Sherbrooke** *Que.* Can.
116 B3 **Shereiq** Sudan
136 B2 **Sheridan** U.S.A.
139 D2 **Sherman** U.S.A.
100 B2 **'s-Hertogenbosch** Neth.
96 □ **Shetland Islands** *is* U.K.
76 B2 **Shetpe** Kazakh.
Shevchenko Kazakh. *see* Aktau
137 D1 **Sheyenne** *r.* U.S.A.
79 B3 **Shibām** Yemen
66 D2 **Shibetsu** Japan
71 B3 **Shicheng** China
96 B2 **Shiel, Loch** *l.* U.K.
77 E2 **Shihezi** China
Shijiao China *see* **Fogang**
70 B2 **Shijiazhuang** China
74 A2 **Shikarpur** Pak.
67 B4 **Shikoku** *i.* Japan
66 D2 **Shikotsu-ko** *l.* Japan
86 D2 **Shilega** Rus. Fed.
75 C2 **Shiliguri** India
75 D2 **Shillong** India
89 F3 **Shilovo** Rus. Fed.
117 C3 **Shimbiris** *mt.* Somalia
67 C3 **Shimizu** Japan
73 B3 **Shimoga** India
67 B4 **Shimonoseki** Japan
96 B1 **Shin, Loch** *l.* U.K.
67 C4 **Shingū** Japan
123 D1 **Shingwedzi** S. Africa
123 D1 **Shingwedzi** *r.* S. Africa
119 D3 **Shinyanga** Tanz.
67 C4 **Shiono-misaki** *c.* Japan
138 B1 **Shiprock** U.S.A.
71 A3 **Shiqian** China
70 A2 **Shiquan** China
Shiquanhe China *see* **Gar**
Shiquan He *r.* China/Pak. *see* Indus
67 C3 **Shirane-san** *mt.* Japan
81 D3 **Shīrāz** Iran
66 D2 **Shiretoko-misaki** *c.* Japan
66 D2 **Shiriya-zaki** *c.* Japan
74 B2 **Shiv** India
75 B2 **Shivpuri** India
70 B2 **Shiyan** China
70 A2 **Shizuishan** China
67 C4 **Shizuoka** Japan
89 D3 **Shklow** Belarus
109 C2 **Shkodër** Albania
83 H1 **Shmidta, Ostrov** *i.* Rus. Fed.
135 C3 **Shoshone** U.S.A.
135 C3 **Shoshone Mountains** *mts* U.S.A.
123 C1 **Shoshong** Botswana
91 C1 **Shostka** Ukr.
70 B2 **Shouxian** China
138 A2 **Show Low** U.S.A.
91 C2 **Shpola** Ukr.
142 B2 **Shreveport** U.S.A.
99 B2 **Shrewsbury** U.K.
62 A1 **Shuangjiang** China
87 E4 **Shubarkuduk** Kazakh.
116 B1 **Shubrā al Khaymah** Egypt
89 D2 **Shugozero** Rus. Fed.
120 B2 **Shumba** Zimbabwe
110 C2 **Shumen** Bulg.
88 C2 **Shumilina** Belarus
89 D3 **Shumyachi** Rus. Fed.
126 A2 **Shungnak** U.S.A.
78 B3 **Shuqrah** Yemen
89 F2 **Shushkodom** Rus. Fed.
81 C2 **Shushtar** Iran
128 C2 **Shuswap Lake** Can.
89 F2 **Shuya** Rus. Fed.
89 F2 **Shuyskoye** Rus. Fed.
62 A1 **Shwebo** Myanmar
62 A1 **Shwedwin** Myanmar
62 A2 **Shwegyin** Myanmar
77 C2 **Shymkent** Kazakh.
91 C2 **Shyroke** Ukr.
59 C3 **Sia** Indon.
74 A2 **Siahan Range** *mts* Pak.
74 B1 **Sialkot** Pak.
64 B2 **Siargao** *i.* Phil.

88 B2 **Šiauliai** Lith.
109 C2 **Šibenik** Croatia
83 H2 **Siberia** *reg.* Rus. Fed.
60 A2 **Siberut** *i.* Indon.
74 A2 **Sibi** Pak.
110 B1 **Sibiu** Romania
60 A1 **Sibolga** Indon.
62 A1 **Sibsagar** India
61 C1 **Sibu** *Sarawak* Malaysia
118 B2 **Sibut** C.A.R.
64 B1 **Sibuyan** *i.* Phil.
64 B1 **Sibuyan Sea** Phil.
128 C2 **Sicamous** Can.
63 A3 **Sichon** Thai.
70 A2 **Sichuan** *prov.* China
70 A3 **Sichuan Pendi** *basin* China
105 D3 **Sicié, Cap** *c.* France
Sicilia *i.* Italy *see* **Sicily**
108 B3 **Sicilian Channel** Italy/Tunisia
108 B3 **Sicily** *i.* Italy
150 A3 **Sicuani** Peru
74 B2 **Siddhapur** India
111 C3 **Sideros, Akra** *pt* Greece
107 D2 **Sidi Aïssa** Alg.
107 D2 **Sidi Ali** Alg.
114 B1 **Sidi Bel Abbès** Alg.
114 A2 **Sidi Ifni** Morocco
60 A1 **Sidikalang** Indon.
96 C2 **Sidlaw Hills** U.K.
99 B3 **Sidmouth** U.K.
134 B1 **Sidney** Can.
136 C1 **Sidney** *MT* U.S.A.
136 C2 **Sidney** *NE* U.S.A.
140 C2 **Sidney** *OH* U.S.A.
143 D2 **Sidney Lanier, Lake** U.S.A.
154 B2 **Sidrolândia** Brazil
103 E1 **Siedlce** Pol.
100 C2 **Sieg** *r.* Ger.
100 D2 **Siegen** Ger.
63 B2 **Siĕmréab** Cambodia
108 B2 **Siena** Italy
103 D1 **Sieradz** Pol.
153 B5 **Sierra Grande** Arg.
114 A4 **Sierra Leone** *country* Africa
144 B2 **Sierra Mojada** Mex.
138 A2 **Sierra Vista** U.S.A.
105 D2 **Sierre** Switz.
111 B3 **Sifnos** *i.* Greece
107 C2 **Sig** Alg.
127 H2 **Sigguup Nunaa** *pen.* Greenland
103 E2 **Sighetu Marmaţiei** Romania
110 B1 **Sighişoara** Romania
60 A1 **Sigli** Indon.
92 □B2 **Siglufjörður** Iceland
102 B2 **Sigmaringen** Ger.
100 B3 **Signy-l'Abbaye** France
106 C1 **Sigüenza** Spain
114 B3 **Siguiri** Guinea
88 B2 **Sigulda** Latvia
63 B2 **Sihanoukville** Cambodia
92 I3 **Siilinjärvi** Fin.
81 C2 **Siirt** Turkey
60 B2 **Sijunjung** Indon.
74 B2 **Sikar** India
114 B3 **Sikasso** Mali
137 F3 **Sikeston** U.S.A.
66 B2 **Sikhote-Alin'** *mts* Rus. Fed.
111 C3 **Sikinos** *i.* Greece
144 B2 **Silao** Mex.
75 D2 **Silchar** India
77 D1 **Siletiteniz, Ozero** *salt l.* Kazakh.
75 C2 **Silgarhi** Nepal
80 B2 **Silifke** Turkey
75 C1 **Siling Co** *salt l.* China
110 C2 **Silistra** Bulg.
80 A1 **Silivri** Turkey
93 F3 **Siljan** *l.* Sweden
93 E4 **Silkeborg** Denmark
88 C2 **Sillamäe** Estonia
142 B1 **Siloam Springs** U.S.A.
123 D2 **Silobela** S. Africa
88 B2 **Šilutė** Lith.
81 C2 **Silvan** Turkey
138 B2 **Silver City** U.S.A.
136 B3 **Silverton** U.S.A.
62 B1 **Simao** China
130 C2 **Simàrd, Lac** *l.* Can.
111 C3 **Simav** Turkey
111 C3 **Simav Dağları** *mts* Turkey
118 C2 **Simba** Dem. Rep. Congo
141 D2 **Simcoe, Lake** Can.
60 A1 **Simeulue** *i.* Indon.
91 C3 **Simferopol'** Ukr.
110 B1 **Şimleu Silvaniei** Romania
100 C3 **Simmern (Hunsrück)** Ger.
129 D2 **Simonhouse** Can.
51 C2 **Simpson Desert** Austr.
93 F4 **Simrishamn** Sweden
60 A1 **Sinabang** Indon.
116 B2 **Sinai** *pen.* Egypt
71 A3 **Sinan** China
65 B2 **Sinanju** N. Korea
62 A1 **Sinbo** Myanmar
150 A1 **Sincelejo** Col.
111 C3 **Sındırgı** Turkey
86 E2 **Sindor** Rus. Fed.
111 C2 **Sinekçi** Turkey
106 B2 **Sines** Port.
106 B2 **Sines, Cabo de** *c.* Port.
75 C2 **Singahi** India
60 B1 **Singapore** *country* Asia
61 C2 **Singaraja** Indon.
119 D3 **Singida** Tanz.
62 A1 **Singkaling Hkamti** Myanmar
61 B1 **Singkawang** Indon.
60 A1 **Singkil** Indon.
53 D2 **Singleton** Austr.
62 A1 **Singu** Myanmar
108 A2 **Siniscola** *Sardinia* Italy
109 C2 **Sinj** Croatia
116 B3 **Sinkat** Sudan
80 B1 **Sinop** Turkey
65 B1 **Sinp'o** N. Korea
61 C1 **Sintang** Indon.
139 D3 **Sinton** U.S.A.
65 A1 **Sinŭiju** N. Korea
103 D2 **Siófok** Hungary
105 D2 **Sion** Switz.
137 D2 **Sioux Center** U.S.A.
137 D2 **Sioux City** U.S.A.
137 D2 **Sioux Falls** U.S.A.
130 A1 **Sioux Lookout** Can.
65 A1 **Siping** China
129 E2 **Sipiwesk Lake** Can.
60 A2 **Sipura** *i.* Indon.
93 E4 **Sira** *r.* Norway
Siracusa Italy *see* **Syracuse**
51 C1 **Sir Edward Pellew Group** *is* Austr.
79 C2 **Sīrīk** Iran
62 B2 **Siri Kit Dam** Thai.
128 B1 **Sir James MacBrien, Mount** Can.
79 C2 **Sīrjān** Iran
81 C2 **Şırnak** Turkey
74 B2 **Sirohi** India
74 B2 **Sirsa** India
115 D1 **Sirte** Libya
115 D1 **Sirte, Gulf of** Libya
88 B2 **Širvintos** Lith.
145 C2 **Sisal** Mex.
122 B2 **Sishen** S. Africa
81 C2 **Sisian** Armenia
129 D2 **Sisipuk Lake** Can.
63 B2 **Sisŏphŏn** Cambodia
105 D3 **Sisteron** France
75 C2 **Sitapur** India
123 D2 **Siteki** Swaziland
128 A2 **Sitka** U.S.A.
62 A2 **Sittang** *r.* Myanmar
100 B2 **Sittard** Neth.
62 A1 **Sittwe** Myanmar
61 C2 **Situbondo** Indon.
80 B2 **Sivas** Turkey
111 C3 **Sivaslı** Turkey
80 B2 **Siverek** Turkey
80 B2 **Sivrihisar** Turkey
116 A2 **Sīwah** Egypt
74 B1 **Siwalik Range** *mts* India/Nepal
105 D3 **Six-Fours-les-Plages** France
70 B2 **Sixian** China
123 C2 **Siyabuswa** S. Africa
93 F4 **Sjælland** *i.* Denmark
109 D2 **Sjenica** Serb. and Mont.
92 G2 **Sjøvegan** Norway
91 C2 **Skadovs'k** Ukr.
93 F4 **Skagen** Denmark
93 E4 **Skagerrak** *str.* Denmark/Norway
134 B1 **Skagit** *r.* U.S.A.
128 A2 **Skagway** U.S.A.
74 B1 **Skardu** Jammu and Kashmir
103 E1 **Skarżysko-Kamienna** Pol.
103 D2 **Skawina** Pol.
128 B2 **Skeena** *r.* Can.
128 B2 **Skeena Mountains** Can.
98 D2 **Skegness** U.K.
92 H3 **Skellefteå** Sweden
92 H3 **Skellefteälven** *r.* Sweden
97 C2 **Skerries** Rep. of Ireland
111 B3 **Skiathos** *i.* Greece
97 B3 **Skibbereen** Rep. of Ireland
92 □B2 **Skíðadals-jökull** *glacier* Iceland
98 B1 **Skiddaw** *hill* U.K.
93 E4 **Skien** Norway
103 E1 **Skierniewice** Pol.
115 C1 **Skikda** Alg.
52 B3 **Skipton** Austr.
98 B2 **Skipton** U.K.
93 E4 **Skive** Denmark
92 H1 **Skjervøy** Norway
111 B3 **Skopelos** *i.* Greece
89 E3 **Skopin** Rus. Fed.
109 D2 **Skopje** Macedonia
93 F4 **Skövde** Sweden
141 F2 **Skowhegan** U.S.A.
88 B2 **Skrunda** Latvia
128 A1 **Skukum, Mount** Can.
123 D1 **Skukuza** S. Africa
88 B2 **Skuodas** Lith.
96 A2 **Skye** *i.* U.K.
111 B3 **Skyros** Greece
111 B3 **Skyros** *i.* Greece
93 F4 **Slagelse** Denmark
97 C2 **Slaney** *r.* Rep. of Ireland
88 C2 **Slantsy** Rus. Fed.
109 C1 **Slatina** Croatia
110 B2 **Slatina** Romania
129 C1 **Slave** *r.* Can.
114 C4 **Slave Coast** Africa
128 C2 **Slave Lake** Can.
82 G3 **Slavgorod** Rus. Fed.
109 C1 **Slavonski Brod** Croatia
90 B1 **Slavuta** Ukr.
90 C1 **Slavutych** Ukr.
91 D2 **Slavyansk-na-Kubani** Rus. Fed.
89 D3 **Slawharad** Belarus
103 D1 **Sławno** Pol.
97 A2 **Slea Head** *hd* Rep. of Ireland
130 C1 **Sleeper Islands** Can.
97 D1 **Slieve Donard** *hill* U.K.
97 B1 **Slieve Gamph** *hills* Rep. of Ireland
97 B1 **Sligo** Rep. of Ireland
97 B1 **Sligo Bay** Rep. of Ireland

93 G4 **Slite** Sweden
110 C2 **Sliven** Bulg.
110 C2 **Slobozia** Romania
128 C3 **Slocan** Can.
88 C3 **Slonim** Belarus
100 B1 **Sloten** Neth.
99 C3 **Slough** U.K.
103 D2 **Slovakia** *country* Europe
108 B1 **Slovenia** *country* Europe
91 D2 **Slov"yans'k** Ukr.
90 B1 **Sluch** *r.* Ukr.
103 D1 **Słupsk** Pol.
88 C3 **Slutsk** Belarus
97 A2 **Slyne Head** *hd* Rep. of Ireland
131 D1 **Smallwood Reservoir** Can.
88 C3 **Smalyavichy** Belarus
88 C3 **Smarhon'** Belarus
129 D2 **Smeaton** Can.
109 D2 **Smederevo** Serb. and Mont.
109 D2 **Smederevska Palanka** Serb. and Mont.
91 C2 **Smila** Ukr.
88 C2 **Smiltene** Latvia
128 B2 **Smithers** Can.
143 E1 **Smithfield** U.S.A.
141 D3 **Smith Mountain Lake** U.S.A.
130 C2 **Smiths Falls** Can.
137 D3 **Smoky Hills** U.S.A.
92 E3 **Smøla** *i.* Norway
89 D3 **Smolensk** Rus. Fed.
110 B2 **Smolyan** Bulg.
130 B2 **Smooth Rock Falls** Can.
Smyrna Turkey *see* **İzmir**
92 □B3 **Snæfell** *mt.* Iceland
98 A1 **Snaefell** *hill* Isle of Man
132 B2 **Snake** *r.* U.S.A.
134 D2 **Snake River Plain** U.S.A.
100 B1 **Sneek** Neth.
97 B3 **Sneem** Rep. of Ireland
122 B3 **Sneeuberge** *mts* S. Africa
108 B1 **Snežnik** *mt.* Slovenia
91 C2 **Snihurivka** Ukr.
93 E3 **Snøhetta** *mt.* Norway
129 D1 **Snowbird Lake** *l.* Can.
98 A2 **Snowdon** *mt.* U.K.
Snowdrift Can. *see* **Łutselk'e**
129 C1 **Snowdrift** *r.* Can.
138 A2 **Snowflake** U.S.A.
129 D2 **Snow Lake** Can.
52 A2 **Snowtown** Austr.
53 C3 **Snowy** *r.* Austr.
53 C3 **Snowy Mountains** Austr.
139 C2 **Snyder** U.S.A.
121 □D2 **Soalala** Madag.
117 B4 **Sobat** *r.* Sudan
100 C3 **Sobernheim** Ger.
89 F2 **Sobinka** Rus. Fed.
151 D3 **Sobradinho, Barragem de** *resr* Brazil
151 D2 **Sobral** Brazil
87 C4 **Sochi** Rus. Fed.
65 B2 **Sŏch'ŏn** S. Korea
49 H5 **Society Islands** French Polynesia
150 A1 **Socorro** Col.
138 B2 **Socorro** U.S.A.
144 A3 **Socorro, Isla** *i.* Mex.
56 B4 **Socotra** *i.* Yemen
63 B3 **Soc Trăng** Vietnam
106 C2 **Socuéllamos** Spain
92 I2 **Sodankylä** Fin.
134 D2 **Soda Springs** U.S.A.
93 G3 **Söderhamn** Sweden
93 G4 **Södertälje** Sweden
116 A3 **Sodiri** Sudan
117 B4 **Sodo** Eth.
93 G3 **Södra Kvarken** *str.* Fin./Sweden
100 D2 **Soest** Ger.
110 B2 **Sofia** Bulg.
Sofiya Bulg. *see* **Sofia**
68 C2 **Sog** China
93 E3 **Sognefjorden** *inlet* Norway
111 D2 **Söğüt** Turkey
100 B2 **Soignies** Belgium
105 C2 **Soissons** France
90 A1 **Sokal'** Ukr.
111 C3 **Söke** Turkey
81 C1 **Sokhumi** Georgia
114 C4 **Sokodé** Togo
89 F2 **Sokol** Rus. Fed.
101 F2 **Sokolov** Czech Rep.
115 C3 **Sokoto** Nigeria
115 C3 **Sokoto** *r.* Nigeria
90 B2 **Sokyryany** Ukr.
73 B3 **Solapur** India
135 B3 **Soledad** U.S.A.
89 F2 **Soligalich** Rus. Fed.
99 C2 **Solihull** U.K.
86 E3 **Solikamsk** Rus. Fed.
87 E3 **Sol'-Iletsk** Rus. Fed.
100 C2 **Solingen** Ger.
92 G3 **Sollefteå** Sweden
93 G4 **Sollentuna** Sweden
101 D2 **Solling** *hills* Ger.
89 E2 **Solnechnogorsk** Rus. Fed.
60 B2 **Solok** Indon.
49 E3 **Solomon Islands** *country* S. Pacific Ocean
48 D3 **Solomon Sea** P.N.G./Solomon Islands
105 D2 **Solothurn** Switz.
101 D1 **Soltau** Ger.
89 D2 **Sol'tsy** Rus. Fed.
96 C3 **Solway Firth** *est.* U.K.
120 B2 **Solwezi** Zambia
111 C3 **Soma** Turkey
117 C4 **Somalia** *country* Africa
120 B1 **Sombo** Angola
109 C1 **Sombor** Serb. and Mont.
144 B2 **Sombrerete** Mex.
140 C3 **Somerset** U.S.A.
123 C3 **Somerset East** S. Africa
126 E2 **Somerset Island** Can.
122 A3 **Somerset West** S. Africa
101 E2 **Sömmerda** Ger.
75 C2 **Son** *r.* India
93 E4 **Sønderborg** Denmark
101 E2 **Sondershausen** Ger.
Søndre Strømfjord *inlet* Greenland *see* **Kangerlussuaq**
62 B1 **Sông Da, Hô** *resr* Vietnam
119 D4 **Songea** Tanz.
65 B1 **Sŏnggan** N. Korea
65 B1 **Songhua Hu** *resr* China
Sŏngjin N. Korea *see* **Kimch'aek**
63 B3 **Songkhla** Thai.
65 B2 **Sŏngnam** S. Korea
65 B2 **Songnim** N. Korea
120 A1 **Songo** Angola
121 C2 **Songo** Moz.
69 E1 **Songyuan** China
Sonid Youqi China *see* **Saihan Tal**
89 E2 **Sonkovo** Rus. Fed.
62 B1 **Sơn La** Vietnam
74 A2 **Sonmiani** Pak.
101 E2 **Sonneberg** Ger.
138 A2 **Sonoita** Mex.
144 A2 **Sonora** *r.* Mex.
135 B3 **Sonora** *CA* U.S.A.
139 C2 **Sonora** *TX* U.S.A.
117 A4 **Sopo** *watercourse* Sudan
103 D2 **Sopron** Hungary
108 B2 **Sora** Italy
130 C2 **Sorel** Can.
51 D4 **Sorell** Austr.
106 C1 **Soria** Spain
76 B2 **Sor Mertvyy Kultuk** *dry lake* Kazakh.
90 B2 **Soroca** Moldova
154 C2 **Sorocaba** Brazil
87 E3 **Sorochinsk** Rus. Fed.
59 D2 **Sorol** *atoll* Micronesia
59 C3 **Sorong** Indon.
119 D2 **Soroti** Uganda
92 H1 **Sørøya** *i.* Norway
92 G2 **Sorsele** Sweden
64 B1 **Sorsogon** Phil.
86 C2 **Sortavala** Rus. Fed.
92 G2 **Sortland** Norway
65 B2 **Sŏsan** S. Korea
123 C2 **Soshanguve** S. Africa
89 E3 **Sosna** *r.* Rus. Fed.
153 B4 **Sosneado** *mt.* Arg.
86 E2 **Sosnogorsk** Rus. Fed.
86 D2 **Sosnovka** Rus. Fed.
88 C2 **Sosnovyy Bor** Rus. Fed.
103 D1 **Sosnowiec** Pol.
91 D2 **Sosyka** *r.* Rus. Fed.
145 C2 **Soto la Marina** Mex.
118 B2 **Souanké** Congo
104 C3 **Souillac** France
Sŏul S. Korea *see* **Seoul**
104 B2 **Soulac-sur-Mer** France
104 B3 **Soulom** France
80 B2 **Soûr** Lebanon
107 D2 **Sour el Ghozlane** Alg.
129 D3 **Souris** *Man.* Can.
131 D2 **Souris** *P.E.I.* Can.
129 E3 **Souris** *r.* Can.
151 E2 **Sousa** Brazil
115 D1 **Sousse** Tunisia
104 B3 **Soustons** France
122 B3 **South Africa, Republic of** *country* Africa
99 C3 **Southampton** U.K.
127 F2 **Southampton Island** Can.
73 D3 **South Andaman** *i.* India
52 A1 **South Australia** *state* Austr.
130 B2 **South Baymouth** Can.
140 B2 **South Bend** U.S.A.
143 D2 **South Carolina** *state* U.S.A.
58 B2 **South China Sea** N. Pacific Ocean
136 C2 **South Dakota** *state* U.S.A.
99 C3 **South Downs** *hills* U.K.
129 D2 **Southend** Can.
99 D3 **Southend-on-Sea** U.K.
54 B2 **Southern Alps** *mts* N.Z.
50 A3 **Southern Cross** Austr.
129 E2 **Southern Indian Lake** Can.
159 **Southern Ocean**
143 E1 **Southern Pines** U.S.A.
96 B3 **Southern Uplands** *hills* U.K.
149 F6 **South Georgia and South Sandwich Islands** *terr.* S. Atlantic Ocean
129 E1 **South Henik Lake** *l.* Can.
54 B2 **South Island** N.Z.
65 B2 **South Korea** *country* Asia
135 B3 **South Lake Tahoe** U.S.A.
128 B1 **South Nahanni** *r.* Can.
55 Q4 **South Orkney Islands** S. Atlantic Ocean
136 C2 **South Platte** *r.* U.S.A.
98 B2 **Southport** U.K.
143 E2 **Southport** U.S.A.
96 C1 **South Ronaldsay** *i.* U.K.
123 D3 **South Sand Bluff** *pt* S. Africa
129 D2 **South Saskatchewan** *r.* Can.
129 E2 **South Seal** *r.* Can.
55 P3 **South Shetland Islands** Antarctica

98 C1 **South Shields** U.K.
54 B1 **South Taranaki Bight** *b.* N.Z.
130 C1 **South Twin Island** Can.
96 A2 **South Uist** *i.* U.K.
53 D2 **South West Rocks** Austr.
99 D2 **Southwold** U.K.
109 C3 **Soverato** Italy
88 B2 **Sovetsk** Rus. Fed.
86 F2 **Sovetskiy** Rus. Fed.
91 C2 **Sovyets'kyy** Ukr.
123 C2 **Soweto** S. Africa
66 D1 **Sōya-misaki** *c.* Japan
90 C1 **Sozh** *r.* Europe
110 C2 **Sozopol** Bulg.
106 C1 **Spain** *country* Europe
99 C2 **Spalding** U.K.
135 D2 **Spanish Fork** U.S.A.
97 B2 **Spanish Point** Rep. of Ireland
108 B3 **Sparagio, Monte** *mt. Sicily* Italy
135 C3 **Sparks** U.S.A.
140 A2 **Sparta** U.S.A.
143 D2 **Spartanburg** U.S.A.
111 B3 **Sparti** Greece
109 C3 **Spartivento, Capo** *c.* Italy
89 D3 **Spas-Demensk** Rus. Fed.
89 F2 **Spas-Klepiki** Rus. Fed.
66 B2 **Spassk-Dal'niy** Rus. Fed.
89 F3 **Spassk-Ryazanskiy** Rus. Fed.
111 B3 **Spatha, Akra** *pt* Greece
136 C2 **Spearfish** U.S.A.
139 C1 **Spearman** U.S.A.
137 D2 **Spencer** U.S.A.
52 A2 **Spencer Gulf** *est.* Austr.
98 C1 **Spennymoor** U.K.
54 B2 **Spenser Mountains** N.Z.
101 D3 **Spessart** *reg.* Ger.
96 C2 **Spey** *r.* U.K.
102 B2 **Speyer** Ger.
100 C1 **Spiekeroog** *i.* Ger.
100 B2 **Spijkenisse** Neth.
128 C2 **Spirit River** Can.
103 E2 **Spišská Nová Ves** Slovakia
82 C1 **Spitsbergen** *i.* Svalbard
102 C2 **Spittal an der Drau** Austria
109 C2 **Split** Croatia
129 E2 **Split Lake** Can.
129 E2 **Split Lake** *l.* Can.
134 C1 **Spokane** U.S.A.
140 A1 **Spooner** U.S.A.
102 C1 **Spree** *r.* Ger.
122 A2 **Springbok** S. Africa
131 E2 **Springdale** Can.
142 B1 **Springdale** U.S.A.
101 D1 **Springe** Ger.
138 C1 **Springer** U.S.A.
138 B2 **Springerville** U.S.A.
136 C3 **Springfield** *CO* U.S.A.
140 B3 **Springfield** *IL* U.S.A.
141 E2 **Springfield** *MA* U.S.A.
137 E3 **Springfield** *MO* U.S.A.
140 C3 **Springfield** *OH* U.S.A.
134 B2 **Springfield** *OR* U.S.A.
123 C3 **Springfontein** S. Africa
131 D2 **Springhill** Can.
143 D3 **Spring Hill** U.S.A.
54 B2 **Springs Junction** N.Z.
98 D2 **Spurn Head** *hd* U.K.
128 B3 **Squamish** Can.
109 C3 **Squillace, Golfo di** *g.* Italy
109 D2 **Srbija** *aut. rep.* Serb. and Mont.
109 C2 **Srebrenica** Bos.-Herz.
110 C2 **Sredets** Bulg.
83 L3 **Sredinnyy Khrebet** *mts* Rus. Fed.
83 L2 **Srednekolymsk** Rus. Fed.
89 E3 **Sredne-Russkaya Vozvyshennost'** *hills* Rus. Fed.
83 I2 **Sredne-Sibirskoye Ploskogor'ye** *plat.* Rus. Fed.
110 B2 **Srednogorie** Bulg.
69 D1 **Sretensk** Rus. Fed.
61 C1 **Sri Aman** *Sarawak* Malaysia
73 B4 **Sri Jayewardenepura Kotte** Sri Lanka
73 C3 **Srikakulam** India
73 C4 **Sri Lanka** *country* Asia
74 B1 **Srinagar** Jammu and Kashmir
73 B3 **Srivardhan** India
101 D1 **Stade** Ger.
101 E1 **Stadensen** Ger.
100 C1 **Stadskanaal** Neth.
101 D2 **Stadtallendorf** Ger.
101 D1 **Stadthagen** Ger.
101 E2 **Staffelstein** Ger.
99 B2 **Stafford** U.K.
99 C3 **Staines** U.K.
91 D2 **Stakhanov** Ukr.
Stalingrad Rus. Fed. *see* **Volgograd**
103 E1 **Stalowa Wola** Pol.
99 C2 **Stamford** U.K.
141 E2 **Stamford** *CT* U.S.A.
139 D2 **Stamford** *TX* U.S.A.
122 A1 **Stampriet** Namibia
92 F2 **Stamsund** Norway
123 C2 **Standerton** S. Africa
140 C2 **Standish** U.S.A.
123 D2 **Stanger** S. Africa
153 C6 **Stanley** Falkland Is
136 C1 **Stanley** U.S.A.
83 I3 **Stanovoye Nagor'ye** *mts* Rus. Fed.
83 J3 **Stanovoy Khrebet** *mts* Rus. Fed.
53 D1 **Stanthorpe** Austr.
103 E1 **Starachowice** Pol.
Stara Planina *mts* Bulg./Serb. and Mont. *see* **Balkan Mountains**
89 D2 **Staraya Russa** Rus. Fed.
89 D2 **Staraya Toropa** Rus. Fed.
110 C2 **Stara Zagora** Bulg.
103 D1 **Stargard Szczeciński** Pol.
142 C2 **Starkville** U.S.A.
91 D2 **Starobil's'k** Ukr.
89 D3 **Starodub** Rus. Fed.
103 D1 **Starogard Gdański** Pol.
90 B2 **Starokostyantyniv** Ukr.
91 D2 **Starominskaya** Rus. Fed.
91 D2 **Staroshcherbinovskaya** Rus. Fed.
91 D2 **Starotitarovskaya** Rus. Fed.
89 F3 **Staroyur'yevo** Rus. Fed.
99 B3 **Start Point** U.K.
88 C3 **Staryya Darohi** Belarus
89 E3 **Staryy Oskol** Rus. Fed.
101 E2 **Staßfurt** Ger.
141 D2 **State College** U.S.A.
143 D2 **Statesboro** U.S.A.
143 D1 **Statesville** U.S.A.
93 E4 **Stavanger** Norway
87 D4 **Stavropol'** Rus. Fed.
87 D4 **Stavropol'skaya Vozvyshennost'** *hills* Rus. Fed.
52 B3 **Stawell** Austr.
123 C2 **Steadville** S. Africa
136 B2 **Steamboat Springs** U.S.A.
101 E2 **Stedten** Ger.
128 C2 **Steen River** Can.
134 C2 **Steens Mountain** U.S.A.
100 C1 **Steenwijk** Neth.
126 D2 **Stefansson Island** Can.
101 E3 **Steigerwald** *mts* Ger.
129 E3 **Steinbach** Can.
100 C1 **Steinfurt** Ger.
120 A3 **Steinhausen** Namibia
92 F3 **Steinkjer** Norway
122 A2 **Steinkopf** S. Africa
122 B2 **Stella** S. Africa
105 D2 **Stenay** France
101 E1 **Stendal** Ger.
Stepanakert Azer. *see* **Xankändi**
131 E2 **Stephenville** Can.
139 D2 **Stephenville** U.S.A.
122 B3 **Sterling** S. Africa
136 C2 **Sterling** *CO* U.S.A.
140 B2 **Sterling** *IL* U.S.A.
87 E3 **Sterlitamak** Rus. Fed.
101 E1 **Sternberg** Ger.
128 C2 **Stettler** Can.
140 C2 **Steubenville** U.S.A.
99 C3 **Stevenage** U.K.
129 E2 **Stevenson Lake** Can.
126 B2 **Stevens Village** U.S.A.
128 B2 **Stewart** Can.
126 B2 **Stewart** *r.* Can.
54 A3 **Stewart Island** N.Z.
127 F2 **Stewart Lake** Can.
102 C2 **Steyr** Austria
122 B3 **Steytlerville** S. Africa
128 A2 **Stikine** *r.* Can.
128 A2 **Stikine Plateau** Can.
122 B3 **Stilbaai** S. Africa
139 D1 **Stillwater** U.S.A.
109 D2 **Štip** Macedonia
96 C2 **Stirling** U.K.
92 F3 **Stjørdalshalsen** Norway
103 D2 **Stockerau** Austria
93 G4 **Stockholm** Sweden
98 B2 **Stockport** U.K.
135 B3 **Stockton** U.S.A.
98 C1 **Stockton-on-Tees** U.K.
63 B2 **Stœng Trêng** Cambodia
96 B1 **Stoer, Point of** U.K.
99 B2 **Stoke-on-Trent** U.K.
109 D2 **Stol** *mt.* Serb. and Mont.
109 C2 **Stolac** Bos.-Herz.
100 C2 **Stolberg (Rheinland)** Ger.
88 C3 **Stolin** Belarus
101 F2 **Stollberg** Ger.
101 D1 **Stolzenau** Ger.
96 C2 **Stonehaven** U.K.
129 E2 **Stonewall** Can.
129 D2 **Stony Rapids** Can.
92 G2 **Storavan** *l.* Sweden
93 F4 **Store Bælt** *sea chan.* Denmark
92 F3 **Støren** Norway
92 F2 **Storforshei** Norway
126 D2 **Storkerson Peninsula** Can.
137 D2 **Storm Lake** U.S.A.
96 A1 **Stornoway** U.K.
86 E2 **Storozhevsk** Rus. Fed.
90 B2 **Storozhynets'** Ukr.
92 F3 **Storsjön** *l.* Sweden
92 H2 **Storslett** Norway
92 G2 **Storuman** Sweden
99 C3 **Stour** *r. England* U.K.
99 C2 **Stour** *r. England* U.K.
130 A1 **Stout Lake** Can.
88 C3 **Stowbtsy** Belarus
97 C1 **Strabane** U.K.
102 C2 **Strakonice** Czech Rep.
102 C1 **Stralsund** Ger.
122 A3 **Strand** S. Africa
93 E3 **Stranda** Norway
97 D1 **Strangford Lough** *inlet* U.K.
96 B3 **Stranraer** U.K.
105 D2 **Strasbourg** France
140 C2 **Stratford** Can.
54 B1 **Stratford** N.Z.
139 C1 **Stratford** U.S.A.
99 C2 **Stratford-upon-Avon** U.K.
128 C2 **Strathmore** Can.
96 C2 **Strathspey** *val.* U.K.

102 C2 **Straubing** Ger.
51 C3 **Streaky Bay** Austr.
140 B2 **Streator** U.S.A.
110 B2 **Strehaia** Romania
111 B2 **Strimonas** *r.* Greece
153 B5 **Stroeder** Arg.
101 D1 **Ströhen** Ger.
109 C3 **Stromboli, Isola** *i.* Italy
96 C1 **Stromness** U.K.
92 G3 **Strömsund** Sweden
96 C1 **Stronsay** *i.* U.K.
53 D2 **Stroud** Austr.
99 B3 **Stroud** U.K.
100 C1 **Strücklingen (Saterland)** Ger.
109 D2 **Struga** Macedonia
88 C2 **Strugi-Krasnyye** Rus. Fed.
122 B3 **Struis Bay** S. Africa
109 D2 **Strumica** Macedonia
122 B2 **Strydenburg** S. Africa
90 A2 **Stryy** Ukr.
128 B2 **Stuart Lake** Can.
130 A1 **Stull Lake** Can.
89 E3 **Stupino** Rus. Fed.
140 B2 **Sturgeon Bay** U.S.A.
130 C2 **Sturgeon Falls** Can.
130 A2 **Sturgeon Lake** Can.
140 B2 **Sturgis** *MI* U.S.A.
136 C2 **Sturgis** *SD* U.S.A.
50 B1 **Sturt Creek** *watercourse* Austr.
52 B1 **Sturt Stony Desert** Austr.
123 C3 **Stutterheim** S. Africa
102 B2 **Stuttgart** Ger.
142 B2 **Stuttgart** U.S.A.
92 □A2 **Stykkishólmur** Iceland
90 B1 **Styr** *r.* Belarus/Ukr.
155 D1 **Suaçuí Grande** *r.* Brazil
116 B3 **Suakin** Sudan
78 A3 **Suara, Mount** Eritrea
109 C1 **Subotica** Serb. and Mont.
110 C1 **Suceava** Romania
97 B2 **Suck** *r.* Rep. of Ireland
152 B2 **Sucre** Bol.
154 B2 **Sucuriú** *r.* Brazil
89 E2 **Suda** Rus. Fed.
91 C3 **Sudak** Ukr.
117 A3 **Sudan** *country* Africa
130 B2 **Sudbury** Can.
117 A4 **Sudd** *swamp* Sudan
89 F2 **Sudislavl'** Rus. Fed.
89 F2 **Sudogda** Rus. Fed.
94 B1 **Suðuroy** *i.* Faroe Is
107 C2 **Sueca** Spain
116 B2 **Suez** Egypt
116 B2 **Suez, Gulf of** Egypt
80 B2 **Suez Canal** Egypt
141 D3 **Suffolk** U.S.A.
79 C2 **Şuḩār** Oman
69 D1 **Sühbaatar** Mongolia
101 E2 **Suhl** Ger.
109 C1 **Suhopolje** Croatia
70 B2 **Suide** China
66 B2 **Suifenhe** China
69 E1 **Suihua** China
70 A2 **Suining** China
70 B2 **Suiping** China
70 B2 **Suiyang** China
70 B2 **Suizhou** China
74 B2 **Sujangarh** India
74 B1 **Sujanpur** India
74 A2 **Sujawal** Pak.
60 B2 **Sukabumi** Indon.
61 B2 **Sukadana** Indon.
61 C2 **Sukaraja** Indon.
89 E3 **Sukhinichi** Rus. Fed.
89 F2 **Sukhona** *r.* Rus. Fed.
62 A2 **Sukhothai** Thai.
74 A2 **Sukkur** Pak.
89 E2 **Sukromny** Rus. Fed.
59 C3 **Sula, Kepulauan** *is* Indon.
74 A1 **Sulaiman Range** *mts* Pak.
58 C3 **Sulawesi** *i.* Indon.
150 A2 **Sullana** Peru
137 E3 **Sullivan** U.S.A.
139 D2 **Sulphur Springs** U.S.A.
64 B2 **Sulu Archipelago** *is* Phil.
64 A2 **Sulu Sea** N. Pacific Ocean
101 E3 **Sulzbach-Rosenberg** Ger.
79 C2 **Sumāil** Oman
Sumatera *i.* Indon. *see* Sumatra
60 A1 **Sumatra** *i.* Indon.
58 C3 **Sumba** *i.* Indon.
61 C2 **Sumbawa** *i.* Indon.
61 C2 **Sumbawabesar** Indon.
119 D3 **Sumbawanga** Tanz.
120 A2 **Sumbe** Angola
96 □ **Sumburgh** U.K.
96 □ **Sumburgh Head** *hd* U.K.
61 C2 **Sumenep** Indon.
67 D4 **Sumisu-jima** *i.* Japan
131 D2 **Summerside** Can.
140 C3 **Summersville** U.S.A.
128 B2 **Summit Lake** Can.
103 D2 **Šumperk** Czech Rep.
81 C1 **Sumqayıt** Azer.
143 D2 **Sumter** U.S.A.
91 C1 **Sumy** Ukr.
75 D2 **Sunamganj** Bangl.
65 B2 **Sunan** N. Korea
79 C2 **Şunaynah** Oman
52 B3 **Sunbury** Austr.
141 D2 **Sunbury** U.S.A.
65 B2 **Sunch'ŏn** N. Korea
65 B3 **Sunch'ŏn** S. Korea
123 C2 **Sun City** S. Africa
60 B2 **Sunda, Selat** *str.* Indon.
136 C2 **Sundance** U.S.A.
75 C2 **Sundarbans** *reg.* Bangl./India
98 C1 **Sunderland** U.K.
128 C2 **Sundre** Can.
93 G3 **Sundsvall** Sweden
123 D2 **Sundumbili** S. Africa
60 B2 **Sungailiat** Indon.
60 B2 **Sungaipenuh** Indon.
60 B1 **Sungei Petani** Malaysia
80 B1 **Sungurlu** Turkey
93 E3 **Sunndalsøra** Norway
134 C1 **Sunnyside** U.S.A.
135 B3 **Sunnyvale** U.S.A.
83 I2 **Suntar** Rus. Fed.
74 A2 **Suntsar** Pak.
114 B4 **Sunyani** Ghana
82 D2 **Suoyarvi** Rus. Fed.
138 A2 **Superior** *AZ* U.S.A.
137 D2 **Superior** *NE* U.S.A.
140 A1 **Superior** *WI* U.S.A.
140 B1 **Superior, Lake** Can./U.S.A.
89 D3 **Suponevo** Rus. Fed.
81 C2 **Sūq ash Shuyūkh** Iraq
70 B2 **Suqian** China
78 A2 **Sūq Suwayq** Saudi Arabia
79 C2 **Şūr** Oman
74 A2 **Surab** Pak.
61 C2 **Surabaya** Indon.
61 C2 **Surakarta** Indon.
74 B2 **Surat** India
74 B2 **Suratgarh** India
63 A3 **Surat Thani** Thai.
89 D3 **Surazh** Rus. Fed.
109 D2 **Surdulica** Serb. and Mont.
74 B2 **Surendranagar** India
82 F2 **Surgut** Rus. Fed.
64 B2 **Surigao** Phil.
63 B2 **Surin** Thai.
151 C1 **Suriname** *country* S. America
Surt Libya *see* **Sirte**
Surt, Khalīj *g.* Libya *see* **Sirte, Gulf of**
60 B2 **Surulangun** Indon.
89 F2 **Susanino** Rus. Fed.
135 B2 **Susanville** U.S.A.
80 B1 **Suşehri** Turkey
131 D2 **Sussex** Can.
101 D1 **Süstedt** Ger.
100 C1 **Sustrum** Ger.
83 K2 **Susuman** Rus. Fed.
111 C3 **Susurluk** Turkey
75 B1 **Sutak** Jammu and Kashmir
122 B3 **Sutherland** S. Africa
99 C2 **Sutton Coldfield** U.K.
66 D2 **Suttsu** Japan
49 F4 **Suva** Fiji
89 E3 **Suvorov** Rus. Fed.
103 E1 **Suwałki** Pol.
63 B2 **Suwannaphum** Thai.
143 D3 **Suwannee** *r.* U.S.A.
Suweis, Qanâ el *canal* Egypt *see* **Suez Canal**
65 B2 **Suwŏn** S. Korea
79 C2 **Sūzā** Iran
89 F2 **Suzdal'** Rus. Fed.
70 B2 **Suzhou** *Anhui* China
70 C2 **Suzhou** *Jiangsu* China
67 C3 **Suzu** Japan
67 C3 **Suzu-misaki** *pt* Japan
82 B1 **Svalbard** *terr.* Arctic Ocean
91 D2 **Svatove** Ukr.
63 B2 **Svay Riĕng** Cambodia
93 F3 **Sveg** Sweden
88 C2 **Švenčionys** Lith.
93 F4 **Svendborg** Denmark
Sverdlovsk Rus. Fed. *see* **Yekaterinburg**
109 D2 **Sveti Nikole** Macedonia
88 B3 **Svetlogorsk** Rus. Fed.
88 B3 **Svetlyy** Rus. Fed.
93 I3 **Svetogorsk** Rus. Fed.
110 C2 **Svilengrad** Bulg.
110 B2 **Svinecea Mare, Vârful** *mt.* Romania
110 C2 **Svishtov** Bulg.
103 D2 **Svitavy** Czech Rep.
91 C2 **Svitlovods'k** Ukr.
69 E1 **Svobodnyy** Rus. Fed.
92 F2 **Svolvær** Norway
88 C3 **Svyetlahorsk** Belarus
143 D2 **Swainsboro** U.S.A.
120 A3 **Swakopmund** Namibia
52 B3 **Swan Hill** Austr.
128 C2 **Swan Hills** Can.
129 D2 **Swan Lake** *l.* Can.
129 D2 **Swan River** Can.
53 D2 **Swansea** Austr.
99 B3 **Swansea** U.K.
123 C2 **Swartruggens** S. Africa
Swatow China *see* **Shantou**
123 D2 **Swaziland** *country* Africa
93 G3 **Sweden** *country* Europe
139 C2 **Sweetwater** U.S.A.
136 B2 **Sweetwater** *r.* U.S.A.
122 B3 **Swellendam** S. Africa
103 D1 **Świdnica** Pol.
103 D1 **Świdwin** Pol.
103 D1 **Świebodzin** Pol.
103 D1 **Świecie** Pol.
129 D2 **Swift Current** Can.
97 C1 **Swilly, Lough** *inlet* Rep. of Ireland
99 C3 **Swindon** U.K.
102 C1 **Świnoujście** Pol.
105 D2 **Switzerland** *country* Europe
97 C2 **Swords** Rep. of Ireland
88 C3 **Syanno** Belarus
89 D2 **Sychevka** Rus. Fed.
53 D2 **Sydney** Austr.
131 D2 **Sydney** Can.
131 D2 **Sydney Mines** Can.
91 D2 **Syeverodonets'k** Ukr.

86 E2 **Syktyvkar** Rus. Fed.
142 C2 **Sylacauga** U.S.A.
75 D2 **Sylhet** Bangl.
102 B1 **Sylt** *i.* Ger.
111 C3 **Symi** *i.* Greece
91 D2 **Synel'nykove** Ukr.
109 C3 **Syracuse** *Sicily* Italy
136 C3 **Syracuse** *KS* U.S.A.
141 D2 **Syracuse** *NY* U.S.A.
77 C2 **Syrdar'ya** *r.* Asia
80 B2 **Syria** *country* Asia
63 A2 **Syriam** Myanmar
Syrian Desert Asia *see* **Bādiyat ash Shām**
111 B3 **Syros** *i.* Greece
87 D3 **Syzran'** Rus. Fed.
102 C1 **Szczecin** Pol.
103 D1 **Szczecinek** Pol.
103 E1 **Szczytno** Pol.
103 E2 **Szeged** Hungary
103 D2 **Székesfehérvár** Hungary
103 D2 **Szekszárd** Hungary
103 E2 **Szentes** Hungary
103 D2 **Szentgotthárd** Hungary
103 D2 **Szigetvár** Hungary
103 E2 **Szolnok** Hungary
103 D2 **Szombathely** Hungary

T

78 B2 **Tābah** Saudi Arabia
76 B3 **Ţabas** Iran
81 D3 **Tābask, Kūh-e** *mt.* Iran
150 B2 **Tabatinga** Brazil
114 B2 **Tabelbala** Alg.
129 C3 **Taber** Can.
102 C2 **Tábor** Czech Rep.
119 D3 **Tabora** Tanz.
114 B4 **Tabou** Côte d'Ivoire
81 C2 **Tabrīz** Iran
78 A2 **Tabūk** Saudi Arabia
77 E2 **Tacheng** China
102 C2 **Tachov** Czech Rep.
64 B1 **Tacloban** Phil.
150 A3 **Tacna** Peru
134 B1 **Tacoma** U.S.A.
152 C4 **Tacuarembó** Uru.
138 B3 **Tacupeto** Mex.
117 C3 **Tadjoura** Djibouti
80 B2 **Tadmur** Syria
129 E2 **Tadoule Lake** Can.
65 B2 **Taegu** S. Korea
65 B2 **Taejŏn** S. Korea
65 B3 **Taejŏng** S. Korea
65 B2 **T'aepaek** S. Korea
69 E1 **Ta'erqi** China
107 C1 **Tafalla** Spain
152 B3 **Tafí Viejo** Arg.
79 D2 **Taftān, Kūh-e** *mt.* Iran
91 D2 **Taganrog** Rus. Fed.
91 D2 **Taganrog, Gulf of** Rus. Fed./Ukr.
62 A1 **Tagaung** Myanmar
64 B1 **Tagaytay City** Phil.
64 B2 **Tagbilaran** Phil.
64 B1 **Tagudin** Phil.
64 B2 **Tagum** Phil.
106 B2 **Tagus** *r.* Port./Spain
60 B1 **Tahan, Gunung** *mt.* Malaysia
115 C2 **Tahat, Mont** *mt.* Alg.
69 E1 **Tahe** China
49 H5 **Tahiti** *i.* French Polynesia
139 E1 **Tahlequah** U.S.A.
135 B3 **Tahoe, Lake** U.S.A.
135 B3 **Tahoe City** U.S.A.
126 D2 **Tahoe Lake** Can.
115 C3 **Tahoua** Niger
79 C2 **Tahrūd** Iran
128 B3 **Tahsis** Can.
70 B2 **Tai'an** China
Taibus Qi China *see* **Baochang**
71 C3 **T'aichung** Taiwan
54 C1 **Taihape** N.Z.
70 C2 **Tai Hu** *l.* China
52 A3 **Tailem Bend** Austr.
71 C3 **T'ainan** Taiwan
155 D1 **Taiobeiras** Brazil
71 C3 **T'aipei** Taiwan
60 B1 **Taiping** Malaysia
71 B3 **Taishan** China
153 A5 **Taitao, Península de** *pen.* Chile
71 C3 **T'aitung** Taiwan
92 I2 **Taivalkoski** Fin.
92 H2 **Taivaskero** *hill* Fin.
71 C3 **Taiwan** *country* Asia
71 B3 **Taiwan Strait** China/Taiwan
70 B2 **Taiyuan** China
70 B2 **Taizhou** *Jiangsu* China
71 C3 **Taizhou** *Zhejiang* China
78 B3 **Ta'izz** Yemen
77 D3 **Tajikistan** *country* Asia
75 B2 **Taj Mahal** India
Tajo *r.* Port. *see* **Tagus**
58 A1 **Tak** Thai.
54 B2 **Takaka** N.Z.
67 B4 **Takamatsu** Japan
67 C3 **Takaoka** Japan
54 B1 **Takapuna** N.Z.
67 C3 **Takasaki** Japan
122 B1 **Takatokwane** Botswana
67 C3 **Takayama** Japan
67 C3 **Takefu** Japan
60 A1 **Takengon** Indon.
63 B2 **Takêv** Cambodia
63 B2 **Ta Khmau** Cambodia
66 D2 **Takikawa** Japan
128 B2 **Takla Lake** Can.
128 B2 **Takla Landing** Can.
77 E3 **Taklimakan Shamo** *des.* China
128 A2 **Taku** *r.* Can./U.S.A.
63 A3 **Takua Pa** Thai.
115 C4 **Takum** Nigeria
88 C3 **Talachyn** Belarus
74 B1 **Talagang** Pak.
150 A2 **Talara** Peru
74 A2 **Talar-i-Band** *mts* Pak.
59 C2 **Talaud, Kepulauan** *is* Indon.
106 C2 **Talavera de la Reina** Spain
153 A4 **Talca** Chile
153 A4 **Talcahuano** Chile
89 E2 **Taldom** Rus. Fed.
77 D2 **Taldykorgan** Kazakh.
59 C3 **Taliabu** *i.* Indon.
64 B1 **Talisay** Phil.
61 C2 **Taliwang** Indon.
81 C2 **Tall 'Afar** Iraq
143 D2 **Tallahassee** U.S.A.
88 B2 **Tallinn** Estonia
142 B2 **Tallulah** U.S.A.
104 B2 **Talmont-St-Hilaire** France
90 C2 **Tal'ne** Ukr.
117 B3 **Talodi** Sudan
91 E1 **Talovaya** Rus. Fed.
126 E2 **Taloyoak** Can.
88 B2 **Talsi** Latvia
152 A3 **Taltal** Chile
129 C1 **Taltson** *r.* Can.
60 A1 **Talu** Indon.
53 C1 **Talwood** Austr.
114 B4 **Tamale** Ghana
115 C2 **Tamanrasset** Alg.
99 A3 **Tamar** *r.* U.K.
145 C2 **Tamazunchale** Mex.
114 A3 **Tambacounda** Senegal
61 B1 **Tambelan, Kepulauan** *is* Indon.
91 E1 **Tambov** Rus. Fed.
145 C2 **Tamiahua, Laguna de** *lag.* Mex.
143 D3 **Tampa** U.S.A.
143 D3 **Tampa Bay** U.S.A.
93 H3 **Tampere** Fin.
145 C2 **Tampico** Mex.
69 D1 **Tamsagbulag** Mongolia
102 C2 **Tamsweg** Austria
53 D2 **Tamworth** Austr.
99 C2 **Tamworth** U.K.
119 E3 **Tana** *r.* Kenya
67 C4 **Tanabe** Japan
92 I1 **Tana Bru** Norway
117 B3 **T'ana Hāyk'** *l.* Eth.
61 C2 **Tanahgrogot** Indon.
58 C3 **Tanahjampea** *i.* Indon.
50 C1 **Tanami Desert** Austr.
126 A2 **Tanana** U.S.A.
108 A1 **Tanaro** *r.* Italy
65 B1 **Tanch'ŏn** N. Korea
64 B2 **Tandag** Phil.
110 C2 **Ţăndărei** Romania
153 C4 **Tandil** Arg.
74 A2 **Tando Adam** Pak.
74 A2 **Tando Muhammmad Khan** Pak.
114 B2 **Tanezrouft** *reg.* Alg./Mali
119 D3 **Tanga** Tanz.
119 C3 **Tanganyika, Lake** Africa
Tanger Morocco *see* **Tangier**
101 E1 **Tangermünde** Ger.
75 C1 **Tanggula Shan** *mts* China
114 B1 **Tangier** Morocco
75 C1 **Tangra Yumco** *salt l.* China
70 B2 **Tangshan** China
68 C2 **Taniantaweng Shan** *mts* China
59 C3 **Tanimbar, Kepulauan** *is* Indon.
64 B2 **Tanjay** Phil.
60 A1 **Tanjungbalai** Indon.
61 B2 **Tanjungpandan** Indon.
60 B1 **Tanjungpinang** Indon.
61 C1 **Tanjungredeb** Indon.
61 C1 **Tanjungselor** Indon.
74 B1 **Tank** Pak.
115 C3 **Tanout** Niger
75 C2 **Tansen** Nepal
116 B1 **Ţanţā** Egypt
119 D3 **Tanzania** *country* Africa
69 E1 **Taonan** China
138 B1 **Taos** U.S.A.
114 B2 **Taoudenni** Mali
88 C2 **Tapa** Estonia
145 C3 **Tapachula** Mex.
151 C2 **Tapajós** *r.* Brazil
60 A1 **Tapaktuan** Indon.
145 C3 **Tapanatepec** Mex.
150 B2 **Tapauá** Brazil
114 B4 **Tapeta** Liberia
74 B2 **Tapi** *r.* India
141 D3 **Tappahannock** U.S.A.
150 B2 **Tapurucuara** Brazil
154 B1 **Taquarí** Brazil
154 A1 **Taquarí** *r.* Brazil
154 B1 **Taquari, Serra do** *hills* Brazil
154 C2 **Taquaritinga** Brazil
115 D4 **Taraba** *r.* Nigeria
Ţarābulus Libya *see* **Tripoli**
61 C1 **Tarakan** Indon.
88 A3 **Taran, Mys** *pt* Rus. Fed.
54 B1 **Taranaki, Mount** *vol.* N.Z.
106 C1 **Tarancón** Spain
109 C2 **Taranto** Italy
109 C2 **Taranto, Golfo di** *g.* Italy
150 A2 **Tarapoto** Peru
91 E2 **Tarasovskiy** Rus. Fed.

150 A2 **Tarauacá** Brazil
150 B2 **Tarauacá** *r.* Brazil
77 D2 **Taraz** Kazakh.
107 C1 **Tarazona** Spain
77 E2 **Tarbagatay, Khrebet** *mts* Kazakh.
96 A2 **Tarbert** *Scotland* U.K.
96 B3 **Tarbert** *Scotland* U.K.
104 C3 **Tarbes** France
96 B2 **Tarbet** U.K.
51 C3 **Tarcoola** Austr.
53 D2 **Taree** Austr.
110 C2 **Târgoviște** Romania
110 B1 **Târgu Jiu** Romania
110 B1 **Târgu Mureș** Romania
110 C1 **Târgu Neamț** Romania
79 C2 **Tarif** U.A.E.
152 B3 **Tarija** Bol.
79 B3 **Tarīm** Yemen
77 E2 **Tarim He** *r.* China
77 E3 **Tarim Pendi** *basin* China
59 D3 **Taritatu** *r.* Indon.
82 G2 **Tarko-Sale** Rus. Fed.
114 B4 **Tarkwa** Ghana
64 B1 **Tarlac** Phil.
92 G2 **Tärnaby** Sweden
77 C3 **Tarnak** *r.* Afgh.
110 B1 **Târnăveni** Romania
103 E1 **Tarnobrzeg** Pol.
103 E1 **Tarnów** Pol.
114 B1 **Taroudannt** Morocco
108 B2 **Tarquinia** Italy
107 D1 **Tarragona** Spain
107 D1 **Tàrrega** Spain
80 B2 **Tarsus** Turkey
152 B3 **Tartagal** Arg.
104 B3 **Tartas** France
88 C2 **Tartu** Estonia
80 B2 **Ţarţūs** Syria
155 D1 **Tarumirim** Brazil
89 E3 **Tarusa** Rus. Fed.
108 B1 **Tarvisio** Italy
81 D3 **Tashk, Daryācheh-ye** *l.* Iran
77 C2 **Tashkent** Uzbek.
131 D1 **Tasiujaq** Can.
77 E2 **Taskesken** Kazakh.
54 B2 **Tasman Bay** N.Z.
51 D4 **Tasmania** *state* Austr.
54 B2 **Tasman Mountains** N.Z.
156 D8 **Tasman Sea** S. Pacific Ocean
115 C2 **Tassili du Hoggar** *plat.* Alg.
115 C2 **Tassili n'Ajjer** *plat.* Alg.
103 D2 **Tatabánya** Hungary
90 B2 **Tatarbunary** Ukr.
83 K3 **Tatarskiy Proliv** *str.* Rus. Fed.
67 C4 **Tateyama** Japan
128 C1 **Tathlina Lake** Can.
78 B3 **Tathlīth** Saudi Arabia
78 B2 **Tathlīth, Wādī** *watercourse* Saudi Arabia
53 C3 **Tathra** Austr.
62 A1 **Tatkon** Myanmar
128 B2 **Tatla Lake** Can.
103 D2 **Tatra Mountains** Poland
74 A2 **Tatta** Pak.
154 C2 **Tatuí** Brazil
139 C2 **Tatum** U.S.A.
81 C2 **Tatvan** Turkey
151 D2 **Taua** Brazil
155 C2 **Taubaté** Brazil
101 D3 **Tauberbischofsheim** Ger.
54 C1 **Taumarunui** N.Z.
62 A1 **Taunggyi** Myanmar
62 A2 **Taungup** Myanmar
99 B3 **Taunton** U.K.
100 C2 **Taunus** *hills* Ger.
54 C1 **Taupo** N.Z.
54 C1 **Taupo, Lake** N.Z.
88 B2 **Tauragė** Lith.
54 C1 **Tauranga** N.Z.
111 C3 **Tavas** Turkey
86 F3 **Tavda** Rus. Fed.
106 B2 **Tavira** Port.
99 A3 **Tavistock** U.K.
63 A2 **Tavoy** Myanmar
111 C3 **Tavşanlı** Turkey
99 A3 **Taw** *r.* U.K.
140 C2 **Tawas City** U.S.A.
61 C1 **Tawau** *Sabah* Malaysia
64 A2 **Tawitawi** *i.* Phil.
145 C3 **Taxco** Mex.
77 D3 **Taxkorgan** China
96 C2 **Tay** *r.* U.K.
96 C2 **Tay, Firth of** *est.* U.K.
96 B2 **Tay, Loch** *l.* U.K.
128 B2 **Taylor** Can.
139 D2 **Taylor** U.S.A.
140 B3 **Taylorville** U.S.A.
78 A2 **Taymā'** Saudi Arabia
83 H2 **Taymura** *r.* Rus. Fed.
83 H2 **Taymyr, Ozero** *l.* Rus. Fed.
83 G2 **Taymyr, Poluostrov** *pen.* Rus. Fed.
63 B2 **Tây Ninh** Vietnam
64 A1 **Taytay** Phil.
82 G2 **Taz** *r.* Rus. Fed.
114 B1 **Taza** Morocco
129 D2 **Tazin Lake** Can.
86 G2 **Tazovskaya Guba** *sea chan.* Rus. Fed.
81 C1 **T'bilisi** Georgia
91 E2 **Tbilisskaya** Rus. Fed.
118 B3 **Tchibanga** Gabon
118 B2 **Tcholliré** Cameroon
103 D1 **Tczew** Pol.
144 B2 **Teacapán** Mex.
54 A3 **Te Anau** N.Z.
54 A3 **Te Anau, Lake** N.Z.
145 C3 **Teapa** Mex.
54 C1 **Te Awamutu** N.Z.
115 C1 **Tébessa** Alg.
60 B2 **Tebingtinggi** *Sumatera* Indon.
60 A1 **Tebingtinggi** *Sumatera* Indon.
114 B4 **Techiman** Ghana
144 B3 **Tecomán** Mex.
144 B2 **Tecoripa** Mex.
145 B3 **Técpan** Mex.
144 B2 **Tecuala** Mex.
110 C1 **Tecuci** Romania
76 C3 **Tedzhen** Turkm.
76 C3 **Tedzhen** *r.* Turkm.
68 C1 **Teeli** Rus. Fed.
98 C1 **Tees** *r.* U.K.
111 C3 **Tefenni** Turkey
61 B2 **Tegal** Indon.
146 B3 **Tegucigalpa** Hond.
115 C3 **Teguidda-n-Tessoumt** Niger
114 B4 **Téhini** Côte d'Ivoire
81 D2 **Tehrān** Iran
145 C3 **Tehuacán** Mex.
145 C3 **Tehuantepec, Golfo de** *g.* Mex.
145 C3 **Tehuantepec, Istmo de** *isth.* Mex.
99 A2 **Teifi** *r.* U.K.
Tejo *r.* Spain *see* **Tagus**
145 B3 **Tejupilco** Mex.
54 B2 **Tekapo, Lake** N.Z.
145 D2 **Tekax** Mex.
116 B3 **Tekezē Wenz** *r.* Eritrea/Eth.
111 C2 **Tekirdağ** Turkey
54 C1 **Te Kuiti** N.Z.
75 C2 **Tel** *r.* India
81 C1 **T'elavi** Georgia
80 B2 **Tel Aviv-Yafo** Israel
145 D2 **Telchac Puerto** Mex.
128 A2 **Telegraph Creek** Can.
154 B2 **Telêmaco Borba** Brazil
99 B2 **Telford** U.K.
60 A2 **Telo** Indon.
86 E2 **Tel'pos-Iz, Gora** *mt.* Rus. Fed.
88 B2 **Telšiai** Lith.
60 B1 **Teluk Anson** Malaysia
61 B2 **Telukbatang** Indon.
60 A1 **Telukdalam** Indon.
130 C2 **Temagami Lake** Can.
61 C2 **Temanggung** Indon.
123 C2 **Temba** S. Africa
60 B2 **Tembilahan** Indon.
120 A1 **Tembo Aluma** Angola
99 B2 **Teme** *r.* U.K.
60 B1 **Temerluh** Malaysia
77 D1 **Temirtau** Kazakh.
53 C2 **Temora** Austr.
139 D2 **Temple** U.S.A.
97 C2 **Templemore** Rep. of Ireland
145 C2 **Tempoal** Mex.
91 D2 **Temryuk** Rus. Fed.
153 A4 **Temuco** Chile
54 B2 **Temuka** N.Z.
145 C2 **Tenabo** Mex.
73 C3 **Tenali** India
63 A2 **Tenasserim** Myanmar
99 A3 **Tenby** U.K.
117 C3 **Tendaho** Eth.
105 D3 **Tende** France
108 A2 **Tende, Col de** *pass* France/Italy
73 D4 **Ten Degree Channel** India
67 D3 **Tendō** Japan
114 B3 **Ténenkou** Mali
115 D2 **Ténéré du Tafassâsset** *des.* Niger
114 A2 **Tenerife** *i.* Canary Is
107 D2 **Ténès** Alg.
61 C2 **Tengah, Kepulauan** *is* Indon.
62 A1 **Tengchong** China
61 C2 **Tenggarong** Indon.
70 A2 **Tengger Shamo** *des.* China
77 C1 **Tengiz, Ozero** *salt l.* Kazakh.
71 B3 **Tengxian** China
119 C4 **Tenke** Dem. Rep. Congo
114 B3 **Tenkodogo** Burkina
51 C1 **Tennant Creek** Austr.
142 C1 **Tennessee** *r.* U.S.A.
142 C1 **Tennessee** *state* U.S.A.
145 C3 **Tenosique** Mex.
53 D1 **Tenterfield** Austr.
154 B2 **Teodoro Sampaio** Brazil
155 D1 **Teófilo Otôni** Brazil
145 C3 **Teopisca** Mex.
144 B2 **Tepache** Mex.
54 B1 **Te Paki** N.Z.
144 B3 **Tepalcatepec** Mex.
144 B2 **Tepatitlán** Mex.
144 B2 **Tepehuanes** Mex.
109 D2 **Tepelenë** Albania
144 B2 **Tepic** Mex.
102 C1 **Teplice** Czech Rep.
89 E3 **Teploye** Rus. Fed.
144 B2 **Tequila** Mex.
108 B2 **Teramo** Italy
89 E3 **Terbuny** Rus. Fed.
90 B2 **Terebovlya** Ukr.
87 D4 **Terek** *r.* Rus. Fed.
151 D2 **Teresina** Brazil
155 D2 **Teresópolis** Brazil
63 A3 **Teressa Island** India
80 B1 **Terme** Turkey
77 C3 **Termez** Uzbek.
108 B3 **Termini Imerese** *Sicily* Italy
145 C3 **Términos, Laguna de** *lag.* Mex.
109 B2 **Termoli** Italy
59 C2 **Ternate** Indon.
100 A2 **Terneuzen** Neth.
108 B2 **Terni** Italy

90 B2 **Ternopil'** Ukr.
128 B2 **Terrace** Can.
130 B2 **Terrace Bay** Can.
122 B2 **Terra Firma** S. Africa
140 B3 **Terre Haute** U.S.A.
131 E2 **Terrenceville** Can.
100 B1 **Terschelling** *i.* Neth.
108 A3 **Tertenia** *Sardinia* Italy
107 C1 **Teruel** Spain
92 H2 **Tervola** Fin.
109 C2 **Tešanj** Bos.-Herz.
116 B3 **Teseney** Eritrea
66 D2 **Teshio-gawa** *r.* Japan
128 A1 **Teslin** Can.
128 A1 **Teslin Lake** Can.
154 B1 **Tesouro** Brazil
115 C3 **Tessaoua** Niger
121 C2 **Tete** Moz.
90 C1 **Teteriv** *r.* Ukr.
101 F1 **Teterow** Ger.
90 B2 **Tetiyiv** Ukr.
114 B1 **Tétouan** Morocco
109 D2 **Tetovo** Macedonia
152 B3 **Teuco** *r.* Arg.
144 B2 **Teul de González Ortega** Mex.
101 D1 **Teutoburger Wald** *hills* Ger.
108 B2 **Tevere** *r.* Italy
54 A3 **Teviot** N.Z.
51 E2 **Tewantin** Austr.
54 C2 **Te Wharau** N.Z.
139 E2 **Texarkana** U.S.A.
53 D1 **Texas** Austr.
139 D2 **Texas** *state* U.S.A.
139 E3 **Texas City** U.S.A.
100 B1 **Texel** *i.* Neth.
139 D2 **Texoma, Lake** U.S.A.
123 C2 **Teyateyaneng** Lesotho
89 F2 **Teykovo** Rus. Fed.
89 F2 **Teza** *r.* Rus. Fed.
75 D2 **Tezpur** India
62 A1 **Tezu** India
129 E1 **Tha-anne** *r.* Can.
123 C2 **Thabana-Ntlenyana** *mt.* Lesotho
123 C2 **Thaba Putsoa** *mt.* Lesotho
123 C1 **Thabazimbi** S. Africa
123 C2 **Thabong** S. Africa
63 A2 **Thagyettaw** Myanmar
62 B1 **Thai Binh** Vietnam
63 B2 **Thailand** *country* Asia
63 B2 **Thailand, Gulf of** Asia
62 B1 **Thai Nguyên** Vietnam
63 A3 **Thalang** Thai.
74 B1 **Thal Desert** Pak.
101 E2 **Thale (Harz)** Ger.
62 B2 **Tha Li** Thai.
123 C1 **Thamaga** Botswana
116 C3 **Thamar, Jabal** *mt.* Yemen
79 C3 **Thamarīt** Oman
130 B2 **Thames** *r.* Can.
54 C1 **Thames** N.Z.
99 D3 **Thames** *est.* U.K.
99 D3 **Thames** *r.* U.K.
63 A2 **Thanbyuzayat** Myanmar
62 B2 **Thanh Hoa** Vietnam
73 B3 **Thanjavur** India
74 A2 **Thano Bula Khan** Pak.
62 B1 **Than Uyen** Vietnam
74 A2 **Thar Desert** India/Pak.
52 B1 **Thargomindah** Austr.
62 A2 **Tharrawaddy** Myanmar
81 C2 **Tharthār, Buḩayrat ath** *l.* Iraq
111 B2 **Thasos** *i.* Greece
62 B1 **Thât Khê** Vietnam
62 A2 **Thaton** Myanmar
62 A1 **Thaungdut** Myanmar
62 A2 **Thayetmyo** Myanmar
62 A1 **Thazi** Myanmar
146 C2 **The Bahamas** *country* West Indies
98 B1 **The Cheviot** *hill* U.K.
134 B1 **The Dalles** U.S.A.
99 C2 **The Fens** *reg.* U.K.
114 A3 **The Gambia** *country* Africa
The Great Oasis Egypt *see* **Khārijah, Wāḩāt al**
79 C2 **The Gulf** Asia
100 B1 **The Hague** Neth.
129 E1 **Thelon** *r.* Can.
101 E2 **Themar** Ger.
96 A1 **The Minch** *sea chan.* U.K.
150 B2 **Theodore Roosevelt** *r.* Brazil
129 D2 **The Pas** Can.
111 B2 **Thermaïkos Kolpos** *g.* Greece
136 B2 **Thermopolis** U.S.A.
53 C3 **The Rock** Austr.
130 B2 **Thessalon** Can.
111 B2 **Thessaloniki** Greece
99 D2 **Thetford** U.K.
131 C2 **Thetford Mines** Can.
62 A1 **The Triangle** *mts* Myanmar
131 D1 **Thévenet, Lac** *l.* Can.
99 D2 **The Wash** *b.* U.K.
139 D2 **The Woodlands** U.S.A.
142 B3 **Thibodaux** U.S.A.
129 E2 **Thicket Portage** Can.
137 D1 **Thief River Falls** U.S.A.
105 C2 **Thiers** France
119 D3 **Thika** Kenya
73 B4 **Thiladhunmathee Atoll** Maldives
75 C2 **Thimphu** Bhutan
105 D2 **Thionville** France
111 C3 **Thira** *i.* Greece
98 C1 **Thirsk** U.K.
Thiruvananthapuram India *see* **Trivandrum**
93 E4 **Thisted** Denmark
129 E1 **Thlewiaza** *r.* Can.
62 A2 **Thoen** Thai.
123 D1 **Thohoyandou** S. Africa
101 E1 **Thomasburg** Ger.
97 C2 **Thomastown** Rep. of Ireland
143 D2 **Thomasville** U.S.A.
100 C2 **Thommen** Belgium
129 E2 **Thompson** Can.
128 E3 **Thompson** *r.* U.S.A.
134 C1 **Thompson Falls** U.S.A.
128 B2 **Thompson Sound** Can.
96 C3 **Thornhill** U.K.
55 C2 **Thorshavnheiane** *reg.* Antarctica
104 B2 **Thouars** France
128 C2 **Three Hills** Can.
63 A2 **Three Pagodas Pass** Myanmar/Thai.
114 B4 **Three Points, Cape** Ghana
63 B2 **Thu Dâu Môt** Vietnam
100 B2 **Thuin** Belgium
Thule Greenland *see* **Qaanaaq**
121 B3 **Thuli** Zimbabwe
130 B2 **Thunder Bay** Can.
63 A3 **Thung Song** Thai.
101 E2 **Thüringer Becken** *reg.* Ger.
101 E2 **Thüringer Wald** *mts* Ger.
97 C2 **Thurles** Rep. of Ireland
96 C1 **Thurso** U.K.
96 C1 **Thurso** *r.* U.K.
151 D2 **Tianguá** Brazil
70 B2 **Tianjin** China
70 B2 **Tianjin** *mun.* China
71 A3 **Tianlin** China
70 B2 **Tianmen** China
70 A2 **Tianshui** China
154 B2 **Tibagi** *r.* Brazil
118 B2 **Tibati** Cameroon
Tiberias, Lake *l.* Israel *see* **Galilee, Sea of**
115 D2 **Tibesti** *mts* Chad
Tibet *aut. reg.* China *see* **Xizang Zizhiqu**
68 B2 **Tibet** *reg.* China
Tibet, Plateau of China *see* **Qingzang Gaoyuan**
52 B1 **Tibooburra** Austr.
144 A2 **Tiburón, Isla** *i.* Mex.
114 B3 **Tîchît** Maur.
114 A2 **Tichla** Western Sahara
145 D2 **Ticul** Mex.
114 A3 **Tidjikja** Maur.
100 B2 **Tiel** Neth.
65 A1 **Tieling** China
100 A2 **Tielt** Belgium
100 B2 **Tienen** Belgium
68 B2 **Tien Shan** *mts* China/Kyrg.
Tientsin China *see* **Tianjin**
93 G3 **Tierp** Sweden
145 C3 **Tierra Blanca** Mex.
145 C3 **Tierra Colorada** Mex.
153 B6 **Tierra del Fuego, Isla Grande de** *i.* Arg./Chile
154 C2 **Tietê** Brazil
Tiflis Georgia *see* **T'bilisi**
143 D2 **Tifton** U.S.A.
90 B2 **Tighina** Moldova
131 D2 **Tignish** Can.
150 A2 **Tigre** *r.* Ecuador/Peru
81 C2 **Tigris** *r.* Asia
145 C2 **Tihuatlán** Mex.
144 A1 **Tijuana** Mex.
91 E2 **Tikhoretsk** Rus. Fed.
89 D2 **Tikhvin** Rus. Fed.
89 D2 **Tikhvinskaya Gryada** *ridge* Rus. Fed.
54 C1 **Tikokino** N.Z.
81 C2 **Tikrīt** Iraq
83 J2 **Tiksi** Rus. Fed.
100 B2 **Tilburg** Neth.
152 B3 **Tilcara** Arg.
52 B1 **Tilcha** Austr.
114 C3 **Tillabéri** Niger
134 B1 **Tillamook** U.S.A.
63 A3 **Tillanchong Island** India
111 C3 **Tilos** *i.* Greece
52 B2 **Tilpa** Austr.
86 F2 **Til'tim** Rus. Fed.
89 E3 **Tim** Rus. Fed.
86 D2 **Timanskiy Kryazh** *ridge* Rus. Fed.
54 B2 **Timaru** N.Z.
91 D2 **Timashevsk** Rus. Fed.
114 B3 **Timbedgha** Maur.
50 C1 **Timber Creek** Austr.
Timbuktu Mali *see* **Tombouctou**
114 C2 **Timimoun** Alg.
110 B1 **Timiș** *r.* Romania
110 B1 **Timișoara** Romania
130 B2 **Timmins** Can.
89 E2 **Timokhino** Rus. Fed.
151 D2 **Timon** Brazil
59 C3 **Timor** *i.* Indon.
58 C3 **Timor Sea** Austr./Indon.
93 G3 **Timrå** Sweden
114 B2 **Tindouf** Alg.
75 C2 **Tingri** China
93 F4 **Tingsryd** Sweden
59 D2 **Tinian** *i.* N. Mariana Is
152 B3 **Tinogasta** Arg.
111 C3 **Tinos** Greece
111 C3 **Tinos** *i.* Greece
115 C2 **Tinrhert, Plateau du** Alg.
62 A1 **Tinsukia** India
107 D2 **Tipasa** Alg.
97 B2 **Tipperary** Rep. of Ireland
109 C2 **Tirana** Albania

Tiranë Albania see Tirana
108 B1 Tirano Italy
90 B2 Tiraspol Moldova
111 C3 Tire Turkey
96 A2 Tiree i. U.K.
74 B1 Tirich Mir mt. Pak.
73 B3 Tiruchchirappalli India
73 B4 Tirunelveli India
73 B3 Tirupati India
73 B3 Tiruppattur India
73 B3 Tiruppur India
109 D1 Tisa r. Europe
129 D2 Tisdale Can.
107 D2 Tissemsilt Alg.
152 B2 Titicaca, Lago l. Bol./Peru
75 C2 Titlagarh India
110 C2 Titu Romania
143 D3 Titusville U.S.A.
99 B3 Tiverton U.K.
108 B2 Tivoli Italy
79 C2 Ţīwī Oman
145 D2 Tizimín Mex.
107 D2 Tizi Ouzou Alg.
114 B2 Tiznit Morocco
145 C3 Tlacotalpán Mex.
144 B2 Tlahualilo Mex.
145 C3 Tlapa Mex.
145 C3 Tlaxcala Mex.
145 C3 Tlaxiaco Mex.
114 B1 Tlemcen Alg.
123 C1 Tlokweng Botswana
128 B2 Toad River Can.
121 □D2 Toamasina Madag.
60 A1 Toba, Danau l. Indon.
74 A1 Toba and Kakar Ranges mts Pak.
147 D3 Tobago i. Trin. and Tob.
59 C2 Tobelo Indon.
130 B2 Tobermory Can.
96 A2 Tobermory U.K.
129 D2 Tobin Lake l. Can.
60 B2 Toboali Indon.
76 C1 Tobol r. Kazakh./Rus. Fed.
86 F3 Tobol'sk Rus. Fed.
151 D2 Tocantinópolis Brazil
151 D2 Tocantins r. Brazil
143 D2 Toccoa U.S.A.
108 A1 Toce r. Italy
152 A3 Tocopilla Chile
53 C3 Tocumwal Austr.
144 A2 Todos Santos Mex.
128 B3 Tofino Can.
96 □ Toft U.K.
59 C3 Togian, Kepulauan is Indon.
114 C4 Togo country Africa
74 B2 Tohana India
126 B2 Tok U.S.A.
116 B3 Tokar Sudan
69 E3 Tokara-rettō is Japan
91 E1 Tokarevka Rus. Fed.
49 G3 Tokelau terr. S. Pacific Ocean
91 D2 Tokmak Ukr.
77 D2 Tokmok Kyrg.
54 C1 Tokoroa N.Z.
68 B2 Toksun China
67 B4 Tokushima Japan
67 C3 Tōkyō Japan
121 □D3 Tôlañaro Madag.
154 B2 Toledo Brazil
106 C2 Toledo Spain
140 C2 Toledo U.S.A.
106 C2 Toledo, Montes de mts Spain
142 B2 Toledo Bend Reservoir U.S.A.
121 □D3 Toliara Madag.
58 C2 Tolitoli Indon.
108 B1 Tolmezzo Italy
104 B3 Tolosa Spain
145 C3 Toluca Mex.
87 D3 Tol'yatti Rus. Fed.
140 A2 Tomah U.S.A.
66 D2 Tomakomai Japan
106 B2 Tomar Port.
103 E1 Tomaszów Lubelski Pol.
103 E1 Tomaszów Mazowiecki Pol.
144 B3 Tomatlán Mex.
142 C2 Tombigbee r. U.S.A.
155 D2 Tombos Brazil
114 B3 Tombouctou Mali
120 A2 Tombua Angola
123 C1 Tom Burke S. Africa
53 C2 Tomingley Austr.
58 C3 Tomini, Teluk g. Indon.
109 C2 Tomislavgrad Bos.-Herz.
50 A2 Tom Price Austr.
82 G3 Tomsk Rus. Fed.
93 F4 Tomtabacken hill Sweden
145 C3 Tonalá Mex.
150 B2 Tonantins Brazil
59 C2 Tondano Indon.
49 G4 Tonga country S. Pacific Ocean
71 B3 Tongcheng China
70 A2 Tongchuan China
71 A3 Tongdao China
65 B2 Tongduch'ŏn S. Korea
100 B2 Tongeren Belgium
65 B2 Tonghae S. Korea
62 B1 Tonghai China
65 B1 Tonghua China
65 B2 Tongjosŏn-man b. N. Korea
62 B1 Tongking, Gulf of China/Vietnam
69 E2 Tongliao China
70 B2 Tongling China
52 B2 Tongo Austr.
71 A3 Tongren China
70 B2 Tongshan China
71 A4 Tongshi China
Tongtian He r. China see Yangtze
96 B1 Tongue U.K.
65 B3 T'ongyŏng S. Korea
69 E2 Tongyu China
65 A1 Tongyuanpu China
74 B2 Tonk India
63 B2 Tônlé Sab l. Cambodia
135 C3 Tonopah U.S.A.
93 F4 Tønsberg Norway
135 D2 Tooele U.S.A.
52 B3 Tooleybuc Austr.
53 D1 Toowoomba Austr.
137 D3 Topeka U.S.A.
144 B2 Topia Mex.
144 B2 Topolobampo Mex.
86 C2 Topozero, Ozero l. Rus. Fed.
134 B1 Toppenish U.S.A.
111 C3 Torbalı Turkey
76 B3 Torbat-e Heydarīyeh Iran
76 C3 Torbat-e Jām Iran
106 C1 Tordesillas Spain
107 C1 Tordesilos Spain
107 D1 Torelló Spain
101 F2 Torgau Ger.
100 A2 Torhout Belgium
Torino Italy see Turin
154 B1 Torixoreu Brazil
106 B1 Tormes r. Spain
92 H2 Torneälven r. Sweden
127 G3 Torngat Mountains Can.
92 H2 Tornio Fin.
106 B1 Toro Spain
130 C2 Toronto Can.
119 D2 Tororo Uganda
80 B2 Toros Dağları mts Turkey
99 B3 Torquay U.K.
106 B2 Torrão Port.
106 B1 Torre mt. Port.
107 D1 Torreblanca Spain
106 C1 Torrecerredo mt. Spain
106 B1 Torre de Moncorvo Port.
106 C1 Torrelavega Spain
106 C2 Torremolinos Spain
52 A2 Torrens, Lake salt flat Austr.
107 C2 Torrent Spain
144 B2 Torreón Mex.
106 B2 Torres Novas Port.
106 B2 Torres Vedras Port.
107 C2 Torrevieja Spain
96 B2 Torridon U.K.
106 C2 Torrijos Spain
141 E2 Torrington CT U.S.A.
136 C2 Torrington WY U.S.A.
107 D1 Torroella de Montgrí Spain
94 B1 Tórshavn Faroe Is
108 A3 Tortolì Sardinia Italy
107 D1 Tortosa Spain
103 D1 Toruń Pol.
97 B1 Tory Island Rep. of Ireland
89 D2 Torzhok Rus. Fed.
122 B2 Tosca S. Africa
89 D2 Tosno Rus. Fed.
152 B3 Tostado Arg.
101 D1 Tostedt Ger.
80 B1 Tosya Turkey
86 D3 Tot'ma Rus. Fed.
67 B3 Tottori Japan
114 B4 Touba Côte d'Ivoire
114 B1 Toubkal, Jbel mt. Morocco
114 B3 Tougan Burkina
115 C1 Touggourt Alg.
105 D2 Toul France
71 C3 Touliu Taiwan
105 D3 Toulon France
104 C3 Toulouse France
62 A2 Toungoo Myanmar
100 A2 Tournai Belgium
105 C2 Tournus France
151 E2 Touros Brazil
104 C2 Tours France
115 D2 Tousside, Pic mt. Chad
122 B3 Touwsrivier S. Africa
66 D2 Towada Japan
134 D1 Townsend U.S.A.
51 D1 Townsville Austr.
77 E2 Toxkan He r. China
66 D2 Tōya-ko l. Japan
67 C3 Toyama Japan
67 C3 Toyota Japan
115 C1 Tozeur Tunisia
81 C1 Tqvarch'eli Georgia
80 B2 Trâblous Lebanon
80 B1 Trabzon Turkey
106 B2 Trafalgar, Cabo c. Spain
128 C3 Trail Can.
88 B3 Trakai Lith.
97 B2 Tralee Rep. of Ireland
97 C2 Tramore Rep. of Ireland
63 A3 Trang Thai.
59 C3 Trangan i. Indon.
55 I2 Transantarctic Mountains Antarctica
Transylvanian Alps mts Romania see Carpații Meridionali
108 B3 Trapani Sicily Italy
53 C3 Traralgon Austr.
63 B2 Trat Thai.
102 C2 Traunstein Ger.
140 B2 Traverse City U.S.A.
103 D2 Třebíč Czech Rep.
109 C2 Trebinje Bos.-Herz.
103 E2 Trebišov Slovakia
109 C1 Trebnje Slovenia
153 C4 Treinta y Tres Uru.
153 B5 Trelew Arg.
93 F4 Trelleborg Sweden
130 C2 Tremblant, Mont hill Can.

109 C2 **Tremiti, Isole** *is* Italy
134 D2 **Tremonton** U.S.A.
107 D1 **Tremp** Spain
103 D2 **Trenčín** Slovakia
153 B4 **Trenque Lauquén** Arg.
98 C2 **Trent** *r.* U.K.
108 B1 **Trento** Italy
141 D2 **Trenton** Can.
137 E2 **Trenton** *MO* U.S.A.
141 E2 **Trenton** *NJ* U.S.A.
131 E2 **Trepassey** Can.
153 B4 **Tres Arroyos** Arg.
155 C2 **Três Corações** Brazil
154 B2 **Três Lagoas** Brazil
153 A5 **Tres Lagos** Arg.
155 C1 **Três Marias, Represa** *resr* Brazil
155 C2 **Três Pontas** Brazil
153 B5 **Tres Puntas, Cabo** *c.* Arg.
155 D2 **Três Rios** Brazil
101 F1 **Treuenbrietzen** Ger.
108 A1 **Treviglio** Italy
108 B1 **Treviso** Italy
99 A3 **Trevose Head** *hd* U.K.
109 C3 **Tricase** Italy
73 B3 **Trichur** India
53 C2 **Trida** Austr.
100 C3 **Trier** Ger.
108 B1 **Trieste** Italy
108 B1 **Triglav** *mt.* Slovenia
59 D3 **Trikora, Puncak** *mt.* Indon.
97 C2 **Trim** Rep. of Ireland
73 C4 **Trincomalee** Sri Lanka
154 C1 **Trindade** Brazil
152 B2 **Trinidad** Bol.
147 D3 **Trinidad** *i.* Trin. and Tob.
136 C3 **Trinidad** U.S.A.
147 D3 **Trinidad and Tobago** *country* West Indies
131 E2 **Trinity Bay** Can.
111 B3 **Tripoli** Greece
Tripoli Lebanon *see* **Trâblous**
115 D1 **Tripoli** Libya
149 G5 **Tristan da Cunha** *i.* S. Atlantic Ocean
73 B4 **Trivandrum** India
108 B2 **Trivento** Italy
103 D2 **Trnava** Slovakia
109 C2 **Trogir** Croatia
109 C2 **Troia** Italy
100 C2 **Troisdorf** Ger.
131 C2 **Trois-Rivières** Can.
86 E2 **Troitsko-Pechorsk** Rus. Fed.
151 C2 **Trombetas** *r.* Brazil
123 C3 **Trompsburg** S. Africa
92 G2 **Tromsø** Norway
92 F3 **Trondheim** Norway
128 C2 **Trout Lake** Can.
128 B1 **Trout Lake** *l. N.W.T.* Can.
130 A1 **Trout Lake** *l. Ont.* Can.
99 B3 **Trowbridge** U.K.
142 C2 **Troy** *AL* U.S.A.
141 E2 **Troy** *NY* U.S.A.
105 C2 **Troyes** France
109 D2 **Trstenik** Serb. and Mont.
89 D3 **Trubchevsk** Rus. Fed.
106 B1 **Truchas** Spain
79 C2 **Trucial Coast** U.A.E.
146 B3 **Trujillo** Hond.
150 A2 **Trujillo** Peru
106 B2 **Trujillo** Spain
147 C4 **Trujillo** Venez.
142 B1 **Trumann** U.S.A.
131 D2 **Truro** Can.
99 A3 **Truro** U.K.
138 B2 **Truth or Consequences** U.S.A.
103 D1 **Trutnov** Czech Rep.
93 F3 **Trysil** Norway
103 D1 **Trzebiatów** Pol.
68 B1 **Tsagaannuur** Mongolia
121 □D2 **Tsaratanana, Massif du** *mts* Madag.
110 C2 **Tsarevo** Bulg.
122 A2 **Tses** Namibia
122 B1 **Tsetseng** Botswana
68 C1 **Tsetserleg** Mongolia
122 B2 **Tshabong** Botswana
122 B1 **Tshane** Botswana
91 D2 **Tshchikskoye Vodokhranilishche** *resr* Rus. Fed.
118 B3 **Tshela** Dem. Rep. Congo
118 C3 **Tshikapa** Dem. Rep. Congo
118 C3 **Tshikapa** *r.* Dem. Rep. Congo
123 D1 **Tshipise** S. Africa
118 C3 **Tshitanzu** Dem. Rep. Congo
118 C3 **Tshuapa** *r.* Dem. Rep. Congo
87 D4 **Tsimlyanskoye Vodokhranilishche** *resr* Rus. Fed.
Tsingtao China *see* **Qingdao**
Tsining China *see* **Jining**
121 □D2 **Tsiroanomandidy** Madag.
123 C3 **Tsomo** S. Africa
67 C4 **Tsu** Japan
67 D3 **Tsuchiura** Japan
66 D2 **Tsugaru-kaikyō** *str.* Japan
120 A2 **Tsumeb** Namibia
122 A1 **Tsumis Park** Namibia
120 B2 **Tsumkwe** Namibia
67 C3 **Tsuruga** Japan
66 C3 **Tsuruoka** Japan
67 A4 **Tsushima** *is* Japan
Tsushima-kaikyō *str.* Japan/S. Korea *see* **Korea Strait**
67 B3 **Tsuyama** Japan
123 C2 **Tswelelang** S. Africa
91 C2 **Tsyurupyns'k** Ukr.
Tthenaagoo Can. *see* **Nahanni Butte**
59 C3 **Tual** Indon.
97 B2 **Tuam** Rep. of Ireland
49 H5 **Tuamotu Archipelago** French Polynesia
91 D3 **Tuapse** Rus. Fed.
54 A3 **Tuatapere** N.Z.
96 A1 **Tuath, Loch a'** U.K.
138 A1 **Tuba City** U.S.A.
61 C2 **Tuban** Indon.
152 D3 **Tubarão** Brazil
102 B2 **Tübingen** Ger.
115 E1 **Tubruq** Libya
144 A1 **Tubutama** Mex.
152 C2 **Tucavaca** Bol.
128 B1 **Tuchitua** Can.
138 A2 **Tucson** U.S.A.
139 C1 **Tucumcari** U.S.A.
150 D1 **Tucupita** Venez.
151 D2 **Tucuruí** Brazil
151 D2 **Tucuruí, Represa** *resr* Brazil
107 C1 **Tudela** Spain
106 B1 **Tuela** *r.* Port.
62 A1 **Tuensang** India
123 D2 **Tugela** *r.* S. Africa
64 B1 **Tuguegarao** Phil.
106 B1 **Tui** Spain
59 C3 **Tukangbesi, Kepulauan** *is* Indon.
126 C2 **Tuktoyaktuk** Can.
88 B2 **Tukums** Latvia
145 C2 **Tula** Mex.
89 E3 **Tula** Rus. Fed.
145 C2 **Tulancingo** Mex.
135 C3 **Tulare** U.S.A.
138 B2 **Tularosa** U.S.A.
110 C1 **Tulcea** Romania
90 B2 **Tul'chyn** Ukr.
129 E1 **Tulemalu Lake** Can.
139 C2 **Tulia** U.S.A.
142 C1 **Tullahoma** U.S.A.
97 C2 **Tullamore** Rep. of Ireland
104 C2 **Tulle** France
51 D1 **Tully** Austr.
139 D1 **Tulsa** U.S.A.
150 A1 **Tumaco** Col.
123 C2 **Tumahole** S. Africa
93 G4 **Tumba** Sweden
118 B3 **Tumba, Lac** *l.* Dem. Rep. Congo
53 C3 **Tumbarumba** Austr.
150 A2 **Tumbes** Peru
128 B2 **Tumbler Ridge** Can.
52 A2 **Tumby Bay** Austr.
65 B1 **Tumen** China
150 B1 **Tumereng** Guyana
64 A2 **Tumindao** *i.* Phil.
74 A2 **Tump** Pak.
151 C1 **Tumucumaque, Serra** *hills* Brazil
53 C3 **Tumut** Austr.
99 D3 **Tunbridge Wells, Royal** U.K.
80 B2 **Tunceli** Turkey
53 D2 **Tuncurry** Austr.
119 D4 **Tunduru** Tanz.
110 C2 **Tundzha** *r.* Bulg.
128 B1 **Tungsten** Can.
115 D1 **Tunis** Tunisia
115 C1 **Tunisia** *country* Africa
150 A1 **Tunja** Col.
92 F3 **Tunnsjøen** *l.* Norway
Tunxi China *see* **Huangshan**
154 B2 **Tupã** Brazil
154 C1 **Tupaciguara** Brazil
142 C2 **Tupelo** U.S.A.
152 B3 **Tupiza** Bol.
83 H2 **Tura** Rus. Fed.
86 F3 **Tura** *r.* Rus. Fed.
78 B2 **Turabah** Saudi Arabia
83 J3 **Turana, Khrebet** *mts* Rus. Fed.
54 C1 **Turangi** N.Z.
76 B2 **Turan Lowland** Asia
78 A1 **Turayf** Saudi Arabia
88 B2 **Turba** Estonia
74 A2 **Turbat** Pak.
150 A1 **Turbo** Col.
110 B1 **Turda** Romania
Turfan China *see* **Turpan**
76 C2 **Turgay** Kazakh.
111 C3 **Turgutlu** Turkey
80 B1 **Turhal** Turkey
107 C2 **Turia** *r.* Spain
108 A1 **Turin** Italy
86 F3 **Turinsk** Rus. Fed.
90 A1 **Turiys'k** Ukr.
119 D2 **Turkana, Lake** *salt l.* Eth./Kenya
77 C2 **Turkestan** Kazakh.
80 B2 **Turkey** *country* Asia
76 C3 **Turkmenabat** Turkm.
76 B2 **Turkmenbashi** Turkm.
76 B2 **Turkmenistan** *country* Asia
147 C2 **Turks and Caicos Islands** *terr.* West Indies
93 H3 **Turku** Fin.
135 B3 **Turlock** U.S.A.
54 C2 **Turnagain, Cape** N.Z.
100 B2 **Turnhout** Belgium
129 D2 **Turnor Lake** Can.
110 B2 **Turnu Măgurele** Romania
68 B2 **Turpan** China
77 D2 **Turugart Pass** China/Kyrg.
142 C2 **Tuscaloosa** U.S.A.
142 C2 **Tuskegee** U.S.A.
73 B4 **Tuticorin** India
120 B3 **Tutume** Botswana
49 F3 **Tuvalu** *country* S. Pacific Ocean

78 B2 **Tuwayq, Jabal** *hills* Saudi Arabia
78 B2 **Tuwayq, Jabal** *mts* Saudi Arabia
78 A2 **Tuwwal** Saudi Arabia
144 B2 **Tuxpan** *Nayarit* Mex.
145 C2 **Tuxpan** *Veracruz* Mex.
145 C3 **Tuxtla Gutiérrez** Mex.
62 B1 **Tuyên Quang** Vietnam
63 B2 **Tuy Hoa** Vietnam
80 B2 **Tuz Gölü** *salt l.* Turkey
81 C2 **Tuz Khurmātū** Iraq
109 C2 **Tuzla** Bos.-Herz.
91 E2 **Tuzlov** *r.* Rus. Fed.
89 E2 **Tver'** Rus. Fed.
98 B1 **Tweed** *r.* U.K.
122 A2 **Twee Rivier** Namibia
135 C4 **Twentynine Palms** U.S.A.
131 E2 **Twillingate** Can.
134 D2 **Twin Falls** U.S.A.
54 B2 **Twizel** N.Z.
137 E1 **Two Harbors** U.S.A.
129 C2 **Two Hills** Can.
139 D2 **Tyler** U.S.A.
83 J3 **Tynda** Rus. Fed.
93 F3 **Tynset** Norway
111 B3 **Tyrnavos** Greece
52 B3 **Tyrrell, Lake** *dry lake* Austr.
108 B2 **Tyrrhenian Sea** France/Italy
76 B2 **Tyub-Karagan, Mys** *pt* Kazakh.
87 E3 **Tyul'gan** Rus. Fed.
86 F3 **Tyumen'** Rus. Fed.
83 J2 **Tyung** *r.* Rus. Fed.
99 A3 **Tywi** *r.* U.K.
123 D1 **Tzaneen** S. Africa

U

120 B2 **Uamanda** Angola
150 B2 **Uaupés** Brazil
155 D2 **Ubá** Brazil
155 D1 **Ubaí** Brazil
151 E3 **Ubaitaba** Brazil
118 B3 **Ubangi** *r.* C.A.R./Dem. Rep. Congo
67 B4 **Ube** Japan
106 C2 **Úbeda** Spain
154 C1 **Uberaba** Brazil
154 C1 **Uberlândia** Brazil
123 D2 **Ubombo** S. Africa
63 B2 **Ubon Ratchathani** Thai.
119 C3 **Ubundu** Dem. Rep. Congo
150 A2 **Ucayali** *r.* Peru
74 B2 **Uch** Pak.
77 E2 **Ucharal** Kazakh.
66 D2 **Uchiura-wan** *b.* Japan
83 J3 **Uchur** *r.* Rus. Fed.
128 B3 **Ucluelet** Can.
74 B2 **Udaipur** India
91 C1 **Uday** *r.* Ukr.
93 F4 **Uddevalla** Sweden
92 G2 **Uddjaure** *l.* Sweden
100 B2 **Uden** Neth.
74 B1 **Udhampur** Jammu and Kashmir
108 B1 **Udine** Italy
89 E2 **Udomlya** Rus. Fed.
62 B2 **Udon Thani** Thai.
73 B3 **Udupi** India
83 K3 **Udyl', Ozero** *l.* Rus. Fed.
67 C3 **Ueda** Japan
58 C3 **Uekuli** Indon.
118 C2 **Uele** *r.* Dem. Rep. Congo
101 E1 **Uelzen** Ger.
119 C2 **Uere** *r.* Dem. Rep. Congo
87 E3 **Ufa** Rus. Fed.
119 D3 **Ugalla** *r.* Tanz.
119 D2 **Uganda** *country* Africa
89 E2 **Uglich** Rus. Fed.
89 D2 **Uglovka** Rus. Fed.
89 D3 **Ugra** Rus. Fed.
103 D2 **Uherské Hradiště** Czech Rep.
101 E2 **Uichteritz** Ger.
96 A2 **Uig** U.K.
120 A1 **Uíge** Angola
65 B2 **Ŭijŏngbu** S. Korea
135 D2 **Uinta Mountains** U.S.A.
120 A3 **Uis Mine** Namibia
65 B2 **Ŭisŏng** S. Korea
123 C3 **Uitenhage** S. Africa
100 C1 **Uithuizen** Neth.
74 B2 **Ujjain** India
Ujung Padang Indon. *see* Makassar
89 F3 **Ukholovo** Rus. Fed.
62 A1 **Ukhrul** India
86 E2 **Ukhta** Rus. Fed.
135 B3 **Ukiah** U.S.A.
127 H2 **Ukkusissat** Greenland
88 B2 **Ukmergė** Lith.
90 C2 **Ukraine** *country* Europe
69 D1 **Ulaanbaatar** Mongolia
68 C1 **Ulaangom** Mongolia
Ulan Bator Mongolia *see* Ulaanbaatar
Ulanhad China *see* **Chifeng**
69 E1 **Ulanhot** China
87 D4 **Ulan-Khol** Rus. Fed.
69 D1 **Ulan-Ude** Rus. Fed.
75 D1 **Ulan Ul Hu** *l.* China
65 B2 **Ulchin** S. Korea
Uleåborg Fin. *see* **Oulu**
88 C2 **Ülenurme** Estonia
73 B3 **Ulhasnagar** India
69 D1 **Uliastai** China
68 C1 **Uliastay** Mongolia
59 D2 **Ulithi** *atoll* Micronesia
53 D3 **Ulladulla** Austr.
96 B2 **Ullapool** U.K.
98 B1 **Ullswater** *l.* U.K.
65 C2 **Ullŭng-do** *i.* S. Korea
102 B2 **Ulm** Ger.
65 B2 **Ulsan** S. Korea
96 □ **Ulsta** U.K.
97 C1 **Ulster** *reg.* Rep. of Ireland/U.K.
52 B3 **Ultima** Austr.
111 C3 **Ulubey** Turkey
111 C2 **Uludağ** *mt.* Turkey
123 D2 **Ulundi** S. Africa
77 E2 **Ulungur Hu** *l.* China
50 C2 **Uluru** *hill* Austr.
98 B1 **Ulverston** U.K.
87 D3 **Ul'yanovsk** Rus. Fed.
136 C3 **Ulysses** U.S.A.
90 C2 **Uman'** Ukr.
86 C2 **Umba** Rus. Fed.
59 D3 **Umboi** *i.* P.N.G.
92 H3 **Umeå** Sweden
92 H3 **Umeälven** *r.* Sweden
127 I2 **Umiiviip Kangertiva** *inlet* Greenland
126 D2 **Umingmaktok** Can.
123 D2 **Umlazi** S. Africa
117 A3 **Umm Keddada** Sudan
78 A2 **Umm Lajj** Saudi Arabia
117 B3 **Umm Ruwaba** Sudan
115 E1 **Umm Sa'ad** Libya
134 B2 **Umpqua** *r.* U.S.A.
120 A2 **Umpulo** Angola
123 C3 **Umtata** S. Africa
154 B2 **Umuarama** Brazil
109 C1 **Una** *r.* Bos.-Herz./Croatia
155 E1 **Una** Brazil
154 C1 **Unaí** Brazil
78 B2 **'Unayzah** Saudi Arabia
136 C1 **Underwood** U.S.A.
89 D3 **Unecha** Rus. Fed.
53 C2 **Ungarie** Austr.
52 A2 **Ungarra** Austr.
127 G2 **Ungava, Péninsule d'** *pen.* Can.
127 G3 **Ungava Bay** Can.
65 C1 **Unggi** N. Korea
90 B2 **Ungheni** Moldova
Unguja *i.* Tanz. *see* **Zanzibar Island**
154 B3 **União da Vitória** Brazil
150 B2 **Unini** *r.* Brazil
142 C1 **Union City** U.S.A.
122 B3 **Uniondale** S. Africa
141 D3 **Uniontown** U.S.A.
79 C2 **United Arab Emirates** *country* Asia
95 C3 **United Kingdom** *country* Europe
132 D3 **United States of America** *country* N. America
129 D2 **Unity** Can.
96 □ **Unst** *i.* U.K.
101 E2 **Unstrut** *r.* Ger.
89 E3 **Upa** *r.* Rus. Fed.
119 C3 **Upemba, Lac** *l.* Dem. Rep. Congo
122 B2 **Upington** S. Africa
134 B2 **Upper Alkali Lake** U.S.A.
128 C2 **Upper Arrow Lake** Can.
134 B2 **Upper Klamath Lake** U.S.A.
128 B1 **Upper Liard** Can.
97 C1 **Upper Lough Erne** *l.* U.K.
93 G4 **Uppsala** Sweden
78 B2 **'Uqlat aş Şuqūr** Saudi Arabia
Urad Qianqi China *see* **Xishanzui**
76 B2 **Ural** *r.* Kazakh./Rus. Fed.
53 D2 **Uralla** Austr.
87 E3 **Ural Mountains** Rus. Fed.
76 B1 **Ural'sk** Kazakh.
Ural'skiy Khrebet *mts* Rus. Fed. *see* **Ural Mountains**
119 D3 **Urambo** Tanz.
53 C3 **Urana** Austr.
129 D2 **Uranium City** Can.
86 F2 **Uray** Rus. Fed.
98 C1 **Ure** *r.* U.K.
86 D3 **Uren'** Rus. Fed.
144 A2 **Ures** Mex.
76 C2 **Urgench** Uzbek.
100 B1 **Urk** Neth.
111 C3 **Urla** Turkey
109 D2 **Uroševac** Serb. and Mont.
144 B2 **Uruáchic** Mex.
151 D3 **Uruaçu** Brazil
144 B3 **Uruapan** Mex.
150 A3 **Urubamba** *r.* Peru
151 C2 **Urucara** Brazil
151 D2 **Uruçuí** Brazil
151 C2 **Urucurituba** Brazil
152 C3 **Uruguaiana** Brazil
153 C4 **Uruguay** *country* S. America
Urumchi China *see* **Ürümqi**
68 B2 **Ürümqi** China
53 D2 **Urunga** Austr.
110 C2 **Urziceni** Romania
67 B4 **Usa** Japan
82 E2 **Usa** *r.* Rus. Fed.
111 C3 **Uşak** Turkey
82 G1 **Ushakova, Ostrov** *i.* Rus. Fed.
77 D2 **Ushtobe** Kazakh.
153 B6 **Ushuaia** Arg.
86 E2 **Usinsk** Rus. Fed.
88 C3 **Uskhodni** Belarus
89 E3 **Usman'** Rus. Fed.

86 D2 **Usogorsk** Rus. Fed.
104 C2 **Ussel** France
66 B2 **Ussuriysk** Rus. Fed.
108 B3 **Ustica, Isola di** *i. Sicily* Italy
83 H3 **Ust'-Ilimsk** Rus. Fed.
86 E2 **Ust'-Ilych** Rus. Fed.
103 D1 **Ustka** Pol.
83 L3 **Ust'-Kamchatsk** Rus. Fed.
77 E2 **Ust'-Kamenogorsk** Kazakh.
86 F2 **Ust'-Kara** Rus. Fed.
86 E2 **Ust'-Kulom** Rus. Fed.
83 I3 **Ust'-Kut** Rus. Fed.
91 D2 **Ust'-Labinsk** Rus. Fed.
88 C2 **Ust'-Luga** Rus. Fed.
86 E2 **Ust'-Nem** Rus. Fed.
83 K2 **Ust'-Nera** Rus. Fed.
83 K2 **Ust'-Omchug** Rus. Fed.
83 H3 **Ust'-Ordynskiy** Rus. Fed.
86 E2 **Ust'-Tsil'ma** Rus. Fed.
86 D2 **Ust'-Ura** Rus. Fed.
76 B2 **Ustyurt Plateau** Kazakh./Uzbek.
89 E2 **Ustyuzhna** Rus. Fed.
89 D2 **Usvyaty** Rus. Fed.
135 D3 **Utah** *state* U.S.A.
135 D2 **Utah Lake** U.S.A.
93 I4 **Utena** Lith.
141 D2 **Utica** U.S.A.
107 C2 **Utiel** Spain
128 C2 **Utikuma Lake** Can.
100 B1 **Utrecht** Neth.
106 B2 **Utrera** Spain
92 I2 **Utsjoki** Fin.
67 C3 **Utsunomiya** Japan
87 D4 **Utta** Rus. Fed.
62 B2 **Uttaradit** Thai.
127 G1 **Uummannaq** Greenland
127 H2 **Uummannaq Fjord** *inlet* Greenland
93 H3 **Uusikaupunki** Fin.
139 D3 **Uvalde** U.S.A.
119 D3 **Uvinza** Tanz.
68 C1 **Uvs Nuur** *salt l.* Mongolia
67 B4 **Uwajima** Japan
78 A2 **'Uwayrid, Harrat al** *lava field* Saudi Arabia
116 A2 **Uweinat, Jebel** *mt.* Sudan
83 H3 **Uyar** Rus. Fed.
115 C4 **Uyo** Nigeria
152 B3 **Uyuni, Salar de** *salt flat* Bol.
76 C2 **Uzbekistan** *country* Asia
104 C2 **Uzerche** France
105 C3 **Uzès** France
90 C1 **Uzh** *r.* Ukr.
90 A2 **Uzhhorod** Ukr.
109 C2 **Užice** Serb. and Mont.
80 E3 **Uzlovaya** Rus. Fed.
111 C3 **Üzümlü** Turkey
111 C2 **Uzunköprü** Turkey

V

123 B2 **Vaal** *r.* S. Africa
123 C2 **Vaal Dam** S. Africa
123 C1 **Vaalwater** S. Africa
92 H3 **Vaasa** Fin.
103 D2 **Vác** Hungary
152 C3 **Vacaria** Brazil
154 B2 **Vacaria, Serra** *hills* Brazil
135 B3 **Vacaville** U.S.A.
74 B2 **Vadodara** India
92 I1 **Vadsø** Norway
105 D2 **Vaduz** Liechtenstein
94 B1 **Vágar** *i.* Faroe Is
94 B1 **Vágur** Faroe Is
103 D2 **Váh** *r.* Slovakia
49 F3 **Vaiaku** Tuvalu
88 B2 **Vaida** Estonia
136 B3 **Vail** U.S.A.
79 C2 **Vakīlābād** Iran
108 B1 **Valdagno** Italy
89 D2 **Valday** Rus. Fed.
89 D2 **Valdayskaya Vozvyshennost'** *hills* Rus. Fed.
106 B2 **Valdecañas, Embalse de** *resr* Spain
93 G4 **Valdemarsvik** Sweden
105 D2 **Val-de-Meuse** France
106 C2 **Valdepeñas** Spain
153 B5 **Valdés, Península** *pen.* Arg.
153 A4 **Valdivia** Chile
130 C2 **Val-d'Or** Can.
143 D2 **Valdosta** U.S.A.
128 C2 **Valemount** Can.
105 C3 **Valence** France
107 C2 **Valencia** Spain
150 B1 **Valencia** Venez.
107 D2 **Valencia, Golfo de** *g.* Spain
100 A2 **Valenciennes** France
136 C2 **Valentine** U.S.A.
64 B1 **Valenzuela** Phil.
150 A1 **Valera** Venez.
109 C2 **Valjevo** Serb. and Mont.
88 C2 **Valka** Latvia
93 H3 **Valkeakoski** Fin.
100 B2 **Valkenswaard** Neth.
91 D2 **Valky** Ukr.
55 D2 **Valkyrie Dome** *ice feature* Antarctica
145 D2 **Valladolid** Mex.
106 C1 **Valladolid** Spain
107 C2 **Vall de Uxó** Spain
93 E4 **Valle** Norway
145 C2 **Vallecillos** Mex.
150 B1 **Valle de la Pascua** Venez.
150 A1 **Valledupar** Col.
145 C2 **Valle Hermoso** Mex.
135 B3 **Vallejo** U.S.A.
152 A3 **Vallenar** Chile
85 E6 **Valletta** Malta
137 D1 **Valley City** U.S.A.
134 B2 **Valley Falls** U.S.A.
128 C2 **Valleyview** Can.
107 D1 **Valls** Spain
129 D3 **Val Marie** Can.
88 C2 **Valmiera** Latvia
88 C3 **Valozhyn** Belarus
154 B2 **Valparaíso** Brazil
153 A4 **Valparaíso** Chile
105 C3 **Valréas** France
59 D3 **Vals, Tanjung** *c.* Indon.
74 B2 **Valsad** India
122 B2 **Valspan** S. Africa
91 D1 **Valuyki** Rus. Fed.
106 B2 **Valverde del Camino** Spain
81 C2 **Van** Turkey
141 F1 **Van Buren** U.S.A.
128 B3 **Vancouver** Can.
134 B1 **Vancouver** U.S.A.
128 B3 **Vancouver Island** Can.
140 B3 **Vandalia** U.S.A.
123 C2 **Vanderbijlpark** S. Africa
128 B2 **Vanderhoof** Can.
88 C2 **Vändra** Estonia
93 F4 **Vänern** *l.* Sweden
93 F4 **Vänersborg** Sweden
121 □D3 **Vangaindrano** Madag.
81 C2 **Van Gölü** *salt l.* Turkey
138 C2 **Van Horn** U.S.A.
59 D3 **Vanimo** P.N.G.
83 K3 **Vanino** Rus. Fed.
104 B2 **Vannes** France
59 D3 **Van Rees, Pegunungan** *mts* Indon.
122 A3 **Vanrhynsdorp** S. Africa
93 H3 **Vantaa** Fin.
49 F4 **Vanua Levu** *i.* Fiji
49 E4 **Vanuatu** *country* S. Pacific Ocean
140 C2 **Van Wert** U.S.A.
122 B3 **Vanwyksvlei** S. Africa
122 B2 **Van Zylsrus** S. Africa
75 C2 **Varanasi** India
92 I1 **Varangerfjorden** *sea chan.* Norway
92 I1 **Varanger Halvøya** *pen.* Norway
109 C1 **Varaždin** Croatia
93 F4 **Varberg** Sweden
109 D2 **Vardar** *r.* Macedonia
93 E4 **Varde** Denmark
92 J1 **Vardø** Norway
100 D1 **Varel** Ger.
88 B3 **Varėna** Lith.
108 A1 **Varese** Italy
155 C2 **Varginha** Brazil
93 I3 **Varkaus** Fin.
110 C2 **Varna** Bulg.
93 F4 **Värnamo** Sweden
155 D1 **Várzea da Palma** Brazil
86 C2 **Varzino** Rus. Fed.
Vasa Fin. *see* **Vaasa**
88 C2 **Vasknarva** Estonia
110 C1 **Vaslui** Romania
93 G4 **Västerås** Sweden
93 G3 **Västerdalälven** *r.* Sweden
88 A2 **Västerhaninge** Sweden
93 G4 **Västervik** Sweden
108 B2 **Vasto** Italy
90 C1 **Vasyl'kiv** Ukr.
104 C2 **Vatan** France
108 B2 **Vatican City** Europe
92 □B3 **Vatnajökull** *ice cap* Iceland
110 C1 **Vatra Dornei** Romania
93 F4 **Vättern** *l.* Sweden
138 B2 **Vaughn** U.S.A.
105 C3 **Vauvert** France
88 B3 **Vawkavysk** Belarus
93 F4 **Växjö** Sweden
86 E1 **Vaygach, Ostrov** *i.* Rus. Fed.
101 D1 **Vechta** Ger.
110 C2 **Vedea** *r.* Romania
100 C1 **Veendam** Neth.
100 B1 **Veenendaal** Neth.
129 C2 **Vegreville** Can.
106 B2 **Vejer de la Frontera** Spain
93 E4 **Vejle** Denmark
109 D2 **Velbŭzhdki Prokhod** *pass* Macedonia
100 B2 **Veldhoven** Neth.
109 B2 **Velebit** *mts* Croatia
100 C2 **Velen** Ger.
109 C1 **Velenje** Slovenia
109 D2 **Veles** Macedonia
106 C2 **Vélez-Málaga** Spain
155 D1 **Velhas** *r.* Brazil
109 D2 **Velika Plana** Serb. and Mont.
88 C2 **Velikaya** *r.* Rus. Fed.
89 D2 **Velikiye Luki** Rus. Fed.
89 D2 **Velikiy Novgorod** Rus. Fed.
86 D2 **Velikiy Ustyug** Rus. Fed.
110 C2 **Veliko Tŭrnovo** Bulg.
108 B2 **Veli Lošinj** Croatia
89 D2 **Velizh** Rus. Fed.
86 D2 **Vel'sk** Rus. Fed.
101 F1 **Velten** Ger.
91 D1 **Velykyy Burluk** Ukr.
108 B2 **Venafro** Italy
154 C2 **Venceslau Bráz** Brazil
104 C2 **Vendôme** France
89 E3 **Venev** Rus. Fed.
Venezia Italy *see* **Venice**
150 B1 **Venezuela** *country* S. America
150 A1 **Venezuela, Golfo de** *g.* Venez.

108 B1 **Venice** Italy
143 D3 **Venice** U.S.A.
108 B1 **Venice, Gulf of** Europe
100 C2 **Venlo** Neth.
100 B2 **Venray** Neth.
88 B2 **Venta** *r.* Latvia/Lith.
88 B2 **Venta** Lith.
123 C3 **Venterstad** S. Africa
99 C3 **Ventnor** U.K.
88 B2 **Ventspils** Latvia
135 C4 **Ventura** U.S.A.
139 C3 **Venustiano Carranza, Presa** *resr* Mex.
107 C2 **Vera** Spain
145 C3 **Veracruz** Mex.
74 B2 **Veraval** India
108 A1 **Verbania** Italy
108 A1 **Vercelli** Italy
105 D3 **Vercors** *reg.* France
92 F3 **Verdalsøra** Norway
154 B1 **Verde** *r. Goiás* Brazil
154 B2 **Verde** *r. Mato Grosso do Sul* Brazil
144 B2 **Verde** *r.* Mex.
138 A2 **Verde** *r.* U.S.A.
155 D1 **Verde Grande** *r.* Brazil
101 D1 **Verden (Aller)** Ger.
154 B1 **Verdinho, Serra do** *mts* Brazil
108 A2 **Verdon** *r.* France
105 D2 **Verdun** France
123 C2 **Vereeniging** S. Africa
106 B1 **Verín** Spain
91 D3 **Verkhnebakanskiy** Rus. Fed.
92 J2 **Verkhnetulomskiy** Rus. Fed.
91 E1 **Verkhniy Mamon** Rus. Fed.
89 E3 **Verkhov'ye** Rus. Fed.
90 A2 **Verkhovyna** Ukr.
83 J2 **Verkhoyanskiy Khrebet** *mts* Rus. Fed.
129 C2 **Vermilion** Can.
137 D2 **Vermillion** U.S.A.
130 A2 **Vermillion Bay** Can.
141 E2 **Vermont** *state* U.S.A.
135 E2 **Vernal** U.S.A.
128 C2 **Vernon** Can.
139 D2 **Vernon** U.S.A.
143 D3 **Vero Beach** U.S.A.
111 B2 **Veroia** Greece
108 B1 **Verona** Italy
104 C2 **Versailles** France
104 B2 **Vertou** France
123 D2 **Verulam** S. Africa
100 B2 **Verviers** Belgium
105 C2 **Vervins** France
105 D3 **Vescovato** *Corsica* France
87 E3 **Veselaya, Gora** *mt.* Rus. Fed.
91 C2 **Vesele** Ukr.
105 D2 **Vesoul** France
92 F2 **Vesterålen** *is* Norway
92 F2 **Vestfjorden** *sea chan.* Norway
94 B1 **Vestmanna** Faroe Is
93 E3 **Vestnes** Norway
108 B2 **Vesuvio** *vol.* Italy
89 E2 **Ves'yegonsk** Rus. Fed.
93 G4 **Vetlanda** Sweden
86 D3 **Vetluga** Rus. Fed.
100 A2 **Veurne** Belgium
105 D2 **Vevey** Switz.
91 D1 **Veydelevka** Rus. Fed.
80 B1 **Vezirköprü** Turkey
151 D2 **Viana** Brazil
106 B1 **Viana do Castelo** Port.
Viangchan Laos *see* Vientiane
62 B1 **Viangphoukha** Laos
154 C1 **Vianópolis** Brazil
108 B2 **Viareggio** Italy
93 E4 **Viborg** Denmark
109 C3 **Vibo Valentia** Italy
107 D1 **Vic** Spain
144 A1 **Vicente Guerrero** Mex.
108 B1 **Vicenza** Italy
105 C2 **Vichy** France
142 B2 **Vicksburg** U.S.A.
155 D2 **Viçosa** Brazil
52 A3 **Victor Harbor** Austr.
50 C1 **Victoria** *r.* Austr.
52 B3 **Victoria** *state* Austr.
128 B3 **Victoria** Can.
153 A4 **Victoria** Chile
113 H4 **Victoria** Seychelles
139 D3 **Victoria** U.S.A.
119 D3 **Victoria, Lake** Africa
52 B2 **Victoria, Lake** Austr.
62 A1 **Victoria, Mount** Myanmar
59 D3 **Victoria, Mount** P.N.G.
120 B2 **Victoria Falls** *waterfall* Zambia/Zimbabwe
126 D2 **Victoria Island** Can.
50 C1 **Victoria River Downs** Austr.
122 B3 **Victoria West** S. Africa
135 C4 **Victorville** U.S.A.
110 C2 **Videle** Romania
92 □A2 **Víðidalsá** Iceland
153 B5 **Viedma** Arg.
153 A5 **Viedma, Lago** *l.* Arg.
100 B2 **Vielsalm** Belgium
101 E2 **Vienenburg** Ger.
103 D2 **Vienna** Austria
105 C2 **Vienne** France
104 C2 **Vienne** *r.* France
62 B2 **Vientiane** Laos
100 C2 **Viersen** Ger.
104 C2 **Vierzon** France
144 B2 **Viesca** Mex.
109 C2 **Vieste** Italy
62 B2 **Vietnam** *country* Asia
62 B1 **Viêt Tri** Vietnam
64 B1 **Vigan** Phil.
108 A1 **Vigevano** Italy
106 B1 **Vigo** Spain
73 C3 **Vijayawada** India
92 □B3 **Vík** Iceland
110 B2 **Vikhren** *mt.* Bulg.
129 C2 **Viking** Can.
106 B2 **Vila Franca de Xira** Port.
106 B1 **Vilagarcía de Arousa** Spain
106 B1 **Vilalba** Spain
106 B1 **Vila Nova de Gaia** Port.
107 D1 **Vilanova i la Geltrú** Spain
106 B1 **Vila Real** Port.
106 B1 **Vilar Formoso** Port.
155 D2 **Vila Velha** Brazil
150 A3 **Vilcabamba, Cordillera** *mts* Peru
92 G3 **Vilhelmina** Sweden
150 B3 **Vilhena** Brazil
88 C2 **Viljandi** Estonia
88 B3 **Vilkaviškis** Lith.
83 H1 **Vil'kitskogo, Proliv** *str.* Rus. Fed.
144 B1 **Villa Ahumada** Mex.
106 B1 **Villablino** Spain
102 C2 **Villach** Austria
144 B2 **Villa de Cos** Mex.
152 B4 **Villa Dolores** Arg.
145 C3 **Villa Flores** Mex.
145 C2 **Villagrán** Mex.
145 C3 **Villahermosa** Mex.
144 A2 **Villa Insurgentes** Mex.
152 B4 **Villa María** Arg.
152 B3 **Villa Montes** Bol.
144 B2 **Villanueva** Mex.
106 B2 **Villanueva de la Serena** Spain
106 C2 **Villanueva de los Infantes** Spain
152 C3 **Villa Ocampo** Arg.
108 A3 **Villaputzu** *Sardinia* Italy
152 C3 **Villarrica** Para.
106 C2 **Villarrobledo** Spain
152 B3 **Villa Unión** Arg.
144 B2 **Villa Unión** *Durango* Mex.
144 B2 **Villa Unión** *Sinaloa* Mex.
150 A1 **Villavicencio** Col.
152 B3 **Villazon** Bol.
107 C2 **Villena** Spain
104 C3 **Villeneuve-sur-Lot** France
142 B2 **Ville Platte** U.S.A.
105 C2 **Villeurbanne** France
102 B2 **Villingen** Ger.
88 C3 **Vilnius** Lith.
91 C2 **Vil'nohirs'k** Ukr.
91 D2 **Vil'nyans'k** Ukr.
100 B2 **Vilvoorde** Belgium
88 C3 **Vilyeyka** Belarus
83 J2 **Vilyuy** *r.* Rus. Fed.
93 G4 **Vimmerby** Sweden
153 A4 **Viña del Mar** Chile
107 D1 **Vinaròs** Spain
140 B3 **Vincennes** U.S.A.
55 G3 **Vincennes Bay** Antarctica
141 D3 **Vineland** U.S.A.
62 B2 **Vinh** Vietnam
63 B2 **Vinh Long** Vietnam
139 D1 **Vinita** U.S.A.
90 B2 **Vinnytsya** Ukr.
55 O2 **Vinson Massif** *mt* Antarctica
93 E3 **Vinstra** Norway
108 B1 **Vipiteno** Italy
64 B1 **Virac** Phil.
129 D3 **Virden** Can.
104 B2 **Vire** France
120 A2 **Virei** Angola
155 D1 **Virgem da Lapa** Brazil
138 A1 **Virgin** *r.* U.S.A.
123 C2 **Virginia** S. Africa
137 E1 **Virginia** U.S.A.
141 D3 **Virginia** *state* U.S.A.
141 D3 **Virginia Beach** U.S.A.
135 C3 **Virginia City** U.S.A.
147 D3 **Virgin Islands (U.K.)** *terr.* West Indies
147 D3 **Virgin Islands (U.S.A.)** *terr.* West Indies
63 B2 **Virôchey** Cambodia
109 C1 **Virovitica** Croatia
100 B3 **Virton** Belgium
88 B2 **Virtsu** Estonia
109 C2 **Vis** *i.* Croatia
88 C2 **Visaginas** Lith.
135 C3 **Visalia** U.S.A.
74 B2 **Visavadar** India
64 B1 **Visayan Sea** Phil.
93 G4 **Visby** Sweden
126 D2 **Viscount Melville Sound** *sea chan.* Can.
151 D2 **Viseu** Brazil
106 B1 **Viseu** Port.
73 C3 **Vishakhapatnam** India
88 C2 **Višķi** Latvia
109 C2 **Visoko** Bos.-Herz.
108 B2 **Viterbo** Italy
49 F4 **Viti Levu** *i.* Fiji
83 I3 **Vitim** *r.* Rus. Fed.
155 D2 **Vitória** Brazil
151 D3 **Vitória da Conquista** Brazil
106 C1 **Vitoria-Gasteiz** Spain
104 B2 **Vitré** France
105 C2 **Vitry-le-François** France
89 D2 **Vitsyebsk** Belarus
105 D2 **Vittel** France
108 B3 **Vittoria** *Sicily* Italy
108 B1 **Vittorio Veneto** Italy
106 B1 **Viveiro** Spain
144 A2 **Vizcaíno, Sierra** *mts* Mex.
110 C2 **Vize** Turkey

73 C3 **Vizianagaram** India
100 B2 **Vlaardingen** Neth.
87 D4 **Vladikavkaz** Rus. Fed.
89 F2 **Vladimir** Rus. Fed.
66 B2 **Vladivostok** Rus. Fed.
109 D2 **Vlasotince** Serb. and Mont.
100 B1 **Vlieland** *i.* Neth.
100 A2 **Vlissingen** Neth.
109 C2 **Vlorë** Albania
102 C2 **Vöcklabruck** Austria
101 D2 **Vogelsberg** *hills* Ger.
119 D3 **Voi** Kenya
105 D2 **Voiron** France
131 D1 **Voisey Bay** Can.
109 C1 **Vojvodina** *prov.* Serb. and Mont.
92 J3 **Voknavolok** Rus. Fed.
Volcano Bay *b.* Japan *see* **Uchiura-wan**
89 E2 **Volga** Rus. Fed.
89 F2 **Volga** *r.* Rus. Fed.
87 D4 **Volgodonsk** Rus. Fed.
87 D4 **Volgograd** Rus. Fed.
89 D2 **Volkhov** Rus. Fed.
89 D1 **Volkhov** *r.* Rus. Fed.
101 E2 **Volkstedt** Ger.
91 D2 **Volnovakha** Ukr.
90 B2 **Volochys'k** Ukr.
91 D2 **Volodars'ke** Ukr.
90 B1 **Volodars'k-Volyns'kyy** Ukr.
90 B1 **Volodymyrets'** Ukr.
90 A1 **Volodymyr-Volyns'kyy** Ukr.
89 E2 **Vologda** Rus. Fed.
89 E2 **Volokolamsk** Rus. Fed.
91 D1 **Volokonovka** Rus. Fed.
111 B3 **Volos** Greece
88 C2 **Volosovo** Rus. Fed.
89 D2 **Volot** Rus. Fed.
89 E3 **Volovo** Rus. Fed.
87 D3 **Vol'sk** Rus. Fed.
114 C4 **Volta, Lake** *resr* Ghana
155 D2 **Volta Redonda** Brazil
87 D4 **Volzhskiy** Rus. Fed.
92 □C2 **Vopnafjörður** Iceland
88 C3 **Voranava** Belarus
86 F2 **Vorkuta** Rus. Fed.
88 B2 **Vormsi** *i.* Estonia
89 E3 **Voronezh** Rus. Fed.
89 E3 **Voronezh** *r.* Rus. Fed.
91 E1 **Vorontsovka** Rus. Fed.
91 C2 **Vorskla** *r.* Rus. Fed.
88 C2 **Võrtsjärv** *l.* Estonia
88 C2 **Võru** Estonia
122 B3 **Vosburg** S. Africa
105 D2 **Vosges** *mts* France
89 E2 **Voskresensk** Rus. Fed.
93 E3 **Voss** Norway
83 H3 **Vostochnyy Sayan** *mts* Rus. Fed.
86 E3 **Votkinsk** Rus. Fed.
154 C2 **Votuporanga** Brazil
100 B3 **Vouziers** France
92 J2 **Voynitsa** Rus. Fed.
91 C2 **Voznesens'k** Ukr.
93 E4 **Vrådal** Norway
66 B2 **Vrangel'** Rus. Fed.
83 N2 **Vrangelya, Ostrov** *i.* Rus. Fed.
109 D2 **Vranje** Serb. and Mont.
110 C2 **Vratnik** *pass* Bulg.
110 B2 **Vratsa** Bulg.
109 C1 **Vrbas** *r.* Bos.-Herz.
109 C1 **Vrbas** Serb. and Mont.
122 A3 **Vredenburg** S. Africa
122 A3 **Vredendal** S. Africa
100 B3 **Vresse** Belgium
109 D1 **Vršac** Serb. and Mont.
122 B2 **Vryburg** S. Africa
123 D2 **Vryheid** S. Africa
89 D1 **Vsevolozhsk** Rus. Fed.
109 D2 **Vučitrn** Serb. and Mont.
109 C1 **Vukovar** Croatia
86 E2 **Vuktyl'** Rus. Fed.
123 C2 **Vukuzakhe** S. Africa
109 B3 **Vulcano, Isola** *i.* Italy
63 B2 **Vung Tau** Vietnam
74 B2 **Vyara** India
Vyatka Rus. Fed. *see* **Kirov**
89 D2 **Vyaz'ma** Rus. Fed.
93 I3 **Vyborg** Rus. Fed.
88 C2 **Vyerkhnyadzvinsk** Belarus
87 D3 **Vyksa** Rus. Fed.
90 B2 **Vylkove** Ukr.
90 A2 **Vynohradiv** Ukr.
89 D2 **Vypolzovo** Rus. Fed.
89 D2 **Vyritsa** Rus. Fed.
91 D2 **Vyselki** Rus. Fed.
90 C1 **Vyshhorod** Ukr.
89 D2 **Vyshniy-Volochek** Rus. Fed.
103 D2 **Vyškov** Czech Rep.
86 C2 **Vytegra** Rus. Fed.

W

114 B3 **Wa** Ghana
100 B2 **Waal** *r.* Neth.
100 B2 **Waalwijk** Neth.
128 C2 **Wabasca** *r.* Can.
128 C2 **Wabasca-Desmarais** Can.
140 B3 **Wabash** *r.* U.S.A.
117 C4 **Wabē Gestro** *r.* Eth.
117 C4 **Wabē Shebelē Wenz** *r.* Eth.
129 E2 **Wabowden** Can.
143 D3 **Waccasassa Bay** U.S.A.
101 D2 **Wächtersbach** Ger.
139 D2 **Waco** U.S.A.
74 A2 **Wad** Pak.
115 D2 **Waddan** Libya
100 B1 **Waddenzee** *sea chan.* Neth.
128 B2 **Waddington, Mount** Can.
100 B1 **Waddinxveen** Neth.
129 D2 **Wadena** Can.
137 D1 **Wadena** U.S.A.
116 B2 **Wadi Halfa** Sudan
116 B3 **Wad Medani** Sudan
70 C2 **Wafangdian** China
100 B2 **Wageningen** Neth.
127 F2 **Wager Bay** Can.
53 C3 **Wagga Wagga** Austr.
137 D2 **Wahoo** U.S.A.
137 D1 **Wahpeton** U.S.A.
54 B2 **Waiau** *r.* N.Z.
59 C3 **Waigeo** *i.* Indon.
58 B3 **Waikabubak** Indon.
52 A2 **Waikerie** Austr.
54 B2 **Waimate** N.Z.
75 B3 **Wainganga** *r.* India
58 C3 **Waingapu** Indon.
129 C2 **Wainwright** Can.
54 C1 **Waiouru** N.Z.
54 B2 **Waipara** N.Z.
54 C1 **Waipawa** N.Z.
54 B2 **Wairau** *r.* N.Z.
54 C1 **Wairoa** N.Z.
54 B2 **Waitaki** *r.* N.Z.
54 B1 **Waitara** N.Z.
54 B1 **Waiuku** N.Z.
119 E2 **Wajir** Kenya
67 C3 **Wakasa-wan** *b.* Japan
54 A3 **Wakatipu, Lake** N.Z.
129 D2 **Wakaw** Can.
67 C4 **Wakayama** Japan
136 D3 **WaKeeney** U.S.A.
54 B2 **Wakefield** N.Z.
98 C2 **Wakefield** U.K.
66 D1 **Wakkanai** Japan
123 D2 **Wakkerstroom** S. Africa
103 D1 **Wałbrzych** Pol.
53 D2 **Walcha** Austr.
100 C1 **Walchum** Ger.
103 D1 **Wałcz** Pol.
99 B2 **Wales** *admin. div.* U.K.
53 C2 **Walgett** Austr.
119 C3 **Walikale** Dem. Rep. Congo
135 C3 **Walker Lake** *l.* U.S.A.
52 A2 **Wallaroo** Austr.
98 B2 **Wallasey** U.K.
134 C1 **Walla Walla** U.S.A.
101 D3 **Walldürn** Ger.
53 C2 **Wallendbeen** Austr.
49 F4 **Wallis and Futuna Islands** *terr.* S. Pacific Ocean
96 □ **Walls** U.K.
98 B1 **Walney, Isle of** *i.* U.K.
99 C2 **Walsall** U.K.
136 C3 **Walsenburg** U.S.A.
101 D1 **Walsrode** Ger.
143 D2 **Walterboro** U.S.A.
120 A3 **Walvis Bay** Namibia
119 C2 **Wamba** Dem. Rep. Congo
52 B1 **Wanaaring** Austr.
54 A2 **Wanaka** N.Z.
54 A2 **Wanaka, Lake** N.Z.
130 B2 **Wanapitei Lake** Can.
154 B3 **Wanda** Arg.
66 B1 **Wanda Shan** *mts* China
62 A1 **Wanding** China
54 C1 **Wanganui** N.Z.
53 C3 **Wangaratta** Austr.
65 B1 **Wangqing** China
62 A1 **Wan Hsa-la** Myanmar
71 B4 **Wanning** China
100 B2 **Wanroij** Neth.
99 C3 **Wantage** U.K.
70 A2 **Wanxian** China
70 A2 **Wanyuan** China
73 B3 **Warangal** India
101 D2 **Warburg** Ger.
50 B2 **Warburton** Austr.
52 A1 **Warburton** *watercourse* Austr.
75 B2 **Wardha** India
96 C1 **Ward Hill** U.K.
128 B2 **Ware** Can.
101 F1 **Waren** Ger.
100 C2 **Warendorf** Ger.
53 D1 **Warialda** Austr.
122 A2 **Warmbad** Namibia
135 C3 **Warm Springs** U.S.A.
134 C2 **Warner Lakes** U.S.A.
143 D2 **Warner Robins** U.S.A.
152 B2 **Warnes** Bol.
52 B3 **Warracknabeal** Austr.
53 C2 **Warrego** *r.* Austr.
53 C2 **Warren** Austr.
142 B2 **Warren** *AR* U.S.A.
140 C2 **Warren** *OH* U.S.A.
141 D2 **Warren** *PA* U.S.A.
97 C1 **Warrenpoint** U.K.
137 E3 **Warrensburg** U.S.A.
122 B2 **Warrenton** S. Africa
115 C4 **Warri** Nigeria
98 B2 **Warrington** U.K.
52 B3 **Warrnambool** Austr.
103 E1 **Warsaw** Pol.
Warszawa Pol. *see* **Warsaw**
103 C1 **Warta** *r.* Pol.
53 D1 **Warwick** Austr.
99 C2 **Warwick** U.K.
135 C3 **Wasco** U.S.A.
136 C1 **Washburn** U.S.A.
141 D3 **Washington** *DC* U.S.A.
137 E2 **Washington** *IA* U.S.A.
140 B3 **Washington** *IN* U.S.A.
137 E3 **Washington** *MO* U.S.A.
143 E1 **Washington** *NC* U.S.A.
140 C2 **Washington** *PA* U.S.A.
134 B1 **Washington** *state* U.S.A.

141 E2 **Washington, Mount** U.S.A.
140 C3 **Washington Court House** U.S.A.
74 A2 **Washuk** Pak.
130 C1 **Waskaganish** Can.
129 E2 **Waskaiowaka Lake** Can.
122 A2 **Wasser** Namibia
130 C2 **Waswanipi, Lac** *l.* Can.
58 C3 **Watampone** Indon.
141 E2 **Waterbury** U.S.A.
129 D2 **Waterbury Lake** Can.
97 C2 **Waterford** Rep. of Ireland
97 C2 **Waterford Harbour** Rep. of Ireland
137 E2 **Waterloo** U.S.A.
123 C1 **Waterpoort** S. Africa
141 D2 **Watertown** *NY* U.S.A.
137 D2 **Watertown** *SD* U.S.A.
140 B2 **Watertown** *WI* U.S.A.
141 F2 **Waterville** U.S.A.
99 C3 **Watford** U.K.
136 C1 **Watford City** U.S.A.
129 D2 **Wathaman** *r.* Can.
139 D1 **Watonga** U.S.A.
129 D2 **Watrous** Can.
119 C2 **Watsa** Dem. Rep. Congo
140 B2 **Watseka** U.S.A.
118 C3 **Watsi Kengo** Dem. Rep. Congo
128 B1 **Watson Lake** Can.
135 B3 **Watsonville** U.S.A.
59 C3 **Watubela, Kepulauan** *is* Indon.
59 D3 **Wau** P.N.G.
117 A4 **Wau** Sudan
53 D2 **Wauchope** Austr.
140 B2 **Waukegan** U.S.A.
139 D2 **Waurika** U.S.A.
140 B2 **Wausau** U.S.A.
99 D2 **Waveney** *r.* U.K.
137 E2 **Waverly** U.S.A.
143 D2 **Waycross** U.S.A.
137 D2 **Wayne** U.S.A.
143 D2 **Waynesboro** *GA* U.S.A.
141 D3 **Waynesboro** *VA* U.S.A.
143 D1 **Waynesville** U.S.A.
74 B1 **Wazirabad** Pak.
98 C1 **Wear** *r.* U.K.
139 D2 **Weatherford** U.S.A.
134 B2 **Weaverville** U.S.A.
130 B1 **Webequie** Can.
117 C4 **Webi Shabeelle** *r.* Somalia
137 D1 **Webster** U.S.A.
137 E2 **Webster City** U.S.A.
55 Q2 **Weddell Sea** Antarctica
100 B2 **Weert** Neth.
53 C2 **Wee Waa** Austr.
100 C2 **Wegberg** Ger.
103 E1 **Węgorzewo** Pol.
101 F3 **Weiden in der Oberpfalz** Ger.
70 B2 **Weifang** China
70 C2 **Weihai** China
53 C1 **Weilmoringle** Austr.
101 E2 **Weimar** Ger.
70 A2 **Weinan** China
51 D1 **Weipa** Austr.
53 C1 **Weir** *r.* Austr.
140 C2 **Weirton** U.S.A.
62 B1 **Weishan** China
101 E2 **Weißenfels** Ger.
102 C2 **Weißkugel** *mt.* Austria/Italy
103 D1 **Wejherowo** Pol.
128 C1 **Wekweti** Can.
140 C3 **Welch** U.S.A.
117 B3 **Weldiya** Eth.
123 C2 **Welkom** S. Africa
99 C2 **Welland** *r.* U.K.
51 C1 **Wellesley Islands** Austr.
53 C2 **Wellington** Austr.
54 B2 **Wellington** N.Z.
122 A3 **Wellington** S. Africa
137 D3 **Wellington** U.S.A.
153 A5 **Wellington, Isla** *i.* Chile
53 C3 **Wellington, Lake** Austr.
128 B2 **Wells** Can.
99 B3 **Wells** U.K.
134 D2 **Wells** U.S.A.
50 B2 **Wells, Lake** *salt flat* Austr.
54 B1 **Wellsford** N.Z.
98 D2 **Wells-next-the-Sea** U.K.
102 C2 **Wels** Austria
99 B2 **Welshpool** U.K.
123 C2 **Wembesi** S. Africa
130 C1 **Wemindji** Can.
134 B1 **Wenatchee** U.S.A.
71 B4 **Wenchang** China
114 B4 **Wenchi** Ghana
70 C2 **Wendeng** China
101 E1 **Wendisch Evern** Ger.
117 B4 **Wendo** Eth.
134 D2 **Wendover** U.S.A.
71 B3 **Wengyuan** China
71 C3 **Wenling** China
71 A3 **Wenshan** China
52 B2 **Wentworth** Austr.
71 C3 **Wenzhou** China
123 C2 **Wepener** S. Africa
122 B2 **Werda** Botswana
101 F2 **Werdau** Ger.
101 F1 **Werder** Ger.
101 F3 **Wernberg-Köblitz** Ger.
101 E2 **Wernigerode** Ger.
101 D2 **Werra** *r.* Ger.
53 D2 **Werris Creek** Austr.
101 D3 **Wertheim** Ger.
100 C2 **Wesel** Ger.
101 E1 **Wesendorf** Ger.
101 D1 **Weser** *r.* Ger.
101 D1 **Weser** *sea chan.* Ger.
51 C1 **Wessel, Cape** Austr.
51 C1 **Wessel Islands** Austr.
123 C2 **Wesselton** S. Africa
80 B2 **West Bank** *terr.* Asia
140 B2 **West Bend** U.S.A.
99 C2 **West Bromwich** U.K.
100 C2 **Westerburg** Ger.
100 C1 **Westerholt** Ger.
50 B2 **Western Australia** *state* Austr.
122 B3 **Western Cape** *prov.* S. Africa
Western Desert *des.* Egypt *see* **Aş Şaḩrā' al Gharbīyah**
73 B3 **Western Ghats** *mts* India
114 A2 **Western Sahara** *terr.* Africa
Western Samoa *country* S. Pacific Ocean *see* **Samoa**
100 A2 **Westerschelde** *est.* Neth.
100 C1 **Westerstede** Ger.
100 C2 **Westerwald** *hills* Ger.
153 B6 **West Falkland** *i.* Falkland Is
140 B3 **West Frankfort** U.S.A.
100 B1 **West Frisian Islands** Neth.
147 D2 **West Indies** N. America
96 A1 **West Loch Roag** *b.* U.K.
128 C2 **Westlock** Can.
100 B2 **Westmalle** Belgium
142 B1 **West Memphis** U.S.A.
140 C3 **Weston** U.S.A.
99 B3 **Weston-super-Mare** U.K.
143 D3 **West Palm Beach** U.S.A.
137 E3 **West Plains** U.S.A.
137 D2 **West Point** U.S.A.
54 B2 **Westport** N.Z.
97 B2 **Westport** Rep. of Ireland
129 D2 **Westray** Can.
96 C1 **Westray** *i.* U.K.
100 B1 **West-Terschelling** Neth.
97 B1 **West Town** Rep. of Ireland
140 C3 **West Virginia** *state* U.S.A.
53 C2 **West Wyalong** Austr.
134 D2 **West Yellowstone** U.S.A.
59 C3 **Wetar** *i.* Indon.
128 C2 **Wetaskiwin** Can.
101 D2 **Wetzlar** Ger.
59 D3 **Wewak** P.N.G.
97 C2 **Wexford** Rep. of Ireland
129 D2 **Weyakwin** Can.
129 D3 **Weyburn** Can.
101 D1 **Weyhe** Ger.
99 B3 **Weymouth** U.K.
54 C1 **Whakatane** N.Z.
129 E1 **Whale Cove** Can.
96 □ **Whalsay** *i.* U.K.
54 B1 **Whangarei** N.Z.
98 C2 **Wharfe** *r.* U.K.
139 D3 **Wharton** U.S.A.
128 C1 **Wha Ti** Can.
136 B2 **Wheatland** U.S.A.
138 B1 **Wheeler Peak** *NM* U.S.A.
135 D3 **Wheeler Peak** *NV* U.S.A.
140 C2 **Wheeling** U.S.A.
98 B1 **Whernside** *hill* U.K.
128 B2 **Whistler** Can.
98 C1 **Whitby** U.K.
142 B2 **White** *r.* U.S.A.
50 B2 **White, Lake** *salt flat* Austr.
131 E2 **White Bay** Can.
136 C1 **White Butte** *mt.* U.S.A.
52 B2 **White Cliffs** Austr.
128 C2 **Whitecourt** Can.
134 D1 **Whitefish** U.S.A.
98 B1 **Whitehaven** U.K.
97 D1 **Whitehead** U.K.
128 A1 **Whitehorse** Can.
142 B3 **White Lake** *l.* U.S.A.
135 C3 **White Mountain Peak** U.S.A.
116 B3 **White Nile** *r.* Sudan/Uganda
86 C2 **White Sea** Rus. Fed.
134 D1 **White Sulphur Springs** U.S.A.
143 E2 **Whiteville** U.S.A.
114 B3 **White Volta** *watercourse* Burkina/Ghana
138 B2 **Whitewater Baldy** *mt.* U.S.A.
130 B1 **Whitewater Lake** Can.
129 D2 **Whitewood** Can.
96 B3 **Whithorn** U.K.
54 C1 **Whitianga** N.Z.
135 C3 **Whitney, Mount** U.S.A.
51 D2 **Whitsunday Island** Austr.
52 A2 **Whyalla** Austr.
100 A2 **Wichelen** Belgium
137 D3 **Wichita** U.S.A.
139 D2 **Wichita Falls** U.S.A.
96 C1 **Wick** U.K.
138 A2 **Wickenburg** U.S.A.
97 C2 **Wicklow** Rep. of Ireland
97 D2 **Wicklow Head** *hd* Rep. of Ireland
97 C2 **Wicklow Mountains** Rep. of Ireland
98 B2 **Widnes** U.K.
101 D1 **Wiehengebirge** *hills* Ger.
100 C2 **Wiehl** Ger.
103 D1 **Wieluń** Pol.
Wien Austria *see* **Vienna**
103 D2 **Wiener Neustadt** Austria
100 B1 **Wieringerwerf** Neth.
100 D2 **Wiesbaden** Ger.
100 C1 **Wiesmoor** Ger.
103 D1 **Wieżyca** *hill* Pol.
99 C3 **Wight, Isle of** *i.* U.K.
96 B3 **Wigtown** U.K.
100 B2 **Wijchen** Neth.
52 B2 **Wilcannia** Austr.
123 C3 **Wild Coast** S. Africa
123 C2 **Wilge** *r.* S. Africa
100 D1 **Wilhelmshaven** Ger.

141 D2 **Wilkes-Barre** U.S.A.
55 H3 **Wilkes Land** *reg.* Antarctica
129 D2 **Wilkie** Can.
138 B2 **Willcox** U.S.A.
100 B2 **Willebroek** Belgium
147 D3 **Willemstad** Neth. Antilles
52 B3 **William, Mount** Austr.
52 A1 **William Creek** Austr.
138 A1 **Williams** U.S.A.
141 D3 **Williamsburg** U.S.A.
128 B2 **Williams Lake** Can.
140 C3 **Williamson** U.S.A.
141 D2 **Williamsport** U.S.A.
143 E1 **Williamston** U.S.A.
122 B3 **Williston** S. Africa
136 C1 **Williston** U.S.A.
128 B2 **Williston Lake** Can.
135 B3 **Willits** U.S.A.
137 D1 **Willmar** U.S.A.
122 B3 **Willowmore** S. Africa
123 C3 **Willowvale** S. Africa
50 B2 **Wills, Lake** *salt flat* Austr.
52 A3 **Willunga** Austr.
52 A2 **Wilmington** Austr.
141 D3 **Wilmington** *DE* U.S.A.
143 E2 **Wilmington** *NC* U.S.A.
100 D2 **Wilnsdorf** Ger.
143 E1 **Wilson** U.S.A.
53 C3 **Wilson's Promontory** *pen.* Austr.
100 B3 **Wiltz** Lux.
50 B2 **Wiluna** Austr.
99 C3 **Winchester** U.K.
140 C3 **Winchester** *KY* U.S.A.
141 D3 **Winchester** *VA* U.S.A.
98 B1 **Windermere** *l.* U.K.
120 A3 **Windhoek** Namibia
137 D2 **Windom** U.S.A.
51 D2 **Windorah** Austr.
130 D2 **Wind River Range** *mts* U.S.A.
53 D2 **Windsor** Austr.
130 B2 **Windsor** Can.
147 D3 **Windward Islands** Caribbean Sea
147 C3 **Windward Passage** Cuba/Haiti
137 D3 **Winfield** U.S.A.
100 A2 **Wingene** Belgium
53 D2 **Wingham** Austr.
130 B1 **Winisk** Can.
130 B1 **Winisk** *r.* Can.
130 B1 **Winisk Lake** Can.
63 A2 **Winkana** Myanmar
129 E3 **Winkler** Can.
114 B4 **Winneba** Ghana
140 B2 **Winnebago, Lake** U.S.A.
134 C2 **Winnemucca** U.S.A.
136 C2 **Winner** U.S.A.
142 B2 **Winnfield** U.S.A.
137 E1 **Winnibigoshish, Lake** U.S.A.
129 E3 **Winnipeg** Can.
129 E2 **Winnipeg** *r.* Can.
129 E2 **Winnipeg, Lake** Can.
129 D2 **Winnipegosis, Lake** Can.
141 E2 **Winnipesaukee, Lake** U.S.A.
142 B2 **Winnsboro** U.S.A.
137 E2 **Winona** *MN* U.S.A.
142 C2 **Winona** *MS* U.S.A.
100 C1 **Winschoten** Neth.
101 D1 **Winsen (Aller)** Ger.
101 E1 **Winsen (Luhe)** Ger.
138 A1 **Winslow** U.S.A.
143 D1 **Winston-Salem** U.S.A.
101 D2 **Winterberg** Ger.
143 D3 **Winter Haven** U.S.A.
100 C2 **Winterswijk** Neth.
105 D2 **Winterthur** Switz.
51 D2 **Winton** Austr.
54 A3 **Winton** N.Z.
52 A2 **Wirrabara** Austr.
99 D2 **Wisbech** U.K.
140 A2 **Wisconsin** *r.* U.S.A.
140 B2 **Wisconsin** *state* U.S.A.
140 B2 **Wisconsin Rapids** U.S.A.
103 D1 **Wisła** *r.* Pol.
101 E1 **Wismar** Ger.
123 C2 **Witbank** S. Africa
98 D2 **Withernsea** U.K.
100 B1 **Witmarsum** Neth.
99 C3 **Witney** U.K.
123 D2 **Witrivier** S. Africa
101 E1 **Wittenberge** Ger.
101 E1 **Wittenburg** Ger.
101 E1 **Wittingen** Ger.
100 C3 **Wittlich** Ger.
100 C1 **Wittmund** Ger.
101 F1 **Wittstock** Ger.
120 A3 **Witvlei** Namibia
101 D2 **Witzenhausen** Ger.
103 D1 **Władysławowo** Pol.
103 D1 **Włocławek** Pol.
53 C3 **Wodonga** Austr.
59 C3 **Wokam** *i.* Indon.
99 C3 **Woking** U.K.
101 F2 **Wolfen** Ger.
101 E1 **Wolfenbüttel** Ger.
101 D2 **Wolfhagen** Ger.
136 B1 **Wolf Point** U.S.A.
101 E1 **Wolfsburg** Ger.
100 C3 **Wolfstein** Ger.
131 D2 **Wolfville** Can.
102 C1 **Wolgast** Ger.
102 C1 **Wolin** Pol.
129 D2 **Wollaston Lake** Can.
129 D2 **Wollaston Lake** *l.* Can.
126 D2 **Wollaston Peninsula** Can.
53 D2 **Wollongong** Austr.
101 E2 **Wolmirsleben** Ger.
101 E1 **Wolmirstedt** Ger.
100 C1 **Wolvega** Neth.
99 B2 **Wolverhampton** U.K.
65 B2 **Wŏnju** S. Korea
128 B2 **Wonowon** Can.
65 B2 **Wŏnsan** N. Korea
53 C3 **Wonthaggi** Austr.
52 A2 **Woocalla** Austr.
51 C1 **Woodah, Isle** *i.* Austr.
99 D2 **Woodbridge** U.K.
136 B3 **Woodland Park** U.S.A.
50 C2 **Woodroffe, Mount** Austr.
51 C1 **Woods, Lake** *salt flat* Austr.
129 E3 **Woods, Lake of the** Can./U.S.A.
53 C3 **Woods Point** Austr.
131 D2 **Woodstock** *N.B.* Can.
140 C2 **Woodstock** *Ont.* Can.
54 C2 **Woodville** N.Z.
139 D1 **Woodward** U.S.A.
53 D2 **Woolgoolga** Austr.
52 A2 **Woomera** Austr.
140 C2 **Wooster** U.S.A.
122 A3 **Worcester** S. Africa
99 B2 **Worcester** U.K.
141 E2 **Worcester** U.S.A.
102 C2 **Wörgl** Austria
98 B1 **Workington** U.K.
98 C2 **Worksop** U.K.
136 B2 **Worland** U.S.A.
101 D3 **Worms** Ger.
99 C3 **Worthing** U.K.
137 D2 **Worthington** U.S.A.
58 C3 **Wotu** Indon.
59 C3 **Wowoni** *i.* Indon.
Wrangel Island Rus. Fed. *see* **Vrangelya, Ostrov**
128 A2 **Wrangell** U.S.A.
96 B1 **Wrath, Cape** U.K.
136 C2 **Wray** U.S.A.
122 A2 **Wreck Point** S. Africa
98 B2 **Wrexham** U.K.
136 B2 **Wright** U.S.A.
63 A2 **Wrightmyo** India
128 B1 **Wrigley** Can.
103 D1 **Wrocław** Pol.
103 D1 **Września** Pol.
70 B2 **Wu'an** China
70 A2 **Wudu** China
70 A2 **Wuhai** China
70 B2 **Wuhan** China
70 B2 **Wuhu** China
Wujin China *see* **Changzhou**
115 C4 **Wukari** Nigeria
62 B1 **Wuliang Shan** *mts* China
59 C3 **Wuliaru** *i.* Indon.
71 A3 **Wumeng Shan** *mts* China
130 B1 **Wunnummin Lake** Can.
101 F2 **Wunsiedel** Ger.
101 D1 **Wunstorf** Ger.
62 A1 **Wuntho** Myanmar
100 C2 **Wuppertal** Ger.
122 A3 **Wuppertal** S. Africa
101 E2 **Wurzbach** Ger.
101 D3 **Würzburg** Ger.
101 F2 **Wurzen** Ger.
68 C2 **Wuwei** China
70 A2 **Wuxi** *Chongqing* China
70 C2 **Wuxi** *Jiangsu* China
Wuxing China *see* **Huzhou**
71 A3 **Wuxuan** China
Wuyang China *see* **Zhenyuan**
69 E1 **Wuyiling** China
71 B3 **Wuyishan** China
71 B3 **Wuyi Shan** *mts* China
70 A1 **Wuyuan** China
70 A2 **Wuzhong** China
71 B3 **Wuzhou** China
53 C2 **Wyangala Reservoir** Austr.
52 B3 **Wycheproof** Austr.
99 B3 **Wye** *r.* U.K.
50 B1 **Wyndham** Austr.
142 B1 **Wynne** U.S.A.
129 D2 **Wynyard** Can.
136 B2 **Wyoming** *state* U.S.A.
103 E1 **Wyszków** Pol.
140 C3 **Wytheville** U.S.A.

X

117 D3 **Xaafuun** Somalia
121 C3 **Xai-Xai** Moz.
70 A1 **Xamba** China
62 B1 **Xam Hua** Laos
120 A2 **Xangongo** Angola
81 C2 **Xankändi** Azer.
111 B2 **Xanthi** Greece
150 B3 **Xapuri** Brazil
107 C2 **Xátiva** Spain
Xiaguan China *see* **Dali**
71 B3 **Xiamen** China
70 A2 **Xi'an** China
70 A3 **Xianfeng** China
70 B2 **Xiangfan** China
Xiangjiang China *see* **Huichang**
62 B2 **Xiangkhoang** Laos
71 B3 **Xiangtan** China
Xiangyang China *see* **Xiangfan**
70 B2 **Xiantao** China
70 A2 **Xianyang** China
70 B2 **Xiaogan** China
69 E1 **Xiao Hinggan Ling** *mts* China
70 C2 **Xiaoshan** China
62 B1 **Xichang** China
145 C2 **Xicohténcatl** Mex.

70 A2 **Xifeng** *Gansu* China
71 A3 **Xifeng** *Guizhou* China
75 C2 **Xigazê** China
83 I4 **Xilinhot** China
70 B2 **Xincai** China
68 C2 **Xinghai** China
70 B2 **Xinghua** China
71 B3 **Xingning** China
70 A2 **Xingping** China
70 B2 **Xingtai** China
151 C2 **Xingu** *r.* Brazil
71 A3 **Xingyi** China
71 B3 **Xinhua** China
68 C2 **Xining** China
68 B2 **Xinjiang** *reg.* China
Xinjing China *see* **Jingxi**
65 A1 **Xinmin** China
71 B3 **Xinning** China
70 B2 **Xintai** China
70 B2 **Xinxiang** China
70 B2 **Xinyang** China
71 B3 **Xinyu** China
70 B2 **Xinzhou** *Shanxi* China
69 D2 **Xinzhou** *Shanxi* China
106 B1 **Xinzo de Limia** Spain
Xiongshan China *see* Zhenghe
68 C2 **Xiqing Shan** *mts* China
151 D3 **Xique Xique** Brazil
70 A1 **Xishanzui** China
71 A3 **Xiushan** China
71 B3 **Xiuying** China
70 B2 **Xixia** China
75 C1 **Xizang Zizhiqu** *aut. reg.* China
71 A3 **Xuanwei** China
70 B2 **Xuanzhou** China
70 B2 **Xuchang** China
Xucheng China *see* **Xuwen**
117 C4 **Xuddur** Somalia
Xujiang China *see* Guangchang
71 B3 **Xun Jiang** *r.* China
71 B3 **Xunwu** China
71 B3 **Xuwen** China
71 A3 **Xuyong** China

Y

117 B4 **Yabēlo** Eth.
69 D1 **Yablonovyy Khrebet** *mts* Rus. Fed.
143 D1 **Yadkin** *r.* U.S.A.
75 C2 **Yadong** China
89 E2 **Yagnitsa** Rus. Fed.
118 B1 **Yagoua** Cameroon
128 C3 **Yahk** Can.
144 B2 **Yahualica** Mex.
80 B2 **Yahyalı** Turkey
67 C4 **Yaizu** Japan
134 B1 **Yakima** U.S.A.
114 B3 **Yako** Burkina
66 D2 **Yakumo** Japan
126 B3 **Yakutat** U.S.A.
83 J2 **Yakutsk** Rus. Fed.
91 D2 **Yakymivka** Ukr.
63 B3 **Yala** Thai.
53 C3 **Yallourn** Austr.
111 C2 **Yalova** Turkey
91 C3 **Yalta** Ukr.
65 A1 **Yalu Jiang** *r.* China/N. Korea
67 D3 **Yamagata** Japan
67 B4 **Yamaguchi** Japan
86 F1 **Yamal, Poluostrov** *pen.* Rus. Fed.
53 D1 **Yamba** Austr.
117 A4 **Yambio** Sudan
110 C2 **Yambol** Bulg.
86 G2 **Yamburg** Rus. Fed.
62 A1 **Yamethin** Myanmar
114 B4 **Yamoussoukro** Côte d'Ivoire
90 B2 **Yampil'** Ukr.
75 C2 **Yamuna** *r.* India
75 D2 **Yamzho Yumco** *l.* China
83 K2 **Yana** *r.* Rus. Fed.
70 A2 **Yan'an** China
150 A3 **Yanaoca** Peru
78 A2 **Yanbu' al Baḩr** Saudi Arabia
70 C2 **Yancheng** China
50 A3 **Yanchep** Austr.
70 B2 **Yangcheng** China
71 B3 **Yangchun** China
65 B2 **Yangdok** N. Korea
71 B3 **Yangjiang** China
Yangôn Myanmar *see* Rangoon
70 B2 **Yangquan** China
71 B3 **Yangshuo** China
70 C3 **Yangtze** *r.* China
69 E2 **Yangtze, Mouths of the** China
65 B1 **Yanji** China
137 D2 **Yankton** U.S.A.
83 K2 **Yano-Indigirskaya Nizmennost'** *lowland* Rus. Fed.
83 K2 **Yanskiy Zaliv** *g.* Rus. Fed.
53 C1 **Yantabulla** Austr.
70 C2 **Yantai** China
118 B2 **Yaoundé** Cameroon
59 D2 **Yap** *i.* Micronesia
59 D3 **Yapen** *i.* Indon.
59 D3 **Yapen, Selat** *sea chan.* Indon.
144 A2 **Yaqui** *r.* Mex.
51 D2 **Yaraka** Austr.
86 D3 **Yaransk** Rus. Fed.
49 E2 **Yaren** Nauru
78 B3 **Yarīm** Yemen
77 D3 **Yarkant He** *r.* China
75 D2 **Yarlung Zangbo** *r.* China
131 D2 **Yarmouth** Can.
86 F2 **Yarongo** Rus. Fed.
89 E2 **Yaroslavl'** Rus. Fed.
66 B2 **Yaroslavskiy** Rus. Fed.
53 C3 **Yarram** Austr.
89 D2 **Yartsevo** Rus. Fed.
89 E3 **Yasnogorsk** Rus. Fed.
63 B2 **Yasothon** Thai.
53 C2 **Yass** Austr.
111 C3 **Yatağan** Turkey
129 E1 **Yathkyed Lake** Can.
67 B4 **Yatsushiro** Japan
150 B2 **Yavari** *r.* Brazil/Peru
75 B2 **Yavatmal** India
90 A2 **Yavoriv** Ukr.
67 B4 **Yawatahama** Japan
81 D2 **Yazd** Iran
142 B2 **Yazoo City** U.S.A.
111 B3 **Ydra** *i.* Greece
63 A2 **Ye** Myanmar
77 D3 **Yecheng** China
144 B2 **Yécora** Mex.
89 E3 **Yefremov** Rus. Fed.
89 E2 **Yegor'yevsk** Rus. Fed.
117 B4 **Yei** Sudan
86 F3 **Yekaterinburg** Rus. Fed.
89 E3 **Yelets** Rus. Fed.
114 A3 **Yélimané** Mali
96 □ **Yell** *i.* U.K.
128 C1 **Yellowknife** Can.
Yellow River *r.* China *see* Huang He
69 E2 **Yellow Sea** N. Pacific Ocean
136 C1 **Yellowstone** *r.* U.S.A.
136 A2 **Yellowstone Lake** U.S.A.
88 C3 **Yel'sk** Belarus
78 B3 **Yemen** *country* Asia
86 E2 **Yemva** Rus. Fed.
91 D2 **Yenakiyeve** Ukr.
62 A1 **Yenangyaung** Myanmar
62 B1 **Yên Bai** Vietnam
114 B4 **Yendi** Ghana
111 C3 **Yenice** Turkey
111 C3 **Yenifoça** Turkey
68 C1 **Yenisey** *r.* Rus. Fed.
53 C2 **Yeoval** Austr.
99 B3 **Yeovil** U.K.
51 E2 **Yeppoon** Austr.
83 I2 **Yerbogachen** Rus. Fed.
81 C1 **Yerevan** Armenia
77 D1 **Yereymentau** Kazakh.
87 D3 **Yershov** Rus. Fed.
65 B2 **Yesan** S. Korea
77 C1 **Yesil'** Kazakh.
111 C3 **Yeşilova** Turkey
99 A3 **Yes Tor** *hill* U.K.
53 D1 **Yetman** Austr.
62 A1 **Yeu** Myanmar
104 B2 **Yeu, Île d'** *i.* France
91 C2 **Yevpatoriya** Ukr.
91 D2 **Yeysk** Rus. Fed.
88 C2 **Yezyaryshcha** Belarus
71 A3 **Yibin** China
70 B2 **Yichang** China
69 E1 **Yichun** *Heilong.* China
71 B3 **Yichun** *Jiangxi* China
70 B2 **Yidu** China
110 C2 **Yıldız Dağları** *mts* Turkey
80 B2 **Yıldızeli** Turkey
70 A2 **Yinchuan** China
65 B1 **Yingchengzi** China
71 B3 **Yingde** China
70 C1 **Yingkou** China
70 B2 **Yingshan** *Hubei* China
70 A2 **Yingshan** *Sichuan* China
71 B3 **Yingtan** China
77 E2 **Yining** China
117 B4 **Yirga Alem** Eth.
70 B2 **Yishui** China
68 C2 **Yiwu** China
71 B3 **Yiyang** China
71 A3 **Yizhou** China
92 I2 **Yli-Kitka** *l.* Fin.
92 H2 **Ylitornio** Fin.
92 H3 **Ylivieska** Fin.
61 C2 **Yogyakarta** Indon.
118 B2 **Yoko** Cameroon
67 C3 **Yokohama** Japan
115 D4 **Yola** Nigeria
67 D3 **Yonezawa** Japan
71 B3 **Yong'an** China
71 B3 **Yongchun** China
70 A2 **Yongdeng** China
65 B2 **Yŏngdŏk** S. Korea
71 C3 **Yongkang** China
62 B1 **Yongsheng** China
71 B3 **Yongzhou** China
150 A1 **Yopal** Col.
50 A3 **York** Austr.
98 C2 **York** U.K.
137 D2 **York** *NE* U.S.A.
141 D3 **York** *PA* U.S.A.
51 D1 **York, Cape** Austr.
52 A3 **Yorke Peninsula** Austr.
52 A3 **Yorketown** Austr.
98 C2 **Yorkshire Wolds** *hills* U.K.
129 D2 **Yorkton** Can.
87 D3 **Yoshkar-Ola** Rus. Fed.
97 C3 **Youghal** Rep. of Ireland
53 C2 **Young** Austr.
52 A3 **Younghusband Peninsula** Austr.
140 C2 **Youngstown** U.S.A.
114 B3 **Youvarou** Mali
77 E2 **Youyi Feng** *mt.* China/Rus. Fed.

80 B2 **Yozgat** Turkey
134 B2 **Yreka** U.S.A.
Yr Wyddfa *mt.* U.K. *see* **Snowdon**
105 C2 **Yssingeaux** France
93 F4 **Ystad** Sweden
Ysyk-Köl Kyrg. *see* **Balykchy**
77 D2 **Ysyk-Köl** *salt l.* Kyrg.
92 □A3 **Ytri-Rangá** *r.* Iceland
62 B1 **Yuanjiang** China
62 B1 **Yuan Jiang** *r.* China
62 B1 **Yuanmou** China
135 B3 **Yuba City** U.S.A.
66 D2 **Yūbari** Japan
145 C3 **Yucatán** *pen.* Mex.
146 B2 **Yucatan Channel** Cuba/Mex.
50 C2 **Yuendumu** Austr.
71 B3 **Yueyang** China
86 F2 **Yugorsk** Rus. Fed.
Yugoslavia *country* Europe *see* **Serbia and Montenegro**
83 L2 **Yukagirskoye Ploskogor'ye** *plat.* Rus. Fed.
126 A2 **Yukon** *r.* Can./U.S.A.
128 A1 **Yukon Territory** *admin. div.* Can.
71 B3 **Yulin** *Guangxi* China
70 A2 **Yulin** *Shaanxi* China
62 B1 **Yulong Xueshan** *mt.* China
138 A2 **Yuma** *AZ* U.S.A.
136 C2 **Yuma** *CO* U.S.A.
68 C2 **Yumen** China
80 B2 **Yunak** Turkey
70 B2 **Yuncheng** China
71 B3 **Yunfu** China
62 B1 **Yunnan** *prov.* China
52 A2 **Yunta** Austr.
70 B2 **Yunyang** China
150 A2 **Yurimaguas** Peru
77 E3 **Yurungkax He** *r.* China
71 C3 **Yü Shan** *mt.* Taiwan
68 C2 **Yushu** China
Yushuwan China *see* **Huaihua**
81 C1 **Yusufeli** Turkey
77 E3 **Yutian** China
62 B1 **Yuxi** China
66 D2 **Yuzhno-Kuril'sk** Rus. Fed.
83 K3 **Yuzhno-Sakhalinsk** Rus. Fed.
91 C2 **Yuzhnoukrayinsk** Ukr.
104 C2 **Yvetot** France

Z

100 B1 **Zaandam** Neth.
69 D1 **Zabaykal'sk** Rus. Fed.
78 B3 **Zabīd** Yemen
76 C3 **Zābol** Iran
79 D2 **Zābolī** Iran
144 B3 **Zacapu** Mex.
144 B2 **Zacatecas** Mex.
145 C3 **Zacatepec** Mex.
145 C3 **Zacatlán** Mex.
111 B3 **Zacharo** Greece
144 B2 **Zacoalco** Mex.
145 C2 **Zacualtipán** Mex.
109 C2 **Zadar** Croatia
63 A3 **Zadetkyi Kyun** *i.* Myanmar
89 E3 **Zadonsk** Rus. Fed.
106 B2 **Zafra** Spain
109 C1 **Zagreb** Croatia
81 C2 **Zagros, Kūhhā-ye** *mts* Iran
79 D2 **Zāhedān** Iran
80 B2 **Zahlé** Lebanon
78 B3 **Ẓaḩrān** Saudi Arabia
Zaire *country* Africa *see* **Congo, Democratic Republic of**
109 D2 **Zaječar** Serb. and Mont.
89 E3 **Zakharovo** Rus. Fed.
81 C2 **Zākhō** Iraq
111 B3 **Zakynthos** Greece
111 B3 **Zakynthos** *i.* Greece
103 D2 **Zalaegerszeg** Hungary
110 B1 **Zalău** Romania
78 B2 **Ẓalim** Saudi Arabia
117 A3 **Zalingei** Sudan
78 A2 **Ẓalmā, Jabal aẓ** *mt.* Saudi Arabia
128 C2 **Zama City** Can.
Zambeze *r.* Moz. *see* **Zambezi** *r.* Zambia
120 B2 **Zambezi** Zambia
120 C2 **Zambezi** *r.* Zambia
120 B2 **Zambia** *country* Africa
64 B2 **Zamboanga** Phil.
64 B2 **Zamboanga Peninsula** Phil.
106 B1 **Zamora** Spain
144 B3 **Zamora de Hidalgo** Mex.
103 E1 **Zamość** Pol.
75 B1 **Zanda** China
100 B2 **Zandvliet** Belgium
140 C3 **Zanesville** U.S.A.
81 C2 **Zanjān** Iran
Zante *i.* Greece *see* **Zakynthos**
119 D3 **Zanzibar** Tanz.
119 D3 **Zanzibar Island** Tanz.
89 E3 **Zaokskiy** Rus. Fed.
115 C2 **Zaouatallaz** Alg.
70 B2 **Zaozhuang** China
89 D2 **Zapadnaya Dvina** *r.* Europe
89 D2 **Zapadnaya Dvina** Rus. Fed.
68 B1 **Zapadnyy Sayan** *reg.* Rus. Fed.
139 D3 **Zapata** U.S.A.
92 J2 **Zapolyarnyy** Rus. Fed.
91 D2 **Zaporizhzhya** Ukr.
101 E2 **Zappendorf** Ger.
80 B2 **Zara** Turkey
145 B2 **Zaragoza** Mex.
107 C1 **Zaragoza** Spain
76 B3 **Zarand** Iran
76 C3 **Zaranj** Afgh.
88 C2 **Zarasai** Lith.
89 E3 **Zaraysk** Rus. Fed.
150 B1 **Zaraza** Venez.
115 C3 **Zaria** Nigeria
90 B1 **Zarichne** Ukr.
81 D3 **Zarqān** Iran
66 B2 **Zarubino** Rus. Fed.
103 D1 **Żary** Pol.
115 D1 **Zarzis** Tunisia
75 B1 **Zanskar Mountains** India
123 C3 **Zastron** S. Africa
69 E1 **Zavitinsk** Rus. Fed.
103 D1 **Zawiercie** Pol.
77 E2 **Zaysan, Ozero** *l.* Kazakh.
68 C3 **Zayü** China
90 B1 **Zdolbuniv** Ukr.
Zealand *i.* Denmark *see* **Sjælland**
100 A2 **Zeebrugge** Belgium
123 C2 **Zeerust** S. Africa
50 C2 **Zeil, Mount** Austr.
101 F2 **Zeitz** Ger.
88 B3 **Zelenogradsk** Rus. Fed.
82 E1 **Zemlya Aleksandry** *i.* Rus. Fed.
82 F1 **Zemlya Vil'cheka** *i.* Rus. Fed.
107 D2 **Zemmora** Alg.
145 C3 **Zempoaltépetl, Nudo de** *mt.* Mex.
65 B1 **Zengfeng Shan** *mt.* China
105 D2 **Zermatt** Switz.
91 E2 **Zernograd** Rus. Fed.
101 E2 **Zeulenroda** Ger.
101 D1 **Zeven** Ger.
100 C2 **Zevenaar** Neth.
83 J3 **Zeya** Rus. Fed.
79 C2 **Zeydābād** Iran
83 J3 **Zeyskoye Vodokhranilishche** *resr* Rus. Fed.
103 D1 **Zgierz** Pol.
88 B3 **Zhabinka** Belarus
76 A2 **Zhalpaktal** Kazakh.
77 C1 **Zhaltyr** Kazakh.
76 B2 **Zhanaozen** Kazakh.
Zhangde China *see* **Anyang**
70 B1 **Zhangjiakou** China
71 B3 **Zhangping** China
71 B3 **Zhangshu** China
68 C2 **Zhangye** China
71 B3 **Zhangzhou** China
71 B3 **Zhangjiajie** China
87 D4 **Zhanibek** Kazakh.
71 B3 **Zhanjiang** China
71 B3 **Zhao'an** China
71 B3 **Zhaoqing** China
71 A3 **Zhaotong** China
75 C1 **Zhari Namco** *salt l.* China
77 E2 **Zharkent** Kazakh.
89 D2 **Zharkovskiy** Rus. Fed.
77 E2 **Zharma** Kazakh.
90 C2 **Zhashkiv** Ukr.
71 C3 **Zhejiang** *prov.* China
82 F1 **Zhelaniya, Mys** *c.* Rus. Fed.
89 E3 **Zheleznogorsk** Rus. Fed.
70 A2 **Zhenba** China
71 A3 **Zheng'an** China
71 B3 **Zhenghe** China
70 B2 **Zhengzhou** China
71 A3 **Zhenyuan** China
91 E1 **Zherdevka** Rus. Fed.
86 D2 **Zheshart** Rus. Fed.
77 C2 **Zhezkazgan** *Karagandinskaya Oblast'* Kazakh.
77 C2 **Zhezkazgan** *Karagandinskaya Oblast'* Kazakh.
83 J2 **Zhigansk** Rus. Fed.
Zhi Qu *r.* China *see* **Yangtze**
76 C1 **Zhitikara** Kazakh.
88 D3 **Zhlobin** Belarus
90 B2 **Zhmerynka** Ukr.
74 A1 **Zhob** Pak.
83 L1 **Zhokhova, Ostrov** *i.* Rus. Fed.
75 C2 **Zhongba** China
62 A1 **Zhongdian** China
Zhonghe China *see* **Xiushan**
70 A2 **Zhongning** China
71 B3 **Zhongshan** China
Zhongshan China *see* **Lupanshui**
70 A2 **Zhongwei** China
Zhongxin China *see* **Zhongdian**
70 B2 **Zhoukou** China
70 C2 **Zhoushan** China
91 C2 **Zhovti Vody** Ukr.
65 A2 **Zhuanghe** China
70 B2 **Zhucheng** China
89 D3 **Zhukovka** Rus. Fed.
89 E2 **Zhukovskiy** Rus. Fed.
70 B2 **Zhumadian** China
Zhuoyang China *see* **Suiping**
71 B3 **Zhuzhou** *Hunan* China
71 B3 **Zhuzhou** *Hunan* China
90 A2 **Zhydachiv** Ukr.
88 C3 **Zhytkavichy** Belarus
90 B1 **Zhytomyr** Ukr.

103 D2 **Žiar nad Hronom** Slovakia
70 B2 **Zibo** China
103 D1 **Zielona Góra** Pol.
62 A1 **Zigaing** Myanmar
71 A3 **Zigong** China
114 A3 **Ziguinchor** Senegal
144 B3 **Zihuatanejo** Mex.
103 D2 **Žilina** Slovakia
83 H3 **Zima** Rus. Fed.
145 C2 **Zimapán** Mex.
121 B2 **Zimbabwe** *country* Africa
114 A4 **Zimmi** Sierra Leone
110 C2 **Zimnicea** Romania
115 C3 **Zinder** Niger
78 B3 **Zinjibār** Yemen
103 D2 **Zirc** Hungary
62 A1 **Ziro** India
79 C2 **Zīr Rūd** Iran
103 D2 **Zistersdorf** Austria
145 B3 **Zitácuaro** Mex.
103 C1 **Zittau** Ger.
87 E3 **Zlatoust** Rus. Fed.
103 D2 **Zlín** Czech Rep.
89 D3 **Zlynka** Rus. Fed.
89 E3 **Zmiyevka** Rus. Fed.
91 D2 **Zmiyiv** Ukr.
89 E3 **Znamenka** *Orlovskaya Oblast'* Rus. Fed.
91 E1 **Znamenka** *Tambovskaya Oblast'* Rus. Fed.
91 C2 **Znam"yanka** Ukr.
103 D2 **Znojmo** Czech Rep.
91 D1 **Zolochiv** *Kharkivs'ka Oblast'* Ukr.
90 A2 **Zolochiv** *L'vivs'ka Oblast'* Ukr.
91 C2 **Zolotonosha** Ukr.
89 E3 **Zolotukhino** Rus. Fed.
121 C2 **Zomba** Malawi
80 B1 **Zonguldak** Turkey
105 D3 **Zonza** *Corsica* France
114 B4 **Zorzor** Liberia
115 D2 **Zouar** Chad
114 A2 **Zouérat** Maur.
109 D1 **Zrenjanin** Serb. and Mont.
89 D2 **Zubtsov** Rus. Fed.
105 D2 **Zug** Switz.
81 C1 **Zugdidi** Georgia
106 B2 **Zújar** *r.* Spain
100 C2 **Zülpich** Ger.
121 C2 **Zumbo** Moz.
145 C3 **Zumpango** Mex.
138 B1 **Zuni Mountains** U.S.A.
71 A3 **Zunyi** China
109 C1 **Županja** Croatia
105 D2 **Zürich** Switz.
100 C1 **Zutphen** Neth.
115 D1 **Zuwārah** Libya
90 C2 **Zvenyhorodka** Ukr.
121 C3 **Zvishavane** Zimbabwe
103 D2 **Zvolen** Slovakia
109 C2 **Zvornik** Bos.-Herz.
114 B4 **Zwedru** Liberia
123 C3 **Zwelitsha** S. Africa
103 D2 **Zwettl** Austria
101 F2 **Zwickau** Ger.
100 C1 **Zwolle** Neth.
83 L2 **Zyryanka** Rus. Fed.